SHŌKAN

SHŌKAN
HIROHITO'S SAMURAI

ARMS AND
ARMOUR

**DEDICATED TO
THE 'FORGOTTEN' ALLIED FORCES IN BURMA
WHO NEVER RECEIVED THE OFFICIAL RECOGNITION
THEY DESERVED
and
TO MY GOOD FRIEND AND MENTOR, RON GREGORY
(whose encouragement brought this project
to fruition)**

Arms and Armour Press
A Cassell Imprint
Villiers House, 41–47 Strand, London WC2N 5JE.

Distributed in the USA by Sterling Publishing Co. Inc., 387 Park Avenue South, New York, NY 10016-8810.

Distributed in Australia by Capricorn Link (Australia) Pty. Ltd., P.O. Box 665, Lane Cove, New South Wales 2066.

British Library Cataloguing in Publication Data
Fuller, Richard
Shōkan – Hirohito's samurai: leaders of the Japanese armed forces 1926–1945
I. Title
305.52
ISBN 1-85409-151-4

Maps and charts drawn by the author. Designed and edited by DAG Publications Ltd. Designed by David Gibbons; edited by Michael Boxall; typeset by Ronset Typesetters, Darwen, Lancashire; camerawork by M&E Reproductions, North Fambridge, Essex; printed and bound in Great Britain by Hartnolls Ltd, Bodmin.

Acknowledgements

Particular thanks must go to my friends Trevor Duffin and Ron Gregory for the provision of much additional material; and to all others who contributed historical and photographic material including Brian Cleevely, Andrew MacMillan, numerous Regimental and Military museums, the Imperial War Museum and the Australian War Memorial.

Grateful acknowledgement is also made to the author's friends and fellow sword collectors abroad who have made research and collecting a pleasure; in particular Trevor Duffin, Herb Gopstein, Leo Monson Jr., Cheyenne Noda, Curt Peritz, Clarence Siman, George Trotter and Brenton Williams.

The photographic assistance of Dave Gardner is also greatly appreciated.

Richard Fuller
Bristol, England.
1991

Contents

Introduction	7
1 Japan at War, 1931–45: A Chronology	23
2 Surrender Ceremonies	34
3 Organization of Japanese Armed Forces at the End of the Second World War	49
4 Biographical Details	76
Imperial Japanese Army General Officers, c. 1926–45	78
Imperial Japanese Navy Flag Officers, 1926–45	244
Bibliography	308
Indexes	311

Introduction

THE IDEA of assembling an index of Japanese Generals and Admirals was prompted by an interest in collecting Japanese military swords of the Second World War. Their use and subsequent surrender by named officers, where such information was available, is of great historical significance to the collector. In general it appeared impossible to track down service records and surrender details of low–ranking officers, and indeed, even those up to the rank of Colonel. However, the names of Generals and Admirals kept appearing in various English language military campaign books dealing with the Far Eastern war. In many cases there appeared to be confusion over their romanized names and commands. It therefore became necessary to keep lists compiled from the various books to confirm details and identification, especially of the participants of the various formal surrender ceremonies which occurred in 1945 and 1946. As the relevant information grew it became necessary to expand to a card index for flexibility and it is this which forms the main part of this publication. Names, ranks and commands alone were inadequate so campaign details, when located, were also added.

This work is, perhaps, unique in English because of the sheer number of officers listed. Generally reference works that include biographies only refer to the more famous officers and omit the less important officers who also participated or who commanded supply bases, military police, transport, commisariat, etc. Without them no armed force could function.[1]

Since the various entries are drawn from English-language sources, many are fragmentary and do not cover the entire number who served in the Japanese military campaigns from 1931 to 1945. Such coverage would indeed be a daunting task. Apologies are offered if, through the lack of corroborating evidence, a General or Flag Officer rank has inadvertently been given when in fact this rank was not actually attained until after the war through service with the current Japanese Self-Defence Force or Japanese Maritime Self-Defence Force. Similarly apologies are also given for any omissions and errors in fact or sequence which must inevitably occur in a work of this kind.

The Japanese army and navy had separate air forces, but it has not been possible to provide separate sections for these because the respective commanders could be transferred to normal army or naval duties during their careers. However, the entries have been divided into army Generals and naval Flag Officers (Admirals) to facilitate a breakdown of these arms.

Although there are 820 General Officers and 258 Admirals listed, they are, as previously stated, only a small number of the total who served from the 'Manchurian Incident' in September 1931 up to the Japanese surrender in August 1945. The following figures given in KOGUN – The Japanese Army in the Pacific (see Bibliography) indicate the active and authorized number of Generals as of 15 August 1945:

Rank	Regulars	Reserves, recalled & retired	Total on active duty	Full authorized total
Generals	19	2	21	21
(and Field Marshals)				
Lieutenants-General	384	100	484	560
Majors-General	623	473	1,096	1,432

This gives a total of 1,601 General Officers on active duty as against an authorized total of 2,013. (Note that: This does not include Flag Officers of the navy, and their totals have not been located.)

148 Generals alone surrendered to the Russians in Manchuria.

The total composition of an Army was usually smaller than that used in the west, so the use of two or more Army Corps (each consisting of two or more divisions) to form an Army was not utilized.

The navy remained autonomous and virtually never came under army command until the last months of the war because of intense rivalry and, indeed, dislike. Naval losses by November 1944 were so high that the command structure was reduced, most surface fleets ceased to exist in strength and the Naval Air Fleets (land-based) became the most potent force left. The navy lost a much greater proportion of men and *matériel* in comparison to the army.

In late 1941 the Imperial Japanese Navy was the largest naval force in the Far East. It consisted of 10 battleships, 18 heavy cruisers, 20 light cruisers, 6 fleet carriers, 4 light carriers, 112 fleet-type destroyers and 65 submarines; total 235 ships. These were divided among the Combined Fleet, which under the Commander-in-Chief, Vice-Admiral YAMAMOTO Isoroku, comprised:

1st Fleet (Battle Fleet), Vice-Admiral YAMAMOTO Isoroku; Hiroshima, Japan.

2nd Fleet (Scouting Fleet), Vice-Admiral KONDO Nobutake; Hainan Island, off southern China.

3rd Fleet (Blockade and Transport Fleet), Vice-Admiral TAKAHASHI Ibo; Formosa.

4th Fleet[2] (Mandates Fleet), Vice-Admiral INOUYE Shigeyoshi; Truk, Caroline Islands.

5th Fleet (Northern Fleet), Vice-Admiral HOSOGAYA Boshiro; Maizuru and Ominato, Japan.

6th Fleet (Submarine Fleet), Vice-Admiral SHIMIZU Mitsumi; Kwajalein Atoll, Marshall Islands.

1st Air Fleet (Carrier Fleet), Vice-Admiral NAGUMO Chuichi; Kure, Japan.

11th Air Fleet (land based), Vice-Admiral TSUKUHARA Nishio; Formosa and Indo-China.

Home Islands, Naval Districts and Naval Guard Districts

Vice- or Rear-Admiral responsible for the coastal and harbour defence of Japan and adjoining territory (normally with a naval Air Group attached). Principally responsible for the main Naval Bases where they were located.

District	Location
Kure Naval District	Kure, southern Honshu, Japan
Maizuru Naval District	Maizuru, north-western Honshu, Japan
Sasebo Naval District	Sasebo, north-western Kyushu, Japan
Yokosuka Naval District	Yokosuka, south-eastern Honshu, Japan

Chinkai Guard District	Chinkai, Korea
Hainan Guard District	Hainan Island, off southern China
Ominato Guard District	Ominato, northern Honshu, Japan
Osaka Guard District	Osaka, southern Honshu, Japan
Ryojun (Port Arthur) Guard District	Ryojun (Port Arthur), Manchuria
Takao Guard District	Takao, Formosa

GENERAL GUIDE TO THE COMMAND STRUCTURE OF THE IMPERIAL JAPANESE ARMY AND ARMY AIR FORCE

Imperial General Headquarters
Tokyo

Army Group
(Usually named, e.g., China Expeditionary Army, Southern Army)
Two or more Area Armies
Field Marshal or General

Area Army
(Either named, e.g., Burma Area Army, or enumerated, e.g., 14th Area Army)
Usually two or more Armies and one Air Army
General or Lieutenant-General

Army	**Air Army**
(enumerated)	(enumerated)
Two or more Divisions	Two Air Divisions
Lieutenant-General	Lieutenant-General
Division	**Air Division**
(enumerated)	(enumerated)
Full operational strength	No fixed size
18,000-20,000	Strength dependent upon the task
but considerably reduced	Lieutenant-General
by the end of the war	
Lieutenant-General	
Brigade	**Air Brigade**
(enumerated)	(enumerated)
Infantry Group of a Division	Four Flying Regiments
or acting independently	80-160 aircraft of
Strength approx. 6,000	the same type or mixed
Major-General	Major-General

Naval Base Forces (by late 1944)
Vice- or Rear-Admiral or Captain. BF = Base Force; SBF = Special Base Force.

Area Fleet	Fleet	Base Force	Location
Unclassified		Amoy SBF	Amoy, China
		Bako SBF	Bako
		Hongkong Area SBF	Hongkong, China
		Okinawa Area BF	Ryukyu Islands
		Ryojun (Port Arthur) SBF	Manchuria
		Shanghai SBF	China
		Tsingtao SBF	China
		Yangstze River SBF	China
		Chichijima Area SBF	Bonin Islands
		Rashin SBF	North Korea?
		Kuriles Area BF	Kataoka Bay

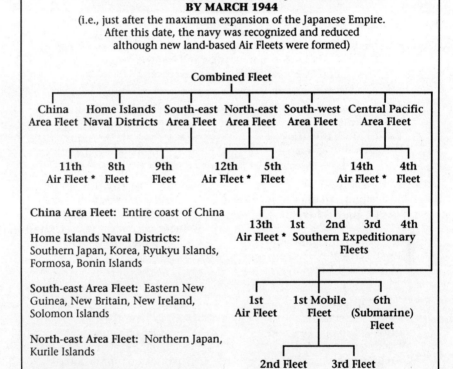

ORGANIZATION OF THE IMPERIAL JAPANESE NAVY BY MARCH 1944
(i.e., just after the maximum expansion of the Japanese Empire. After this date, the navy was recognized and reduced although new land-based Air Fleets were formed)

Combined Fleet

China Area Fleet — Home Islands Naval Districts — South-east Area Fleet — North-east Area Fleet — South-west Area Fleet — Central Pacific Area Fleet

11th Air Fleet * — 8th Fleet — 9th Fleet — 12th Air Fleet * — 5th Fleet — 14th Air Fleet * — 4th Fleet

13th Air Fleet * — 1st, 2nd, 3rd, 4th Southern Expeditionary Fleets

1st Air Fleet — 1st Mobile Fleet — 6th (Submarine) Fleet

2nd Fleet (Battleships) — 3rd Fleet (Carriers)

China Area Fleet: Entire coast of China

Home Islands Naval Districts: Southern Japan, Korea, Ryukyu Islands, Formosa, Bonin Islands

South-east Area Fleet: Eastern New Guinea, New Britain, New Ireland, Solomon Islands

North-east Area Fleet: Northern Japan, Kurile Islands

South-west Area Fleet: Burma, Malaya, French Indo-China, Netherlands East Indies and Philippines

Central Pacific Fleet: Marshall Islands, Caroline Islands, Mariana Islands

Note: All these units formed Striking Forces used to assist the Area Fleets when necessary

* Land-based

Area Fleet	Fleet	Base Force	Location
South-east Area Fleet		1st BF	Buin on Bougainville, Solomon Islands
		2nd SBF	Wewak, New Guinea (Absorbed by 27th SBF, March 1944)
		7th BF	Sio, New Guinea? (Absorbed by 27th SBF, March 1944)
		8th BF	Rabaul, New Britain
		14th BF	Kavieng, New Ireland
North-east Area Fleet		Kuriles BF	Kurile Islands
South-west Area Fleet	1st Southern Expeditionary Fleet	9th BF	Sabang, Sumatra
		10th SBF	Singapore, Malaya
		11th SBF	Saigon, Indo-China
		12th SBF	Port Blair, Andaman Islands
		13th BF	Rangoon, Burma
		15th SBF	Prai, opposite Penang Island, Malaya
	2nd Southern Expeditionary Fleet	21st SBF	Surabaya, Java
		22nd SBF	Balikpapan, Borneo
		23rd SBF	Macassar, Celebes
		24th SBF	Ende, Flores Islands
	3rd Southern Expeditionary Fleet	31st BF	Manila on Luzon, Philippines
		32nd SBF	Davao on Mindanao, Philippines
		33rd BF	Central Philippines
	4th Southern Expeditionary Fleet	25th SBF	Ambon Island, off Ceram
		26th SBF	Kau? (Possibly Kai Island, off south New Guinea)
		27th SBF	Wewak, New Guinea
		28th BF	New Guinea
Central Pacific Fleet		4th BF	Truk, Caroline Islands
		5th BF	Saipan, Mariana Islands (Rendered ineffective July 1944)
		30th BF	Palau Islands

Note: 3rd BF rendered ineffective on Tarawa, January 1944; 6th BF rendered ineffective on Kwajalein, February 1944.

[1] The military police were the *Kempei* ('*Kempeitai*' means the military police corps as a whole) which is also the same as the 'gendarmerie'.

[2] 4th Fleet was activated on 15 November 1939 with the primary duty of defending Japanese territory granted to her by mandate after the First World War. It was not an orthodox combat fleet. It remained in being until the end of the Second War.

During the period December 1941 to September 1945 the number of warships in service almost doubled to 451 (including submarines), but as can be seen from the following the total losses were 332 (73.6 per cent).[3] It is therefore not surprising that the navy turned to *Kamikaze* (suicide) tactics as their last form of attack.[4] The following breakdown shows that by September 1945 only 37 vessels (8.2 per cent) remained operational.

12 Battleships	11 sunk, 1 heavily damaged
26 Carriers	20 sunk, 5 heavily damaged, 1 not commissioned
18 Heavy cruisers	16 sunk, 2 heavily damaged
22 Light cruisers	21 sunk, 1 heavily damaged
3 Training cruisers	2 sunk, 1 operational
179 Destroyers	133 sunk, 27 heavily damaged, 7 operational, 12 unmanned, decommissioned, target ships, etc.
191 Submarines *I, RO, HA* classes	129 sunk, 1 damaged, 29 operational, 28 de-commissioned, 3 captured, 1 not commissioned
451 Total	

Note: Midget submarines and various suicide craft are not included in these figures.

As a matter of interest the only war-time ship that served in the post-war navy (Maritime Self-Defence Force) was the destroyer *Nashi*, which was sunk off Kure in July 1945 but raised in 1955.

Many (or perhaps most) of the Generals and Admirals who served in China and the Pacific war were not of samurai descent. It was, however, an inherent principle of the Japanese officer corps that the old samurai code of *bushidō*[5] be taught and obeyed without question, even though the samurai caste had effectively disappeared from Japanese society by 1877. This code of ethics was not part of Army Regulations, but was considered as being incorporated into them. Its best known principle was death before dishonour, with absolute loyalty to the Emperor. This was also a fundamental teaching for all ranks.

Attack with no retreat (unless ordered, although it would no doubt be termed a tactical withdrawal) and death before surrender were the accepted norm for all Japanese military forces, much to the chagrin of the Western Allies who could not reconcile this belief with their own traditions of warfare. Similarly the Japanese could not accept the failure of the enemy to adopt and adhere to a similar policy. The atrocious cruelty and ill-treatment of Allied prisoners cannot be excused, but the reason for it is explicable when the *bushidō* code is considered.

As the war progressed with severe Japanese losses of men, territory and *matériel*, the principle of no surrender among other ranks began to waver with the realization that final victory, or even an honourable settlement, was a mere dream of the high command. Consequently, Japanese prisoners began to be taken in increasing numbers. The officer class, however, adhered to the no surrender doctrine with a few exceptions among Company officer ranks.[6] The author can

---

[3]Summarized from 'The United States at War – Final Official Report to the Secretary of the Navy 1945' by Fleet Admiral E. J. King, C in C US Fleet and Chief of Naval Operations.

[4]'*Kamikaze*', literally 'divine wind', was the name given to the great storm which destroyed the Mongol fleet in 1281, thus saving Japan from invasion. The use of aircraft as suicide weapons would, it was thought, achieve the same result. Thus the name seemed appropriate for such forces and was suggested in October 1944 by Captain Inoguchi Rikihei, IJN, who was Senior Staff Officer to 1st Air Fleet. It was officially adopted, becoming synonymous in the West for any form of suicide attack.

[5]Literally *Bushi* (samurai, warrior) *DŌ* (way, morality, moral doctrine), i.e., 'way of the warrior'.

[6]It is believed that the highest rank of officer taken alive before August 1945 was that of Major, but this is open to correction if necessary.

find no record of the capture or surrender of officers of Field and General's rank before the official cessation of hostilities in August 1945. This also applies to senior officers of the Imperial Japanese Navy. Such officers preferred suicide to capture in accordance with the *bushidō* code and the subsequent disgrace that this would bring to themselves, their families, country and Emperor.

The Emperor's broadcast of August 1945[7] announcing the Japanese surrender was too much to bear for a number of senior Generals and Admirals, who also chose suicide. However, although there was dissension among many whether to accept it or fight on, they decided to adhere to Allied orders and surrender where and when specified upon receiving written confirmation from IGHQ, Tokyo or verbally from their superiors.

There were those in Japanese-held areas who would not accept the surrender in any circumstances and the shame they thought it brought. Thus they continued to resist or hide until long after the war. They were individuals or small bands who, in some cases, refused to believe Japan had actually surrendered despite the dropping of leaflets and even personal entreaties from their families. They were few in numbers and were mostly other ranks, NCOs or junior officers. The most famous is Second Lieutenant Onoda Hiroo who held out on Lubang Island, Philippines, until 1974.[8]

Even now (forty-five years later) there are still reports of former Japanese soldiers surrendering. Tanaka Kiyoaki, aged 77 and Hashimoto Shigeyuki, aged 71, have finally given themselves up and returned to their families in Japan.[9] They refused to surrender to the Allies at the end of the war, preferring instead to join the Malayan Communists fighting for the Chinese Peoples Communist Party on the Thai–Malayan borders.

[7]The renouncement of his 'deity' status and change to that of a 'human being' did not occur until January 1946.

[8]He refused to give up since it conflicted with the orders given to him in 1945 to fight a guerrilla action until the Japanese army returned. His former commanding officer had to be flown in from Japan to order him to surrender.

[9]They gave themselves up to Thai authorities on 9 January 1990 after an amnesty for Communists. However, it is now alleged that they were both guilty of war crimes, having been engineers on the Burma Railway and directly responsible for the death of Allied prisoners.

Japanese Military and Civilian Government Organization 1926–45

Emperor Hirohito
(Head of State and Supreme Commander of all Armed Forces)

Palace Institutions

Imperial Family Councillors: All adult male members of the imperial family down to fifth generation in descent from an Emperor; through most of Hirohito's reign, 25 princes: to advise Emperor on matters affecting family, e.g., property, marriages, princely peccadillos, major decisions of state

Privy Councillors: 26 elder statesmen appointed by Emperor on advice of prime minister: to advise Emperor on any question he referred to it for opinion. (They were known as 'Jushin'.)

Lord Privy Seal: to give Emperor day-to-day political advice. Secretary and staff: to keep track of imperial seals and all documents of state to which they were affixed
Imperial tombs and shrines
Imperial archives

General Staffs

Army Chief of Staff HQ
General Affairs Bureau:
Organization and Mobilization Section
First Bureau: Operations
Second Bureau: Intelligence
Third Bureau: Transport and Communications
Forth Bureau: Historical
General Staff College
Land Survey Department

Armies:
Kwantung Army
China Expeditionary Army
*Korean Army
*North China Army
Southern Army
*Taiwan Army
Home Armies
Various Area Armies
Tokyo Guard
War College

Navy Chief of Staff HQ
First Department: Operations
Second Department: Intelli-

Cabinet

Prime Minister: appointed by Emperor on advice of Prince Saionji and elder statesmen; until 1932, often the head of a political party

Foreign Minister:
Foreign Ministry
Ambassadors

Home Minister:
Thought Police
Tokyo (Metropolitan) Police
Prefectural governors and prefectural police

Finance Minister:
Board of the Budget
Bank of Japan
Yokohama Specie Bank

War Minister (for Army):
Military Affairs Bureau
Personnel Bureau
Military Administration Bureau
Economic Mobilization Bureau
Ordnance Bureau
Intendance Bureau

Diet
(Parliament)
(Function: to approve or veto increases in national budget and to discuss legislation presented by prime minister to Emperor)

House of Representatives (Lower House):
466 politicians elected by some 14 million eligible male voters (out of population of 70 million, 1940)

House of Peers:
to guide House of Representatives: included:
66 rich men elected by the 6,000 highest taxpayers in Japan
150 of lesser nobility elected by the 1,000-odd adult male members of same
all princes and marquises
125 imperial nominees selected for knowledge or meritorious service

houses

Peers' and Peeresses' Schools

Code Research Institute

Spy Service Directorship, to co-ordinate and keep track of all Japanese espionage; roughly equivalent to C.I.A.

Grand Chamberlain: to advise Emperor on matters of his personal health and recreation and, in practice, on matters of international diplomacy

Board of Chamberlains: stewards, butlers, grooms, etc.

Board of Ceremonials

Court Physicians' Bureau

Bureau of Imperial Cuisine

Imperial Stables Bureau

Imperial Poetry Bureau

Imperial Recreations Board

Households of Crown Prince, Empress, Empress Dowager

Imperial Household Minister: to supervise and manage imperial fortune: investments, rents from 3.2 million acres of crown lands, upkeep of 23 secondary palaces

Imperial Treasury

Maintenance and Works Bureau

Board of Imperial Auditors

bined Fleet, First Fleet, Second Fleet, etc.

Naval Staff College

Inspectorships

Inspector-General of Military Education:

Military Academy

Tank, Signal, Infantry, other specialized schools

Military preparatory schools

Inspector-General of Military Aviation:

Air Schools, research institutes, cartel liaison committees

(*Until absorbed by formation of Army Groups and Area Armies)

Army Investigation Committee

Press Relations Squad

Secret Police: semi-autonomous, responsible to commanders overseas and expected to work with Home and Justice

Prisoner-of-War Administration (founded 1942)

Navy Minister:

Naval affairs administered through bureaucracy similar to War Minister's

Justice Minister:

Courts

Judges

Prosecutors

Education Minister:

Schools

Government publications and propaganda

Commerce and Industry Minister

Agriculture and Forestry Minister

Transportation Minister

CONTINUED

Palace Institutions

Chief Imperial Aide-de-Camp: to advise Emperor on military matters
Imperial Naval Aide-de-Camp
Other aides-de-camp

Supreme War Council: High-ranking Army and Navy officers appointed by Emperor—the military counterpart of the Privy Council
Board of Field Marshals and Fleet Admirals (Acted in an advisory capacity only)

Imperial Headquarters: Established 1937 to centralize Emperor's command functions in palace; top ministers and bureau chiefs from General Staff and War and Navy ministries plus permanent palace staff to co-ordinate all war plans and maps for Emperor's reference. Comprised:
Army Chief of Staff
War Minister
Inspector-General of Military Education
Inspector-General of Military Aviation
Navy Chief of Staff
Navy Minister

Cabinet

Overseas Affairs Minister (Colonisation):
Prosperous Asia Institute: semi-autonomous, to administer occupied areas in China
South Sea Development Board: semi-autonomous, to administer conquests in South-east Asia

Welfare Minister:
National health
Food rationing

Cabinet Planning Board: to write all legislation discussed by Diet (began as inspection board, 1935: became planning board, 1941, and took charge of all domestic legislation and mobilization for the war)

Munitions Minister

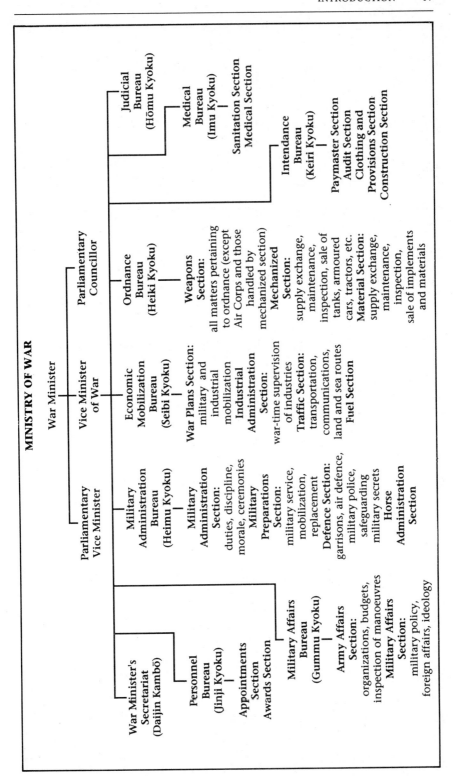

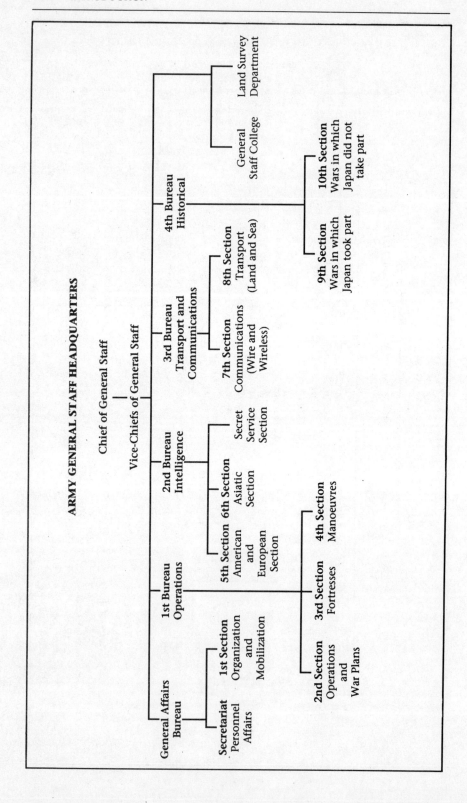

ARMY GENERAL STAFF HEADQUARTERS

Chief of General Staff

Vice-Chiefs of General Staff

General Affairs Bureau

Secretariat
Personnel Affairs

1st Bureau
Operations

1st Section
Organization and Mobilization

2nd Section
Operations and War Plans

3rd Section
Fortresses

4th Section
Manoeuvres

2nd Bureau
Intelligence

5th Section
American and European Section

6th Section
Asiatic Section

Secret Service Section

3rd Bureau
Transport and Communications

7th Section
Communications (Wire and Wireless)

8th Section
Transport (Land and Sea)

4th Bureau
Historical

9th Section
Wars in which Japan took part

10th Section
Wars in which Japan did not take part

General Staff College

Land Survey Department

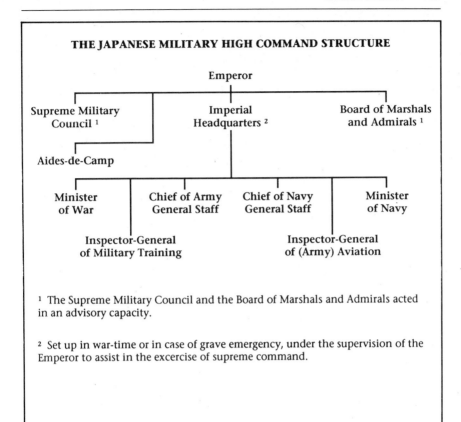

THE JAPANESE MILITARY HIGH COMMAND STRUCTURE

¹ The Supreme Military Council and the Board of Marshals and Admirals acted in an advisory capacity.

² Set up in war-time or in case of grave emergency, under the supervision of the Emperor to assist in the excercise of supreme command.

Japanese Governments from 1932 to 1945

Military involvement in Japanese politics is not surprising when it is noted that nine out of eleven Prime Ministers from May 1932 to August 1945 were generals or admirals. There were, however, thirteen cabinets; Prince Konoye headed three of them.

1927–9: Prime Minister General TANAKA Giichi.
1929–31: Prime Minister Hamaguchi Osachi; shot 14 November 1930 (acting premier Shidehara Kijuro).
1931: Prime Minister Wakatsukuki Reijiro.
December? 1931 to assassination 15 May 1932: Prime Minister Inukai Tsuyoshi.
26 May 1932–4 July 1934: Prime Minister Admiral Viscount SAITO Makoto (Military-dominated cabinet which effectively ended democratic government in Japan).
7 July 1934–March 1936: Prime Minister Admiral OKADA Keisuke.
9 March 1936–10 February 1937: Prime Minister Hirota Koki.
February–30 April 1937: Prime Minister Lieutenant-General HAYASHI Senjuro.
3 June 1937–4 January 1939: Prime Minister Prince Konoye Fumimaro. (First government).

5 January–28 August 1939: Prime Minister General Baron HIRANUMA Kiichiro.
30 August 1939–January 1940: Prime Minister General ABE Nobuyuki.
14 January–June 1940: Prime Minister Admiral YONAI Mitsumasa.
21 June–16 July 1940: Prime Minister Prince Konoye Fumimaro. (Second government). Cabinet resigned but he stayed to form next.
16 July 1940–16 October 1941: Prime Minister Prince Konoye Fumimaro. (Third government).
18 October 1941–18 July 1944: Prime Minister General TOJO Hideki.
22 July 1944–4 April 1945: Prime Minister General KOISO Kuniaki.
5 April–15 August 1945: Prime Minister Admiral Baron SUZUKI Kantaro.
16 August–28 September 1945: Prime Minister Field Marshal Prince HIGA-SHIKUNI Naruhiko.
30 August 1945: American occupation and administration of Japan commences.
October 1945–April 1946: Prime Minister Baron Shidehara Kijuro (first transitional government)

Imperial Japanese Army and Navy Commissioned Officer Ranks

Class	Army Rank	Naval Rank	Japanese Equivalent
Marshal[1] (Gensui) 元帥	Field Marshal	Admiral of the Fleet (Fleet Admiral)	Gensui 元帥
General officer (Shōkan) 將官	General	Admiral	Taishō 大將
	Lieutenant-General	Vice-Admiral	Chūjō 中將
	Major-General	Rear-Admiral	Shōshō 少將
Field officer (Sakan) 佐官	Colonel	Captain	Taisa 大佐
	Lieutenant-Colonel	Commander	Chūsa 中佐
	Major	Lieutenant-Commander	Shōsa 少佐
Company officer (Ikan) 尉官	Captain	First Lieutenant	Taii 大尉
	First Lieutenant	Lieutenant Junior Grade. (Sub-Lieutenant)	Chūi 中尉
	Second Lieutenant	Acting Sub-Lieutenant	Shōi 少尉

Officers of the Army Airforce and Navy Airforce retained their respective army and naval ranks, there being no separate ranking system as was used in the Royal Air Force. The Japanese did not use the ranks of Brigadier, Brigadier-General or Commodore.

[1] An honorary rank bestowed by the Emperor, but rarely awarded. It did not affect the command held.

The Minister of War (who also represented the Army) and Minister of the Navy had to be Generals and Admirals, respectively, on the active service list. If on the reserve list at the time of appointment they had to be reinstated to the active list before taking up either post. Their appointment had to be approved by the Army or Navy Chiefs of Staff. The Army or Navy could prevent the formation of a cabinet or bring about its downfall by failure to nominate a candidate or by instructing either of the Ministers to resign. These ministers were thus an integral part of any government and could strongly influence military policy. The Army and Navy Chiefs of Staff, however, were not allowed to attend cabinet meetings.

Generals and Admirals who became Prime Ministers were normally on the retired or reserve lists but there were exceptions who remained on the active list. General TOJO Hideki concurrently held the post of War Minister and thus had to remain on the active list. Field Marshal Prince HIGASHIKUNI Naruhiko was very rapidly appointed Prime Minister to bring about the speedy Japanese surrender.

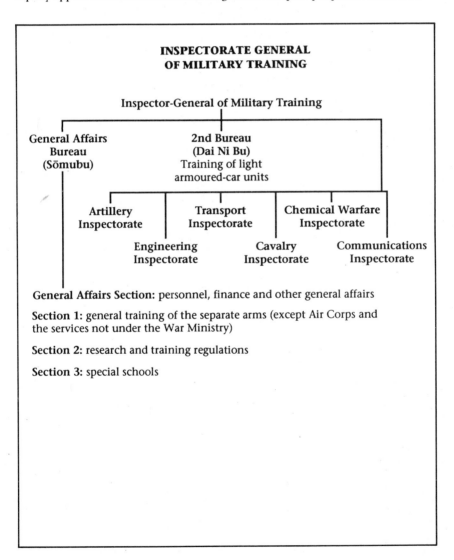

INSPECTORATE GENERAL OF MILITARY TRAINING

Inspector-General of Military Training

General Affairs Bureau (Sōmubu)

2nd Bureau (Dai Ni Bu) Training of light armoured-car units

Artillery Inspectorate

Transport Inspectorate

Chemical Warfare Inspectorate

Engineering Inspectorate

Cavalry Inspectorate

Communications Inspectorate

General Affairs Section: personnel, finance and other general affairs

Section 1: general training of the separate arms (except Air Corps and the services not under the War Ministry)

Section 2: research and training regulations

Section 3: special schools

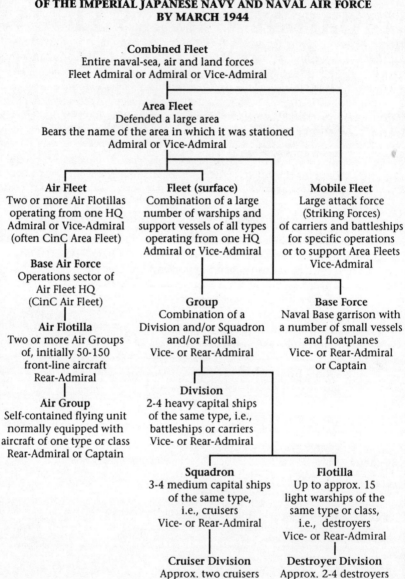

**GENERAL GUIDE TO THE COMMAND STRUCTURE
OF THE IMPERIAL JAPANESE NAVY AND NAVAL AIR FORCE
BY MARCH 1944**

Combined Fleet
Entire naval-sea, air and land forces
Fleet Admiral or Admiral or Vice-Admiral

Area Fleet
Defended a large area
Bears the name of the area in which it was stationed
Admiral or Vice-Admiral

Air Fleet
Two or more Air Flotillas
operating from one HQ
Admiral or Vice-Admiral
(often CinC Area Fleet)

Base Air Force
Operations sector of
Air Fleet HQ
(CinC Air Fleet)

Air Flotilla
Two or more Air Groups
of, initially 50-150
front-line aircraft
Rear-Admiral

Air Group
Self-contained flying unit
normally equipped with
aircraft of one type or class
Rear-Admiral or Captain

Fleet (surface)
Combination of a large
number of warships and
support vessels of all types
operating from one HQ
Admiral or Vice-Admiral

Group
Combination of a
Division and/or Squadron
and/or Flotilla
Vice- or Rear-Admiral

Division
2-4 heavy capital ships
of the same type, i.e.,
battleships or carriers
Vice- or Rear-Admiral

Squadron
3-4 medium capital ships
of the same type,
i.e., cruisers
Vice- or Rear-Admiral

Cruiser Division
Approx. two cruisers

Mobile Fleet
Large attack force
(Striking Forces)
of carriers and battleships
for specific operations
or to support Area Fleets
Vice-Admiral

Base Force
Naval Base garrison with
a number of small vessels
and floatplanes
Vice- or Rear-Admiral
or Captain

Flotilla
Up to approx. 15
light warships of the
same type or class,
i.e., destroyers
Vice- or Rear-Admiral

Destroyer Division
Approx. 2-4 destroyers

Notes:
1. Submarines were under 6th Fleet which was directly under the command of
Combined Fleet.
2. The rank of Commodore was not used in the Japanese Navy.
3. The Japanese word SENTAI means 'Flotilla' and 'Squadron', which implies
that there was no distinction between the two.

Chapter 1.
Japan at War, 1931–45:
A Chronology

1905: Japan defeats Russia and now controls Formosa, Kwantung Peninsula (southern tip of Manchuria) and south Sakhalin Island.

1910: Japan annexes Korea.

1926: Emperor Hirohito crowned. Takes the reign name of *shōwa* meaning 'radiant peace'.

1931:
September
18/19 'Manchurian (or Mukden) Incident. Kwantung Army in Manchuria precipitates military action against China by dynamiting a short section of South Manchurian Railway and blaming it on the Chinese. (Kwantung Army HQ at Port Arthur. Total force 10,400).
19 Mukden in south Manchuria occupied by Japanese after they have bombed it.
30 Japan promises League of Nations that it will withdraw from disputed Manchurian areas (but later they refuse).
November
4 'Nonni Bridge Incident', Manchuria. Fighting between Chinese and Japanese at an important bridge.
18 Japanese occupy Tsitsihar after establishment of government of Liaoning (Fengten) province.
December Kwantung Army strength increases to 64,900 plus a small air force.

1932:
January
4 Occupation of south Manchuria completed by Kwantung Army.
9 Assassination attempt on Emperor Hirohito by Korean nationalist. Chinese official newspaper expresses regret that Emperor was not killed. Japanese community in Shanghai demand official apology. Japanese nationals subsequently attacked and Japanese goods boycotted.
29 Japanese army and naval units bomb Chapei section of Shanghai and then invade. The 'First Shanghai Incident'.
February
1 Nanking shelled by Japanese navy.
5 Occupation of Manchuria extended, including areas recently dominated by Russia.
March
18 Manchuria renamed 'Manchukuo' and becomes Japanese puppet state.

September

15   Japan formally recognizes Manchukuo and forms Manchurian Defence Force under command of C in C of Kwantung Army.

1933:
February

24   Japan withdraws from League of Nations after censure over aggression in China.

March

4   Jehol province, Inner Mongolia occupied by Japanese.

1934:
March

1   Henry Pu-Yi (deposed Manchu Emperor of China) crowned Kang-Te, Emperor of Manchukuo.

December

29   Washington Naval Treaty of 1922 (imposing limitations on British, French, Italian, Japanese and US fleet sizes) declared no longer acceptable by Japan.

1935:
January

18   Japanese and Manchurian troops cross into demilitarized zone between Jehol and Chahar provinces, Inner Mongolia.

May

30   Demand by the Japanese military that anti-Japanese activities in China be stopped.

June

10   China yields to Japanese demands to remove Nationalist forces from Tienstsin and Peking.

1936:
January

15   Japan declares Washington Naval Treaty will be void after 31 December 1936.

September

22   Pakhoi and Hankow invaded by Japanese marines.

November

25   Japan and Germany sign Anti-Comitern Pact (to oppose Russian interference abroad).

1937:
July

7–8   'Marco Polo Bridge (or China) Incident'. Death of a Japanese soldier becomes cause for demand to search Wanping, a suburb of Peking. Chinese refusal leads to Japanese attack across Marco Polo Bridge over Hun River. This precipitates full-scale Sino-Japanese War which lasts, until 1945.

11   Marco Polo Bridge Incident tentatively settled but Japanese implement a huge build-up of their troops in China.

25   Japanese army advances along Tientsin – Peking Railway, capturing Langfang.

30   Tientsin captured by Japanese.

31   Peking captured by Japanese.

August

13   'Second Shanghai Incident'. Commencement of Japanese attack on
            Shanghai, China.

25   Chinese ports up to 800 miles south of Shanghai are blockaded by
            Japanese navy.

September

25   First Chinese victory over Japanese Army at Pinghsingkwan,
            northern Shansi province.

November

12   Shanghai finally occupied by Japanese after 92-day battle.

December

6   Japanese 10th Army and Shanghai Expeditionary Force link up
            outside Nanking.

13   Infamous 'Rape of Nanking' by Japanese army with estimated
            260,000–300,000 Chinese civilians and prisoners of war being killed.

24   Hangchow, Chekiang province, China, occupied by Japanese.

1938:

January

10   Tsingtao occupied by Japanese without resistance.

15   Commencement of continuous bombing raids on Chunking (seat of
            Chinese government).

March

6   Yellow River reached by Japanese.

25   Battle of Taierchuang, southern Shantung province, China. Begins
            this day, lasting two weeks. 16,000 Japanese killed (out of 18,000) by
            Chinese. First major Japanese defeat in modern times.

28   Puppet government of China established under Wang Chang-wei by
            the Japanese at Nanking.

May

15   Chinese forces in retreat after series of defeats in Honan province.

June

10   Massive offensive launched by Japanese Central China Expedition-
            ary Army involving 400,000 Japanese troops to capture Nationalist
            Chinese temporary capital of Hankow.

July

11   'Lake Khasan Incident'. Fighting commences between Japanese
            Kwantung Army and Russians at Changkufeng (near border of
            Manchurian, Siberia and Korea) culminating in humiliating
            Japanese defeat.

October

25   Hankow captured by Japanese.

1939:

May

12   'Nomonhan (or Khalkhyn-Gol) Incident'. Begins this day between
            Manchurian and Mongolian forces which clash on Manchurian –
            Outer Mongolian border. It escalates into major battles between
            Japanese and Russians, again culminating in Japanese defeat.

18   Russians attacked by Japanese 23rd Division on Khalka River on
            Outer Mongolian and Manchurian border. Japanese are victorious.

28   Renewed fighting on Khalka River until mid June but Russians again
            fail to oust the Japanese.

August

20–25   Soviet Far Eastern Army attacks Kwantung Army along Khalka River with biggest tank battle in history (up to this time). Japanese suffer biggest defeat to date.

September

1   Germany invades Poland. Commencement of Second World War.

30   Japanese forces withdraw from Hunan province, south China, after major defeat by Nationalist Chinese army at First Battle of Changsha (which began in August).

October

29   US Military Attaché in China reports 100,000 armed Chinese are supporting Japanese forces.

1940:

May

1   Japanese offensive recommences in western Hupeh province to assert pressure on Nationalist Chinese temporary seat of government at Chungking, Szechwan province, western China.

June

17   Japanese suffer 20,000 casualties in Hupeh campaign.

July

2   Japan conscripts 1,000,000 for military service and almost doubles strength of Kwantung Army.

26   US government commences partial embargo on aviation fuel, iron and steel to Japan.

August

3   Aviation fuel embargo causes Japanese protest to America.

September

22   French Indo-China permits Japanese occupation of all airfields, railways and ports.

27   Tripartite Pact signed between Germany, Italy and Japan to guarantee 10-year military and economic military assistance.

November

30   Pro-Japanese Chinese government and Japan conclude peace treaty at Nanking.

1941:

April

2   End of 17-day Battle of Shangkao, China with major Japanese defeat.

13   Russia and Japan sign 5-year neutrality pact.

21   Foochow, capital of Fukien province, China, occupied by Japanese.

July

21   Military bases in French Indo-China occupied by Japanese.

26   US freezes Japanese assets. Britain does likewise.

28   Japan retaliates by freezing American, British and Dutch assets. Japanese troops land in Indo-China.

September

17   Second Battle of Changsha (capital of Hunan province), China, commences with Japanese attempt to advance in Hunan province.

30   Second Battle of Changsha concludes with major victory for China.

November

6   Japanese Southern Army ordered to prepare for war.

7	Imperial Japanese Navy high command informed of date of Pearl Harbor attack.

December

7	Japanese navy attacks Pearl Harbor, the main Pacific base for the US Fleet (8 December Japanese time).
8	Philippines, Malaya, Siam, Singapore, Hong Kong and Guam, Midway, Wake Islands attacked and bombed by Japanese.
9	Japanese occupy Bangkok, Siam and invade Tarawa and Makin Islands. China at last formally declares war on Japan.
10	British naval force of *Prince of Wales* (battleship) and *Repulse* (battle-cruiser) sunk by Japanese naval aircraft off Malaya.
12	First Japanese landings in Philippines.
16	British Borneo invaded by Japanese.
19	Japanese invasion of Hong Kong commences.
22	Main Japanese force (14th Army) lands in Philippines.
23	Rangoon, capital of Burma, bombed by Japanese. Wake Island captured by Japanese. Sarawak, Borneo, invaded by Japanese.
25	Hong Kong surrenders to Japanese army forces.
30	US and Filipino forces withdraw to Bataan, Luzon, Philippines.

1942:

January

3–12	Third Battle of Changsha, China, results in defeat of Japanese.
16	Burma invasion by Japanese (15th Army) commences.
19	British North Borneo formally surrenders to Japanese.
23	New Britain, New Ireland, Dutch Borneo and Solomon Islands invaded by Japanese.
30	Malaya occupied by Japanese (except for Singapore Island).

February

14–16	Japanese invade Sumatra.
15	Singapore surrenders to Japanese 25th Army (Greatest British defeat in history).
19	Portugese Timor in the East Indies invaded by Japanese.
23	Japanese submarine shells oil refinery on American mainland near Santa Barbara, California.
27–1 March	Battle of Java Sea. Virtually entire Allied fleet sunk by Japanese Navy.
28	Java invaded by Japanese 16th Army.

March

4	Broome, Western Australia, attacked by Japanese aircraft.
8	Rangoon, capital of Burma, captured by Japanese Army.
9	Java capitulates to Japanese.
12	US Army lands large forces at Noumea, New Caledonia.
21	US and Filipino troops forced to defend last stronghold of Corregidor in Manila Bay, Luzon, Philippines.

April

9	British naval base at Trincomalee, Ceylon, attacked by Japanese naval aircraft.
18	First bombing raid on mainland Japan. 'Doolittle' raid on Tokyo launched from US navy carriers.
29	Burma Road into China closed when Lashio, Burma, captured by Japanese.

May

4–8   Battle of Coral Sea. First defeat of Japanese navy by US Fleet with loss
         of one Japanese carrier.

6   Entire Philippines under Japanese control with surrender of
         Corregidor.

8   Myitkyina, northern Burma, captured by Japanese.

15   All of Burma conquered by Japanese army.

31   Sydney Harbour, New South Wales, Australia, attacked by Japanese
         midget submarines.

June

4–6   Battle of Midway. Japanese lose four carriers in major naval battle
         with US Fleet. First naval battle when two fleets are not in sight of
         each other since entire engagement consists of aircraft to ship attack.
         (This is regarded as the turning-point of the war in favour of the
         Allies).

17   Aleutian Islands, US territory near Alaska, invaded by Japanese.

22–23   Japanese 18th Army invades New Guinea, landing at Buna.

August

7   First major offensive by USA with invasion of Guadalcanal and
         Solomon Islands.

9   Battle of Savo Island. Major defeat for Allied naval forces between
         Guadalcanal and Florida Islands in Solomon Islands.

24–25   Battle of Eastern Solomons. Japanese reinforcement transports and
         naval escorts for Guadalcanal defeated with loss of one Japanese
         carrier.

31   Japanese forces in New Guinea forced on defensive.

September

3   Lanchi in China recaptured by Chinese.

October

11–12   Battle of Cape Esperance, Solomon Islands, results in US naval
         victory.

25   Naval battle off Santa Cruz Islands, Solomons.

December

16   British offensive in Burma launched by 14th Indian Division in
         attempt to capture Akyab on Arakan coast.

1943:

January

2   Japanese attempt to take Port Moresby, New Guinea, is stopped.

22   Major Allied victory at Papua, south-eastern New Guinea.

February

18   Japanese complete evacuation of Guadalcanal after six months' fierce
         land and sea battles.

         First 'Chindit' raid. British and Empire troops cross Chindwin River,
         Burma, to fight behind enemy lines.

March

2–5   Battle of the Bismarck Sea. Last Japanese reinforcement convoy to
         Lae, New Guinea, sunk by US naval forces.

13   Japanese forces pushed back across Yangtze River, China, after
         crossing on 8 March.

16–19   British forces outflanked in the Arakan, Burma, and forced to
         withdraw.

April

18   Death of Admiral YAMAMOTO Isoroku, CinC of Japanese Combined
          Fleet in air ambush by US aircraft off Bougainville, Solomon Islands.

May

2   Japanese bomb Darwin, Northern Territories, Australia.

12   British campaign to recapture Arakan, Burma, fails with evacuation
          of Maungdaw.

18   New Japanese offensive across Yangtze River, China, to drive on
          Chungking.

30   Attu Island in Aleutians finally occupied by US troops.

June

30   Commencement of Allied amphibious operations against Japanese-
          held islands in south-west Pacific (Operation 'Cartwheel').

July

5–6   Naval battle of Kula Gulf off Kolombangara, Solomon Islands.

August

25   New Georgia Island, Solomons, occupied by US troops.

September

8   Italy surrenders.

October

3   Japanese Army launches offensive along a broad front in central
          China.

November

2   Naval battle of Empress Augusta Bay, Bougainville, Solomon Islands.
          Japanese reinforcements stopped.

20   US invasion of Tarawa and Makin Islands in Gilbert Islands.

28   Tarawa occupied after bitter fighting.

1944:

January

8   Maungdaw in the Arakan, Burma, recaptured by British forces.

31   Kwajalein in Marshall Islands invaded by US troops. (Captured 4
          February.)

February

4   Major offensive in Arakan, Burma, by Japanese to repell British.
          Hukawng Valley in north Burma attacked by Chinese troops.

10   Truk, Caroline Islands, abandoned as main Japanese naval base in
          Pacific.

15–20   Japanese forces in Solomon Islands cut off by Allies.

19   US troops land on Eniwetok Atoll (cleared by 21st) and Engebi
          Island, Marshall Islands.

March

5   Second 'Chindit' raid. Three brigades of British and Empire troops
          dropped behind Japanese lines in Burma.

7   Operation 'U-GO' to invade Assam, India, launched by Japanese 15th
          Army.

31   CinC of Japanese Combined Fleet, Admiral KOGA Mineichi, killed in
          aircraft crash during a storm off Cebu Island, Philippines.

April

4   Japanese attack Kohima in Assam, India.

17	Japanese launch offensive over Yellow River, Honan Province, China. (Last major Japanese offensive in China.)

May

10	Chinese cross Salween River in force in attempt to take northern Burma.
16	Japanese turned at Kohima. (Limit of Japanese expansion in Burma.)
17	Myitkyina airport, northern Burma, captured by US 'Merrill's Marauders'.
18	Admiralty Islands cleared by US forces.

June

2	Japanese successfully complete offensive operations in Honan province, China, and halt their advance.
16	Saipan in Mariana Islands invaded by US marines.
17	Fourth Battle of Changsha – Hengyang, China. Changsha city, Hunan province, occupied by Japanese.[1]
18–20	Battle of Philippine Sea ('Great Marianas Turkey Shoot'). Japanese fleet loses three carriers and many aircraft, effectively preventing it from carrying out future offensive operations.
22	Japanese 15th Army repulsed at Imphal, Manipur State, India. (Commencement of Japanese retreat through north-west Burma.)

July

24	US troops invade Tinian, Mariana Islands.
25	US marines invade Guam, Mariana Islands.
26	Saipan regarded as secure by US forces. (First campaign where Japanese surrender in large numbers.)

August

3	Myitkyina town, northern Burma, taken by Allies.
4	Japanese capture Hengyang city, Hunan province, China.
11	Guam occupied by US forces.
12	Tinian occupied by US forces.
20	Biak Island, off New Guinea, taken by US troops after three months' fighting.

September

5	Chinese armies link up to open land route between China and Burma.
15	Peleliu Island, Palau Group, invaded by US marines.
22	Ulithi Atoll, western Carolines, occupied and used as major anchorage by US Pacific Fleet.

October

14	Peleliu occupied by US troops.
17	US forces commence landings on islands in Leyte Gulf, Philippines.
20	US forces make major landings in the Philippines.
23–26	Battle of Leyte Gulf, Philippines. Greatest naval battle of the war. Japanese Fleet decisively defeated by US Fleet with loss of four Japanese carriers and three battleships. Japanese naval power completely broken.
27	First *Kamikaze* (suicide aircraft) attack on US naval Task Force off Philippines.

---

[1] This is referred to as the Third Battle of Changsha in *World War II Almanac* by R. Goralski. However that occurred in late December 1941–mid January 1942 (ref: *History of Sino-Japanese War, 1937–45. See* Bibliography).

November

17	Japanese offensive to take Kweiyang, Kwei Chow province, China, on the way to Kunming and wartime capital of Chungking, Szechwan province.
24	Nanning, Kwangsi province, China, captured by Japanese in an attempt to link up with their forces in Indo-China.
25	General retreat ordered for Japanese armies in Burma.
15	Bhamo, north-east Burma, captured by Chinese.

1945:
January

2	Akyab in Arakan, Burma, captured by British Commonwealth forces.
9	US landings at Lingayen Gulf, Philippines.
22	Burma Road to China opened.
25	Japanese China Expeditionary Army ordered to concentrate on defence of coast and north China and discontinue offensive operations in the interior of China.
31	China effectively split in two by Japanese capture of Kukong (Shaokuan).

February

7	Allied air base at Kanchow, China, taken by Japanese.
12	First successful crossing of Irrawaddy River, Burma, by British forces.
19	Iwo Jima Island, Bonin (Ogasawara) Group, invaded by US marines.
25	First fire raids (night bombing) on large Japanese cities by US air force.

March

1	US Forces attack Ryukyu Islands.
2	Corregidor, Philippines, finally recaptured by US forces.
3	Manila, capital of Philippines, taken by US forces after massacres by Japanese naval troops.
4	Important Japanese communications centre of Meiktila, central Burma, taken by British and Empire forces.
9	Remaining Vichy French garrisons in Indo-China attacked by Japanese. Massive fire bomb attack on Tokyo by US air force.
18	First US naval attacks on mainland Japan at Kobe and Kure.
20	Mandalay, Central Burma, occupied by British Empire forces.
21	'Okha' (piloted flying suicide bombs) first used by Japanese against US naval forces.
26	Iwo Jima finally cleared of last Japanese resistance.
28	Burma National Army changes sides and fights for British.

April

1	Okinawa in Ryukyu Islands, invaded by US forces.
5	Russia repudiates Russian–Japanese Neutrality Pact signed in 1941.
7	Battle of East China Sea. Majority of remaining ships in Japanese navy sunk by US aircraft in an attempted suicide attack on the US fleets off Okinawa.
13	Chinese offensives in Honan and Hupeh provinces. Japanese attempt to take Chinchiang.
14–15	Attempted *coup* in Tokyo by Army officers who fear the emperor has recorded a surrender statement.

17	Last major landing by US forces to secure the Philippines (made on Mindanao).

May

2	Rangoon, capital of Burma, abandoned by Japanese.
6	Lord Mountbatten declares Burma campaign effectively over.
8	VE Day, war in Europe ends.
17	Last surface naval battle of the war at Malacca Strait, between Malaya and Sumatra, ends with a Japanese heavy cruiser sunk by Royal Navy.
20	Japanese begin to evacuate forces from Kwangsi province, China, to reinforce home-defence armies in Japan.
26–27	Nanning, capital of Kwangsi province, retaken by Chinese and isolating up to 200,000 Japanese troops from Indo-China.

June

10	Brunei Bay, Borneo, invaded by Australian forces.
12	Visayan Islands occupied by US troops.
15	Chinese advance on a broad front in Kwangsi province, China.
17	Japanese withdraw northwards from south China.
19	Siam invaded from Burma by British Empire forces.
20	All of southern Philippines occupied by US forces.
22	Okinawa declared secure by US forces.

July

12	Japan requests Russia to act as mediator between herself and the Allies.
16	Withdrawal of Japanese troops from Amoy in southern China.

August

3	Last organized Japanese forces in Burma captured or killed.
5	Atomic bomb dropped on Hiroshima.
8	Russia declares war on Japan.
9	Atomic bomb dropped on Nagasaki. Russia invades Manchuria and begins to annihilate the Japanese Kwantung Army.
10	Japan announces it will surrender provided the Allies guarantee the Emperor's person and position.
14	Japan agrees to unconditional surrender.
15	Emperor's surrender broadcast. VJ Day. End of Second World War.
19	Japanese military delegation arrives at Manila, Philippines, to receive surrender instructions.
21	Kwantung Army, Manchuria, surrenders to Russians.
22–29	Japanese military forces in various theatres announce their surrender.
28	First landing by US military personnel on Japanese soil at Atsugi airbase, south-east of Tokyo.

September

2	Japan signs formal instrument of surrender to Allies aboard USS *Missouri* in Tokyo Bay, Japan.
September–November	Fully armed Japanese troops used by European Allies to police various former colonies, such as Indo-China, and to fight Communist nationalist insurgents. Formal Japanese surrenders organized.

1946:

February	Last of formal Japanese surrender ceremonies. Many Japanese troops repatriated to Japan.

Map 1. Timescale of Japanese expansion in the Far East 1895–1945

Chapter 2.
Surrender Ceremonies

AFTER THE SURRENDER proclamation by the Emperor on 15 August 1945, the Japanese armed services began to surrender; in occupied territories they surrendered to representatives of the Allies when they arrived at the numerous Japanese bases, garrisons and headquarters. Since it was impossible to send enough representatives, many units were ordered to assemble at a single location for convenience. In some cases, units on remote islands or inaccessible sites could not be reached for a considerable time. There was also the fear for the Allied officer sent on such a task that the Japanese had not heard of the surrender or would refuse to obey it.

Officially constituted surrender ceremonies were ordered. Initially they were local with a unit commander surrendering to the first authorized Allied officer who arrived. Later, major ceremonies were organized for the official surrender of commanders of Area Armies, Armies and their divisional commanders to high-ranking Allied officers. Only officers of Britain (and designated Empire forces), America, China and Russia were empowered officially to accept Japanese surrenders.

At least four main surrenders were signed:

(a) Surrender of all Japanese armed forces throughout the Far East and Japan, aboard USS *Missouri*, Tokyo Bay, 2 September 1945.
(b) Surrender of all Japanese forces in China, North Indo-China and Formosa at Nanking, 9 September 1945.
(c) Surrender of all Japanese forces in South-East Asia at Singapore, Malaya, 12 September 1945.
(d) Surrender of all Japanese forces in Manchuria, north Korea, south Sakahlin and Kurile Islands at Hsinking, Manchuria, 21 August 1945.

It is estimated that there were approximately 5,500,000 Japanese under arms at the time of surrender (including those on mainland Japan). In China alone there were 1,283,240[1] with 680,879 in South-East Asia.[2]

General MacArthur, Supreme Commander of Allied Powers, thought Japanese officers should retain their swords rather than risk loss of face and possible loss of control over their men. Lord Louis Mountbatten, Supreme Allied Commander of South-East Asia (SEAC) totally disagreed and ordered that all swords be surrendered. This was done in his theatre of operations and soon accepted by American and other Allied commanders who followed suit.

Ceremonies were constituted to sign various local or major surrender documents and/or to hand over swords. In general British (and Empire) ceremonies followed the same procedures. The Japanese officers, wearing swords, were paraded under the watchful eyes of armed British troops with invited civilians present to witness the event. After the disarming order had been read by

[1] *History of the Sino-Japanese War* (see Bibliography).
[2] *The life and times of Lord Mountbatten* by J. Terraine.

the presiding British officer (usually the senior officer commanding the area), the senior Japanese officer was ordered to come forward and place his sword on a table, normally draped with the Union Jack, or present it personally to his opposite number. Any documents were normally signed before handing over his sword. Staff officers, if present, would then hand over their swords. The remaining officers then unclipped their swords and, either singly or in ranks, stepped forward and laid them on the ground or on large mats. The swords were collected and stored under guard until their fate was decided (either destruction or distributed as souvenirs).

At major surrenders, the presiding British officer would allow other senior officers to accept swords from surrendering Japanese officers. Distribution of these trophies was done either at the same time or at special parades when awards could be made to Allied officers in order of precedence, civilians involved in the war effort and then troops from NCOs downwards. It should be noted that swords were not handed over at every surrender.

The following official document is an account of a typical surrender ceremony:

FROM   THE NAVAL OFFICER IN CHARGE, RANGOON.
DATE   20TH. OCTOBER, 1945.
TO   THE COMMANDER IN CHIEF, EAST INDIES STATION.
REF. NO. 194 / 4093 / 239.

SUBJECT.   FORMAL SURRENDER OF JAPANESE
                    NAVAL FORCES, BURMA.

1. The Imperial Japanese Naval Forces remaining in Burma have been concentrated at Mergui, on the Tenasserim Coast.
2. This force, consisting of Port Parties, Landing, Patrol and harbour craft crews, numbers 60 Officers and 913 ratings, is designated the "17th. Naval Guard", which, together with small detachments still at Moulmein, Tavoy and Victoria Point, has been commanded by Captain TSUNEKI CHIYOJI, I.J.N. – the Japanese S.N.O., Burma area.
3. Consequently, as Captain TSUNEKI and his force at Mergui constitute my "opposite numbers", and in view of your signal 29 1048. September (indicating the policy concerning the surrender of swords by Japanese Naval Officers), and my own pending relinquishment of command, I resolved, after consultation with the General Officer, C. in C., 12th. Army, to take the formal surrender of the Japanese Naval Forces in my area on 19th. October.
4. As reported in my signal 17 1454, October, I therefore arranged to proceed to Mergui, with a representative party of 10 officers and 50 ratings of H.M.S "CHINTHE", in H.M.S. "JED", who was about to complete her last voyage to the Tenasserim Coast with Army (including C.A.S. (B)) personnel, mails and stores for the garrison.
5. The G.O., C. in C., 12th. Army, Lieutenant-General Sir MONTAGU STOPFORD, K.B.E. kindly arranged that he be represented by his G.S.O. I, Colonel H. LASH, Rifle Brigade; that the G.O.C. the 17th. Indian Division, Major-General CROWTHER, be represented by Brigadier C. HAYES–NEWINGTON, D.S.O., commanding the Moulmein area, and that an Army Press Officer and Sergeant photographer should accompany the Naval Party – which they did, together with

several other officers with C.A.S. (B) business to transact in Mergui.

6. The two senior officers were of great assistance to me in planning the surrender ceremony, arranging inter-service conferences, and in passing the resulting requirements to the Mergui garrison commander, Lieutenant-Colonel BROCKENHURST, Frontier Force Regiment, by signal.

7. "JED" arrived and anchored at the northern end of the Mergui harbour minefield, eight miles from the port, at 09.30 on 19th. October in accordance with the programme, but the three Japanese landing craft ordered to meet the ship failed to arrive until 1100 – this reported to be due to Japanese misunderstanding of the rendezvous.

The landing party, including a Naval Guard of Officers and 50 ratings drawn from "JED" together with stores and mails, were embarked and landed at Mergui at 1315, where I was received by the Garrison Commander, Lieutenant-Colonel BROCKENHURST, and a guard of honour.

8. The ceremonial surrender parade was mounted at 1415, on a football field at the outskirts of the town. A most suitable theatre, fringed as it is by trees and pagodas and then surrounded, at a distance, by a fair number of the very assorted population.

9. The parade consisted of two guards of honour; the Naval guard provided by "JED" and the Army guard by the Frontier Force Regiment, with Officers and men spectators of both Services appropriately placed.

The Japanese Naval force of some 40 Officers and 800 ratings were drawn up in three ranks along the side of the field, smartly dressed (in both senses) with Officers correctly posted, the Commanding Officer, Captain TSUNEKI, in the centre front, he alone wearing his sword.

10. At 1430, accompanied by Brigadier HAYES-NEWINGTON, Colonel LASH, Commander L. JAMES, R.N., my C.S.O., and Lieutenant Commander R. S. MILLER, R.N.R. the Commanding Officer of "JED", I arrived at the parade.

The White Ensign was broken and I took the salute from and inspected the guards of honour – both of which were a credit to their Services.

11. Proceeding to a table in the centre of the ground, flanked by the senior officers, and facing the Japanese Captain, I delivered the attached declaration and order through an interpreter. Captain TSUNEKI, after a momentary pause and slight shrug, unbuckled his sword, advanced and with correct military punctilio surrendered the sword to me.

12. The Japanese force was then marched smartly past the White Ensign, saluting by sections as they went, and the surrender parade thus ended. Simple as it was, I share the opinion of other senior officers that this ceremony was most impressive and, I hope, effective.

The strict parade ground bearing of the Japanese Naval Officers and ratings throughout the preliminary wait and the ceremony itself is worthy of special comment. There was no outward sign of dejection or realization of utter defeat and, to those who know them but little, they appeared to preserve their usual enigmatical expression – though I observed the Commanding Officer and his two senior officers to be under great mental strain.

13. Introductions to local notables, a drive round the town – to inspect the devastation caused by R.A.F. bombing –, and a tea party given by the Mayor (designate) was followed by talks at Garrison Head Quarters.

The visiting party returned to "JED" by 1900, and that night, in celebration of the occasion, I entertained to dinner a party of 12 officers representative of both Services.

Having disembarked guests, "JED" sailed for Rangoon at 0900, 20th. October.

14. All Japanese Naval officers, with the exception of Captain TSUNEKI, had been disarmed prior to my arrival. I therefore arranged with the Garrison Commander for the Naval swords and dirks thus collected to be transferred to me.

Those totalled 52 swords and 8 dirks of various shapes, sizes and degrees of rank, which I took on charge and transferred to Rangoon.

15. After consultation with the Army Authorities as to their policy adopted for the distribution and disposal of these trophies, I arranged and carried out a presentation of swords as follows:-

A.   To Army Officers, in appreciation of their close
      co-operation in the work of opening and
      developing the Port of Rangoon:-
      Brigadier C. HERBERT. 12th. Army.
         Director of Transport, Burma.
      Brigadier L. WOODHOUSE.
         Commander, No. 1 Area. S.E.A.C.
      Colonel B. HARPER. R.A.S.C.
         Port Commandant, Rangoon.
B.   To H.M. Ships, concerned:-
      H.M.S. "JED", for the ship.
      H.M.S. "JED", Lieutenant Commander R. S.
         MILLER., R.N.R. Commanding Officer.
      H.M.S. "JED", Lieutenant E. S. HUTCHINSON.,
      R.N.R. First Lieut. and Officer of the Guard.
      H.M.S. "BEACON", for the ship.
         Pilot Vessel Rangoon.
B.   H.M.S. "BARBRAKE", for the ship.
         Representing the Boom Defence Vessels
         recently employed at Rangoon.
      H.M.S. "CLEOPATRA", for the ship.
         To commemorate her part in the return of
         H.E. The Governor of Burma to Rangoon.
         (Not yet presented)
C.   To attached Naval Units:-
      Captain K. LYLE., R.N. Commanding Officer,
      Burma R.N.V.R.
      Lieut. Commander A. CAMPBELL, Burma
      R.N.V.R. C.O. Coastal Forces, Burma.
      To the Senior Officers of each of the four Coastal
         Force Flotillas.
D.   To the Heads of Departments and particularly

outstanding Officers of the Port Party.

E.   To Mr. WITCHER, Chairman, Rangoon Port
Commissioners. For the Port Commissioners,
to commemorate the transfer of the Port to
Civil Authority.

N.B.   The detailed list of the presentations in Sections
C. and D. above, will be forwarded.

16. After the above distributions there remain 19 swords and 4 dirks,
graded A. B. and C., according to rank, in equal proportions. These
trophies were set aside and will be taken by me in "JED" to Colombo
for special distribution as you see fit.

(Armament Supply Note attached)

CAPTAIN. ROYAL NAVY.

APPENDIX.
JAPANESE NAVAL SURRENDER AT MERGUI – 19th. October, 1945.
TEXT OF DECLARATION AND ORDER.

I, Captain H. J. MURPHY, R.N. of His Britannic Majesty's Fleet, the
Senior R.N. Officer, Burma Area, have the honour to represent
Admiral Sir Arthur John POWER, the Commander-in-Chief of the
East Indies Station, and through him, Admiral Lord Louis MOUNT-
BATTEN, the Supreme Allied Commander, South East Asia.

2. In that capacity it is my duty to accept from you Captain Chiyoji
TSUNEKI of the Imperial Japanese Navy, the Japanese Senior Naval
Officer commanding the Burma Area, the formal outward sign of
unconditional surrender.

3. Therefore, in token of such surrender, and in open and permanent
acknowledgement of the complete and utter defeat of the Imperial
Japanese Navy at sea and in the air over the sea by the Navies of the
Allied Nations, I order you Captain TSUNEKI to now advance and to
surrender to me your sword.

This ceremony was unique in that it was the only naval surrender to have taken
place in the Burma theatre. Captain Tsuneki's sword is a *kai-guntō* with his family
mon (badge or crest) on the hilt and a shōwa period (post-1926) blade inscribed
'NŌSHŪ SEKI (NO) JU KANEMITSU SAKU', i.e., 'Made by Kanemitsu living at
Seki in Nōshū (Mino province)'. This sword is now in the Ron Gregory collection.

Some Japanese officers, particularly those who were retained in a working
capacity by the Allies, kept their swords until repatriation. Even those who had
assisted in policing (until civil administration had been restored) or had even
fought Communist guerrillas while under Allied command, were still required to
give up their swords to their opposite numbers. This was done at official
ceremonies or through military channels. Often this was accompanied by a letter
from a Japanese officer to his Allied counterpart explaining the history of the
sword and expressing his personal views of its loss.

The following letters are typical examples and indicate the sentiment and
strong feelings of the officers involved no matter what the rank or age of blade
concerned. It is interesting to note that the tone is most respectful and may even
express admiration for the Allied officers with whom they worked.[3]

[3]These and other letters are also published in *Military Swords of Japan, 1868–1945* by Richard Fuller and
Ron Gregory (*see* Bibliography).

Johore Bahru, 8th June 1946.

Brigadier M.S.K. Maunsell DSO OBE,
Commander, British Inter-Service Mission
            to French Indo-China.
Sir,

I have the honour of presenting to you, in fulfilment of my promise of last year, my treasured Japanese sword, which I have cherished during all my campaigns in 1937–45, and which by your sufferance I have retained to date.

An excellent specimen of the eighteenth century Japanese sword-smiths' art, it is not unworthy, I believe, of presentation to a true representative of British Army, who by his highminded conduct and truly chivalrous actions has commanded my highest respect and admiration during the months of our contest in French Indo-China. I am very glad to bequeath my treasured possession to so gallant a gentleman as your good self.

With the kindest personal regard, I remain,   Faithfully yours,
                                                 (signed)
                                                 Takazo Numata,
                                                 Lieut.-General.

Colonel D. S. C. Rossier
Commander Sub-Area Padang
ALF Sumatra
Sir,

Being informed that you have been appointed Commander Sub-Area Padang, I have a pleasure to present you here this sword of mine, and express hearty congratulations for your promotion of rank and position.

The sword I am presenting to you bears the name KANEMOTO, most famously called SEKI NO MAGOROKU which is well authorized by the historians of Japanese swords. This sword was made approximately 350 years ago, and is classified as the later 'old sword'. KANEMOTO is the name of the maker of this sword, and he lived in 'Mino', or the present 'Gifu' prefecture, in central or the most mountainous region in Japan, as one of the most famous sword-makers of that age. It was an age just at the end of long and destructive days of war and conflict.

The shape of this sword is an even bow-curve, and shows a good deal of lustre. The pretty edge-waves are generally called the 'sanbon sugi' (or a variation of three cryptomerias), and they are comparatively narrow in shape. The sanbon sugi is a notable feature of this sword. And an 'old sword' in general, we say reminds us of the dark blue firmament at night of profound peace and silence. I hope that you would appreciate the gracefulness and at the same time severity of the Japanese Samurai spirit seen through the sword. To my regret, however, the scabbard of this sword is more or less delapidated, mostly due to the days of operations as a regiment commander at the Indian and Burmese fronts, but it will by no means lessen the value of the sword itself.

I, the Commanding Officer of the Japanese 25th Independent Brigade, representing the whole Japanese forces in Central Sumatra, wish to send you a word of sincere goodwill, and expect as ever your fair considerations towards the coming various matters concerning our army.

> Sincerely yours,
> (signed)
>
> Kimio Omota,
> Major-General
> Officer Com-
> manding
> Japanese
> 25th Inde-
> pendent Mixed
> Brigade

Padang, Sumatra,
25th March 1946.

This sword is now in the Royal Lincolnshire Regiment Museum.

> Japanese Central Contact Bureau.
> Padang. 15th April 1946.

To: Officer Allied Land Forces
     PADANG. SUMATRA.
NIPPON-TŌ The Japanese SAMURAI SWORD

The swords we are handing over to you here are ones that formerly belonged to the ablest officers in our 25th Independent Brigade. Most of them were made about 250 to 300 years ago in districts where our famous sword-makers lived. They are all precious ones and some of them are those that the great old Japanese feudal lords possessed for themselves, and duly deserve to be a national treasure. For example, the MAGOROKU, the MUTSU-NO-KANESADA, OSAFUNE-NO-SUKESADA, KUNINORI, BIZEN-NO-KUNIMATSU, etc.

From the old Japanese SAMURAI (at present age Japanese Soldiers especially characterised in officers) has respected their swords as their spirits, and it was common for them to make promises 'in the name of their swords', which means they will commit 'Harakiri' suicide, and die together with his sword, his spirit if he should break the promise. They love it and respect it most deeply and solemnly, and make it a rule to keep it always within the reach of their hand. We can well imagine how deep their sorrow was when they at last had to part with them which their ancestors went to war, and with which they themselves had been together all the way through this long war. But nevertheless, since the sword and its owner is traditionally and spiritually one, even though it may happen to part temporarily with his master will safely return to him again in the long run, it is believed.

I, as Chief Negotiator with Allied Officer in Central Sumatra Area, representing all the owners of these forty swords expect from the bottom of my heart that these SAMURAI SWORDS will always be loved and respected by you, their new masters, on behalf of Japanese Officers, their former owners. It needs to be an expert to appreciate the swords properly, but it is a good thing to try to see the mysterious solemnity, its long history and the technical meaning it bears in itself.

We can well say here that the NIPPON-TŌ is one of the first and foremost symbol of the Japanese soldier's spirit.

In reliance, entrusting everything to your high virtue and gentlemanship.

Yours sincerely,
(signed)

(SHIGEMI OHNO, Captain.)
Officer Commanding.
Japanese Central Contact Bureau.

The following Japanese surrenders represent only a small proportion of the total that must have occurred:

Andaman and Nicobar Islands 9 October 1945. Surrender of these islands by Vice-Admiral HARA Tisia, 12th Naval Special Base Force Commander, to Captain J. H. Blair, RNR, and Major-General SATO Tamenori, GOC of 37th IMB to Brigadier J. A. Salamons at Port Blair.

Borneo:
Balikpapan 8 September 1945. Rear-Admiral KAMADA Michiaki, 22nd Naval Special Base Force Commander surrendered to Major-General L. J. Milford, GOC, 7th Australian Division on HMS *Burdekim*.
Bandjermasin 17 September 1945. Major-General UNO surrendered 2,500 troops to Australian Lieutenant-Colonel Robson.
Jesselton 6 October 1945. No details.
Kuching (North Borneo) 11 September 1945. Major-General YAMAMURA, Garrison commander, surrendered to Australian Brigadier T. C. Eastick.
Labuan (South Borneo) 10 September 1945. Lieutenant-General BABA Masao, C in C 37th Army, surrendered to Major-General Wotten, GOC, Australian 9th Division.
Penadjam September 1945. Captain Endo, IJN, surrendered to Brigadier F. G. Wood, OC, 25th Brigade. (Possibly this is related to, or the same as, the Tempadeong ceremony).
Tempadeong 10 September 1945. Rear-Admiral NOMIYA, (Balikpapan garrison commander?) surrendered to Brigadier F. G. Wood, OC, 25th Brigade.
Tenom 15 September 1945. Major-General AKASHI, GOC, 56th IMB (Independent Mixed Brigade), surrendered to Brigadier S. W. H. C. Porter, GOC, 24th Australian Infantry Brigade.

Bonin Islands:
Chichi Jima 3 September 1945. Major-General TACHIBANA Yoshio surrendered Bonin Islands to Commodore J .H. Magruder, USN, on USS *Dunlap*.
Chichi Jima 13 December 1945. Vice-Admiral KUNIZO Morio, surrendered to Colonel Presley M. Rixley, USMC.

Burma:
Abya 30 August 1945. Major Hisanori Wako, Staff Officer to 28th Army surrendered his sword to Lieutenant-Colonel C. N. Smyth, 1/10 Gurkha Regiment.
Mergui 19 October 1945. Captain Tsuneki Chiyoji, IJN, 17th Naval Guard Force

Commander, surrendered the remaining naval forces in Burma to Captain H. J.
Murphy, RN.

Paung 28 October 1945. Swords surrendered to 1/10th Gurkhas at HQ of
Japanese 54th, 55th Divisions, 28th Army by: Major-General NAGAZAWA
Kanichi, Commander of 55th Division Infantry Group; Major-General KOBA
Toba, Commander of 54th Division Infantry Group; Lieutenant-General
MIYAZAKI Shigesaburo, GOC 54th Division; Major-General SEI.C., Commander
of 14th Transport Service HQ.

Rangoon 28 August 1945. Rear-Admiral CHUDO Kaigye and Lieutenant-
Colonel Tomuria Moro, signed local surrender at Government House to
Lieutenant-General F. A. M. Browning, C of S to Lord Louis Mountbatten.

Rangoon 13 September 1945. Major-General ICHIDA Jiro, Vice C of S to Burma
Area Army signed surrender of all Japanese forces in Burma to Brig. E. F. E.
Armstrong at Government House.

Rangoon 24 October 1945. Swords surrendered at ceremony presided over by
Lieutenant-General Sir Montagu Stopford, GOC, 12th Army at Judson College:
General KIMURA Heitaro, C in C, Burma Area Army to Brigadier E. F. E.
Armstrong; Lieutenant-General SAKURAI Shozo, C in C 28th Army to Brigadier
J. D. Shapland; Major-General ICHIDA Jiro, Vice C of S to Burma Area Army to
Brigadier R. I. Jones; plus Major Kono, Colonel Ashikawa and Captain Hiroshi,
IJN.

Thaton 25 October 1945. Lieutenant-General HONDA Masaki, C in C 33rd Army
surrendered to Major-General W. A. Crowther, GOC, 17th Indian Division.

Thaton Last week of October 1945. Possibly same ceremony as last: Lieutenant-
General KAWADA Tsuchitaro, GOC, 31st Division and Lieutenant-General
TAKEHARA Saburo, GOC, 49th Division surrendered swords to Major-General
W. A. Crowther, GOC, 17th Indian Division.

Caroline Islands:
Truk 2 September 1945. *See* Truk.
Ponape Island (Pakin Atoll) September 1945. Surrender to Lieutenant A. C.
Thies, USN, aboard USS *Hyman* of 9,000 army and naval personnel with their
arms.
Woleai (Central Carolines) 19 December 1945. No details.

Celebes:
Menado (North Celebes). No details.
Macassar (South Celebes). Vice-Admiral OSUGI Morikazu surrendered to
Brigadier I. N. Dougherty.
Note *see also* Morotai, in the Moluccas.

China and North Korea:
Nanking 9 September 1945. General OKAMURA Yasutsugu, C in C, China
Expeditionary Army and Vice-Admiral FUKUDA Ryōzō, C in C, China Area Fleet
surrendered all Japanese armed forces in China, North Indo-China and Formosa
to Chinese General Ho Ying-chin, C in C, all Chinese Armed Forces (also present
was American Lieutenant-General A. C. Wedemeyer).

The following ceremonies occurred from 11 September to mid October 1945:

Canton Lieutenant-General TANAKA Hisaichi, C in C, 23rd Army surrendered
23rd Army plus 129th, 130th Divisions and other units to Chinese General Chang

Fa-kuei, C in C, 2nd Front Army.

Changsha Lieutenant-General SAKANISHI Ichiro, C in C, 20th Army surrendered 20th Army plus 64th Division and other units to Chinese General Wang Yao-wu, C in C, 4th Front Army.

Hangchow Lieutenant-General MATSUI Takuro, C in C, 13th Army surrendered 133rd Division and other units to Chinese General Ku Chu-tung, C in C, 3rd War Area.

Hankow C in C, 6th Area Army (probably General OKABE Nosaburo) surrendered 6th Area Army (which included 132nd Division and other units) to Chinese General Sun Wei-ju, C in C, 6th War Area.

Hsuchow Lieutenant-General SOGAWA Jiro, C in C, 6th Army surrendered 65th, 70th Divisions and other units to Chinese General Li Pin-hsien, C in C, 10th War Area.

Kueisui Lieutenant-General NEMOTO Hiroshi, C in C, Mongolian Garrison Army surrendered small number of units to Chinese General Fu Tso-yi, C in C, 12th War Area.

Loyang Lieutenant-General TAKAMORI Takashi, C in C, 12th Army surrendered 12th Army with 22nd, 110th Division and other units to Chinese General Hu Tsung-nan, C in C, 1st War Area.

Nanking Lieutenant-General SOGAWA Jiro, C in C, 6th Army surrendered 6th Army plus 3rd, 34th, 161st Divisions to Chinese General Tang En-po, C in C, 3rd Front Army.

Nanchang Lieutenant-General KASAHARA Yukio, C in C, 11th Army surrendered 13th, 58th Divisions and other units to Chinese General Hsueh Yueh, C in C, 9th War Area.

Peiping (Peking) Lieutenant-General NEMOTO Hiroshi, C in C, Mongolian Garrison Army surrendered North China Special Garrison Force, Mongolian Garrison Army, 118th Division and other units to Chinese General Sun Lien-chung of 11th War Area.

Saigon Lieutenant-General TSUCHIHASHI Yuitsu, C in C 38th Army, surrendered 38th Army and Japanese troops in northern Indo-China to Chinese General Lu Han, C in C 1st Front Army.

Shanghai Lieutenant-General MATSUI Takuro, C in C, 13th Army surrendered 13th Army plus 27th, 60th, 61st, 69th Divisions and other units to Chinese General Tang En-po, C in C, 3rd Front Army.

Swatow Lieutenant-General TANAKA Hisaichi, C in C 23rd Army surrendered 104th Division and other units to Chinese General Yu Han-mou, C in C 7th War Army.

Taiyuan Lieutenant-General SUMIDA Raishiro, C in C, 1st Army surrendered 1st Army plus 114th Division and other units to Chinese General Yen Hsi-shan, C in C, 2nd War Area.

Tsinan Lieutenant-General HOSOKAWA Tadayasu, C in C, 43rd Army surrendered 43rd Army plus 47th Division and other units to Chinese General Li Yen-nien of 11th War Area.

Tsingtao Major-General NAGANO Kameichiro, GOC, 4th Division Infantry Group surrendered to Chinese Lieutenant-General Chen Pao Tsang (and Major-General Sheppard).

Yencheng Lieutenant-General TAKAMORI Takashi, C in C, 12th Army surrendered 15th Division and other units to Chinese General Liu Chih, C in C, 5th War Area.

Formosa: General ANDO Rikichi, C in C, 10th Area Army surrendered 10th Area Army on Formosa (with six divisions and other units) together with the Penghu Garrison Force to Chinese General Chen Yi.

Hong Kong: 16 September 1945. Major-General OKADA Umekichi, Occupation Commander, and Vice-Admiral Ruitaro, C in C, South China Fleet signed surrender of Hong Kong (and surrendered their swords) to Rear-Admiral Sir Cecil Harcourt, RN, at Government House.

Indo-China (South of 16° Latitude): ? 26 August 1945. No details; ? 13 September 1945. No details.
Saigon 26 November 1945. Kempeitai officers surrendered swords to Subahdar Major Chatter Singh at ceremony presided over by Major-General D. D. Gracey, Chief of Allied Control Commission.
Saigon 30 November 1945. Field Marshal TERAUCHI Hisaichi, C in C, Southern Army, surrendered two swords to Lord Louis Mountbatten, Supreme Commander South-East Asia.

Indo-China (North of 16° Latitude): *See* CHINA: Nanking.

Japan
Ominato 10 September 1945. Vice-Admiral UGAKI Kenji, Commander of Ominato Naval Guard District, surrendered to Vice-Admiral Frank J. Fletcher on USS *Panamint*, Ominato anchorage, northern Honshu.

Tokyo Bay 2nd September 1945. General UMEZU Yoshijiro, Chief of the Army General Staff, on behalf of the armed forces, and Foreign Minister Shigemitsu Mamoru, on behalf of the Emperor, signed the Instrument of Surrender with General Douglas MacArthur, Supreme Commander Allied Powers, and nine Allied representatives on USS *Missouri*.

Yokosuka 30 August 1945. Vice-Admiral TOTSUKA Mitsutaro, Commander of Yokosuka Naval District Base, surrendered to Rear-Admiral Robert B. Carney, USN, C of S to US 3rd Fleet.

Java:
Bandoeng? 16 January 1946. Surrender of 540 Japanese troops to 3/5th Royal Gurkha Regiment (approx. 80 swords surrendered).
Batavia October 1945. Lieutenant-General NAGANO Yuichiro, C in C, 16th Army and Major-General YAMAMOTO Shigeichi, C of S to 16th Army, surrendered their swords to Major-General D. C. Hawthorn, GOC, 23rd Indian Division at Div. HQ (Both were immediately arrested and relieved of command). Location unknown, 1946. Major-General MABUCHI Itsuo, replacement C in C, 16th Army, surrendered sword to Major-General Allons, Royal Netherlands Army.

Kairiru and Muschu Islands (off New Guinea): 10 September 1945. Rear-Admiral SATO Shiro surrendered these islands to Lieutenant-General Sir H. Robertson.

Korea (North of 38° lat): Under Kwantung Army. See MANCHURIA.

Korea (South of 38° lat.):
Keijo (Seoul) 9 September 1945. Lieutenant-General KOZUKI Yoshio, C in C, 17th Army, Vice-Admiral YAMAGUCHI Gisaburo, General ABE Nobuyuki, acting Governor-General of Korea, surrendered to General J. R. Hodge and Admiral T. C. Kinkaid, USN, in the throne room of Government House.
Cheju-Do (Island off tip of South Korea) 30 September 1945. Lieutenant-General TOYAMA, C in C, 58th Army surrendered army and naval troops to US 24th Army Corps.

Malaya:
Bahau 21 September 1945. Surrender of 2,500 Japanese troops to 37th Indian Brigade (260 swords were surrendered).
Bentong, Pahang 20 September 1945. Major- or Lieutenant-General TAMOTO surrendered a sword to Lieutenant-Colonel Crookshank, 6th Mahrattas (possibly the same officer as at Raub).
Bidor, Perak 18 September 1945. Lieutenant-General NOMURA, Governor of Perak, and Major-General ODA, Military Commander of Perak, surrendered with 4,500 men.
Ipoe (Ipoh) 16 September 1945. Surrender of a tank battalion with 22 tanks.
Kuala Kangsar 18 September 1945. Surrender of a unit with 19 armoured cars.
Kuala Lumpur 13 September 1945. Lieutenant-General ISHIGURO Teizo, C in C, 29th Army, surrendered all Japanese forces in Malaya (excluding Singapore, Johore, Penang) to Lieutenant-General O. L. Roberts, C in C, 34th Corps.
Kuala Lumpur 14 September 1945. Colonel Aoki surrendered 6,000 troops.
Kuala Lumpur 22 February 1946. General ITAGAKI Seishiro, C in C, 7th Area Army, surrendered a sword to Lieutenant-General F. W. Messervy, GOC, Malaya Command. Lieutenant-General AYABE, C of S to 7th Area Army, surrendered a sword to Brigadier C. P. Jones.
Penang Island 2 September 1945. Rear-Admiral UOZUMI Jisaku, Governor of Penang Island, and Rear-Admiral BAZUDI, Military Commander of Penang Island, surrendered to Vice-Admiral H. T. C. Walker, RN, on HMS *Nelson*.
Raub, Pahang 21 September 1945. Japanese forces surrendered swords to Colonel Cruikshank, 4/5th Mahrattas.
Singapore September 1945. Lieutenant-General NUMATA Takazo, C of S to Southern Army, surrendered to Lieutenant-General F. A. M. Browning, C of S to Lord Louis Mountbatten.
Singapore 4 September 1945. General ITAGAKI Seishiro, C in C, 7th Area Army, and Vice-Admiral FUKUDOME Shigeru, C in C, 10th Area Fleet (on behalf of the subordinate 1st Southern Expeditionary Fleet), signed surrender of Singapore and Johore on HMS *Sussex*.
Singapore 12 September 1945. Surrender of all Japanese forces in South-East Asia to Lord Louis Mountbatten, Supreme Commander of South-East Asia Command, and other Allied representatives at Municipal Council Chamber. Japanese representatives were: General ITAGAKI Seishiro, C in C, 7th Area Army; General KIMURA Heitaro, C in C, Burma Area Army; Lieutenant-General KINOSHITA Bin, C in C, 3rd Air Army; Lieutenant-General NAKAMURA Akita, C in C, 18th Area Army; Lieutenant-General NUMATA Takazo, C of S to Southern Army; Vice-Admiral FUKUDOME Shigeru, C in C, 10th Area Fleet; Vice-Admiral SHIBATA, C in C, 2nd Southern Expeditionary Fleet.
Sungei Patani 8 October 1945. Major-General INOUYE, GOC, 94th Division,

with 1,400 officers and men, surrendered to Major-General G. E. Woods.
Tampoi (Johore State) 25 February 1946. Army Captain Okazaki Tomeiki with
other officers of 37th Army HQ surrendered swords to Major-General Nicholson,
GOC, British 2nd Division.
Kluang 1945. Two General officers surrendered swords to Brigadier D. W.
Jackson of 1st Battalion, the Devonshire Regiment (Possibly they were the GOC
and C of S to 46th Division).

Manchuria (and North Korea):
Harbin 13 September 1945. A surrender to Russian Major-General Shalkov.
Hsinking (Changchun) 21 August 1945. General YAMADA Otozo, C in C,
Kwantung Army, formally surrendered all Japanese forces in Manchuria, North
Korea, South Sakhalin and Kurile Islands.
Jaliho? 19 August 1945. Lieutenant-General HATA Hikosaburō, C of S,
Kwantung Army, negotiated surrender terms for Kwantung Army with Marshal
Alexander M. Vasilevsky, C in C, Soviet Far Eastern Armies.

Marcus Island: 31 August 1945. Rear-Admiral MATSUBARA, Commander of
Marcus Island, surrendered to Rear Admiral Whiting, USN, on US destroyer
Bagley.

Moluccas:
Ceram Major-General KOBORI, GOC 5th Division, surrendered to Australian
Brigadier Steele at Piros Base on Ceram.

Morotai: 9 September 1945. Lieutenant-General TESHIMA Fusataro, C in C, 2nd
Army, signed surrender at HQ of Australian General Sir Thomas Blamey.

Morotai: Major- or Lieutenant-General ICHI formally surrendered all Japanese
forces in the Celebes.

Nauru Island: 14 September 1945. Captain Soeda Hisayuki surrendered 3,700
men to Brigadier J. R. Stevenson on HMAS *Diamantina.*

New Britain:
Rabaul 6 September 1945. General IMAMURA Hitoshi, C in C, 8th Area Army,
and Vice-Admiral KUSAKA Jinichi, C in C, South-East Area Fleet, signed
surrender of armed forces in South-East Pacific area to Lieutenant-General
Vernon Sturdee, C in C, 1st Australian Army on HMS *Glory.*

New Guinea (Dutch):
Cape Wom 13 September 1945. Lieutenant-General ADACHI Hatazo, C in C,
18th Army, surrendered 17,000 troops in New Guinea to Major-General H. C. H.
Robertson.

New Ireland: 19 September 1945. Lieutenant-General ITO Takeo, GOC 40th
IMB and Rear-Admiral TAMURA Ryukichi surrendered swords to Lieutenant-
General K. W. Eather, GOC, Australian 11th Division on HMS *Swan* at Fangelawa
Bay.

Ocean Island:
Mili 2 October 1945. Lieutenant-Commander Suzuki Nahoomi, IJN, surrendered

his sword and all forces on Ocean Island to Brigadier J. R. Stevenson, DSO, on
HMAS *Diamantina*.

Palau Islands:
Pelelieu 2 September 1945. Lieutenant-General INOUE Sadao, GOC, 14th
Division, surrendered to Brigadier General P. Rogers, USMC.

Philippines:
Baguio on Luzon 3 September 1945. General YAMASHITA Tomoyuki, C in C,
14th Area Army, and Vice-Admiral OKOCHI Denshichi, C in C, South-West Fleet,
surrendered to American Major General W. H. Gill, GOC, 32nd Division at
Government House.
Manila on Luzon 31 August 1945. Surrender on USS *Missouri*.

Ryukyu Islands:
Okinawa 7 September 1945. 105,000 army and naval troops in Ryukyu Islands
were surrendered to General J. Stilwell, C in C, American 10th Army by two
Japanese Generals and one Admiral.

Siam (Thailand):
Bangkok 11 January 1946. Surrender of all Japanese forces in Siam to Major-
General G. C. Evans, GOC, 7th Indian Division. The following 22 senior
commanders all surrendered their swords at this time in the order given:
Lieutenant-General NAKAMURA Akita, C in C, 18th Area Army; Lieutenant-
General HANAYA Tadashi, C of S to 18th Area Army; Lieutenant-General
KATAMURA Shihachi, C in C 15th Army. Lieutenant-General KIMURA
Matsujiro, GOC, 4th Division; Lieutenant-General HIRATA Masachika, GOC,
22nd Division; Lieutenant-General TANAKA Nobuo, GOC, 33rd Division;
Lieutenant-General SATO Kenryo, GOC, 37th Division; Lieutenant-General
MATSUYAMA Yuzo, GOC, 56th Division; Vice-Admiral TANAKA Raizo,
Commander, 13th Naval Base Force; Rear-Admiral SATO Katsuya, C of S to 13th
Naval Base Force; Major-General KAMADA Mitsugi, Chief of 18th Area Army
Medical Dept; Major-General OHARA Reizo, HQ 18th Area Army; Major-General
NUMATA Ken, Chief of 18th Area Army Ordnance Dept; Major-General
MACHINO Kazuo, Chief of 18th Area Army Intendance Dept; Major-General
YOSHIDA Gonpachi, C of S to 15th Army; Major-General SHIMAZU Kiyoshi,
Chief of 15th Army Medical Dept; Major-General SATO Gonpachi, GOC 29th
Mixed Brigade; Major-General KOBAYASHI Shigekichi, GOC, 5th Engineer
Corps; Major-General KASUYA Tomekichi, GOC, 2nd Field Transport Corps;
Major-General KOURI Katsuhiro, GOC, Field Railway Corps; Major-General
HAMADA Minoru, Second Superindendent of Railways; Major-General ADACHI
Katsumi, GOC, 4th Special Railway Corps. (Note. This is the largest single
surrender ceremony of senior Japanese Commanders yet located but, strangely,
neither the Imperial War Museum nor Australian War Memorial Museum have
any photographs of this event.
Banpong 25 September 1945. Major-General YOSHIDA Gonpachi, C of S to 15th
Army, and Major-General ADACHI Katsumi, GOC, 4th Special Railway Corps,
surrendered a dirk and sword respectively to Colonel L. M. Coffey, British
Intelligence Corps.
Hadyai (Ha'Adyai) Sword surrendered by an unknown Japanese Admiral to
Major M. Goodall.

Ubon Lieutenant-General HIRATA Masachika, GOC, 22nd Division surrendered
a sword to Major D. de Smiley, Force 136.

Solomon Islands:
Torokina (on Bougainville) 8 September 1945. Lieutenant-General KANDA
Masatane, C in C, 17th Army, and Vice-Admiral Baron SAMEJIMA Tomoshige,
surrendered to Lieutenant-General Savige, GOC, 2nd Australian Corps.
Numa Numa (on Bougainville) 18 September 1945. Major-General KIJIMA
Kesao, GOC, 38th Independent Mixed Brigade, surrendered his sword to Captain
W. Davies, Australian Army, on the *Deborah*.

Sumatra:
Koeta Radja (in Atjek province) December 1945. Major-General INO
Shezaburo, Governor of Atjek province, northern Sumatra, surrendered to Major
Esmond-Jones, CO 2nd Battalion, Durham Light Infantry.
Padang Island 21 October 1945. Lieutenant-General TANABE Moritake, C in C,
25th Army, and Vice-Admiral HIROSE Sueto, Commander of 9th Naval Base
Force, formally surrendered Sumatra to Major-General H. M. Chambers, GOC,
26th Indian Division.
Padang Island 25 March 1946. Major-General OMOTA Kimio, GOC, 25th IMB,
surrendered sword to Colonel D. S. C. Rossiter, Commander of Sub-Area Padang.

Timor: 11 September 1945. Colonel Kaida Tatsuichi surrendered to Australian
Brigadier L. G. H. Dyke on HMAS *Moresby*.

Truk: 2 September 1945. Lieutenant-General MUGIKURA Shunsaburō, C in C,
31st Army, and Rear-Admiral HARA Chuichi, Commander of Truk naval forces,
surrendered 130,000 personnel on Truk and most of Caroline Islands to Vice-
Admiral G. P. Murray, USN, on USS *Portland*.

Wake Island: September 1945. 1,262 troops surrendered to Brigadier General L.
H. M. Sanderson, USMC, on destroyer USS *Levy*.

Chapter 3. Organization of Japanese Armed Forces at the end of the Second World War

THIS CHAPTER is an attempt to tabulate as closely as possible the organization of Japanese army units (from various Brigade types up to Area Armies) at the time of the surrender in August/September 1945.

Because of Japanese military reverses, a number of Divisions and Brigades had recently transferred to commands other than those they had fought under for a number of years. Immediately after the surrender many units assembled together for ease of disarming and thus came out of their normal sphere of control. The time under consideration is one of shifting command structures and responsibilities, consequently it is difficult to document with certainty. The following tables are therefore not necessarily complete and there may be unintentional errors. However, it forms a comprehensive guide for those interested in locating army units during this period. The names and ranks of unit commanders, where identified, have been given. They are those who are known to have surrendered, with the exception of Japan, where they are recorded as being in command in about June 1945.

It has not been possible to determine the organization of the widely scattered units of the Imperial Japanese Navy in such a way as to show some semblance of a command structure, although this information must be available. However, Mountbatten's Report to the Combined Chiefs of Staff — South-East Asia 1943–1945 (see Bibliography) does reproduce the organization of the 10th Area Fleet which came under the control of Southern Army in 1945. This is tabulated at the end of the Japanese Army Forces charts. Although prior to the time under consideration, details of garrisons defeated at Biak, Iwo Jima, Kwajalein, Makin, Okinawa and Tarawa have been included out of interest.

Units listed in the following charts are as follows:

Groups:
China Expeditionary Army; First General Army; Second General Army; Kwan-tung Army; Southern Army; Air General Army; Burma Area Army.

Area Armies: 1, 2, 3, 5, 6, 7, 8, 10, 11, 12, 13, 14, 15, 16, 17, 18, North China.

Armies: 1, 2, 3, 4, 5, 6, 11, 12, 13, 14, 15, 16, 17, 18, 20, 23, 25, 27, 28, 29, 30, 31, 32, 33, 34, 35, 36, 37, 38, 39, 40, 41, 43, 44, 50, 51, 52, 53, 54, 55, 56, 57, 58, 59, Mongolia Garrison, Tokyo Defence, Tokyo Bay Army Corps.

Air Armies 1, 2, 3, 4, 5, 6,

Divisions: 1, 2, 3, 4, 5, 6, 7, 8, 9, 10, 11, 12, 13, 14, 15, 16, 17, 18, 19, 20, 21, 22, 23, 24, 25, 26, 27, 28, 29, 30, 31, 32, 33, 34, 35, 36, 37, 38, 39, 40, 41, 42, 43, 44, 46, 47, 48, 49, 50, 51, 52, 53, 54, 55, 56, 57, 58, 59, 60, 61, 62, 63, 64, 65, 66, 68, 69, 70, 71, 72, 73, 77, 79, 81, 84, 86, 88, 89, 91, 93, 94, 96, 100, 102, 103, 104, 105, 107, 108, 109, 110, 111, 112, 114, 115, 116, 117, 118, 119, 120, 121, 122, 123, 124, 125, 126, 127, 128, 129, 130, 131, 132, 133, 134, 135, 136, 137, 138, 139, 140, 142, 143, 144, 145, 146, 147, 148, 149, 150, 151, 152, 153, 154, 155, 156, 157, 160, 161, 201, 202, 205, 206, 209, 212, 214, 216, 221, 222, 224, 225, 229, 230, 231, 234, 303, 308, 312, 316, 320, 321, 322, 344, 351, 354, 355.

Imperial Guards 1, 2, 3.

Armoured 1, 2, 3, 4.

Air Divisions 1, 2, 4, 5, 7, 8, 9, 10, 11, 12, 13, 51, 52, 53, 55.

Independent Mixed Brigades (IMB): 1, 2, 3, 4, 5, 6, 8, 9, 12, 17, 19, 21, 22, 23, 24, 25, 26, 27, 28, 29, 34, 35, 36, 37, 38, 39, 40, 43, 44, 49, 50, 51, 52, 53, 54, 55, 56, 57, 58, 61, 62, 65, 66, 68, 69, 70, 71, 72, 75, 76, 80, 81, 84, 85, 86, 87, 88, 89, 90, 91, 92, 98, 102, 103, 104, 105, 107, 109, 118, 122, 125, 126.

Independent Infantry Brigades (IIB): 1, 2, 5, 6, 7, 8, 10, 11, 12, 13, 14.

Independent Garrison Units (IGU): 2, 3, 4, 5, 6, 7, 9, 11, 12, 13.

49

Organization of Japanese Army Forces at end of the Second World War

Location	Group	Area Army	Army	Division	No. Divs
Aitape	See Central Pacific				
Amboina	See North Australian Front				
Andaman Islands	See Southern Army Operations (Location 4)				
Betio Islands	See Tarawa Atoll				
Biak Island (off New Guinea) June 1944		2nd Area Army (deactivated 13 June 1945)		Temporary Garrison Commander Lieutenant-General NUMATA Takazo (Southern Army Chief of Staff – left 15 June 1944) Garrison Commander Colonel Kuzume Nasyiki (Committed suicide 22 June 1944) Comprised: 222nd Infantry Regiment Light Tank Company 19th Naval Guard Unit 28th Naval Special Base Force	11,400 men, wiped out June 1944
Batavia, (Java)	See Southern Army Operations (Location 4)				
Bonin Islands	See Central Pacific				
Borneo	See Southern Army Operations (Location 4)				
Burma	See Southern Army Operations (Location 7)				

(Indonesia)	Operations (Location 3)		
Central Pacific (Mandates)	31st Army Formally surrendered to US Forces: Truk, Wake, the Palaus, Mortlock, Mille, Ponape, Kusaie, Jaluit, Maloelap, Wotje, Enderby, Mereyon, Rota, Pagan (4th Fleet Commander surrendered bases of Namorik, Nauru, Ocean Island)	31st Army Lieutenant-General MUGIKURA Shunsaburō (Note: 49th, 50th, 51st, 52nd, 53rd I.M.Bs believed to be in this command area)	52nd (Truk District Group, Caroline Islands) Lieutenant-General MUGIKURA Shunsaburō (Con-currently C in C, 31st Army) 14th (Palau District Group) Lieutenant-General INOUE Sade (Division destroyed on Palau) 29th (Southern Marianas District Group) Lieutenant-General TAKASHINA Hyo (Division destroyed on Guam, August 1944) 43rd (Northern Marianas District Group) Lieutenant-General SAITO Yoshitsugu HQ Saipan (killed with garrison 7 July 1944) 109th (Bonin District Group) Major-General TACHIBANA Yoshio, HQ Chichi Jima (Note: Lieutenant-General KURIBAYASHI Tadamichi, HQ Iwo Jima, died with garrison, 27 March 1945)
Chichi Jima Island	*See* Central Pacific		

Location	Group	Area Army	Army	Division	No. Divs
China	China Expeditionary Army General OKAMURA Yasuji HQ Nanking, Kiangsu province (Note: The 90th and 91st IMBs were also in the China theatre)	6th Area Army (Wide area from Wuchang-Hankow to Hengyang areas)		Under direct 6th Area Army control: 27th 47th 64th? 68th?	
		General OKABE Nosaburō (Note: 22nd IMB and 7th IIB believed to be in this command area)	11th Army (Hupeh province area) Lieutenant-General KASAHARA Yukio	Possibly 34th 132nd 85th IMB 88th? IMB 5th IIB 11th IIB 12th IIB	
			20th Army (activated September 1941 Area between Hengyang and Wunchang-Hankow) HQ Hengyang, Hunan province Lieutenant-General SAKANISHI Ichiro	13th 58th 116th 81st IMB 86th IMB 87th? IMB 2nd IGU	
		North China Area Army General SHIMOMURA Sadamu HQ Peiping (Peking)	1st Army (HQ Taiyuan in Shanshi province) Lieutenant-General SUMIDA Raishiro	114th Lieutenant-General MIURA Saburō 3rd IMB 14th IIB 5th IGU	
		Possibly replaced by Lieutenant-General NEMOTO Hiroshi before surrender	12th Army (HQ Chengchow in Honan province) Lieutenant-General TAKAMORI Takashi	110th 115th? 92nd IMB 4th Cavalry Brigade 6th IGU 13th IGU	

Command	Units
	118th (Tientsin) 3rd Armoured 1st, 8th, 21st IMBs
(Note: 66th? IMB and 2nd, 10th, IIBs believed to be in this command area)	
43rd Army (HQ Tsinan in Shantung province) Lieutenant-General HOSOKAWA Tadayasu	5th IMB 9th IMB 1st IIB 9th, 11th, 12th IGUs
Mongolia Garrison Army (HQ Kalgan on Chinese–Mongolian border) Lieutenant-General NEMOTO Hiroshi	North China Special Garrison Force 2nd IMB 4th IGU
China Expeditionary Army HQ (Note: 6th IIB believed to be in this command area)	
13th Army (Shangai–Lower Yangtze River area) Lieutenant-General MATSUI Takuro	60th 61st 69th 70th 133rd 6th, 62nd, 89th? IMBs
6th Army (Around Nanking) Lieutenant-General TANAKA Hisaichi	3rd 34th (Possibly in 11th Army) 40th 65th 161st? 84th IMB

Location	Group	Area Army	Army	Division	No. Divs
			23rd Army (HQ Canton, Kwantung province) Lieutenant-General TANAKA Hisaichi	Hong Kong Defence Force 104th 129th 130th 131st Hainan Island Garrison Force 19th, 22nd, 23rd IMBs 8th, 13th IIBs	
				13th Air Division also in China	
Formosa	10th Area Army Lieutenant-General ANDO Rikichi (also controlled Okinawa and Ryukyu Islands)	10th Area Army		9th 12th 50th 66th 71st 8th Air 12th, 75th, 76th, 102nd, 103rd IMBs	
Guam	See Central Pacific				
Hollandia	See Central Pacific				
Indian Ocean	See Southern Army Operations (Location 4)				
Indo-China	See Southern Army Operations (Location 5)				
Indonesia	See Southern Army Operations (Location 4)				
Iwo Jima	See Central Pacific				
Japan	5th Area Army (formerly Northern	5th Area Army	27th Army Lieutenant-General	7th (Obihiro, Hokkaido) 42nd (Shinshiru Island)	

Hokkaido, Sakhalin and Kurile Islands

69th IMB

			Divisions	No./Type
First General Army GHQ Tokyo Field Marshal SUGIYAMA Gen (Responsible for north-eastern, eastern and north coast districts of Japan). Sugiyama committed suicide upon Japan's surrender, September 1945 and was replaced by General DOHIHARA Kenji until late September 1945. General KAWABE Masakazu from late September 1945 to deactivation.	**11th Area Army** (HQ Sendai) General FUJIE Keisuke Note: There were two IMBs in this command area (Formerly North-eastern District Army)	**50th Army** (HQ Aomori) Lieutenant-General HOSHINO Toshimoto	157th (Sanbongi) 308th (Shimokita)	2 Infantry
		Under direct control of 11th Area Army: 72nd (Fukushima) 142nd (Yoshioka) 222nd (Kurosawajiri) 322nd (Ogawara)		4 Infantry
	12th Area Army (HQ Tokyo) General TANAKA Shizuichi (March–August 1945) Replaced by General DOHIHARA Kenji (August–September 1945)	**36th Army** (HQ Urawa) Lieutenant-General KANIMURA Toshimichi (Remained as a reserve)	81st (South of Utsunomiya) 93rd (near Chiba) 201st (Kawagoe) 202nd (Maebashi) 209th (moving from Kanazawa) 214th (Utsunomiya) 1st Armoured (near Tochigi) 4th Armoured (Chiba)	6 Infantry 2 Armoured
		51st Army (HQ Mito) Lieutenant-General NODA Kengo Note: There were seven IMBs in this command area (Formerly Eastern District Army)	44th (southern coast of Kashimanada) 151st (east of Kasumigaura) 221st (Ota)	3 Infantry

Note: Japanese home defence known as General Defence Command was deactivated in April 1945 and the District Armies reorganized as Area Armies under General Armies until the surrender

Location	Group	Area Army	Army	Division	No. Divs
			52nd Army HQ at Susui in Chiba prefecture Lieutenant-General SHIGETA Tokumatsu	3rd Imperial Guards (near Naruto) 147th (Ichinomiyu) 152nd (near Yokaichiba) 234th (near Oami)	4 Infantry
			53rd Army HQ Tamagawa in Kanagawa prefecture Lieutenant-General AKASHIBA Yaezo	84th (Matsuda) 140th (Fujisawa) 316th (west of Ischaramachi)	3 Infantry
			Tokyo Defence Army HQ Tokyo Lieutenant-General IIMURA Jo (under IGHQ control)	1st Imperial Guards Lieutenant-General MORI Takeshi (Tokyo) (assassinated 15 August 1945)	
			Tokyo Bay Army Corps HQ Tateyama Lieutenant-General OBA Shihei	354th (Tateyama)	1 Infantry
				Under direct control of 12th Area Army: 321st (Oshima)	1 Infantry
		13th Area Army HQ Nagoya Lieutenant-General OKADA Tasuku	54th Army HQ Shinshiromachi, north of Toyohashi Lieutenant-General KOBAYASHI Nobuo	73rd (Kokubu) 143rd (near Kanesashimachi) 224th (in transit) 355th (in transit)	4 Infantry
		Note: There were three IMBs under this		Under direct control of 13th Area Army:	2

Second General Army	Area Army	Army	Units		
Second General Army GHQ at Hiroshima Field Marshal HATA Shunroku (Responsible for western districts of Honshu, Shikoku and Kyushu)	15th Area Army HQ Osaka Lieutenant-General UCHIYAMA Eitaro	55th Army HQ Shinkai, northern suburb of Kochi Lieutenant-General HARADA Kumakichi	11th (near Kochi) 155th (near Kochi) 205th (near Kochi) 344th (Sukumo and Nakamura)	4	Infantry
	Note: There were four IMBs in this command area	59th Army HQ Hiroshima Lieutenant-General FUJII Yoji	230th (coast of Yamaguchi Prefecture) 231st (Yonago)	2	Infantry
	(Formerly Central District Army)		Under direct control of 15th Area Army: 144th (Wakayama) 255th (Tatsuno)	2	Infantry
	16th Area Army HQ Fukuoka Lieutenant-General YOKOYAMA Isamu	56th Army HQ Iizuka Lieutenant-General SHICHIDA Ichiro	145th (Ashiya) 351st (Fukuoka) 312th (Imari)	3	Infantry
	Note: 4th, 98th, 107th, 118th, 122nd, 125th, 126th IMBs were in this command area	57th Army HQ Takarabe Lieutenant-General NISHIHARA Kanji	86th (Ariake Bay) 154th (Miyazaki front) 156th (Miyazaki front) 212th (Miyazaki front)	4	Infantry
	(Formerly Western District Army)	40th Army HQ Ijuin (transferred from Formosa May 1945) Lieutenant-General NAKAZAWA Mitsuo	77th (Kajiki) 146th (southern Satsuma Peninsula) 206th (Izaku, Western Satsuma Peninsula) 303rd (Sendai front)	4	Infantry
			Under direct control of 16th Area Army: 25th (Kobayashi) 216th (Kumamoto) 57th (Fukuoka)	3	Infantry

Location	Group	Area Army	Army	Division	No. Divs
	Air General Army GHQ Tokyo General KAWABE Masakazu	Air General Army	1st Air Army HQ Tokyo Lieutenant-General YASUDA Takeo	10th Air division (in 12th Area Army area) 30th Fighter Group	
			6th Air Army HQ Fukuoka Lieutenant-General SUGIWARA Michio	12th Air division (in 16th Area Army area) 53rd Air training division	
			5th Air Army HQ Seoul, Korea Lieutenant-General SHIMOYAMA Takuma	Under direct control of Air General Army: 11th Air division (in 15th Area Army area) 51st Air training division 52nd Air training division	

Total Army and Airforce Forces for Defence of Japan 2,300,000 Officers and Men

Location	Group	Area Army	Army	Division	No. Divs
Java (Indonesia) Johore	See Southern Army Operations (Location 4) See Southern Army Operations (Location 4)				
Korea (South)	17th Area Army Lieutenant-General KOZUKI Yoshio (Functioned as a Group until subordinated to	17th Area Army	58th Army HQ Cheju-do Island Lieutenant-General TOYAMA	96th 111th 121st	3 Infantry
(Total forces in				Under direct control of 17th Area Army?:	

Location						Notes
	5th Air Army HQ Seoul Lieutenant-General SHIMOYAMA Takuma (defence of Japan)					*See* Japan
Korea (North)	*See* Manchuria					
Kwajalein (Marshall Islands)						3,500–3,800 troops of 6th Naval Base Force concentrated on Roi Namur. US troops landed February 1944. Only 265 Japanese survivors.
Leyte	*See* Southern Army Operations (Location 2)					
Makin Island (Gilbert Islands)	(Naval Garrison)		Under Commander of Gilbert Islands (*See* Tarawa Atoll)			Attacked by US Forces 20 November 1943. Garrison of 830 men (Only 1 Japanese sailor and 104 Koreans survived)
Malaya	*See* Southern Army Operations (Location 4)					
Manchuria and Korea	Kwantung Army (HQ Hsinking) General YAMADA Otozo (Total forces excluding North Korea, 780,000 men)	1st Area Army (HQ Mutanchiang) defence of East Manchuria General KITA Seiichi	3rd Army (HQ Yenchi) defence of Hsinking-Tumen railway Lieutenant-General MURAKAMI Keisaku	79th 112th Lieutenant-General NAKAMURA Jizio 127th 128th Lieutenant-General MIZUHARA Yoshishige		

Location	Group	Area Army	Army	Division	No. Divs
				Under direct control of 1st Area Army: 122nd 134th 139th	
			5th Army (HQ Mutanchiang) area between Mutanchiang Plain and Tungan Lieutenant-General SHIMIZU Noritsune	124th Lieutenant-General SHINA Masatake 126th 135th	
			4th Army (HQ Tsitsihar) North Manchuria area Lieutenant-General UEMURA Mikio	119th 123rd 149th 80th IMB	
		3rd Area Army HQ Mukden (defence of south and west Manchuria) General USHIROKU Jun	30th Army HQ Hsinking (defence of West Manchuria) Lieutenant-General IIDA Shojiro	39th 125th 138th 148th	
			44th Army HQ Liaoyuan (defence of west Manchuria)	63rd 107th 117th	

Defence Army, being renamed 5 June 1945)

Under direct control of 3rd Area Army: 108th   136th

2nd Air Army

5 Air squadrons

59th
137th

34th Army HQ
Hamhung, North Korea
Lieutenant-General
KUSHIBUCHI Senichi

See Korea (South)

See Korea (South)

17th Area Army
Lieutenant-General
KOZUKI Yoshio
South Korea
(Subordinated to
Kwantung Army 9
August 1945)

See Korea (South)

Marianas	*See* Central Pacific
Moluccas	*See* Southern Army Operations (Location 3)
Mongolia	*See* China
New Britain	*See* South-East Pacific
New Georgia	*See* South-East Pacific
New Guinea	*See* Southern Army Operations (Location 1)
Nicobar Islands	*See* Southern Army Operations (Location 4)
North Australia Front	*See* Southern Army Operations (Location 3)

Location	Group	Area Army	Army	Division	No. Divs
Okinawa in Ryukyu Islands (Defence of April 1945) See also Ryukyu Islands	10th Area Army (HQ Formosa) Lieutenant-General ANDO Rikichi (also controlled Formosa and Ryukyu Islands)	10th Area Army	32nd Army Lieutenant-General USHIJIMA Mitsuru (suicide 22 June 1945)	24th Lieutenant-General AMAMIYA Tatsumi 62nd Lieutenant-General FUJIOKA Takeo 44th IMB Major-General SUZUKI Shigeji (Shigeru) 5th Artillery Command Major-General WADA Kosuke Okinawa Home Guard Okinawa Naval Special Base Force Rear-Admiral OTA Minoru	
Palau Philippines Rendova, Munda, Kolombangara, New Georgia	See Central Pacific See Southern Army Organization (Location 2) See South-East Pacific				
Ryukyu Islands (included Okinawa)	10th Area Army (HQ Formosa) Lieutenant-General ANDO Rikichi (also controlled Formosa)	10th Area Army	32nd Army Lieutenant-General USHIJIMA Mitsuru (suicide 22 June 1945) All 32nd Army Units had been	24th } See Okinawa 62nd } 28th (in Sakishima Group) 45th IMB 59th IMB 60th IMB	3 Infantry

Operations (Location 6)				3 Infantry
South-East Pacific (included New Britain, New Ireland, Bougainville in Solomons)	8th Area Army (HQ Rabaul, New Britain) General IMAMURA Hitoshi	8th Area Army		
		17th Army (HQ Bougainville, Solomon Islands) Lieutenant-General KANDA Masatane	6th (in Bougainville) Lieutenant-General AKINAGA Tsutomi	
			17th (in New Britain) Lieutenant-General SAKAI Yasushi	
			38th (in New Britain)	
			38th IMB (in Bougainville) Major-General KIJIMA Kesao	
			40th IMB (in New Ireland) Lieutenant-General ITO Takeo	
			65th IMB (in New Britain)	
		(Note: 39th IMB believed to be in this command area)		
			'Nanto' (south-east) Detachment (New Georgia) Major-General SASAKI Minoru (Unit destroyed by October 1943)	
Operations Controlled by Southern Army:	Southern Army (HQ Saigon, 1,500 men) Field Marshal Count TERAUCHI Hisaichi			
(1) New Guinea		2nd Area Army (deactivated 13 June 1945)		
		18th Army Lieutenant-General ADACHI Hatazo	20th (Aitape, New Guinea) Lieutenant-General NAKAI Masutaro	
			41st (New Guinea) Lieutenant-General MANO Goro	
			51st (Hollandia, New Guinea) Lieutenant-General NAKANO Hidemitsu	

Location	Group	Area Army	Army	Division	No. Divs
(2) Philippine Islands		14th Area Army (Promoted from 14th Army status, August 1944) General YAMASHITA Tomoyuki (Note: 61st IMB believed to be in this command area)	Southern Area: 35th Army HQ Cebu (defended southern half of Philippines area. Area south of Masbate and Panay Islands) Lieutenant-General MOROZUMI Gyosaku (from June 1945)	16th (Leyte) Lieutenant-General MAKINO Shiro; 30th (Cagayan on Mindanao); 100th (Davao on Mindanao) Lieutenant-General MOROZUMI Gyosaku; 1st Lieutenant-General KATAOKA Kaoru; 102nd (Visayas) Lieutenant-General FUKUEI Shinpei; 26th Lieutenant-General YAMAGATA Kurihanao; 54th IMB (Zamboagna on Mindanao); 55th IMB (Jolo Islands); 68th IMB Major-General KURUSU Takeo	
			Northern Area (Luzon): As from December 1944 the northern area was split into three groups: 'Shobu' Group (Northern Luzon) General YAMASHITA Tomoyuki, 14th Area Army Commander, took personal control	23rd (Lingayen Gulf sector – arrived end of November 1944); 58th IMB (Lingayen Gulf sector); 10th (San Jose sector)	152,000

		103rd (Aparri sector) 19th (San Fernando area)	
	'Kembu' Group (West of Clark Field) Lieutenant-General TSUKADA Rikichi	1st Raiding Group Lieutenant-General TSUKADA Rikichi One Regiment of 10th Division (39th Infantry Reg?) 2nd Mobile Infantry Naval Combat and Service Troops (15,000 men)	30,000 men
	41st Army ('Shimbu' Group – East of Manila) Lieutenant-General YOKOYAMA Shizuo	8th Lieutenant-General YOKOYAMA Shizuo 105th Manila Naval Defence Force (16,000 men – committed atrocities) Rear-Admiral IWABUCHI Sanji	80,000 men
	4th Air Army (whole of Philippines) Lieutenant-General TOMINAGA Kyoji (Rendered ineffective by April 1945)	2nd Air 4th Air	
(3) North Australian Front	2nd Army HQ near Macassar in the Celebes Lieutenant-General TESHIMA Fusataro (2nd Army remained responsible for garrison	5th (Ceram-Aru-Ambon) 32nd (Halmahera) 35th (Western New Guinea) 36th (Western New Guinea) 57th IMB (Northern Celebes)	

Location	Group	Area Army	Army	Division	No. Divs
	Southern Army (Cont.)		duties after deactivation of 2nd Area Army on 13 June 1945)	The following were transferred to 2nd Army Command from 7th Area Army after the ceasefire: 37th Army (Borneo) Lieutenant-General BABA Masao 48th Div. (Timor & Lesser Sundas) Lieutenant-General YAMADA Kunitaro	
(4) Indian Ocean:		7th Area Army (HQ Singapore – moved to Rengam after surrender) Lieutenant-General ITAGAKI Seishiro			
Borneo			37th Army (South Borneo)[1] Lieutenant-General BABA Masao	56th IMB (North Borneo) Major-General AKASHI 71st IMB (South Borneo) Major-General YAMAMURA H	
Java			16th Army (HQ Batavia) Lieutenant-General NAGANO Yuichiro until about October 1945; Major-General MABUCHI Itsuo from about October 1945	48th (Timor and Lesser Sundas) Lieutenant-General YAMADA Kunitaro[1] 27th IMB (Bandoeng) 28th IMB (Surabaya) Major-General IWABE Shigeo	
Sumatra			25th Army (HQ Fort de Kock) Lieutenant-	2nd Imperial Guards (Medan) 25th IMB (Padang) – Major-	

Johore)	to 2nd Army command after the ceasefire)	ISAGORO Teizo (Reinforced by 37th Division, but the bulk was still in Bangkok, Siam)	35th IMB (Port Blair, Andaman Islands) 36th IMB (Car Nicobar, Nicobar Islands) 37th IMB (Camorta, Nicobar Islands) Major-General SATO Tamenori 70th IMB (Kuala Kangsar)
Johore	(The unit marked[2] was under direct command of 7th Area Army)		Under direct control of 7th Area Army: 26th IMB (Singapore) 46th IMB (Kluang) Possibly Lieutenant-General KOKUBU Shinshichiro
	3rd Air Army (HQ Singapore) Lieutenant-General KINOSHITA Bin		5th Air (Phom Penh, Cambodia) Lieutenant-General HATTORI 7th Air (Malang) 9th Air (Palembang, Sumatra) 55th Air (Singapore)
(5) Indo-China (Note: for the surrender, the Allies split Indo-China along Latitutde 16° with units in the north (marked[3])		38th Army HQ Saigon Lieutenant-General TSUCHIHASHI Yuitsu	2nd (less detachment; HQ Saigon – 8,000 men) Lieutenant-General MANAGI Keishin 21st (Hanoi. Surrendered at Haiphong)[3] 55th (Phnom Penh) Lieutenant-General SAKUMA Takenobu 22nd – Portion only surrendered at Haiphong[3]

Location	Group	Area Army	Army	Division	No. Divs
surrendering to the Chinese and those in the south to SEAC)				34th IMB (Tourane, Vietnam)[3] 2,500 Naval personnel in Saigon	
(6) Siam (Thailand)		18th Area Army (activated July 1945) Lieutenant-General NAKAMURA Akito (Known as 39th Army until July 1945) HQ Bangkok (The unit marked[4] was technically under 29th Army command, Malaya)		4th less detachment (Lampang) Lieutenant-General KIMURA Matsujiro (Placed under 15th Army command) 22nd (Bangkok)—surrendered (less a portion) at Ubon Lieutenant-General HIRATA Masachika 37th (Nakon Nayok) Lieutenant-General SATO Kenryo[4] 29th IMB (Prachuap Khirikan) Major-General SATO Gonpachi 1st Air Service Corps Bangkok Garrison	
(7) Burma		Burma Area Army (HQ Moulmein) General KIMURA Heitarō	15th Army (Lampang, Siam) Lieutenant-General KATAMURA Shihachi[5]	15th (Kanchanabari, Siam)[5] 33rd (Nakon Pathom, Siam) Lieutenant-General TANAKA Nobuo[5] 56th (Khunyuam, Siam) Lieutenant-General MATSUYAMA Yuzo[5]	
		(Units marked[5] retreated from Siam into Siam and came under 18th	28th Army (Paung, Burma) Lieutenant-General	54th Lieutenant-General MIYAZAKI Shigesaburō 55th (HQ only – see 38th Army)	

General HONDA Masaki			18th (Kyaikto, Burma) Lieutenant-General NAKA Eitaro 49th (Thaton, Burma) Lieutenant-General TAKEHARA Saburō 53rd (Kaywe, Burma) Lieutenant-General HAYASHI Yoshihide Detachments from 2nd and 4th 105th IMB (Thaton, Burma) Lieutenant-General MATSUI Hideji Under direct control of Burma Area Army: 24th IMB (Thanbyuzayat, Burma) 72nd IMB (Hnipadaw, Burma) Major-General YAMAMOTO Tsunoru
Sumatra (Indonesia)	*See* Southern Army Operations (Location 4)		
Tarawa Atoll (Betio Island) in Gilbert Islands	(Naval Garrison)	Commander of Gilbert Islands Rear-Admiral SHIBASAKI Keiji (killed 21 or 24 November 1943 on Betio Island Tarawa Atoll)	Sasebo 7th Special Naval Landing Force (1,497 men) Commander Sugai Takeo 3rd Naval Base Force (1,122 men) 11th Pioneers (1,246 men) 4th Fleet Construction Engineers (970 men) (US forces attacked Tarawa, 21 November 1943. Only 17 Japanese and 129 Koreans survived)

Location	Group	Area Army	Army	Division	No. Divs
Thailand	See Southern Army Operations (Location 6)				
Timor	See North Australian Front				
Tinian Island (Marianas)				5th Infantry Regiment Colonel Ogata Keishi (killed July or August? 1944) (US forces attacked Tinian, 24 July 1944)	
Truk	See Central Pacific				
Visayas	See Southern Army Operations (Location 2)				

ORGANIZATION OF THE IMPERIAL JAPANESE NAVY IN SOUTH-EAST ASIA, AUGUST 1945

SOUTHERN ARMY (Saigon) - Field Marshal Count TERAUCHI Hisaichi

10th AREA FLEET (Singapore) - Vice-Admiral FUKUDOME Shigeru

1st Southern Expeditionary Fleet
Vice-Admiral FUKUDOME Shigeru
(Singapore)

2nd Southern Expeditionary Fleet
Vice-Admiral SHIBATA
(Surabaya, Java)

13th Naval Air Fleet
(Singapore)

9th Base Force
(Sabang, Sumatra)
Rear-Admiral
HIROSE Sueto

10th Special
Base Force
(Singapore)

11th Special
Base Force
(Saigon, Indo-China)

12th Special
Base Force
(Port Blair,
Andaman Islands)

13th Base Force
(Bangkok, Siam)
Rear-Admiral
TANAKA Raizo

15th Special
Base Force
(Penang, Malaya)

17th Naval
Guard Force
(Mergui, Burma)
Captain

SOUTHERN ARMY
CinC Field Marshal TERAUCHI Hisaichi

BURMA AREA ARMY
(Formed March 1943)
1. CinC Lt-Gen KAWABE Masakazu (from formation-30 August 1944)
1a. CofS Lt-Gen NAKA Eitaro (from formation-30 August 1944)
2. CinC Lt-Gen KIMURA Hyotaro (30 August/early September 1944-end of war)
2a. CofS Lt-Gen TANAKA Shinichi (30 August/early September 1944-May 1945)
2b. CofS Lt-Gen SHIDEI Tsunamasa (c. May 1945-killed 18 August 1945)

5th AIR DIVISION
1. GOC Maj-Gen TAZOE Noboru
2. GOC Lt-Gen HATTORI

under direct command of
BURMA AREA ARMY

49th Division
Stategic reserve
Arrived July 1944
Transferred to 33rd Army, March 1945

2nd Division
Stategic reserve
Transferred from 28th Army, May 1944
Transferred to 38th Army, French Indo-China, January/February 1945

105th Independent Mixed Brigade
Formed to defend Rangoon, April 1945
Transferred to 33rd Army by August/September 1945

33rd ARMY
Formed April 1944
1. CinC Lt-Gen HONDA Masaki (from formation-end of war)
1a. CofS Maj-Gen KATAKURA Tadashi (from formation-late 1944)
1b. CofS Maj-Gen YAMAMOTO Seiei (late 1944-December 1944/January 1945?)
1c. CofS Maj-Gen SAWAMOTO Rikichi (January 1945-end of war)

18th Division
Transferred from 15th Army, April or May 1944-end of war
(Last GOC Lt-Gen NAKA Eitaro)

53rd Division
Formed April/May 1944-end of war
(Last GOC Lt-Gen HAYASHI Yoshihide)

56th Division
Transferred from 15th Army, April or May 1944
Transferred back to 15th Army, July/August 1945

28th ARMY
Formed late 1943 or January 1944 for defence of Arakan
1. CinC Lt-Gen SAKURAI Shōzō (from formation-end of war)
1a. CofS Maj-Gen IWAKURO Hideo (from formation-end of war)

55th Division
Transferred from 15th Army, November? 1943
Transferred to 38th Army, Indo-China by August 1945 (HQ only remained in Burma)
(Last GOC Lt-Gen SAKUMA Takenobu)

54th Division
Arrived January 1944-end of war
(Last GOC Lt-Gen MIYAZAKI Shigesaburō)

2nd Division
Arrived February/March 1944-end of war
Transferred to direct B.A.A. command, May 1944

15th ARMY *
Formed for invasion of Burma-January 1942
1. CinC Lt-Gen IIDA Shojiro (from formation-March 1943)
1a. CofS Maj-Gen ISAYAMA Haruki (from formation?-March 1943)
2. CinC Lt-Gen MUTAGUCHI Renya (March 1943-30 August 1944)
2a. CofS Maj-Gen OBATA Nobuyoshi (March, April or May 1943)
2b. CofS Maj-Gen KUNOMURA Todai (April or May 1943-30 August/early September 1944)
3. CinC L-Gen KATAMURA Shihachi (30 August/early September 1944-end of war)
3a. CofS Maj-Gen YOSHIDA Gonpachi (September? 1944-end of war)

33rd Division *
From invasion of Burma, January 1942 Attacked Imphal from south, 1944
(Last GOC Lt-Gen TANAKA Nobuo)

55th Division
From invasion of Burma,
January 1942-end of war
Transferred to 28th Army,
Siam, November 1943

18th Division
Arrived at Rangoon,
March/April 1942-end of war
Transferred to 33rd Army,
April or May 1944

56th Division *
Arrived at Rangoon,
March/April 1942
Transferred to 33rd Army,
April or May 1944
Transferred back to 15th Army,
July/August 1945
(Last GOC Lt-Gen MATSUYAMA Yuzo)

31st Division
Ordered to Burma, 17 June 1943
but delayed in Siam until late 1943?
Northern column in Kohima attack, 1944
Transferred to 33rd Army by August 1945

15th Division *
Arrived in Burma, 1944
Attacked Kohima from south
and Imphal from north, 1944

72nd Independent Mixed Brigade
Formed December 1944
Came under 55th Division control
Transferred to direct B.A.A. command
by August 1945

49th Division
Transferred from B.A.A. control,
March 1945-end of war
(Last GOC Lt-Gen TAKEHARA Saburo)

31st Division
Transferred from 15th Army
by August 1945
(Last GOC Lt-Gen KAWADA Tsuchitaro)

24th Independent Mixed Brigade
Transferred to direct B.A.A. command
by August 1945

105th Independent Mixed Brigade
Transferred from direct B.A.A. command
by August/September 1945
(Last GOC Lt-Gen MATSUI Hideji)

72nd Independent Mixed Brigade
Transferred from 28th Army
by August 1945
(Last GOC probably
Maj-Gen YAMAMOTO Tsunoru)

24th Independent Mixed Brigade
Transferred from 33rd Army
by August 1945

Note:
National units assisting Japanese:
INDIAN NATIONAL ARMY
Took part in Kohima-Imphal campaign, 1
(Commander Subhas Chandra Bose)
BURMA NATIONAL ARMY
Affiliated to 55th Division during
initial invasion of Burma, January 1942
Changed sides and joined British,
28 March 1945
(Last commander Aung San)

* 15th Army HQ, 15th,33rd & 56th Divisions
were transferred to 18th Area Army command
after retreating into Siam, August/September 1945

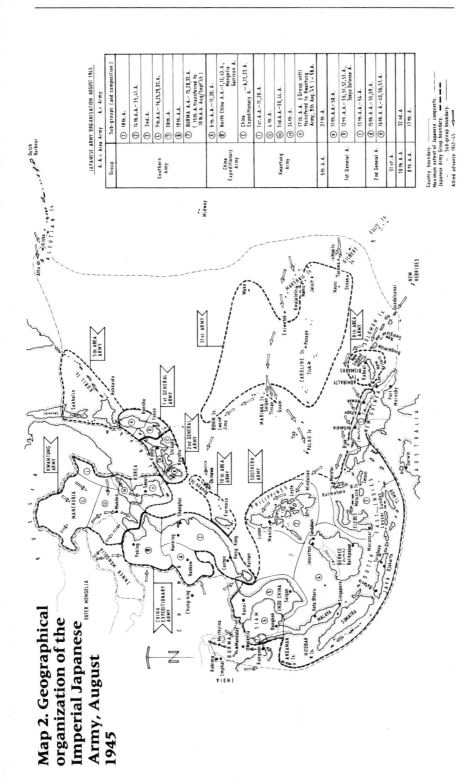

Map 2. Geographical organization of the Imperial Japanese Army, August 1945

JAPANESE ARMY ORGANISATION AUGUST 1945		
Group	\multicolumn{2}{l}{Sub-groups (and composition)}
Southern Army	①	18th A.
	②	14th A.A.—35,41.A.
	③	2nd A.
	④	7th A.A.—16,25,29,37.A.
	⑤	38th A.
	⑥	18th A.A.
	⑦	BURMA A.A.—15,28,33.A. (15th A.transferred to 18 th A.A Aug/Sept'45)
China Expeditionary Army	⑧	6 th.A.A.—11,20. A.
	⑨	North China A.A.—1,12 A.A., Mongolia Garrison A.
	⑩	China Expeditionary A.— 6,13,23. A.
Kwantung Army	⑪	1st. A.A.—11,20. A.
	⑫	4 th. A.
	⑬	3rd A.A.—30, 44. A.
	⑭	17th .A. A. (Group until transferred to Kwantung Army, 5th Aug,'45)—5B.A.
5th. A.A.	⑮	27th A.
1st General A.	⑯	11th A.A.—50 A.
	⑰	12th.A.A.—36,51,52,53. A., Tokyo Defence A.
2nd General A.	⑱	13th A.A.—54. A.
	⑲	15th A.A.—55,59.A.
	⑳	16th A. A.—40,56,57.A.
31st.A.		
10th.A.A.		
8th.A.A.		32 nd. A.
		17th A.

A.A.= Area Army   A.= Army

Country boundary. ···········
Maximum extent of Japanese conquests. ————
Japanese Army Group boundary. ————
Sub-group boundary. ————
Allied advance 1943–45. ⟹

**Map 3. Disposition of the Japanese Army in China
prior to official surrender, 9 September 1945, and in
Manchuria prior to Soviet invasion, 8 August 1945**

Map 4. Assembly Areas of Japanese forces for formal surrender to Chinese, from 11 September to mid-October 1945

Chapter 4.
Biographical Details

THE JAPANESE LANGUAGE is comprised of thousands of Chinese ideographs (*kanji*). Each character may have several meanings and readings. Each name normally consists of two such characters, but in some cases, more. It is usually accepted that two characters used in combination as a name may be read in a commonly accepted form but variations from the norm occur.

The personal name of an adult Japanese male is almost never spoken and even good friends use formal address, prefixing the surname with 'Mr'. A man's parents would obviously know the intended meaning of the ideographs they had chosen for a name, but friends or associates may not. Even in later life it may not be clear. For example TOJO Hideki was listed as TOJO Eiki, and TADA Hayao is often given as TADA Shun.

During the Second World War captured Japanese documents were translated for Intelligence purposes by Japanese-speaking westerners or American 'nisei' (second-generation American–Japanese). They would give an officer's name in the way they thought was the most likely romanized (English) reading. The same name occurring elsewhere and translated by another person could be given a different reading either wholly or in part. Such variations can thus be found in post-war English language military histories or campaign reports which, in turn, leads to confusion when several such references are consulted. Strange spellings are also found which do not appear in romanized names. Often they cannot be corrected without access to the original *kanji*. Examples encountered are FUPRUDZO, OKUVA, TIDZYAKI.

The most common name forms encountered, rightly or wrongly are given as the main entries in the indexes with variations in surnames or forenames given in parenthesis. Sometimes just a simple spelling difference accounts for a different name, e.g., IMAI, IMAYE; FUJIE, FUJII; YANAGIDA, YANAGITA; MINAKAMI, MIZUKAMI. Such differences often occur because written English attempts to reproduce the sounds of Japanese words using the Roman alphabet, and different authors use different spellings, e.g., HARA, WARA or RYU, RIU.

There is also confusion over male personal names and surnames since they sound totally indistinguishable to an English speaker. The Japanese put the surname first and personal name last. However a number of English-speaking writers have apparently assumed the last name must be a surname and thus entered it in their works. For example ANAN Tadaki is incorrect since TADAKI is the surname. The reader is thus advised to look under both names in these indexes if in doubt. Complications have arisen when both names could be used for surnames. Without a second name being given, problems can arise in identifying unit commanders. For example eight generals with the surname YAMAMOTO are listed. Even with a location it is often difficult especially if the rank given is non-specific. For example one often sees a reference to General YAMAMOTO in Burma. There were in fact at least two who played important parts in the Burma campaign: Major-General YAMAMOTO Seiei, Chief of Staff to 33rd Army, and Major-General YAMAMOTO Tsunoru, Infantry Group commander of 33rd Division. In this instance both unit designations are '33' which in itself can present further difficulties.

Information given may be fragmentary and may also lead to unintentional duplication of entries. If a reference is found to officers with the same or similar name at widely spaced dates and different locations and commands, they will be given separately unless corroborating evidence has been located to confirm the same identity.

Dates given are, where possible, those when the post or command was assumed. In full biological entries these may be correct, but in fragmentary entries they may represent the date when the officer was engaged in that particular appointment. There may also be unintentional gaps between two posts when an officer assumed a, so far, unrecorded position.

Cross-indexing of names has also been utilized, whenever possible, to assist the reader in following leadership changes of a particular command or isolating participants involved in particular campaigns.

The variation in naval terminology creates problems in quantifying and identifying individual units or forces. For example the terms flotilla, squadron, division or group are often used by different historians for the same unit of warships in a particular battle or fleet. The correct term may only be clarified when the unit commander is known. Similarly the use of the terms escort, support, guard or covering force can create problems when attempting to clarify the composition of fleet units given by different references for the same force.

It has not always been possible to rationalize such terms in the biographical details of admirals, and apologies are offered where this seems apparent.

It is often thought that all Japanese, especially senior officers, were cruel and callous to Allied prisoners and, indeed, even their own men. Some were humane in their way, given the restraints of indoctrination, tradition and regulations. Often they were overwhelmed by the sheer number of prisoners suddenly delivered into their hands by the Allied collapse in 1942. Those accused of war crimes and crimes against humanity were tried by Allied tribunals throughout the Far East and sentenced accordingly. There is now not much doubt that at least two senior generals (HONMA Masaharu and YAMASHITA Tomoyuki) were tried and executed as scapegoats to placate General MacArthur and American opinion of the time. The number of Japanese tried for war crimes was relatively small in comparison to the number of Germans charged.

In comparison it may be noted that no member of the Imperial family was tried for war crimes. For example Field Marshal Prince NASHIMOTO Morimasa was held for a time as a suspected war criminal but then released, and Lieutenant-General Prince ASAKA Yasuhiko, who apparently ordered the massacre at Nanking, was never charged with any crime. The Supreme Commander of the Japanese Armed Forces, Emperor Hirohito, was never charged with waging an aggressive war or crimes against humanity despite demands from many Allied parties. It is certainly arguable that the Emperor was not a passive figurehead and, in fact, supported the war effort with full control of the main strategy movements and attacks which he ratified at imperial conferences. He had absolute power, if he cared to exercise it, to prosecute or stop the war at any time by imperial decree. He also failed to ensure the protection and well-being of Allied prisoners of war.

The refusal to indict was directly attributable to General Douglas MacArthur who was Military Governor of Japan during the American occupation. He met the

Emperor and, so it was reported, came to respect him. The American prosecutor at the International Military Tribunal for the Far East war crimes trials was instructed to ensure that the Emperor had not been implicated and, indeed, attempted to elicit statements from those on trial that Hirohito was not in any way to blame for the outbreak and prosecution of the war. This did not meet with the success hoped for and was almost undermined by the testimony of TOJO Hideki who refused to confirm it.

The reason for MacArthur's decision was probably due to a fear of unfavourable Japanese reaction and possible rebellion if the throne were threatened. The status of the Emperor was ensured as part of Japan's acceptance of the surrender. Members of the Imperial family were presumably not promised amnesty, but MacArthur probably considered them as being in the same position as the Emperor as far as Japanese public opinion was concerned.

Military personnel abroad who had not been tried were generally repatriated to Japan by 1946 or 1947 except for those in Russian hands who sometimes died in captivity or were not released until the middle or late 1950s. Senior officers together with their men were held without trial in Siberia and were subjected to hard labour for the duration.

Swords were carried by all officers as both weapons and symbols of authority. The loss of one's sword was regarded as a supreme disgrace. Lord Mountbatten ordered the disarming of all Japanese officers within his theatre of command and before repatriation as a punishment for ill-treatment of Allied prisoners of war. Details of such surrender ceremonies are given in Chapter 2.

Many senior officers owned two or more swords and may have surrendered them at different times. Where records of such surrenders have been located, the relevant details are given.

Up to the early 1930s, army and naval officers carried variations of a sword known as a *kyu-guntō* (proto-military sword) which has a European-style hilt with knucklebow and traditional style Japanese blade.* This was superseded, c.1933, by a new pattern based on the traditional style samurai sword (*tachi*) with tape bound hilt and known as *shin-guntō* (new-military sword) for the army and *kai-guntō* (naval or sea-military sword) for the navy. The latter two patterns were the most common and brought home as souvenirs by returning Allied troops.

* For details of such swords the reader should refer to *Military Swords of Japan 1868 – 1945* by Richard Fuller and Ron Gregory (see Bibliography).

Imperial Japanese Army General Officers c. 1926–45

ABE Heisuke
Lieutenant-General; Commander of 41st Division (under 18th Army), New Guinea; Died of disease at Wewak, New Guinea, September 1943.

ABE Koichi
Major-General; Infantry Brigade Commander of 48th Division (under Y. TSUCHIHASHI) during the invasion of the Philippines which landed late December 1941; Led first Japanese forces into Manila; Transferred with division

for invasion of Java, 1942; Lieutenant-General; Commander of 107th Division, Manchuria, September 1944.

ABE Nobuyuki

General; Prime Minister (replacing Baron Hiranuma), 30 August 1939; Concurrently Foreign Minister until October 1939; Forced to resign after a vote of 'no confidence' was passed by the entire Diet (Parliament), 14 January 1940; (Replaced by Admiral M. YONAI); Became a Jushin (elder statesman and Privy Councillor) and adviser to the Emperor, c.1941; Agreed at a conference with the Emperor and seven other Jushin that war was the only course left for Japan, 29 November 1941; Concurrently President of Imperial Rule Assistance Association (totalitarian party formed to replace pre-war Japanese political parties), 1942; Only Jushin to support Premier H. TOJO when others forced his resignation, 17 July 1944; Governor-General of Korea by the end of the war; Signed the surrender of South Korea (south of Latitude 38°) together with Y. KOZUKI (C in C 17th Army) and Vice-Admiral G. YAMAGUCHI (Commander of Port Arthur Naval Base) to Lieutenant-General John R. Hodge, US Army, and Admiral T. C. Kinkaid, USN, in the throne room of Government House, Keijo (Seoul) Korea, 9 September 1945; Arrested as a suspected Class A war criminal and held in Sugamao prison, Tokyo; Granted amnesty before war crimes trials, 29 April 1946.*

* The sole reason for amnesty was that only enough seats in the court room for 26 of the 28 named Class A war criminals were available. The other given amnesty was J. MAZAKI.

ADACHI Hatazo

2nd Lieutenant (infantry), December 1910; Graduated from War College, November 1922; Member of Army General Staff, May 1925; Major, March 1926; Member of Army General Staff, December 1928; Lieutenant-Colonel, August 1930; Official duty in Europe, September 1932; Attached to Kwantung Army HQ, Manchuria, March 1933; Commander of Kwantung Army Railway Command, April 1934; Colonel, August 1934; Section Chief in Army General Staff, August 1935; Commander of 12th Infantry Regiment, December 1936; Major-General, Attached to Kwantung Army HQ, March 1938; Lieutenant-General; Commander of 37th Division, August 1940; Chief of Staff to North China Area Army, November 1941; Commander of 18th Army (under 2nd Area Army), New Guinea, November 1942, consisting of 41st Division (G. MANO); Withdrew to Buna, Gona and Sananda on north coast with 6,000 troops and 1,300 reinforcements by December 1942; Lost Gona (see also T. HORII, K. ODA); Decided Salamaua and Lae were strategically important and must be held at all costs; Reinforced by 20th Division (J. AOKI, M. NAKAI) and 51st Division (H. NAKANO), January 1943; Strengthened Salamaua at expense of Lae defence, July? 1942; Evacuated Salamaua to reinforce Lae, 6 September 1943; Salamaua occupied by Americans, 11 September 1943; American and Australian sea-borne attack against Lae (4 September) which they captured by 16 September 1943; Forced into a retreat; Hoped to get the army to Hollandia, Dutch New Guinea, before it was invaded by the Allies; Lost Kaiapit in Markham Valley and Dumpu in Ramu River valley, 2 October 1943; Finschhafen Harbour lost (see S. KATAGIRI), 2 October 1943; Established base at Wewak with 30,000 men to cross the Sepic River, April 1944; Hollandia taken by Americans, cutting off the army in Wewek–Aitape area, April 1944; Launched attack against American forces at

Wewak, 10–11 July 1944; Counter-attack by Americans forced a retreat; Maprik district made main resistance area but it was lost, May 1945; Driven away from the coast in the Aitape–Wewak campaign and enclosed in the mountains, May 1945; Issued various 'last stand' orders; Finally ordered a 'last stand' in the Nyakombi–Sassuia area with 20th Division in centre, 51st and 41st Divisions on the wings (total strength about 13,500), July 1945; Formally surrendered to Major-General H. C. H. Robertson at Cape Wom airstrip, Wewak, Dutch New Guinea, 13 September 1945 (where he surrendered at least one sword at this time); Charged with war crimes including killing prisoners; Sentenced to life imprisonment, 12 July 1947; Committed suicide by hanging in prison on Manus Island, Admiralty Islands, 10 September 1947.

Note: There are two swords in the Australian War Memorial Museum given by Major-General H. C. H. Robertson and said to have been taken from H. ADACHI:
Cat.no.OL.15. A *shin-guntō* with a blade by Yosazaemonjo Sukesada of Osafune dated 1511 but it is apparently a fake signature.
Cat.no.AWM 31261. A *shin-guntō* with a high-quality Meiji-period (1868–1912) blade forged in koto period (pre-1596) style. Said to have a 'staff officer tassel' which implies it is not ADACHI'S personal sword but one from a member of his staff who also surrendered their swords at the same time.

ADACHI Juro
Major-General; Commander of Hong Kong Defence Unit, January 1942.

ADACHI Katsumi
Major-General; Commander of 4th Special Railway Corps, Siam, c.1945; Appears to have surrendered to Lieutenant-Colonel L. M. Coffey of British Intelligence Corps at Banpong, Siam, September 1945; [1] Participated in formal surrender of 18th Army (under A. NAKAMURA) at Bangkok, Siam, 11 January 1946.[2]

[1] Surrendered a *shin-guntō* with brown metal scabbard which has a silver plate inscribed 'Presented to Lieut. Colonel L. M. Coffey. British Int. Corps. by Maj. General Katsumi Adachi. Cmdr 4th Special Railway Corps at the Disarmament Ceremony, Banpong, Siam, Sept. 12th 1945'. Showa-period blade (post-1926) signed SEKI ICHIMONJI. Now in a private collection in Australia. (*See also* G. YOSHIDA).
[2] Surrendered a sword (together with nineteen generals and two admirals) at formal surrender of Japanese forces in Siam to Major-General G. C. Evans, GOC of 7th Indian Division at Bangkok, 11 January 1946. It was almost certainly passed on to one of the senior Allied officers who were also present.

AIDA Toshiji
Major-General; Infantry Group Commander of 18th Division (under S. TANAKA), Burma, from September 1943.

AKASHI
Major-General; Commander of 56th Independent Mixed Brigade (under 37th Army – M. BABA) based at Tenom, Borneo; Surrendered to Brigadier S. W. H. C. Porter, OC Australian 24th Infantry Brigade at the officers' club, Beaufort, Borneo, 15 September 1945.

AKASHIBA Yaezo
2nd Lieutenant (infantry), December 1912; Major, March 1928; Staff Officer in 1st Division, March 1928; Attached to Personnel Bureau at War Ministry, April 1932; Lieutenant-Colonel, August 1932; Member of Personnel Bureau at War

Ministry, August 1935; Official duty in Europe, February 1936, Colonel, August 1936; Commander of 10th Infantry Regiment, July 1936; Commanding Officer of Cadet Unit at Military Academy, July 1938; Major-General, March 1939; Director of Military Academy, October 1941; Lieutenant-General; Commander of 25th Division, October 1942; Commander of 1st Imperial Guards Division, Tokyo, October 1943; Commander of 53rd Army (for defence of Japan) at HQ Tamagawa, Kanagawa prefecture, Japan, April 1945.

AKASHITA Tsutomu (Riichi, Tsutani)
Lieutenant-General; Commander of 13th Division (under 11th Army – I. YOKOYAMA) in Battle of Western Hupei, China, late April 1943; Absent when divisional HQ was captured by Chinese 6th Provisional Division, 7 June 1943; Battle of Changsha–Hengyang, late May–early August 1944; Battle of Kweilin–Liuchow, early September–mid December 1944.

AKIFUSA (AKIGUSA) Shun
Major-General; Commander of 4th Border Garrison Unit at Futo, Tungan province, Manchuria, December 1942; Chief of Harbin Military Mission, Manchuria, c.1945; Directly controlled Hogoin Camp 'Scientific Research Division' containing 150 Soviet citizens arrested in Manchurian territory. Escapees and wrongdoers were sent to 'Detachment 731' (see S. ISHII) for biological experiments and certain death.

AKIHATA
Major-General; Ex-priest; Chief of Staff to an unknown unit.

AKIJIKA Tadashi
Lieutenant-General; Commander of 13th Division, China, from August 1942.

AKINAGA Tsutomi (Tsutomu)
Major-General; Chief of Staff to 17th Army (under H. HYAKUTAKE) on Bougainville, Solomon Islands, September 1943, Lieutenant-General; Commander of 6th Division (replacing M. KANDA) in 17th Army (under M. KANDA), Bougainville, February 1945; Killed, 22 May 1945.

Personal facts. Strict disciplinarian and ardent militarist. Not used to active command. He was considered a poor divisional commander.

AMAGASU Jutarō
Lieutenant-General; Commander of 33rd Division (under 11th Army) during First Battle of Changsha, China, early August–October 1939.

AMAKASU Shigetarō
A General officer; Testified on behalf of 14th Area Army Commander T. YAMASHITA at war crimes trials in Manila, Philippines, 1945.

AMAMIYA Tatsumi
Lieutenant-General; Commander of 24th Division, February 1944; Division at Tungan, Manchuria, until July 1944; Division stripped of men to reinforce other fronts before transfer via Fusan and Moji to Okinawa, Ryukyu Islands (coming under 32nd Army – M. USHIJIMA), late 1944; Brought up to full strength and

organized for the defence of Okinawa retaining 42nd Field Artillery unit; Dispersed in southern sector for defence against expected American attack from the south-east, in the Mintogawa area, which did not materialize; American landings in mid north-west of the island, 1 April 1945; Division ordered to concentrate in Shuri defence area because of American pressure from the north and to abandon defence of south-eastern coast by 27 April 1945; Ordered to form vanguard of 32nd Army all-out counter-attack against American forces (*see* M. USHIJIMA for campaign details), 4 May 1945; Attack failed with very heavy losses, 5 May 1945; Forced back to Shuri area; Division ordered to withdraw to Kiyamu Peninsula; Withdrawal to extreme south coast undertaken, 23–30 May 1945; Formed defensive line with 44th Independent Mixed Brigade on high ground in the Madeera area with 89th Regiment in Yaeju Dake area; Army split up by 19 June 1945; Encouraged his few remaining forces to fight to the last man, 20 June 1945; Division completely destroyed; Dead (suicide or killed) by the time Okinawa was declared secure by American forces, 22 June 1945.

AMANO Morikazu
Major-General; Chief of 1st Section of Army General Staff by 1945; Member of the delegation to Manila, Philippines (together with T. KAWABE and Rear-Admiral I. YOKOYAMA), to receive Allied requirements for the execution of surrender terms, 19–20 August 1945.

AMAYA Shojikiro
Lieutenant-General; Commander of 40th Division (under 11th Army) at Battle of Tsaoyang–Ichang, China, mid April 1940.

ANAMI Korechika
Born February 1887; Major, February 1922; Staff Officer in Sakhalin Expeditionary Army, August 1923; Member of Army General Staff, May 1925; Lieutenant-Colonel, August 1925; Official visit to France, August 1927; Depot Unit Commander of 45th Infantry Regiment, August 1928; Aide-de-camp to Emperor Hirohito, August 1929;* Colonel, August 1930; Regimental Commander in 2nd Imperial Guards Division, August 1933; Superintendent of Tokyo Military Preparatory School, August 1934; Major-General, March 1935; Chief of Military Administration Bureau in War Ministry, March 1937, Lieutenant-General, March 1938; Commander of 109th Division, Shansi province, central China, November 1938; Vice Minister of War, October 1939; Commander of 11th Army, Central China, April 1941; Commander-in-Chief of 2nd Area Army, Manchuria, July 1942; General, May 1943; HQ Tsitsihar, Manchuria; Transferred with 2nd Area Army HQ (and 2nd Army HQ – F. TESHIMA) to direct operations in New Guinea and Halmahera area, November 1943; HQ at Davao, Philippines and later Menado, Celebes; Controlled 2nd Army (F. TESHIMA), 19th Army (K. KITANO), 18th Army (H. ADACHI) and 4th Air Army (K. TOMINAGA); Inspector-General of Army Aviation; Concurrently Military Councillor and Chief of Army Aeronautical Department, December 1944; War Minister in Admiral K. SUZUKI cabinet (replacing G. SUGIYAMA) from 7 April 1945; Agreed with Admiral M. YONAI's proposal that Russia should be requested to mediate for peace on Japan's behalf, 12 May 1945; Refused to accept Allied Potsdam declaration for unconditional Japanese surrender even after dropping of atomic bombs and Russian invasion of Manchuria, 9 August 1945; Wanted to fight on even after Japanese acceptance of the Potsdam declaration, 13 August 1945; Ordered

Eastern Army District Commander S. TANAKA to tighten security and ensure public order before the official surrender was broadcast by the Emperor, 14 August 1945; Requested to join attempted *coup* by rebel army officers to prevent the surrender announcement but refused although taking to action to prevent it, 15 August 1945; Committed tradional suicide (*seppuku*) on the night of 15 August 1945.

Note: His sword, a *shin-guntō*, is now in the Yasukuni Shrine museum, Tokyo. He has also been photographed with an army *kyu-guntō*.

* Said to have been the Emperor's favourite aide-de-camp.

ANDO Chuichiro
Major-General; Commander of 9th Independent Garrison Unit, March 1942.

ANDO Kisaburō
General; Minister without Portfolio in charge of propaganda in H. TOJO cabinet, appointed 9 June 1942 aged 65.

ANDO Rikichi
2nd Lieutenant (infantry), November 1914; Graduated from War College, December 1914?; Resident Officer in England, January 1919; Major, August 1929; Official duty in Europe, September 1921; Lieutenant-Colonel, August 1924; Military Attaché in India, August 1925; Member of Army General Staff, April 1927; Colonel; Commander of 13th Infantry Regiment, March 1928; Chief of Staff to 5th Division, May 1930; Chief of Military Administration Section of Military Administration Bureau at War Ministry, March 1931; Military Attaché to England, May 1932; Major-General; Commander of 1st Infantry Brigade, December 1934; Superintendent of Toyama Army School, August 1935; Commander of 5th Independent Garrison Unit, April 1936; Vice Chief of Inspectorate General of Military Training, August 1937; Lieutenant-General; Commander of 5th Division, May 1938; Commander of 21st Army, November 1938; Commander-in-Chief of South China Area Army, February 1940; Prematurely invaded northern Indo–China, October 1940; Transferred to reserve list (as punishment for the invasion), January 1941; Recalled to active duty and promoted to General as Commander-in-Chief of 10th Area Army, Taihoku, Formosa, November 1941 – end of the war; Controlled all forces in Formosa plus the Ryukyu Islands (32nd Army. *See* M. USHIJIMA), Sakishima Islands (28th Division), Amami and Daito Islands; Surrendered Formosa and Penghu complex to Chinese General Chen Yi upon Japan's surrender, September 1945.

ANDO Saburō
Lieutenant-General; Retired; President of Imperial Rule Assistance Association (totalitarian party formed to replace pre-war Japanese political parties); Ordered arrested by American occupation forces in Tokyo as a suspected war criminal, 2 December 1945.

ANZAI – Same as SAKANISI Ichiro

AOKI Jusei
Lieutenant-General; Commander of 20th Division (under 18th Army), New Guinea; Died of disease while withdrawing towards Aitape, April? 1944. Replaced (by M. NAKAI).

AOKI Seiichi

Lieutenant-General; Commander of 40th Division (under 11th Army), China, August 1941; Engaged in second Battle of Changsha, September–October 1941; Third Battle of Changsha, December 1941–January 1942; Assistant Chief of Staff to Southern Army (under H. TERAUCHI) at HQ Saigon, Indo–China; Official representative of H. TERAUCHI at Japan's victory parade in Manila after conquest of the Philippines, 5 January 1942; Replaced 2 August 1944; Commander of 2nd Depot Division (supplying 2nd, 13th, 22nd, 42nd, 72nd Divisions and 3rd, 24th, 43rd, 54th Independent Mixed Brigades), Sendai, Japan, September 1944; Concurrently Commander of Home Stations for various army units at Osaka, Sakai, Shinodayama and Takatsuki (all in Osaka Regimental District), March 1945.

AOTSU (AOZU) Kikutaro

Major-General Infantry Group commander in 41st Division (under G. MANO), New Guinea, August or September 1944: Commander of 237th Regiment and other detachments (directly under 18th Army command – H. ADACHI) ordered to delay and repulse any Australian advance along the New Guinea coast between Anumb and Danmap, October 1944; Reinforced by part of 80th and 239th Regiments plus III/115th Battalion, January 1945; Ordered to withdraw intact to 20th Division position and placed under its control, 10 February 1945; III/115th Battalion heavily defeated at Nambut Hill and Sowom; HQ moved to Shisso Mountain, March 1945.

ARAKI Masatsugu

Major-General; Commander of 79th Infantry Brigade in 103rd Division (under Y. MURAOKA), Baguio on Luzon, Philippines, July 1944?

Baron ARAKI Sadao

Born 26 May 1877; Company Commander in 1st Infantry Regiment of Imperial Guards during Russo–Japanese war, 1904–5; Major, July 1918; Staff Officer at Siberian Expeditionary Army HQ Vladivostock, November 1918; Commander of 23rd Infantry Regiment, July 1919; Army General Staff, April 1921; Major-General; Commander of 8th Infantry Brigade, March 1923; Provost Marshal General, January 1924; Bureau Chief of Army General Staff, May 1925; Lieutenant-General, July 1927; Commandant of Army Staff College, August 1928; Commander of 6th Division, August 1929; Inspector-General of Military Training, August 1931; Leading army expert on Russian affairs and principal advocate of 'strike north' policy (i.e., against Russia); Minister of War in Inukai cabinet (replacing J. MINAMI), December 1931; Thought another Russo–Japanese war was inevitable so strengthened Japanese forces in Manchuria; Ardent imperialist and leader of 'Imperial Way' faction; Advocated a tough foreign policy; Continued as War Minister in Admiral M. SAITO cabinet, 1932; General, October 1933; Failed to gain support for militaristic policies; Resigned as War Minister obstensibly on the grounds of ill health (replaced by S. HAYASHI), 22 January 1934; Baron, 1935; Retired to inactive list (after '2–26 Insurrection'), March 1936; Education Minister in Prince Konoye cabinet in charge of propaganda, 1938–9;* Advocate of militaristic education and 'Imperial Way'; Arrested as a Class A war criminal; Tried by the International Tribunal for the Far East, Tokyo, 26 April 1946–12 November 1948; Found guilty (for waging an aggressive war against China) and sentenced to life imprisonment; Released for health reasons, June 1955; Died 1967.

Personal facts: Idealistic. Fiery temperament.

* The 'Imperial Way' (*Kodo-ha*) faction was an ultra-nationalist organization which wanted to sweep away the 'corrupting influence of big business and political parties' to restore 'traditional Japanese virtues' under the Emperor.

ARIKAWA Keiichi
Major-General; Said to be Commander of 62nd Division, Manchuria, but possibly Infantry Group Commander or acting divisional commander if there was a delay between the commands of Y. HONGO and T. FUJIOKA after the division's arrival in Okinawa (i.e., September 1944 to March 1945).*

* The article 'Okinawa' by Charles J. Leonard in *After the Battle* magazine, No. 42 implies ARIKAWA was in command during the Okinawa campaign of 1945. However *Okinawa – Touchstone to Victory* by Benis M. Frank (*see* Bibliography) implies that T. FUJIOKA was in command at the time of the division's arrival in September 1944. The 'Japanese Order of Battle' for 1945 gives T. FUJIOKA as being in command from February 1945 which coincides with 32nd Army internal reorganization date. He is not mentioned in *Okinawa 1945* by Ian Gow (*See* Bibliography).

ARIMINA
Major-General; Commandant of Changi Jail, Singapore, November 1943–March 1944.

ARISUE
Major-General; Chief of Staff to 23rd Army (*see* T. SAKAI, R. ISOGAI), Hong Kong, December 1941; Ordered execution of four escaped Canadian POWs, August 1942.

ARISUE Seizo
Major-General; Chief of 2nd Bureau (Intelligence) of Army General Staff, August 1942 – end of war; Lieutenant-General, March 1945; Visited Hiroshima after dropping of the atomic bomb, 7 August 1945; Met American advance party of occupation forces at Atsugi airbase, south-east of Tokyo, 28 August 1945.

ARITOMI Jiro
Major General; Commander of 56th Infantry Brigade (in 60th Division), Shanghai – Soochow – Kashing area, China, May 1944.

Prince ASAKA Yasuhiko
Born 1887; Uncle of Emperor Hirohito and half-brother of Princes N. HIGA-SHIKUNI, T. KAYA, M. NASHIMOTO; Commander of 1st Imperial Guards (Division ?), c.1934; Lieutenant-General; Commander of forces which attacked Nanking, China (probably 10th Army) which combined with the Shanghai Expeditionary Force to form Central China Area Army (under I. MATSUI) outside Nanking, 2–6 December 1937; Attacked Nanking, 8 December 1937; Nanking fell, 12–13 December 1937; Ordered the death of all prisoners in the infamous 'Rape of Nanking'* when an estimated 260,000–300,000 military prisoners and civilians were slaughtered (see also K. NAKAJIMA, I. MATSUI, I. CHO, H. YANAGAWA), 12 December 1937–10 February 1938; Recalled to Tokyo after massacres became known (but not disciplined) and retired, 1938; Member of Supreme War Council, 1938–45; General, in the reserve by 1941; Became one of Tokyo's best-known golfers in post-war Japan.

* Presumably because of his royal blood, he does not seem to have been tried as a war criminal. The blame for the massacre was laid on the C in C Central China Area Army, I. MATSUI.

ASAMI Kikuo

Major-General; Chief of Staff to 39th Division, Tangyang area, Hupeh province, Central China, December 1942.

ASANO Takeshi

Major-General; Commander of a Fuel Storage Depot, south Sumatra, March 1944; At Palembang, Sumatra, April 1944.

ASHIDATE

Major-General; Presided over a trial of British POWs at Hong Kong, December 1943.

ASHIZUKA Chozo

Major-General; Concurrently Commander of six Home Stations for various army and air units at Chiba, Ichikawa, Kashiwa, Narashino, Narimasu and Sakura, in Tokyo and Chiba Regimental Districts, March 1945.

AYABE Kitsuji

Born 1894; Graduated from Military Academy, May 1915, 2nd Lieutenant (cavalry), attached to 12th Cavalry Regiment, December 1915; Army Cavalry School (equitation student), October 1917; In Siberian Expeditionary Army, August 1918–July 1919; Lieutenant, April 1919; Army Cavalry School (long-term student of equitation), August 1919; Graduated from Army Cavalry School, July 1920; Captain, March 1924; Graduated from War College, November 1924; Company Commander in 12th Cavalry Regiment, January 1925; Attached to Military Affairs Bureau of War Ministry, October 1926; Military Student in Poland and Soviet Union, September 1928; Major, August 1930; Member of Army Affairs Section at War Ministry, November 1930; Concurrently Instructor at War College, August 1931; Member of Army General Staff, November 1933; Lieutenant-Colonel, August 1934; Staff Officer in Kwantung Army, Manchuria, August 1935; Colonel; August 1935; Engaged in Chahar area operations as a Staff Officer in Kwantung Army, North China Detachment, August–October 1937; Section Chief (Organization and Mobilization) of Army General Staff, October 1937; Commander of 25th Cavalry Regiment, Central China, March 1939; Staff Officer to 3rd Army, Manchuria, March 1940; Major-General; Deputy Chief of Staff to 3rd Army, August 1940; Army General Staff, October 1940; Member of Military Observer Mission to Germany and Italy (under T. YAMASHITA), December 1940–July 1941; Chief of Staff to Kwantung Army, Manchuria, July 1941; Chief of Staff to 1st Area Army, Manchuria, July 1942; Chief of 1st Bureau of Army General Staff and a Staff Officer to IGHQ, Tokyo, December 1942; Lieutenant-General, October 1943; Vice Chief of Staff to Southern Army (under H. TERAUCHI), HQ Singapore (replacing M. INADA), 11 October 1943; Attended final war games for invasion of Imphal, India, at Rangoon, Burma, 23 December 1943; Sent to Tokyo to persuade IGHQ to accept the plan which was authorized by H. TOJO with Order no.1776, January 1944; Hospitalized in Java after an air accident, February 1944; Assigned to 7th Area Army HQ Singapore, April 1944; Chief of Staff to 7th Area Army (under S. ITAGAKI), June 1944 – end of war. Surrendered a sword to Brigadier C. P. Jones (at the same ceremony as S. ITAGAKI), Kuala Lumpur, Malaya, 22 February 1946.*

* This is now in the Royal Engineers Museum. A *shin-guntō* with brown metal scabbard and a General Officer's tassel. Blade details are unknown.

BABA Hideo

Lieutenant-General; Commander of Army Maritime Transport Command, HQ Hiroshima, Japan, 1945, Survived the dropping of the atomic bomb (but lost his family), 5 August 1945.

BABA Masao (Matsuo) 馬 場 正 郎

Lieutenant-General; Commander of 4th Division, Sumatra, c. August 1944; Commander of 37th Army, Borneo (replacing M. YAMAWAKI), effective from 21 January 1945; Did not countermand order given by his predecessor M. YAMAWAKI to march Australian and British POWs from Sandakan to Ranau which resulted in the 'Sandakan death marches';[1] Sent columns into the interior to attack Australian Special Forces (Force 136) which had organized considerable resistance utilizing various native tribes, May–June 1945; HQ Weston, June 1945; Command consisted of 56th IMB in north Borneo, 71st IMB in south Borneo and 25th Independent Regiment at Jesselton; Formed a base at Pensiagan, north Borneo; Advanced to Sapong Estate with approximately 2,000 men but lost about 400 through guerrilla attacks; Brunei Bay area invaded by the 9th Australian Division, 10 June 1945; 56th IMB forced to retreat. Balikpapan attacked by the 7th Australian Division, 1 July 1945; Sent another column against Australian Special Forces by advancing towards Sapong from the coast reaching upper reaches of Limbang River; Reached Trusan Valley by the end of the war, 15 August 1945; Negotiated surrender terms from Sapong, 4–9 September 1945; Surrendered at Labuan, south Borneo, to Major-General G. F. Wotton, G.O.C. 9th Australian Division (surrendering his sword at this time), 10 September 1945;[2] The Japanese column in Trusan Valley refused to surrender until receiving his written order to do so which reached them on 10 October 1945; Tried for war crimes by Australian Military Court at Rabaul, New Britain, which included the 'Sandakan death marches' and sentenced to death, 5 June 1947; Hanged.

[1] Emaciated and brutalized prisoners were force-marched 165 miles across rugged country from Sandakan to Ranau in three separate batches:
First march – 455 prisoners in nine groups left 29 January–6 February 1945. Only 230 reached Ranau.
Second march – 566 prisoners departed 29 May but only 203 arrived at Ranau.
Third march – 75 prisoners departed in July but none arrived at Ranau. All sick left behind at Sandakan were executed.
By 1 August 1945 only 32 prisoners were still alive at Ranau, but they were all shot because they were unfit for forced labour in Japan. Only two escapees survived the war out of the entire original Sandakan camp complement of prisoners.
[2] This sword is now in the Australian War Memorial Museum cat.no. AWM 31262. It is a scarce cavalry officer's pattern with shin-guntō-type General Officer's tassel. The blade is by KANENOBU of Mino province, c.1650.

BAN Takeo (Yoshio)

Lieutenant-General; Commander of 34th Division, Nanchang, China, March 1943; Moved to Hunan, early 1944; Engaged in Battle Changsha–Hengyang (under 11th Army), late May–early August 1944, Battle of Western Hunan (under 20th Army), April–early June 1945.

BANZAI Kazuyoshi (Ichiryo)

Lieutenant-General; Commander of 20th Army, Hengyang area, Central China, c. April 1944.

BANZAI Richachiro 坂西 利八郎

Colonel; Military adviser to Chinese General Yuan Shikan, c. 1906; Acted as chief umpire at the second Chinese grand manoeuvres, 1906; Adviser to the Chinese Ministry of War, c. 1913; Lieutenant-General; Head of espionage network in China; Retired, 1932; Executive Director of Japan's civilian espionage network, 1930s.

BUTO Nobuyoshi – Same as MUTO Nobuyoshi

CHICHIWA Koji

Major-General; Commander of Iki Fortress at Mushozu in Iki, Nagasaki prefecture, Japan, February 1944.

CHIJISIMA

Lieutenant-General; Governor of Indo–China; Chief of Staff in Java, Second World War.

CHIKU

Major-General; Commander of northern section of Elebante area, Bougainville Island, Solomons, c.1945.

CHO Isamu

Colonel in 16th Division and Chief of Staff to Prince Y. ASAKA; Said to have issued orders for the execution of all prisoners at Nanking on instructions of Y. ASAKA, December 1937; Commander of 74th Regiment (in 19th Division) during Lake Khasan incident, Korean–Siberian border, July–August 1938; Commanded an army observer team in Hanoi, Indo–China (replacing I. NISHIMURA), August 1940; Major-General; Vice Chief of Staff to T. YAMASHITA during 'Strike South' exercises, Manchuria, July–December 1942; On Southern Army HQ staff (under H. TERAUCHI), December 1941; Commander of 10th Division, Manchuria, February 1942; Southern Army officer to 14th Army, Manila, Philippines, April 1942; Lieutenant-General Chief of Staff to 32nd Army (under M. USHIJIMA), Okinawa, August 1944; An advocate of underground defensive fortifications; HQ Shuri Castle in the south of the island; American forces landed in the Hagushi area, mid-northwest of the island, 1 April 1945 (see M. USHIJIMA for campaign details); Convinced that an all-out counter-attack by the whole army with 24th Division (T. AMAMIYA) in the van should be launched and persuaded M. USHIJIMA to agree; Attack launched, 4 May 1945: Complete failure with very heavy losses, 5 May 1945; Agreed with the decision to withdraw to an area full of caves in the Kiyamu Peninsula for the final defence of the island; Withdrew, 23– 30 May 1945, HQ at Mabumi; Army split up and Mabumi attacked by the American 7th Division, 19 June 1945; Committed traditional suicide (*seppuku*) with a dagger and then was decapitated with a sword by the HQ adjutant (together with M. USHIJIMA) in their cave HQ, evening of 21 June 1945; He was aged 51 at the time of his death. Personal facts: Short-tempered and slapped subordinates. Smoked and drank to excess. Liked intrigue.

DOHIHARA (DOIHARA) Kenji 土 肥 原

Graduated from War College, November 1912; Captain, August 1913; Member of Army General Staff, June 1918; Military Adviser to the Chinese Government,

November 1918; Major, July 1919; Member of Army General Staff, January 1920; Official duty in Europe, May 1921; Official duty in China, December 1922 (where he ran espionage missions to eastern Siberia and north China during 1920s); Lieutenant-Colonel, August 1923; In 3rd Infantry Regiment, China, March 1927; Colonel, July 1927; Military adviser to Chinese warlord Chang Tso-Lin who controlled the eastern province of Manchuria, March 1928–March 1929; Commander of 30th Infantry Regiment, March 1929; Attached to Army General Staff, December 1930;[1] Major-General; Attached to Kwantung Army HQ, Manchuria, August 1932; Took charge of the Special Service Agency (i.e., Army Intelligence Branch) at Mukden, Manchuria, and declared himself Mayor of the city (after the outbreak of the 'Manchurian Incident'), 19 September 1931; Organized establishment of former Chinese Ch'ing dynasty Emperor Pu-Yi as ruler of a separate Manchuria (Manchukuo) who was proclaimed by the Kwantung Army in March 1932;[2] Commander of 9th Infantry Brigade, April 1932; Appointed to buy the allegiance of Chinese and Mongolian leaders during the Japanese attack on Jehol province, Inner Mongolia, February 1933; Attached to Kwantung Army HQ, October 1933; Believed to be Chief of Staff to China Garrison Army, c. 1934; Forced the Chinese Governor of Chahar province, Inner Mongolia, to relinquish control to the Japanese after complaining that one of his officers had been imprisoned by the Chinese, 1935; Attempted to persuade Chinese warlords in five northernmost Chinese provinces to break from China and form an autonomous government under Japanese army protection, 1935; Nicknamed 'The Lawrence of Manchuria' by western newsmen; Unofficially commenced the occupation of the northern Chinese provinces with 5,000 men on the pretext that they were to protect Japanese merchants from bandits, 1936; Lieutenant-General, May 1936; At 1st Division HQ, May 1936; Commander of 14th Division, China, March 1937; Commander of 5th Army, northern China, May 1939; Military Councillor, September 1940; Principal of Military Academy, October 1940; General, April 1941; Inspector-General of Army Aviation, June 1941, Commander-in-Chief of Eastern District Army, Japan, May 1943; Commander-in-Chief of 7th Area Army, HQ Singapore, Malaya, March 1944–April 1945;[3] (replaced by S. ITAGAKI); Inspector-General of Military Training, April 1945; Commander-in-Chief of 12th Area Army, Japan, August 1945, Commander-in-Chief of 1st General Army, Japan (replacing G. SUGIYAMA) with American approval following the Japanese surrender, 12 September 1945;[4] Ordered arrested as a Class A war criminal by American occupation forces, 21 September 1945; Tried by the International Military Tribunal for the Far East in Tokyo, 26 April 1946 – 12 November 1948; Found guilty and hanged in Sugamo prison, Tokyo, 23 December 1948.

[1] Expert on Asia and believed in 'Asia for the Asiatics'.
[2] Pu-Yi was not officially recognized as Emperor of Manchukwo by the Japanese government until 15 November 1932. He was crowned Kang-Te on 1 March 1933.
[3] 7th Area Army controlled 29th Army (defence of Malaya, Andaman and Nicobar Islands), 25th Army (Sumatra), 16th Army (Java) and 37th Army (Borneo).
[4] *Kogun – The Japanese Army in the Pacific war* (*see* Bibliography) gives K. DOHIHARA and M.KAWABE as having this post at the same time. A contemporary newspaper account confirms the above dating of DOHIHARA's appointment. Possibly M. KAWABE replaced him after his removal for the war crimes trial and until the Japanese war machine was run down.

EBASHI Eiji

Lieutenant-General; Commander of Provisional Air Command (Army airforce units based in China after the opening of the Sino–Japanese war in 1937), c.1939;

Command consisted of 1st, 3rd, 7th Air Groups; Commander of 2nd Joint Air Group (consisting of 2nd, 9th, 12th Air Groups in Manchuria and Provisional Air Group in China), September 1939 (replacing T. GIGA); Attacked Russian air base near Boir Nor, Mongolia 14–15 September 1939.

EDA Minoru
Lieutenant-General; Chief of Staff to 59th Division (under T. HOSOKAWA), Tsinan in Shantung province, China, June 1943.

ENBU (ENJU) Katsuichiro
Lieutenant- or full? General; Commander of 11th Army (replacing Y. OKA-MURA), China, late 1939; Engaged in Battle of Southern Hunan (with 3rd, part of 4th, 15th, 17th, 39th Divisions), early January 1940; Battle of Tsaoyang–Ichang (with 3rd, 4th, 6th, 13th, 30th, 40th Divisions), mid April 1940; Replaced (by A. TADAKI), 1940 or 1941.

ENDO
Major-General; Commander of the light bomber group of 3rd Air Group (under (M. SUGAWARA) during invasion of Malaya, HQ Sungei Patani, northwest Malaya, December 1941; Ground support for 25th Army (under T. YAMASHITA); HQ Kuala Lumpur airfield, Malaya, January 1942; Main force transferred to support the invasion of the East Indies, January 1942.

ENDO Harunobu
Major-General; Commander of Home Station for various army and air units at Morioka, Japan, March 1945.

ENDO Saburo
Lieutenant-General; Director General of Aviation Weaponry Bureau in Ammunition Ministry, c.1944; Wanted Saipan in the Marianas defended to the death and suggested super battleships *Musashi* and *Yamato* be run aground by the navy to act as gun platforms.

ENDO Shinichi
Major-General; Commander of 57th Independent Mixed Brigade from its activation, Japan, July 1944; Brigade transferred to Menado, Celebes, October 1944.

ETO Genkuro
Major-General; Purged from the army in the 1920s; Member of the House of Peers in 1930s.

FUJIE Keisuke
2nd Lieutenant (artillery), June 1900; Graduated from War College, November 1914; Attached to Army General Staff, August 1915; Member of Army General Staff, April 1916; Assistant Military Attaché to France, August 1917; Attached to Army General Staff, October 1919; Instructor at War College, April 1922; Lieutenant-Colonel, March 1926; Colonel, August 1929; Member of Japanese delegation to General Disarmament Conference, Geneva, August 1931; Commander of 2nd Heavy Field Artillery Regiment, August 1933; Major-General; Director of Artillery School, August 1934; Commander of 4th Heavy Field

Artillery Brigade, August 1935; Chief of General Affairs Bureau – Military Police, HQ Kwantung Army, Manchuria, August 1936; Commander of Kwantung Military Police, March 1937; Lieutenant-General, November 1937; Commander of 16th Division, July 1938; Attached to Army General Staff, August 1939; Superintendent of War College, December 1939; Commander-in-Chief of Western District Army, Japan, April 1941; General, February 1943; Commander-in-Chief of Eastern District Army, Japan, March 1944; Commander-in-Chief of 12th Area Army, Japan, and concurrently Commander-in-Chief of Eastern District Army, February 1945; Retired, April 1945; Recalled to active duty as Commander-in-Chief of 11th Area Army (for defence of Japan), HQ Sendai, Japan, and concurrently Commander of Tohoku District Army, June 1945.

FUJII Yoji

Lieutenant General; Commander of 59th Army (under 2nd General Army – S. HATA), responsible for Hiroshima Military District (with 230th, 231rd Divisions), HQ Hiroshima Castle, Japan, 1945; killed by the atomic bomb blast while leaving his house in Hiroshima, 5 August 1945 (his burnt sword was found alongside his charred remains). (see also S. MATSUMURA, YAMAMOTO).

FUJII Yonekuchi

Major-General; Concurrently Commander of Fukuyama (infantry and shipping), Hiroshima (various) and Ujina (shipping and signals) Home Stations, Japan, March 1945.

FUJIMURA Masuzo

Major-General; Chief of Staff to East Central District Army (under T. OKADA), Nagoya? Japan, February 1945.

FUJIMURA Yuzuru

Major-General; Commander of 8th Artillery Group (in 8th Division), Suiyang, Manchuria, March 1943.

FUJIOKA Takeo

Lieutenant-General; Commander of 62nd Division when it arrived in Okinawa (under 32nd Army – M. USHIJIMA), 1 March 1945 (replacing Y. HONGO);* Defended area north-west of Shuri, southern Okinawa; American forces landed in mid-west of island, 1 April 1945; Division forced to retreat with heavy losses, concentrating in south on left flank of 32nd Army (see M. USHIJIMA for campaign details); Held defensive positions; All-out counter-attack with 32nd Army commenced 4 May 1945; Attack repulsed with very heavy losses, 5 May 1945; Disagreed with M. USHIJIMA about withdrawal to Kiyamu Peninsula but was overruled, 22 May 1945; Remnant withdrew to defensive positions in Kiyamu Peninsula, 23–30 May 1945; Army split up by 19 June 1945; Division destroyed; Committed suicide by 22 June 1945.

*See also K. ARIKAWA.

FUJISAWA Shigezo

Major-General; Commander of 2nd Air Signals Unit, August 1943, Possibly absorbed by 2nd Air Signals Brigade, July 1944.

FUJITA Shinichi

Lieutenant-General; Commander of 3rd Division (under 11th Army) during first Battle of Changsha, China, August–October 1939.

FUJIWARA Shigeo

Lieutenant-General; c. Second World War.

FUKEI (FUKUYU, FUKUE) Shinpei (Shempei, Shimpei, Simpei, Sanehira)

Major-General; Commander of Prisoner of War camps in Singapore (and possibly the whole of Malaya), August 1942; Authorized the issue of 'promise not to escape' forms to POWs at Changi Jail, Singapore, late August 1942;* Authorized the execution of four escapees from Changi, early September 1942; Replaced (probably by M. SAITO), March 1944; Lieutenant-General; Commander of 102nd Division (under 35th Army – S. SUZUKI) from its activation in June 1944 with responsibility for Panay, Negros, Bohol and HQ on Cebu in Central Visayas, Philippines; HQ Iloito, August 1944; HQ and five battalions sent to defend Leyte Island (under 35th Army), October–November 1944; fought American invasion forces, suffering heavy losses and forced to retreat by December 1944, Informed 35th Army that he intended to evacuate the remains of his division to Cebu Island (without official approval) if transportation could be found, 29 December 1944; Ordered to report to 35th Army HQ to explain this unauthorized action but refused to go; Sailed with his staff to Cebu Island, 1 January 1945; Relieved of command pending permission for a court-martial from IGHQ, Tokyo, and ordered to remain on Cebu; Reluctantly reinstated because IGHQ failed to reply (Remnant of division was still in the central Visayas by the end of the war); Presumably still on Cebu at the time of the Japanese surrender, August 1945; Returned by the Allies to Singapore and held in Changi Jail pending trial for war crimes; Tried and sentenced to death for the execution of escapees in 1942 and executed by firing-squad.

*This was a direct contravention of the Hague Convention which did not require a POW to renounce his right to attempts to escape captivity; The consequent ill treatment of POWs *en masse* caused the signing of these forms 'under duress' in September 1942.

FUKUDA Hikosuke

Lieutenant-General; Commander of reinforcements to Tsingtao to protect Japanese nationals against possible attack from Chiang Kai-shek's 'Army of Liberation' and massacred 7,000 Chinese, May 1928.

FUKUNAGA Utata

Major-General; Commander of 16th Field Transport Command, Malay Peninsula, November 1944.

FUNABIKI Masayuki

Lieutenant-General; Commander of 64th Division, Central Kiangsu province, China, from its activation in June 1943.

FUPRUDZO

A General officer; Head of Military Operations Department of General Staff, Tokyo, Japan, c.1931.
Note. This is a very doubtful spelling since it is not a recognizable Japanese name and does not seem to equate to anything similar.

FUROME
Major- or Lieutenant-General; Commander of army airforce based at Macassar, Celebes (under 2nd Army or 2nd Area Army).

FURUNO
Major- or Lieutenant-General; Quartermaster of Kwantung Army, Manchuria, c.1943.

FURUSHIMA Chiichi
Lieutenant-General; Concurrently Commander of Shimoseki (air and artillery) and Yamaguchi (infantry) Home Stations, Japan, March 1945?

FURUSHO Mikio
Lieutenant-General; Aviation expert; Vice Minister of War, c.1935.

FUSATARO Teshima – Same as TESHIMA Fusataro

FUSE Yasumasa
Major-General; Commander of 41st Garrison Unit, Korea, January 1944?

FUTAMI Akisaburō
Major-General; Chief of Staff to 17th Army (under H. HYAKUTAKE), HQ Rabaul, New Britain, 1942; Stated that reinforcing Guadalcanal after the defeat of K. KAWAGUCHI was futile, September 1942: Suffered from ill health; Replaced (by S. MIYAZAKI) for his defeatist attitude, September 1942.

GIGA Tetsuji
Lieutenant-General; Commander of 2nd Joint Air Group (consisting of 7th, 9th, 12th Air Groups), Manchuria, c.1939; Personally led air attack on Russian air base at Tomsk in Mongolia during fighting at the Khalka River, 27 June 1939; Replaced (by E. EBASHI), September 1939.

GONDO
Lieutenant-General; Director* of 9th Army Technical Research Institute at Noborito, near Kawasaki City, Kanagawa prefecture, Japan, c.1944; Developed the 'mother and daughter' bomb (secret weapon), 1944.

*There was apparently no 9th Army so this must refer to the 9th Technical Research Institute.

GONDO Hakaru
Major-General; Commander of 13th Shipping Group, Kowloon, China, February 1945.

GOTO Juro
Major-General; Commander of Kofu Home Station (infantry), Tokyo, Japan, April 1945.

HAGI Saburo
Major-General; Chief of Staff to 26th Division, North China, March 1942; Chief of Staff to 5th Area Army, Sapporo, Japan, February 1945.

HAGISU

Lieutenant General; Commander of 30th Division, China, c.1939;* (Probably replaced by K. MURAKAMI, c.1940).

*There appears to be some variance of dating for the service of this division. *Japanese Armed Forces Order of Battle* Vol. 1. (*see* Bibliography) gives the activation of 30th Division as June 1943 in Korea. However *History of the Sino-Japanese War* (*see* Bibliography) specifies this division as part of 11th Army in China, May–June 1940, at the Battle of Tsaoyang–Ichang. This entry is taken from *Imperial Japanese Army and Navy Uniforms and Equipment* by Nakata (Arms & Armour Press, 1973) which gives the date 1939 and a reference to Nanking and Hankow.

HAMADA (HOMADA) Hitoshi (Minoru, Someo)

Major-General; Deputy Chief Supervisor of Allied Prisoner of War Information Bureau (under S. UEMURA); Chief of Staff to 39th Army (under A. NAKAMURA), Siam, November 1944; Deputy Chief of Staff to 18th Area Army (which was upgraded 39th Army) under A. NAKAMURA, July 1945; (Concurrently?) Second Superintendent of Railways responsible for the area between Prachaub and the Malayan border; Arrested by the British after the surrender for war crimes (forced use of POWs on railway building) but committed suicide to avoid trial.

Note. Surrendered a sword to General Auchlineck at Bangkok, September 1945. Surrendered another sword (together with nineteen Generals and two Admirals) to Major-General G. C. Evans, GOC 7th Indian Division, at Bangkok, 11 January 1946.

HANAMOTO Kisaburō 浜 本 喜三郎

Lieutenant-General; Commander-in-Chief of Northern Army, Japan, c.1942.

HANAYA (HANATANI) Tadashi

Major; Head of Special Duties Organization, Mukden, Manchuria; Involved in blowing up a section of track of the South Manchurian Railway to provoke Japan into hostilities with China (the Manchurian Incident), 16 September 1931; Served in China; Lieutenant-General; Commander of 55th Division (replacing T. KOGA), Burma, upon the transfer of the division from 15th Army to 28th Army (under S. SAKURAI) control, November 1943; The division was to invade Bengal, India, to draw off British reserves which would otherwise oppose the invasion of Imphal (*see* R. MUTAGUCHI) in Operation 'HA-GO' (or 'Z'); The operation began 11 January 1944; Attacked British 7th Division with some success but was forced to withdraw near Sinzweya with heavy losses at the Battle of the Admin. Box (*see* S. SAKURAI, T. SAKURAI), 22 February 1944; Defence of the Irrawaddy River delta area of Arakan, July? 1944; Three infantry battalions were formed into 'Shinbu Force' (under K. NAGAZAWA) for a retreat while he personally commanded the remainder, 'Chu Force', to stop the Allied advance between Meiktila and Rangoon, December? 1944; Replaced (by T. SAKUMA), late 1944 or early 1945; Chief of Staff to 18th Area Army (under A. NAKAMURA), HQ Bangkok, Siam, July? 1945; Attended a debate on the Japanese surrender, after the official announcement, at Southern Army HQ, Saigon, with C in C H. TERAUCHI and commanders of other Area Armies, 16 August 1945; Surrendered a sword (together with A. NAKAMURA, eighteen Generals and two Admirals) to Major-General G. C. Evans, GOC 7th Indian Division, at Bangkok, 11 January 1946.

Personal facts: Disliked by subordinate officers. A bully. Berated and even beat senior officers under his command. Sympathetic and fatherly to other ranks.

HARA Kumakichi

Major- or Lieutenant-General; Chief of Staff to Shanghai Expeditionary Force (under I. MATSUI) during the Battle of Shanghai, mid August–mid December 1937; Lieutenant-General; Commander of 16th Army, Batavia, Java, 1942–5? (Possibly replaced by Y. NAGANO); Commander of 55th Army (for defence of Japan), HQ at Shinkai in city of Kochi, Japan, 1945.

HARA Mamoru

Lieutenant-General; Commander of 9th Division, from August 1942; HQ at Mutanchiang province, Manchuria; Deputy Vice Minister of Japanese Demobilization Ministry (which replaced the War Ministry after the American occupation), 1946.

HARADA

Major-General?; Air adviser to T. YAMASHITA in a military mission to Europe and obtained secret radar information from Germans, December 1940–June 1941.

HARADA Hisao

Major-General; Commander of Home Station for one infantry unit at Matsumoto in Nagano Regimental District, Japan, March 1945.

HARADA Jiro

Lieutenant-General; Commander of 10th Division (under 35th Army); Commander of 100th Division (under 35th Army, see S. SUZUKI) from its activation in June 1944; Davao area, Mindanao, Philippines; Replaced (possibly by G. MOROZUMI).

HARADA Susumu

Major-General; Commander of 3rd Brigade of Tokyo Guards at the time of the Japanese surrender, August 1945.

HARADA Yoshikazu

Major-General; Commander of 2nd South Seas Detachment, Kusaie, Caroline Islands, April 1944.

HASE

Lieutenant-General; Commander of 6th Division (in Central China Area Army under I. MATSUI) which attacked Nanking and participated in the massacres, December 1937; Tried by a Chinese court for war crimes and publicly executed outside Nanking, end of April 1947.

HASEGAWA Miyoji

Lieutenant-General; Commander of 5th Depot Division (supplying 5th, 39th, 64th, 70th, 105th Divisions and 27th IMB), Hiroshima, Japan, October 1941.

HASHIMOTO Gen (Gun)

Major-General; Chief of Staff to North China Garrison Army, HQ Peking, c.1937; Signed local peace agreement with Chinese General Sung Chi-yuen after the 'Marco Polo Bridge Incident', Peking, 7–11 July 1937; marched on Nanking, November–December 1937; Member of Imperial GHQ liaison team present at the Battle of Xuzhow, China, 1938.

HASHIMOTO (HASIMOTO) Mure
Lieutenant-General; Used poison gas in Shansi province, China (probably under 1st Army), 1939.

HASHIMOTO Toranosuke
Lieutenant-General; Commander of Secret Police in Manchuria, August 1932 – August 1933; Vice Minister of War, January 1934.

HASUNUMA Shigeru
General; Chief aide-de-camp to Emperor Hirohito, c.1942–end of the war; Present at an Imperial Conference to ratify peace proposals and the surrender, 14 August 1945.

HATA Eitaro
(Full?) General; Elder brother of Field Marshal S. HATA.

HATA Hikosaburo
Colonel; Military Attaché to embassy in Russia (he had a high opinion of Russian military capability); Lieutenant-General; Vice Chief of Army General Staff, Tokyo, c.1943; Visited Southern Army regions to report on campaigns; Visited Southern Army HQ (under H. TERAUCHI) at Manila, Philippines, April 1944; Visited Burma Area Army HQ (under M. KAWABE), Rangoon, 1–2 May 1944, and then returned to Tokyo; Reported to Premier H. TOJO that he considered the Imphal–Kohima operation by Burma Area Army would fail and was accused of defeatism; Chief of Staff to Kwantung Army (under O. YAMADA), HQ Hsinking, Manchuria; Present at a conference to discuss the Emperor's surrender broadcast and recommended that the Kwantung Army accept it, 16 August 1945; Flew in a Soviet aircraft from Harbin to HQ of 1st Red Banner Army near the Soviet–Manchurian border (at Jaliho?), north–east of Vladivostock where he agreed surrender terms for Kwantung Army with Marshal Alexander M. Vasilivsky, C in C Soviet Far Eastern Armies, 19 August 1945; Ordered arrested by American occupation forces in Tokyo as a suspected war criminal, 2 December 1945.

HATA Shunroku
Born 1879; younger brother of E. HATA; 2nd Lieutenant (artillery), June 1901; Graduated from War College with 'top scholarly rank', November 1910; Army General Staff, December 1910; Military Student in Germany, March 1912; Major, July 1914; Official duty in Europe, September 1914; Lieutenant-Colonel, July 1918; Official Duty in Europe, December 1918; Member of Plenipotentiary's Suite at Peace Conference, February 1919; Colonel and Commander of 16th Field Artillery Regiment, July 1921; Major-General, March 1926; Commander of 4th Heavy Field Artillery Brigade, March 1926; Chief of 4th Bureau of Army General Staff, July 1927; Chief of 1st Bureau of Army General Staff, August 1928; Lieutenant-General; Inspector-General of Artillery Training, August 1931; Commander of 14th Division, August 1933; Chief of Army Aeronautical Department, December 1935; Commander of Formosa Army, August 1936; Military Councillor, August 1937; (Concurrently?) Inspector-General of Military Training, August 1937; General, November 1937; Commander of Central China Expeditionary Army, February 1938; Military Councillor, December 1938; Senior aide-de-camp to Emperor Hirohito, May 1939; War Minister in N. ABE cabinet from August 1939 and continued in the post in Admiral M. YONAI cabinet;

Forced to resign by Army Chief of Staff Prince K. KANIN to bring down the M. YONAI government because the army did not agree with the policy of improving relationships with Britain and America, June 1940; Military Councillor, July 1940; Commander-in-Chief of China Expeditionary Army, March 1942–November 1944; Replaced (by Y. OKAMURA); Field Marshal, June 1943; Inspector-General of Military Education, November 1944; Commander-in-Chief of 2nd General Army, activated by IGHQ (controlling 15th & 16th Armies), April 1945; GHQ Hiroshima Castle;* Responsible for the defence of Kyushu, Shikoku and western Honshu, Japan; instructed by IGHQ to prepare for Operation 'KETSU-GO' (expulsion of Allied invasion forces before consolidation of a beach-head), July 1945; Coastal defences less than 70 per cent complete by August 1945; Agreed with other senior army leaders that the army would act in accordance with the Emperor's wishes for peace and requested War Minister K. ANAMI that he would be allowed to give up his rank of Field Marshal (presumably as atonement for the defeat), 14 August 1945; Arrested as a Class A war criminal; Tried by the International Tribunal for the Far East, Tokyo, 26 April 1946–12 November 1948; Found guilty and sentenced to life imprisonment; Died 1962.

* GHQ Hiroshima Castle was destroyed by the atomic bomb, 5 August 1945. He was probably in Tokyo at the time but the subordinate 59th Army Commander Y.FUJII was killed.

HATTORI
Major-General; Commander of Railway Unit attached to 25th Army (under T. YAMASHITA) for invasion of Malaya, 1941–2.

HATTORI
Lieutenant-General; Commander of 5th Air Division, Cambodia, c.1945; Reported, together with T. SAKUMA, to HQ Allied Land Forces, Phnom Penh, to receive surrender orders, October 1945.

HATTORI Hisashi
Major-General; Commander of 2nd Independent Infantry Brigade, Shihchi-achuang province, China, January 1945?.

HATTORI Naomi
Major-General; Commander of 60th Infantry Brigade (in 69th Division), Taiyuan, Shansi province, China, December 1942; At Linfan by April 1944; At Yuncheng, Shansi province, late 1944.

HAYASHI (HAYASI)
Lieutenant-General; Commander of 1st Division, c.1931.

HAYASHI Senjuro
Lieutenant-General; Commander of Japanese Army (Chōsen Army) in Korea, 1931 (Possibly replacing J. MINAMI); Acted in support of Kwantung Army (see S. HONJO) and without the approval of the Japanese cabinet by attacking along the South Manchurian Railway from Changchun to Port Arthur, September 1931;* War Minister in Admiral K. OKADA cabinet (replacing S. ARAKI), July 1934; Purged 'Strike North' (i.e., against Russia) advocates from the Kwantung Army; Resigned (replaced by Y. KAWASHITA), 3 September 1935; Prime Minister (replacing Hirota), 4 February 1937; Immediately dissolved the Diet (parliament)

hoping new elections would strengthen the Showakai Party (which was backed by the army) but this failed; Resigned because the newly elected Diet opposed army expansionist policies, 30 April 1937 (replaced by Prince Konoye); Became a Jushin (elder statesman) and adviser to throne, c.1941; Agreed at a conference with seven other Jushin and the Emperor that war was the only course left open for Japan, 29 November 1941.

*This disobeyed the order that an army commander would not use troops outside his area without direct order from the Emperor.

HAYASHI (HYASHI) Yoshihide (Gishu)

Masterminded 'Nonni Bridge Incident' which precipitated the Japanese invasion of northern Manchuria, November 1931; Colonel; Commanded an army research team 'Unit 82' (under T. YAMASHITA) on Formosa to collect data on tropical warfare and to study the feasibility of attacking South East Asia, Philippines, Malaya, etc. (i.e., 'Strike South'), late 1940; Major-General; Director General of the Japanese Military Administration of the Philippines, 1933-34; Commander of the 24th Independent Mixed Brigade, Burma (formed for Tenasserim coast garrison duties under Burma Area Army – M. KAWABE) with four battalions; Strength 5,495 by 1 January 1944; Brigade moved north via Mandalay, arriving at Indaw (placed under direct command of 15th Army – R. MUTAGUCHI), 18 March 1944; Went straight into battle against British 'Chindit' operations (second raid) which threatened supplies and communications to 15th Army forces heading for Imphal; reinforced by three battalions from 15th, 18th, 56th Divisions (strength increased to 20,000), mid–late March 1944; Attacked by British from their 'Aberdeen' base, 26 March 1944; British attack failed; Attacked British 'White City' base (British 77th Brigade) near Mawlu, north of Indaw; Reinforced to 9 battalions, 6th April 1944; Launched numerous attacks but eventually repulsed after prolonged heavy fighting and numerous casualties (more than 3,000 against only several hundred British casualties); Retreated by 16 April 1944; Ordered by GOC 53rd Division K. TAKEDA to garrison Indaw area with remnant, mid May 1944;[1] Replaced (by T. SAKUMA), c.1944; Lieutenant-General; Commander of 53rd Division (replacing K. TAKEDA) under 33rd Army (M. HONDA), Burma, c.1944; Covered crossing of Sittang River for units of 28th Army (under S. SAKURAI) when they attempted to break out from Pegu Yomas into Tenasserim, July 1945;[2] At 53rd Division HQ, Shanywa, to greet 28th Army Commander S. SAKURAI when the formal announcement of the Japanese surrender was made, 15 August 1945; HQ at Kaywe for the formal surrender.

[1] Indaw was the main supply depot for 33rd Division plus rations and ammunition for 15th Division. It also had an airfield. Thus it was very important for the Japanese.
[2] One reference says he was killed on 10 April 1945 but this has not been substantiated elsewhere.

HAYASHI Yoshitaro

Lieutenant-General; Commander of 110th Division, Layang, Honan province, China, from August 1942.

HAYASHIDA Hirotsugu

Major-General; Commander of 84th Infantry Brigade (in 114th Division), Linfen, Shansi province, China, November 1944.

Prince HIGASHIKUNI Naruhiko (Toshihiko) 東久爾 稔彦

Born December 1887; Uncle of Emperor Hirohito and brother of princes Y. ASAKA and M. NASHIMOTO; Established the 'House of Higashikuni' by order of

Emperor Meiji, November 1906; Graduated from Military Academy, 1908; Graduated from War College, 1914; Captain; Company Commander in 29th Infantry Regiment, 1915; Major and Battalion Commander in 7th Division, July 1918; Resident Officer in France studying military tactics, April 1920; Staff Officer at Army General Staff HQ; Major-General, December 1929; Commander of 5th Infantry Brigade, 1930; Lieutenant-General and Commander of 4th Division, August 1934; Military Councillor, December 1935; Commander of Japanese Army Air Force (Army Aeronautical Department); Ordered the bombing of civilians in China, August 1937; Commander of 2nd Army, China, April 1938; Personally commanded four divisions in attack on Hankow from the rear, April–October 1938; Military Councillor, January 1939; General, August 1939; served in China; Awarded Order of the Golden Kite First Class, 1940; Concurrently Commander of Defence Command and Member of Supreme War Council, December 1941–July 1944;* Military Councillor, April 1945;' Field Marshal during last period; Suddenly appointed Prime Minister (replacing K. SUZUKI) to conclude rapidly the Japanese surrender, 16 August 1945; Instructed by the Emperor to kerb army indiscipline by those opposed to the surrender; (General MacArthur landed in Japan, 30 August 1945); Official surrender of all Japanese armed forces signed on behalf of the Japanese government by Foreign Minister Shigemitsu Mamoru on board the USS *Missouri*, Tokyo Bay, 2 September 1945; Reverted to commoner status, November 1945; Operated provisions, second-hand goods and dressmakers shops; Formed new religious order (Higashikuni-Kyo) which was banned.

Note: He signed official documents NARUHIKO-Ō, i.e., NARUHIKO–Prince.

* He was approached to form a government to replace Premier Prince Konoye (and make the decision for or against war with America) but was against the involvement of members of the royal family in politics so declined. He finally accepted the position of Prime Mnister because of a personal request from the Emperor to bring the war to a conclusion.

HIGUCHI Kiichiro

2nd Lieutenant (infantry), December 1909; Graduated from War College, November 1918; Member of Army General Staff, April 1922; Staff Officer to Korea army, December 1923; Major, August 1924; Military Attaché to Japanese Legation in Poland, May 1925; Attached to 34th Infantry Regiment, February 1928; Lieutenant-Colonel, August 1928; Attached to Army Technical Department, August 1930; Staff Officer to Tokyo Garrison HQ, August 1932; Colonel, March 1933; Commander of 41st Infantry Regiment, August 1933; Chief of Staff to 3rd Division, August 1935; Army General Staff, March 1937; Major-General; Kwantung Army HQ, Manchuria, August 1937; Chief of 2nd Bureau of Army General Staff, July 1938; Lieutenant-General, October 1939; Commander of 9th Division, December 1939; Commander-in-Chief, Northern District Army, Japan, August 1942; Commander-in-Chief, Northern Army, Japan, February 1943; Commander-in-Chief, 5th Area Army (upgraded Northern Army), HQ Sapporo, Japan, March or April 1944; Concurrently Commander-in-Chief of Northern District Army Command, February 1945; Held both posts until the end of the war.

HIJI Kata

Major-General; Military Commander of west Java, 1942.

HIRANO Shozo

Major-General; Commander of 2nd Engineers Unit, Manchuria, March 1943.

HIRANO Toyoji

Major-General; Commander of Military Police (Kempeitai) Unit of 25th Army, March 1943; Sumatra, March 1944.

Baron HIRANUMA Kiichirō

General; Retired; Ultra nationalist; Minister of Justice; President of Privy Council, 1936-9; Helped to form 'Kokuhon-sha' (organization for spreading nationalist propaganda among the young); Prime Minister, January 1939; Told the Diet (parliament) that those Chinese who failed to understand (i.e., co-operate with) the Japanese must be exterminated; Failed to slow army expansionist policy in China; Not informed by the Japanese navy of their occupation of the Chinese island of Hainan until after it occurred; Resigned as a result of the signing of the German–Soviet non-aggression pact which violated the 1936 Anti-Comitern Pact (to oppose Russian interference abroad) which had been signed by Germany and Japan, 28 August 1939; Became a Jushin (elder statesman); Opposed war with America, 1941; President of Privy Council, 5 April 1945 – until the end of the war; Recommended at an Imperial Conference that negotiations for peace should be pursued (after dropping of the first atomic bomb), August 1945; Insisted that the Emperor's position must be protected; Narrowly escaped assassination attempt by army officers opposed to the surrender, 14 August 1945; Held in Sugamo prison, Tokyo, as a suspected war criminal, September 1945; Tried by the International Tribunal for the Far East, 1946-48; Sentenced to life imprisonment, 1948.

HIRAOKA Chikara

Major-General; Chief of Military Affairs Department of 1st Guards Division, Tokyo, c.May 1944.

HIRAOKA Kiyoshi

Major-General; Commander of 11th Field Transport Command, October 1941; Central China, February 1944.

HIRATA Juzo

Major-General; Concurrently Commander of three Home Stations for infantry and army units at Shibata, Muramatsu and Takeda, all in Niigata Regimental District, March 1945?

HIRATA (HIRADA) Masachika (Shokoku)

Major-General; Member of an IGHQ liaison team to 22nd Division, China, 1941; Lieutenant-General; Commander of 22nd Division, January 1944; Division at Canton, China; Moved south to Pingsiang near Indo–China border, January 1945; Under 18th Area Army (A. NAKAMURA) command, Siam, by end of the war; Surrendered at Ubon, Siam, 1945.

Note: Surrendered a sword (together with A. NAKAMURA, eighteen Generals and two Admirals) to Major-General G. C. Evans, GOC 7th Indian Division, at Bangkok, Siam, 11 January 1946.

HISHIKARI Taka

General; Ambassador to Manchukuo and Commander of Kwantung Army (replacing N. MUTO), Manchuria, July 1933.

HISHIKI Tomejiro

Major-General; Commander of Home Station for one infantry unit at Wakamatsu in Fukushima Regimental District, March 1945.

HITOMI Hidezo

Lieutenant-General; Commander of 12th Division, October 1943; Division at Mutanchiang province, Manchuria, until December 1944; Transferred to Formosa, January–February 1945.

HOJO (HOJYO, HOKUJO) Takichi (Tokichi)

Major-General; Commander of 54th Independent Mixed Brigade from its activation in June 1944; Defended Zamboagna Peninsula, Mindanao, Philippines (under 35th Army – S. SUZUKI) with nearly 9,000 army (and naval) troops, 1945; American 41st Division landed, 10 May 1945; fought from heavily defended positions inland from the beaches but was driven further inland from the peninsula with nearly 50 per cent losses by April 1945; Units scattered, being hunted by American and Filippino guerrillas; Only about 2,000 survived by the time of the surrender; Possibly a Lieutenant-General by the end of the war.

HONDA Atsushi

Major-General; Commander of 1st Airfield Unit, January 1944.

HONDA Masaki (Seizai)

Born 1889 in Iida, Nagano prefecture, Japan; Entered school at Nagano but sent to Military Cadet School while in his second year of school; Entered Military Academy and graduated; 2nd Lieutenant (infantry) in the 4th Regiment of Imperial Guards Division, 1910; Staff Captain on Imperial General Staff by 1918; Military Attaché in Paris for three years; Major in the infantry, 1925; Commander of a battalion of 22nd Infantry Regiment, 1926; Senior lecturer at the Infantry School, 1930; On staff of Military Education Branch, 1932; Colonel; Commander of 22nd Infantry Regiment, 1934; Major-General, 1937; Vice Commander of Infantry School, 1938; Lieutenant-General; Chief of Staff to China Expeditionary Army, December 1939; Commander of 8th Division, Manchuria, October 1940; Chief of Armoured Warfare Department in Military Education Branch, 1941–3; Commander of 20th Army, Manchuria, 1943; Commander of 33rd Army, Burma (under Burma Area Army – M. KAWABE), from its activation, April 1944; Comprised 18th Division (S. TANAKA), 56th Division, 53rd Division, (K. TAKEDA) and controlled north-east Burma; Ordered 18th Division to withdraw from Mogaung Valley to Sahmaw, June 1944; Ordered 53rd Division to reinforce Myitkyina but then diverted it to reinforce 18th Division, June 1944 (Myitkyina airfield already taken by the Allies in mid May 1944); 18th Division (E. NAKA) sent to relieve Meiktila but failed to arrive before its capture by the Allies (see E. NAKA, T. KASUYA); 49th Division (S. TAKEHARA) added to 33rd Army command, March 1945; Given personal command of forces to recapture Meiktila with 18th and 49th Divisions plus two regiments from 33rd and 53rd Divisions; Temporarily formed a separate army called 'The Army of the Decisive Battle' (Kesshōgun), 18 March 1945 (Caretaker of 33rd Army in his absence from HQ was Y. MATSUYAMA); Japanese attacks met with limited success but were repulsed with heavy losses by 27 March 1945; Ordered by Burma Area Army Chief of Staff (S. TANAKA) to turn 33rd Army from offensive to defensive role by protecting the retreat of 15th Army (S. KATAMURA), late March 1945;

Attempted to prevent British push from Meiktila with depleted 18th and 49th Divisions; HQ near Pyawbwe and just missed capture when it was overrun by British and Indian troops, 10? April 1945; Battle of Pyawbwe (resulted in this area being cleared of Japanese by 11 April 1945) allowed the British to advance on Rangoon; 33rd Army reduced to only approximately 8,000 (18th, 49th, 53rd Divisions plus four regiments from 2nd Division), 14 April 1945; Formed a defensive position with 18th and 49th Divisions at Sinthe Chaung, south of Yamethin plus 53rd Division and elements of 55th Division (T. HANAYA), with HQ near Pyinmana; HQ attacked and destroyed by British tanks but he escaped on foot, 19 April 1945; Army broken up and scattered; Ordered by Burma Area Army (H. KIMURA) to mount an offensive to retake Rangoon and help 28th Army (S. SAKURAI) break out from Pegu Yomas hills into Tenasserim but he refused since the army was only capable of delaying tactics (33rd Army strength was only: 18th Division – 2,000, 55th Division elements – 1,000, 56th Division – 1,600, 49th Division – 300), end of May 1945; Set up supply dumps for 28th Army if they succeeded in the breakout; Launched limited attack at Nyaungkashe and Abya in the Sittang River bend area with 18th and 53rd Divisions which was 10 days premature (Battle of Sittang Bend) in support of 28th Army crossing, 3 July 1945; HQ at Bilin, Burma, August 1945; Surrendered at British Twelfth Army HQ, Rangoon, to General Sir Montagu Stopford, 25 August 1945;[1] Formally surrendered a sword to Major-General Crowther, GOC 17th Indian Division, at Thaton, Burma, 25 October 1945;[2] Commanded all Japanese POWs in Burma from 1945 until repatriation; Returned to Japan; 1947; Died, 17 July 1964 aged 75.

Personal facts: Attractive to women. Loved fishing and sakē. Did not gamble. Fairly academic and conducted his personal life and career with 'studied correctness'. Renowned for his kindness to the private soldier. Unusually, for a man of his rank, he told filthy stories even to private soldiers (probably to boost morale).

[1] This is accordng to *The Four Samurai* by Arthur Swinson (*see* Bibliography) but it has not been verified elsewhere. He is also said to have surrendered a sword at this ceremony.
[2] The blade is signed 'OMI DAIJO FUJIWARA TADAHIRO', i.e., Fujiwara Tadahiro, lord of Omi. Probably Tadahiro of Hizen, c.1650. *Shin-guntō* mounts. Now in the National Army Museum, London. Cat.no. 6003–32. Major-General Crowther received the sword on behalf of Lieutenant-General Sir Montagu Stopford, C in C, Twelfth Army, who in turn presented it to Lieutenant-General Sir Frank Messervy, Commander of IVth Corps. He gave it to the museum.

HONDŌ

Major-General; Head of the Japanese Army Negotiating Committee which concluded a cease-fire agreement with the Russians, ending the fighting on the Manchurian – Mongolian border, 15 September 1939.

HONGO Yoshio

Lieutenant-General; Commander of 62nd Division from its activation in June 1943; Located in Shansi province, China; Moved to Honan province, May 1944, then back to Shansi; Division transferred to Okinawa (under 32nd Army), arriving September 1944; Replaced by T. FUJIOKA, March 1945 (*see also* K. ARIKAWA), 1944 or 1945; Commander of 44th Army (under 3rd Area Army – J. USHIROKU)* for defence of western Manchuria (comprising 63rd, 107th, 117th Divisions); HQ Liaoyuan; Russians invaded Manchuria, 9 August 1945; 107th

Division defending the Halung–Taoan railway was isolated by 13 August 1945; 63rd and 117th Divisions suffered heavy losses; Taoan captured by the Russians, 14 August 1945; Believed to have surrendered at the cessation of hostilities.

* Formerly Kwantung Defence Army but renamed, 5 June 1945. 63rd and 117th Divisions were transferred from China.

Baron HONJO Shigeru

Expert on China and spoke fluent Chinese; Military adviser to north China warlord Chang Tso-lin, 1921-4; Commander of 10th Division, HQ Osaka, Japan, 1931; General; Commander-in-Chief of Kwantung Army, HQ Port Arthur, Manchuria, August 1931; Away from HQ during 'Manchurian Incident' (see S. IZAGAKI) and was not consulted about the mobilization of the army and the subsequent military action, 18–19 September 1931; Captured Mukden and south Manchuria with HQ being moved to Mukden, September 1931; Invaded north Manchuria and captured Tsitshihar, November 1931; Recalled to Tokyo and replaced (by N. MUTO), August 1932; Elevated to the Peerage, late 1932; Member of Supreme War Council; Chief aide-de-camp to Emperor Hirohito, 6 April 1933; Resigned because of his son-in-law's involvement in the '2–26' insurrection, April 1936; retired to first reserve, 22 April 1936; President of the organization for the relief of demobilized soldiers by 1945; Committed ritual suicide (seppuku), Tokyo, 20 November 1945, after reading a newspaper report that he was to be arrested and tried as a war criminal (for instigating the 'Manchurian' or 'Mukden Incident' which precipitated the Japanese invasion of Manchuria).

HONMA (HOMMA) Masaharu 本間　雅晴

Born 27 November 1887; 2nd Lieutenant (infantry), November 1907; Graduated from War College, December 1915; Captain; Attached to Army General Staff, August 1917; Military student attached to East Lancashire Regiment, England, and served as an observer with British Second Army HQ in France during First World War; Awarded the British Military Cross, 1918; Devoted all his spare time to studying English; Assistant Military Attaché in London, 1920; Instructor at War College, Japan, June 1921; Resident Officer in India, 1922–4; Army General Staff, August 1925; Aide-de-camp to, and protégé of, Prince Chichibu, January 1927; Military Attaché to Britain, June 1930–2; Acknowledged expert on British affairs and pro-British; Army General Staff, May 1932; Chief of War Ministry Press Relations Squad, 1932; Commander of 1st Infantry Regiment, August 1933; Major-General; Commander of 32nd Infantry Brigade, August 1935; Army General Staff, December 1936; Accompanied Prince Chichibu to London for the coronation of George VI, 1937; Chief of 2nd Bureau (Intelligence) of Army General Staff, July 1937; Sent to Nanking, China, to assess reports of Japanese massacres, January 1938; Lieutenant-General; Commander of 27th Division, China, July 1938; Commander of Japanese blockading force of Tientsin foreign concessions, China, 1939; Commander of 14th Army (under Southern Expeditionary Army – H. TERAUCHI) comprising 16th Division (S. MORIOKA), 48th Division (Y. TSUCHIHASHI) for the invasion of the Philippines, November 1941; Main invasion force landed between Agoo and Bauang, Lingayen Gulf, Luzon, 22–23 December 1941; Drove back the Filipino and American forces 50 miles in six days; Army entered Manila, 2 January 1942; 48th Division and most of 5th Air Group were removed from his command for the invasion of Java but 65th Brigade (A. NAKA) arrived as reinforcements; Forced Allied retreat into Bataan, 26

January 1942; Broke off offensive to rest and reorganize, 8 February 1942;[1] Reproved by the Emperor for his failure to capture Bataan on schedule and his command authority was pre-empted by a group of staff officers from Southern Army HQ with Imperial orders; Reinforced with 4th Division (K. KITANO); Recommenced attack, 3 April 1942; Bataan surrendered, 9 April 1942; Corregidor (the last Allied stronghold) surrendered, 6 May 1942; Recalled to Tokyo and given a 'conquering general's welcome' although still in disgrace for his time failure;[2] Replaced (by S. TANAKA); Transferred to first reserve list, August 1943 – end of war; Tried as a Class A war criminal by an American military tribunal, Manila, Philippines; Charged with 'violating rules of war' including responsibility for the 'Bataan Death March'[3] (see also Y. KAWANE) although he retained only nominal command at the time, December 1945–April 1946; Executed by firing squad (as a soldier while his subordinates were hanged) at Los Banos, Luzon, 3 April 1946; His name was 'cleared' and removed from the list of war criminals by the Japanese Government, 1952.

Personal facts: Graduated from Staff College with a high pass mark. Regarded by his contemporaries as the senior Lieutenant-General in the Japanese army. Recognized as a superb strategist. Had a cold and aristocratic manner. Wrote prose and verse. A fine linguist, being fluent in spoken and written English. Tall for a Japanese, being nearly 5 feet 10 inches.

[1] His failure to attack without reinforcements was regarded by many generals as a breach of the samurai code of *bushido* which warranted dismissal. He was expected to attack in accordance with orders regardless of the likely outcome whether it be defeat or victory.
[2] However, according to *The Rising Sun* by J. Toland (*see* Bibliography) he was refused permission to make the traditional conqueror's report to the Emperor, which compounded his disgrace.
[3] Refused to allow ill-treatment of Filipinos and did not accept that the Americans had exploited the Philippines. Certain staff officers (notably Lieutenant-Colonel Tsuji Masanobu) issued orders in his name and without his knowledge for the execution of all prisoners of war and countermanded his lenient policies. The C in C Southern Army, H. TERAUCHI, also forwarded an unfavourable report to Tokyo about his liberal attitude. HONMA ordered the release of all Filipino soldiers captured after the invasion against the advice of his staff.

HORII Tomitaro

2nd Lieutenant (infantry), December 1911; Attached to Shanghai Expeditionary Army HQ, February 1932; Battalion Commander in 68th regiment, August 1932; Lieutenant-Colonel; Attached to 3rd Infantry Regiment and Training Officer at Wasede University, August 1933; Attached to 12th Independent Infantry Regiment, January 1935; Colonel, August 1937; Attached to HQ of 8th Depot Division, October 1937; Commander of 82nd Infantry Regiment, July 1938; Major General; Attached to HQ of 11th Depot Division, March 1940; Commander of South Seas Detached Force (Nankai Shitai) from its activation, November 1941, (formed from units of 55th Division for independent missions); Sailed from the Bonin Islands, 23 November 1941; Invaded Guam, 10 December 1941; Invaded Rabaul, New Britain, 23 January 1942; Unit involved in massacre of Australian prisoners at Rabaul; Detachment captured Salamaua, New Guinea, 8 March 1942; Sailed from Rabaul with Port Moresby Invasion Force but returned after the Japanese naval defeat at the Battle of the Coral Sea, 7 May 1942; Advance unit (of 15th Independent Engineer Unit – Colonel Yokoyama) landed at Gona, north-east coast of New Guinea, 21 July 1942; Advanced along the difficult Kokoda trail (across Owen Stanley mountains to Port Moresby); Kokoda plateau captured in 1st Battle of Kokoda, 28–29 July 1942; Kokoda taken by the Australians without a fight; Retaken by Japanese at 2nd Battle of Kokoda, 10 August 1942; HORII sailed with main body of South Seas Detached Force from Rabaul, 17 August 1942; Landed at Basabua between Gona and Buna, 18 August 1942;[1] 7,626 troops landed at three sites, 29 July–22 August 1942; SSDF placed under control of 18th Army; Reached Kokoda and inspected the front line at Deniki, 24 August 1942; Captured Isurava Valley, 26 August 1942; Battle of Isurava, 26–30 August 1942, suffering severe losses but the Australians were forced to withdraw; Occupied Alola, 30 August 1942; Issued the order that shortages forced economies of ammunition and supplies, 1 September 1942; Myola occupied after the Australians were forced to withdraw, 3 September 1942; Japanese advanced to Efogi with establishment of HQ there, 7 September 1942; HQ moved to Nauro but with only minimal supplies, mid September 1942; Battle of Ioraibaiwa Ridge (within sight of Port Moresby) forced an Australian withdrawal to Imita Ridge but Japanese strength had reduced to only 50 per cent and food was almost nil, 12–18 September 1942; Ordered a withdrawal from Ioraibaiwa (limit of the advance) because of food shortages, lack of ammunition and sickness compounded by 18th Army withdrawing units to defend Buna against expected American landings, 25 September 1942; General fighting retreat along Kokoda trail towards Buna on the coast with strong rearguard actions;[2] Kokoda retaken by Australians, 2 November 1942; Suffered 580 killed at the Battle of Oivi, 10 November 1942; Drowned with his Chief of Staff and two other officers while attempting to cross the Kumusi River, 11 or 12 November 1942 (Remnant reached original beach-head. *See also* K. ODA).

[1] By 20 August 1942 the force consisted of: HQ, two battalions of 144th Infantry Regiment, 55th Mountain Artillery, 47th Field Anti-Artillery, 5th Sasebo Naval Landing Force, two battalions of 41st Infantry Regiment and ancillaries.
[2] The advancing Australians found examples of atrocities and canabalism on Australian captives perpetrated by the starving retreating Japanese.

HOSHINO Toshimoto
Lieutenant-General; Commander of 1st Armoured Division (under Kwantung Army), Ningan, Manchuria, September 1944; Commander of 50th Army (under 11th Area Army) for defence of Japan, HQ Aomori, Japan, 1945.

HOSOKAWA Tadayasu
Lieutenant-General; Commander of 59th Division, Tsinan, Shantung province, China, March 1943; Commander of 43rd Army, HQ Tsinan, China, by 1945; Surrendered 43rd Army, 47th Division and other units to Chinese General Hu Tsung-nan of 1st War Area at Tsinan upon the cessation of hostilities, September 1945.

HOSOMI Koreo
Major-General; Commander of 1st Tank Brigade (in 1st Armoured Division – T. HOSHINO), Ningan, Manchuria, December 1944.

HSUO Mabutsi – Same as MABUCHI Itsuo

HYAKUTAKE Seikichi (Haruyoshi, Harukichi)
Younger brother of Admiral HYAKUTAKE Saburo; 2nd Lieutenant (infantry), December 1909; Graduated from War College, December 1921; Attached to Army General Staff, December 1922; Member of latter, June 1923; Major, August 1923; Resident Officer in Poland, December 1925; Lieutenant-Colonel, August 1928;

Attached to Kwantung Army HQ, Manchuria, August 1931; Colonel; Attached to Army Signal School, August 1932; Section Chief in Army General Staff, February 1933; Commander of 78th infantry Regiment, March 1935; Superintendent of Hiroshima Military Preparatory School, April 1936; Major-General, March 1937; Superintendent of Army Signal School, August 1937; Commander of 4th Independent Mixed Brigade, March 1939; Lieutenant-General, August 1939; Inspector-General of Signal Training, April 1940; Commander of 17th Army, May 1942; Controlled New Guinea, Dutch East Indies, Guam and Solomons; Ordered by IGHQ, Tokyo to reoccupy Guadalcanal and Tulagi from the invading American forces, August 1942; Ordered Operation 'KA' to prevent the occupation of Guadalcanal by American marines with 28th Infantry Regiment (under Colonel KICHIKI) landing advance unit on 18 August 1942; Battle of Tenaru (Ilu) resulted in a Japanese defeat with the loss of 800 men (ICHIKI shot himself at Taivu), 21 August 1942; Reinforcement under K. KAWAGUCHI were landed by reinforce-ment-convoy 'Tokyo Express'; Operation failed because of the Japanese in-sistence on full frontal attack (*banzai* charges) which resulted in heavy losses; HYAKUTAKE took personal command of Guadalcanal operations; Sailed with reinforcements of 230th Regiment from 38th Division, 16th Regiment from 2nd Division (*see* M. MARUYAMA, Y. NASU) and 17th Army Artillery Section (*see* T. SUMIYOSHI) plus a large naval escort; Landed with staff, 10 October 1942; Main force landed at Tassafaronga, 15 October 1942 (Total strength now brought up to about 20,000 which was approx. equal to American forces); Planned a full-scale attack on Henderson airfield which was scheduled for 23 October 1942; Two-pronged attack with a diversionary attack was launched but failed with heavy losses; General retreat but reinforcements were landed east of American positions, 1 November 1942; 350 Japanese killed at Battle of Gavaga Creek, 10 November 1942; Retreated inland; Reinforcements and supplies landed 2–10 November 1942; Reinforced with remnant of 38th Division (under T. SANO) after loss of transports carrying them, 15 November 1942; 8th Area Army (under H. IMAMURA) was formed which subordinated and relegated 17th Army to the Guadalcanal area, December 1942 or January 1943; IGHQ, Tokyo, issued orders for the withdrawal of all Japanese forces on Guadalcanal, 4 January 1943; HQ moved to Tassafaronga, 10 January 1943; Last reinforcements arrived, 13 January 1943; The American build-up, lack of supplies and heavy losses caused the Japanese campaign to fail; American forces took Mount Austen after bitter fighting, 18 January 1943; Orders for evacuation brought personally by 8th Area Army staff officers, 14 January 1943; all units withdrawn slowly towards Cape Esperance (troops were not told of the evacuation plan and the Americans did not find out); remnant of 38th Division (T. SANO) evacuated by destroyers at Cape Esperance, night of 12 February 1943; He evacuated the island with his staff and remnant of 2nd Division (M. MARUYAMA), night of 4/5 February 1943; Rearguard of 3,000 men evacuated, 7–8 February 1943 (A total of 11,000– 12,000 men were evacuated without detection by American army or naval forces. Only stragglers remained); Directed operations on Bougainville Island, Solomons; 17th Army now consisted of 6th Division and 38th IMB plus naval troops including 87th Garrison Force in Buka area, 6th Sasebo Special Naval Landing Force and 7th Kure Landing Force in the south; HQ in Buin–Faisi area, 1944; Ordered evacuation of Shortland and Fauro Islands, December 1944; Suffered a paralysis on his left side and was replaced (by M. KANDA), February 1945; Appears to have remained incapacitated on Bougainville until the cessation of hostilities, August 1945; Returned to Japan, February 1946; Died 10 March 1947.

ICHI
Major- or Lieutenant-General; Flown by the Australians to Morotai Island, Moluccas, formally to surrender all Japanese forces in the Celebes, 1945.

ICHIDA (ICHITA, ICHINA, ISHIDA) Jiro
Major-General; Vice Chief of Staff to Burma Area Army (under H. KIMURA); At 53rd Division HQ during the official announcement of Japan's surrender, Shanywa, Burma, 15 August 1945; Signed surrender of the Japanese forces under the command of Burma Area Army on behalf of H. KIMURA to Brigadier E. F. E. Armstrong of Twelfth Army at Government House, Rangoon, Burma, 13 September 1945; Surrendered a sword to Brigadier R. I. Jones of Twelfth Army Staff at Judson College, Rangoon, 24 October 1945 (This ceremony was presided over by Lieutenant-General Sir Montagu Stopford, C in C Twelfth Army. H. KIMURA, S. SAKURAI also surrendered their swords at this time).

ICHIKI
Major-General; Head of the Secretariat (Administrative Department) to the Governor-General of Hong Kong, 1942–5, possibly replacing YAMAZAKI.

ICHIKI Kiyonao
2nd Lieutenant (infantry), December 1916; Attached to Army Infantry School, February 1935; Instructor at Army Infantry School, April 1935; Lieutenant-Colonel, March 1938; Member of Research Branch of Toyama Army School, September 1939; Instructor at Army Infantry School, August 1940; Colonel, March 1941; Commander of 28th Infantry Regiment, July 1941; Formed advance unit of 17th Army (under S. HYAKUTAKE) for Operation 'KA' to repulse American marines from Guadalcanal; Landed on Guadalcanal, 18 August 1942; Defeated (with loss of 800 men) at Battle of Tenaru (Ilu); Committed suicide by shooting, 21 August 1942; Said to be a Major-General by this time, but it could have been a posthumous promotion.

IGA Tachibana – same as TACHIBANA Yoshio

IGATU
Lieutenant-General; Superior of S. KOH* who was Commander of Internee and POW camps in the Philippines; Apparently directly responsible to C in C 14th Area Army T. YAMASHITA, 1945.

* Possibly S. KOH was commander of all camps on Luzon while IGATU was responsible for all camps in the Philippines, but this is conjectural.

IGETA Keiji
Major-General; Chief of Staff to 31st Army (under H. OBATA) HQ Saipan Island, Marianas; The Americans landed on Saipan, 16 June 1945 (*see* Y. SAITO for campaign details); Confirmed to IGHQ, Tokyo, and to 31st Army HQ, Guam, that all forces would fight to the death, 25 June 1944; Decided at a meeting with Y. SAITO and Vice-Admiral C. NAGUMO to form a defensive line across the northern part of the island after being pushed back; Line broken by Americans; Committed suicide (*seppuku*) in a cave together with Y. SAITO, Vice-Admiral C. NAGUMO and Rear-Admiral K. IGETA, dawn on 7 July 1944.

IHARA Junjiro

Major-General; Chief of Staff to 34th Army (under S. KUSHIBUCHI), Korea, July 1942; Received American General Hodge, head of occupation forces for south Korea, on Getsubi Island, Inchon, Korea, 8 September 1945.

IIDA Shojiro

Born 1888; 2nd Lieutenant in 42nd Infantry Regiment, December 1908; 1st Lieutenant, December 1911; Graduated from War College, December 1915; Army Ordnance Department, October 1916; Captain, December 1918; Participated in Siberian Expedition, February 1919; Attached to 42nd Infantry Regiment, June 1921; Instructor at Infantry School, August 1922; Major, March 1924; Battalion Commander in 44th Infantry Regiment, August 1926; Instructor at Infantry School, December 1927; Lieutenant-Colonel, August 1928; Staff Officer in 4th Division, March 1930; Colonel and Instructor at Infantry School, August 1932; Commander of 4th Infantry Regiment in Guards Division, August 1934; Chief of Staff to 4th Division, August 1935; Chief of Military Administration Bureau of War Ministry; Major-General, March 1937; Chief of Staff to 1st Army, January 1938; Commander of Formosa Mixed Brigade, October 1938; Lieutenant-General, August 1939; Commander of 2nd Imperial Guards Division, October 1939, Commander of 25th Army, Saigon, Indo–China, July 1941; Replaced (by T. YAMASHITA), November 1941; Commander of 15th Army (under Burma Area Army) consisting of 33rd Division (S. SAKURAI), 55th Division (Y. TAKEUCHI) and 5th Air Division (H. OBATA), November 1941; Invaded Tanasserim coast, 11 December 1941; Moulmein captured, 31 January 1942; Ordered to take Rangoon as a priority; Rangoon captured, 8 March 1942; Reinforced with 18th and 56th Divisions which landed at Rangoon, early March 1942; Lashio (terminus of Burma Road) captured, 27 April 1942; Myitkyina occupied, 8 May 1942; Ordered 56th and 18th Divisions to halt at Salween River rather than advance into Yunnan province, China, 26 April 1942; Shwegyin on Chindwin River captured by 33rd Division, 9 May 1942; Final withdrawal of British Army from Burma, 20 May 1942 (with 13,000 British casualties against 4,000 Japanese); Ordered by C in C Southern Army, H. TERAUCHI, to plan Operation '21' to capture northern Assam in India with 18th and 33rd Divisions, but the idea was dropped because of his opposition and that of his divisional commanders, 25 October 1942; Employed 18th, 33rd and 56th Divisions to repulse the first 'Chindit' raid, from February 1943; Replaced (by R. MUTAGUCHI), 18 March 1943; Assigned to General Defence Command, Japan, April 1943; Retired, December 1944; Recalled as Commander of 30th Army (under 3rd Area Army – J. USHIROKU) for defence of south-western Manchuria, July 1945; HQ Hsinking (Changchun); Army consisted of 39th, 125th, 138th, 148th Divisions; Russia invaded Manchuria, 9 August 1945; Ordered by J. USHIROKU to move all forces to Hsinking (against 3rd Area Army policy) instead of forming pre-determined defensive positions; Arrived at Hsinking, 12 August 1945; Believed to have surrendered at the cessation of hostilities.

IIMURA Jo

Born 1888; 2nd Lieutenant (infantry) in 3rd Imperial Guard Infantry Regiment, December 1909; 1st Lieutenant, February 1913; Company Commander in 3rd Imperial Guard Infantry Regiment and Captain, June 1919; Graduated from War College, December 1921; Member of Army General Staff HQ, August 1923; Major, August 1924; Assigned to Korea Army HQ (with duty station in

Manchuria), October 1924; Instructor at War College, December 1926; Lieutenant-Colonel, August 1928; Military Attaché to Turkey, January 1930; Colonel, August 1932; Instructor at War College, September 1932; Section Chief at Army General Staff HQ, March 1933; Commander of 61st Infantry Regiment, March 1935; Major General; Member of Research Staff at War College, March 1937; Deputy Commandant of War College, March 1938; Commandant of War College, March 1939; Lieutenant-General, August 1939; Chief of Staff to Kwantung Army, Manchuria, September 1939 (after the 'Nomonhan Incident'); Army General Staff HQ, October 1940; Chief of Total Warfare Research Institute, January 1941; Commander of 5th Army, Manchuria, October 1941; Commandant of War College, October 1943; Extensive trip throughout East Asia to collect 'instructional material', February 1944; Chief of Staff to Southern army (under H. TERAUCHI), Saigon, March 1944; Thought Imphal–Kohima operation in Burma should be cancelled because it had a 80–85 per cent chance of success but he was overruled, May 1944; Sent to Philippines to convey order to C in C 14th Area Army T. YAMASHITA that Leyte Island was to be reinforced at all costs; Agreed with T. YAMASHITA that the defence of Luzon should be paramount at the expense of Leyte because of the American landings at Mindoro; Returned to Saigon with a report that he had changed operational instructions without Southern Army sanction and was sacked on the spot by H. TERAUCHI; Transferred to become C in C 2nd Area Army (regarded as non-operational), Pirang, Celebes (replacing K. ANAMI), December 1944; Commander of Toyko Defence Army (under IGHQ), activated June 1945; Concurrently Commander of Tokyo Divisional District, 1945; Instructed to defend Tokyo to the death but had only 20,000 men and no major defences by August 1945.

IIZUKA Keinosuke
Major-General; Commander of a Home Station for an infantry unit at Akita, Japan, March 1945.

IJUIN Kanenobu
Major-General; Commander of 51st Independent Mixed Brigade from its activation, Truk, Caroline Islands, May 1944.

IKEDA Naozo
Major-General; Commander of 20th Separate Composite Brigade* under 11th Army (A. TADAKI) during the Battle of Shangkao, early March 1941.

* This may be the same as an Independent Mixed Brigade.

IKEDA Renji
Lieutenant-General; Commander of 56th Depot Division (which supplied 12th, 18th, 56th, 86th Divisions and 19th IMB) Kurume, Japan, August 1944.

IKEDA Shunkichi
Lieutenant-General; Commander of 35th Division, March 1944; Division in Kaifeng area, north China until March 1944 then transferred via Manila to Halmahera Island, Moluccas, off north-west New Guinea (under 2nd Army) where it suffered heavy losses.

IKEDA Sumihisa

Lieutenant-General; Director of Imperial Cabinet Planning Board (or Bureau), July 1945; Attended last surrender meeting in the Emperor's bunker, 9 August 1945; Lead other former Japanese army officers serving Emperor Haile Selassie of Ethiopia 1953–62.

IKEGAMI Kenkichi

Major-General; Commander of 9th Independent Brigade (under 11th Army) during the third Battle of Changsha, China, late December 1941 – mid January 1942.

IKEHAMA Seiji

Major-General; Concurrently Commander of two Home Stations for an infantry unit at Ashigawa and an anti-aircraft unit at Obihiro, both in Kushiro Regimental District, Japan, March 1945.

IKUTA Torao

Major-General; Commander of a Garrison Unit which arrived on Luzon, Philippines, just before the fall of Bataan, April 1942; Verbally informed by 14th Army staff officers (see M. HONMA) that all prisoners of war must be executed, but he refused to comply without written orders; Manila Garrison Commander, 1942; 1st Garrison Unit Commander, eastern Japan, January 1944; Commander of 7th Independent Infantry Brigade, November 1944; Brigade located in Nanchang, Kiansi province, China.

IMADA Shintaro

Major-General; Chief of Staff to 36th Division, March 1936; Division in Shansi, China, until November 1943, then transferred to Halmahera, Moluccas, off western New Guinea.

IMAGAWA Issaku

Major-General; Commander of 59th Sentai (fighters), c.1939;* Fought in Nomonhan campaign against Russian aircraft on the Mongolian–Manchurian border, May–September 1939.

*A 'Sentai' was an airforce battle corps adopted in 1937, consisting of 3 or 4 squadrons each equipped with 40 fighters or 30 bombers or reconnaissance aircraft.

IMAI Kiyoshi

Lieutenant-General; Vice Chief of Army General Staff, c.1937.

IMAI Takeo

Colonel; Intermediary between Premier Prince Konoye and Wang Chang-wei (Chinese defector from the Kumintang Government who formed a puppet Chinese Government under the Japanese on 28 March 1938); Tried to organize direct contact with Chinese Nationalist Government (under Chiang Kai-shek) to reach an equitable agreement between Japan and China, 1940; Commander of a Regiment in 65th Infantry Brigade[1] (under A. NAKA) during the invasion of the Philippines, from November 1941; Brigade sent to front line to relieve 48th Division on the Bataan peninsula, 9 January 1942; The regiment attacked Filipinos down the coast road but was repulsed with one-third losses, 13 January 1942; Broke through Abucay defence line when a Filipino counter-attack overreached itself, 16 January 1942; Captured Mount Limay, 8 April 1942; Verbally informed that all prisoners of war must be executed after the fall of Bataan but he refused without confirmation by written orders;[2] Actually ordered the release of 1,000 prisoners, April 1942; Major-General; Deputy Chief of Staff to China Expeditionary Army (under Y. OKAMURA), HQ Nanking, China; Flew from Nanking to Chihkiang, Honan province, to receive the surrender orders for all Japanese troops in China, Formosa and northern Indo–China from Chinese Lieutenant-General Hsiao I-su, Army Affairs Chief of Staff, 21–23 August 1945.

[1] Probably 148th Regiment but also given as 9th Regiment.
[2] A 14th Army staff officer, Lieutenant-Colonel Tsuji Masanobu, convinced some fellow officers that a massacre of prisoners was necessary because of racist principles. They in turn persuaded some field commanders that it was an official order although it was without the knowledge, and against the principles, of the 14th Army Commander, M. HONMA.

IMAMURA Hitoshi (Kinichi) 今村 勾

Born 1886; 2nd Lieutenant (infantry), December 1907; Graduated from War College, December 1915; Captain, May 1917; member of Military Affairs Bureau of War Ministry, May 1917; Military student in England, April 1918; Assistant Military Attaché in England, October 1918; Official duty in Europe, August 1920; Army General Staff, August 1921; Major, August 1922; Lieutenant-Colonel, August 1926; Resident Officer in India, April 1927; Colonel; Section chief in Military Affairs Bureau of War Ministry, August 1930; Section Chief on Army General Staff, August 1931; Commander of 57th Infantry Regiment, April 1932; Commandant of Narashino Army School, August 1933; Major-General and Commander of 40th Infantry Brigade, March 1935; Deputy Chief of Staff to Kwantung Army, Manchuria, March 1936; Commandant of Army Infantry School, August 1937; Chief of Army Administration Bureau of War Ministry, January 1938; Lieutenant-General, March 1938; Commander of 5th Division, China, 1938 or 1939 – January 1940; Deputy Chief of Inspectorate General of Military Training, March 1940; Commander of 23rd Army, June 1941; Commander of 16th Army (under Southern Army – H. TERAUCHI) formed for the invasion of Java and the Dutch East Indies; Java invaded, February 1942; Forced to jump into the sea in Bantam Bay when his ships (plus three other transports) was sunk in error by four torpedoes from the cruiser *Chikuma* which missed the cruiser USS *Houston*, February 1942; Captured Java and Dutch East Indies, March 1942; Adopted a liberal attitude in order to establish order with a minimum of force much to the consternation of Southern Army HQ and IGHQ, Tokyo; Released Indonesian nationalist Achmed Sukarno from captivity; Commander-in-Chief of 8th Area Army (with responsibility for south-east Pacific area) from its activation, December 1942 or January 1943;[1] HQ Rabaul, New Britain; Command consisted of 17th Division (Y. SAKAI), 38th Division and 65th IMB in New Britain, 17th Army (S. HYAKUTAKE) on Bougainville, Solomons, and 18th Army (H. ADACHI) in New Guinea; Ordered reinforcement of Lae and Salamaua, New Guinea, but lost most of the 6,400 troops when their transports were sunk in the Battle of the Bismarck Sea, 1 March 1943; Ordered by IGHQ, Tokyo, to secure New Guinea at the expense of other areas such as the Solomons, 25 March 1943; General, May 1943; New Georgia lost (*see* M. SASAKI), August 1943; New Britain became isolated with subsequent loss of control of subordinate units; 18th Army (H. ADACHI) in New Guinea and 4th Air Army (K. TOMINAGA) were transferred to 2nd Area Army (K. ANAMI) control; Signed the surrender of 'all Japanese forces in New Guinea, New Britain, New Ireland,

Bougainville and adjacent islands'[2] (together with Vice-Admiral J. KUSAKA) to Australian Lieutenant-General A. H. Sturdee, C in C Australian First Army, on board HMS *Glory* off Rabaul, New Britain, 6 September 1945; Surrendered a sword at this time;[3] Delegate at the formal surrender of all Japanese forces in SEAC area to Lord Mountbatten, Singapore, 12 September 1945.

[1] Formation date may be slightly prior since he is said to have arrived at his HQ on 22 November 1942.
[2] Quoted from the formal Instrument of Surrender signed at that time.
[3] His *shin-guntō* with a General's sword knot was presented by Lady Sturdee to the Australian War Memorial Museum in 1982. Cat.no. ACC 7102. Unsigned blade attributed to either Kanenori Miyamoto or Gassan Sadakatsu, *c.*1918; The *habaki* (blade collar) is gold and inscribed 'Onishi' which means 'Imperial Gift'. Blade shape is *unokubi-zukuri*.

IMAMURA Hōsaku
Major- or Lieutenant-General; China, *c.*1945; Remained in command of armed Japanese troops who stayed after the Japanese surrender and fought for the Chinese Nationalists against the Communists in Shansi province, China, 1945–9; Defeated and committed suicide by poison rather than be captured, April 1949.

IMAMURA Teiji
Lieutenant-General; Commander of Tsushima Fortress, Tsushima Island, between Kyushu, Japan, and Korea, June 1943.

IMANISHI
Major-General; Attached to the Army Air Service; Trained 'Manda' Squadron which was designated as one of the first 'Kamikaze' units, *c.*October 1944; This unit was sent to the Philippines under 4th Air Army. November 1944.

IMAYE
Major-General; Lecturer at War College, Tokyo; Chief of Staff to 2nd Imperial Guards Division (under T. NISHIMURA) during the invasion of Malaya, December 1941; Supported T. NISHIMURA in his disobedience to and dislike of 25th Army Commander T. YAMASHITA; Demoted to Colonel after the removal of T. NISHIMURA and transferred as a regimental commander in Manchuria, 1942; Captured by the Russians, 1945; Died in a Siberian prison camp.

IMOTO
Major-General; Attached to Imperial GHQ, Tokyo, *c.*1942; Visited 14th Army HQ (under M. HONMA), Philippines, to consider the delay in the capture of the Bataan peninsula, 5 January 1942.

INABA Masazumi
Major-General; Commander of 3rd Shipping Transport Command, Singapore, Malaya, March 1945.

Note: Possibly the same as INADA Masazumi.

INABA Shiro
Lieutenant-General; Commander of 6th Division (under 11th Army) during the battle of Nanchang, China, mid February–early May 1939.

INADA Masazumi

Major-General; Vice Chief of Staff to Southern Army (under H. TERAUCHI), HQ Singapore, Malaya, c.1942; Visited 15th Army HQ at Maymyo, Burma, to discuss the projected invasion of Imphal and Assam, India, with R. MUTAGUCHI, 17 May 1943; Attended war games on the operation (to be called Operation 'U-GO') at Burma Area Army HQ (see M. KAWABE, T. KATAKURA, R. MUTAGUCHI), 24–27 June 1943; Opposed the military soundness of the plan but accepted the political implications in establishing a base in India for the 'Free India' movement; Chairman of a senior officers' meeting to discuss 15th Army invasion plan at Southern Army HQ, Singapore; Bitterly opposed the operation without modifications but he was transferred before he could finally block it;* Replaced (by K. AYABE) and transferred to 19th Army, HQ Ceram Island, Moluccas; 11 October 1943.

Note: Possibly the same as INABA Masazumi.

*He was signatory of a formal agreement with the Siamese, whereby Japan promised to increase Siamese territory, which was not honoured. He was unfairly blamed for this and removed by the Chief of the Personnel Bureau K. TOMINAGA, who disliked him, at the behest of H. TOJO.

INAMURA Toyojiro

Major-General; Commander of Karafuto Mixed Brigade, Karafuto, Japan, December 1942.

INKAI Moto

Major-General; Commander of Korean Gendarmerie (Military Police), 1945; Ordered arrested by the American occupation forces in Tokyo as a suspected war criminal, 2 December 1945.

INO Shezaburo

Major-General; Governor of Atjek province, northern Sumatra; Surrendered a sword* to Major E. Esmond-Jones, OC 'D' Company, 2nd Battalion Durham Light Infantry at Koetaradja (northern point of Sumatra), 19 December 1945; Evacuated by the DLI together with Rear-Admiral HIROSE and 9th Naval Shore Force (3,776 army and naval personnel).

* This sword is now in the Durham Light Infantry Museum. Cat.no. 143. It is a *shin-guntō* with *koto* or *shinto*-period blade, having a shortened tang so only the word 'OSHU' (i.e., Mutsu province) remains of the signature.

INOUE (INOUYE)

Lieutenant-General; Commander of 94th Division (under 29th Army – T. ISHIGURO), northern Malaya; Surrendered the division with 1,400 officers and 8,000–9,000 men to Major-General G. E. Woods, GOC 25th Indian Division, Sungei Patani, 24 miles north of Butterworth in north Malaya, 8 October 1945; He surrendered a sword to Major Woods at this time.

INOUE (INOUYE) Kazutsugu

Lieutenant-General or General; Believed c. 1920s or 1930s.

INOUE Sadao (Sadae)

Lieutenant-General; Commander of 14th Division, April 1944; Division transferred from Manchuria to Palau Islands, Pacific, mid 1944; Palau Sector

Commander (under 31st Army); Peleliu (southernmost island) defensively strengthened under its local commander Colonel Nakagawa Kunio); Peleliu invaded by Americans, 15 September 1944; The island was captured, after virtually the entire 11,000-man garrison had died, 28 September 1944; Command area isolated until the end of the war; Surrendered on Peleliu to Brigadier General P. Rogers, USMC, 2 September 1945.

INOUE Tadanori
Major-General; Believed c.1920s or 1930s.

INOUE Yoshisuke
Major-General; Commander of 35th Independent Mixed Brigade, Andaman Islands, from its activation in February or March 1944.

ISA Kazuo
Lieutenant-General; Commander of 86th Division (under 57th Army), Ariake Bay, Japan, from its activation in April 1944.

ISAYAMA Haruki (Haruke, Shunju)
Major-General; Chief of Staff to 15th Army (under S. IIDA) during the invasion of Burma, probably from its formation in January 1942; Replaced (by N. OBATA), March 1943; Lieutenant-General; Shanghai, China; Tried as a war criminal in China and sentenced to life imprisonment.

ISETANI
Lieutenant-General; Military Attaché to the Japanese Embassy in China by 1935; Outspoken and anti-Chinese government.

ISHIDA Eikuma
Major-General; Commander of Southern Army Field Railway Command, HQ Bangkok, Siam, February 1944; Lieutenant-General by the end of the war; Tried at Singapore, Malaya (with four of his senior officers) by British Military Authorities, charged with inflicting 'inhuman treatment' on POWs and use of POW labour in Building the Burma Railway, 1946; Sentenced to 10 years' imprisonment.

ISHIDA Jiro – Same as ICHIDA Jiro

ISHIGURO Teizo 石黒
Lieutenant-General; Commander of 29th Army (under 7th Area Army – S. ITAGAKI) responsible for the whole of Malaya (except Singapore) and the Andaman and Nicobar Islands, c.1945; Army consisted of 46th, 94th Divisions and 70th IMB in Malaya and 35th, 36th, 37th IMBs in Andaman and Nicobar Islands; Relieved of responsibility for Penang and Johore, Malaya,* by 7th Area Army with the transfer of 9th Division but reinforced by 37th Division which came from Indo–China via Bangkok, Siam, 27 July 1945; Surrendered all forces in Malaya (except Singapore, Johore and Penang) to Lieutenant-General O. L. Roberts, C in C British 34th Corps, at Kuala Lumpur, Malaya, 13 September 1945.

* The bulk of 37th Division had not reached Malaya from Bangkok by the time of the surrender. It therefore surrendered there.

ISHIHARA (ISHIWARA) Kanji

Born 1889; 2nd Lieutenant in 65th Infantry Regiment, December 1909; 1st Lieutenant, February 1913; Graduated from War College, November 1918; Captain in 65th Infantry Regiment, April 1919; Office of Military Training, July 1919; Central China Expeditionary Army HQ, April 1920; Instructor at War College, July 1921; Language Officer in Germany, July 1922; Major, August 1924; Instructor at War College, October 1925; Lieutenant-Colonel, August 1928; Staff Officer in Kwantung Army, Manchuria; Involved in the murder of Chinese warlord Marshal Chang Tso-lin, Mukden, Manchuria, 4 June 1928; Envisaged Manchuria as an autonomous state colonized by the Japanese; Acted with co-conspirators (including S. ITAGAKI) to involve the Kwantung Army with the seizure of all Manchuria against the wishes of the Cabinet and Army General Staff; Involved with (or organized) the 'Manchurian Incident' (which culminated in the occupation of the whole of Manchuria), 18–19 September 1931; Colonel, August 1932; Co-founder of the Great East Asia League (Toa Renmei) to unite Asia and Japan as equals; Member of the Japanese delegation to the Geneva Conference, October 1932; Commander of 4th Infantry Regiment, March 1933; Section Head of Operations Bureau of Army General Staff, August 1935; Supervised war planning for the conquest of central China (but actually he opposed it); Major-General; Chief of Operations of the Army General Staff, March 1937; Reluctantly agreed to reinforce insurgent forces in North China (after the 'Marco Polo Bridge Incident') with 3 divisions and 2 brigades, July 1937; A local peace agreement allowed the cancellation of the reinforcements, late July 1937; Bitter opponent of H. TOJO but was appointed as his Deputy Chief of Staff in the Kwantung Army as a punishment for a failure to pass on instructions to Army General Staff, August 1937; Replaced (by S. SHIMOMURA), approx. November 1937; Relegated to garrison commander for loudly criticizing Imperial policy; Commander of Maizuru Fortified Zone, Japan, December 1937; Warned Premier Prince Konoye that the policy of dealing only with pro-Japanese Chinese and the Nationalists would inevitably lead to prolonged hostilities in China, 1938; Retired 1938; Recalled to active duty as Commander of 16th Division (Manchuria? or Japan?), September 1939–March 1941;[1] Retired to the reserve as a Lieutenant-General, March 1941;[2] Special Cabinet Adviser to the government (under Premier Prince N. HIGASHIKUNI), appointed 16 August 1945; Cancer of the bladder, 1946; Illness prevented him attending the Tokyo International Military Tribunal as a witness in war crimes trials, so a special court was set up in Sugata City for him to give evidence; Died 1949.

Personal facts: Flamboyant character. Full of ideas and a great strategist. Known as the 'genius of the army'.

[1] Must have been a Lieutenant-General for this appointment, i.e., before his retirement to the reserve.
[2] According to *Singapore – the Japanese Version* by Masanobu Tsuji (see Bibliography) he was Commander of the Kyoto Garrison, Japan, before his retirement in 1941.

ISHII Kaho

Lieutenant-General; Commander of 32nd Division (under 2nd Army), Halmahera Island, Moluccas, October 1944.

ISHII Masayoshi

Major-General; Chief of Staff to North-eastern District Army (under T. YOSHI-TOMO), Sendai?, Japan, February 1945.

ISHII Shiro

Born 1883 in Chiba prefecture; From a family of wealthy land-owners; Graduated from the College of Medicine of Imperial University in Kyoto, 1919–29; Entered the army as a volunteer; Applied for regular service; Commissioned Lieutenant as an army physician; Transferred to First Military Hospital, Tokyo, c.1922; Postgraduate student of pathology and bacteriology at Imperial University, Kyoto, April 1926–April 1928; Sent on foreign mission visiting Europe and Russia, 1928–late 1930; Instructor of epidemiology at Army Military Medical Academy, Tokyo, 1931–6; Strongly advocated bacteriological warfare; Commander of secret bacteriological warfare centre 'Ei', Nanking, China (see also S. SATO), 1939–40? Major-General by 1940; Twice Commander of bacteriological warfare centre 'Water Supply and Prophylaxis Administration Centre of the Kwantung Army', Manchuria (set up in 1935–6) and code-named 'Detachment 731', 1941; The proper name was 'Manshu Detachment 731', i.e., 731st Manchurian Detachment of the Kwantung Army see also M. KITANO, Y. WAKAMATSU) formed to research bacteriological weapons; Located near Pingfan Station, 20 kilometres from Harbin and divided into eight sections with approx. 3,000 personnel and complete with its own air force unit near Anta Station; Four other '731' branches were established at Hailin, Linkow, Sunwu and Hailar in the 1940s; It was the largest of all such 'Detachments' (see also S. SATO) and was under the direct control of C in C Kwantung Army (Y. UMEZU, O. YAMADA); Chief of 'Detachment 731' for the second time (replacing M. KITANO), March–August 1945; Lieutenant-General before or during this appointment; Controlled and ordered lethal bacteria and freezing experiments on human subjects; At least 3,000 people were killed between 1940–45;[1] Devised a 'plague bomb' to be dropped from aircraft; Deliberately caused a plague epidemic with infected fleas in the Nimpo area, central China, summer 1940; Deliberately contaminated the ground to infect advancing Chinese at Chekang, July 1942; Prepared plans to release high-altitude balloons carrying plague-infected rats to land in America; Upon the Russian invasion of Manchuria he destroyed the establishment, killed 400–500 prisoners, released plague-infected rats and shipped all the equipment to Korea, August 1945; Fled south with his subordinate commanders but was captured five weeks later in Nanking, China; American Defense Department officials granted him (and his colleagues) immunity for revealing research data since it was considered that 'publicity must be avoided in the interests of defense and national security of the USA'.[2] The data was considered to be of considerable value and should not be revealed to other nations.[3] Said to have lectured on the human testing of infectious organisms at a special camp (Fort Detrick), America, 1948;[3] Later suffered from chronic dysentery; Died from cancer of the throat.

[1] Some American captives were apparently among those killed by experimentation.
[2] This was ratified with the full approval of General MacArthur.
[3] Head of the 'frostbite research team' Yoshimura Hisato and the head of the vivisection team were both teaching at Japanese universities after the war. See also M. KITANO. Staff of other similar establishments who were captured by the Russians were tried and sentenced as war criminals.

ISHIKAWA Tadao

Major-General; Commander of Military Affairs Department of 47th Division, Hirosaki Divisional District, Japan, from June 1943.

ISHIKAWA Takuma

Major-General; Commander of Fusan (Chinkai Bay) Fortress, Korea, May 1944.

ISHIMOTO Sadanao
Lieutenant-General; Commander of 50th Division, Formosa, from its activation in May 1944; The division was continuously stationed in Formosa until the end of the war.

ISHINO Yoshio
Major-General; Commander of 1st Garrison Unit, Mukden, Manchuria, June 1942.

ISHIRI
Major- or Lieutenant-General; Stationed on Halmahera Island, Moluccas, c.1945, but his post has not been established.

ISHITANI Jinzaburo
Major-General; Concurrently Commander of three Home Stations for an infantry unit at Tsu, an Air Signals unit at Ujiyamada and a meteorological unit at Yokkaichi, all in Tsu Regimental District, Japan, March 1945.

ISODA
Major-General?; Chief of 'Hikari Kikan' (Lightning Organization) liaising between IGHQ, Tokyo and the Indian National Army (after its reforming in October? 1943 under Subhas Chandra Bose – see also H. IWAKURO), Burma, April 1945; Arrived with lorries for the retreating INA from Moulmein, late April 1945, and arrived back in Moulmein, 1 May 1945; Possibly withdrew with Chandra Bose to Bangkok, Siam, May 1945; Gave evidence at the trial of Indian National Army Generals at Delhi, India, November 1945.

ISOGAI (ISOGA, ISOYA) Rensuke (Renosuke)
Born 1886; Major-General; Served in China; Attempted negotiations with Chinese Premier Chiang Kai-shek to gain Japanese control of north China, March–May 1935; Lieutenant-General; Commander of 10th Division, China, 1937; Commander-in-Chief of Kwantung Army, Manchuria; Accepted responsibility for the Japanese defeat by the Russians during the 'Nomonhan Incident' on the Manchurian – Outer Mongolian border, May 1939; Governor-General of Hong Kong (replacing T. SAKAI), January 1942; Replaced (by H. TANAKA), 1945? Tried and found guilty of war crimes by the Chinese but pardoned by Chiang Kai-shek; Tried for war crimes in Japan and sentenced to life imprisonment;* Died 1967.

*According to At the going down of the Sun by O. Lindsay (see Bibliography).

ISOMURA Takeakira (Buryō)
Colonel; Senior Staff Officer to Burma Area Army, Rangoon, c.1943; Major-General; Deputy Chief of Staff to Burma Area Army (under M. KAWABE), Rangoon, c.1944.

ISOMURA Toshi
Lieutenant-General or General, 1930s.

ITABANA
Major- or Lieutenant-General; Commander of 6th Air District Command, Hollandia, Dutch New Guinea, c.1944; Replaced, April 1944.

ITADA

Major-General; Commander of 121st Brigade (in 105th Division?) under North China Area Army during the Battle of Hsuchow, China, late December 1937–May 1938; Lieutenant-General; Probable Commander of 105th Division, c.1938.

ITADA (ITADO) Teiko

Lieutenant-General; Commander of 'Konoe' Division* (under Central China Expeditionary Army) during the Battle for Hsuchow, China, late December 1937–May 1938.

* This is according to the *History of the Sino–Japanese War 1937–1945* (*see* Bibliography). However 'Konoe' means 'Imperial Guards' which was known as the 'Guards Division' from its activation in 1867 until being renamed the 2nd Guards Division in 1943 (at the same time the 1st Guards Division was formed). No record of this division serving outside Tokyo, Japan, from 1867 to 1940 has been located to confirm this entry.

ITAGAKI Seishirō 板垣 征四郎

2nd Lieutenant (infantry), November 1904; Graduated from War College, November 1916; Staff Officer to Central China Expeditionary Unit, July 1919; Major, April 1920; Battalion Commander in 20th Infantry Regiment, April 1921; Lieutenant-Colonel, August 1923; Assistant Military Attaché to China, June 1924; Dispatched to China, 1927; Colonel and Commander of 33rd Infantry Regiment, March 1928; Involved with the murder of Chinese warlord Marshal Chang Tso-lin, Mukden, Manchuria, 4 June 1928; Senior Staff Officer to Kwantung Army, Manchuria, May 1929; Envisaged Manchuria as an autonomous state with Japanese colonization; Involved with the organization of the 'Manchurian Incident' (*see also* K. ISHIHARA) and ordered the mobilization of the Kwantung Army (without orders from CinC S. HONJO) which launched a premature attack on Mukden, 18–19 September 1931; Ensured that Army General Staff orders to restrict punitive action were ignored; Major-General and attached to Kwantung Army, August 1932; Deputy Chief of Staff to Kwantung Army, December 1934; Chief of Staff to Kwantung Army, March 1936; Lieutenant-General, April 1936; Commander of 5th Division (under North China Area Army), March 1937; War Minister in Prince Konoye cabinet, June 1938; Presided over Japanese army defeats by the Russians at Lake Khasan, 11 July 1938, and 'Nomonhan Incident', 12 May 1939; Chief of Staff to China Expeditionary Army (under J. NISHIO), HQ Nanking, China, 12 September 1939; General; Commander of Chosen (Korea) Army, July 1941; Commander of 17th Army (with Korea District Army Command), February 1945; Commander-in-Chief of 7th Area Army (replacing K. DOHIHARA), HQ Singapore, Malaya (controlling Java, Sumatra, Malaya, Borneo, Andaman and Nicobar Islands) under Southern Army (H. TERAUCHI), April 1945 – Japanese surrender, September 1945; Formally surrendered Singapore and Johore, Malaya (together with Vice-Admiral S. FUKUDOME) on board HMS *Sussex* to Lieutenant-General Sir Philip Christison, C in C XV Corps, at Singapore, 4 September 1945; Signed the formal surrender of all Japanese army, naval, air and auxiliary forces (total of 738,400 men) in South East Asia under Southern Army control on behalf of H. TERAUCHI (who was too ill to attend) at Singapore, 12 September 1945;[1] Surrendered a sword (together with K. AYABE) to Lieutenant-General Messervy at Kuala Lumpur, Malaya, 22 February 1946;[2] Arrested as a Class A war criminal, charged with war crimes relating to the deaths and maltreatment of POWs and civilian internees; Tried by the International tribunal for the Far East, Tokyo, 26

April 1946–November 1948; Found guilty and hanged at Sugamo prison, Tokyo, 23 December 1948.

Personal facts: A born organizer.

[1] Surrendered a sword on behalf of H. TERAUCHI to Lord Louis Mountbatten at this ceremony. Also present were H. KIMURA, B. KINOSHITA, A. NAKAMURA, T. NUMATA and Vice-Admirals S. FUKUDOME, SHIBATA.

[2] This sword is now in the British Museum. It is a *shin-gunto* with a blade signed KANEMOTO (of Seki. c.1450. Kanemoto II). There is a *shin-gunto* in the National Army Museum (Cat.no. 6107–5–1) which is said to have belonged to S. ITAGAKI but it is recognized that the provenance is doubtful.

ITAMI Masakichi
Major-General; Governor-General of Penang, Malaya, by October 1943.

ITATSU Naotoshi
Major-General; Commander of 10th Independent Infantry Brigade, Yangchuang, Shansi province, China, January 1944.

ITO
Major-General; Envoy to Burma Area Army HQ Rangoon, with a message from IGHQ, Tokyo, stating that the Imphal invasion operation 'must succeed whatever the cost', May 1944.

ITO Shinobu
Major-General; Commander of 2nd Shipping Transport Command, Shanghai, China, February 1944.

ITO Takeo
Major-General; Served in China; Commander of 38th Division Infantry Group (under T. SANO) with 228th Regiment (Colonel Doi), 229th Regiment (R. TANAKA), 230th Regiment (Colonel Shoji); Held in reserve by 23rd Army Commander (T. SAKAI) for the main attack on Hong Kong Island which commenced 18 December 1941; Heavy losses on both sides with the Japanese committing atrocities on civilians and POWs; The British garrison surrendered, 25 December 1941; Commander of 'Ito Detachment' (part of South Seas Detachment), assisting in the capture of Amboina and Timor, 1942; Commander of 40th Independent Mixed Brigade, garrisoning New Ireland with HQ at Namanatai (or Namatanai) from its activation in July 1944; Possibly Lieutenant-General by the end of the war; Surrendered a sword (together with his staff) to Lieutenant-General K. W. Eather, GOC 11th Australian Division, on board HMAS *Swan* at Namanatai, morning of 19 September 1945 (There was a naval surrender on the same day. *See* Rear-Admiral R. TAMURA); Sentenced to death at Rabaul War Crimes trial but the sentence was not confirmed, 24 May 1946.

ITSUKI Toshio
Major-General; Commander of 36th Independent Mixed Brigade, Nicobar Islands, from its activation in February 1944.

IWABE Shigeo
Major-General; Commander of 28th Independent Mixed Brigade (under 16th Army – Y. NAGANO), Surabaya, Java, July 1944?; Prevented armed nationalists from seizing Army HQ without bloodshed after the main Japanese forces had

been dispersed in accordance with Allied surrender orders, 1 October 1945; Arrested by orders of Southern Army GHQ for handing over arms (or not preventing it) to Indonesian nationalists in contravention of Allied surrender orders (*see also* Y. NAGANO, NAKAMURA, S. YAMAMOTO), October 1945.

Note: Said, but not confirmed, to have surrendered the east Java garrison and his sword to a Dutch naval officer, Captain P. J. G. Huyer, who had no official sanction from SEAC to accept such a surrender, only to deliver surrender terms.

IWAI Torajiro
Lieutenant-General; Commander of 108th Division (under direct control of 3rd Area Army), Manchuria, September 1944.

IWAKIRI Hide
Major-General; Commander of 69th Infantry Brigade (in 64th Division under M. FUNABIKI), China, June 1943.

IWAKURO Hideo
Lieutenant-Colonel; Drew up influential Japanese army policy in Manchuria ('The Guiding Principle of Manchukuo'), 1932; On the staff of Military Affairs Bureau of the War Ministry (under A. MUTO), Tokyo, c.1935; Colonel; Lecturer at Nakano (espionage and saboteur) School, Nakano, Tokyo, from about 1937; Believed that to maintain peace with America was to Japan's advantage; Conceived the idea of flooding China with counterfeit banknotes to wreck its economy; Sent to America by Premier H. TOJO to assist Ambassador Admiral K. NOMURA in an attempt to reconcile the differences between Japan and America, 30 March–August 1941; Attempted to persuade various Japanese political, military and industrial groups to urge continuation of negotiations with America to avoid war; Transferred to operational duties in Cambodia on orders from H. TOJO for voicing his personal and statistical objections to war and left Tokyo on 28 August 1941; Commander of 5th Guards Regiment in Malaya and involved in the attack on Singapore, February 1942; Major-General; Chief of 'Iwakuro Kikan' (formerly 'Fujiwara Kikan') which was an organization liaising between the Indian National Army (Under Mohan Singh) and IGHQ, Tokyo, June, 1942; Name changed to 'Hikari Kikan' (Lightning Organization); Mohan Singh was arrested after becoming disillusioned by Japanese promises and the INA temporarily disbanded, December 1942 (*see also* ISODA); Member of Military Government in Sumatra; Chief of Staff to 55th Division (under T. HANAYA), Burma; Chief of Staff to 28th Army (under S. SAKURAI) from its activation, late 1943 (garrisoning the Arakan), Burma; Controlled 28th Army espionage and intelligence sections; Involved with organizing 28th Army retreat across the Irrawaddy River into Pegu Yomas and then across the Sittang River, April–August 1945.

IWANAKA
Major-General; Casualty in the Battle of Shangkao, China,* when 34th Division and 20th Independent Brigade were encircled by the Chinese with Japanese battle casualties of 15,000 troops and the loss of ten heavy guns and more than 1,000 rifles, 15 March–April 1941.

* This battle marked the first major tactical victory for the Chinese army in four years' fighting.

IWANAKA (IWANAGA) O.
Lieutenant-General; Commander of 116th Division, China, June 1943; HQ Anking (under 11th Army), January 1944; Tungting Lake operations, January 1944; Battle of Changsha–Hengyang, late May–early August 1944; HQ at Paoching, Hunan province, Battle of Kweilin–Liuchow, early September–mid December 1944.

IWANAKA Yoshiharu
Lieutenant-General; Commander of 2nd Armoured Division (under 14th Area Army – T. YAMASHITA), Luzon, Philippines, September 1944; HQ San Miguel, central Luzon; moved against American invasion forces landing at Lingayen Gulf but suffered heavy losses through air attacks before it could start, January 1945; Came under 41st Army control (S. YOKOYAMA), March 1945; Armoured strength destroyed by the time of the Japanese surrender, 2 September 1945.

IWASA Masao
Major General; Commander of Home Station for various army units, Utsuno-miya, Japan, March 1945?

IWASA Rokuro
General; Commander-in-Chief of all 'Kempeitai' (military police) Forces, HQ Tokyo, Japan, c.1936.

IWASA Shun
Major General; Infantry Group Commander of 6th Division (under M. KANA), Bougainville, Solomons, from July 1943.

IWASAKI Tamio
Lieutenant-General; Commander of 111th Division (under 58th Army), Man-churia, from its activation in July 1944.

KABURAGI Masataka
Major-General; Chief of Staff to 34th Army (under T. SANO), Hankow, China, c.1944; Sentenced to death by American Military Commission for torture and strangulation of three American airmen at Hankow in December 1944; Hanged at Ward Road Jail, Shanghai, China, with four of his subordinates, 22 April 1946.

KAGESA Sadaaki
Lieutenant-General; Commander of 38th Division, Rabaul, New Britain, June 1943 (Some divisional units were on Guadalacanal and New Georgia).

KAJISUKA Ryuji
Born 1881 in Tajiri, Japan; Joined the army in 1914; Lieutenant in medical service of the army, 1915; Worked in First Military Hospital; Doctor of Medicine, March 1924; Teacher at Military Medical Academy in Tokyo; Chief of Sanitary Division of Medical Administration of War Ministry, 1933–7; Chief of Medical Division of the Army in China, 1937; Major-General in Medical Service, 1937; Chief of Medical Division of 2nd Army, 1937; Chief of Medical Administration of Chosen (Korea) Army, 1938; Chief of Medical Administration of Kwantung Army, Manchuria, December 1939 (until Japanese surrender, September 1945); Lieutenant-General August 1940; Supporter of bacteriological warfare; Took

active part in formation of bacteriological warfare centres (*see* S. ISHII, K. KAWASHIMA, Y. WAKAMATSU); Supplied equipment and trained staff for these centres; Captured by the Russians, September 1945; Tried by Russian Military Tribunal at Khabarovsk for war crimes relating to bacteriological warfare and sentenced to 25 years in a labour correction camp, December 1949.

KAKUWA Zensuke
Major-General; Commander of 13th Field Transport Command, August 1943; Central and southern China by November 1944.

KAMADA Mitsugi
Major-General; Chief of Medical Department of 18th Area Army (under A. NAKAMURA), Siam, 1945; Surrendered a sword to Major-General G. C. Evans, GOC 7th Indian Division (together with A. NAKAMURA, eighteen Generals and two Admirals) at Bangkok, Siam, 11 January 1946.

KAMIMURA Toshimichi
Lieutenant-General; Commander of 36th Division or Army?

KAMIYA
Major- or Lieutenant-General; Under 14th Army, Philippines, 1942; Presided over the execution of ten American POWs as a reprisal for Filipino guerrilla attack in Laguna province, Luzon, Philippines, 12 June 1942.

KANAYA Hanzo
General; Chief of Army General Staff, c.1930; Supported the invasion of Manchuria after the 'Manchurian Incident', 18–19 September 1931; Had to apologize personally to the Emperor for the actions of the Kwantung Army in the Manchurian Incident;* Resigned or replaced (by Prince K. KANIN), 1931 or 1932.

* The 'Manchurian Incident' was the blowing up of a short stretch of the South Manchuria Railway (which was Japanese owned) by Chinese soldiers. However this was staged by the Japanese as an excuse to precipitate the invasion of Manchuria.

KANDA Masatane
2nd Lieutenant (infantry) in 18th Infantry Regiment, December 1991; 1st Lieutenant, December 1914; Army General Staff, April 1916; Captain, December 1920; Member of Army General Staff, May 1921; Kwantung Army HQ Manchuria, October 1922; Army General Staff, March 1924; Member of Army General Staff, October 1924; Kwantung Army HQ, May 1925; Major, August 1926; 39th Infantry Regiment, December 1927; Battalion Commander in 39th Infantry Regiment, August 1928; Staff Officer to Chosen (Korea) Army, December 1929; Lieutenant-Colonel, August 1930; Army General Staff, November 1931; Military Attaché to Turkey, May 1932; Member of Army General Staff, March 1934; Colonel and Section Head of Army General Staff, March 1935; Commander of 45th Infantry Regiment, March 1936; Major-General; Department Head of Inspectorate of Military Training, July 1938; Lieutenant-General, March 1941; Commander of 6th Division, China, April 1941; Engaged in 2nd Battle of Changsha, September-October 1941; 3rd Battle of Changsha, December 1941–January 1942; Division on Bougainville, Solomons (under 17th Army HYAKUTAKE), December 1942; Commander of 17th Army (replacing H. HYAKUTAKE with 6th Division command taken by T. AKINAGA), 17 February

1945, HQ Buin – Faisi area, Bougainville; Assumed command of all naval troops on the island (except for 8th Fleet HQ), June 1945; Issued order for a final battle against Australian troops, 31 July 1945; Ordered to surrender by Lieutenant-General Savige, GOC Australian II Corps, at Torokina (together with I. MAKATA and Vice-Admiral Baron T. SAMEJIMA), 8 February 1945;* All handed over swords at this time.

Personal facts: Professional soldier who was ruthless, hard, shrewd, fussy, steeped in tradition and a very capable field commander.

* His sword is now in the Australian War Memorial Museum, Cat.no. AWM 20314. A *shin-guntō*, it has a showa period (post-1926) blade signed 'EMURA SAKU' (i.e., Made by Emura).

Prince KANIN Kotohito

Born 1865; Great Uncle of Empress Nakago and senior member of the Imperial family from 1923; Professional army officer; Youngest Field Marshal in the Japanese Army; Chief of Army General Staff (replacing H. KANAYA), December 1931 or 1932; Forced the resignation of War Minister S. HATA from the Admiral M. YONAI cabinet because the army did not agree with the government policy of improving relationships with America and Britain (and refused to appoint a replacement) thus bringing down the government, July 1940; Resigned (replaced by H. SUGIYAMA), 3 October 1940;* Member of Supreme War Council and senior adviser to the Emperor on army matters; Said to have died from haemorrhoids, 1945.

* He resigned in protest against the Military Supreme Command decision to force Vichy France to allow Japanese air bases in northern Indo–China which he thought would lead to British and American retaliation.

KASAHARA Kahei

Major-General; Commander of Akrashan (Ajisan) Garrison, October 1942.

KASAHARA Yukio (Sachiro)

Lieutenant-General; Chief of Staff to Kwantung Army (under O. YAMADA), Hsinking, Manchuria, c.1942; Commander of 11th Army, China, comprising 3rd, 13th, 22nd, 27th (part), 58th Divisions; Launched a counter-offensive against the Chinese in the Kweilin–Liuchow area, late April 1945; Surrendered 11th Army and 13th, 58th Divisions plus other units to Chinese General Hsueh Yeuh, of 9th War Area, at Nanchang, upon the Japan's surrender, September 1945.

KASHI (KASHII) Kohei

Lieutenant-General; Appointed Military Commander of Tokyo (Martial Law Forces) during the '2–26 Insurrection', 26 February 1926;* Negotiated with insurgents to lay down their arms, finally threatening them with military action which would brand them as traitors (since they had disobeyed a direct order from the Emperor to surrender); They surrendered on 29 February 1926.

* Rebellion by some young army officers and 1,400 soldiers of the 1st and 3rd Infantry Regiments of the 1st Division in an attempt to return to full imperial rule directly under the Emperor without the influence of politicians or big business. They murdered several statesman including Premier Admiral K.OKADA.

KASUYA (KATSUYA, KATSUDANI) Tomekichi

Major-General; Commander of 2nd Field Transport Command, June 1943; Unit transferred to Burma, January 1945; HQ Meiktila, Burma, which was an important road, rail and air centre with four airfields and a supply base for 15th and 33rd Armies; Assumed defence command when the British broke through forward army units, late February 1945; Defence consisted of scratch units;* His command was confirmed by 15th Army (S. KATAMURA) but reinforcements were to be sent comprising 18th Division plus two regiments and 168th Regiment from 49th Division; British attacks commenced, 28 February 1945; Only 168th Regiment arrived but nearly all of it was destroyed in fighting; Gave orders to fight to the death but rescinded the order and evacuated with survivors to Thazi then Kemapyu where he commanded the communications line from the Shan states; Meiktila was captured with 2,000 Japanese dead in the town and 47 taken prisoner, 3 March 1945; Remained as Commander of 2nd Field Transport Command in Siam until the end of the war, September 1945.

Note: Surrendered a sword (together with nineteen Generals and two Admirals) to Major-General G. C. Evans, GOC 7th Indian Division, Bangkok, Siam, 11 January 1946.

* Strangely Burma Area Army had no defence plans for such an important town.

KATAGIRI Goro
Major-General; Commander of Home Station for one infantry unit, Tottori, Japan, March 1945?

KATAGIRI Shigeru
Lieutenant-General; Commander of 20th Division under 18th Army – H. ADACHI), Gali, New Guinea, September 1943; Marched 200 miles to reinforce Finschhafen harbour (see E. YAMADA), arriving at Sattelburg, 10 October 1943; Launched seaborne counter-attack on Australia but was repulsed, 17 October 1943; Forced to abandon Sattelberg, 25 October 1943.

KATAKURA (KITAMURA) Tadashi (Chu, Saichi)
Served in China; Colonel; Senior Staff Officer to Chief of Staff (E. NAKA) of Burma Area Army, HQ Rangoon, c.1943; Present at war games when 15th Army Commander R. MUTAGUCHI proposed the invasion of India which he bitterly opposed, 24–27 June 1943; After the removal of the Vice Chief of Staff to Southern Army M. INADA he dropped his opposition, October 1943; Major-General and Chief of Staff to 33rd Army (under M. HONDA) from its inception, April 1944; HQ Maymyo, Burma, controlling 18th Division (E. NAKA) and 56th Division (T. MATSUYAMA); Ordered to attempt to cut the India–China road link and hold a line from Lashio to Monglong Mountains, north-east of Mandalay (Operation 'DAN'), October 1944; Replaced (by S. YAMAMOTO), late 1944; Gave evidence at the trials of Indian National Army Generals, Delhi, India, November 1945.

KATAMURA Shihachi
Lieutenant-General; Commander of 54th Division, August 1941; Based at Himeji Divisional District, Japan, until March 1943; Division moved to Java and then to Burma, arriving January 1944; Under 28th Army (S. SAKURAI) command for defence of the Arakan coast including Ramree and Cheduba Islands; Gradually forced to retreat from the Arakan; Replaced (by S. MIYAZAKI), late August 1944; Commander of 15th Army (replacing R. MUTAGUCHI), 30 August–early September 1944; Army consisted of 15th Division (R. SHIBATA), 31st Division (T.

KAWADA), 33rd Division (N. TANAKA); Ordered to stop enemy advance on the banks of the Irrawaddy River and secure the area north of Madaya, Sagaing bridgehead and Pakokku area (Operation 'BAN'), October 1944; Reinforced by 53rd Division (transferred from 33rd Army); Decided not to fight pitched battle for Shwebo, ordering 31st Division to Irrawaddy River with minor losses, 7 January 1945; Shwebo taken by British 33rd Corps; Ordered by C in C Burma Area Army H. KIMURA to defend Mandalay so ordered 15th Division (under S. YAMAMOTO) to defend it to the death, March 1945; Rescinded the order and allowed a withdrawal, 18 March 1945; Weakened Irrawaddy defence by having to reinforce the defence of Meiktila by sending 18th Division (S. TANAKA) and a regiment each from 15th and 33rd Divisions (see also T. KASUYA); Ordered by Burma Area Army to form defence of Toungoo if 33rd Army (M. HONDA) were defeated at Pyawbwe, April 1945; Ordered to withdraw to Toungoo–Pegu area in south; Suffered heavy losses and command structure broke down, April 1945; HQ at Pyinamana, April 1945; Remnant of 15th Army plus 33rd Army held Sittang River mouth and Tenasserim coastal strip to maintain an escape route, May 1945; Retreated into Siam (placed under 18th Area Army Command); HQ Lampang, Siam, August 1945; Surrendered a sword (together with nineteen Generals and two Admirals) to Major-General G. C. Evans GOC 7th Indian Division, Bangkok, Siam, 11 January 1946.

KATAOKA Tadasu (Kaoru)
2nd Lieutenant (cavalry), December 1915; Graduated from War College, November 1925; Army General Staff, December 1926; Member of Army General Staff, December 1927; Instructor at War College, March 1931; Attached to Military Affairs Bureau of War Ministry, February 1932; Member of Army General Staff, December 1932; Lieutenant-Colonel and Staff Officer to Cavalry Group, August 1934; Instructor at Army Cavalry School, March 1937; Attached to Military Affairs Bureau of War Ministry, March 1937; Attached to 4th Depot Division HQ, April 1937; Staff Officer in 4th Depot Division, November 1937; Colonel, March 1938; Chief of Staff to 104th Division, July 1938; Commander of Imperial Guard Cavalry Regiment, April 1939; Commander of Imperial Guard Reconnaissance Regiment, December 1940; Major-General; Commander of 3rd Cavalry Brigade, March 1941; Chief of Staff to 5th Army February 1943; Acting Commander of 1st Division, China, August 1944; Lieutenant-General; Commander of 1st Division which transferred from Shanghai to reinforce Leyte, Philippines (under 35th Army – S. SUZUKI), landing at Ormoc, 2 November 1944; Immediately ordered to prepare for offensive action against American invasion forces, south-east of Carigara; Division strength reduced to 25 per cent by 17 November 1944; Retreated to mountains near San Isidro in north-west part of the island; Evacuated with staff to Cebu Island, 12 January 1945; Only 743 men from 1st Division reached Cebu out of original strength of 11,000.

KATAYAMA Shotaro
Lieutenant-General; Governor of Selangor State, Malaya; Personally crowned the new Sultan, Raja Musa, 5 November 1943; Still in this post in February 1945.

KATO
Lieutenant-Colonel; Commander of the 'Hayabusa' Sentai (Squadron of Hayabusa-type fighters), Kwang Tung Airfield, China, April 1941; Unit moved to Fukouko Island, southern French Indo–China; Supported 15th Army landings in

Malaya, December 1941; Attacked various Malayan airfields; Participated in air battles over Batavia, Bantoeng and Java; Unit moved to Siam and attacked various air bases in Burma, 1942; The *Syonan Shimbum* (Singapore newspaper) says he was 'the only army officer ever to have been conferred seven times with the Testimonial of Gallantry' for actions in air battles over various battle fronts, which on each occasion was brought to the personal attention of the Emperor; Killed in Burma, 1942;[1] Promoted two ranks to Major-General.[2]

[1] In 1944 his story was made into a Japanese feature film called 'Kato Hayabusa Sentotai'. He was apparently 'much respected by all the airmen of the Nippon Air Force as the "God of the Air Battles".'
[2] It is uncertain if this was before or after his death, but he is always referred to by this rank. A two-rank promotion was normally posthumous.

KATO Akira
Major-General; Commander of 8th Independent Infantry Brigade, Canton area, Kwantung province, China, January 1944.

KATO Hakujiro
Major-General; Commander of North China Special Garrison Unit, August 1943; Peiping, (i.e., Peking), Hopeh province, China, September 1944; Concurrently Commander of North China Expeditionary Force Military Police.

KATO Reizo
Lieutenant-General; Commander of 25th Division, Manchuria from October 1943.

KATO Rinpei
Lieutenant-General; Chief of Staff to 8th Area Army (under H. IMAMURA), Rabaul, New Britain, November 1942.

KATO Sadamu
Major-General; Infantry Group Commander of 25th Division (under R. KATO), Manchuria, from August 1943.

KATSUDANI Tomechika – Same as KASUYA Tomechika

KATSUKI (KOTOKUI, KOTOUKI, KOZUKI) Kiyoshi (Kiyoji)
Lieutenant-General; Commander of North China Garrison Army (replacing T. KASHIRO) consisting of 5th, 20th Divisions, three brigades and the collaborating Chinese Eastern Hopei Army; Concentrated on the Peiping (i.e., Peking) Railway; Responsible for Peiping – Tientsin operations and launched a punitive attack against Chinese forces around the Peking area (even though a local truce was in force – *see* G. HASHIMOTO), early July–August 1937; Commander of 1st Army consisting of 5th (part), 6th, 14th, 20th, 108th Divisions (under North China Area Army – H. TERAUCHI) being involved with operations along the northern section of the Peiping – Hankow Railway, mid August 1937; Involved in operations in northern and eastern Honan, China, January 1938; Replaced, July 1938.

KATSUYA – Same as KASUYA Tomechika.

KAWABE Masakazu (Shozo)
Born 1886; Elder brother of KAWABE Torashiro; 2nd Lieutenant in 35th Infantry Regiment, December 1907; 1st Lieutenant, November 1910; Graduated from War

College, 1915; Captain and Company Commander in 35th Infantry Regiment, August 1917; Resident Officer in Switzerland, April 1918; Section Member of Inspectorate General of Military Training, June 1921; Major, August 1923; Member of Army General Staff, June 1925; Lieutenant-General, July 1927; Military Attaché to Germany, August 1929; Colonel, August, 1931; Commander of 6th Infantry Regiment, April 1922; Commander of Training Regiment of Infantry School, August 1933; Chief of 1st Section of Inspectorate General of Military Training, March 1934; Major-General attached to same Inspectorate, March 1936; Infantry Brigade Commander in north China, April 1936; Assistant Chief of Staff to North China Area Army, April 1936; Assistant Chief of Staff to Central China Expeditionary Army, February 1938; Chief of Main Department of Inspectorate General of Military Training, January 1939; Lieutenant-General, March 1939; Acting Inspector General of Military Training for about one month, October 1939; Commander of 12th Division, March 1940; Commander of 3rd Army, March 1941; Chief of Staff to China Expeditionary Army, August 1942; Commander-in-Chief of Burma Area Army from its activation, March? 1943, HQ Rangoon; Agreed with plan (Operation 'U-GO') to advance to the Indian border; Held war games to study the feasibility of an advance to the Indian border and the forming of a defensive line, with senior officers present including M. INADA, R. MUTAGUCHI, E. NAKA and Lieutenant-Colonel Prince Takeda (the Emperor's brother) who represented IGHQ, Tokyo; R. MUTAGUCHI proposed an advance into Assam, India (rather than halting to form a defence line) without consultation with M. KAWABE; objections were raised but this modified plan was accepted, 24–27 June 1943; Formed 28th Army (under S. SAKURAI), late 1943; Operation 'U-GO' to take Kohima and Imphal, India, commenced by 15th Army (under R. MUTAGUCHI), 7–8 March 1944; Launched diversionary attacks into Bengal, India, from the Arakan (see T. HANAYA) to draw off British reserves, late March 1944; 33rd Army (under M. HONDA) was formed in April 1944; Unhappy with the progress of Operation 'U-GO' but assured IGHQ, Tokyo, that it had an 80–85 per cent chance of success, 2 May 1944; Chinese counter-attack across the Salween River against 18th Division (S. TANAKA), 11 May 1944; Myitkyina airfield taken by the Allies, mid May 1944; Visited 15th Army HQ at Indaingyyi although ill from amoebic dysentery, 5 May 1944; Notified IGHQ, Tokyo, that Operation 'U-GO' was facing problems, 9 June 1944; Returned to HQ, Rangoon, but found he could not cancel the Operation because of pressure from C in C Southern Army H. TERAUCHI; Ordered 15th Army (R. MUTAGUCHI) to maintain the offensive despite requests from MUTAGUCHI to cancel it, late June 1944; Finally ordered by Southern Army GHQ to cancel the operation because of a fear of a Chinese advance from Yunnan and Hukawng Valley in the north and, instead, to concentrate on cutting the India–China road link, 2 July 1944; Commanding from his sick bed by this time; Suffered heavy losses in all units; Ordered the retreat from Kohima – Imphal front, 9 July 1944; Lost Myitkyina (see G. MINAKAMI), 1 August 1944; Replaced (by H. KIMURA), 11 September 1944; Commander-in-Chief of Central District Army, Japan, December 1944; Commander-in-Chief of 15th Area Army, Japan, retaining Central District Army Command, February 1945; General, March 1945; Commander-in-Chief of Air General Army, HQ Tokyo, for the defence of Japan, Korea and Ryukyus, 8 April 1945; Comprising 1st, 6th Air Armies in Japan, 2nd Air Army, Manchuria, 5th Air Army, China and 1st, 51st, 52nd Air Divisions; formed army air force 'special units' (Kamikaze), May–1 July 1945; Given 10th, 11th, 12th Air Divisions, July 1945; Concluded air defence plan (in Operation 'KETSU-GO') in combination with the navy air arm to throw 1,000 regular and 1,600 suicide army aircraft with 5,225 navy aircraft (plus others from Korea and Manchuria) against any seaborne invasion forces likely to invade the areas of Shikoku, Kyushu and Kanto, Japan, July 1945;[1] Commander-in-Chief of 1st General Army, Japan, after the Japanese surrender, September 1945.[2]

[1] Total estimated at 2,500 regular and 7,500 suicide aeroplanes.

[2] *Kogun – The Japanese Army in the Pacific War* (*see* Bibliography) gives M. KAWABE and K. DOHIHARA as having this post at the same time. But a contemporary newspaper account confirms DOHIHARA's appointment as 12 September 1945 following the suicide of G. SUGIYAMA. However he was arrested as a war criminal on 21 September 1945 and was thus probably replaced by M. KAWABE until the army was disbanded.

KAWABE Torashiro

Younger brother of KAWABE Masakazu; Graduated from Military Academy, May 1912; 2nd Lieutenant (artillery), December 1912; Captain, August 1920; Graduated from War College, November 1921; Operations Section of Army General Staff HQ, December 1922–August 1925; Resident Officer at Riga, Latvia, studying Soviet military affairs, January 1926–September 1928; Major, March 1927; Instructor (tactics) at War College, December 1928–April 1929; Operations Section of Army General Staff HQ, April 1929–January 1932; Lieutenant-Colonel, August 1931; Military Attaché to Russia, February 1932–April 1934; Staff Officer (Operations and Intelligence) in Kwantung Army, Manchuria, August 1934–March 1936; Colonel, March 1935; Commander of a Field Artillery Regiment in the Imperial Guards Division, March 1936–February 1937; Chief of Operations Section of Army General Staff HQ, March 1937–February 1938; Colonel in Army Air Force, August 1937; Hamamatsu Flying School, Japan, March–September 1938; Major-General, July 1938; Military Attaché to Germany, October 1938–February 1940; Concurrently Military Attaché to Hungary, August 1939; Commander of 7th Air Brigade, September 1940 (in Manchuria and then Canton, China, From February 1941)–July 1941; Chief of Staff to General Defence Command, Japan, July–November 1941; Lieutenant-Colonel, October 1941; Chief of General Affairs Bureau of Inspectorate General of the Air Force, December 1941–May 1943; Commander of 2nd Air Army, Manchuria, May 1943–August 1944; Deputy Chief of Inspectorate General of the Air Force, August 1944–April 1945; Deputy Chief of Army General Staff at IGHQ, Tokyo, April 1945–end of war; Lead a delegation on behalf of the Emperor, Government and armed forces to receive the terms for the Japanese surrender from General Douglas MacArthur at Manila, Philippines;* Received Allied requirements for execution of surrender terms from General Sutherland (Chief of Staff to MacArthur), 19–20 August 1945; Flew back to Japan but his Mitsubishi bomber crash-landed on a Japanese beach; however he escaped uninjured.

* Also accompanied by M. AMANO, Rear-Admiral YOKOYAMA and staff.

KAWABURO Shizuma

Major-General; Commander of 51st Infantry Group (in 51st Division), eastern New Guinea, February 1944 (*see also* H. NAKANO).

KAWADA Suesaburo

Lieutenant-General; Commander of 73rd Division, Nagoya, Japan, October 1944.

KAWADA Tsuchitato (Tshuitaro)

Lieutenant-General; Commander of 31st Division (under 15th Army – R. MUTAGUCHI), Burma (replacing K. SATO) effective from 7 July 1944; The starving remnant of the division were in retreat; Received some reinforcements but was still under strength, October? 1944; Ordered not to defend Shwebo in a pitched battle and withdrew with minor losses, 7 January 1945; Ordered by 15th Army to withdraw to the Irrawaddy River, 18 January 1945; Remained in command until the cessation of hostilities, September 1945; By the time of the surrender the division command had transferred to 33rd Army; surrendered a sword (together with S. TAKEHARA) to Major-General W. A. Crowther at Thaton, Burma, last week of October 1945.

KAWAGISHI (KAWAKISHI) Bunzaburo

Lieutenant-General; An aide-de-camp to Emperor Hirohito, c.1935; Appointed to a command in Korea, December 1936; Commander of 20th Division, China, under Garrison Forces (K. KATSUKI) on Peiping Railway; Engaged in Peiping (Peking) – Tientsin operations, July–early August 1937; Replaced (by J. KAWAMINE), 1937.

KAWAGUCHI Kiyotake (Seiken)

2nd Lieutenant (infantry), December 1914, Graduated from War College, November 1922; Captain, August 1923; Attached to Army General Staff, November 1923; Staff Officer in 4th Division, May 1925; Staff Officer in Formosa Army, August 1928; Major and Instructor at Army Heavy Artillery School, August 1929; Member of Military Affairs Bureau of War Ministry, September 1930; Adjutant at same Ministry, August 1931; Staff Officer in China Garrison Army, August 1933; Lieutenant-Colonel, March 1934; Attached to 4th Division HQ, March 1935; Staff Officer to Tokyo Bay Fortress, March 1937; Colonel and attached to North China Area Army, December 1938; Staff Officer in Central Defence Army, Japan, March 1939; Staff Officer in Central District Army, Japan, August 1940; Major-General; Commander of 35th Infantry Brigade, December 1940; Brigade under the command of 25th Army (T. YAMASHITA) in the attack on Singapore, Malaya, December 1941; Borneo invasion, 23 December 1941– January 1942; Commander of Japanese forces on Visayan Islands, Philippines, (under 14th Army – M. HONMA), HQ Cebu Island, January 1942; Transferred with Brigade to 17th Army (under H. HYAKUTAKE), HQ Koror Island, Palaus; Reinforced Guadalcanal, Solomons, with 35th Infantry Brigade and remainder of 28th Infantry Regiment (approx. 6,000 men) under 17th Army after initial failure of advance units of 28th Regiment (under Colonel ICHIKI) to expel invading American marines; Landed with his troops, 29 August–11 September 1942; Attempted to capture Henderson airfield in a three-pronged attack; Defeated at 'Bloody Ridge' and forced to retreat westwards having lost 700 dead, 13 September 1942; Defended west bank of Matanikau River; Evacuated to Rabaul, New Britain, to report personally the reason for failure to 17th Army Commander H. HYAKUTAKE; Returned to Guadalcanal with major reinforcements under the personal command of H. HYAKUTAKE (consisting of 17th Army HQ and 2nd Division – M. MARUYAMA); Landed at Tassafaronga Point, 9–10 October 1942; Commanded a unit of 2nd Division (under M. MARUYAMA) but was detached to form right wing of an attack on Henderson airfield with three infantry battalions and three machine-gun and mortar battalions; Thought he would have more chance of success if he attacked from the south-east but M. MARUYAMA was not informed; Consequently the attack from the designated position was not forthcoming or on time; Immediately relieved of command and replaced by Colonel Shoji Toshinari, 24 October 1942 (see also Y. NASU, T. SUMIYOSHI); Left Guadalcanal in disgrace, 4 November 1942; Hospitalized in Manila, Philippines, suffering from malnutrition and malaria; Assigned to Eastern District Army HQ, Japan, November 1942; Unassigned list, March 1943; Transferred to first reserve list, April 1943; Recalled as Commander of Tsushima Fortress probably until the end of the war.

KAWAHARA Tadaichi
Major-General; Commander of 27th Independent Mixed Brigade, Java, February 1945.

KAWAI Kiyoshi
Major-General; Commander of Anti-aircraft Artillery Defence Group, Central Japan, May 1944, Renamed Anti-aircraft Artillery Group, November 1944?

KAWAMATA Osato
Military Attaché in Latvia and Russia; Head of Russian Section of Army GHQ, Tokyo; Major-General; Principal of Nakano (espionage and saboteur) School with branches in Nakano, Tokyo and Tomioka City (replacing R. TANAKA), October 1941;* Another branch was formed at Futamata in Iwata City, August 1944; Replaced (by B. YAMAMOTO), March 1945.

* The three branches were ostensibly for clandestine activities against: Soviet Union (Nakano branch): Guerrilla warfare in the south-west Pacific (Tomoioka branch): Guerrilla warfare in south-east Asia and China (Futamata branch).

KAWAME Taro
Major-General; Chief of Staff to 20th Army (under I. BANZAI), Hengyang area, central China, February 1944.

KAWAMINE Josaburo
Lieutenant-General; Commander of 20th Division (replacing B. KAWAGISHI), China, 1937; Division under 1st Army (K. KATSUKI) in operations along the northern sector of the Peiping (Peking) – Hankow Railway, mid August 1937.

KAWAMURA Kaoru
Major-General; Commander of Home Station for infantry and engineers at Okayama, Japan, March 1945.

KAWAMURA Saburō (Sanro)
Military Attaché in London; Major-General; Commander of Infantry Group (9th Infantry Brigade) of 5th Division (under T. MATSUI); Landed at Singora, Siam, for Malayan invasion, 8 December 1941; Moved across Malayan border, 9 December 1941; Broke through British Jitra defence line by 10 December 1941; Entered Alor Star, 11-12 December 1941 (see T. MATSUI) for campaign details); Attacked Gemas defence line, southern Malaya, and broke through after heavy fighting, 16–19 January 1942; Captured Kahang airfield, 25 January 1942; Part of centre attack forces on Singapore island, 9–15 February 1942; Commander of Singapore Garrison Army (consisting of 2nd Field Kempeitai and 2nd Garrison Unit) occupying 4th sector (south) of Singapore Island, i.e., Singapore City;

Involved in a purge of local Chinese who were thought to have anti-Japanese attitudes, 1942; Chief of Staff to 38th Army (under Y. TSUCHIHASHI), Saigon, Indo–China, December 1944–end of war, September 1945; Tried (together with T. NISHIMURA) as a war criminal by a British Military Court for the massacres of several thousand Chinese civilians at Singapore between 18 February–3 March 1942; Sentenced to death by hanging, 1947.

KAWANE Yoshitaka

Major-General; Commander of North China Field Motor Transport Depot; Transportation Officer of 14th Army (under M. HONMA) for invasion of the Philippines, December 1941; Ordered to land and organize transportation for prisoners taken after the fall of Bataan on Luzon (25,000 were expected) in two phases; Assumed prisoners could walk sixteen miles to Balanga using their own rations; Provided 200 trucks for transportation 35 miles from Balanga to rail centre at San Fernando, and then by train for 40 miles to Capas with a final walk of eight miles to (prison) Camp O'Donnell; In Fact, 75,000 troops surrendered; they were starving and had had no rations; Many took three days to walk the first sixteen miles; Approximately half had to continue walking to San Fernando before rail transport was provided; An estimated 7,000–10,000 died of weakness, starvation and brutality, April 1942. This was the infamous 'Bataan Death March'.

KAWARADA Takane

Major-General; Commander of 92nd Independent Mixed Brigade, Yencheng area, Honan province, north China, June 1945.

KAWASHIMA Kiyoshi

Born 1893 in Hasunuma village, Chiba prefecture, Japan; Joined the army in 1916; Doctor of Medical Sciences; Lieutenant-Colonel; Instructor in hygiene at Preparatory Department of Military School, Tokyo; Transferred to Peking, China; Chief of General Division of 'Detachment 731' (see S. ISHII), near Harbin, Manchuria, April 1939–June 1941; Head of 4th Section (known as 'Production Division') of 'Detachment 731' for mass production of bacteria for warfare, June 1941–March 1945; Chief of Medical Service at First Front HQ of Kwantung Army, Manchuria, March 1945–end of war, August 1945; Major-General by end of war; Captured by the Russians, 20 August 1945; Tried by Russian Military Tribunal at Khabarovsk, for crimes relating to bacteriological warfare and sentenced to 25 years in a labour correction camp, December 1949 (see also S. ISHII, R. KAJISUKA, Y. WAKAMATSU).

KAWASHIMA Osamu

Major-General; Commander of 82nd Infantry Brigade (in 105th Division – Y. TSUDA) Luzon, Philippines, from its activation in July 1944.

KAWASHIMA Yoshiyuki

General; War Minister in Admiral K. OKADA cabinet (replacing S. HAYASHI), September 1935; Berated by army officers to bring about the social and political reforms required by those in the '2–26 Insurrection' (rebellion of some young army officers in Tokyo) on 26 February 1936; Demanded, and got, a declaration of martial law to end the rebellion; Resigned with the fall of the cabinet, March 1936.

KAWAZOE Muraji
Major-General; Commander of 75th Infantry Brigade (in 100th Division – J. HARADA), Mindanao, Philippines, from its activation in June 1944.

Prince KAYA Tsunenori
Born 1900; Elder brother of Princes Y. ASAKA and N. HIGASHIKUNI; Childhood playmate, and near twin in appearance, of Emperor Hirohito; First cousin of Empress Nagako; Major; European tour and State Visit to Germany (after which he strongly advocated a German–Japanese alliance), March–August 1934; Toured north China and Manchukuo (Manchuria), April–May 1935; Emperor's envoy to captured Nanking, China, 10 January 1938; Returned to Japan to report to Emperor Hirohito, 16 January 1938; Major-General; Supervisor of War Strategy at Army Staff College, 1943; Lieutenant-General, 1943; Commander of 3rd Imperial Guards Division, Tokyo, 1944; Accepted sinecures in the Taisho and Nisshin Life Insurance Companies after the war.

KAYASHIMA Kōichi
Major-General; Commander of 18th Independent (or Composite?) Brigade (under 11th Army) during the Battle of Tsaoyang–Ichang, China, Early May–late June 1940; Commander of 18th Brigade and part of 40th Division which comprised 'Kayashima Force' which formed one of five major forces for operations in central Hupei, China, November 1940.

KAYASHIMA Takashi
Lieutenant-General; Commander of 6th Depot Division, Kumamoto, Japan, November 1943; Supplied 6th, 23rd?, 37th, 46th, 58th, 102nd, 103rd Divisions and 59th IMB.

KENJO Gohachiro
Major-General; Infantry Group Commander of 12th Division, Manchuria, from October 1943.

KIDO
Major-General; Artillery Group Commander of 17th Army, Solomons, c.1945.

KIDO Kanji
Major-General; Commander of 99th Infantry Brigade (in 133rd Division – K. MOJI), Hangchow area, Chekiang province, China, April 1945.

KIJIMA Kesao
Major-General; Commander of 38th Independent Mixed Brigade (formed around 81st Regiment) under 17th Army (M. KANDA), Bougainville, Solomons, from its activation, June 1944; HQ Numa Numa on the northern coast by November 1944; Converted Pearl Ridge (on central Emperor Mountain Range) to a fortress to resist attack by the Australian 7th Brigade but lost it after three days' heavy fighting, 30 December 1944–1 January 1945; Strength about 1,600, March 1945; Suffered heavy losses from Australian attacks but reinforced by about 1,500 men from December 1944–July 1945; Suggested to C in C 17th Army M. KANDA that 38th IMB be withdrawn to the south because of a possible Australian combined land and sea attack against Numa Numa but permission was refused (on the grounds that the troops were unfit for a long march so must stay and fight), July

1945; Grouped at Numa Numa and remained there until the end of the war, September 1945; Surrendered a sword to Captain W. Davies, Australian Army, aboard the *Deborah* in Numa Numa harbour, 18 September 1945.

KIKUCHI

Lieutenant-General; Formosa, 1941; Instructor in military geography at War College, Tokyo; Governor-General's Department, Formosa (i.e., Taiwan), c.1941; Assisted Formosa Army No. 82 Unit (Formosa Army Research Section) in planning attack strategy and logistics for the invasion of Malaya and East Indies, early 1941.

Note: Possibly the same as Baron KIKUCHI Takeo.

KIKUCHI Hitoshi

Major-General;[1] Head of 1st Section of 'Detachment 731', near Pingfan Station, 20 kilometres from Harbin, Manchuria, 1942-5.*

* 'Detachment 731' was the 731st Manchurian Detachment of the Kwantung Army set up to research and produce bacteriological weapons. *See* S. ISHII.

Baron KIKUCHI Takeo

(Full?) General; Held in Sugamo prison, Tokyo, as a suspected war criminal but released without trial, 31 August 1947.

Note: Possibly the same as KIKUCHI.

KIMURA

Lieutenant-General; Chief of Staff to Kwantung Army (under Y. UMEZU), Manchuria. Later became a full General.

Note: Possibly the same as KIMURA Heitarō.

KIMURA Heitarō (Hyotaro, Kyotaro)

Born 28 September 1888; 2nd Lieutenant (artillery) in 16th Artillery Regiment, December 1908; 1st Lieutenant, December 1911; Graduated from War College, November 1916; Army General Staff, September 1917; Captain, July 1918; Staff Officer at 3rd Division HQ and participated in Siberian Expedition, August 1918; Returned to Japan, April 1919; Resident Officer in Germany, January 1923; Major, August 1923; Army General Staff, May 1925; Instructor at War College, October 1925; Battalion Commander in 24th Artillery Regiment, August 1926; Artillery Department at Office of Military Training, July 1927; Lieutenant-Colonel, March 1928; Member of Japanese Delegation at London Conference, 1929–May 1930; Colonel and Commander of 22nd Artillery Regiment, August 1931; Instructor at Field Artillery School, August 1932; Section Chief at Economics and Mobilization Bureau of War Ministry, March 1935; Chief of Military Administration Bureau of War Ministry, March 1936; Major-General, August 1936; Lieutenant-General; Vice Minister of War, April 1941–March 1943; Member of Planning Board and Total War Institute, Tokyo; Possibly Chief of Staff to Southern Army (under H. TERAUCHI), c.1944; Head of Ordnance Administration HQ, Tokyo; Commander-in-Chief of Burma Area Army (replacing M. KAWABE), HQ Rangoon, September 1944; Took command as all forces in the north and west were in retreat; Forces comprised 15th Army (S. KATAMURA) –

centre, 28th Army (S. SAKURAI) – south, 33rd Army (M. HONDA) – north-east, and 2nd, 49th Divisions as strategic reserves plus seven battalions of the Burma National Army and Indian National Army, September 1944; For a time some units were transferred from Burma although reinforcements arrived; Instructed by Southern Army that no further reinforcements and bulk supplies could be sent; Lost Bhamo, mid December 1944; Ordered defence of Mandalay for purely prestige reasons although it was decided only southern Burma should be defended; British forces crossed the Irrawaddy River in the Nyaungu – Pagan area on the border of 15th and 28th Armies' operation sectors, 12–15 February 1945; Mandalay lost, 19 March 1945; Concentrated on defence of central Burma at the cost of losing southern and northern areas, February 1945; Meiktila (important road, rail and air centre plus supply base for 15th and 33rd Armies) was lost, 3 March 1945; (see also T. KASUYA); Ordered the recapture of Meiktila but Japanese forces were repulsed, 28 March 1945; Ordered a general withdrawal from the Irrawaddy Valley, late March 1945; Ordered a stand at Pyawbwe (last heavily defended area before Rangoon) by 33rd Army (M. HONDA) but the British broke through, inflicting heavy Japanese losses by 11 April 1945; Ordered 54th Division (S. KATAMURA) to Toungoo for a second line of defence; Lost effective control over 15th and 33rd Armies, April 1945; Ordered the formation of 105th independent Mixed Brigade (H. MATSUI) to defend Rangoon, April 1945; Ordered by C in C Southern Army H. TERAUCHI to defend Rangoon, 20 April 1945, but instead decided to defend south-east Burma to protect Siam (but was opposed by his Chief of Staff S. TANAKA); Abandoned Rangoon by 26 April 1945; Transferred HQ to Moulmein; General, May 1945; Ordered 15th Army (S. KATAMURA) and 33rd Army (M. HONDA) to protect the breakout of 28th Army (S. SAKURAI) from the Pegu Yomas across the Sittang River into Tenasserim after it was cut off by the abandonment of Rangoon, July–August 1945; Command of 15th Army HQ, 15th and 33rd Divisions was taken by 18th Area Army (A. NAKAMURA) after these units retreated into Siam, August 1945; Issued cease-fire orders at HQ Moulmein to all units under his command, 20–23 August 1945; Delegate at the formal surrender of all Japanese forces in South East Asia to Lord Louis Mountbatten, Singapore, Malaya, 12 September 1945; Tried as a Class A war criminal by the International Military Tribunal for the Far East, Tokyo, for atrocities committed by troops under his command and for waging an aggressive war while Vice Minister of War, 26 April 1946–12 November 1948; Found guilty and hanged at Sugamo prison, Tokyo, 23 December 1948.

Note: Appears to have surrendered at least two swords:
(a) Surrendered a sword to C in C Fourteenth Army, General Slim at Singapore, 12 September 1945. A shin-guntō with a General Officer's sword knot.
(b) Surrendered a sword to Brigadier E. F. E. Armstrong, Twelfth Army, who immediately handed it to Lieutenant-General Sir Montagu Stopford, C in C Twelfth Army, at Judson College, Rangoon, Burma, 24 October 1945. Same ceremony as J. ICHIDA, S. SAKURAI.

KIMURA Matsujiro
Lieutenant-General; Commander of 4th Division (under 18th Area Army – A. NAKAMURA), Siam, c.1945; Assembled for surrender at Lampang, Siam and placed under 15th Army HQ Command (which had come from Burma); Surrendered a sword to Major-General G. C. Evans, GOC 7th Indian Division, at

Bangkok, Siam (together with nineteen Generals and two Admirals), 11 January 1946.

KIMURA Naoki

Major-General; Commander of 2,500-strong detachment (under 14th Army – M. HONMA) which landed at Legaspi, southern Luzon, Philippines, 12 December 1941; Secured airfield and Manila railway; Attacked American General Wainwright's defensive line in the Bataan peninsula with 5,000 men, 17 January 1942; One of his units (700 infantrymen) circled the Filipino–American right flank and reached the sea so cutting off Wainright's front-line forces, 21 January 1942; Commanded amphibious attacks against Bataan but was eventually defeated, 23 January 1942; Concurrently Commander of three Home Stations for various army units at Fuchiyama, Kyoto and Maizuru, all in Kyoto Regimental District, Japan, June 1944.

KIMURA Tsunehiro

Lieutenant-General; Commander of 110th Division, Hopeh province, North China, September 1944; Moved to Loyang, Honan province, September 1944.

KINOSHITA Bin (H.)

Lieutenant-General; Commander of 3rd Air Army (under Southern Army – H. TERAUCHI) consisting of 5th, 7th, 9th, 55th Air Divisions, HQ Singapore, Malaya, 1945; Delegate at formal surrender of all Japanese forces in South East Asia to Lord Louis Mountbatten, Supreme Commander SEAC, Singapore, September 1945.

KINOSHITA Eiichi

Major-General; Commander of Eastern District Military Police, Japan, 1945; Ordered arrested by the American Occupation Forces as a suspected war criminal, 2 December 1945.

KINOSHITA Satoshi

Lieutenant-General; Commander of army forces in eastern Singapore (under 7th Area Army), c.1945; Attended a conference with C in C Southern Army H. TERAUCHI and other Area Army Commanders to discuss the surrender announcement, Saigon, 16 August 1945.

KIRA Goichi

Major-General; Commander of Supply Services for 14th Area Army (under T. YAMASHITA), Philippines, c.1944–5; Survived the war.

KISHIGAWA Kenichi

Major-General; Commander of 17th Independent Mixed Brigade, Yochow area, Hunan province, China, October 1943.

KITA Seiichi

Born 1886; 2nd Lieutenant in 36th Infantry Regiment, December 1907; Attached to 68th Infantry Regiment, February 1908; 1st Lieutenant, November 1910; Tientsin Garrison Infantry Unit, June 1911; Captain in 68th Infantry Regiment, April 1918; Graduated from War College, November 1919; Army General Staff, April 1920; Resident Officer in China, February 1931; Major, August 1923; Army

General Staff, May 1925; Instructor at War College, February 1926; Resident Officer in China, May 1927; Resident Officer in England, September 1927; Lieutenant-Colonel, October 1927; Army General Staff, August 1928; Colonel and Commander of 37th Infantry Regiment, August 1931; Shanghai Expeditionary Army HQ, February 1931; Staff Officer in Kwantung Army, Manchuria, August 1933; Chief of 7th Section of Army General Staff, August 1934; Resident Officer in China, June 1935; Military Attaché to China, March 1936; Major-General; Lieutenant-General; Commander of 12th Army, north China; Later assigned to Army General Staff; Commander-in-Chief of 1st Area Army (under Kwantung Army – O. YAMADA) consisting of 3rd Army (K. MURAKAMI), 5th Army (N. SHIMIZU) and three division under direct Area Army control; HQ Mutanchiang; Responsible for defence of eastern Manchuria; Constructed fortifications along the Siberian border; Russia invaded Manchuria, 9 August 1945; Defence lines shattered with heavy losses after heavy fighting; His forces had no artillery or aircraft to counter the Russian armour; Mutanchiang attacked, 13 August 1945; Suffered 40,000 dead and wounded by the end of the war; Surrendered at the cessation of hostilities; Believed to have died in a Soviet prison camp in about 1951.

KITAGAWA Kazuo
Lieutenant-General; Commander of 66th Division, Formosa, September 1944.

KITAJIMA
Artillery officer; Lieutenant-General; Military Commander of Kong Kong, c.1942.

Note: Possibly same as KITAJIMA Kineo.

KITAJIMA Kineo
Lieutenant-General; Commander of 1st Artillery Corps; Arrived in Philippines to reinforce 14th Army (under M. HONMA), March 1942; Bombarded front line of Bataan peninsular defence with 241 guns for seven hours, 3 April 1942; Commander of Takao Fortress, Formosa, April 1944.

KITAMURA Katsuzo
Major-General; Commander of 50th Independent Mixed Brigade, Woleai Island, Carolines, June 1944.

KITANO (KITAMURA) Kenzo
2nd Lieutenant (infantry) attached to 38th Infantry Regiment, December 1910; 1st Lieutenant, December 1913; Assigned to Army General Staff, January 1915; Attached to 38th Infantry Regiment, May 1916; Graduated from War College, December 1919; Captain and Company Commander in 38th Infantry Regiment, April 1920; Attached to Inspectorate-General of Military Training and became a section member, December 1920; Attached to latter again, July 1922; Resident Officer in Germany, September 1922; Major, August 1925; Attached to Inspectorate-General of Military Training, October 1925; Section member of last, December 1928; Battalion Commander in 3rd Infantry Regiment, March 1929; Lieutenant-Colonel and section member of Inspectorate-General of Military Training, August 1929; Member of Personnel Affairs Bureau of War Ministry, August 1930; Colonel and Commander of Senior-Course Cadet Unit at Military Academy, August 1933; Commander of 37th Infantry Regiment, March 1935;

Major-General and Hunchun Garrison Commander, Manchuria, August 1937; Chief of Staff to Korea Army, March 1938; Chief of Military Police in China, September 1939; Lieutenant-General; Commander of 4th Division, China 1940;* Transferred with the division to Manchuria, May–June 1940; Transferred with division via Shanghai to the Philippines for the invasion under 14th Army (M. HONMA), February 1942; Transferred to Osaka, Japan, July 1942; Commandant of Kunchuling Army School, Manchuria, July 1942; Commander of 19th Army (under 2nd Area Army – K. ANAMI), HQ Amboina Island, Moluccas, October 1943; attached to Army General Staff HQ, March 1945; Commandant of Military Academy, March 1945.

* It is uncertain if he was already a Lieutenant-General for the post of Chief of Military Police in China.

KITANO Masaji (Masazo)

Professor at the University of Manchuria; Major-General; Commander of secret bacteriological warfare centre 'Detachment 731', near Pingfan Station, 20 kilometres from Harbin, Manchuria, August 1942? or 1944? – March 1945; Replaced (by S. ISHII); Remained as Deputy Commander under S. ISHII; Proposed the use of plague-infected fleas as a weapon; Deliberately caused plague epidemics and controlled lethal experiments on human beings; Fled south with S. ISHII from the Russian advance, August 1945; Captured five weeks later at Nanking, China; Given immunity from the war crimes prosecutions by the American Defense Department for giving the research data to the Americans; See also S. ISHII; After the war he served as President and Chairman of Green Cross (Japanese pharmaceutical firm developing artificial blood); Still alive in 1982, a revered man in his 90s.

KITANO Norimoto

Major-? General; Commanded a portion of 6th Division (under 11th Army) during the Battle of Tsaoyang–Ichang, China, early May–late June 1940.

KITAZONO Toyozo

Major-General; Commander of 3rd Field Transport Command, December 1942; Located in Philippines, October 1944.

KOBA Toba (Tomotoki)

Colonel; Commander of 55th Infantry Regiment (under 18th Division – R. MUTAGUCHI); Division arrived in Burma, March–April 1942; Garrisoned central Burma with regimental responsibility for the area of the Zibyu Range (Homalin to Mawlaik) – Katha on the Irrawaddy River – Bhamo; Fought against first 'Chindit' raid 17 February–early May 1943; Major-General; Infantry Group Commander of 54th Division (under S. MIYAZAKI), Arakan, Burma; Commanded an Independent Force of 54th Division (consisting of two infantry battalions and two companies of 4inch guns) to form northern column (KOBA Force) during the retreat; Defeated at Shandathyki–Taungdaw, 9–12 May 1945; Moved his unit from Mount Popa to protect the Irrawaddy River crossing by the rest of 54th Division; Crossed the Irrawaddy into Pegu Yomas with heavy losses, late May 1945; Moved eastwards to Toungoo, 22 July 1945; Protected crossing of the Sittang River but again suffered heavy losses, 23 July 1945; Rejoined main divisional forces in Tenasserim, 25–28 July 1945; Surrendered a sword at the formal surrender of 28th Army HQ and 54th Division (see also S. MIYAZAKI, K. NAGAZAWA, C. SEI) to 1/10th Ghurka Rifles at Paung, Burma, 28 October 1945.

KOBAYASHI Asasaburō
Lieutenant-General; Chief of Staff to China Expeditionary Army (under Y. OKAMURA), Nanking, central China, February 1945.

KOBAYASHI Nobuo
Lieutenant-General; Commander of 60th Division, Shanghai–Soochow–Kashing area, Kiangsu province, China, from its activation in April 1942; Commander of 54th Army (defence of Japan), HQ Shimshiromachi, north of Toyohashi, Japan, c.1945.

KOBAYASHI Shigekichi
Major-General; Commander of 5th Engineer Corps (under 18th Area Army – A. NAKAMURA), Siam, c.1945; Surrendered a sword (together with A. NAKA-MURA, eighteen Generals and two Admirals) to Major-General G. C. Evans, GOC 7th Indian Division, Bangkok, Siam, 11 January 1946.

KOBAYASHI Takashi
Major-General; Infantry Group Commander of 2nd Imperial Guards (under T. NISHIMURA) during the invasion of Malaya, December 1941–February 1942; Commander of 6th Border Garrison Force, Aigun, Heiho province, Manchuria, December 1942.

KOBORI
Major-General; Commander of 5th Division (under 2nd Army – F. TESHIMA) in Ceram–Aru–Ambon area of the Moluccas; Received surrender orders on Ambon Island (together with Vice-Admiral ICHISE), September 1945; Surrendered to Australian Brigadier Steel at Piros Base, Ceram Island, where he had been transferred by order of the Australians.

KOBORI Kinjo
Major-General; Commander of a Fuel Storage Depot, Surabaya, Java, March 1944.

KOGA Ryutaro
Major-General; Commander of 52nd Infantry Brigade (in 58th Division), Hengyang–Kweilin area, Kwangsi province, China, March 1942.

KOGA Takeshi
Lieutenant-General; Commander of 55th Division (replacing Y. TAKEUCHI) under 15th Army (S. IIDA), Burma, late 1942; Division was only at two-thirds strength because 144th Regiment had been transferred to New Guinea; Ordered to the Arakan (western coastal area of Burma) to relieve 215th Regiment (under 33rd Division) which was engaged with the first British–Indian offensive, January 1943; The division travelled 600 miles across Arakan Yomas arriving late March 1943; Defended Donbaik in Mayu peninsula with 143rd Regiment against the British attack; Main bulk of the division arrived, 3 April 1943; 112th Regiment captured British 6th Brigade Commander and staff at Indin Village, 3 April 1943; British forced to retreat with heavy losses; Ordered the capture of Bauthidaung and Maungdaw by 112th, 143rd, 213th Regiments, 2nd Battalion of 214th Regiment plus artillery, 20 April 1943; Bauthidaung captured, 8 May 1943; Maungdaw captured, 14 May 1943; British–Indian offensive stopped and they

were forced into retreat arriving back at their original positions, May 1943; (British losses 5,057, Japanese losses 1,775); Division transferred to 28th Army (S. SAKURAI) command, July? 1943; Replaced (by T. HANAYA), November 1943; Commander of 81st Division, Utsunomiya, Japan, from its activation in April 1944.

KOH (KUO) Shiyoku
Lieutenant-General; Commander of internees and POW camps in the Philippines (under IGATU), c.1945; Tried by a Military Tribunal for mistreatment of POWs and civilian internees, Manila, 1946; Sentenced to death by hanging, 18 April 1946.*

* Stated at the trial of C in C 14th Area Army T. YAMASHITA that he accepted full responsibility for the administration of the camps but he declined to testify at his own trial.

KOISO Kuniaki
Born 1880; 2nd Lieutenant in 30th Infantry Regiment, June 1901; 1st Lieutenant, November 1903; Battalion Adjutant in 30th Infantry Regiment, September 1904; Company Commander of same regiment, March 1905; Captain, June 1905; Graduated from War College, November 1910; Army Staff Officer to Kwantung Government-General, September 1912; Major and Battalion Commander in 2nd Infantry Regiment, August 1914; Army General Staff HQ, June 1915; Emissary to Inner Mongolia; Arranged for the Mongolian invasion of Manchuria which was co-ordinated with a Japanese attempt on the life of Chinese warlord Chang Tso-lin; Lieutenant-Colonel, July 1918; Staff Officer in 12th Division, August 1918; Chief of Staff (LOC) to 12th Division, September 1918; Army General Staff HQ, April 1919; Army Air Service (ensuring aviation Intelligence gathered from Europe was fully utilized by the Air Force), July 1921; Colonel, February 1922; Official duty in Europe, June 1922; Commander of 51st Infantry Regiment, August 1923; Section Chief on Army General Staff, May 1925; Major-General and Instructor at War College, December 1926; Chief of Administration Division of Army Aeronautical Department, July 1927; Chief of Material Mobilization Bureau of War Ministry, August 1929; Chief of Military Affairs Bureau of War Ministry, August 1930; Masterminded 'March 1931 plot' to incriminate War Minister K. UGAKI which succeeded in removing him; Lieutenant-General, August 1931; Vice Minister of War, February 1932; Chief of Staff to Kwantung Army, Manchuria, and concurrently Chief of Special Service Department of the same army, August 1932; Commander of 5th Division, HQ Hiroshima, Japan, March 1934; Commander of Chosen (Korea) Army and known as the 'Tiger of Korea', December 1935; General 1937; Army General Staff, July 1938; Retired to first reserve list, July 1938; Minister of Overseas Affairs (with control of overseas colonization), April–August 1939; Minister of Overseas Affairs again, January–July 1940; Governor-General of Korea, May 1942; Prime Minister (replacing H. TOJO), 22 July 1942;* Adopted an aggressive policy of prosecuting the war; Formed 'Supreme War Council' to discuss important military matters in the presence of the Emperor, from 8 August 1944; Philippines invaded and Japanese naval power shattered in the Battle of Leyte Gulf; Okinawa invaded; Defence policies and an attempt to obtain a clandestine peace with the Nationalist Chinese were a failure; Did not receive army backing; Resigned, 4 April 1945; replaced (by Admiral K. SUZUKI); Ordered arrested as a Class A war criminal by the occupying forces, 1945; Tried by the International Tribunal for the

Far East, Tokyo, 26 April 1946–12 November 1948; Found guilty and sentenced to life imprisonment; Died in prison aged 70, 1950.

* Also wished for the concurrent post of War Minister but this was blocked by the army.

KOITO Gyoichi
Lieutenant-General; Commander of 7th Division, November 1941; Home Depot, Asahigawa, Japan; Some units sent to the Kuriles, spring 1944; but the main strength was in Hokkaido, Japan.

KOIZUMI Chikahiko
Lieutenant-General; Army Surgeon-General; Health Minister in H. TOJO cabinet, October 1941–July 1944.*

* Presumably had retired by this time.

KOKUBU (KOKOBU) Shinshichiro
Lieutenant-General; Commander of 46th Division (under 19th Army), Lesser Sundas, November 1944; Division transferred to Johore, Malaya (under 7th Area Army), HQ Kluang, by August 1945.*

* May not have been in command at this time. Reported to have been military Governor of Java but the time period is unconfirmed.

KOMATSUBARA Michitaro
Lieutenant-General; Supporter of 'Strike North' policy (i.e., against Russia); Expert on Russian affairs; Commander of 23rd Division, April 1938; Fought in Nomonhan (Nomonghan) campaign against Russian and Mongolian forces along the Khalka River on the Mongolian – Manchurian border which began on 11 May 1939; The division was defeated with 73 per cent losses;* Informed the Emperor of the losses at the conclusion of the fighting, 16 September 1939; Returned to Japan and committed suicide as expiation for his defeat.

* These losses were kept from the Japanese public who were told it was a great victory.

KOMATSUZAKI Rikio
Major-General; Commander of 1st Independent Mixed Brigade, Hanton, Hopeh province, China, August 1942.

KONDO Gonpachi
Lieutenant-Colonel; Attached to Imperial GHQ, Tokyo, Japan; Attended war games as IGHQ representative (together with Lieutenant-Colonel Prince Takeda) to decide the feasibility of the invasion of Imphal, Manipur State and Kohima, Assam, in India, at Burma Area Army HQ, Rangoon (see also M. INADA, M. KAWABE, R. MUTAGUCHI), 24–27 June 1943;* Believed to have been a Lieutenant-General by the end of the war.

* Burma – The Longest War by Louis Allen (see Bibliography) gives his rank as Lieutenant-Colonel at this conference but he is given as a Lieutenant-General in the index. Therefore this entry may be in error.

KONDO Kanetoshi
Major-General; Commander of 3rd Airfield Unit, Tachiarai, (Japan?), January 1944.

KONDO Shihachi

Major-General; Commander of 19th Independent Mixed Brigade, Swatow area, Kwantung province, China, November 1944.*

* Kwantung province is on the south coast of China and must not be confused with the Japanese 'Kwantung' Army in Manchuria.

KONO Takeishi

Major-General; Commander of 77th Infantry Brigade (in 102nd Division – S. FUKUEI), central Visayas, Philippines, July 1944; Commanded 13,500 air force and ground troops (either under 35th Army or 4th Air Army) protecting eight airfields on Negros Island, Visaya Group, Philippines, 1945; American 40th Division landed on the north-west coast of Negros, 29 March 1945; Fought using delaying tactics since short of weapons and ammunition; Americans entered Bacolod City after the Japanese withdrawal (and destruction of part of it before they left), 30 March 1945; Concentrated in northern Negros mountains; Suffered heavy losses and retreated south, April 1945; Northern Negros taken by the Americans, early June 1945; Remnant ordered further into Negros mountains; Fought on until the cessation of hostilities; Only 6,000 troops survived.

KONUMA Harao (Haruo)

Colonel; Chief of Strategy and Tactics Section of Army General Staff, c.1942; Chief Staff Officer to 17th Army (under H. HYAKUTAKE), HQ Rabaul, New Britain, by September 1942; Initially opposed reinforcement of Guadalcanal, Solomons, after the American landings but was persuaded to accept the idea and organized large reinforcements by dispatching 17th Army HQ (directly under the C in C H. HYAKUTAKE) and 2nd Division; Sailed with the force which landed at Tassafaronga Point, 9–10 October 1942; Remained with 17th Army HQ to act as Chief of Staff for Guadalcanal forces;* After heavy fighting in October he devised guerrilla tactics of fighting to the death from fox-holes, November 1942; Personally visited the Commanders of 2nd and 38th Divisions to advise them of 17th Army Orders to evacuate the army from Guadalcanal, but the troops were told it was a 'strategic withdrawal', late January 1943; Major-General; Deputy Chief of Staff to 14th Area Army (under T. YAMASHITA) during the defence of the Philippines (replacing T. NISHIMURA), 11 December 1944–cessation of hostilities, September 1945.

* This must have been in a temporary acting capacity while 17th Army Chief of Staff S. MIYAZAKI was at the front line.

KOURI Katsuhiro

Major-General; Commander of Field Railway Corps (under 18th Area Army – A. NAKAMURA), Siam, c.1945; Surrendered a sword (together with A. NAKA-MURA, eighteen Generals and two Admirals) to Major-General G. C. Evans, GOC 7th Indian Division, Bangkok, Siam, 11 January 1946.

KOZUKI Kiyoshi – Same as KATSUKI Kiyoshi

KOZUKI Yoshi

Lieutenant-General by the end of Second World War; Vice Minister of the Japanese Demobilization Ministry (which replaced the abolished War Ministry), Tokyo, 1946.

Note: Possibly the same as KOZUKI Yoshio.

KOZUKI (KOTSUKI) Yoshio

Born 1886; 2nd Lieutenant (infantry) in 4th Infantry Regiment of Imperial Guards Division, December 1909; Lieutenant, February 1913; Graduated from War College and assigned to Army General Staff, August 1918; Captain and Adjutant at War Ministry, July 1919; Language Officer in Germany, November 1921; Major, August 1924; Assigned to Military Affairs Bureau, August 1925; Lieutenant-Colonel, August 1928; Assigned to Military Administration Bureau (of War Ministry?), December 1930; Colonel, August 1932; Commander of 11th Infantry Regiment, March 1935; Major-General and Commander of 40th Infantry Brigade, August 1937; Chief of Military Administration Bureau, July 1938; Lieutenant-General, August 1939; Commander of Shipping Transportation HQ, March 1940; Commander of 19th Division, August 1940; Commander of 2nd Army, July 1942; Commander of Mongolia Army, June 1943; Commander of 11th Army, China, November 1944; Commander-in-Chief of 17th Area Army, Keijo, Korea, April 1945; Signed the surrender of South Korea (south of 38° latitude) which comprised 360,000 troops (together with Vice-Admiral G. YAMAGUCHI) to Lieutenant General J. R. Hodge, American Army, and Admiral T. C. Kinkaid, USN, in the Throne Room, Government House, Keijo (Seoul), 9 September 1945.

Note: Possibly the same as KOZUKI Yoshi.

KUBO

Probably Major-General; Vice Chief of Staff to 34th Army (under S. KUSHI-BUCHI), Korea, at the time of the Japanese surrender, August 1945.

KUBOTA Takajiro

Major-General; Commander of 72nd Infantry Brigade (in 65th Division), Hsuchow, Kiangsu province, central China, September 1944?

KUDO Ryoichi

Major-General; Chief of Staff to 6th Army (under J. SOGAWA), Hailar, Manchuria, February 1944.

KUMABE

Major-General; Chief of Staff to 3rd Air Group (under M. SUGAWARA); Arrived at Saigon, Indo–China, late October 1941; 3rd Air Group supported the invasion of Malaya by 25th Army (under T. YAMASHITA) from 8 December 1941.

KUNITAKE Michio

Major-General; Chief of Staff to Central District Army, Osaka, Japan, December 1942.

KUNO Seiichi

Lieutenant-General; Commander of 25th Army (replacing H. IMAMURA), China, from January 1940; Engaged in Battle of southern Kwangsi which lasted until late February 1940; Defended Nanning but lost it, 30 December 1940.

KUNOMURA Todai (Momoyo)

Major-General; Chief of Staff to 15th Army (under R. MUTAGUCHI) at HQ Maymyo, Burma (replacing N. OBATA), April–May 1943; Present at war games to decide the feasibility of the invasion of Imphal and Assam, India (*see also* M. KAWABE, R. MUTAGUCHI, E. NAKA) at Burma Area Army HQ, Rangoon, 24–27 June 1943; Completely compliant with the wishes of R. MUTAGUCHI; Chairman of a tactical exercise (table-top type) at HQ Maymyo with E. NAKA present, 12 August 1943; Attended senior officers' conference at Southern Army HQ, Singapore, to discuss the plan; Tried to persuade Southern Army Chief of Staff S. INADA to give it full support; Sent to 31st Division (K. SATO) HQ on Kohima front to deliver orders, 21 June 1944; Lieutenant-General and transferred as Commander of 2nd Guards Division, HQ Medan, Sumatra (under 25th Army), 30 August or early September 1944.

KURIBAYASHI Tadamichi

2nd Lieutenant (cavalry), December 1914; Graduated from War College, November 1923; Resident Officer in America, September 1927; Major, March 1930; Military Attaché to Canada, April 1930; Lieutenant-Colonel, August 1933; Member of Military Affairs Bureau of War Ministry, December 1933; Commander of 7th Cavalry Regiment, August 1936; Section Chief (cavalry) of Military Administration Bureau at War Ministry and Colonel, August 1937; Major-General and Commander of 2nd Cavalry Brigade, March 1940; Commander of 1st Cavalry Brigade, December 1940; Chief of Staff to 23rd Army, September 1941; Lieutenant-General and Commander of 2nd Imperial Guard Depot Division, June 1943; Commander of 109th Division from its activation to defend the Bonin Islands (which included Iwo Jima and Chichi Jima), 30 June 1944;[1] Concentrated on the defence of Iwo Jima (which had vital airfields in range of Japan) with a total of approx 14,000 troops comprising 109th Division, 2nd Independent Mixed Brigade (K. OSUGA, S. SENDA), 145th Regiment and 26th Tank Regiment (plus approx 7,000 naval personnel under Rear-Admiral T. ICHIMARU); Decided to leave beaches undefended against the wishes of his subordinates and the naval commander; Concentrated defence inland and on Mount Suribachi; The island was heavily bombarded by American naval forces for six weeks, January–February 1945; American 4th and 5th Marines landed, 19 February 1945; Mount Suribachi was surrounded by American forces, 22 February 1945; Suribachi captured by the Americans with heavy Japanese losses, 24 February 1945; Centre of island captured by American with 50 per cent losses of Japanese front-line troops, 25 February 1945; HQ in a cave; Ordered the flag of the 145th Regiment to be burnt to prevent its capture, 14 March 1945; 145th Regiment and 2nd IMB (S. SENDA) wiped out by 16 March 1945;[2] Moved HQ to another cave but was wounded; Committed suicide by traditional *seppuku*, aged 60, 27 March 1945; Posthumous promotion to full General.

Note: Reported to have left two swords in Japan. One of which was presented by, or on behalf of, the Emperor Taisho when he graduated second in his class at War College, 1923.

[1] Under direct command of IGHQ, Tokyo.
[2] By the end of the campaign approx. 18,000 Japanese had been killed and only 216 prisoners taken (rising to 867) against 4,554 US marines and 363 US naval personnel killed.

KURIOWA Yoshikatsu

Lieutenant-General; Commander of Kochi Home Station (infantry), Japan, March 1945.

KURODA

Major-General; Attached to 37th Army HQ (under M. YAMAWAKI), Borneo, c.1944; Gave evidence in war crimes trial of two Japanese army captains involved in the 'Sandakan death marches'.

KURODA Shigenori

Born 1887; 2nd Lieutenant (infantry) in 47th Infantry Regiment, December 1909; 1st Lieutenant, February 1913; Graduated from War College, November 1916; Office of Military Training, August 1917; Amur Railway Detachment HQ, Manchuria, August 1918; Company Commander in 47th Infantry Regiment; Captain, June 1919; Office of Military Training, August 1919; Resident Officer in England, January 1922; Major, August 1924; Office of Military Training, May 1925; Battalion Commander in 57th Infantry Regiment, March 1928; Lieutenant-Colonel, August 1928; Office of Military Training, August 1929; Colonel and Commander of 59th Infantry Regiment, August 1932; Section Chief (conscription) at War Ministry, August 1933; Military Attaché to India, August 1935; Major-General; March 1937; Army General Staff, May 1937; Lieutenant-General and Bureau Chief at Office of Military Training, July 1941; Chief of Staff to Southern Army (under H. TERAUCHI), June 1942; Commander of Japanese forces in Java by October 1943; Commander of 14th Army, Philippines (replacing S. TANAKA?), 1943?; Upgraded to 14th Area Army, July 1944; Regarded the Philippines as indefensible and so took no action to safeguard them; Allowed discipline to become lax and roads and railways to fall into disrepair; Unpopular with his senior officers; Disagreed with the policy of IGHQ, Tokyo; Liked his personal pleasures including golf; Removed when his protector, Premier H. TOJO, fell from power (replaced by T. YAMASHITA), September 1944.

KUROSE Heiichi

Major-General; Commander of 57th Infantry Brigade (in 68th Division), Hengyang area, Hunan province, China, April 1945?

KURUSU Takeo

Major-General; Commander of 68th Independent Mixed Brigade (under 35th Army – S. SUZUKI), Philippines, 1944–5.

KUSABA

Lieutenant-General; Commander of Field Railway Command of the Kwantung Army, Manchuria, c.1940.

KUSABA Sueyoshi

Major-General; Commander of the FU-GO Project, Japan, November 1944–March 1945.*

* This was the building and launching of balloons carrying explosive charges which were launched into the upper winds blowing across the Pacific to take them to the west coast of America. Success was minimal with one reported forest fire and apparently injury to some civilians who found unexploded charges.

KUSABA Tatsumi

Lieutenant-General; Commander of 25th Army (possibly replacing T. YAMASHITA), Malaya, 1942; Presumably in Manchuria by the end of the war since he committed suicide on a Russian aircraft en route to a war crimes trial (for atrocities committed in Malaya), 1945.

KUSHIBUCHI (KUCHIFUCHI) Senichi
Lieutenant-General; Commander of 28th Division (under 1st Area Army), Manchuria, March 1943; Division came under 3rd Area Army command, Manchuria, February 1944; Commander of 34th Army (consisting of 59th, 137th Divisions), HQ Hamhung, Korea (replacing T. SANO), under Kwantung Army, c.1945; 34th Army survived virtually intact after the Russian invasion of Manchuria, 9–15 August 1945.

KUWADA Teizo
Major-General; Commander of 3rd Cavalry Brigade, Paoching area, Tungan province, Manchuria, August 1944.

KUWAKI Takaaki
A General officer; Retired 1942.

KUWAORI Katsuhiro
Major-General; Commander of 4th Railway Transport Command, Bandoeng, Java, November 1944.

MABUCHI (MARUCHI, MABUTSI) Itsuo (Hsuo)
Major-General; Chief of Staff to 5th Division ; Division moved to Ambon Island – Dutch New Guinea area, late 1942; Moved to Kai Island – Aru Islands, off southwest New Guinea, early 1944; (Acting?) Commander of 16th Army (replacing Y. NAGANO), Java (under 7th Area Army – S. ITAGAKI), October 1945; Commanded Japanese troops serving under the Dutch against nationalist insurgents until repatriation in 1946.

Note: (a) Said to have surrendered a sword to Major-General J. J. Mojet, Royal Netherlands Army.
(b) Surrendered a sword to Major-General Allons, Royal Netherlands Army after serving under him until repatriation, 1946, A *shin-guntō* with a blade signed 'TAIRA NAGAMORI' of Bungo province. Koto period (pre-1596). Now in the Netherlands Army Museum. Leyden, Holland.

Viscount MACHIJIRI Kazumoto
Born 1889; Married the first cousin of Empress Nagako; Commander of the Imperial Guards artillery, 1926; Aide-de-camp and liaison officer to Emperor Hirohito, 1930–7; Lieutenant-General; Chief of Staff to 2nd Army (and concurrently a Bureau Chief?), north China, April 1938; Commander of the Chemical Weapons Branch of the Army, June–December 1941; Commander of (French) Indo–China Garrison Army, 1942–4; Retired, May 1945; Died 1950.

MACHIMURA Kingo
(Full?) General; Superintendent of Tokyo Metropolitan Police Department by August 1945.

MACHINO Kazuo

Major-General; Chief of Intendance Department of 18th Area Army (under A. NAKAMURA), Siam, 1945; Surrendered a sword (together with A. NAKAMURA, eighteen Generals and two Admirals) to Major-General G. C. Evans, GOC 7th Indian Division, Bangkok, Siam, January 1946.

MAEDA Masami

Lieutenant-General; Chief of Staff to 14th Army (under M. HONMA) during the invasion of the Philippines, 1941; Supported the plan to blockade the Bataan peninsula to starve out the American and Filipino forces and prepared a report to this effect for IGHQ, Tokyo, 10 February 1942; Sacked by Chief of Army General Staff G. SUGIYAMA for defeatist reports and also for reports that he was living in luxury away from the front, March 1942; Replaced (by T. WACHI).

MAKATA (MAGATA) Isaoshi

Major-General; Chief of Staff to 17th Army (under M. KANDA), Bougainville Island, Solomons, 1945; Surrendered to Lieutenant-General Savige, GOC Australian II Corps, at Torokina on Bougainville (together with M. KANDA and Vice-Admiral Baron T. SAMEJIMA); All handed over swords at this ceremony.

MAKINO Shira

2nd Lieutenant (infantry), December 1914; Graduated from War College, November 1922; Instructor at Military Academy, August 1928; Major, August 1930; Battalion Commander in 4th Imperial Guard Infantry Regiment, March 1931; Lieutenant-Colonel and Instructor at War College, August 1933; Staff Officer in 12th Division, December 1935; Colonel, August 1937; Attached to Military Preparatory Academy, November 1937; Commander of 35th Infantry Regiment, July 1938; Major-General and Chief of Staff to 5th Army, March 1940; Senior Instructor at Military Preparatory Academy, 1941; Director of last, October 1941; Superintendent of same, December 1942; Lieutenant-General, June 1943; Commander of 16th Division (under 35th Army – S. SUZUKI) as garrison of Leyte Island, Philippines; He had no combat experience and the division consisted mainly of conscripts; HQ Tacloban; American forces landed near Dulag, 20 October 1944; Moved HQ inland; Most of Tacloban occupied by the Americans, 21 October 1944; Split division into Southern and Northern Leyte Defence Forces; Southern Force pushed back across the coastal plain to foothills of the mountains; Reinforced by 1st Division (under T. KATAOKA) which landed at Ormoc, early November 1944; Division destroyed by December 1944; Remained (or trapped?) on the island after the evacuation of the remnant of 35th Army, early January 1945; Reported to have died on Leyte, early 1945.

MANAGI (MANAKI) Keishin (Takanobu)

Lieutenant-General; Deputy Chief of Staff to 25th Army (under T. YAMASHITA), Malaya, December 1941; Acting Commander of 2nd Division (replacing S. OKAZAKI) under direct command of Burma Area Army, Burma, January– February 1945; Division transferred to southern Indo–China about this time (under 38th Army – Y. TSUCHIHASHI); HQ established at Phom Penh, Cambodia, March 1945; HQ at Saigon by the time of the Japanese surrender, August 1945; Attended surrender negotiations with Major-General D. Gracey, Head of Allied Control Commission, Saigon, August? 1945

MANJŌME Takeo

Major-General; Commander of 12,000 troops (possibly 162nd Division) defending Cebu City (under 35th Army – S. SUZUKI), Cebu Island, Philippines, 1945; Concentrated on the defence of the northern part of the island; The American 'Americal' Division landed near Cebu City, 26 March 1945; Abandoned the beaches and Cebu City to concentrate defence in nearby hills; Cebu City taken by the Americans after its destruction by the retreating Japanese, 27 March 1945; American pressure and heavy fighting drove the remaining forces into the mountains of the northern part of the island; Effective resistance broken by mid June 1945; Remnant fought in small isolated groups until the cessation of hostilities, August 1945.

MANO Goro

Lieutenant-General; Commander of 41st Division (under 18th Army), Wewak, New Guinea, June 1943; Moved south-east, October 1943; Medang area, January 1944; Suffered heavy losses withdrawing north-west, March 1944; Hansa Bay, April 1944; Aitape–Hollandia area suffering heavy losses, May 1944; Deployed from Anumb river to Balif, October 1944; Again suffered heavy losses against Australians; Remnant withdrew north-west to Wora, April 1945; HQ at Winge, July 1945; HQ attacked by Australians but he escaped; Surrendered at Wewak to Australian Major-General Roy King, acting GOC 6th Division.

Note: His sword is in Australia (private collection?). It has a blade signed 'MASAMUNE' but not of Sagmi (one of at least sixteen smiths of this name).

MARUYAMA Masao

Lieutenant-General; Commander of 2nd Division, China and Manchuria, c.1937–1940; Division transferred to Japan 1940–January 1942; Division transferred to Java for the invasion, March–August 1942; Division transferred to Rabaul, New Britain, September 1942; Division transferred as reinforcements to Guadalcanal, Solomons, and personally commanded units of 16th Infantry Regiment in 2nd Division (under 17th Army – H. HYAKUTAKE) which landed 9–10 October 1942; Ordered to take Henderson airfield in a pincer movement; Split the division with K. KAWAGUCHI (29th Infantry Regiment) on right and stayed with Y. NASU and Divisional HQ on the left; Advance slowed by the jungle conditions and lack of maps reaching position near 'Bloody Ridge' behind schedule, 23 October 1942; Not informed that K. KAWAGUCHI had changed his plan and his time of attack so relieved him of command which caused another delay; Heavy Artillery Commander T. SUMIYOSHI was not informed of the delays so launched an abortive attack at the correct time, 23 October 1942; Finally launched a night attack on Henderson airfield with initial success and even informed C in C 17th Army H. HYAKUTAKE that the plan has succeeded, but instead it was repulsed by American marines with more than 900 Japanese dead, 23–24 October 1942; Forced to retreat; Informed of the plan to evacuate Guadalcanal, 17 January 1943; Evacuated with the remnant of his force, night of 4/5 February 1943; Landed at Rabaul, New Britain; Division transferred to Philippines for reorganization; Replaced (by S. OKAZAKI) before the division was transferred to Singapore by November 1943; Survived the war.

MASAI Yoshihito
Major-General; Commander of Army Artillery Unit, Western District Army HQ Kokura, Japan, June 1942.

MASKA (MASUOKA, MATSUOKA) Kenshichi
Major-General; Commander of Kempeitai forces, Philippines; Sentenced to ten years' hard labour at Manila, Philippines, after a war crimes trial.

MATSUDA Iwao
Major-General; Commander of 65th Independent Mixed Brigade, New Britain, October 1943.

MATSUI Hideji
Colonel; Commander of 113th Regiment in 56th Division, north Burma; Major-General; Commander of 105th Independent Mixed Brigade (KAN-I Force) formed for the defence of Rangoon (directly under Burma Area Army command – H. KIMURA) from every available Japanese including clerks, civilians, anti-aircraft troops, 13th Naval Guard Force, etc., April 1945; Ordered to defend Payagi and Pegu (if these were lost Rangoon would be cut off from Japanese troops in the Tenasserim area), 27 April 1945; Arrived at Pegu and took personal command, 28 April 1945; Fought hard and was ordered by H. KIMURA to abandon Pegu after attempting to destroy the port installations and withdrew to defend Rangoon to the death, 30 April 1945; Not told of the abandonment of Rangoon by Burma Area Army four days previously (i.e., 26 April); Defence orders were changed to waging guerrilla warfare. He ordered the transfer of fit POWs towards the Sittang River but said they could be released if enemy opposition were met and actually released all unfit POWs, 30 April 1945; Avoided the destruction of his forces by moving into the Pegu Yomas hills; Attempted to break out across the Sittang Valley into Tenasserim and crossed the Sittang River c. 22–24 July 1945; Believed to have survived until the Japanese surrender, August 1945.

MATSUI Iwane (Iwace, Sekiakon)
General; Commander of Formosa Garrison Army; Retired, 1933; Leading figure in DAI ASIA KYOKAI (Great Asia Association) of Japan supporting 'Asia for the Asians' with Japan as the driving force, touring Asian capitals to gain support, August 1933; Tried to prevent war with China, 1935; Accepted such a war was inevitable; Recalled to active duty (aged 60) and appointed Commander of the Shanghai Expeditionary Force, 15 August 1937;[1] Landed at Shanghai, China, 23 August 1937; Stated that he wanted to advance as far as Nanking and requested army and political support for the idea; Suffered from tuberculosis by this time; Moved against Nanking; Commander-in-Chief of Central China Area Army (formed from 10th Army and the Shanghai Expeditionary Force after the link-up of the two forces outside Nanking), 2–6 December 1937; Attacked Nanking, 8 December 1937; Nanking captured, 12–13 December 1937; Conducted the campaign from his sick bed; Entered Nanking in a triumphal parade as the infamous 'Rape of Nanking' began;[2] Returned to HQ, Shanghai, 17 December 1937;[3] Recalled to Japan (but not disciplined) and retired, February 1938;[4] Arrested as a Class A war criminal, 1945; Tried for the Nanking atrocities by the International Military Tribunal for the Far East, Tokyo, 26 April 1946–12 November 1948; Known as the 'Butcher of Nanking'; Hospitalized with a

stomach ailment during the trial investigation of the Nanking massacres so could not personally defend himself; Found guilty, sentenced to death and hanged at Sugamo prison, Tokyo, 23 December 1948.

[1] Before assuming command he stated that he wished to 'protect and patronise Chinese officials and people as far as possible'.
[2] After the fall of Nanking he issued strict orders that only picked units should go in and that they must 'refrain from acts which would disgrace military honour'. The Japanese forces massacred an estimated 260,000–300,000 prisoners and civilians. Although he did not order the slaughter (see K. NAKAJIMA, H. YANAGAWA) he could not countermand the order to commit such killings, although given by a subordinate, because it was given by the Imperial Prince Y. ASAKA who was the uncle of Emperor Hirohito.
[3] Upon returning to Shanghai he issued orders to Nanking commanders that 'anyone guilty of misconduct must be severely punished'. All his orders were ignored.
[4] Believed to have been a member of the Admiral M. YONAI cabinet, 1940.

MATSUI Setsu
Major-General; Commander of 10th Field Replacement Unit, Kanazawa?, Japan, April 1944; Unit located in Yincheng, central China, July 1944.

MATSUI Takuro (Kyutaro)
Lieutenant-General; Commander of 5th Division (under 25th Army – T. YAMASHITA) with approx. 16,000 men; Assembled at Samah Port, Hainan Island, off south China, for embarkation for the Malaya invasion, sailing 4 December 1941; Landed at Singora, Siam, 8 December 1941; (See also S. KAWAMURA); Other units of 5th Division (42nd Infantry Regiment and Artillery) landed at Patani, Siam, 8 December 1945; Rapidly destroyed British defences, taking Alor Star, Malaya, 11–12 December 1941; Attacked Penang Island but met no resistance, 15 December 1941; Held up at the Perak River but forced a crossing, 26 December 1941; Battle of Slim River, seizing an intact bridge, 7 January 1942; Entered Kuala Lampur, the capital of the Malayan States, 11 January 1942; Divisional strength reduced but not allowed to rest; Attacked Gemas defence line and broke through after heavy fighting, 16–19 January 1942; Captured Kluang, 25 January 1942; Entered Johore Bahru, 31 January 1942; Assigned the centre position for the attack on Singapore Island across the Singapore Strait, which commenced 9 February 1942; Combined with 18th Division (see R. MUTAGUCHI) for a night attack on Bukit Timah heights, 10/11 February 1942; Attacking Singapore Island reservoir defences; The British surrendered, 15 February 1942; Commander of 13th Army, Lower Yangtze River area, China, by the end of the war, August 1945; Surrendered 13th Army, 27th, 60th, 61st, 69th Divisions and other units to Chinese General Tang En-po of 3rd Front Army at Shanghai, September 1945; Also surrendered 133rd Division and other units to Chinese General Ku Chu-tung of 3rd War Area at Hangchow, China, about the same time.

MATSUMOTO Kenji
Major-General; Personal aide-de-camp to Field Marshal Prince N. HIGASHIKUNI, c.1943.

MATSUMURA Shūitsu
Served in China; Major-General; Attached to IGHQ, Tokyo, 1945; Chief of Staff to 59th Army (under Y. FUJII), HQ Hiroshima Castle, Japan, July 1945; Injured in his house by the atomic bomb blast, 5 August 1945.

Note: The explosion's epicentre was only 1,000 yards from his house, at about 1,500 feet above ground level, and the temperature beneath it was 5,000°C, but he survived with only a bad cut and numerous lacerations from glass, and was able to make his way to Lieutenant-General YAMAMOTO's house outside the city.

MATSUMURA Tomokatsu
Born 1899 in Tokyo; Graduated from Military Academy, 1928; Platoon commander in 38th Infantry Regiment, 1928–9; Assigned to Army General Staff in 1st Section of General Affairs Bureau, 1929–December 1932; Mission abroad, 1932–6; Instructor in military history at Military Academy, 1936–7; Attached to Formation (Organization and Mobilization?) Section of Army General Staff, 1937–October 1939; Member of 4th Bureau (Historical) of Army General Staff, October 1941–August 1943; Chief of 1st Operations Division of Kwantung Army and then chief of a section, October 1939–October 1941; Head of 5th Section (America and Europe) in 2nd Bureau (Intelligence) of Army General Staff, (replacing Y. TAMURA), Manchuria, August 1943–March 1945; Assistant Deputy Chief of Staff to Kwantung Army, March 1945–end of war, August 1945; Final rank Major-General.

MATSUO Eiichi
Major-General; Concurrently Commander of two Home Stations : a signals unit at Aomori and an infantry unit at Asahigawa, both in Hakodate Regimental District, Japan, March 1945.

MATSURA Atsuo
Lieutenant-General; Commander of 106th Division, China, from its activation, 1938?; Battle of Nanchang (under 11th Army), mid February–early May 1939; Replaced (by R. NAKAI); Reported killed in China, believed 20 April 1942.

MATSURA Hoichi
Major-General; Concurrently Commander of two Home Stations: an infantry unit at Omura and an artillery unit at Sasebo, both in Nagasaki Regimental District, May 1945.

MATSUYAMA Yuzo (Sukezo, Suteza, Takezo)
Lieutenant-General; Commander of 56th Division, China; Division transferred to Burma, landing at Rangoon, March–April 1942; Under 15th Army (S. IIDA); Ordered to loop east through Taunggyi and advance north through the Shan States to cut the road to China; Advance guard sent to join 55th Division (under Y. TAKEUCHI) to assist in the attack on Toungoo; 148th Regiment captured Lashio, 29 April 1942; Ordered by 15th Army to halt at the Salween River, 26 April 1942; Ordered to co-operate with 18th Division (R. MUTAGUCHI) and 33rd Division (S. SAKURAI) to repulse the first British 'Chindit' raid, central Burma, February–May 1943; Division transferred to 33rd Army (M. HONDA) control, April 1944; 56th Division Infantry Group of 1,500 men (under G. MIZUKAMI) detached to reinforce Myitkyina, June 1944; Remainder of the division left to defend the north-eastern front alone against three Chinese divisions and 'Mars' Brigade after a policy decision by C in C Burma Area Army H. KIMURA to concentrate on the defence of central Burma, February 1945; Suffered heavy losses at Myitson on the Shweli River, 19 February 1945; Appears to have been

concurrently acting commander of 33rd Army (HQ?) for a short time during the absence of M. HONDA, March 1945; Division withdrawn from the Chinese border to garrison the southern Shan States in place of the whole of 15th Army, May? 1945; Formed 'Matsuyama Force' with 15th, 56th, 55th(part) Divisions to cover Burma Area Army breakout across the Sittang River, July 1945; Retreated into Siam and came under 15th Army (S. KATAMURA) control which had also retreated there, July–August 1945; HQ at Khunyuam, Siam, August 1945; Participant in at least two surrender ceremonies; Died soon after the war.

Notes: (a) Surrendered a sword to Sir Montagu Stopford, C in C Twelfth Army, possibly at Rangoon, Burma, 1945 (exact date unknown). Blade tang signed 'YASUTSUGU WO MOTTE NAMBAN TETSU NI OITE BUSHŪ EDO SAKU KORE WO' (i.e., Yasutsugu made this using foreign iron at Edo in Bushū). Hollyhock mon. Blade engraved with a *bonji* and dragon *horimono* with engraver's details on the tang 'YAMASHIRO NO KAMI FUJIWARA KUNIHIRO' (i.e., Fujiwara Kunihiro, lord of Yamashiro). Blade dated to *c*.1605. This sword was subsequently presented to Lieutenant-General Sir Francis Festing, GOC 36th Division (during the period 16 November 1943–29 August 1945) which was the main opponent of the Japanese 56th Division. After the war he had it re-polished in Tokyo and the blade mounted in *shira-saya* (plain wooden keeper mounts) and the military mounts fitted with a wooden blade. It was then presented to MATSUYAMA's widow 'as a token of respect from a one-time opponent', 6 January 1954.
(b) Surrendered a sword (together with nineteen Generals and two Admirals) to Major-General G. C. Evans, GOC 7th Indian Division, Bangkok, Siam, 11 January 1946.

MAZAKI (MASAKI) Jinsaburo
Born 1876; Graduated from Military Academy, November 1897; 2nd Lieutenant in 46th Infantry Regiment, June 1898; Tsushima Guard Battalion (infantry), May 1899; 1st Lieutenant in 46th Infantry Regiment, November 1900; Instructor of Training Unit at Military Academy, December 1900; Captain, June 1904; Graduated from War College, December 1905; Military Affairs Bureau of the War Ministry, November 1907; Major, January 1909; Language Officer in Germany, May 1911; Battalion Commander in 42nd Infantry Regiment, June 1914; Lieutenant-General, November 1914; Section Chief in Office of Military Training, November 1916; Colonel, January 1918; Commander of 1st Infantry Regiment in Imperial Guards Division, HQ Tokyo, July 1921; Favoured 'Strike North' policy (i.e., against Russia); Major-General; Commander of 1st infantry Brigade, August 1922; Commandant of Military Academy, August 1923; Lieutenant-General, March 1937; Commander of 8th Division, August 1927; Commander of 1st Division, July 1929; Deputy Chief of Army General Staff (under S. ARAKI), January 1932; Sent to China to curb Kwantung Army's attacks into northern China, April 1933; General and Military Councillor, June 1933; Inspector-General of Military Training, January 1934; Member of 'Imperial Way' (Kodo-ha) faction supporting 'Strike North' policy; Forced to resign because of his support for these policies (and replaced by J. WATANABE), July 1935; Military Councillor, July 1935; Retired, March 1936; Held by the American occupying forces in Sugamo prison, Tokyo, for a year and a half for complicity in the '2–26 Insurrection' (26 February 1936) but released without prosecution, 31 August 1947; Withdrew from public life to his estate in Kyushu until his death, 31 August 1956.

MAZAKI Kumao

Major-General; Commander of 3rd Air Signals Unit, August 1943; Located at Singapore, Malaya, October 1944.

MIHARA Shunji

Major-General; Commander of 1st Railway Transport Command, Japan, August 1943.

MIKAMI Kizo

Major-General; Commander of 22nd Air Brigade (under 14th Army), Philippines, 1942.

MIKUNI Naotomi

Lieutenant-General; Commander of 21st Division (French) Indo–China, March 1943.

MINAKAMI (MIZUKAMI) Genzo

Major-General; Infantry Group Commander of 56th Division (under Y. MATSUYAMA), Burma, c.1944; Detached from division with orders to reinforce Myitkyina with the Infantry Group of 1,500 men and assumed command of the defence against the attack by 'Merill's Marauders' and Chinese troops, 17 May 1944; (Myitkyina was already garrisoned by 114th Regiment under Colonel Maruyama with 3,000 men); Myitkyina airfields already lost by mid May 1944; Ordered to hold the town for three months; Strength reduced to 2,500 with some artillery by 31 May 1944; Recaptured Charpate and Namkwi villages by 26 May 1944; Allied assault temporarily halted, end of May 1944; Fresh Allied attacks forced a withdrawal back to Myitkyina town with 790 Japanese killed and 1,180 wounded by mid July 1944; Ordered by 33rd Army to defend Myitkyina to the death, 10 July 1944; Put up a strong defence but suffered heavy losses; Promoted two grades to full General;[1] Held Myitkyina for 76 days although outnumbered approx. 15:1; Ordered Colonel Maruyama to withdraw the remnant (about 700 men) across the Irrawaddy River by night, 1–3 August 1944; Withdrew to the mid-stream island of Nonthalon and then committed suicide by shooting himself after ordering that the regimental flag be saved, 3 August 1944;[2] His sword, ashes and regimental colours were brought out by his adjutant and given to 33rd Army Commander M. HONDA at army HQ Bhamo (and presumably returned to Japan).

[1] Promotion of two grades was normally only posthumous, so he knew he was 'expected' to die.
[2] He was still within the Myitkyina area so did not leave alive.

MINAMI (MIRAMI) Jiro

Born 1874; 2nd Lieutenant (cavalry), 1895; Company Commander in 1st Cavalry Regiment during Russo–Japanese War (taking part in the assault on Port Arthur), 1904–5; Major, 1905; Major-General, 1919; Commander of a garrison unit in China; Director of Cavalry School; Lieutenant-General; Commander of 16th Division; Vice Chief of Army General Staff, 1927; Commander of Korea (Chosen) Army, 1929; Replaced (by S. HAYASHI), 1930; General, 1930; War Minister in Wakutsuki cabinet (replacing K. UGAKI), 1931;* Believed in Japanese territorial expansion; Supported the Japanese invasion of Manchuria after the 'Manchurian Incident', 19 September 1931; Resigned (and replaced by S. ARAKI), late 1931; Concurrently Commander-in-Chief of Kwantung Army, Manchuria, and Ambassador to 'Manchukuo', 1934; Placed on reserve list after '2–26 Insurrection' (rebellion of young army officers in Tokyo) 26 February 1936; Governor-General of Korea, 1936–42; Member of Privy Council, 1942; Arrested as a Class A war criminal and tried by the International Tribunal for the Far East, Tokyo, 26 April 1946–12 November 1948; Found guilty and sentenced to life imprisonment; Released for health reasons; Died 1957.

Note: A sword blade only is now in the US Naval Academy Museum, Annapolis. The tang is signed and is said to read 'General Jiro Mirami got this sword (on) a good day in early summer, 1932. Hideaki of Muroran, 1912'. Cat.no.71.64

*In 1931 he addressed divisional commanders, encouraging them to take part in political activities provided they were favourable to the army.

MINE Komatsu
Major-General; Head of Secret Police, HQ Tokyo; Supplied Russian-made bombs for the assassination of the Chinese warlord Chang Tso-lin (*see also* Y. TATEKAWA) and was subsequently appointed to investigate the murder, supplying a 'whitewash' report on Japanese involvement, August 1928.

MINEKI Juichiro
Major-General; Commander of 'Hokkai' (North Seas) Garrison Unit, c.Second World War.

MISHIMA Giichiro
Major-General; Commander of 3rd Artillery Group in 3rd Division (under M. YAMAMOTO), China, from February 1944.

MIURA Chujiro (Makio)
Lieutenant-General; Commander of 69th Division, Linfen, China, May 1944; Moved to Yuncheng, Shansi province, China, late 1944; Engaged in the Battle of western Honan – northern Hopeh (under 12th Army), late March–late May 1945.

MIURA Saburō
Lieutenant-General; Commander of 114th Division (under 1st Army – R. SUMIDA), Shansi province, China, January 1945–end of the war, August 1945; negotiated an agreement with Chinese General Wang Ching-kuo that units under his command would not be disarmed after the surrender provided that they stayed and fought against the Communists (which many did from 1945 to 1949).

MIWA Tetsuji
Lieutenant-General; Concurrently Commander of two Home Stations for army units at Sabae and Tsuruga, both in Fukui Regimental District, Japan, March 1945.

MIYAKAWA (MIYAGAWA) Seizo (SEISHIRO)
Lieutenant-General; Commander of 3rd Division (replacing S. AOKI) under 11th Army, China, 2 August 1944; Engaged in the Battle of Kweilin–Liuchow, September–mid December 1944.

MIYAKE Kōji
Major- or Lieutenant-General; Chief of Staff to Kwantung Army, Manchuria, c.1931.

MIYAKE Sadahiro (Sadahiko)

Major-General; 20th Infantry Group Commander (in 20th Division), eastern New Guinea, April or May 1944; Group detached to form 'Miyake Force' in a counter-attack towards Malik but ordered to withdraw to Jamei after the Australians made a southern approach, 19 March 1945; 'Miyake Force' returned to 20th Division Command but Jamei lost to the Australians, 25 May 1945; Withdrew to Ulupu and then to Aoniaru.

MIYAMOTO Kiyokazu

Major-General; Chief of Staff to 22nd Division, China, January 1943; Division moved to Canton via Shanghai; Division moved south to Pingsiang, near Indo–China border, January 1945; Believed to have retained the post at this time.

MIYASHITA Fumio (Takeo)

Major-General; Commander of 11th Independent Infantry Brigade, Yingshan, Hupeh province, China, February 1944; Engaged in Battle of western Honan–northern Hopah, China, late March–late May 1945.

MIYASHITA Kenichiro

Major-General; Commander of 1st Independent Infantry Brigade, Yengchow, Shangtung province, China, January 1944.

MIYAZAKI Shigesaburō 宮崎 繁三郎

Younger brother of MIYAZAKI Shuichi; Major-General; Infantry Group Commander (basically 58th Regiment) of 31st Division (under S. KATO) from the division's activation in China, March 1943; Division transferred to Burma and arrived by September 1943; Division moved against Kohima in Assam, India, as part of 15th Army (R. MUTAGUCHI); Deviated from Ukhrul to attack a British brigade at Shangshak (ten miles south) but was repulsed, 23 March 1944; Reinforced by 60th Regiment from 15th Division (which was supposed to attack Shangshak but was delayed) 23–25 March 1944; The British abandoned Shangshak after heavy losses on both sides, 26 March 1944; March on Kohima village recommenced, 28 March 1944; Attack on Kohima commenced, 4 April 1944; Numerous attacks followed which failed; British garrison relieved, 18 April 1944; HQ Barrack Hill; Dislodged from Kohima Ridge with heavy losses, 13 May 1944; Ordered by K. SATO to withdraw, 31 May 1944; Tried to block Kohima–Imphal road but failed, June 1944; Infantry Group placed under direct command of 15th Army (R. MUTAGUCHI), 4 June 1944; Lieutenant-General and Commander of 54th Division (replacing S. KATAMURA) under 28th Army (S. SAKURAI), 30 August–early September 1944; Garrisoned the Arakan between Irrawaddy River and coast, December 1944; HQ at Taungup–Maudaing area; Division suffered heavy losses by 1945; Split into two main groups to defend Dalet Chaung area and An-Minbu road, Arakan, February 1945; Ordered to concentrate north of Yenangyaung in Irrawaddy Valley, February 1945; HQ Kolan, February–March 1945; Crossed the Irrawaddy River into Pegu Yomas at Kama, losing most of his artillery and transport with 1,400 men killed, 26–31 May 1945; Formed northern shield for 28th Army (S. SAKURAI) breakout across the Sittang River; Concentrated at Zalon, north of Prome, to try to escape from Pegu Yomas but failed; Moved out from Pegu Yomas, 16 June 1945; Split into columns (see T. KOBA); Reached assembly point for breakout near Pyu, 17 July 1945; Crossed Sittang River while in flood and under British gunfire, suffering heavy losses, 24–

25 July 1945; Reassembled in Tenasserim with only 4,000 men remaining, early August 1945; HQ at Paung, Burma, August–Japanese surrender in September 1945; Formally surrendered a sword at the divisional surrender (*see also* T. KOBA, K. NAGAZAWA, C. SEI) at Paung to the 1/10th Ghurka Rifles, 28 October 1945.

MIYAZAKI Shuichi 宮 崎

Elder brother of MIYAZAKI Shigesaburō; 2nd Lieutenant in 17th Infantry Regiment, December 1916; 1st Lieutenant, April 1920; Attached to Cadet Unit of Military Academy Preparatory School, February 1921; Captain, August 1925; Company Commander in 17th infantry Regiment, December 1927; Army General Staff HQ, February 1929; Military Instructor at War College, June 1932; Major, August 1932; Lieutenant-Colonel, August 1935; Colonel, March 1938; Staff Officer in 11th Army, China, August 1938; Commander of 26th Infantry Regiment, October 1939; Military Instructor at War College, October 1940; Major-General, October 1941; Chief of Staff to 17th Army (under H. HYAKU-TAKE), HQ Rabaul, New Britain (replacing A. FUTAMI), October 1942; Transferred with H. HYAKUTAKE to Guadalcanal, Solomons, landing October 1942; Operated from 17th Army HQ, Guadalcanal, October 1942–February 1943;* Opposed orders from C in C 8th Area Army H. IMMAMURA to evacuate Guadalcanal; Evacuated from Guadalcanal, arriving on Bougainville, Solomon Islands, February 1943; Chief of 4th Bureau (Historical) of Army General Staff HQ, Tokyo, May 1943; Deputy Commandant of War College, August 1943; Chief of Staff to 6th Area Army, China, August 1944; Lieutenant-General, October 1944; Chief of 1st Bureau (Operations) of Army General Staff HQ, Tokyo, December 1944; Attended operational liaison conference between IGHQ, Southern Army and 14th Area Army (to discuss the abandonment of Leyte Island), Manila, Philippines, December 1944; Gave details of Army General Staff initial preparations to deal with an American assault on the Japanese home islands at a secret conference, 6 February 1945; Blocked transfer of 84th Division to reinforce 32nd Army (M. USHIJIMA) on Okinawa, January 1945; Believed 'decisive' battle would be for Japan and not Okinawa; Admitted at an IGHQ conference to Premier K. KOISO that America was expected to invade Japan after Okinawa fell, 2 April 1945; Remained in the post until the end of the war.

*See also H. KONUMA.

MIYAZAKI Takeshi

Major-General; Commander of 45th Independent Mixed Brigade from its activation in Formosa, May 1944; Brigade moved to Ishigaki in the Ryuku Islands.

MIYOSHI

Lieutenant?-General; Commander of army airforce TOKUBETSU (Special) Units for *Kamikaze* attacks (under 6th Air Army – M. SUGIWARA) during the defence of Okinawa but based in Kyushu, Japan, 1945; 6th Air Army placed under the overall control of Vice-Admiral M. UGAKI for co-ordination of army and navy conventional and *Kamikaze* air attacks, March–15 August 1945.

MIZUHARA Yoshishige

Lieutenant-General; Commander of 128th Division (under 3rd Army – K. MURAKAMI), north-eastern Manchuria; Attacked by the invading Russian 5th Army but put up a strong resistance, 9 August 1945; Held up the Russian advance but suffered heavy losses, 13 August 1945; Believed to have surrendered at the cessation of hostilities, 15 August 1945.

MIZUKAMI – See MINAKAMI Genzo

MOJI Kahei
Lieutenant-General; Commander of 133rd Division from its activation, Hangchow area, Chekiang province, China, March 1945.

MONONOBE Choho
Lieutenant-General; Commander of 2nd Guards Depot Division, Tokyo, September 1944; Supplied 1st, 2nd, 3rd Guards Divisions, 27th, 28th, 31st, 32nd, 35th, 59th, 61st, 114th?, 117th Divisions and 8th, 9th, 17th, 22nd, 35th, 36th, IMBs.

MORI Suehiro (Suichiro)
Lieutenant-General; Commander of 58th Division (under 11th Army), China, July 1944; Engaged in Battle of Kweilin–Liuchow, early September–mid December 1944; Believed to be still in China at the time of the cessation of hostilities, August 1945.

MORI Takeshi (Nuzo)
2nd Lieutenant (cavalry), December 1916; Captain, August 1925; Graduated from War College, December 1927; Company Commander in 13th Cavalry Regiment, January 1928; Attached to Army General Staff, April 1929; Member of Army General Staff, December 1929; Attached to Army General Staff and dispatched to China, March 1931; Major, August 1931; Staff Officer in Kwantung Army, Manchuria, February 1932; Instructor at Cavalry School, August 1933; Instructor at War College, June 1935; Lieutenant-Colonel, August 1935; Staff Officer in 1st Army, August 1937; Colonel, March 1938; Instructor at War College, July 1938; Deputy Chief of Staff to 6th Army, Manchuria, July 1941; Major-General, August 1941; Chief of Staff to 6th Army, Manchuria, July 1942; Deputy Chief of Military Police HQ, February 1943; Chief of Staff to 19th Army (controlling the region north of Australia), January 1944; Lieutenant-General and attached to Eastern District Army, Japan, March 1945; Commander of 1st Imperial Guards Division, Tokyo, April 1945; Entrusted with the defence of the Imperial Palace under the direct command of the Emperor; Attempted (with S. TANAKA) to organize fire-fighting at the palace after American bombing, 24–25 May 1945; Was asked to join the attempted *coup d'état* by rebel army officers who wanted to continue the war and prevent the Emperor's surrender broadcast but he said he could not betray the Emperor's decision; Assassinated during the attempted *coup* and false orders were issued under his name, early hours of 15 August 1945.

MORIMOTO Yukio
Major-General; Commander of a Home Station for a headquarters and infantry unit, Nara, Japan, March 1945?

MORIMURA Tsunetaro
Major-General; Commander of 1st Field Replacement Unit, Utsunomiya, Japan, April 1944; Located in Siangton area, Hunan province, China, November 1944.

MORIOKA Susumu

Lieutenant-General; Commander of 16th Division[1] (under 14th Army – M. HONMA) for the invasion of the Philippines, November 1941; Two units under N. KIMURA (and possibly S. SAKAGUCHI) landed at Legaspi on Luzon and Davao on Mindanao respectively with the main divisional force landing at Lamon Bay, southern Luzon, 24 December 1942;[2] Delayed by the stubborn defence of the Bataan peninsula and weakened by sickness; Carried out a diversionary attack to support attack by 65th Brigade (see A. NAKA), 3 April 1942; Bataan surrendered, 8 April 1942.

[1] Regarded as a poor division.
[2] According to *Singapore and After* by Lord Strabogli (published in 1942) MORIOKA was primarily responsible for heavy bombing raids on Manila (after General MacArthur had declared it an open city and removed all anti-aircraft guns) 27 and 28 December 1941. Civilian casualties were extremely heavy.

MORITA Norimasa

Major-General; Commander of Home Station for one infantry unit, Toyama, Japan, March 1945.

MOROZUMI Gyosaku

Lieutenant-General; Commander of 30th Division, March 1944; Division in Korea until May 1944; Division transferred via Manila, Philippines, to Mindanao Island, Philippines, with HQ at Suriago (under 35th Army – S. SUZUKI), June 1944; HQ at Cagayan, September 1944; Strength reduced by the transfer of 41st and 77th Regiments for Leyte Island defence, October–November 1944; HQ Impalutao, December 1944; American invasion of Philippines forced HQ to Malaybalay, January 1945; Concurrently acting Commander of 35th Army (under 14 Area Army – T. YAMASHITA) during the absence of S. SUZUKI (who was fighting on Leyte and Cebu Islands); Bulk of 35th Army (approx 43,000 men) were based on Mindanao Island with 100th Division (under J. HARADA) and naval troops concentrated around Davao Port and south-eastern section plus 30th Division in the central mountains and the rest of the island; Americans landed unopposed at Illana Bay, Mindanao (and moved east), 17 April 1945; Kakaban, in centre of island, captured by the Americans, severing the link between 100th and 30th Divisions, 23 April 1945; American 24th Division captured Davao Port, 3 May 1945; Southern Mindanao isolated; Heavy fighting by 100th Division* in the hills and north-east of Davao slowed the American advance; Three additional landings by American troops in the north and south-west by 10 May 1945; The American 31st Division attacking from the south and 40th Division from the north met at Impalutao, 23 May 1945; Japanese forced back to northern mountains by the American advance from the east and west, mid June 1945; Probably confirmed as full Commander of 35th Army (upon the death of S. SUZUKI), 14 June 1945; Army split and forced into the jungle of the interior to fight in isolated pockets with approx 20 per cent total losses and the remainder mainly sick, starving and with very little ammunition by July 1945; Surrendered, August 1945.

*Believed to be concurrently commander of 100th Division (possibly replacing J. HARADA) by the end of the war.

MOTOGAWA Shozo

Major-General; Commander of 105th Brigade (under North China Area Army) during the Battle of Hsuchow, late December 1937.

MUGIKURA (MUKIGURA, MAGIKURA) Shunsaburo (Shunzabura)

Lieutenant-General; Commander of 52nd Division, December 1941; Division remained at home depot, Kanazawa, Japan, until November 1943; Transferred with division to Caroline Islands; Commander of 31st Army, Truk District Group, and concurrently 52nd Division Commander, January 1945; Signed the surrender of the Caroline Islands to Vice Admiral George Murray, USN, on board USS *Portland*.

MURA Takaiki

Major-General; Infantry Group Commander of 14th Division, Tsitsihar, Manchuria, June 1943.

MURAI Kenjiro

Major-General; Envoy from the Imperial Palace office of Aides-de-Camps to assist Colonel Nakagawa Kunio, Commander of Peleliu in Palau Islands; Peleliu Island invaded by American marines, 15 September 1944; Garrison destroyed; Peleliu occupied by Americans, 14 October 1944; Retreated into a cave where both committed suicide, 24 or 25 November? 1944.*

* Possibly this should be October.

MURAI Toshio

Lieutenant-General; Concurrently Commander of three Home Stations for army and air units at Chofu, Tachikawa and Tokyo, all in Tokyo Regimental District, March 1945.

MURAJI Toshio

Major-General; Commander of 2nd Field Railway Command, Peiping (Peking), China, December 1944.

MURAKAMI (MURAGAMI) Keisaku

Lieutenant-General; Commander of 30th Division (under 11th Army) during the Battle of Tsaoyang – Ichang, China, early May–late June 1940;* Commander of 39th Division, China; Formed 'Murakami Force' with 39th Division and other non-infantry units as part of five major forces in operations in central Hupeh, China, November 1940; Commander of 3rd Army (under Kwantung Army – O. YAMADA) consisting of 79th, 112th (J. NAKAMURA), 127th, 128th (Y. MIZUHARA) Divisions; Responsible for the defence of south-eastern Manchuria and defence of the Hsinking–Tumen railway; Attacked by Russian 5th Army, 9th August 1945; Believed to have surrendered at the cessation of hostilities.

* See footnote to HAGISU entry.

MURAKAMI Makoto

Major-General; Head of Military Affairs Department of the 3rd Guards Division (under Prince T. KAYA), Tokyo, May 1944.

MURAKAMI Soji

Major-General; Commander of 72nd Infantry Brigade in 65th Division (under Y. OTA) from the division's activation in June 1943; Located in Hsuchow, Kiangsu province, central China; Replaced (possibly by T. KUBOTA), September 1944?

MURAOKA Chotarō
(Full?) General; Commander-in-Chief of Kwantung Army, Manchuria, c.1927.

MURAOKA Yoshitake (Yutaka)
Lieutenant-General; Commander of 103rd Division (under 41st Army – S. YOKOYAMA) from its activation, July 1944; Located at Baguio, Luzon Island, Philippines; The division had been virtually destroyed by the time hostilities ceased, August 1945.

MURATA Takaiki
Major-General; Commander of 12th Independent Infantry Brigade, Sienning area, Hupeh province, China, February 1944.

MUROYA Chuichi
Major-General; Attached to 51st Division (possibly as Chief of Staff or Infantry Group Commander).

MUTAGUCHI Renya
Born 1888 in Saga prefecture, Japan; 2nd Lieutenant (infantry) in 13th Infantry Regiment, December 1910; 1st Lieutenant, December 1913; Graduated from War College, November 1917; Army General Staff, July 1918; Captain, April 1920; (Company Commander?) in 4th Infantry Regiment, March 1921; Major and attached to Military Affairs Bureau of War Ministry, May 1927; Resident Officer in France, December 1928; Instructor at War College, November 1929; Lieutenant-Colonel, August 1930; Section Chief of Army General Staff, January 1933; Colonel, March 1934; Commander of Peiping (Peking) Garrison Infantry Unit, China, February 1936; Regimental Commander and involved with the 'Marco Polo Bridge Incident', 7 July 1937; Major-General and assigned to Kwantung Army HQ, Manchuria, March 1938; Chief of Staff to 4th Army, July 1938; Commandant of Military Academy, April 1939; Lieutenant-General; Commander of 18th Division, China, April 1941; Part of the division (approx. 13,000 men) was transferred for the invasion of Malaya (under 25th Army – T. YAMASHITA), November 1941; Main body (HQ and two regiments) were held in reserve in Canton, China; Two units ('Takuma' Detachment and 'Koba' Regiment) took part in the initial invasion landing at Kota Bharu, 8 December 1941; Divisional main body embarked from Canton and landed at Singora, Malaya, 23 January 1942; Advanced down west side of Malaya; Broke through Gemas defence line, 15–19 January 1942; Divisional forces reunited at Kluang, 28 January 1942; Assigned right wing of attack on Singapore Island across the straits, which commenced 9 February 1942; Wounded in left shoulder after crossing the Singapore Strait; Combined with 5th Division (T. MATSUI) for a night attack on Bukit Timah heights, 10–11 February 1942; The British surrendered, 15 February 1942; Division transferred to the Philippines (under 14th Army – M. HONMA), February 1942; Division transferred to Burma, landing at Rangoon, March–April 1942; Held in reserve (under 15th Army – S. IIDA) in the Sittang Valley area and followed the advance of 55th Division; Ordered by 15th Army to halt at the Salween River, 26 April 1942; Garrisoned Shan States, Central Burma, HQ Maymyo; Ordered to co-operate with 33rd Division (S. SAKURAI) and 56th Division (Y. MATSUYAMA) to repulse the first British 'Chindit' raid, February–May 1943; Strongly favoured a Japanese advance to capture northern Assam and Imphal (Manipur State) in India after previous rejection of 'Operation 21' (see S.

IIDA); Replaced (by S. TANAKA), March 1943; Commander of 15th Army (replacing S. IIDA) under Burma Area Army (M. KAWABE); HQ Maymyo, Shan States, 15 April 1943; 15th Army consisted of 18th (S. TANAKA), 33rd (S. SAKURAI), 55th (T. KOGA), 56th (Y. MATSUYAMA) Divisions; Attended war games at Burma Area Army HQ (see M. KAWABE) to press for full support of his own plan to attack Imphal and Assam (Operation 'U-GO' or 'C') instead of advancing just to form a new defence line as was proposed; Submitted his own plan without prior approval of C in C Burma Area Army M. KAWABE; There were objections by some senior officers present but the plan was accepted, 23–27 June 1943; Tactical exercise (table-top type) held at HQ Maymyo, 12 August 1943; Final war games at Rangoon, 23 December 1943; IGHQ, Tokyo, gave authorization for the occupation of a zone around the Imphal area with Order no.1776, 7 January 1944; Operation 'U-GO' offensive commenced, 7–8 March 1944;* 33rd Division (M. YANAGIDA) moved against Imphal, 15th Division (M. YAMAUCHI) was added in January 1944 to cut off the road to Kohima and 31st Division (K. SATO) moved against Kohima; HQ moved west to Indainggy (five miles north-east of Kalemyo) because of communications difficulties, 29 April 1944; Relieved divisional commanders M. YAMAUCHI (15th Div.) and M. YANAGIDA (33rd Div.) of their commands, late May 1944; Ordered 31st Division not to withdraw from Kohima (see K. SATO), 28 May 1944; HQ at Kuntaung, 7 June 1944; Ordered 31st Division to change attack from Kohima to Imphal but divisional commander K. SATO refused, 21 June 1944; 31st Division retreated against his direct orders (consequently K. SATO was dismissed, 10 July 1944); With heavy losses and failures, he finally ordered all divisions to retreat, 9 July 1944; Transferred for failure of Operation 'U-GO' (replaced by S. KATAKURA) to General Staff HQ, Tokyo effective from 30 August 1944; Retired, December 1944; Director of Junior Course at Military Academy until the cessation of hostilities, August 1945; Died aged 76, 2 August 1966.

Personal facts: Reputation for personal bravery. Deeply believed in the samurai code of *Bushido*. Acted quickly; Respected but was generally disliked. Loved sex and sakē. Liked newspaper publicity.

* The estimated time for the capture of Imphal was three weeks.

MUTO Akira

2nd Lieutenant (infantry) in 72nd Infantry Regiment, December 1913; Member of Oita POW Internment Camp Staff, December 1914; Graduated from War College, November 1920; Assigned to Military Academy, April 1921; Assigned to Inspectorate General of Military Training, December 1922; Major, August 1928; Member of Army General Staff, November 1930; Lieutenant-Colonel, August 1932; Assigned to 1st Infantry Regiment, March 1934; Military Affairs Bureau in War Ministry, March 1935; Staff Officer in Kwantung Army, Manchuria, June 1936; Colonel, August 1936; Section Chief (Operations) at Army General Staff HQ, March 1937; Vice Chief of Staff to Shanghai Expeditionary Army (under I. MATSUI), China, 1937; Billeting commander at Nanking and involved in looting, rape and massacres, 12 December 1937–February 1938; Major-General, March 1939; Chief of Military Affairs Bureau of War Ministry and concurrently Chief Secretary of Supreme War Council, September 1939; Wanted Premier H. TOJO replaced, 1941; Lieutenant-General, October 1941; Commander of 2nd Imperial Guards Division (replacing T. NISHIMURA), Singapore, Malaya, April 1942;

The S. Hayashi Cabinet (February 1937) Standing (left to right): Industry and Commerce Minister, Godo Takuo; Navy Minister, Vice-Admiral Yonai Mitsumasa; War Minister, General Nakamura Kotaro; Home Minister, Kawarada Kakichi; Justice Minister, Shiono Suehiko. Seated (left to right): Finance Minister, Yuki Toyataro; Prime Minister (and concurrently Foreign and Education Ministers), Lieutenant-General Hayashi Senjuro; Agriculture and Forestry Minister, Yamazaki Iatsunosuki.

Left: Vice-Admiral Hasegawa Kiyoshi (p. 252). Right: General Matsui Iwane
(Iwace, Sekiakon) (p. 148).

General Okamura Yasutsugu, CinC of the China Expeditionary army, handing over surrender document to Nationalist Chinese General Ho Ying Chin at Nanking, China, 9 September 1945. General Ching has a nationalist officer's dagger in a leather frog. (IWM CBI77603) (See p. 179)

Surrender of Andaman and Nicobar Islands at Port Blair, South Andaman Island, October 1945. Japanese representatives at surrender ceremony (left to right): Staff Captain Shimazaki, IJN; Vice-Admiral Hara Kanezo (Teizo, Tisia), 12th Naval Special Base Force Commander (p. 251); Major-General SATO Tamenori, GOC of 37th Independent Mixed Brigade (p. 192); Lieutenant-Colonel Tazawa. (IWM SE5221)

Lieutenant-General Kawada Tsuchitaro, 31st Division Commander (33rd Army), surrenders his sword (*shin-guntō* with General Officer's sword knot) to Major-General W. A. Crowther, DSO, 17th Division commander at Thaton, Burma, last week of October 1945. (IWM IND4902) (See p. 129)

Saigon, Indo-China, November 1945. A party of Japanese Kempeitai lay their swords on the ground. (IWM SE5691)
Army General Officers

Adachi Hatazo (p. 79)

Anami Korechika (p. 82)

Araki Sadao (p. 84)

Ayabe Kitsuji (p. 86)

Baba Masao (p. 87) Cho Isamu (p. 88)

Dohihara (Doihara)
Kenji (p. 88)

Hamada Minoru (Someo) (p. 94)

Hata Shunroku (p. 96)

Baron Hiranuma Kiichirō (p. 100)

Honda Masaki (Seizai) (p. 101)   Honma (Homma) Masaharu (p. 103)

Hyakutake Seikichi (Haruyoshi, Harukichi) (p. 105)   Inouye Kazutsugu (p. 113)

Inoue Tadanori (p. 114)   Ishiguro Teizo (p. 114)

Isogai (Isoga, Isoya) Rensuke (Renosuke) (p. 117)   Isomura Toshi (p. 117)

Itagaki Seishirō (p. 118)

Kanda Masatane (p. 122)

Kawabe Masakazu
(Shozo) (p. 126)

Koiso Kuniaki (p. 139)

Mori Takeshi (Nuzo) (p. 156)

Mutaguchi Renya (p. 159)

Muto Akira (p. 160)

Muto (Buto) Nobuyoshi (p. 161)

Nakai Takezo (p. 165)

Nakamura Akihito (p. 166)

Nakayama Nobuyoshi (p. 168)

Prince Nashimoto Morimasa (p. 169)

Numata Takazo (p. 174)

Sakamoto Sueo (p. 186)

Sugiyama Gen (Hajime) (p. 199)   Suzuki Sōsaku (p. 201)

Tachibana (Iga)
Yoshio (p. 203)

Tanaka Giichi (p. 209)   Tanaka Kunishige (p. 210)

Tanaka Shizuichi
(Seiichi, Seiji) (p. 212)

Count Terauchi Hisaichi (Juichi) (p. 215)

Tojo Hideki (Eiki) (p. 218)

Left: Ueda Kenkichi (p. 224). Right: Minami Jiro (p. 152)

Ugaki Kazushige (p. 225)

Umezu Yoshijirō (p. 225)

Yamashita Tomoyuki (Hobun) (p. 236)

Yokoyama Shizuo (p. 241)

Eguchi Rinroku (p. 247)

Fukodome Shigeru (p. 248)

Prince Fushimi Hiroyasu (p. 250)

Hara Kenzaburo (p. 251)

Ikeda Iwasaburo (p. 255)

Inouye (Inoue) Shigeyoshi (Shigemi, Seibei) (p. 256)

Koga Mineichi (p. 262)

Kondo Nobutake (p. 264)

Kurita Takeo (p. 266)

Kusaka Jinichi (Ninichi) (p. 267)

Kususe Kumagi (p. 269)

Matsubara (p. 270)

Matsumura Junichi (p. 270)

Mikawa Gunichi (p. 270)

Nagano Osami (Shūshin) (p. 272)

Nagumo Chuichi (p. 273)

Nishimura Shoji (Teiji) (p. 275)

Oikawa (Oyokawa, Okawa) Koshirō (p. 277)

Okada Keisuke (p. 278)

Onishi (Ohnishi) Takijirō (Takujiro, Kakijiro) (p. 280)   Ozawa Jisaburō (p. 282)

Sakonju Naomasa (in the uniform of a Captain) (p. 284)

Shibasaki Keiji (Keichi) (p. 286)

Shima Kiyohide (p. 286)

Shimada Shigetarō (p. 287)   Suzuki Kantarō (p. 289)

Tanaka Raizo (p. 293)

Takarabe (Takarobe) Takeshi
(Takeishi) (p. 292)

Count Tōgō Heihachirō (p. 294)

Toyoda Soemu (p. 296)

Tsukahara Nishio (Nishizo, Fushizo) (p. 297)

Yamaguchi Tamon (p. 301)

Yamamoto Isoroku (p. 301)

Yoshida Zengo (p. 306)

Yonai Mitsumasa (p. 305)

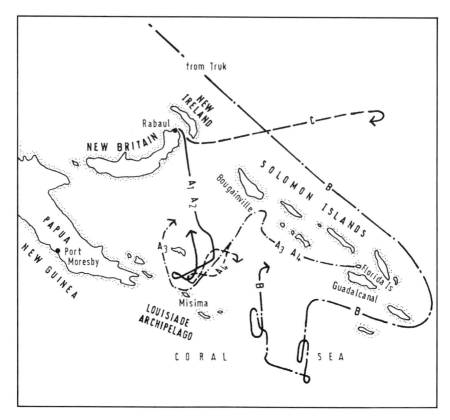

Fig. 1. *JAPANESE FLEET MOVEMENTS IN:*
OPERATION 'MO' – INVASION OF PORT MORESBY AND BATTLE OF CORAL
SEA, MAY 1942.

CinC 4th Fleet and CinC Operation 'MO' – Vice-Admiral INOUYE Shigeyoshi
(stayed in Rabaul).

A_1 – Port Moresby Invasion Force – Rear-Admiral KAJIOKA Sadamichi.
A_2 – Transport Force – Rear-Admiral ABE Koso.
A_3 – Support Group – Rear-Admiral MARUSHIGE Kuninori.
A_4 – Covering Force – Rear-Admiral GOTO Aritomo.
(withdrew 7 May 1942).

B – Carrier Strike Force – Vice-Admiral TAKAGI Takeo including Carrier Division
– Rear-Admiral HARA Chuichi.
(Battle of Coral Sea – 8 May 1942. Withdrew to Truk 11-15 May).
C – Ocean and Nauru Islands Invasion Force – Rear-Admiral SHIMA Kiyohide.
(Sailed 10 May. Recalled 15 May 1942).

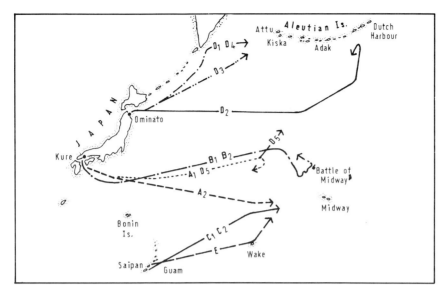

Fig. 2. *JAPANESE FLEET MOVEMENTS IN*:
OPERATIONS 'MI' AND 'AL' – INVASIONS OF MIDWAY AND ALEUTIANS MAY-JUNE 1942

CinC Combined Fleet and CinC Operations 'MI' and 'AL' – Admiral YAMAMOTO Isoroku.

OPERATION 'MI' (Invasion of Midway – Failed).
A_1 – 1st Fleet – Admiral YAMAMOTO Isoroku.
A_2 – 2nd Fleet (Invasion Force Main Body) – Vice-Admiral KONDO Nobutake.
(Sailed 29 May. Withdrew 5 June 1942).

B_1 – 1st Air Fleet (1st Carrier Striking Force) – Vice-Admiral NAGUMO Chuichi.
B_2 – Support Group – Rear-Admiral ABE Hiroaki.
(Sailed 27 May. Battle of Midway, 4-5 June 1942. Lost four carriers).

C_1 – (2nd Fleet) Close Support Group – Rear-Admiral KURITA Takeo.
C_2 – (2nd Fleet) Midway Occupation and Escort Force – Rear-Admiral TANAKA Raizo.
(Sailed 28 May. Withdrew 6 June 1942).
E – Minesweeping Group.

OPERATION 'AL' (Invasion of Aleutians – Succeeded).
D_1 – 5th Fleet Invasion Force – Vice-Admiral HOSOGAYA Boshiro.
(Sailed 28 May).
D_2 – 2nd Carrier Striking Force – Rear-Admiral KAKUTA Kakuji.
(Sailed 26 May. Withdrew 3 June 1942).
D_3 – Attu Island Occupation Force – Rear-Admiral OMORI Sentaro.
(Landed 7 June 1942).
D_4 – Kiska Island Occupation Force – Captain Ono Takeji.
(Landed 7 June 1942).
D_5 – Aleutian Support (Guard) Force – Vice-Admiral TAKASU Shiro.

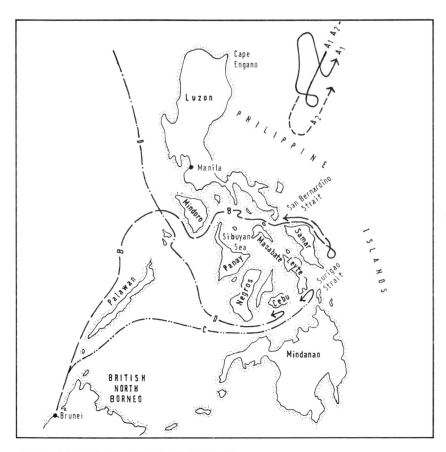

Fig. 3. *JAPANESE FLEET MOVEMENTS IN*:
OPERATION 'SHO 1' — BATTLE OF LEYTE GULF, PHILIPPINES. 23-6 OCTOBER 1944

CinC Combined Fleet — Admiral TOYODA Soemu.
A_1 — Mobile Strike (carrier) Force — Vice-Admiral OZAWA Jisaburo.
A_2 — Covering Force (battleships) — Rear?-Admiral MATSUDA.
These formed the decoy force to lure away US 3rd Fleet.
(Battle of Cape Engano — 25 October 1944).

B — 5th Fleet 1st Division — Vice-Admiral KURITA Takeo.
(Battle off Samar — 25 October 1944).

C — Southern Force (detached from B) — Vice-Admiral NISHIMURA Shoji. Sailed 22 October 1944.
(Battle of Surigao Strait — 25 October 1944).

D — 2nd Diversion Attack Force — Vice-Admiral SHIMA Kiyohide.
(Attached to C and 40 miles behind).

Southern Area Guard Force — Vice-Admiral SAKONJU Naomasa.
(Landed reinforcements on Leyte — 26 October 1944).

Transferred with the division to Sumatra, June 1944; Chief of Staff to 14th Area Army (under T. YAMASHITA), Philippines, (narrowly escaping death upon arrival when his aircraft crash-landed after an American attack), October 1944–end of war; Held in Bilibid prison for war crimes trial; Classified as a Class A war criminal charged with torture, starvation and murder of POWs and civilian internees, gross breach of the laws of war and partially responsible for the 'Rape of Nanking'; Tried by the International Tribunal for the Far East, 26 April 1946–12 November 1948; Found guilty, sentenced to death and hanged at Sugamo prison, Tokyo, 23 December 1948.

MUTO Kazuhiko
Major-General; Commander of a Home Station for one infantry unit, Oita, Japan, March 1945.

MUTO (BUTO) Nobuyoshi
General; Commander of Manchukuo (Manchuria) Defence Forces with concurrent appointment of Commander-in-Chief of Kwantung Army (replacing S. HONJO), Manchuria, September 1932; (Concurrently?) Japanese proconsul in Mukden with the title of 'Special Ambassador to Manchukuo', 1932; Field Marshal; Died, July 1933; Replaced (by T. HISHIKARI).

NAGAI
Major-General; Military Affairs Bureau, Tokyo, c.1945; Injured in an air raid and replaced, July 1945.

NAGAI Yatsuji
Colonel; Accompanied Foreign Minister Matsuoka on a visit to Germany and Russia as a military adviser, March–April 1941; Lieutenant-General; Present at the signing of the formal Japanese surrender aboard USS *Missouri*, Tokyo Bay, 2 September 1945.

NAGAMOTO Tsugio
Major-General; Commander of Central District Police, Japan, 1945; Ordered arrested by the American occupation forces as a suspected war criminal, 2 December 1945.

NAGANO Eiji
Major-General; Commander of 11th Garrison Unit, central Japan, January 1944.

NAGANO Kameichiro
Major-General; Infantry Group Commander of 4th Division* (under K. KITANO) reinforcing 14th Army during the invasion of the Philippines, March 1942; Remained in reserve during the attack on the Bataan peninsula, 3 April 1942; Surrendered to Major-General Sheppard and Chinese Lieutenant-General Chen Pao Tsang, Tsingtao, Shantung province, China, 1945.

* The Appendix to *Four Samurai* by A. Swinson (see Bibliography) gives this appointment, but in the text he is referred to as a 'Commander of a detachment of 21st Division'. The former is preferred.

NAGANO Yuichiro
Lieutenant-General; Commander of 37th Division, Shansi province, China, October 1941; Division moved to Hunan province, spring 1944; Engaged in drives

on Paoching and Kweilin; Division in Changsha and Kweilin area, January 1945; Division moved into Hanoi–Haiphong area, Indo–China, March 1945; Possibly replaced by K. SATO; Commander of 16th Army (possibly replacing K. HARADA) under 7th Area Army (S. ITAGAKI), HQ Batavia, Java, 1945; Issued formal surrender declaration, 23 August 1945; Surrendered his sword[1] (together with S. YAMAMOTO) to Major-General D. C. Hawthorn, GOC 23rd Indian Division, who had them both immediately arrested, charged that they 'wilfully and dishonour-ably neglected the duties which were assigned to you by the Allies at the time of surrender. You have failed to keep order in Java as I charged you on my arrival. You have unscrupulously handed over your arms and equipment to the disorderly elements in this country, thereby making it possible for them to inflict losses on the troops under my command', Batavia, October 1945;[2] Flown to Singapore, Malaya, for a judicial enquiry; Dismissed from command by order of Japanese Southern Army GHQ and replaced (by I. MABUCHI); *see also* S. IWABE and NAKAMURA.

[1] A photograph of this event shows a 'shin-guntō' with a General officer's sword knot and a lace-up leather hilt cover.
[2] They were held responsible for the 'treachery' of Japanese garrisons under their command that handed over their arms to nationalists who subsequently attacked and murdered Dutch civilians and British military personnel.

NAGASHIMA Tsutomi
Major-General; Commander of 54th Infantry Brigade (in 59th Division), Tsinan, Shantung province, China, April 1942.

NAGATA Tetsuzan
Born 1884; Graduated from Military Academy, October 1904; Graduated from War College, November 1911; Company Commander in 58th Infantry Regiment, August 1913; Language Officer in Germany, October 1913; Office of Military Training, August 1914; Language Officer in Denmark, June 1915; Military Attaché to Sweden, June 1921; Army General Staff, February 1923; Office of Military Training, March 1923; Military Affairs Bureau, December 1924; Section Chief of Economics Mobilization Bureau, October 1926; Colonel, March 1927; Commander of 3rd Infantry Regiment, March 1928; Section Chief at Military Affairs Bureau, August 1930; Major General and Chief of 2nd Bureau (Intelli-gence) of Army General Staff, April 1932; Commander of 1st Infantry Brigade, August 1932; Chief of Military Affairs Bureau, March 1934; Assassinated by Lieutenant-Colonel Aizawa Saburo* for allowing evidence, implicating Emperor Hirohito in the 'March Plot', to fall into the hands of army officers who supported 'Strike North' (i.e., against Russia) policy, July 1935; Postumously promoted to Lieutenant-General.

* The reason for the assassination, which was made public, was for reputably putting the army 'in the paws of high finance'.

NAGATSU Sadashige
Lieutenant-General; Commander of 58th Army (under 17th Area Army – Y. KOZUKI), Cheju Island, off south Korea, 1945; Appears to have been replaced (by TOYAMA) by the end of the war.

NAGATSU Saishige
Lieutenant-General; Commander of 13th Army, Shanghai, China, March 1944.

NAGAZAWA (NAGASAWA) Kanichi 長沢　貫一

Colonel; Commander of 121st Infantry Regiment in 54th Division (under S. MIYAZAKI), Burma, c.1944; Major-General; Infantry Group Commander of 55th Division (under T. HANAYA), Burma (replacing T. SAKURAI), December 1944; Division split up with the Infantry Group being called 'Shinbu Force' and comprising three infantry battalions to garrison the south-west area of the Irrawaddy River delta in the Arakan, Burma; 'Shinbu Force' split up into three columns (Colonel Inoue – north, Colonel Kimura – centre, HQ and Colonel Murayama – south) to cover 28th Army (under S. SAKURAI) breakout across the Sittang River, but his detailed orders were captured by the British and revealed the full plan, 2 July 1945; Moved out from Pegu Yomas, 20 July 1945; Failed to cross the swollen Sittang River until about 9–13 August 1945; Arrived at HQ near Kywegan on the Kyaukkyi and Shwegyin road where 'Kanjo Force' (112th Regiment of 55th Division under Colonel Furuya) was encamped, 19 August 1945 (i.e., four days after the cessation of hostilities); Surrendered a sword at Paung, Burma, to 1/10th Gurkha Rifles (same ceremony as 54th, 55th Divisions and 28th Army HQ – see also T. KOBA, S. MIYAZAKI, C. SEI), 28 October 1945; Retired to Tottori, western Japan, where 121st Regiment had been raised.

NAGINO (NASHINO, NASINO)

Lieutenant-General; Medical Officer to C in C Southern Army H. TERAUCHI (and probably Chief Medical Officer to Southern Army), Saigon, Indo–China, c.1945.

NAGOSHI Tokinaga

Major-General; Commander of a Home Station for infantry and engineer units, Mito, Japan, March 1945?

NAGUMO Shinichiro

Major-General; Commander of Home Station for one infantry unit, Yamagata, Japan, March 1945.

NAGURA Shiori

Major-General; Commander of 4th Armoured Division, Ssupingkaiprea, Manchuria, from its activation in September 1944.

NAKA (NARA) Akira

Educated in America; Graduated from Fort Benning Infantry School, America; Lieutenant-General; Commander of 65th Infantry Brigade on garrison duty, Formosa, 1941;* Transferred with the Brigade (6,500 men) to 14th Army (under M. HONMA) for the invasion of the Philippines; Relieved 48th Division in the front line on the Bataan peninsula, Luzon Island, 9 January 1942; From the north attacked the 2nd Philippine Corps on Mount Natib (see also T. IMAI) forcing them to retreat when 9th Infantry Regiment (from 16th Division) crossed Mount Natib; Forced an American–Filipino retreat towards Bataan but lost heavily (more than 2,000 casualties) by 26 January 1942; Advanced around the west side of Mount Samat during a major Japanese offensive on Bataan, forming the main attack force which was covered by other Japanese units, 2 April 1942; Bataan surrendered, 8 April 1942; He survived the war.

* A second-class unit which was described by him as 'absolutely unfit for combat duty'.

NAKA Eitaro

Lieutenant-General; Vice Minister of War, April 1941–March 1943; Chief of Staff to Burma Area Army (under M. KAWABE), HQ Rangoon, from March? 1943; Present at war games at Rangoon with M. KAWABE, R. MUTAGUCHI, M. INADA for the projected advance to form a defensive barrier within Burma near the border with India, and voiced opposition to the plan by R. MUTAGUCHI actually to invade India, 24–27 June 1943; Attended tactical exercise at 15th Army HQ, Maymyo (see M. KUNOMURA) but dropped all opposition to the India invasion plan, 12 August 1943; Attended senior officers' meeting at Southern Army HQ, Singapore, with M. KUNOMURA to support the plan, September 1943; Replaced (by S. TANAKA), 30 August 1944; Commander of 18th Division (under 33rd Army – M. HONDA), north Burma (replacing S. TANAKA), 30 August–early September 1944; Division was ordered to attack from north Burma (leaving a regiment at Mongmit) to reinforce Meiktila (see T. KASUYA) but arrived too late; Arrived at Kume (coming under 15th Army – S. KATAMURA), 4 March 1945; Ordered to attack Meiktila town from the north-east (in conjunction with the 49th Division – S. TAKEHARA from the north) with regiments from 33rd and 53rd Divisions; Lost more than 400 men and heavy guns in fierce fighting around the west airfield, 10–11 March 1945 (18th and 49th Divisions were placed under the direct command of M. HONDA as a separate army within 33rd Army for this campaign); The division was used as the main defence against a British push from Meiktila, late March 1945; Ordered to delay the British advance until the monsoons, April 1945; Divisional strength reported to be only 3,100 men and four mountain guns by 14 April 1945; Defended Sinthe Chaung, south of Yamethin (together with 49th Division); Formed part of 33rd Army (under M. HONDA) to delay the British advance in order to allow 28th Army to breakout across the Sittang River from Pegu Yomas, end of May 1945; Divisional strength reported to be only 2,000 by this time; Involved in defending the area east of Sittang River, July 1945; Believed to have remained in command until the cessation of hostilities, 15 August 1945.

NAKAI Masutarō

2nd Lieutenant (infantry) in 11th Infantry Regiment, December 1918; Siberian Expedition, 1919–20; Assigned to Manchuria Independent Garrison Unit, April 1924; Captain in 20th Infantry Regiment, December 1926; Graduated from War College, December 1930; Instructor at Military Academy (tactics), December 1931; Resident Officer in China (for two years) from April 1933; Major, August 1933; Staff Officer in China Garrison Army (Intelligence), May 1935; Lieutenant-Colonel, August 1936; Military Attaché in China, August 1937; Staff Officer in 2nd Division, July 1938; South China Expeditionary Army HQ, July 1939; Colonel, August 1939; Staff Officer in South China Expeditionary Army, October 1939; Staff Officer in 23rd Army, March 1940; Staff Officer in French Indo–China Expeditionary Army, November 1940; Instructor at Army Infantry School, December 1940; Chief of Staff to 20th Division, March 1941; Arrived at Wewak, New Guinea, January 1943; Directed landings by rear divisional units at Hansa Bay, March 1943; Major-General and 20th Division Infantry Group Commander, August 1943; Directed road construction in Finisterre Mountain range; 'Nakai Detachment' Commander in Kaiapit sector, September 1943; Covered the withdrawal of 51st Division from Lae and defended the Finisterre range; Attacked Kesewi, December 1943; Covered withdrawal of 20th and 51st (H. NAKANO) Divisions at Cape Gumbi, January 1944; Commander of Sepic River Crossing Unit (when main army forces moved to Wewak sector), April 1944; Commanded advance unit of 20th Division towards Aitape; Acting Commander of 20th Division (after death of J. AOKI), April 1944;* Defended But coast, August 1944; Deployed about But and Dagua airfields and inland to Maprik area, October 1944; Lost both airfields, February 1945; Lieutenant-General, March 1945; Withdrew bulk of division south of mountains and included the command of 'Miyake Force' (see S. MIYAKE), April 1945; HQ east of Wonginara Mission attacked by Australians with the loss of 28 out of 40 staff (but no generals), 2 April 1945; Surrendered with the division at the cessation of hostilities, 1945; Surrendered a sword to Lieutenant-Colonel A. C. Murchinson, Commander of 2nd Papuan New Guinea Infantry Battalion, at Wewak, 23 September 1945.

* Remained as G.O.C. 20th Division until the end of the war so this post must have been ratified as permanent, probably upon promotion to Lieutenant-General, March 1945.

NAKAI Ryotaro
Lieutenant-General; Commander of 106th Division (replacing A. MATSURA) under 11th Army during Battle of Changsha, China, early August–early October 1939 (the division was disbanded in 1940).

NAKAI Takezo
Major-General; Superintendent of Toyohashi Army Non-commissioned Officers' School, Toyohashi, Japan, 1930s.

NAKAJIMA (NAKASHIMA) Kesago (Kesao)
Lieutenant-General; Head of Secret Police in Tokyo, 1936; Commanded 16th Division (under 2nd Army) in the field, China (while the Divisional Commander Y. NAKAOKA remained at divisional HQ, Kyoto, Japan);* Engaged in operations along the northern sector of Peiping (Peking) – Hankow railway, moving from Hsiaofan Chen to Ningchin, October 1937; Engaged in Battle for Shanghai which ended on 12 November 1937; Wounded in attack on Nanking, December 1937; In charge of policing Nanking immediately after its capture and responsible for looting and massacres while under the personal protection of Prince Y. ASAKA), December 1937–February 1938 (see also I. MATSUI); Operations in northern and eastern Honan province, early February–early June 1938; Retired 1939.

Personal facts: Sadistic. Expert marksman.

*This seems unusual if most of the division were in the field. Perhaps Y. NAKAOKA was incapacitated or was Commander of the divisional Home Station.

NAKAJIMA Tetsuzo
Major-General; An aide-de-camp to Emperor Hirohito, c.1937; Vice Chief of Army General Staff, 1939; Sent to Nomonhan on the Manchurian–Mongolian border to end hostilities between Russia and Japan, September 1939.

NAKAJIMA Tokutaro
Major-General; Commander of 63rd Infantry Brigade (in 62nd Division – Y. HONGO), Shansi province, China, from its activation in June 1943; Engaged in the Honan campaign, May–June 1944; Division (under K. ARIKAWA) transferred via Shanghai to Okinawa, Ryukyu Islands, August 1944; May have fought in the Okinawa campaign (under T. FUJIOKA), 1 April–22 June 1945.

NAKAMURA

Major-General; Commander of 12th Brigade (in 5th Division – H. IMAMURA), China; Killed during a Chinese attack on Kun-lun-kuan and Tien-yin, late December 1939.

NAKAMURA

Major-General; Unidentified command under 16th Army (Y. NAGANO), Java, by 1945. Unauthorized surrender to Dutch Naval Captain P. J. G. Huyer, in violation of written British orders, at Surabaya (Soerabaja) naval base, Java, August or September 1945;* Arrested by order of Japanese Southern Army GHQ for failure to ensure Allied orders regarding the disposal of Japanese arms was properly obeyed; Sent to Singapore for trial, September 1945; Presumably removed from command; *see also* S. IWABE, Y. NAGANO, S. YAMAMOTO.

*Captain Huyer had no official authorization from SEAC to accept a surrender, only to deliver surrender terms. Only officers of Britain (and empire), America, China and Russia were empowered to receive Japanese surrenders. As a result arms, ammunition, armoured cars and tanks were taken by Indonesian nationalist supporters from the surrendering Japanese and used against British and Indian troops, from September 1945.

NAKAMURA Akihito

Lieutenant-General; Late 1930s.

NAKAMURA (NAKIMURO) Akita (Aketa, Meijin)

Major-General; Commander of Kempeitai (Military Police), China? Lieutenant-General; Commander of 5th Division; Commander of 39th Army, HQ Bangkok, Siam, 1943 or 1944; Organized defence preparations and counter-Intelligence against Allied infiltrators; Command area also included southern Tenasserim area of Burma; Ordered the defence of Tavoy and Mergui, Burma, against possible Allied seaborne invasion; Reinforced retreating Burma Area Army (under H. KIMURA) with 158th Independent Mixed Brigade without orders from Southern Army GHQ, May 1945; Attempted to make Siam self-sufficient in providing food and clothes for Japanese units stationed there; Commander-in-Chief of 18th Area Army (which was upgraded 39th Army), Bangkok, July 1945; Took overall command of 15th Army HQ (under S. KATAMURA) with 15th, 33rd, 56th Divisions from Burma Area Army which had retreated into Siam, August– September 1945; Delegate at the formal surrender of all Japanese forces in south-east Asia to Supreme Commander SEAC Lord Mountbatten, Singapore, Malaya, 12 September 1945; Formally surrendered all Japanese forces in Siam to Major-General G. C. Evans, GOC 7th Indian Division, at Bangkok, 11 January 1946.

Note: (a) Surrendered a sword to Lieutenant-Colonel Gray of 7th Indian Division, November 1945; Sold at auction in 1978; A *shin-guntō* in civilian 'Katana' scabbard. Signed blade but no details.
(b) Surrendered a sword (together with nineteen Generals and two Admirals) to Major-General G. C. Evans, GOC 7th Indian Division, at Bangkok in accordance with orders from Lord Mountbatten, 11 January 1946. This sword surrender ceremony was probably the largest by Japanese officers of, or above, the rank of Major-General.

NAKAMURA Hannosuke

Major-General; Commander of Home Station for two air units at Yokaichi in Otsu Regimental District, Japan, March 1945.

NAKAMURA Jizio

Lieutenant-General; Commander of 112th Division (under 3rd Army), Man-churia, from its activation in July 1944; Remained in command until the end of the war; Committed suicide after the announcement of the Japanese surrender, August 1945.

NAKAMURA Kotaro

General; Minister of War (replacing H. TERAUCHI) in the S. HAYASHI cabinet, 4 February–30 April 1937; Replaced (by G. SUGIYAMA).

NAKAMURA Tadahide

Major-General; 94th Infantry Group Commander (in 94th Division), Chumphan, Malaya, November 1944.

NAKANO Hidemitsu

2nd Lieutenant (infantry), December 1912; Graduated from War College, November 1920; Attached to Army General Staff, June 1921; Member of Army General Staff, August 1924; Kwantung Army HQ, Manchuria, May 1926; Battalion Commander in 63rd Regiment, August 1928; Member of Army General Staff, August 1929; Member of Military Affairs Bureau at War Ministry, December 1930; Army General Staff, August 1931; 48th Infantry Regiment, August 1933; Kwantung Army HQ, Manchuria, June 1934; China Garrison Army, August 1937; Commander of 13th (or 11th?) Infantry Regiment, March 1938; 21st Army HQ, February 1939; Major-General, March 1939; South China Area Army, February 1940; Commander of 39th Infantry Brigade, March 1940; Kwantung Army HQ, Manchuria, December 1940; Lieutenant-General, October 1941; Commander of 51st Division, Manchuria, November 1941; Division moved to Canton area, south China, December 1941; Division transferred to Rabaul, New Britain (under 2nd Area Army), December 1942, then to Lae on north-east coast of New Guinea (under 18th Army – H. ADACHI), arriving January 1943; Attempted to attack Wau but repulsed from Lababia Ridge; Considered Lae and Salamaua strongholds of vital importance; Salamaua lost to American troops, 11 September 1943; Lae taken by Americans, 16 September 1943; Engaged at Hollandia, March 1944; Suffered such heavy losses that the division virtually ceased to exist, the remnant being supplied as reinforcements to other divisions; HQ in Wewak area, 1945.

NAKOKA Yataka

Lieutenant-General; Commander of 16th Division; Stayed at divisional HQ, Kyoto, Japan, while the main body of the division fought in China (under K. NAKAJIMA).*

* This seems unusual if most of the division were in the field. Perhaps he was incapacitated or was Commander of the divisional Home Station.

NAKASHIMA Keizo

Major-General; Commander of Palembang Defence Command, Palembang, Sumatra, January 1944.

NAKASHIMA Kichisaburo

Major-General; Commander of 1st Border Garrison Unit, Tungning, Manchuria, March 1944.

NAKASHIRO Toyojiro

Lieutenant-General; Commander of 114th Division, north China, September 1944? Major-General?;* Commander of Home Stations for two infantry units, Sapporo, Japan, March 1945.

* The 'Order of Battle for the Japanese Armed Forces' for 1944 and 1945 gives his rank as Lieutenant-General in 1944 and Major-General in 1945. Possibly this is an Intelligence error unless he was demoted.

NAKASONE (NAKASONO)

General officer; Killed in an accident in China, 9 September 1943.

NAKAYAMA Makoto

Lieutenant-General; Commander of 3rd Depot Division, Nagoya, Japan, April 1944; Supplied 3rd, 26th, 38th, 65th, 100th, 104th Divisions and 40th? IMB.

NAKAYAMA Masayasu

Major-General; 24th Artillery Group Commander (in 24th Division – T. AMAMIYA), Tungan province, Manchuria, June 1942; Division transferred via Fusan, Korea, and Moji, Japan, to Okinawa, Ryukyu Islands, July 1944; He may have been transferred before the commencement of the Okinawa campaign, 1 April 1945.

NAKAYAMA Nobuyoshi

Lieutenant-General or General?, 1930s.

NAKAYAMA Sadatake

Major-General; Chief of Staff to 11th Army, Liuchow (or Linchow?), south China, February 1944.

NAKAYAMA Todomu

Major-General; Commander of 14th Independent Brigade (under 11th Army), during the third Battle of Changsha, China, late December 1941–mid January 1942.

NAKAZAWA Mitsuo

2nd Lieutenant (infantry), December 1912; Graduated from War College, December 1920; Member of Army General Staff, March 1922; Graduated from Tokyo Foreign Language School (speciality German), March 1923; Resident Officer in Germany, July 1923; Member of Army General Staff, April 1935; Major, March 1927; Instructor at War College, December 1929; Lieutenant-Colonel, July 1932; Instructor at Military Academy, August 1934; Member of Army General Staff, March 1935; Colonel and Commander of 18th Infantry Regiment, March 1936; Chief of Staff to 16th Division, August 1937; Major-General and Director of Military Preparatory Academy, March 1939; Lieutenant-General and Commander of 1st Division, October 1941; Superintendent of Military Preparatory Academy, March 1944, Commander of 40th Army, HQ Kagi, southern Formosa, January 1945; HQ transferred to Ijuin, southern Kyushu, Japan (for the defence of the Satsuma peninsula), early June 1945.

NAMBU Kijiro

Born 22 September 1869; Father was a provincial judge; Artillery officer; Captain; Assigned to small-arms section of Tokyo Artillery Arsenal, Koishikawa, 1897;

Major; In charge of research and development of an automatic pistol (Type 30 Automatic Pistol Plan); Produced the 8mm 'Nambu' pistol in 1902; Transferred the Army Small Arms Manufacturing Factory, Fukuoka prefecture, 1904; Major-General, 1918; Gained Doctor of Technics degree; Designed Type 11 light machine-gun, 1922; Lieutenant-General and Commander of Tokyo Arsenal, 1922; took early voluntary retirement aged 55, 1924; Established the Nambu Rifle Manufacturing Company, Nakano, Tokyo, February 1927; Repaired small arms for the military; Commenced production of the Type 14 pistol at Kokubunji factory, December 1933; Became sole manufacturer of all approved Japanese military handguns, 1936; Merged with two other companies to form the Chuo Kogyo Co. Ltd., becoming the largest private small-arms manufacturing firm in Japan, 1 December 1936; Remained active in the company designing the Type 99 machine-gun; Died aged 80, May 1949.

NARA Akira – *see* NAKA Akira

NARA Takeji
Born 1868; General; Chief Aide-de-camp to Emperor Hirohito, 1921–33.

Prince NASHIMOTO Morimasa 梨 本
Born 1874; Uncle of Emperor Hirohito and half-brother of Princes Y. ASAKA and N. HIGASHIKUNI; Colonel, 1910; General Officer by 1923; Field Marshal, 1932; Remained completely loyal to Emperor Hirohito during the '2–26 Insurrection', 26 February 1936; Secured the promise of co-operation from remaining dissident 'Strike North' (against Russia) officers in Kwantung Army for a planned war against China, May 1937; Appointed Chief Priest of Ise Shrines, October 1937; Ranked first in the religious field and second only to Prince K. KANIN in the army; Member of Supreme War Council (Fleet Admirals and Field Marshals which advised the Emperor); Retired from the active list aged 70 in 1944; His name was placed on the list of suspected war criminals by the occupying powers, 2 December 1945; Held in Sugamo prison, Tokyo, as a hostage by order of General MacArthur to ensure Emperor Hirohito agreed to legislative reforms; Released without charge, 13 April 1946; Died 1951.

NASHIOKA Hisao
Major-General; Commander of 55th Infantry Brigade (in 60th Division, Shanghai – Soochow–Kashing area, Kiangsu Province, China, October 1944.

NASU Yoshio
Major-General; Director of Military Service Bureau at the War Ministry at the time of the Japanese surrender, August 1945.

NASU Yumio
Major-General; Infantry Group Commander of 2nd Division (under M. MARUYAMA); Transferred with division to reinforce Guadalcanal, Solomons, landing 15 October 1942; Formed vanguard of main force (under C in C 17th Army H. HYAKUTAKE); Advanced on Henderson airfield with 2nd Division; Commanded left flank attack on Henderson airfield (under M. MARUYAMA) with 29th Regiment but lost approx. 50 per cent of his troops and was repulsed by the Americans, 23–4 October 1942; Launched second attack with 16th Regiment and remnant of 29th Regiment but was again repulsed; Mortally wounded by a rifle bullet, he died at divisional HQ, 25 October 1942.

NEMOTO Hiroshi
Colonel; In charge of Army Press relations, c.1935; Lieutenant-General; Commander of Mongolian Garrison Army (under North China Area Army – S. SHIMOMURA), HQ Kalgan; Possibly (concurrently?) Commander-in-Chief of North China Area Army (replacing S. SHIMOMURA?) before the end of the war; Surrendered Mongolian Army, North China Special Garrison Unit and 118th Division, etc., to Chinese General Sun Lein-chung of 11th War Area of Peiping (Peking), north China, September or October 1945; Also surrendered minor Japanese units to Chinese General Fu Tso-yi of 12th War Area at Kueisui, September or October 1945; Became a recruiting agent for Nationalist Chinese leader Chiang Kai-shek on Formosa (Taiwan) after the war.

NISHI Yoshikazu (Gi-ichi)
General; Inspector-General of Military Education, March 1936.

NISHIDA Yoshima
Major-General; Commander of 1st Amphibious Brigade (under 29th Division); Components of brigade transferred from Manchuria to Eniwetok Atoll, Marshal Islands, arriving 4 January 1944; Brigade split into three for the defence of three main islands being Brown, Parry and Engebi; HQ located in centre of Parry Island (1,347 men on Parry); American forces invaded, 18 February 1944; Engebi secured by Americans, 18 February; Eniwetok Island captured, 21 February, and Parry considered secure, 22 February 1944; Killed when HQ captured, 23 February 1944.

NISHIFUJI Kinsaku
Major-General; Commander of 6th Field Transport Command, August 1942; Unit located in Manchuria by October 1942.

NISHIHARA Issaku
Major-General; Commander of an observer team in Hanoi, Indo–China, 1940; Replaced (by I. CHO), 1940.

NISHIHARA Kanji
2nd Lieutenant (infantry) in 11th Infantry Regiment, December 1911; 1st Lieutenant, December 1914; Attached to depot unit of 11th Infantry Regiment, June 1919; Captain and Company Commander in 11th infantry Regiment, April 1921; Graduated from War College, November 1921; Assigned to Military Affairs Bureau of War Ministry, December 1922; Attached to 11th Infantry Regiment, December 1922; Section Member in Military Affairs Bureau of War Ministry, August 1923; Resident Officer in France, February 1926; Major, March 1927; Section Member of Military Affairs Bureau of War Ministry, September 1928; Lieutenant-Colonel attached to Army Technical Department, August 1930; Section Member of Military Affairs Bureau of War Ministry and concurrently Instructor at War College, September 1930; Staff Officer in Korea Army, May 1931; Director of Research Department of Infantry School, December 1933; Colonel, December 1934; Deputy Commandant of Narashino Army School, March 1935; Commander of 31st Infantry Regiment, August 1936; Chief of Staff to 8th Division, October 1937; Major-General and Deputy Commandant of Narashino Army School, July 1938; Commandant of last, December 1938; Lieutenant-General and Commander of 23rd Division, March 1941; Inspector-General of Chemical Warfare, November 1942; Acting Deputy Chief of Inspector-

ate General of Military Training, May 1943; Commander of 4th Army, Sunwu, Manchuria, February 1944; Attached to Western Army District HQ, Japan, March 1945; Commander of 57th Army, HQ Takarabe, southern Kyushu, Japan (in charge of defence operations in southern Kyushu), April 1945.

NISHIMURA

Major-General; Head of General Affairs Department of Military Government of Java (under 16th Army – Y. NAGANO, I. MABUCHI); Received surrender order (together with S. YAMAMOTO and Rear-Admiral M. MAEDA) from Rear-Admiral W. R. Patterson, Commander of 5th Cruiser Squadron, aboard HMS *Cumberland* at Tandjoepriok, Java, 16 September 1945.

NISHIMURA Takuma (Takamu)

Presiding judge at the court-martial of army officers involved in the assassination of Premier Inukai, 1932 (all were given light sentences); Lieutenant-General; Commander of 2nd ('Konoe') Imperial Guards Division under 15th Army (S. IIDA), Indo–China, c.1941;* Allocated to 25th Army (under T. YAMASHITA) with approx. 13,000 men for the invasion of Malaya; Invaded Siam, 8 December 1941; Entered Bangkok, 9 December 1941; Crossed the border into Malaya; Followed the advance of 5th Division; Reached Taiping, 23 December 1941; Supported 5th Division (T. MATSUI) in Perak River crossing although only one-third of the division had reached the front; Crossed Perak River and advanced down the east coast, 26 December 1941; Took Ipoh, 26 December 1941; Advanced into Johore State; Engaged in battles of Bakrit–Parit Sulong, mid January 1942; Regarded as petulant and unco-operative by C in C 25th Army T. YAMASHITA; Had a personal feud with T. YAMASHITA over an appointment of a regimental commander; Demanded the Guards Division have an equal share in the attack on Singapore Island rather than be held in reserve; Placed on left wing for the attack across the Singapore Strait; Ordered into the Kranji River swamps and to capture and cross the causeway across the strait; Captured Ubin Island, 7 February 1942; Divisional artillery bombarded Changi Fortress, 8 February 1942; Overreacted to a report (which turned out to be exaggerated) that a regiment had been destroyed by flaming oil during a causeway attack, and complained to T. YAMASHITA who censured him; Delayed attack because of the fear of flaming oil on the water, but ordered to comply, suffering heavy losses due to a rising tide which brought in flaming oil; Ordered to attack Mandai heights but deliberately delayed assembly for the final attack, 10 February 1942; Crossed the causeway to Singapore Island, 14 February 1942; British surrender, 15 February 1942; Deliberately held a separate memorial service for the dead of his division knowing that 25th Army was to hold one later; C in C Southern Army H. TERAUCHI was appraised of his unco-operative activities, etc., and refused to grant the Emperor's Victory Citation to the Imperial Guards which was a supreme disgrace; Relieved of command (replaced by A. MUTO), April 1942; *see also* IMAYE: Forcibly retired to Japan until the end of the war; Brought back to Singapore by the Allies; Tried as a war criminal (together with S. KAWAMURA) by a British Military Court for beheading 200 wounded Allied prisoners at the Maur River and the execution of several thousand Chinese civilians at Singapore 18 February–3 March 1942; Hanged or life imprisonment (accounts vary).

*This division was regarded as a ceremonial unit and, except for two regiments sent to China in 1940, had seen no action. Many senior officers thought it a mistake to use them in the Malayan campaign. However they acquitted themselves well. Often referred to as the 'Konoe' Division which means 'Imperial Guards' Division.

NISHIMURA Toshio

Major-General; Deputy Chief of Staff to 14th Area Army, Philippines, September–11 December 1944; Replaced (by H. KONUMA). *See also* UTSONOMIYA.

NISHIO Juzo (Toshizo)

Born 1881; Lieutenant during Russo–Japanese War; Captain, December 1909; Major, November 1916; Lieutenant-General, August 1920; Colonel and Instructor at War College, April 1923; Commander of 40th Infantry Regiment, March 1925; Section Chief in Office of Military Training, March 1926; Major-General and Commander of 39th Infantry Brigade, August 1929; Chief of 4th Bureau (Historical) of Army General Staff, April 1932; Lieutenant-General, August 1933; Chief of Staff to Kwantung Army, Manchuria, March 1934; Deputy Chief of Army General Staff and a 'Strike South' policy supporter, March 1936; Commander of 2nd Army (under North China Area Army) during operations along northern sector of Peiping (Peking) – Hankow railway, August–early December 1937; Operations in northern and eastern Honan province from early February to early June 1938; Commander-in-Chief of North China Area Army (replacing H. TERAUCHI) during Battle of Hsuchow, August 1937–late May 1938; General; Commander-in-Chief of China Expeditionary Army, unifying military and civil command of 11th, 13th, 21st Armies and North China Garrison Army (including 1st, 12th Armies and Japanese forces in Mongolia), 12 September 1939–March 1941; Military Councillor, 1941; Placed on reserve list, 1942; Governor of Tokyo Metropolis, 1944–Japanese surrender, September 1945.

Note: He had a sword blade made for him in 1940 by the swordsmith Moriwaki Masatake. This was awarded the 'Prime Minister's Prize'. Its whereabouts are unknown. In the same year Masataka became the head instructor at a forge for sword blade making established by the Imperial navy at the Minatogawa-jinja (a shinto shrine) near Kobe.

NISHIOEDA Yutaka

Born 1893; 2nd Lieutenant (infantry) in 4th Infantry Regiment, Sendai, Japan, 1913; 1st Lieutenant, 1919; Graduated from Army college, 1923; Captain and attached to the office of the Army Chief of Staff, 1925; Staff Officer to 3rd Infantry Division, 1927; Division served in China, Shantung province, China; Major and Staff Officer in Kwantung Army, Manchuria, 1932; took part in Jehol province operations, Inner Mongolia; Lieutenant-Colonel and member of Equipment Bureau at War Ministry, 1935; Colonel and Commander of 40th Infantry Regiment, stationed in north and central China, 1938; Chief of Staff to Imperial Guards Division, 1939; Division served at Nanning, southern China; Major-General and Commander of a Mixed Brigade on the Manchurian–Mongolian border, 1941; Chief of Staff to 25th Army (under Y. SAITO), HQ Singapore, Malaya, 1942; Concurrently Military Civil Administrator (Gunseikan) of Malaya and Sumatra; Lieutenant-General and Deputy Chief of Staff to Southern Army (under H. TERAUCHI), 1944; HQ Manila, Philippines, May 1944; HQ Saigon, Indo-China, 30 November 1944–Japanese surrender, September 1945; Acted in the dual capacity as Commanding General of the Japanese army in southern Indo–China and Malaya during the Allied reoccupation, 1945; Repatriated to Japan, 1947; Died 1958.

Note: Surrendered a sword, probably to Major-General, D. Gracey, GOC 20th Indian Division, April or early May 1946. Now in a private collection in Holland.

A *shin-guntō* with a General Officer's knot. Blade signed 'OSAFUNE (NO) JU MORIKAGE', i.e., Morikage living in Osafune. It is a nearly straight blade, c.1400, but the signature is not thought to be genuine. Unusually NISHIOEDA's name is inscribed on the pierced *tsuba* (guard), *dai-seppa*, all other *seppa*, *fuchi* and spring clip. Dragon and Ken *menuki* (hilt ornaments) are stated by him to be made by a shōwa period (post-1926) artisan.

NISHIWAKI Sokichi
Major-General; Commander of 61st Infantry Brigade (in 70th Division – T. UCHIDA), China, July 1942.

NISHIYAMA Fukutaro
2nd Lieutenant (infantry), March 1912; Graduated from War College, December 1925; Instructor at Military Academy, November 1927; Staff Officer in 2nd Division, August 1929; Lieutenant-Colonel and Instructor at Military Academy, August 1932; Attached to an Independent Garrison Unit, December 1933; Colonel and Staff Officer in 1st Depot Division, August 1936; Commander of 12th Infantry Regiment, March 1938; Major-General and Commander of 107th Infantry Brigade, March 1939; Lieutenant-General, June 1943; Commander of 23rd Division, Manchuria, January 1944; Division transferred to San Fernando and Manila, Philippines (under 14th Area Army – T. YAMASHITA), December 1944; Suffered heavy losses in limited counter-attacks against American forces in the Lingayen Gulf area, January 1945; Came under 41st Army (S. YOKOYAMA) control, March 1945; Division virtually destroyed with the remnant located north-east of Baguio by the time of the 14th Area Army surrender, 2 September 1945.

NODA Kengo
2nd Lieutenant (infantry), December 1912; Graduated from War College, November 1920; Army General Staff, September 1922; Staff Officer in Korea Army, March 1925; Major, October 1926; Battalion Commander in 14th Infantry Regiment, August 1927; Member of Army General Staff, August 1929; Lieu-tenant-Colonel, August 1931; Instructor at Infantry School, April 1932; Member of Military Affairs Bureau at War Ministry, August 1933; Official duty in Europe, December 1934; Colonel, August 1935; Commander of 33rd Infantry Regiment, August 1936; Commanding Officer of Training Unit at Infantry School, January 1938; Major-General and Chief of 2nd Bureau of Inspectorate General of Military Training, July 1938; Chief of Personnel Bureau at War Ministry, October 1939; Deputy Chief of Staff to China Expeditionary Army, April 1941; Lieutenant-General, August 1941; Commander of 14th Division, Tsitsihar, Manchuria, December 1942; Deputy Chief of Inspectorate General of Military Training, October 1943; Commander of 51st Army, HQ Mito, Japan, April 1945.

NOGUCHI Susumu
Major-General; Commander of 81st Infantry Brigade (in 105th Division – Y. TSUDA), Luzon, Philippines, from its activation in July 1944.

NOMI Toshio
Major-General; Commander of Formosan Police (see also M. TSUKAMOTO), Formosa, c.1945; Ordered arrested by American occupation forces as a suspected war criminal, 2 December 1945.

NOMIZO Kazuhiko

Major-General; Commander of 51st Infantry Brigade (in 58th Division), China, from July 1942.

NOMURA

Lieutenant-General; Military Governor of Perak, Malaya, c.1945; Surrendered (together with Major-General ODA and 4,500 men) at Bidor, Malaya, 18 September 1945.

NONAKA

Major-General; Commander of 27th Air Group, Kodama, Japan, at the time of the cessation of hostilities, August 1945.

NOZOE Masanori

Lieutenant-General; Commander of 63rd Division, HQ Peiping (Peking), north China, from its activation in June 1943; Honan campaign, May 1944; Division returned to Peiping.

NUKATA Hiroshi

Lieutenant-General; Chief? of 2nd Bureau (Intelligence) of Army General Staff HQ, Tokyo; Chief? of 4th Bureau (Historical) of last.

NUKATA (NUKADA) Tan (Mamoru)

Lieutenant-General; Chief of 3rd Bureau (Transport and Communications) of Army General Staff HQ, Tokyo; Chief of General Affairs Bureau; Chief of Personnel (Bureau?) at War Ministry.

NUMATA Ken

Major-General; Chief of Ordnance Depot of 18th Area Army (under A. NAKAMURA), Siam, by 1945; Surrendered a sword (together with A. NAKAMURA, eighteen Generals and two Admirals) to Major-General G. C. Evans, GOC 7th Indian Division, at Bangkok, 11 January 1946.

NUMATA Takazo

Lieutenant-General; Chief of Staff to 2nd Area Army (under K. ANAMI), HQ Menado, Celebes, by 1944; Visited Biak Island, off northern coast of Dutch New Guinea; Present on Biak during the American invasion, 27 May 1944; Assumed personal command of the defence from the garrison commander Colonel Kuzume Nasiyuki with 11,000 men in prepared defences; Put up a strong resistance; Received some reinforcements during June 1944; left the island before it fell, 15 July 1944;* Replaced (as Chief of Staff to 2nd Army by R. SAKUMA), December? 1944; Chief of Staff to Southern Army (under H. TERAUCHI), HQ Saigon, Indo–China, December 1944; Attended an important meeting at Meiktila, Burma, to decide the defence policy for southern Burma (*see also* S. TANAKA), 24 February 1945; At Southern Army HQ, Saigon, when the surrender broadcast was made by the Emperor, 15 August 1945; Head of a delegation (with Rear-Admiral K. CHUDO and Lieutenant-Colonel Moro Tomuria) which was ordered to Rangoon, Burma, to sign the preliminary agreement for the surrender of all Japanese forces in the Allied SEAC area with Lord Mountbatten's representatives headed by Lieutenant-General F. A. M. Browning, Joint Chief of Staff to SEAC, and representatives of America, Australia, China, France and Netherlands;

Arrived at Rangoon, 26 August 1945; Signed the agreement, 28 August 1945; Delegate at the formal surrender of all Japanese forces in south-east Asia (*see also* S. ITAGAKI) to Lord Mountbatten, Supreme Commander SEAC, at Singapore, Malaya, 12 September 1945; Arranged to protect the sick C in C Southern Army H. TERAUCHI from British harassment and accompanied him to Rengam, near Johore Bahru, Malaya, March 1946; Retained his office until June 1946, being in charge of evacuation and repatriation of Japanese troops in Southern Regions, Malaya, Siam, Indo–China and Dutch East Indies.

Note: (a) Surrendered a sword to Lieutenant-General Frederick Browning, Joint Chief of Staff to SEAC, at Singapore, September 1945; This was returned to him by Browning in September 1952.
(b) Surrendered a sword through military channels to Brigadier M. S. K. Munsell, Commander of British Inter-Service Mission to French Indo–China, 8 June 1946. An accompanying letter confirms it is 'my treasured Japanese sword, which I have cherished during all my campaigns in 1937–45'. Now in a private collection in England. A *shin-guntō* with General Officer's knot. Unsigned blade, stated by Numata to be by SUKENAGA of Bizen (middle 18th century).

* Biak fell and Colonel Kuzume committed suicide, 20 August 1944.

OBA Shihei
2nd Lieutenant (infantry), December 1910; Attached to Military Preparatory Academy, August 1924; Attached to 1st Infantry Regiment, August 1927; Lieutenant-Colonel, August 1931; Attached to Toyohashi Army Reserve Officer School, August 1933; Colonel and Commander of the Depot Unit of 7th Infantry Regiment, August 1936; Commander of Infantry Unit at Toyohashi Army Reserve Officer School, August 1938; Major-General attached to 10th Depot Division HQ, August 1939; Commander of 10th Division Infantry Group, 1940; Lieutenant-General and Commander of 16th Division, August 1942; Attached to Army General Staff, March 1944; Commander of Tokyo Bay Fortress, Japan, June 1944; Concurrently Commander of Tokyo Bay Group HQ at Tateyama, April 1945.

OBARA Kazuaki
Major-General; Commander of 3rd Independent Mixed Brigade, Yuanping area, Shansi province, China, March 1944.

OBATA Hideyoshi (Eiryo)
2nd Lieutenant (cavalry), December 1911; Graduated from War College, December 1919; Instructor at War College, April 1921; Military Student in England, April 1923; Major, March 1926; Instructor at War College, May 1926; Resident Officer in India, November 1927; Member of Military Affairs Bureau at War Ministry, August 1929; Lieutenant-Colonel in Army General Staff, August 1930; Colonel, August 1934; Commander of 14th Cavalry Regiment, December 1935; Attached to 2nd Air Group HQ, August 1937; Commandant of Akeno Air School, November 1937; Major-General and Commanding General of Akeno Air School, March 1938; Lieutenant-General and Commander of 5th Air Group, December 1940; Group attacked the Philippines from 9 December 1941; Transferred to Siam (controlling 10th Air Brigade) to support 15th Army attack on Burma; Commenced bombing raids on Rangoon, 23 December 1941; Suffered heavy losses of aircraft by late February 1942; Commander of 3rd Air Army, March 1943; Army General Staff, December 1943; Commander of 31st Army,

Central Pacific area[1] (controlling Marianas, Bonins, Marshals and Caroline Islands), HQ Saipan in Marianas, early 1944; Away on inspection tour of the Palaus when the Americans invaded Saipan, 11 June 1944; (*see also* K. IGETA, Y. SAITO, Vice-Admiral C. NAGUMO); Vowed to defend the Pacific, and in particular Saipan, or die; Unable to return to Saipan so established new HQ on Guam, in Marianas, 15 June 1944; Americans invaded Guam (which was under the tactical command of T. TAKESHI), 2 July 1944; Took over tactical command of the island's defence upon the death of T. TAKESHI (*see* that entry for campaign details) although Japanese forces had been virtually destroyed by this time, 28 July 1944; Remnant forced back to cliffs on the northern coast by 10 August 1944; Sent last message to IGHQ, Tokyo, saying the defence of Guam was hopeless, 10 August 1945; Launched a final attack and committed suicide, 11 August 1944;[2] Posthumous promotion to full General; Japanese losses estimated at 17,300 killed and 485 taken prisoner; American losses 1,989 with 7,122 wounded.

[1] In theory he was placed under overall command of Vice-Admiral C. NAGUMO but orders to this effect were vague.
[2] Accounts vary. Also said to have been killed in action with a confirmed date of September 1945 but this dating is unlikely.

OBATA Nobuyoshi (Shinryo)
Colonel; Instructor at War College, March 1939; Commander of Transport Regiment in Imperial Guards Division, May 1940; Transferred with division for invasion of French Indo–China, Malaya and Sumatra, 1941–2; Major-General, March 1943; Chief of Staff to 15th Army (under R. MUTAGUCHI), Burma (replacing H. ISAYAMA), March 1943; Sacked by R. MUTAGUCHI for opposing the plans to invade Imphal and Kohima in India (Operation 'U-GO'); Replaced (by M. KUNOMURA), April or May 1943; Chief of Harbin Special Intelligence Agency in Kwantung Army, Manchuria, May 1943; Chief of Staff to Kwantung Defence Army, Manchuria, October 1944; Chief of Staff to 44th Army, Manchuria, June 1945; Captured by, or surrendered to, the Russians after their invasion of Manchuria, 9–15 August 1945, Repatriated to Japan, 1956.

OBATA Toshihiro (Binshiro)
Born 1885; An aristocrat; Graduated 5th in class at Military Academy, 1904; Graduated 1st in class at Staff College, being recognized as a brilliant strategist, 1911; Stationed in Russia during the Revolution, 1917; Chief of Operations Section in Army General Staff, 1928; Leading 'Strike North' supporter (i.e., against Russia); Chief of Operations Bureau of Army General Staff 1932; Major-General, April 1932; Visited Kwantung Army, Manchuria, to report on the League of Nations Commission of Enquiry headed by Lord Lytton, April 1932; Posted as active Brigade Commander in a purge of 'Strike North' supporters, 1934;* Deputy Commandant of War College, 1935–6; Lieutenant-General, 7 March 1936; Retired to reserve list, 1 August 1936; Recalled to active duty, 1937; (Commander?) 14th Division, China, 1937; Minister without Portfolio in N. HIGASHIKUNI cabinet, 16 August–24 September 1945.

[1] Presumably to remove him from any position of influence.

OCHIAI Chukichi
Lieutenant-General; Commander of 77th Division, Sapporo, Japan, from its activation in April 1944.

OCHIAI Jinkuro

Lieutenant-General; Commander of 24th Division (under 11th Army), September 1944; Engaged in Hengyang–Kweilin campaign, central China, Moved south to Canton area, April 1945.

OCHIAI Matsujiro

Major-General; Commander of 13th Independent Infantry Brigade, Wuchow area, Kwangsi province, China, February 1944.

ODA

Major-General; Military Commander in Perak, Malaya, Surrendered (together with Lieutenant-General NOMURA and 4,500 men) at Bidor, Malaya, 18 September 1945.

ODA Kensuku

Major-General; Commander of 5th South Seas Detachment (replacing T. HORII) with elements of 229th Regiment, a detachment of 47th Anti-Aircraft Battalion and Yokosuka No.5 Special Naval Landing Force (under 18th Army – H. ADACHI) at Buna, New Guinea; Protected the beach-head against expected American landings; Also commanded the defence of Gona and Sanananda, early November 1942; Attacked by the Australian 7th Division (and later the American 41st Division) which captured Gona Village, 30 November 1942; Reinforced with 21st Independent Mixed Brigade (under R. YAMAGATA), early December 1942; Buna village captured by the Allies, 14 December 1942; Defended Sanananda but was surrounded; Committed suicide by the time Sanananda fell, 14 January 1943; Japanese resistance ceased by 22 January 1943.

ODA Masato

Major-General; Commander of 70th Independent Mixed Brigade, French Indo–China, August 1944.

ODAKA Kamezō

Lieutenant-General; Commander of 19th Division, Korea, 1937.

OGA Shigeru

Lieutenant-General; Commander of 34th Division (under 11th Army), China; Engaged in third Battle of Changsha, Late December 1941–mid January 1942; Commander of 72nd Division, Sendai, Japan, from its activation in April 1944.

OGASAWARA Kazuo

Lieutenant-General; In the airforce, 1938; Died, or killed, in China.

OGASHI Seikichi

Lieutenant-General; Commander of Home Station for infantry and signals unit, Saga, Japan, March 1945?

OGAWA Yasuzaburo

Major-General; Chief of Staff to 21st Division, October 1941; Division in south Shantung and north Kiangsu, China, until the end of 1941; Division transferred to Hanoi area, Indo–China; One-third of the division landed at Lingayen, Luzon Island, Philippines, February 1942, while the rest remained in Hanoi; Returned to Hanoi, early 1943; He is thought to have remained in this post during this period.

OGAWA Zensho

Major-General; Concurrently Commander of two Home Stations for infantry and air units at Hamada and Matsue, both in Matsue Regimental District area, Japan, March 1945.

OGISU Ryūhei (Rippo)

Lieutenant-General; Commander of 84th Division, Himeji, Japan, October 1944.

OHARA Reizo

Major-General; Attached to HQ of 18th Area Army (under A. NAKAMURA), Siam, by 1945; Surrendered a sword to Major-General G. C. Evans, GOC 7th Indian Division at Bangkok (together with nineteen Generals and two Admirals), 11 January 1946.

OHTANI Keijiro

Head of Secret Police in Chiba area, China, 1935; Major?-General; Commandant of Secret Police (replacing K. TASHIRO), 1936.

OIDADA Tokaku (Kakuzō)

Major-General; Commander of 83rd Infantry Brigade (in 114th Division), Linfen, Shansi province, China, October 1944.

OKABE Nosaburo

General; Commander-in-Chief of 6th Area Army (replacing Y. OKAMURA), China, November 1944; Controlled a wide area from Wuchang–Hankow to Hengyang with 11th Army (Y. KASAHARA) and 20th Army (I. SAKANISHI); Believed to be in command at the cessation of hostilities, 15 August 1945.

Note: The Commander of 6th Area Army surrendered to Chinese General Sun Wei-ju, C in C 6th War Area, at Hankow, 11 September–mid October 1945.

OKABE Toru

Major-General; Commander of 32nd Garrison Unit (Japan?), February 1944.

OKADA Kikusaburo

Major-General; Chief of Staff to 15th Division (under M. YAMAUCHI), Burma, c.1944; Division formed southern attack column on Kohima and northern column for attack on Imphal; Crossed the Chindwin River, mid March 1944;* Cut the Imphal–Kohima road at Kangpokpi, 3 April 1944; Disagreed with M. YAMAUCHI (who thought the British were retreating) and ordered an attempt at encirclement which failed; Imphal attack stopped by British tanks on Nungishigum Hill, 6–13 April 1944; Presumed to have retreated with the division.

* Appears to have dealt directly with C in C 15th Army R. MUTAGUCHI who refused to deal with GOC 15th Division M. YAMAUCHI who was accused of delaying and cowardice.

OKADA Tasuku

2nd Lieutenant (infantry), December 1911; Graduated from War College, November 1922; Member of Army General Staff, December 1924; Assistant Military Attaché to Britain, November 1927; Major, May 1927; Instructor at War College, March 1928; Attached to 3rd Division HQ, January 1929; Aide-de-camp to Prince K. KANIN, June 1930; Lieutenant-Colonel and Member of Inspectorate

General of Military Training, August 1933; Colonel and Commander of 80th Infantry Regiment, March 1935; Chief of Staff to 4th Division, March 1937; Major-General and Commander of 8th Infantry Brigade, July 1938; Superintendent of Army Tank School, October 1939; Chief of Sagami Army Arsenal, Japan, September 1940; Lieutenant-General, March 1941; Commander of 2nd Armoured Division, September 1942; Commander-in-Chief of 13th Area Army, eastern and central districts of Japan, and concurrently Commander of Tokai District Army HQ at Nagoya, Japan, February 1945.

OKADA Umekichi 岡田

Major-General; Military Commander of Hong Kong by 1945; Signed the surrender of Hong Kong (together with Vice-Admiral R. FUJITA) to Rear-Admiral Sir Cecil Harcourt, RN, at Government House, Hong Kong, 16 September 1945.*

* Surrendered a sword to Sir Cecil Harcourt at this time which is now in the National Maritime Museum. A *shin-guntō* with a blade signed 'HIZEN NO KAMI TADAYOSHI' i.e., 'Tadayoshi, lord of Hizen'. General Officer's knot. Cat no. 184.

OKAMOTO Kiyotomi (Seigo)

Major-General; In charge of army peace mission sent to neutral European countries, October 1942; Lieutenant-General; Japanese Military Adviser in Berne, Switzerland, by 1945; Stated that he would be prepared to negotiate for peace with the Americans if they offered to talk; Refused to submit any peace proposals to Tokyo unless the status of the Emperor was guaranteed in writing, early July 1945; persuaded by a Swede, Per Jacobsson, to send a 'strong recommendation' to end the war to Tokyo, mid July 1945; Committed suicide before the cessation of hostilities.

OKAMOTO Yasuyuki

Lieutenant-General; Commander of 10th Division, January 1944; Located in Manchuria, late 1944; Division transferred via Formosa to Luzon Island, Philippines (under 14th Area Army – T. YAMASHITA); Lost men and *matériel* during the sea voyage, arriving considerably understrength; Placed under 41st Army (S. YOKOYAMA) control, March 1945; Ordered to hold San Jose–Tayug defence line against American attack but disobeyed and concentrated elsewhere. Division virtually destroyed by the time of the 14th Area Army formal surrender, 2 September 1945.

OKAMURA

Major-General; Commander of the Ordnance Section of 18th Division (under R. MUTAGUCHI) during the invasion of Malaya which commenced 8 December 1941; Killed during the attack on Burkit Timah heights, Singapore Island, 10–11 February 1942.

OKAMURA Katsumi

Major-General; Commander of 70th Infantry Brigade (in 64th Division – M. FUNABIKI), China, from its activation in June 1943.

OKAMURA Yasutsugu (Yasuji, Keiji)

Born 1884; Of samurai lineage; Graduated from Military Academy with highest honours; 2nd Lieutenant (infantry), November 1904; Graduated from War College as a Captain, November 1913; Adviser to Chinese military leader Sun Chuang-fang, 1920s; Colonel and Commander of 6th Infantry Regiment, July

1927; Section Chief of Army General Staff, August 1928; Chief of Assignment Section of Personnel Bureau at War Ministry, August 1929; Major-General and attached to Army Ordnance, April 1932; Deputy Chief of Staff to Kwantung Army, Manchuria, August 1932; Signed Tangku Truce with a representative of Chinese Nationalist leader Chiang Kai-shek ceding Jehol province, Inner Mongolia, to Japan and establishing a demilitarized zone, 31 May 1933; Member of 2nd Bureau (Intelligence) of Army General Staff, December 1934; Chief of last, March 1935; Dispatched to Dairen, South Manchuria, to explain official government policy of moderation to army representatives but was rebuffed by them, 1935; Lieutenant-General, March 1936;[1] Commander of 2nd Division (in Shanghai Expeditionary Force – I. MATSUI), China; Commander of 11th Army, China, June 1938; Commanded four divisions which attacked Hankow, May–October 1938; Replaced (by K. ENBU), late 1939; Military Councillor, March 1940;[2] General, April 1941; Commander-in-Chief of North China Area Army, July 1941; Commander-in-Chief of 6th Area Army, China, August 1944; Commander-in-Chief of China Expeditionary Army (replacing S. HATA) and responsible for all army forces in China, HQ, Nanking, late November early December 1944; Declared that the Nationalist Chinese forces were barely able to survive, and that the American Air Force in China would soon be exterminated, 1 January 1945; Accepted Chiang Kai-shek's surrender terms, 20 August 1945; Formally surrendered all Japanese forces in China, north Indo–China and Formosa (together with Vice-Admiral R. FUKUDA) to Chinese General Ho Ying-chin, C in C Chinese Armed Forces, at Central Military Academy at Whampoa, Nanking, 9 September 1945; Said to have been appointed Head of 'Rehabilitation HQ of Japanese troops in the Chinese theatre' by Ho Ying-chin; Still in command of 'armed' Japanese troops in Nanking, April 1946;[3] Firm anti-Communist; Wanted by Communist leader Mao Tse-tung for war crimes; Served a brief term in Shanghai jail as a war criminal; Secretly served Chiang Kai-shek as a military adviser in the war against the Communists, 1946–9; Chiang absolved him from war crimes charges to enable him to return to Japan; Returned to Tokyo to assist in the organization of the post-war Japanese Self Defence Force.

Note: (a) Surrendered a sword to Lieutenant General A. C. Wedemeyer, C in C American Forces in China, in 1945. Blade signed 'OSAFUNE TADAMITSU', i.e., 'Tadamitsu of Osafune' and is dated 1505. Now in West Point Museum, America. Aquisition no. 2145.
(b) Surrendered a *shin-guntō* with General Officer's knot at Nanking on 9 September 1945. Now in US Naval Academy Museum, Annapolis, Cat.no.46.42.

[1] Rated by contemporary Japanese officers as one of the outstanding Lieutenant-Generals of that time.
[2] Known as an expert on China because of his distinguished service in Manchuria and China.
[3] Reference: US State Department records.

OKASAKI
Major-General; Chief of Staff to 16th Army, Java, post-1942.

OKAZAKI Seisaburo
Lieutenant-General; Commander of 2nd Division (replacing M. MARUYAMA) probably during reorganization in the Philippines), February–November 1943; Division transferred to Singapore, Malaya, November 1943, then to Burma (under 28th Army – S. SAKURAI), HQ Rangoon, January 1944. Main bulk of division arrived, late February–March 1944; Moved to Lashio; Under direct

command of Burma Area Army from May 1944; Withdrew to central Burma, HQ Thagaya, November 1944; Possibly killed; replaced by acting commander K. MANAGI on withdrawal of division to French Indo-China, January–February 1945.

OKI (OUKI) Kokura

Lieutenant-General; Commander of 110th Division (under 12th Army – T. TAKAMORI) during the Battle of western Honan–northern Hopeh, China, mid March 1945.

OKI Yoshie

Major-General; Commander of Fuel Storage Depot, central Sumatra, March 1944.

OKIDO Sanji

2nd Lieutenant (infantry), December 1913; Graduated from War College, November 1924; Army General Army Staff, December 1925; Member of Army General Staff, December 1926; Instructor at War College, November 1931; Lieutenant-Colonel and Member of Army General Staff, August 1932; Army General Staff, January 1933; Member of Military Affairs Bureau at War Ministry, August 1936; Colonel and attached to 5th division HQ, August 1936; Attached to Army General Staff, January 1937; Staff Officer in China Garrison Army, August 1937; Commander of 76th Infantry Regiment, July 1938; Major-General and Commander of 29th Infantry Brigade, March 1939; Attached to Personnel Bureau at War Ministry, August 1940; Lieutenant-General, November 1941; Commander of 22nd Division, March 1942; Chief of Staff to North China Area Army, November 1942; Commander of Military Police Forces (Kempeitai), HQ Kudan, Tokyo, October 1944–end of war, September 1945; Warned by War Minister K. ANAMI to accept orders only from the War Minister or Vice War Minister to avoid false orders from rebel officers opposed to the surrender, 13 August 1945.

OMOTA (OMOTO) Kimio

Colonel; Commander of 51st Infantry Regiment (in 15th Division), Burma, May 1941; Major-General; Commander of 25th Independent Mixed Brigade (under 25th Army), Sumatra, at the time of the cessation of hostilities, August 1945.

Note: (a) Surrendered a sword to Major P. R. M. Turner, HQ Allied Land forces Sumatra via Major-General N. YAHAGI at Pajakoemboeh, Sumatra, 27 January 1946. A *shin-guntō* with blade signed 'IWAMI NO KAMI FUJIWARA TERUYUKI', i.e., 'Fujiwara Teruyuki, lord of Iwami' (Hawley TER 117), c.1673. Stolen from Maidstone Museum, England, in 1985.
(b) Surrendered a sword to Colonel D. S. C. Rossier, Commander Sub-Area Padang, Sumatra 25 March 1946. A *shin-guntō* with a blade by KANEMOTO (Seki no Magoroku). Now in the Royal Lincolnshire Regiment Museum, England.

ONITAKE Goichi

Major-General; Commander of 7th Independent Garrison Unit, Sunwu, Manchuria, August 1943.

ONODERA Makoto

Major-General; Military Attaché to Sweden, Stockholm, 1945.

OSAKO Michisada

Lieutenant-General; Commander of 47th Division, Hirosaki Divisional District, Japan, from its activation in June 1943; Commander of Home Station for one infantry unit, Kagoshima, Japan, March 1945.

OSHIMA Hiroshi

Born 1886; Graduated from Military Academy, 1906; Graduated from War College, 1915; Major-General; Military Attaché in Berlin, Germany, March 1936; Negotiated Anti-Comitern Pact (whereby Japan and Germany would oppose Russian interference abroad), 1936; Lieutenant-General; Ambassador to Germany, 1938;[1] Pro-Nazi and worked for an alliance between Germany and Japan; Convinced there would never be a pact between Germany and Russia; Extremely embarrassed by the signing of the German–Soviet non-aggression pact and recalled to Japan to explain it, August–September 1939; Returned to Berlin as Ambassador, 1940; Negotiated Tripartite Alliance (between Germany, Italy and Japan to guarantee 10-year military and economic assistance to one another), 1940; Personally presented by Hitler with the Grand Cross of the German Eagle in gold, 14 December 1941;[2] Offered to mediate between Germany and Russia, 1942; Remained as Ambassador until the end of the European war, May 1945; Captured in southern Germany, June? 1945; American secret Naval Operational Intelligence Agency (Op-16-W under Captain Ellis Zacharias) proposed he be sent back to Tokyo by submarine as part of a clandestine peace mission, with the party to be lead by the film actor Douglas Fairbanks Jnr.;[3] This scheme was approved by American Admirals Forrestal (Secretary to the Navy) and King (Joint Chief of Staff) but vetoed by President Truman's close aides, late June 1945; Arrested as a Class A war criminal and tried by the International Tribunal for the Far East, Tokyo, 26 April 1946–12 November 1948; Found guilty and sentenced to life imprisonment; Released in 1955.

[1] Reference: *The Rising Sun* by J. Toland (*see* Bibliography).

[2] This was the prestigious First Grade of the Meritorious Order of the German Eagle and was confirmed on only eight persóns, all of whom were non-Germans.

[3] The following article from the *New York Times* (dated 26 September 1946) is printed in its entirety because of its historical interest and the fact that no mention of this clandestine activity has been found in any of the references consulted for the preparation of this book. It therefore remains unconfirmed:

AXIS PLOT TO KILL STALIN CONFIRMED By Sidney Shalett. Special to the *New York Times*. WASHINGTON, Sept. 21.

As far back as January 1939, the Japanese Ambassador to Berlin secretly informed Heinrich Himmler, Nazi Gestapo Chief, of a Japanese plot to assassinate Premier Stalin. This was revealed in a document of the 'Nazi Conspiracy and Aggression' series, released today by the United States Government.

The volume, second in the series of eight being sponsored by the Office of the United States Chief of Counsel for Prosecution of Axis Criminality, gave further historical highlights on how Japan and Germany had jointly plotted future war moves against the United States, long before the Pearl Harbor attack. The 1,107-page book consists of documents introduced as evidence at the Nuremberg trials, and also numerous documents not previously disclosed.

Himmler on Jan. 31, 1939, conferred with Gen. Hiroshi Oshima, Japanese Ambassador, concerning 'long-range' projects 'aimed at the disintegration of Russia', to become effective in case of war.

Russians Used in Plot

Oshima advised Himmler that he had 'succeeded up to now to send ten Russians with bombs across the Caucasian frontier'. Himmler's report added:

'These Russians had the mission to kill Stalin. A number of additional Russians, who he had also sent across, had been shot at the frontier'.

OSUGA (OHSUGA) Kotoo (Kotau)

Artillery officer; Graduated from Military Academy and War College; Major-General; Commander of Chichi Jima Fortress and responsible for the defence of the Bonin Islands (under 31st Army based on Saipan), March 1944; Commander of 2nd Mixed Brigade (upon the formation of 109th Division – T. KURIBAYASHI which took over the defence of the Bonins), Iwo Jima, from 30 June 1944; HQ near Motoyama village; Disagreed vehemently with T. KURIBAYASHI who ordered the beaches to remain undefended; Voiced his opinion on poor defensive planning; Relieved of command on grounds of ill health (paratyphoid) and hospitalized in an underground field hospital on Iwo Jima, December 1944; Replaced (by S. SENDA); Presumably invalided to Japan before the American invasion in February 1945.

OTA Sadamasa

Major-General; Commander of 58th Infantry Brigade (in 68th Division), Hupeh province, China, from the divisional activation in June 1942; Commander of 19th Depot Division (supplying 19th Division), Ranan, Korea, November 1944; (see also Y. OZAKI).

OTA Yoneo

Lieutenant-General; Commander of 65th Division, Hsuchow, Kiangsu province, central China, from its activation in June 1943; Engaged in Honan operations, spring 1944.

OTSUKA (OHTSUKA) Misao

Major-General; Chief of Judical Affairs Section of 7th Area Army, Singapore; Approved the report of a Japanese prosecutor that ten Allied survivors of the abortive (second) raid to sabotage Japanese shipping in Singapore harbour (Operation 'Rimau' in October 1944) should be court-martialled and sentenced to death, May 1945;* Attended the trial as an observer, 5 July 1945; hanged at Singapore after the war for war crimes (but not connected with Operation 'Rimau').

* All ten men were beheaded in a manner which showed special respect to them since they were regarded as heroic figures by the Japanese, 7 July 1945.

OYAIZU Masao

Lieutenant-General; Director of 6th Army Technical Research Institute, 1941–4.*

* 6th Army was in Manchuria during this period. Possibly this actually refers to the number of the Institute, i.e., 6th Technical Research Institute of the army.

OYOKAWA Furushio

Lieutenant-General; Commander of Army Air Force in the Philippines (4th Air Army?), c.1944; Opposed to the use of suicide tactics; Replaced (by K. TOMINAGA?).

OZAKI Yoshiharu

Lieutenant-General; Commander of 19th Division at home depot, Ranan, Korea, July 1942; Remained at Ranan until 1945 when the division was transferred via Formosa to Luzon Island, Philippines (under 14th Area Army – T. YAMASHITA); Lost men and *matériel* during the sea voyage and arrived considerably understrength; Deployed in Bontac–Sabangan area by mid February 1945; Placed under 41st Army (S. YOKOYAMA) control, March 1945; Division virtually destroyed by the time of 14th Area Army surrender, 2 September 1945; (*see also* S. OTA).

SAITO (SEITO) Masatoshi (Yaheita, Yaheta)

Lieutenant-General; Commander of 101st Division (under 11th Army – Y. OKAMURA), during the Battle of Nanchang, China, mid February – early May 1939; First Battle of Changsha, early August – early October 1939; Commander of 25th Army (under Southern Army – H. TERAUCHI), Sumatra and Malaya (replacing T. YAMASHITA), HQ Singapore, July 1942; Replaced (possibly by M. TANABE), March or April 1943; Posting in Java, 1943-4; Head of all prisoner-of-war camps in Malaya (probably replacing S. FUKUEI), 27 March 1944 – cessation of hostilities, August 1945; Formally surrendered his sword to Lord Mountbatten at Changi Jail, Singapore;* Held at Changi Jail pending trial for war crimes, 1945.

*Mountbatten, upon receiving this sword immediately handed it to his female secretary with words to the effect that she could keep it since he didn't have time for such Japanese trash. This was done as a deliberate insult to SAITO for his treatment of allied POWs. This sword was reported to be still in the hands of the female recipient in England, 1987.

SAITO Tsune

Major-General; Chief of Staff to Kwantung Army, Manchuria, c.1927.

SAITO Yoshitsugu

Cavalryman; Commander of a horse procurement unit; Lieutenant-General; Commander of 43rd Division; Transferred with the division to Saipan Island, Marianas, but lost men and equipment en route, May 1944; Responsible for the Northern Marianas District Group (under 31st Army – H. OBATA), HQ Saipan; Forced to assume command of army defence of Saipan (although not considered an experienced combat commander) since he outranked others including 31st Army Chief of Staff K. IGETA;[1] Forces consisted of 136th Infantry Regiment, 9th Tank Regiment, 47th Independent Mixed Brigade (totals vary from 22,702 to 25,469 men); Combined forces with naval troops (*see* Vice-Admiral C. NAGUMO); American naval forces launched air and sea bombardments from 11 June 1944; American 2nd and 4th Marine Divisions landed at separate beach-heads on the south-west coast, 16 June 1944; Japanese 9th Tank regiment virtually destroyed with the loss of 31 medium tanks during the night of 16 June 1944; American 27th Division landed, 17 June 1944; Americans crossed to east coast by 18 June 1944; Aslito airfield in south captured, 19 June 1944; Island split in two with southern defence restricted to Nafutu Point, 19 June 1944; Troops in Nafutu Point pocket died in a suicide (*banazi*) charge, 26 June 1944;[2] Agreed at a meeting with K. IGETA and Vice-Admiral C. NAGUMO that defence must be restricted to the northern part of the island, 26 June 1944; Japanese forces reduced to approx. 25 per cent; Ordered a last stand on a ridge near Marpi Point, northern tip of the island, but forced to retreat, 27 June 1944; Final HQ at Jingoku-dani (Valley of Hell), 2 July 1944; Wounded by shrapnel and issued orders for a final mass attack with 'each soldier to take seven enemy lives in exchange for his own', although opposed by Vice-Admiral C. Nagumo, 6 July 1944; Launched probably the largest suicide (*banzai*) attack of the war with his remaining forces of about 2,500 army and naval troops (they were all killed or captured for 451 American losses), 7 July 1944; Committed suicide in a cave by traditional *seppuku* (cutting open the stomach) and then shot in the head by his adjutant, dawn of 7 July 1944.[3]

Note: There were less than 1,000 Japanese taken prisoner (out of an original 29,000 to 31,000 army and naval troops) compared with 16,525 American dead and wounded by the time the island was declared secure.

[1] The C in C 31st Army H. OBATA was away on an inspection tour at the time of the American landings so could not take charge.

[2] 'Banzai charge' was an American expression, so called because of the cries of *Banzai* (literally 'Ten Thousand Years', i.e., May the Emperor live that long) before the attack. The correct Japanese name is '*Gyokusai*'.

[3] Chief of Staff K. IGETA, Vice-Admiral C. NAGUMO and Rear-Admiral H. YANO also committed suicide with him, according to an eye-witness account in *Oba, The Last Samurai* (*see* Bibliography).

SAKAGUCHI Shizuo

2nd Lieutenant (infantry), December 1910; Member of Army Central Ordnance Depot, April 1921; Attached to 7th Division HQ, August 1928; Adjutant in 7th Division, August 1930; Lieutenant-Colonel attached to 24th Infantry Regiment, August 1932; Commander of 9th Independent Garrison Battalion, August 1935; Colonel, August 1937; Attached to 16th Division HQ, November 1937; Major-General, August 1938; Commander of 12th Infantry Brigade, September 1939; Commander of Infantry Group of 'Kurume' (18th?) Division, August 1940; Commander of Infantry Group of 56th (or 16th) Division, November 1941; Lieutenant-General; Commander of 'Zentsuji' Division, June 1943; Commander of 65th Division, August 1944; Attached to Western District Army Command, March 1945; Transferred to first reserve list, April 1945.

SAKAI Koji

General officer; On Army General Staff, c.1944; Regarded as a liberal; Told ex-premier Prince Konoye that he wanted to negotiate for peace and have Premier H. TOJO and his cabinet replaced, June 1944.

SAKAI Takashi (Tsutomu)

Lieutenant-General; Commander of 23rd Army with 6,000 men (consisting of units of 18th, 51st, 104th Divisions and 38th Division in reserve), southern China; Ordered to capture Kong Kong in a 10-day campaign by crossing over the Chinese border; Attack commenced, 8 December 1941; Stubborn resistance slowed progress to just the capture of Kowloon by 15 December 1941; First attack on Hong Kong Island repulsed, 15 December 1941; Main attack launched by 38th Division (*see* T. ITO, T. SANO) which had been called in from reserve, 18 December 1941; Heavy losses on both sides with atrocities committed by the Japanese on civilians and POWs; British garrison surrendered, 25 December 1941; Governor-General of Kong Kong until January 1942; Replaced by R. ISOGAI.

SAKAI (SAKI) Yashushi

Lieutenant-General; Commander of 17th Division, January 1943; Division at Hsuchow, Kiangsu province, China, until August 1943; Transferred with division to Solomon Islands (under 8th Area Army – H. IMMAMURA) by October 1943; Main elements in New Britain and a small detachment on Bougainville; Fought in western New Guinea suffering heavy losses; Division transferred to Rabaul, New Britain, spring 1944.

SAKAI Tokutaro

Major-General; Concurrently Commander of two Home Stations for various army units at Nagoya and Toyohashi, both in Nagoya Regimental District, March 1945.

SAKAMOTO Sueo
Major-General; Commander of 39th Independent Mixed Brigade, New Britain, from its activation in July 1944.

SAKAMOTO Yoshitaro
Major-General; Military Affairs Department of 86th Division (under K. ISA), Kurume, Japan, July 1944.

SAKANISHI (ANZAI) Ichiro
Lieutenant-General; Commander of 20th Army, responsible for the area between Hengyang and Wuchang–Hankow, China; Engaged in Battle of western Hunan with 34th, 47th, 64th (part), 68th, 116th Divisions, early April 1945; Surrendered 20th Army and 64th Division to Chinese General Wang Yao-wu of 4th Front Army at Changsha, September 1945.

SAKUMA Ryozo
Major?-General; Chief of Staff to 2nd Area Army (under J. IIMURA), Pinrang, Celebes, December 1944.

SAKUMA Seiichi
Major-General; Infantry Group Commander of 36th Division, Shanshi province, China, October 1941; Commander of 66th Infantry Brigade (in 63rd Division – M. NOZOE), Peiping (Peking), China, October 1943.

SAKUMA (SAKUMI) Takanobu (Takayoshi)
Major-General; Commander of 24th Independent Mixed Brigade (under 33rd Army), Burma (replacing Y. HAYASHI), c.1944; Lieutenant-General; Commander of 55th Division (under 28th Army - S. SAKURAI), Burma, (replacing T. HANAYA), 1944 or 1945; Formed part of 28th Army breakout from Yomas across the Sittang River incurring heavy losses, 8-10 August 1945; Division split up by the end of the war with Rear HQ at Paung, Burma, under 28th Army and the main body at Phnom Penh, Cambodia, under 38th Army, August–September 1945; Reported with GOC 5th Air Division HATTORI to Allied Land Forces, Phnom Penh, to receive surrender orders, October 1945.

SAKURAI Shōzō (Seizō)
Millitary Attaché to France; Served on General Staff at War Ministry during the 'China Incident', 1937; Lieutenant-General; Commander of 33rd Division (under 11th Army) during the Battle of Shangkao, mid March–early April 1941; Engaged in Battle of southern Shansi (under North China Area Army), early May–June 1941; Transferred with division to Siam; Came under the control of 15th Army (S. IIDA) for the invasion of Burma; Crossed the Siam–Burma border, late January 1942; The British retreated because of ineffectual defences; Captured Rangoon (supported by 55th Division – Y. TAKEUCHI), 8 March 1942; 215th Regiment captured Shwedaung (10 miles south of Prome), 24 March 1942; Moved swiftly up the Chindwin River taking Monywa, 3 May 1942; Personally lead the attack on, and capture of, Shwegyin, 9 May 1942; Captured Kalewa (together with huge quantities of stores and munitions), 12 May 1942;[1] Garrisoned the Arakan (western coastal area of Burma) with 215th Regiment which was placed under the direct command of 15th Army; Defended against the British advance, 1942-3; Ordered to co-operate with 18th Division (R. MUTA-

GUCHI) and 56th Division (Y. MATSUYAMA) to repulse the first British 'Chindit' raid in central Burma, February–May 1943; Replaced (by M. YANAGIDA), late 1943; Commander of 28th Army from its activation in late 1943 or January 1944, to defend the Arakan area from possible seaborne invasion; Controlled 55th Division (T. HANAYA and also see T. SAKURAI) and 2nd Division; 54th Division was added, arriving January 1944; Mounted an offensive (Operation 'HA-GO' or 'Z') to invade Bengal, India, in an attempt to draw British reserves which would otherwise block the Imphal invasion (see R. MUTAGUCHI); Operation 'HA-GO' began 11 January 1944; The British mounted an offensive with 5th and 7th Divisions through the Mayu mountain range (Maungdaw retaken by the British by 9 January 1944); 55th Division attack resulted in the capture of the British 7th Division HQ near Sinzweya, 6 February 1944; Attacked the British-held position near Sinzweya (Battle of the 'Admin. Box'), 7 February 1944; The British superiority in artillery and tanks forced a Japanese withdrawal and heavy losses by 22 February 1944; 2nd Division transferred to direct Burma Area Army command, May 1944; Ordered to attack and hold the British advance from Yenangyaung to Rangoon with 54th Division (S. MIYAZAKI), 55th Division (T. HANAYA) and the collaborating Indian National Army in Operation 'KAN', October 1944; Area of command reduced to cover the lower Irrawaddy River area to border on 15th Army (S. KATAKURA) area, early? 1945; Proposed Operation 'MAI' to retreat across the Irrawaddy River, regroup in Pegu Yomas and then cross the Sittang River; Retreated across the Irrawaddy River; Attacked by the British in the Mount Popa area, April 1945; Almost surrounded in front of Yenangyaung oilfields, April 1945; Army cut off in the Pegu Yomas hills after the abandonment of Rangoon by Burma Area Army (see H. KIMURA), 26 April 1945; Planned to break-out across the Sittang Valley into Tenasserim but was delayed during the monsoons with stores and equipment exhausted; HQ Pinmezali (Mezali), June 1945; Breakout date, 20 July 1945 but the British knew of the plan and attempted to destroy the divisions as they crossed the Sittang River which was in flood; Army HQ reached the swollen Sittang and crossed by boat, 28 July 1945; All divisions suffered 50 per cent losses; Reached 53rd Division HQ at Shanywa where he heard of the Japanese surrender, 15 August 1945; Regrouped his remaining forces in Tenasserim and moved to Moulmein, 18 August 1945; Surrendered a sword to Brigadier J.D. Shapland of British Twelfth Army at Judson College, Rangoon, 24 October 1945.[2]

[1] In 127 days 33rd Division had crossed 1,500 miles, fought 34 battles, defeated the British army and captured a country.
[2] J. ICHIDA and H. KIMURA also surrendered their swords at this ceremony which was presided over by Lieutenant-General Sir Montagu Stopford, C in C Twelfth Army.

SAKURAI Tokutaro (Tohutaro, Tokuta)

Major; Intelligence Section of China Expeditionary Army (and a specialist in night combat); Major-General by August 1943; Infantry Group Commander of 55th Division (under T. HANAYA), Arakan area, Burma, August 1943; Division used to defend the Arakan but went on the offensive for Operation 'HA-GO' (or 'Z') to invade Bengal, India (see S. SAKURAI) in an attempt to draw off British reserves from reinforcing the garrisons under attack at Kohima and Imphal; Launched a surprise attack on the 7th Indian Division, Arakan, 3-4 February 1944; Captured 7th Indian Division HQ, one mile north of Sinzweya but the divisional commander escaped, also cutting off 7th Division from XV Corps, 6 February 1944; British forced to stand near Sinzweya (Battle of the 'Admin. Box');

Launched attack, 7 February 1944; Repulsed by British superiority in artillery and tanks which caused heavy losses; Lacked supplies; Withdrawal ordered; Ngak-yedauk Pass recaptured by the British by 23 February 1944; Formed 'Sakura Force' to screen the transfer of 2nd Division out of, and the 55th Division into, the Mayu and Kaladan Valleys, July–September 1944; Replaced (by K. NAGA-ZAWA), December 1944?

Personal facts: Eccentric. Unscrupulous, using rough and ready means to gather Intelligence. Boisterous. Liked personally to lead his men into action.

SANADA Joichiro
2nd Lieutenant (infantry) in 9th Infantry Regiment, December 1919; 1st Lieutenant, December 1922; Captain and Company Commander in 9th Infantry Regiment, August 1928; Staff Officer in Tokyo Garrison Command, August 1929; Adjutant in War Ministry, May 1931; Member of Army Affairs Section at War Ministry, August 1932; Major, August 1934; Official duty in Europe and America, September 1936–September 1937; Assigned to Army Aeronautical Department, March 1937; Member of War Ministry Section (Maintenance), September 1937; Lieutenant-Colonel, November 1937; Secretary to War Minister and concurrently Adjutant in War Ministry, August 1938; Colonel and Commander of 86th Infantry Regiment, August 1939; Staff Officer in China Expeditionary Army and concurrently Staff Officer to China Area Fleet, August 1940; Chief of Army Affairs Section of Military Affairs Bureau at War Ministry, February 1941; Aide to War Minister in IGHQ, Tokyo, November 1941; Chief of Military Affairs Section of Military Affairs Bureau of War Ministry, Tokyo, April 1942; Chief of Second Department at Army General Staff HQ and Staff Officer in IGHQ (Navy Section), December 1942; Major-General, August 1943; Chief of 1st Bureau (Operations) at Army General Staff HQ, October 1943; Chief of Military Affairs Bureau at War Ministry, December 1944; Central District Army HQ, Japan, March 1945; Deputy Chief of Staff to 2nd General Army, GHQ Hiroshima, Japan, April 1945.

SANNOMIYA Mitsuji
Major-General; Commander of Hoyo Fortress, Seganoseki, Oita prefecture, Kyushu, Japan, August 1943.

SANO Tadayoshi
Lieutenant-General; Commander of 38th Division (under 23rd Army – T. SAKAI); Infantry Group (under T. ITO) consisting of 228th, 229th, 230th Regiments was held in reserve for the attack on Hong Kong while other units of 23rd Army commenced attack on Kowloon, 8 December 1941; Formed main attack force against Hong Kong Island which was launched 18 December 1941; Heavy losses on both sides with atrocities committed by the Japanese on civilians and POWs; British garrison surrendered, 25 December 1941; Transferred with division to Rabaul, New Britain, and then used as reinforcements to Guadalcanal (under 17th Army – H. HYAKUTAKE); Convoy attacked with only 4 out of 11 transports surviving to land at Tassafaronga and the divisional strength reduced to only 2,000 men, 15 November 1942; Fought through Guadalcanal campaign against American forces; Informed of plan to evacuate Guadalcanal, 17 January 1943; Evacuated by destroyers to Rabaul, New Britain, with 2,316 men on the night of 1/2 February 1943; Commander of 34th Army, Hankow, central China, July 1944; Army HQ (including 39th, 59th, 63rd, 117th Divisions) were

transferred to Manchuria and North Korea, under Kwantung Army, May 1945; Replaced (by S. KUSHIBUCHI), 1945.

SANO Torata
Lieutenant-General; Commander of 42nd Division, Kurile Islands, March 1944.

SASA (SASSA)
Major-General; Commander of Prisoner of War Camps in Siam, HQ Bampong, 1943; HQ Tarasu, May 1943.

SASA (SASAKI) Shinnosuke
Lieutenant-General; Commander of 39th Division, Tanyang area, northern Hupei province, central China, November 1944; Engaged in the Battle of western Honan–northern Hopeh, March–May 1945.

SASAKI
Lieutenant-General; Commander of 14th Division, HQ Himeji, Japan, c.1940; Refused to assist Captain Hirose* in blowing up the British and American consulates at Kobe, Japan, January 1940.

*Hirose represented Major Ito of the Nakano School for espionage and saboteurs.

SASAKI Isamu
Major-General; Concurrently Commander of two Home Stations for a mortar unit at Numata and an infantry unit at Takasaki, both in Maebashi Regimental District, Japan, March 1945.

SASAKI Minoru (Noboru)
Born 1883; 2nd Lieutenant (cavalry) in 5th Cavalry Regiment, December 1914; 1st Lieutenant, July 1918; Depot Unit of 5th Cavalry Regiment, August 1919; Adjutant of 5th Cavalry Regiment, October 1920; Attached to 5th Cavalry Regiment, January 1921; Captain, August 1923; Company Commander in 5th Cavalry Regiment, December 1923; Military Affairs Bureau at War Ministry, May 1925; Section Member of same Bureau, August 1925; Member of Army Remount Department, October 1926; Military Student in Russia, September 1927; Military Student in Poland and Russia, August 1928; Major, August 1929; Military Affairs Bureau at War Ministry, June 1930; Section Member of Military Affairs Bureau, August 1930; Army Ordnance Main Depot, November 1931; Instructor at War College, December 1932; Lieutenant-Colonel and Director of Research Section of Administration Department (Cavalry), March 1937; Colonel, August 1937; Major-General at Army Ordnance Main Depot, August 1939; Commander of 4th Cavalry Brigade, October 1939; Chief of Staff to 6th Army, China, December 1940; Mechanized Department, August 1942; Commander of 'Nanto' (Southeast) Detachment under 8th Area Army (H. IMAMURA) with 10,000 army and naval troops defending New Georgia, Solomons, 1943; HQ at Munda, north-west New Georgia; Abandoned defence of eastern New Georgia to reinforce the defence of Munda, June 1943; American troops landed at Rendova Island, 30 June 1943, and at Zanana, east of Munda, 2 July 1943; Defended Munda and reinforced with 2,500 troops, 9-10 July 1943; Counter-attacked the American forces but was driven back, 17 July 1943; Lost Munda airfield, 5 August 1943; Formed new defence line from Bairoko Harbour to Sunday Inlet; Bairoko Harbour captured by the Americans; Moved HQ to Kolombangara Island leaving subordinates to defend west New Georgia and the islands of Arundel and Wana

Wana, 8-9 August 1943; New Georgia taken by the Americans, 23 August 1943; Japanese withdrew from Arundel Island, 20-1 September 1943; Kolombangara Island isolated; Withdrew most units to Choiseul Island by 6 October 1943; Choiseul invaded by the Americans who were then withdrawn in favour of isolating and island-hopping; Withdrew to 8th Area Army HQ, Rabaul, New Britain, November 1943; Lieutenant-General, October 1944; He survived the war.

SATAKE Katsuji
Major-General; Commander of 5th Tank Brigade, March 1944.

SATO Bunzo
Major-General; Commander of 58th Independent Mixed Brigade, Lingayen Gulf, Luzon Island, Philippines, December 1944.

SATO Gonpachi
Major-General; Commander of 29th Independent Mixed Brigade (under 18th Area Army – A. NAKAMURA), Siam, by 1945; Surrendered a sword (together with A. NAKAMURA, eighteen Generals and two Admirals) to Major-General G. C. Evans, GOC 7th Indian Division, at Bangkok, Siam, 11 January 1946.

SATO Kennyato (Ken, Kennosuke)
Claimed to be the Managing Editor of the Mainichi Shimbu newspaper, spending 18 months in Australia in an official and semi-official capacity as a journalist, 1935-6;[1] Acted through the Japanese consuls in Melbourne and Sydney to found a 'fifth column' and located pro-Japanese Australians; Claimed to have the names of some leading Australians who would collaborate in the event of a successful Japanese invasion of Australia; Stated that in such an event he would have been the Chief Civil Administrator of Australia;[2] Claimed to have received the honorary rank of Lieutenant-General in the Japanese army during the invasion of north China and Shanghai, 1937; Spoke excellent English; Chief interrogator of captured western foreigners at the fall of Nanking and Hankow, China; Later transferred to a 'Special Detachment of the Navy' to train administrators for the projected invasion of Australia; Claimed the Japanese actually launched invasion forces for Australia (to land midway between Townsville and Brisbane) but were stopped at Rabaul, New Britain, and the Solomon Islands because of a prolonged delay in the capture of Bataan, Philippines, by the army;[3] Further delay and final abandonment of the plan was caused by the Australian resistance in New Guinea, naval Battle of the Coral Sea and the American landings on Guadalcanal; Head of interrogation of Allied POWs at Ofuna Internment Camp near Tokyo, 1942? – 1945; Used brainwashing and torture; Apparently not charged with war crimes after the surrender; At a post-war interview with the Commonwealth Investigation Service he strongly refuted claims made by the Japanese government and military leaders that Australia was never to have been invaded.

Note: This entry was compiled from an article in the *Australasian Post* of 12 December 1985 and from the book *Coffin Boats* by Peggy Warner and Sadao Seno, published by Leo Cooper, 1986.

[1] This newspaper claimed he was only a temporary contributor and held no post.
[2] Possibly a high-ranking *Gunzoku*, i.e., civilian adviser to the army which had its own uniform and ranking system.
[3] It appears that no official Japanese documents confirming an invasion plan for Australia have been located.

SATO Kenryo

Born 1885; Graduated from Military Academy, 1917; Graduated from War College, 1925; Head of War Ministry policy-making team which prepared a 'joint' army and navy statement presented to Premier Hirota demanding electoral and legislative reforms in favour of the armed forces, September 1937; Colonel and Chief of Staff to South China Army; Adviser to War Minister H. TOJO, c.1941; Often served as the official spokesman for army policy; Advised H. TOJO that a 'Strike North' policy against Russia would gain nothing, but a 'Strike South' policy against the East Indies would gain material resources; Major-General; Chief of Military Affairs Bureau by October 1941; Advised Premier H. TOJO that war with America (before diplomatic attempts were abandoned) was folly, 23 October 1941; Opposed the continued reinforcement of Guadalcanal after heavy losses, October – November 1942; Suggested to Premier H. TOJO that the Philippines should be the main battleground at the expense of the Carolines and Marianas but this idea was rejected, February 1944; Advised H. TOJO to request the resignation of his (Tojo's) protégé Admiral S. SHIMADA (Navy Minister and Chief of Naval General Staff) to appease political opponents, 16 July 1944; Tried to persuade Vice-Admiral M. YONAI to replace S. SHIMADA to keep the support of the navy, but failed, and therefore had no alternative but to advise Premier H. TOJO to resign, 17 July 1944; Opposed the navy's plan to launch Operation ' SHO-1' (last-ditch surface attack on American naval forces in Leyte Gulf, Philippines), October 1944; Resigned, or was replaced, 1944; Lieutenant-General and Commander of 37th Division (under 18th Area Army – A. NAKAMURA), Siam, by 1945; HQ Nakon Nayok by the cessation of hostilities, 15 August 1945; Surrendered a sword (together with A. NAKAMURA, eighteen Generals and two Admirals) to Major-General G. C. Evans, GOC 7th Indian Division, at Bangkok, 11 January 1946;* Arrested as a Class A war criminal; Tried by the International Tribunal for the Far East, Tokyo, 26 April 1946 – 12 November 1948; Found guilty and sentenced to life imprisonment; Released in 1956.

*This sword was subsequently presented by Major-General Evans to Lieutenant-Colonel W. C. Walker, HQ Allied Land Forces, Siam (7th Indian Division) together with a presentation certificate which gave the opinion of a Japanese sword judge (Kanteisha) on the blade, Bangkok, 21 January 1946. The blade is unsigned but was attributed to BIZEN OSAFUNE YUKIMITSU (i.e., Yukimitsu of Osafune in Bizen), c.1296. Some of his works are considered National Treasures. The certificate actually states 'Nagafune' which is a misreading of 'Osafune'. The current whereabouts is not recorded.

SATŌ Kōtoku

Lieutenant-General; Commander of 31st Division, China, from its activation in March 1943; Transferred with division to Burma but was delayed in Siam for road building; Arrived in Burma (under 15th Army – R. MUTAGUCHI) by September 1943; HQ Moaugaing, central Burma; Engaged in Operation 'U-GO' (attack on Kohima and Imphal, India); Crossed the Chindwin River as part of a pincer movement against Kohima village, Assam, India (with 15th Division – M. YAMAUCHI); Advanced towards Kohima to form the northern attack force, 15 March 1944; Attack on Kohima commenced, 4 April 1944 (see also S. MIYAZAKI); Attacks failed; British garrison relieved, 18 April 1944; Division suffered heavy losses, lack of ammunition and lack of supplies; Ordered by R. MUTAGUCHI to hold position for ten days, 28 May 1944; Disobeyed and ordered a withdrawal of left and right units to Chadema (two miles east of Kohima), 31 March 1944; Ordered by 15th Army (R. MUTAGUCHI) to change the direction of attack from Kohima to Imphal but refused unless he first received food and supplies, 21 June 1944; Ordered to send units to reinforce 33rd Division Infantry

Group (under T. YAMAMOTO), 7 July 1944; Dismissed from divisional command by R. MUTAGUCHI and replaced (by T. KAWADA), 7 July 1944; Ordered to Burma Area Army HQ, Rangoon, arriving 22 July 1944; Wanted himself court-martialled to expose 15th Army and R. MUTAGUCHI's inability to command;* C in C Burma Area Army M. KAWABE refused the court-martial to avoid embarrassment, so he was judged mentally disturbed because of war stress; Placed on active waiting list, 23 November 1944; Transferred to reserve list and never re-employed.

*R. MUTAGUCHI also wanted him court-martialled for the unheard of act of retreating on his own initiative and in direct contravention of an Army order.

SATO Shunji

Born 1896 in Toyohashi, Aichi prefecture, Japan, Graduated from the Medical Institute, 1923; Joined the army in 1923; Physician and Pathologist; Colonel; Commander of bacteriological warfare centres in central and southern China code-named 'Nami 8604' at Canton, December 1940 – February 1943, and 'Ei 1644' (also known as 'Tama Detachment') at Nanking, February 1943 – March 1944;* Also co-operated with 'Detachments 100 and 731' (see also S. ISHII, Y. WAKAMATSU); Took active part in research and production of bacteriological weapons; Chief of Medical Service of 5th Army (under Kwantung Army), including the supervision of 'Branch 643' and 'Detachment 731'; Issued order to 5th Army units to capture rats for supply to 'Detachment 731' (see S. ISHII) for bacteriological warfare use, May 1945; Final rank Major-General; Captured by the Russians, August 1945; Tried by Russian Miliary Tribunal at Khabarovsk for crimes relating to bacteriological warfare, December 1949; Sentenced to 20 years in a labour correction camp.

*Both centres were formed in 1939 and both were under the control of China Expeditionary Army.

SATO Tadasu

Major-General; Commander of 4th Railway Command, February 1944; Unit at Hankow, China, July 1944.

SATO Tamenori

Major-General; Commander of 37th Independent Mixed Brigade, Andaman and Nicobar Islands, from its activation in February 1944; Remained in command until the end of the war; Surrendered a sword (together with Vice-Admiral T. HARA) to Brigadier J. A. Salamons at Port Blair, South Andaman Island, 9 October 1945.

SAWADA Shigeru

Lieutenant-General; Commander of 13th Army (under China Expeditionary Army – S. HATA), eastern Chekiang, China; Engaged in Battle of Chekiang–Kiangsi, mid May–September 1942; Tried by an American Military Commission for involvement in the execution of three American 'Doolittle Raid' airmen at Shanghai in 1942; Sentence to 5 years' imprisonment, Shanghai, 15 April 1946.

SAWADA Yasutomi

Major-General; Commander of Shipping Force, April 1944; Hiroshima, Japan, May 1944.

SAWAKI Genyu
Major-General; Commander of Home Station for one infantry unit at Tokushima, Japan, March 1945?

SAWAMOTO Rikichi (Rikichiro)
Major-General; Chief Military Adviser to collaborating Burma National Army; Chief of Staff to 33rd Army (under M. HONDA), Burma (replacing S. YAMAMOTO), January? 1945; Visited Burma Area Army (H. KIMURA) HQ at Moulmein when 33rd Army was ordered to retake Rangoon but managed to persuade them that it was impossible because of severe losses already suffered and a lack of armour, late May 1945; Returned to HQ with 20 lorry loads of clothing and weapons; Remained in post until the end of the war and possibly a Lieutenant-General by that time; Present at 53rd Division HQ, Shanywa during the official announcement of the Japanese surrender, 15 August 1945; Surrendered (together with M. HONDA) to Lieutenant-Colonel B. Montgomery, CO, 6th Battalion of the Rajput Regiment, near Thaton, Burma, October 1945; Held at Thaton; Moved to Ahlone camp, Rangoon, 1946; Moved to Kokine camp, 1947; Returned to Japan with last Japanese soldiers detained in Burma, 3 August 1947.

SEGAWA Akitomo
Intelligence Officer in Switzerland, 1919; Aide-de-camp to Imperial Palace, Tokyo, 1920s; Lieutenant-General; Principal of Military Academy; Personal envoy of Emperor Hirohito attached to the Japanese Embassy in Manchuria, May 1932; Critically ill, April 1934.

SEI C. 清
Major-General; Commander of 14th Transport Service HQ (under 28th Army – S. SAKURAI), Burma; Responsible for bringing rations into Pegu Yomas area, April–May 1945; Surrendered a sword at 54th Division and 28th Army HQ formal surrender (*see also* T. KOBA, S. MIYAZAKI, K. NAGAZAWA) to 1/10th Gurkha Rifles at Paung, Burma, 28 October 1945.

SEKI Genroku
Lieutenant-General; Commander of 44th Division, Osaka, Japan, April 1944.

SEKIYA Kiyoshi
Major-General; Commander of Home Station for air and infantry units at Matsuyama, Japan, March 1945.

SENDA Sadasue
Graduated from Military Academy; Major-General; Commandant of Sendai Reserve Academy, Japan, until late 1944; Commander of 2nd Mixed Brigade (under 109th Division – T. KURIBAYASHI), Iwo Jima, Bonin Islands (replacing K. OSUGA), December 1944; HQ near Motoyama Village; Americans landed, 19 February 1945 (*see* T. KURIBAYASHI for campaign details); Suffered heavy losses; HQ in a cave by late February 1945; Requested T. KURABAYASHI for permission to launch a suicide attack in direction of Mount Suribachi but was refused; Disobeyed and launched a small suicide charge in which he killed, 9 March 1945; The Brigade had been wiped out by 16 March 1945.

SEYA
General Officer; Involved in Battle of Taierchuang (possibly in 10th Division), Honan province, China, March–May 1938.

SHIBA Nobutaka

Major-General; Infantry Group Commander of 42nd Division, August 1943; In Japan and then transferred to the Kuriles, early 1944; Commander of 43rd Independent Mixed Brigade, Kurile Islands, from its activation in April 1944.

SHIBASHI Tadaji

Major-General; Commander of 7th Field transport command, August 1942; Unit in Manchuria by February 1943.

SHIBATA Ryūichi (Sotoichi, Uichi)

Lieutenant-General; Commander of 15th Division (under 15th Army – R. MUTAGUCHI), Burma (replacing M. YAMAUCHI) effectively from 10 June 1944; Depleted division engaged in the Imphal campaign at the time of taking command; British 20th and 23rd Divisions drove a wedge between the Japanese 51st and 67th Regiments near Modburg and commenced to annihilate the division piecemeal, early June 1944;* General retreat with heavy losses; Reinforced but still under strength, October? 1944; Division ordered to prevent a British thrust to Mandalay with the additon of 119th Regiment from 53rd Division, January 1945; Replaced (by S. YAMAMOTO) December 1944 or January 1945.

*According to Burma – The Longest War by Louis Allen (see Bibliography) the rare Japanese use of a poison gas grenade against a tank occurred.

SHIBATA Teidan

Major-General; Commander of Clark Field airforce base (under 4th Air Army – K. TOMONAGA), Luzon Island, Philippines, by November 1944.

SHIBAYAMA (SHITAYAMA) Kaneshiro

Lieutenant-General; Vice Minister of War, August 1944 – July 1945; Concurrently Chief of Logistics at IGHQ, Tokyo, May–July 1945; Remained as Chief of the latter from July 1945; Admitted to the Diet (Parliament) that shortages would mean the war could not continue after the spring of 1946.

SHICHIDA Ichiro

2nd Lieutenant (infantry), December 1908; Graduated from War College, November 1919; Member of Army General Staff, December 1920; Major and Battalion Commander in 1st Infantry Regiment, March 1924; Lieutenant-Colonel and Instructor at Infantry School, August 1928; Resident Officer in France, May 1931; Colonel, August 1932; Section Chief of Inspectorate General of Military Training, August 1933; Major-General and Commander of 24th Infantry Brigade, March 1937; Director of Military Academy, November 1937; Lieutenant-General, August 1939; Commander of 20th Division, September 1939; Superintendent of Military Preparatory Academy, April 1941; Commander of Mongolia Garrison Army, March 1942; Commander of 2nd Army, May 1943; Superintendent of Army School of Science, March 1944; Superintendent of Toyama Army School, October 1944; Retired, April 1945; Recalled to active duty as Commander of 56th Army, HQ Iizuka, Japan, April 1945.

SHIDEI Tsunamasa

Lieutenant-General; Chief of Staff to Burma Area Army (under H. KIMURA), replacing S. TANAKA, May? 1945; Killed with Subhas Chandra Bose (Head of the collaborating Indian National Army) in an aircraft crash at Taihoku (Taipei), Formosa, 18 August 1945.

SHIGEMATSU Yoshimasa

Major-General; Commander of 75th Infantry Brigade? (in 65th Division – Y. OTA), central China, from the divisional activation in June 1943.

SHIGETA Tokumatsu

2nd Lieutenant (artillery), December 1912; Graduated from War College, November 1923; Staff Officer in 8th Division, August 1925; Major, December 1927; Battalion Commander in 1st Independent Mountain Artillery Regiment, August 1928; Staff Officer in Tokyo Bay Fortress, March 1931; Lieutenant-Colonel, August 1932; Staff Officer in 2nd Division, August 1934; Commander of 10th Artillery Regiment, March 1936; Colonel, August 1936; Chief of Staff to 6th Division, March 1938; Commander of 1st Field Artillery Brigade, March 1939; Major-General, March 1940; Director of Field Artillery School, April 1941; Superintendent of Field Artillery School, June 1941; Lieutenant-General, October 1941; Commander of 35th Division, March 1942; Inspector General of Artillery Training, March 1943; Commander of 72nd Division, July 1944; Commander of 52nd Army, HQ at Susui, Chiba prefecture, Japan, April 1945.

SHIKATA Ryoji

Educated through boys' school, junior school and senior army cadet school; Commissioned as an infantry officer; Transferred to Military Police (Kempeitai); Aide-de-camp to the Commander of the Kwantung Army Gendarmerie (Military Police) H. TOJO, Manchuria, c.1935 – c.1937; Became a confidant of H. TOJO; Commander of Tokyo Military Police HQ, c.1941 – 1944 (i.e., the fall of H. TOJO from government); Transferred as Commander of Military Police in China, 1944 – end of war, September 1945; Known to be a General officer (Major- or Lieutenant-General); Imprisoned by the Chinese for three years; Then appears to have been tried as a war criminal but acquitted and repatriated to Japan.

SHIMAZU

General officer; Member of Japanese Military Mission to Rome, Italy, 1942.

SHIMAZU Kiyoshi

Major-General; Chief of Medical Department of 15th Army (under S. KATA-MURA), Siam, by 1945; Surrendered a sword (together with S. KATAMURA, eighteen Generals and two Admirals) to Major-General G. C. Evans, GOC 7th Indian Division, at Bangkok, Siam, 11 January 1946.

SHIMIZU Masao

Major-General; Commander of Home Station for various army units at Asahi-gawa, Japan, March 1945.

SHIMIZU (SHIMUZU, SHIMZU) Noritsune

Lieutenant-General; Commander of 5th Army (under 1st Area Army – S. KITA) responsible for the defence of area of Mutanchiang Plain and Tungan, north-eastern Manchuria, September 1944; Army consisted of 124th (M. SHINA), 126th, 135th Divisions; HQ Mutanchiang; Attacked by the invading Russian 1st Banner Army, 9 August 1945; 124th Division lost three battalions and 15th

Border Garrison Unit at Hutou was isolated on the first day, 9 August 1945; Believed to have surrendered after the cessation of hostilities, 15 August 1945.

SHIMOKOBE Kenji
Major-General; Commander of 23rd Independent Mixed Brigade, April 1944; Kwangchowan area, Liuchow Peninsula, south China; Moved to Hainan, China, January 1945.

SHIMOMOTO Kumaya
Lieutenant-General; Commander of 108th Division (under 1st Army) in operations in northern and eastern Honan, China, January 1938.

SHIMOMURA Sadamu (Jo?)
Major?-General; Chief of Operations of Army General Staff (replacing I. KANJI), September 1937; Lieutenant-General; Commander-in-Chief of North China Area Army, Peiping (Peking), north China, November 1944; General; Possibly replaced before the end of the war (by H. NEMOTO); War Minister in last pre-occupation government (under premier Prince N. HIGASHIKUNI), appointed 16 August 1945; Government resigned at the commencement of the American occupation, 24 September 1945.

SHIMOMURA Sadashi
General officer; Signed the execution order for three American airmen captured after the 'Doolittle Raid' over Tokyo, 1942; Arrested as a suspected war criminal, 6 February 1946.

SHIMOTO Kotaro
Major-General; Commander of 9th Artillery Command, June 1944; Rabaul area, New Britain, December 1944.*

*Function unknown. Possibly formed the artillery staff of 8th Area Army.

SHIMOYAMA Takuma
Born 1882; 2nd Lieutenant (infantry) in 1st Infantry Regiment, December 1913; Lieutenant, August 1917; Graduated from War College, November 1921; Captain and Instructor at Military Academy, August 1922; Resident Officer in Germany, March 1925; Officer of Military Training, November 1927; Major, August 1928; Military Administration Bureau at War Ministry, August 1930; Lieutenant-Colonel on Army General Staff, August 1932; Instructor at War College, August 1934; Staff Officer in 11th Division, December 1934; Kwantung Army HQ as adviser to Manchurian Military Administration Bureau, Manchuria, December 1935; Colonel, August 1936; Staff Officer in North China Area Army, August 1937; Commander of 16th Air Regiment, June 1938; Major-General in Army Aeronautical Department, March 1930; Staff Officer in Army Air Force, August 1939; Lieutenant-General; Commander of 5th Air Army,* Seoul, Korea, at the end of the war, August 1945.

*In Okinawa 1945 by Ian Gow (See Bibliography), he is listed as Commander of 5th Navy Air Fleet, which is clearly a mistake.

SHIMURA
Major-General; c. Second World War.

SHINA Masatake (Manatake)

Lieutenant-General; Commander of 20th Depot Division, Keijo (Seoul), Korea, September 1944; Supplied 20th, 49th Divisions; Commander of 124th Division (under 5th Army – N. SHIMIZU), Manchuria; Defended approaches to 5th Army HQ at Mutanchiang; Attacked by invading Russian 1st Red Banner Army and lost three battalions on the first day, 9 August 1945.

SHINOHARA Jiro

Lieutenant-General; Concurrently Commander of four Home Stations for 11th Tank Regiment at Kawanishi, and various army units at Himeji, Kakogawa and Sasayama, all in Kobe Regimental District, Japan, March 1945.

SHINOHARA Saburo

Major-General; Concurrently Commander of four Home Stations for air, artillery and infantry units at Hamamatsu, Iwata, Mishima and Shizuoka, all in Shizuoka Regimental District, Japan, March 1945.

SHINOKURA

General; Commander of all Military Police Forces (Kempeitai) in Japan (and occupied areas?); Committed suicide, Japan, 1945.

SHIROKANE Yoshikata

Lieutenant-General; Commander of 51st Depot Division, Utsunomiya, Japan, September 1944; Supplied 14th, 33rd, 41st, 51st, 63rd, 71st, 81st Divisions and 5th, 53rd IMBs.

SHIROKURA

Major General; Head of Military Police (Kempeitai) in Kwantung Army (under Y. UMEZU), Manchuria, c1943; Ordered escorting of Russian and Chinese prisoners during transit to 'Detachment 731' (see S. ISHII) where they would be subject to lethal biological warfare experimentation.

SHIROKURA Yoshinari

SHOJI (SHOGE)

Major General; At HQ of 'Sepik Force' (under 18th Army), New Guinea; Charged with war crimes.

SHOJI Toshishige

Major-General; Concurrently Commander of three Home Stations for a shipping unit at Ishinomaki, air unit at Koriyama and various army units at Sendai, all in Sendai Regimental District, Japan, March 1945.

SHOKOKU Hirada

Major-General; Commander of 22nd Division (under 23rd Army) during the Battle of Kweilin – Liuchow, China, September–December 1944.

SOGAWA (TOGAWA) Jiro

Lieutenant-General; Commander of 6th Army, Hailar, Manchuria, January 1944; Transferred with army to China (under China Expeditionary Army) by 1945;

Surrendered 6th Army, 3rd, 34th, 40th, 161st Divisions and other units to Chinese General Tang En-po of 3rd Front Army at Nanking, September 1945; Surrendered 65th, 70th Divisions to Chinese General Li Pin-hsien of 10th War Area, at Hsuchow at about the same time.

SUCHIRO Mori
Lieutenant-General; Commander of 58th Division (under 11th Army) during the Battle of Changsha – Hengyang, China, May–August 1944.

SUDO Einosuke
Lieutenant-General; Chief of Staff to General Defence HQ, Japan, February 1945.

SUEFUJI Tomofumi
Lieutenant-General; Commander of 93rd Division, Kanazawa, Japan, September 1944.

SUEMATSU Shigeharu
Lieutenant-General; Commander of 114th Division (under North China Area Army) during the Battle of Hsuchow, China, from late December 1937.

SUGAWARA (SUGIWARA, SUGAHARA) Michio (Michita, Tsuji)
2nd Lieutenant (infantry), December 1909; Graduated from War College, 1919; Major, August 1924; Battalion Commander in 76th Infantry Regiment, March 1925; Major in Air Force, May 1925; Army Aeronautical Department, December 1927; Lieutenant-Colonel in Air Force, August 1928; Colonel and Commander of 6th Air Regiment; Section Chief of Army Aeronautical Department, March 1935; Major-General and Commander of 2nd Air Brigade, August 1937; Commander of 3rd Air Brigade, July 1938; Lieutenant-General, October 1939; Commandant of Shimoshizu Army Air School, December 1939; Commander of 1st Air Group, August 1940; Commander of 3rd Air Group, September 1941; Group transferred to Saigon, Indo-China, arriving late October 1941; Supported 25th Army (under T. YAMASHITA) during the invasion of Malaya (see also ENDO) from 8 December 1941; Destroyed British air power in northern Malaya by mass air attacks on British airfields, 8 December 1941; Bombed supply convoys to Singapore but without success (until the sinking of the *Empress of Asia*, 5 February 1942); Main force transferred to support the invasion of the East Indies, late January 1942; Commander of 3rd Air Army, July 1942; Commandant of Military Academy, May 1943; Deputy Chief of Army Aeronautical Department, April 1944; Chief of same Department, July 1944; Commander of Air Training Army, August 1944; Commander of 6th Air Army (for the defence of the Kanto Plain), HQ Fukuoka, Japan, December 1944; Placed under the overall control of C in C Combined Fleet Admiral S. TOYODA and ordered to deploy in Kyushu, Japan, 21 March–May 1945; 'Special Units' (Tokubetsu) formed for suicide (*Kamikaze*) use; *See also* MIYOSHI and Vice-Admiral M. UGAKI; Engaged in Operation 'TEN-GO' with mass attacks on American naval fleets off Okinawa until the end of the war.

SUGINO Iwao
Major-General; Commander of 73rd Infantry Brigade (in 91st Division – F. TSUTSUMI), Kurile Islands, from the divisional activation in April 1944.

SUGIURA E.
Major-General; Commander of 21st Infantry Brigade (under 25th Army – Y. YAMASHITA) engaged in the attack on Singapore, Malaya, February 1942.

Note: Probably the same as SUGIURA Eikichi.

SUGIURA Eikichi
Major-General; Commander of Military Affairs Department of 42nd Division, August 1943; Division in Japan then transferred to Kurile Islands, early 1944; Lieutenant-General; Commander of 115th Division, Yencheng area, Honan province, China, September 1944.

Note: Probably the same as SUGIURA E.

SUGIYAMA Gen (Hajime)
Born 1880; 2nd Lieutenant (infantry), June 1901; Graduated from War College, November 1910; Army General Staff, December 1910; Official duty in the Philippines, February 1912; Official duty in Singapore, Malaya, October 1912; Major, August 1913; Military Attaché in India, February 1915; Lieutenant-Colonel, August 1917; Commander of 2nd Air Battalion, December 1918; Colonel, June 1921; Chief of Army Affairs Bureau at War Ministry, August 1923; Major-General and Chief of Supply Bureau at Army Aeronautical Department, May 1925; Chief of Military Affairs Bureau, August 1928; Acting Vice Minister of War, June 1930; Lieutenant-General and Vice Minister of War, August 1930; Commander of 12th Division, February 1932; Chief of Army Aeronautical Department, March 1933; General, November 1936; War Minister in first Prince Konoye cabinet (replacing K. NAKAMURA), 3 June 1937; Supported Japanese aggression against China; Persuaded the cabinet to dispatch troops to Peking after the 'Marco Polo Bridge Incident' against the wishes of the moderates (three divisions sent); Agreed with the dispatch of the Shanghai Expeditionary Force (under I. MATSUI), August 1937; Deputy Chief of Army General Staff and concurrently a Military Councillor, June 1938; Commander-in-Chief of North China Area Army, December 1938; Concurrently Commander of Mongolia Garrison Army, August 1939; Member of Supreme War Council, September 1939; Chief of Army General Staff (replacing Prince K. KANIN), October 1940; Vetoed decision to attack Russia and supported 'Strike South' policy if negotiations with America over China and Indo-China failed, 1941; Told Emperor Hirohito that Japan could 'probably' win a war against Britain, Holland and America in an estimated five months, but that attempted diplomacy must come first; Recommended war commence no later than 10 October if diplomacy failed, 5 September 1941; Refused to accept that diplomacy must continue and demanded immediate war, 23 October 1941; Offered only one army concession to America which was that Japanese troops would be pulled out of China in 25 years, i.e., 1966; Stated that war should be declared no later than 13 November, 1 November 1941; Issued orders for attack on Malaya to commence on 8 December (Japanese time), 2 December 1941; Field Marshal, June 1943; Concurrently Member of the Board of Field Marshals and Fleet Admirals (who advised the Emperor), 1944 – end of war; Relieved of post of Chief of Army General Staff (replaced by H. TOJO), 21 February 1944; Inspector-General of Military Training, February 1944; War Minister in K. KOISO cabinet, July 1944; Commander-in-Chief of 1st General Army (under IGHQ) for the defence of eastern Japan (excluding Hokkaido which stayed under direct IGHQ control), from its activation

in April 1945; HQ Tokyo; Controlled 11th, 12th, 13th Area Armies; Instructed by IGHQ to prepare Operation 'KETSU-GO' (expulsion of enemy forces before they could consolidate a beach-head), July 1945; Coastal defences less than 70 per cent complete by August 1945; Committed suicide (together with his wife) upon the Japanese surrender, 15 August 1945; Replaced (by K. DOHIHARA).

SUKUMA (SAKUMA) T.
Lieutenant-General; Commander of 68th Division (under 11th Army – I. YOKOYAMA) during the Battle of Changsha–Hengyang, China, mid May–1 July 1944 when he was replaced (by M. TSUTSUMI).

SUMI Kenshi
Colonel; Commander of 10th Tank Regiment (in 2nd Armoured Division), August 1943; Located in Manchuria until August 1944; Division transferred to Luzon Island, Philippines; Major-General; Chief of Staff to 41st Army (under S. YOKOYAMA), Philippines, March 1945.

SUMIDA
Major-General; Commanded main force of 39th Division (under S. SASA) during the Battle of western Honan – northern Hopeh, China, March–May 1945.

SUMIDA (SUMITA) Raishiro
Lieutenant-General; Commander of 1st Army, Taiyuan, Shansi province, China, November 1944; Surrendered 1st Army, 114th Division and other units to Chinese General Yen Hsi-shan of 2nd War Area, at Taiyuan, September 1945; Became an assistant to the Nationalist Chinese Governor of Shansi province after the war.

SUMIYOSHI Tadashi
Major-General; Commander of Heavy Artillery Section of 17th Army (under H. HYAKUTAKE); Landed on Guadalcanal, Solomons, 15 October 1943; Supported an attack on Henderson airfield by shelling Lunga Point and launching a diversionary attack on the west bank of the Matanikau River with five infantry battalions (*see also* K. KAWAGUCHI, M. MARUYAMA, Y. NASAU); Attacked using tanks around Matanikau River but forced back into the jungle by American forces, 20-1 October 1942; Not informed of the delay in launching the main attack by M. MARUYAMA, so attacked on schedule but was defeated (with 650 dead), 23 October 1942; Launched an evening attack but was defeated by dawn, 24 October 1942; Evacuated with main Japanese forces from Guadalcanal, 1-8 February 1943; Commander of Eastern District Army Artillery Unit, HQ Tokyo, Japan, September 1944.

SUZUKI Harumaki
Lieutenant-General; Concurrently Commander of three Home Stations for signals, artillery and infantry units at Hara-machida, Yokosuka and Kawasaki, all in Yokohama Regimental District, Japan, March 1945.

SUZUKI Heyori
Major-General; Concurrently Commander of two Home Stations for various army units at Aomori and Hirosaki, both in Aomori Regimental District, Japan, March 1945.

SUZUKI Hiraku
Lieutenant-General; Commander of 117th Division, Sinsiang, Honan province, China, September 1944.

SUZUKI Keiji
Lieutenant-Colonel; Staff Officer; Formed MINAMI KIKAN (Organization South) to involve revolutionary groups in Burma in disrupting traffic on the Burma Road (supply route to China) and Haiphong, Indo-China, to Yunnan, China, route, 1940; Sent thirty young Burmese to Hainan Island, off China, for military training;* Remained in Burma and organized the declaration of Burmese independence by the Burma Independence Army at Tavoy, 1942; Sent back to Japan (under orders of 15th Army HQ); Major-General; Chief of Staff to 27th Army, Kurile Islands, March 1944; Returned to Burma by the Allies and held in Rangoon Jail for war crimes trials, 1947.

*Including Aung San, later to become the military head of the Burma National Army.

SUZUKI Sadaji (Teiji)
Lieutenant-General; Commander of 104th Division, Canton area, China, August 1942; Engaged in Battle of Kweilin – Liuchow (under 23rd Army), early September–mid December 1944.

SUZUKI Shigeji (Shigeru)
Major-General; Commander of 44th Independent Mixed Brigade (under 32nd Army – M. WATANABE), Okinawa, Ryukyu Islands, from its activation in May 1944; Remained in command during the Okinawa campaign from 1 April 1945 (see M. USHIJIMA for campaign details). Killed or suicide by late June 1945.

SUZUKI Shigeyasu
Major-General; Commander of 11th Separate Composite Brigade* in operations along the Peiping (Peking) – Suiyuan railway, China, early – late August 1937.

*Possibly the same as an Independent Mixed Brigade.

SUZUKI Soroku
Major-or Lieutenant-General; Cavalry Officer; Visited C in C Kwantung Army S. HONJO as an emissary of Prince K. KANIN before the seizure of Mukden, Manchuria, September 1931.

SUZUKI Sōsaku 鈴木 宗作
2nd Lieutenant (infantry), December 1912; Graduated from War College, November 1919; Army General Staff, April 1920; Member of Army General Staff, November 1921; Resident Officer in Germany, March 1923; Staff Officer on Army General Staff, November 1925; Member of Military Affairs Bureau at War Ministry, December 1928; Lieutenant-Colonel, August 1931; Staff Officer in Kwantung Army, Manchuria, December 1933; Colonel and Commander of 4th Infantry Regiment, August 1935; Chief of 2nd Section of Inspectorate General of Military Training, March 1937; Major-General, July 1938; Deputy Chief of Staff to China Expeditionary Army, September 1939; Chief of 3rd Bureau (Transport and Communications) of Army General Staff, Tokyo, March 1940; Lieutenant-General, March 1941; Chief of Staff to 25th Army (under T. YAMASHITA), November 1941; Remained in post during invasion of Malaya and Sumatra; Concurrently Superintendent of Military Administration of Malaya and Sumatra

(under 25th Army), February–October 1942; Chief of Shipping Department, April 1943; Chief of Central Shipping Transportation HQ, September 1943; Commander of 35th Army (under 14th Area Army – T. YAMASHITA), July 1944;[1] HQ Cebu City, Cebu Island, Philippines (*see also* Y. TOMOCHIKA); Responsible for central and southern Philippines; Ordered to concentrate on the defence of Leyte Island garrisoned by 16th Division (S. MAKINO) and hold it at all costs against an expected American invasion; American 6th Army landed on the east coast of Leyte between Dulag and Tacloban, 20 October 1944, Transferred with HQ to Ormoc Port, Leyte, personally to direct the defence of the island; Garrison reinforced with units of 1st Division (T. KATAOKA), 2 November 1944; Reinforced by 26th Division, early November 1944; Reinforced by 30th, 102nd Divisions but they arrived well understrength because of heavy losses during transit; Suicide tactics used against American tanks; North-eastern Leyte secured by the Americans after heavy fighting, by 30 October 1944; Ordered 1st Division to prevent American advance through Ormoc Valley with resultant stubborn resistance and heavy losses; Units of 16th Division held out in the area west of Dagami in the north but were virtually destroyed by mid November 1944; 35th Army caught in a pincer movement by American advances from the Ormoc Valley in the north and ridges to the south of Ormoc; 26th Division ordered to move east through the central mountains but strength severely depleted having had to reinforce other units; Ordered by 14th Area Army to recapture the airstrips in the east in conjunction with army and naval air offensive (Operation 'WA'), early December 1944; Attacks failed with only a temporary occupation of Buri airstrip by Japanese paratroopers and remnant of 16th Division, 6-9 December 1944; One battalion of 26th Division reached Burauen airfield but was repulsed; Final American offensive began against Ormoc, 5 December 1944; Japanese reinforcements virtually destroyed before being able to land; Ormoc Port captured by the Americans, 10 December 1944; Promoted to General; Japanese forces now trapped on Leyte and forced from Ormoc Valley into western Leyte mountains; Informed by 14th Area Army that no further aid or reinforcements would be sent, 17 December 1944; Ordered to defend southern and central Philippines with remaining forces and garrisons of other islands (*see also* T. HOJO, T. KONO, T. MANJOME), 19 December 1944; Ordered to evacuate as many troops as possible to other central Philippine islands, 25 December 1944; (Leyte forces reduced from 65,000 to approximately 14,500 by 1 January 1945); Escaped to Cebu Island (with approximately 1,000 men), arriving at Cebu City 24 March 1945; Reorganized command structure (*see* T. MANJOME); Americans invaded Cebu Island, landing the 'Americal' Division, 26 March 1945; Main defence centred around Cebu City but abandoned in favour of the northern hills; Cebu City entered by American forces, 27 March 1945; Forced to withdraw north, early April 1945; Japanese forces on Cebu virtually destroyed by mid June 1945; Forced to escape with his staff (and Chief of Staff Y. TOMOCHIKA) in small boats to Mindanao Island; Killed when the boats were attacked by American aircraft, 14 June 1945;[2] Replaced (by G. MOROZUMI).

[1] 35th Army, at its peak during the Leyte fighting, consisted of:
Leyte Island – 1st Div (T. KATAOKA), 16th Div (S. MAKINO), 26th Div (K. YAMAGATA), 30th Div (G. MOROZUMI), 102nd Div (S. FUKUEI).
Mindanao Island – 100th Div (J. HARADA), 54th IMB (T. HOJO).
Jolo Islands – 55th IMB (T. SUZUKI).
Unidentified location – 68th IMB (T. KURUSU).
[2] Accounts of date of death vary but are usually put around 16-19 April 1945. However, 14 June 1945 is, apparently, now confirmed.

SUZUKI Takao
General; Brother of Premier Vice-Admiral Baron SUZUKI Kantaro.

SUZUKI Teiichi
Born 1888; 2nd Lieutenant (infantry), December 1910; Graduated from War College, November 1917; Attached to Army General Staff, July 1918; Captain and Member of Army General Staff, April 1920; Major and attached to 48th Infantry Regiment, December 1925; Battalion Commander in 48th Infantry Regiment, August 1926; Member of Army General Staff, July 1927; Assistant Military Attaché to China, December 1929; Lieutenant-Colonel, March 1930; Member of Military Affairs Bureau in War Ministry, August 1931; Drafted plans for the Japanese Far East Policy, 1932; Colonel, December 1933; Member of Research Division at War College, March 1934; Attached to Military Affairs Bureau and concurrently a Member of Cabinet Research Board, May 1935; Commander of 14th Infantry Regiment, August 1936; Major-General and attached to 16th Division HQ (under Y. NAKAOKA), Kyoto, Japan, November 1937; First Chief of Political Affairs Section of Asia Development Board (China Affairs), December 1938; Responsible for the guidance of the Chinese puppet government under Wang Chang-wei at Nanking, China; Lieutenant-General, August 1940; Acting Secretary-General of the Asia Development Board, December 1940; Transferred to first reserve list; Minister of State (without Portfolio) in the third Prince Konoye cabinet and concurrently Chief of the Cabinet Planning Board co-ordinating the Japanese industrial war effort, April 1941; Stated at an Imperial Conference that Japan's natural resources would be quickly exhausted if negotiations with America were prolonged and would prevent the prosecution of a war, 6 September 1941; Informed the Emperor at an Imperial Conference that Japan's resources were poor and that a quick military victory against America would solve the problem, 5 November 1941; (Served in the 2nd and 3rd Prince Konoye cabinets and the H. TOJO cabinet); Resigned posts, October 1943; Imperial nominee to the House of Peers, 1943; Retired and was given a permanent ministerial rank at court and a full-time assignment for peace planning (contingency planning for Japan's defeat), October 1944; Arrested as a Class A war criminal; Indicted on 49 charges and tried by the International Tribunal for the Far East, Tokyo, 26 April 1946 – 12 November 1948; Found guilty and sentenced to life imprisonment; Released in 1956. Still alive in 1970.

SUZUKI Tetsuzo
Major-General; Commander of 55th independent Mixed Brigade, Jolo Islands, Philippines (under 35th Army), from its activation in July 1944.

SUZUKI Yoshisaburo
Major-General; Commander of 11th Shipping Group, September 1943; Located on Okinawa, February 1945.

TACHIBANA Yoshio (IGA Tachibana)
Major-General; Commander of 1st Mixed Brigade (in 109th Division – T. KURIBAYASHI) from the divisional reactivation in May 1944; Division in Bonin Islands (under 31st Army) until late May 1944; 1st Mixed Brigade on Chichijima; Lieutenant-General by the end of the war, August 1945; Surrendered the Bonin Islands to Commodore John H. Magruder, USN, on board USS *Dunlap* off Chichijima, 3 September 1945;[1] Occupation of the island was delayed until the

garrison of 40,000 men was assembled for repatriation (*see* Vice-Admiral M. KUNIZO); Charged with the execution and cannibalism of American airmen; Tried and executed on Guam.

*Surrendered a sword at this time. A *kyu-guntō* with blade signed 'BISHU OSAFUNE NORIMITSU', i.e., 'Norimitsu of Osafune in Bishu'. Now in the US Marine Corps Museum, Quantico, Virginia, America.

TADA

General; Commander-in-Chief of North China Area Army, c.1941.

TADA Hayao (Shun)

Major-General; Chief Military Adviser to puppet Emperor Pu-Yi of Manchukuo (Manchuria), Hsinking, Manchuria, 1932; Lieutenant-General; Vice Chief of General Staff, Tokyo, Japan, by 1937; Opposed the attack on Nanking, China, but forced to sanction the plan; Arrested as a war criminal, December 1945.

TADA Tamotsu

Major-General; Commander of 6th Independent Mixed Brigade, Anking area, Anhwei province, China, January 1944.

TADAKI Anan

Lieutenant-General or General; Commander of 11th Army (replacing K. ENBU) comprising 33rd, 34th Divisions and 20th IMB, China; Engaged in the Battle of Shankao, China, early March 1941; Reinforced to include four divisions in the 2nd Battle of Changsha, mid August 1941; 3rd Battle of Changsha, mid December 1941; replaced (by TSUKATA), December 1942.

TAGA Tetsuhiro

Major-General; Commander of 23rd Infantry Group (in 23rd Division), August 1942; Division in Manchuria until October or November 1944 (*See* F. NISHI-YAMA for divisional movement after January 1944).

TAGUMI Hachiro

Lieutenant-General; Commander of 36th Division, Halmahera Island, Moluccas, May 1944.

TAJIMA

Major-General; Commander of Batan Island garrison (under 14th Area Army – T. YAMASHITA), off north coast of Luzon Island, Philippines, c.1944;* Tried and convicted by a war crimes tribunal for the killing of three American naval airmen on Batan Island in May 1944; Sentenced to death and hanged at Los Banos, south of Manila, Luzon, Philippines, 3 April 1946.

*Not to be confused with Bataan Peninsula which is in the south of Luzon Island.

TAJIRI Toshio

Lieutenant-General; Concurrently Commander of five Home Stations for various air and army units at Amaki, Fukuoka, Kokura, Kurume and Tachiari, all in Fukuoka Regimental District, Japan, April 1945.

TAKADA Kiyohide

Major-General; Commander of 5th Field Transport Command, August 1943; Located in Burma, February 1945.

TAKAHASHI

Major- or Lieutenant-General; Chief of Staff to North China Area Army, HQ Peiping (Peking), by the cessation of hostilities, August 1945.

TAKAHASHI Mosuke

Major-General; Commander of Shimonoseki Fortress, Japan, March 1943.

TAKAHASHI Takaatsu

Born 1888 in Honze, Akita prefecture, Japan; Joined the army in 1915; Graduated from the Agricultural Department of Imperial University, 1928; Chemist and biologist; Chief of Veterinary Administration of Kwantung Army, Manchuria, 1941 – cessation of hostilities, August 1945; Major-General by 1942; Final rank Lieutenant-General; Directly supervised the activities of bacteriological centre 'Detachment 100' (see Y. WAKAMATSU) with 600–800 personnel; Advocated the use of bacteriological weapons in warfare; Ordered the mass production of bacteria for use as weapons; Captured by the Russians, 1 September 1945; Tried by the Russian Military Tribunal at Khabarovsk for crimes relating to bacteriological warfare and sentenced to 25 years in a labour correction camp, December 1949.

TAKAHASHI Takaji

Lieutenant-General; Commander of 30th Depot Division, Keijo (Seoul), Korea, April 1944; Supplied 30th Division.

TAKAJI W.

Major-General; c. Second World War.

TAKAMORI Takashi

Lieutenant-General; Commander of 11th Division, Hulin, Manchuria, October 1941; Commander of 12th Army comprising 3rd (part), 69th, 110th, 115th, 117th (part) Divisions, China; Engaged in Battle of western Honan – northern Hupeh, March–May 1945; Surrendered 12th Army, 22nd, 110th Divisions and other units to Chinese General Hu Tsung-nan of 1st War Area at Lo-yang, September 1945; Also surrendered 115th Division and other units to Chinese General Liu-chih of 5th War Area at Yen-cheng at about the same time.

TAKANO Naomitsu

Lieutenant-General; Commander of 4th depot Division, Osaka, Japan, September 1944; Supplied 4th, 25th, 34th, 44th, 68th Divisions and 2nd, 25th, 37th IMBs.

TAKASHIMA Tatsuhiko

Major-General; Chief of Staff to 3rd Army, Yeho, Manchuria, March 1943; Chief of Staff to Eastern District Army (under S. TANAKA), HQ Tokyo, Japan; Redesignated as 12th Area Army, April 1945 – September 1945; Requested to join rebellion against acceptance of the surrender but refused and ordered the rebels to withdraw from the Imperial Palace, 14-15 August 1945.

TAKASHINA Hyo – Same as TAKESHI Takashina (Takashina, Hyo)

TAKATSU Toshimitsu

Colonel?; Staff Officer to 14th Army (under M. HONMA) during the invasion of the Philippines, 1941-2; Major-General; Chief of Staff to 23rd Army, Canton, south China, November 1944; Appeared as witness in the war crimes trial of M. HONMA, Manila, Philippines, 1946.

TAKAYAMA Hikoichi
Major?-General; Chief of Staff to 37th Army (under M. BABA), Borneo, by 1945.

TAKEDA
Major-General; On staff of 15th Army (under R. MUTAGUCHI), Burma, c.1944; Personally took ammunition to 31st Division area at Chakahabama on the Kohima front, 24 May 1944.

TAKEDA Hisashi
Major-General; Commander of 1st Field Base Force, October 1943; Located on Halmahera Island, Moluccas, January 1944.

TAKEDA Kaoru
Lieutenant-General; Commander of 53rd Division; Transferred with the division from Kyoto, Japan, to Moulmein, Burma, April 1944; Held in reserve by Southern Army; Ordered to reinforce Burma Area Army for the attack by 15th Army on Kohima and Imphal in India but diverted to 33rd Army (under M. HONDA); Moved north with HQ arriving at Indaw in early May 1944; Responsible for defence of Indaw to Myitkyina railway; Moved against the British 14th Brigade (2nd 'Chindit' operation); Attacked the British 'White City' base after it had been evacuated but lost the leading troops to mines and booby-traps, 11 May 1944; Moved against the British 'Blackpool' base near Namkwin Village; Advanced to relieve Myitkyina garrison (see G. MINAKAMI) by order of 33rd Army to support 18th Division (S. TANAKA) which was defending the Mogaung Valley against Chinese forces, late May 1944; Defended Mogaung Village but was driven out with 1,600 casualties, 27 June 1944; Division placed under the command of 15th Army (S. KATAMURA), October 1944; Forced to retreat; In area south of Singu with strength reduced to 4,000, but ordered to send 119th Regiment to 15th Division (see S. YAMAMOTO) for the defence of Mandalay, January 1945; Remnant in general retreat, arriving at Pyawbwe having lost all the artillery, 6 April 1945; Attacked by British and Indian troops, suffering severely and losing the remaining anti-tank guns, 8 April 1945; Division reported to consist of only 1,600 men by 14 April 1945; Possibly replaced by Y. HAYASHI before the end of the war.

TAKEDA Seiichi
Major-General; Commander of Yura Fortress, Japan, March 1943; Commander of 1st Artillery Command, Sunwu, Manchuria, February 1945.*

*Function unidentified. Possibly formed the artillery staff to an Area Army.

TAKEHARA Saburō 竹原
Major-General, October 1938; Infantry Group Commander of 6th Division, China, April 1941; Lieutenant-General; Commander of 49th Division, Korea, from its activation in January 1944; Transferred with division to Burma (under direct command of Burma Area Army – H. KIMURA), July 1944; Division formed around 106th, 153rd, 168th Infantry Regiments; Division retained as a strategic reserve; HQ Pegu; Regiments sent individually as reinforcements where required; 153rd Regiment fought at Seikpyu, 14 February 1945; 168th Regiment reinforced

56th Division in Yunnan, China, and northern Burma, suffering heavy losses, August 1944–February?1945; Division ordered to reinforce Meiktila, 4 February 1945 (*See also* T. KASUYA); 168th Regiment formed the advance, arriving 27 February 1945; Regiment virtually destroyed by a British attack on Meiktila with the CO, Colonel Yoshida, being killed and the remnant being withdrawn from the town, 2 March 1945; TAKEHARA himself arrived at Minden, four miles south of Pyawbwe, 4 March 1945 (i.e., after the main battle and subsequent loss of the town to the British); 106th Regiment finally arrived, 6 March 1945; Planned the recapture of Meiktila from the south and south-west (in conjunction with 18th Division – E. NAKA, in the north-east and regiments from 33rd Division in north and from 2nd Division in the east); HQ Yindaw; Came under 33rd Army (M. HONDA) command; 49th and 18th Divisions were formed into a separate temporary 'Army of the Decisive Battle' (Kesshogun) for this campaign (being under the personal command of M. HONDA), 18 March 1945; Launched special force (guerrilla unit) attack on the eastern airfield with success, 15-18 March 1945, and other raids into the south-west corner of the town; Heavy losses forced a withdrawal, 27 March 1945; Ordered to hold the road between Pyawbwe and Meiktila, late March 1945; Ordered to delay the British advance until the monsoons, April 1945; Division reported to consist of only 1,600 men and one mountain gun, by late April 1945; Remnant formed defensive position at Sinthe Chaung, south of Yamethin (together with 18th Division); Formed part of 33rd Army to delay British advance while 28th Army (S. SAKURAI) broke out from Pegu Yomas and crossed the Sittang River into Tenasserim, July 1945; (Divisional strength estimated to be only 300 men by this time); Retreated to final HQ at Thaton, Burma, at the time of the cessation of hostilities, 15 August 1945; Formally surrendered (together with T. KAWADA) to Major-General W. A. Crowther, GOC 17th Indian Division, at Thaton, Burma, last week of October 1945.

Note: Owned at least two swords:
(a) Surrendered a *shin-guntō*, with General Officer's knot and civilian *tsuba* (guard), to Major-General W. A. Crowther, GOC 17th Indian Division, at Thaton, Burma, last week of October 1945. This is shown in Imperial War Museum photograph IND 4901. It is believed to have been sold at auction and is now in Japan (which indicates an old blade since war-time military blades are not allowed into Japan).
(b) A *shin-guntō* with General Officer's knot and standard military *tsuba* (guard). This is most unusual in that the blade was specially made for him with his name 'General Takehara' included in the tang inscription and also it underwent a cutting (*tameshigiri*) test. It was made by Kurihara Akihide in November 1942. Now in a private collection in England.

TAKESHI Mori
Major-General; Chief of Staff to 19th Army, Piroe on Ceram Island, Moluccas, January 1944.

TAKESHI Takashina (Takeshina, Hyo)
Lieutenant-General; Commander of 29th Division (under 31st Army – H. OBATA) controlling the Southern Marianas District Group, HQ Guam; Assumed control of the Guam garrison which consisted of 38th Infantry Regiment (of 29th Division), 48th Independent Mixed Brigade, 10th Independent Mixed Regiment,

giving a total of 13,000 army troops (with 5,500 naval personnel concentrated around Orote Peninsula and Apra Harbor under Captain Sugimoto Yutaka, IJN); HQ north of Apra; American marines landed south of Agat on west coast, 2 July 1944; 38th Regiment had been virtually destroyed by mid July 1944; American 77th Division landed south of Agat; 10th Independent Mixed Regiment was attacked in the hills by the American 77th Division; Launched counter-attack against American 3rd Marine Division around Piti on north-east coast, 25 July 1944; Attack broken up with virtual destruction of ten battalions, 26 July 1944; Killed by machine-gun fire from an American tank, 28 July 1944; Command assumed by H. OBATA.

TAKESHITA Yoshiharu
Lieutenant-General; Commander of 27th Division, north China, from November 1942.

TAKEUCHI Yasumori
Major-General; Infantry Group Commander of 8th Division, HQ Suiyang, Manchuria, March 1941; Commander of 8th Independent Mixed Brigade, Tangshan, Hopeh province, China, August 1943.

TAKEUCHI Yiroshi
Lieutenant-General; Commander of 55th Division (under 15th Army – S. IIDA), HQ Bangkok, Siam, by 22 December 1941; Moved HQ to Rahaeng, Siam, to concentrate for the invasion of Tenasserim area of southern Burma, 1 January 1942; Concentrated on Siam – Burma border at Mae Sot, 17 January 1942; Crossed into Burma capturing airfields at Tavoy, Mergui and Victoria Point, 23 January 1942; Attacked Moulmein, 30 January 1942; Division moved north to support 33rd Division (S. SAKURAI) in capturing Rangoon (which was taken 8 March 1942); Moved north and attacked Toungoo, 24 March 1942; Toungoo captured; Division undertook garrison duties in Burma until late 1942; Replaced (by T. KOGA), end of 1942.

TAKEUCHI Zenji
Major-General; Commander of Tsugaru Fortress, Japan, February 1943.

TAKUMI Hiroshi
Major-General; Infantry Group (23rd Infantry Brigade) Commander of 18th Division (under R. MUTAGUCHI), December 1941; Landed at Kota Bahru, Malaya, 8 December 1941; Infiltrated, and went around British and Indian defensive positions, capturing Kota Bahru airfield by afternoon, 8 December 1945; Remained in command during the Malaya campaign.

TAMADA Yoshio
Major-General; Commander of 2nd Amphibious Brigade, north-west New Guinea, March 1944.

TAMAURA Yoshishichi
Major-General; Commander of 6th Railway Transport Command, March 1943; Located in Philippines, October 1944.

TAMOTO

Major- or Lieutenant-General; Surrendered a sword to Lieutenant-Colonel A. K. Crookshank, OC 6th Mahratta Light Infantry, at Bentong, Pahang State, Malaya, 20 September 1945.*

*Sword now in the National Army Museum, London. Cat. no. 6604-27. A *shin-guntō* with blade dated 1940 and signed 'KOA ISSHIN', i.e., 'Asian nations (should unite) as one heart' (to form the Great East Asia Prosperity Sphere) 'MANTETSU SAKU KORE WO', i.e., 'the South Manchurian Railway made this' (at the Mukden arsenal).

TAMURA Hiroshi

Major-General; Commander of 12th Artillery Group (in 12th Division), December 1942; Located in Mutanchiang province, Manchuria, until December 1944; Formosa from January–February 1945.

TAMURA Yoshitomi

Major-General; Chief of 1st Operations Division of Kwantung Army, Manchuria; Replaced (by T. MATSUMURA), August 1943; Chief of Personnel Division of Kwantung Army, HQ Hsinking (Chanchun), Manchuria; Captured by the Russians, 1 September 1945.

TAMURA Yoshitomo

Major-General; Chief of Staff to 31st Army (under H. OBATA), Truk Island, Carolines, July 1944.

TANABE

Major-General; Commander of Army Shipping Transport HQ (supporting 25th Army invasion of Malaya), Samah Port, Hainan Island, off south China, c.1941.

TANABE Moritake

Lieutenant-General; Vice Chief of Army General Staff; Stated he wanted the enemy to be forced into fighting away from their bases and opposed Japanese attacks into enemy-held areas such as Hawaii or Australia which had been recommended by the navy; Mutual agreement reached to attack Port Moresby, New Guinea, by 13 March 1942; Engineered a cabinet decision to abandon the General Staff policy continually reinforcing Guadalcanal, Solomons, by reducing the available shipping tonnage (*see also* S. TANAKA), 5 December 1942;* Commander of 25th Army (under 7th Area Army), Sumatra (possibly replacing M. SAITO), April 1943; HQ Fort de Kock; Army comprised 2nd Imperial Guards Division, 9th Air Division and other units (with a total 71,500 men) by August 1945; Surrendered (together with Vice-Admiral S. HIROSE) to Major-General H. M. Chambers, GOC 26th Indian Division, at Padang, 21 October 1945.

*However this was temporarily revoked by Premier H. TOJO who allowed an increase.

Baron TANAKA Giichi

General officer; Served in China; Retired; Prime Minister; Implemented expansionist policies including the planned seizure of Manchuria but this was prevented by warnings from America, 1927; Requested by the Emperor to provide a detailed report on how the Japanese could undertake military conquests to become a world power* (Report delivered in 1935); Instigated a tough policy against China; ordered Japanese troops into action against Nationalist Chinese in Shantung province on the pretext of protecting local Japanese interests, 1928; Resigned because the Emperor's displeasure was incurred for his failure to punish the Kwantung Army for their involvement in the murder of Chinese warlord and governor Chang Tso-lin, 1929; Held in Sugamo prison, Tokyo, by the occupying powers as a suspected war criminal but released without trial, 31 August 1947.

*According to *Singapore and After* by Lord Stragboli (*see* Bibliography) the contents of this report, known as the 'Tanaka Memorial', was revealed by two Chinese translators employed in the Foreign Office, Tokyo, but its existence was subsequently denied by Japan. However, Japanese expansionist policy apparently followed the leaked report. No original has ever been found and the only known Chinese translated copy is full of errors. It is now widely regarded as a Chinese forgery.

TANAKA Harushige
General officer, c.1933.

TANAKA Hisaichi (Hisakazu, Kyuichi)
Language Officer in America; Instructor at War College; Chief of Staff to Formosa Army; Chief of Staff to Southern Expeditionary Army, Canton, China, 1938; Lieutenant-General; Commander of 21st Division; Commander of 23rd Army Canton, south China, March 1943; Concurrently Governor-General of Hong Kong (replacing R. ISOGAI), 1945?; In Canton at the time of the British re-occupation of Hong Kong, 29 August 1945; Surrendered 23rd Army and 129th, 130th Divisions with other units to Chinese General Fa-Kuei, C in C 2nd Front Army, at Canton, China, September 1945; Also surrendered 103rd (part), 104th Divisions and other units to Chinese General Yu Han-mou of 7th War Area at Swatow at about the same time. Tried in Japan and executed for war crimes.

TANAKA Kunishige
General officer; Probably retired; Head of Higher Ethics Society (Meirinkai), c.1937.*

*A nationalist organization which guided the Reservist Association (about three million army and navy ex-servicemen) 'to develop the military spirit and to promote military efficiency, which in turn will promote social welfare, encourage virtuous customs and habits, and guarantee the stability of national defence'.

TANAKA Nobuichi
Lieutenant-General; Director of HQ Staff Military Operations Section, Tokyo, c.1942; Visited 25th Army HQ (under T. YAMASHITA) at Kluang, Malaya, to discuss the planned attack on Singapore Island, Malaya, late January 1942.

TANAKA Nobuo
Regimental Commander in north China; Major-General; Commander of 29th Independent Mixed Brigade, Siam, c.1944; Ordered to Burma as acting Commander of 33rd Division (replacing M. YANAGIDA), 10 May 1944; Arrived at Rangoon, 13 May 1944; Moved to front where division was engaged in Operation 'U-GO' to capture Imphal, Manipur State, India (under 15th army – R. MUTAGUCHI); HQ Laimanai, 23 May 1944; Confirmed to full command of 33rd Division and promoted to Lieutenant-General, June 1944; 70 per cent of division were killed, wounded or sick by 30 June 1944; Fighting retreat towards the Chinwin River; Division slowly retreated through Kalewa and Shwebo, June–July 1944; Defended the Irrawaddy River crossing for Mandalay, December 1944; 213rd Regiment lost Monwa on Chindwin River, 21 January 1945; Divisional maintenance centre at Taungtha captured by the British, 24 February 1945; Defended Irrawaddy crossing against British 20th Division but lost 953 men (out

of 1,200) in unsuccessful suicide attacks by two battalions against the British beach-head (also lost all tanks to air attacks), middle–late February 1945; Retreated south into Siam; Came under 18th Area Army (A. NAKAMURA) command at Nakon Pathom, Siam, by the time of the cessation of hostilities, 15 August 1945.

Note: Surrendered a sword (together with A. NAKAMURA, eighteen Generals and two Admirals) to Major-General G. C. Evans, GOC 7th Indian Division, at Bangkok, Siam, 11 January 1946. It was later presented to the widow of Major-General D. F. W. Warren, GOC 5th Indian Division (which fought 33rd Division during the Tiddim Road operations in Burma). Blade probably of the Ishido School, greatly shortened (*Ō-suriage*) with *choji hamon*. Sold at Sothebys, London, 21 June 1988.

TANAKA Ryozaburo

Colonel; Commander of 229th Regiment (in 38th Division under T. SANO); Attacked Hong Kong Island, 18 December 1941; Troops involved in atrocities including the murder of fifty-three POWs at Eucliff; British Hong Kong Garrison surrendered, 25 December 1941; Major-General; Tried as a war criminal at Hong Kong and sentenced to 20 years' imprisonment.*

*Hanged according to *The fall of Hong Kong* by Tim Carew (*see* Bibliography), but this seems incorrect.

TANAKA Shinichi (Sumichi)

Born 1893; Section Member of Inspectorate General of Military Training, 1924; Staff Officer in Kwantung Army, Manchuria, April 1932; Army General Staff HQ, Tokyo, December 1933; Attached to 59th infantry Regiment, July 1935; Chief of Military Service Section at War Ministry, April 1936; Chief of Army Affairs Section at War Ministry, March 1937; Chief of Staff to Mongolia Garrison Army, February 1939; Attached to Army General Staff HQ, Tokyo, August 1940; Chief of 1st Bureau (Operations) of Army General Staff and (Concurrently?) Chief of Staff to Inspectorate General, October 1940; Lieutenant-General 1941; Inspection tour of French Indo-China, Siam, Malaya and Philippines, January–February 1942; Vehemently opposed reduction of available shipping tonnage for use by the army which would prevent the continued reinforcement of Guadalcanal, Solomons (*see also* M. TANABE) and insulted Premier H. TOJO (who consequently dismissed him from his post), 6 December 1942; Attached to Southern Army HQ, Saigon, Indo-China, December 1942; Commander of 18th Division (replacing R. MUTAGUCHI), Burma, effective from 13 March 1943; Garrisoned the Shan States with 55th, 56th Regiments in Hukawng Valley and 114th Regiment at Myitkyina (which had been placed under 15th Army – R. MUTAGUCHI); 114th Regiment transferred to 56th Division (but later returned); Ordered to hold the Hukawng Valley; 56th Regiment attempted to repel the 38th Chinese Division on Tanai River but was forced to withdraw with heavy losses, late December 1943; Ordered by 15th Army not to launch an offensive but to delay the Chinese advance, January 1943; Japanese driven from Taro Plain by 30 January 1944; Slowly forced back; Attacked by American 'Merill's Marauders' who linked with the Chinese at Walawbum, 4 March 1944; Ordered a general withdrawal because of the Chinese advance which attacked his HQ; Re-established east–west defensive line in lower Hukawng Valley;[1] Walawbum lost, 7 March 1944; Retreated down Kamaing road in Mogaung Valley; Right flank counter-attacked units of 'Merill's Marauders' at Nhpum Ga and besieged them, 3 March 1944; American relief forced a withdrawal, 9 April 1944; Came under 33rd Army (M. HONDA), April or May 1944; Ordered to hold Kamaing 'at all costs'. Division (consisting of only three depleted regiments) was attacked and almost outflanked by three Chinese divisions near Kamaing, May 1944; Forced to withdraw from Kamaing; Elements of 56th and 114th Regiments were cut off west of Kamaing; Tried to hold Mogaung Valley but ordered to withdraw to Sahmaw (with only 50 per cent of original force left), June 1944; Important Myitkyina airfield captured by 'Merill's Marauders', 17 May 1944; Myitkyina town held by 114th Regiment (Colonel Maruyama); Myitkyina garrison reinforced (see G. MINAKAMI); Main Chinese forces moved down Mogaung Valley, 19 May 1944; Kamaing town taken by the Chinese with the loss of a major Japanese supply depot, 19 May 1944; Mogaung lost to the Japanese, 26 June 1944;[2] Myitkyina town taken by American and Chinese forces after the Japanese abandoned it, 3 August 1944; Replaced (by E. NAKA), early September 1944; Chief of Staff to Burma Area Army (under H. KIMURA), early September 1944 (replacing E. NAKA); Ran an Advanced Tactical HQ at Kalaw, Shan States; Attended important staff meeting (also attended by Chief of Staff Southern Army T. NUMATA) at Meiktila to decide on the defence strategy for southern Burma, 24 February 1945; visited 33rd Army (M. HONDA) HQ at Thazi and, of his own volition, ordered 33rd Army to abandon offensive operations in order to cover the retreat by 15th Army (S. KATAMURA), late March 1945; Visited Toungoo to order its defence by 15th Division (S. YAMAMOTO), mid April 1945; Violently disagreed with C in C Burma Area Army H. KIMURA about the abandonment of Rangoon and refused to sign draft orders to that affect since he (Tanaka) wanted it defended to the last man; However Rangoon was abandoned by 26 April 1945; Thought 33rd Army (M. HONDA) should mount an offensive to retake Rangoon in accordance with the opinion of C in C Southern Army H. TERAUCHI; Replaced (by T. SHIDAI), May 1945; Attached to North-eastern District Army, HQ Sendai, Japan, May 1945; Wounded (by air attack?) and hospitalized, May 1945.

[1] Initially 18th Division resisted three Chinese divisions, then five divisions plus one American Brigade.
[2] Only 5,000 Japanese escaped from the Mogaung Valley.

TANAKA Shìzuichi (Seiichi, Seiji) 田中 静一

2nd Lieutenant (infantry), December 1907; Graduated from War College; Member of Military Affairs Bureau of War Ministry, April 1918; Resident Officer in England, March 1919;* Member of Army General Staff, June 1922; Major, August 1922; Battalion Commander in 22nd Infantry Regiment, December 1924; Military Attaché to the Japanese Embassy in Mexico, May 1926; Lieutenant-Colonel, March 1927; Colonel and Commander of 2nd Infantry Regiment, August 1930; Military Attaché to USA, May 1932; Chief of Staff to 4th Division, August 1924; Major-General and Commander of 5th Infantry Brigade, August 1935; Chief of General Affairs Bureau at Military Police HQ, August 1936; Commander of Kwantung Army Military Police (Kempeitai), Manchuria, August 1937; Lieutenant-General and Commander of Military Police Forces (Kempeitai), Tokyo, Japan, July 1938; Commander of 13th Division (under 11th Army), China, August 1939; Commander of Military Police Forces (Kempeitai), Tokyo, September 1940; Commander of Eastern District Army, Japan, October 1941; Commander of 14th Army (replacing M. HONMA), Philippines, and concurrently Military Governor of the Philippines, October 1942?; Replaced (by S. KURODA?), 1943?; Attached to Army General Staff, May 1943; General, September 1943;

Military Councillor and Superintendent of War College, August 1944; Commander-in-Chief of Eastern District Army (defence of Japan), HQ Tokyo, March 1945; Reorganized as 12th Area Army (under 1st General Army) controlling 51st, 52nd, 53rd Armies, Tokyo Bay Defence Corps, 36th Army (in reserve) and Tokyo Defence Army (which was retained under IGHQ control), April 1945; Attempted (together with T. MORI) to organize fire-fighting at the Imperial Palace, Tokyo, after American bombing, 24-5 May 1945; Offered his resignation to atone for the bombing but it was refused by War Minister K. ANAMI; Ordered by K. ANAMI to tighten security and ensure public order before the official surrender broadcast by the Emperor, 14 August 1945; Took personal command of the 1st Imperial Guards Division after the assassination of its commander (T. MORI) by rebel army officers opposed to the surrender and the rebellion by the division because of the issuing of false orders; Requested to join the attempted *coup d'état* but refused, ordering their withdrawal which was obeyed, thus quashing the rebellion, 15 August 1945; Committed suicide by shooting, 24 August 1945.

*Went to Oxford University and studied Shakespeare.

TANAKA Takayoshi (Ryūkichi, Ryūichi)

Captain; Helped plan, and participated in, the assassination of Chinese warlord Marshal Chang Tso-lin, Mukden, Manchuria, 4 June 1928;[1] Aide to Japanese Consulate in Shanghai, China, 1932; Arranged the murder of a Buddhist priest by Chinese gangsters in Shanghai to divert world attention away from Manchuria; Engineered a military clash in Shanghai between Chinese and Japanese, 1932; Lieutenant-Colonel, 1936; Lead an uprising of Inner Mongolian forces under Mongolian Prince Teh to create an autonomous government (under Japanese domination) but was defeated by Chinese forces at Suiyan, 4 November 1936[2]; Colonel; Regimental Commander in 19th Division during the Lake Khasan incident on the Manchurian–Siberian border, July-August 1938; Major-General; Chief of Military Service Bureau at War Ministry, 1940;[3] Principal of the Nakano (espionage and saboteur) School at Nakano, Tokyo (replacing Lieutenant-Colonel Arisuga Shun);[4] Another branch was set up in Tomioka City, Gunma prefecture, September 1941; Replaced (by O. KAWAMATA), October 1941; Opposed Premier H. TOJO about the attack on America who forced him to retire, 1942; Kept very detailed diaries and testified for both defence and prosecution at the International Tribunal for the Far East war crimes trials, 1946-8.[5]

Personal facts: A tall man with a large head. Nicknamed 'Monster Tanaka' by his contemporaries. A schemer.

[1] Marshal Chang Tso-lin was a powerful warlord and Governor of three eastern provinces of Manchuria. TANAKA accompanied Tso-lin by train to Mukden, Manchuria, but left his carriage just before the bomb exploded. One account says TANAKA was a Colonel by this time but this seems incorrect.
[2] A Japanese puppet state in Inner Mongolia under Prince Teh was actually formed on the 28th October 1937.
[3] This post is given in *War Criminal – The Life and Death of Hirota Koki* (*see* Bibliography) but it did not exist. Probably it was the Military Administration Bureau which contained a Military Service Section. It is known he clashed with A. MUTO, the Chief of the Military Affairs Bureau at this time.
[4] Formed to train operatives for clandestine operations against Russia. The Tomioka branch was formed for guerrilla warfare in the south–west Pacific.
[5] One magazine article (unidentified source) says he was shot as a war criminal but this has not been verified.

TANI (TOSHIO) Hisao

Lieutenant-General; Commander of 6th Division which formed part of the southern attack force on Shanghai (under H. YANAGAWA) and destroyed Sungchiang, China, 1937; Involved in the capture and 'Rape of Nanking', December 1937 (*see also* I. MATSUI); Tried by a Chinese Military Court and sentenced to death for the Nanking massacres, Nanking, China, 10 March 1947.

TANIGUCHI Goro

Major-General; Commander of 12th Field Transport Command, August 1943; Located in Manchuria by December 1944.

TANIGUCHI Hatsuzo

Major-General; Commander of Manila Air Depots, Philippines, September 1944.

TANIGUCHI M.

Lieutenant-General; Commander of 108th Division, Linfen, north China, c.1939.

TASAKA S.

Lieutenant-General; Commander of army forces in western Singapore, Malaya (under 7th Area Army), by August 1945.

TASAKA Yasohachi

Major-General; Commander of 53rd Infantry Brigade (in 59th Division – T. HOSOKAWA), Tsinan, Shantung province, China, March 1943.

TASHIO Taizo

Major-General; Commander of 5th Field Replacement Unit, central China, March 1944.

TASHIRO Kanichiro (Koichiro)

Lieutenant-General; Commandant of Secret Police, China?, 1935; Replaced (by K. OHTANI); Commander of Japanese Garrison Forces on Pei-ning railway, China;[1] Demanded the right to search Wanping, a suburb of Peking, after the death of a Japanese soldier; This was refused by the Chinese, so soldiers of the 'Tanake' (or 'Tanabe') Brigade under his command who were in the area (for 'manoeuvres') attacked at Lukouchiao across the Marco Polo Bridge, 7-8 July 1937;[2] Died mid? July 1937; Replaced (by K. KATSUKI).

[1] Probably this was in fact the North China Garrison Army
[2] This was the 'Marco Polo Bridge Incident' or 'China Incident' which precipitated the Sino-Japanese War of 1937-45. *See also* T. WACHI.

TATEGAWA Yoshitsugi

Lieutenant-General; Commander of 110th Division (under North China Area Army), China; Responsible for the northern sector (Tientsin–Pukow railway) during the Battle of Hsuchow, China, late December 1937 – May 1938.

TATEKAWA Yoshiji

Organized volunteers to fight behind the Russian lines in the Russo-Japanese war, 1904-5; Major-General; Head of European and American Intelligence Section of 2nd Bureau (Intelligence) of Army General Staff; Military Attaché at Japanese Embassy in Peking, China, March 1928; Organized assassination of Chinese warlord Marshal Chang Tso-lin (*see also* T. TANAKA) at Mukden, Manchuria, 4 June 1928; Chief of 2nd Bureau (Intelligence) of Army General Staff, August 1929; Involved in the Japanese capture of Mukden, Manchuria, September 1931; Lieutenant-General; Japanese Ambassador to Russia, late 1940.

TATSUMI E.

General officer; Military Attaché to Japanese Embassy in London, England, c.1940; Survived the war.

Note: Possibly the same as TATSUMI Eiichi

TATSUMI Eiichi

Major-General; Chief of Staff to Eastern District Army, Tokyo, Japan, September 1942.

Note: Possibly the same as TATSUMI E.

TAZOE Noboru

Major- or Lieutenant-General; Commander of Army Air Force in Burma (comprising 4th, 5th, 12th Air Divisions), c.1943; HQ Kalaw, Shan States, c.March 1944; Worried about Allied airborne operations cutting off Japanese forces at Myitkyina and unsuccessfully tried to get 15th Army (R. MUTAGUCHI) to cancel Operation 'U-GO' (Kohima and Imphal campaign) in favour of concentrating Japanese forces on such landings (i.e., against 2nd 'Chindit' operations), 6 March 1944; Japanese airfield at Myitkyina attacked but counter-attack launched on Chindit landing site, 10 and 13 March 1944; Had 161 aircraft (compared with 1,500 available to the British), June 1944.

TERAHIRA

General officer; Commander of a Special Service Corps.

TERAKURA Shozo

Lieutenant-General; Commander of 27th Army (under Northern Army which was renamed 5th Area Army), for the defence of Japan; 27th Army HQ was deactivated when 11th Area Army was organized in 1945.

TERAMOTO Kumaichi

2nd Lieutenant (infantry), December 1910; Graduated from War College, December 1921; Member of Army General Staff, August 1923; Member of Army Aeronautical Department, August 1926; Assistant Military Attaché to USA, December 1928; Lieutenant-Colonel (airforce), March 1930; Attached to Army General Staff, February 1931; Member of Army Aeronautical Department, August 1931; Colonel (airforce) and Commander of 8th Air Regiment, August 1933; Member of Army Aeronautical Department, December 1936; Major-General and Director of Hamamatsu Army Air School, November 1937; Superintendent of same school, August 1939; Lieutenant-General and Commander of 2nd Air Group, August 1940; Commander of 4th Air Army, July 1943; Attached to Army Aeronautical Department, August 1944; Chief of same department, April 1945.

Count TERAUCHI Hisaichi (Juichi) 寺 内 寿 一

Born 1879; Son of Field Marshal, Prime Minister and Governor-General of Korea, Terauchi Masatake; 2nd Lieutenant (infantry), April 1900; Graduated from War

College, December 1903; Major, October 1911; Assistant Military Attaché to Austria, December 1911; Military Student in Germany, February 1913; Lieutenant-Colonel, November 1916; Colonel; Commander of 3rd Imperial Guards Regiment, July 1919; Chief of Staff to Imperial Guards Division, January 1922; Major-General and Commander of 19th Infantry Brigade, February 1924; Chief of Staff to Korea Army, August 1927; Lieutenant-General and Commander of an Independent Garrison Unit, August 1929; Commander of 5th Division, August 1930; Commander of 4th Division, January 1932; Founded 'Army Purification Movement' (non-intervention in politics and strict obedience to orders), 1934; Commander-in-Chief of Formosa Army (organizing 'Strike South' Intelligence-gathering service for a possible attack against Malaya, Java, etc.), August 1934;[1] General, October 1935; Military Councillor, December 1935; Regarded as a 'political innocent' and thus accepted as War Minister in the K. Hirota cabinet but immediately resigned upon being informed of the 'moderates' in other cabinet posts, 6th March 1936; Accepted post after mutual agreement on army demands, 9th March 1936; Persuaded Premier Hirota to carry out a purge of those involved with, or sympathetic to, the '2–26 Insurrection' which involved the forced resignation of all army General Officers in atonement (over 3,000 were reinstated); War Minister in Hirota cabinet (replacing Y. KAWASHIMA), 9 March 1936; Forced to resign and replaced (by K. NAKAMURA), 10 February 1937;[2] Inspector-General of Military Training and, concurrently, Military Councillor, February 1937; Commander of North China Area Army, August 1937; Military Councillor, December 1938; Commander of Southern Army (formed to control all Area Armies and Armies in south-east Asia and the south Pacific), HQ Saigon, Indo-China, from its activation on 6 November 1941; (Supreme Commander of all army invasions, campaigns and occupations in the areas under his control);[3] Field Marshal, June 1943; HQ moved to Manila, Philippines, May 1944; Moved back to Saigon, 30 November 1944; Suffered cerebral haemorrhage but his illness was not reported by his staff to IGHQ, Tokyo, 10 April 1945; Accepted the Emperor's surrender orders after a personal visit by Prince Kanin Haruhito, August 1945;[4] Unable to attend formal surrender of all Japanese forces in South East Asia at Singapore because of ill health (see S. ITAGAKI), 12 September 1945; Personally surrendered to Supreme Commander SEAC, Lord Louis Mountbatten, at Saigon, Indo-China, 30 November 1945; Moved to Rengam, near Johore Bharu, Malaya, by order of Lord Mountbatten and died there of cerebral haemorrhage (second stroke) aged 67, 12 June 1946; Cremated at the Japanese cemetery, Singapore.

Note: (a) General S. ITAGAKI is reported to have surrendered a sword to Lord Mountbatten on behalf of TERAUCHI at Singapore, 12 September 1945. This may have been his army sword (shin-guntō) which had been presented to him by the Emperor on the occasion of his promotion to Field Marshal in 1943. The blade was made by Kotani Yasunori,an instructor at the Nipponto Tanren-kai (Japanese sword forging and tempering society) at the Yasukuni Shrine (for the spirits of all Japanese war dead), Tokyo.
(b) He personally surrendered two of his family swords to Lord Mountbatten at Saigon, 30 November 1945. They were specially flown in from Japan and presented in a wooden box (as a mark of special respect). One is a silver mounted tachi (long sword slung from a belt) with a blade dated 1292. It is now in Mountbatten's home of 'Broadlands', England. The other is a wakizashi (shorter of the two swords carried through the belt of a samurai) with a 15th-century

blade. This was subsequently presented by Mountbatten to King George VI and is now in Windsor Castle.

[1] Given as CinC Korea Army in *War Criminal – The Life and Death of Hirota Koki* (*see* Bibliography), but it appears to be incorrect.

[2] Demanded the resignation of the government because of the criticism of the army in the Diet (parliament) and thus forced the resignation of the Hirota cabinet and himself.

[3] This included all army forces in Indo-China, Siam, Malaya, Sumatra, Java, Borneo, Celebes, Philippines, Burma, New Guinea. Also included 3rd Air Army, HQ Singapore, which controlled all army air operations in south-east Asia. Naval operations were under the separate control command of South West Area Fleet, HQ Penang, Malaya, and subject to Combined Fleet GHQ control in Tokyo. However all naval forces within the Southern Area sphere of operations came under his control in February 1945 when South West Fleet was disbanded and replaced by the formation of 1st Southern Expeditionary Fleet (under Vice-Admiral S. FUKUDOME), HQ Singapore.

The various army campaigns authorized by Southern Army HQ are mentioned under the names of the individual army commanders involved.

[4] He is reported to have ordered the deaths of all POWs in the southern regions if the Allies invaded Japan.

TESHIMA Fusatarō   豊嶋 房太郎

2nd Lieutenant (infantry), December 1910; Graduated from War College, November 1916; Attached to Army Ordnance Department, August 1917; Captain, April, 1920; Member of Military Affairs Bureau at War Ministry, April 1921; Major, August 1925; Attached to 33rd Infantry Regiment, March 1926; Battalion Commander in 33rd Infantry Regiment, March 1927; Member of Military Administration Bureau (Economic Mobilization) at War Ministry, March 1928; Lieutenant-Colonel, August 1929; Attached to Korea Army HQ, August 1931; Colonel and Commander of 33rd Infantry Regiment, March 1934; Chief of Staff to 1st Division, March 1936; Major-General and attached to 12th Depot Division HQ, November 1937; Commander of 27th Infantry Brigade, April 1938; Chief of General Affairs Bureau at Provost Marshal HQ, March 1940; Lieutenant-General and Provost Marshal General, August 1940; Commander of 3rd Division (under 11th Army), China, September 1940; Engaged in the third Battle of Changsha, China, December 1941 – January 1942; Commander of Imperial Guards Division, January 1942; Commander of 2nd Army, HQ Yenichi, Manchuria; Transferred with 2nd Army to the region north of Australia (under 2nd Area Army – K. ANAMI); Army comprised 3rd, 35th, 36th Divisions, occupying the western New Guinea – north Australia front (roughly from Java to Amboina with Timor); HQ near Makassar, Celebes, October 1943; HQ Pinrang, Celebes, August 1945; Given concurrent responsibility for 2nd Area Army command after its deactivation in June 1945; Army now comprised 57th IMB in northern Celebes, 5th Division (KOBORI) in Ceram – Aru – Ambon area, 35th and 36th Divisions in western New Guinea; Given additional command of 37th Army (M. BABA) in Borneo and 48th Division (K. YAMADA) in Timor and Lesser Sundas after the cessation of hostilities, August 1945; Signed the surrender of 'all Japanese Armed Forces under Japanese control in the Netherlands East Indies, east of and exclusive of Lombok, and in Borneo'* to Australian General Sir Thomas Blamey, C in C Australian Military Forces, on Morotai Island, Moluccas, 9 September 1945.

*Quoted from the formal Instrument of Surrender signed at this ceremony. He also surrendered his sword, a *shin-guntō*, to Sir Thomas Blamey at this time.

TODOROKI Morizō
Lieutenant-General; Head? of 'Imperial Way' (Kodo-ha) faction, Japan, 1933.*

*Ultra-nationalist organization wanting to sweep away the corrupting influence of big business and political parties to restore the traditional Japanese virtues under the Emperor. *See also* S. ARAKI.

TŌJŌ Hideki (Eiki) 東條英機
Born 1884; Low caste samurai family; Military Academy Cadet (infantry branch), 1902; Commissioned 2nd Lieutenant (infantry), August 1905; Garrison duty in Manchuria, spring 1905–1906; 1st Lieutenant, 1906?; Captain, 1912?; Staff College until December 1915; Served short period in Siberia with Allied intervention against the Bolsheviks plus General Staff and regimental duties during 1915-18; Official duty in Switzerland, August 1919; Major, August 1929; Military Attaché in Germany, 1919–22; Instructor at Military Staff College, Tokyo; Lieutenant-Colonel, August 1924; Colonel, August 1928; Battalion Commander in 1st Infantry Regiment, Tokyo, August 1929; Major-General, March 1933; Head of General Affairs Bureau at War Office, 1933; Commandant of Military Academy, March 1934; Commander of 24th Infantry Brigade, Kyushu, Japan, August 1934; Commander of Kwantung Army Gendarmerie (Kempeitai), Manchuria, September or October 1935; Instigated a purge of all suspect sympathisers with the '2-26 Insurrection' who were in Manchuria, 1936; Lieutenant-General, December 1936; Founder of the 'Asia Development Union' (Koa-Domei, i.e., Mastery of Japan over Asia); Chief of Staff to Kwantung Army (replacing S. ITAGAKI), Manchuria, March or June 1937; Personally lead an army group in an outflanking movement against Chinese forces in the Peking area, thrusting deep into China, and securing all Inner Mongolia, 1937;[1] Returned to HQ Manchuria; Vice Minister of War (under S. ITAGAKI) in first Prince Konoye cabinet, Tokyo, May 1938; Offended senior industrialists with a speech accusing them of putting profit before the national interest; Quietly removed to the non-political post of Inspector-General of Army Aviation, December 1938; Concurrently held nineteen posts on Boards and Committees; War Minister in second Prince Konoye cabinet, July 1940; Ordered full mobilization after the German attack on Russia; Doubled the strength of the Kwantung Army, Manchuria, 1941; Agreed that negotiations with America over the Japanese occupation of China and Indo-China should cease in favour of war; Continued as War Minister in third Prince Konoye cabinet, July 1941; Forced Prince Konoye to resign, 1941; Prime Minister (replacing Prince Konoye) but remained on the active list, 17 October 1941;[2] General, 18 October 1941; Concurrently Minister for Home Affairs and Minister of War; Fully supported the naval attack on Pearl Harbor, 8 December 1941;[3] Refused to continue with the International Convention Agreement of 1909 which protected the rights of POWs, 1942; Introduced legislation that captured American airmen from the 'Doolittle Raid' over Tokyo be tried as criminals by Military Courts and sentenced to death, 1942; Concurrently Minister of Foreign Affairs, September 1942; Concurrently Minister of Education, April 1943; Concurrently Minister of Commerce and Industry, October 1943; Concurrently Minister of Munitions, November 1943; Concurrently Chief of General Staff controlling both the Army and Navy Chiefs of Staff (thus becoming a modern-day 'Shogun'), 20 February 1944; Refused to admit the war was lost despite severe Japanese defeats, July 1944; Received a vote of no confidence from the Privy Council ('Jushin'), 17 July 1944; Forced to resign, 18 July 1944; Placed on first military retired list, 20 July 1944; Became a 'Jushin' (elder statesman and member of the Privy Council);

Resided at his family house in Setagaya, a suburb of Tokyo, taking up gardening and writing; Part of his property was destroyed by an incendary bomb, 25 May 1945; Continued to maintain that Japan could support her forces in China, Korea and Manchuria, and could remain strong enough to obtain a negotiated peace and not unconditional surrender; Ordered arrested by the American Occupying Forces as a war criminal but attempted suicide by shooting just before the arresting party arrived at his home, 11 September 1945; His life was saved by an American army doctor who had him taken to hospital for recovery before he was taken to Omori POW camp; Transferred to Sugamo prison, Tokyo, 8 December 1945; Tried by the International Tribunal for the Far East, Tokyo, commencing 26 April 1946; Indicted on 50 counts as a Class A war criminal; Judgement issued, 4-12 November 1948; Found guilty and sentenced to death for conspiracy to wage an aggressive war, crimes against peace and atrocities against allied POWs forced to work on the Burma Railway; Executed by hanging at Sugamo prison, 23 December 1948; Cremated together with the bodies of six other executed war criminals at Yokohama and the remains secretly disposed of by Allied officials; Some ashes were secretly kept by Japanese crematoria staff until after the Allied occupation had ended and then were given to the Japanese Repatriation Assistance Bureau who returned them to their families; A joint tomb to TOJO and the other six executed war criminals was unveiled in Aichi prefecture, 17 August 1960; The tombstone reads 'The tomb of the Seven Martyrs'.

Personal facts: Autocratic and a workaholic. Nicknamed 'Kamisori' (the Razor).

Note: Photographed after his suicide attempt with several swords in the background including a *shin-gunto* with a General Officer's knot. As he lay wounded he offered his sword to Lieutenant General Robert Eichelberger, C in C American Eighth Army, who said 'he already had it' (to prevent it being taken as a souvenir by members of the Allied press corps). Presumably it was subsequently handed over to General MacArthur.

The MacArthur Memorial Museum, Norfolk, Virginia, America, has the following swords which were owned by TOJO:
(a) *Tanto* (dirk) blade signed by Masashige, c.1521, in *shira-saya* (plain wooden keeper mounts). Cat. no. 3532.
(b) *Tachi* (long slung sword) blade in *shira-saya* attributed to Yamato province, c.1220. Cat. no. 3511.
(c) *Shin-guntō* with a General officer's knot. Blade signed 'BISHŪ OSAFUNE SUKESADA', i.e., Sukesada of Osafune in Bishū (province) and dated 1507. Cat. no. 3518.

[1] His only combat command.
[2] Stated at a cabinet meeting that he absolutely refused to sanction withdrawal of troops from China to placate America even if that meant that war could be avoided through diplomatic negotiations, 14 October 1941. This precipitated the resignation of Premier Prince Konoye and left him to be the new Prime Minister since the army would not appoint a War Minister if anybody else was chosen. He was ordered by the Emperor to form a cabinet and also to continue diplomatic negotiations (even though opposed to this) which he did until the last minute (however he also ordered war preparations during the same period).
[3] Surprisingly he did not know of the planned Pearl Harbor attack, which had been kept secret by the navy, until after the fleet had sailed, 30 November 1941. He knew only of the planned combined army and navy operations for the invasions of Malaya and the Philippines.

TOKUGAWA (TOGUGAWA) Yoshitoshi

Lieutenant; sent to France to learn to fly, April 1910; returned to Japan with a Henry Farman bi-plane and made the first powered flight in Japan, 19 December

1910; Lieutenant-General; Commander of Army Air Command (i.e., Army Air Force) with eleven Air Wings, Japan, by 1936;* Commander of an Air Division (three Air Regiments with 300+ aircraft) under Central China Expeditionary Army (S. HATA) during the Battle of Wuhan (losing 100 aircraft), early June–mid November 1938.

*The army air force in Manchuria (Kanto Command) was regarded as a separate entity at this time.

TOMIDA

Major-General; Chief of Staff to 23rd Army (under H. TANAKA), Canton, China, by 1945; Refused to allow a British First Aid Group to go on to Hong Kong until the cessation of hostilities had been ratified, 20 August 1945.

TOMINAGA Kyoji

2nd Lieutenant (infantry), December 1913; Graduated from War college, November 1923; Attached to Army General Staff, December 1924; Attached to 23rd Infantry Regiment, February 1925; Attached to Kwantung Army HQ, Manchuria, December 1925; Army General Staff, December 1927; Assistant Military Attaché to Russia, December 1928; Member of Japanese delegation to General Disarmament Conference at Geneva, Switzerland, December 1931; Lieutenant-Colonel on Army General Staff, August 1932; Official duty in Germany, December 1935; Colonel and Section Chief of Army General Staff, August 1936; Staff Officer to Kwantung Army, Manchuria, March 1937; (Commander of?) Infantry Regiment in 2nd Imperial Guards; Major-General and Chief of 4th Bureau (Historical) of Army General Staff, March 1939; Chief of 1st Bureau (Operations) of Army General Staff, September 1939; Attached to Eastern District Army, Japan, September 1939; Commandant of Kunchuling Army Tank School, Manchuria, December 1939; Adviser to South China Army, August 1940; Instigated invasion of northern Indo-China, September 1940; Chief of Personnel Bureau of War Ministry, Tokyo, April 1941 (or possibly October 1940?); Lieutenant-General, December 1941; Vice Minister of War, March 1943; Commander of 4th Air Army (replacing F. OYOKAWA?), Philippines, August 1944; Arrived at Manila, Luzon Island, Philippines, September 1944; Engaged in the air defence of the Philippines; Army aircraft used *Kamikaze* (suicide) tactics in Operation 'SHO' (attacks on American naval forces), 24-6 October 1944; First official army *Kamikaze* units formed by 4th Air Army, November 1944; First official *Kamikaze* action was by aircraft of 'Manda Unit' which rammed American bombers, 5 November 1944; Suffered heavy losses but was reinforced by six *Kamikaze* units, 17 November 1944; Units attacked American fleets off Leyte and Luzon, November 1944 – January 1945; 4th Air Army placed under the control of 14th Area Army (T. YAMASHITA), 1 January 1945; Disagreed with army policy to abandon Manila; Launched *Kamikaze* attacks against American invasion fleet off Lingayen Bay, Luzon Island, 9 January 1945;[1] Initially refused to move HQ from Manila to join C in C 14th Area Army T. YAMASHITA at Baguio, Luzon Island; Obeyed only after receipt of written orders, 8 January 1945; Last organized *Kamikaze* mass attack, 13 January 1945; Entire air strength virtually destroyed by this time; Sick with fever; Ordered his men to fight as infantry with the army; Attempted to get 10th (Area or Air?) Army and 8th Air Division Commanders to fly him to Formosa since he considered it useless to remain without aircraft; Overruled by T. YAMASHITA who still required air reconnaissance; Abandoned his post and flew to Formosa with his senior staff officers, 17

January 1945; T. YAMASHITA accused him of desertion and requested Southern Army HQ to implement a court-martial with the sentence of death; Matter referred to IGHQ, Tokyo; To avoid scandal and because of the influence of his friend, ex-premier H. TOJO, he was demoted and transferred to the first reserve list on Formosa, May 1945;[2] Transferred to active duty as Commander of an infantry division (138th or 139th) which was organized in Manchuria in July 1945; Captured by the Russians and imprisoned in a Siberian labour camp; Released and returned to Japan, 18 April 1955.

[1] Only army *Kamikaze* units were left after 6 January since all naval air units had been destroyed.
[2] It is assumed he was demoted to Major-General but it may have been a demotion in seniority since his command was reduced from an Army to a Division. A division was normally commanded by a Lieutenant-General.

TOMOCHIKA Yoshiharu (Miharu)
Major-General; Chief of Staff to 35th Army (under S. SUZUKI), central and southern Philippines, c.September 1944; HQ Cebu City, Cebu Island; Went with S. SUZUKI to Leyte Island to observe the situation after the American landings, arriving 1 November 1944; Found 16th Division (S. MAKINO) had been routed so ordered the newly arrived 1st Division (T. KATAOKA) to prepare for offensive operations south-east of Carigara; Leyte reinforced by 26th Division (K. YAMAGATA), early November 1944; (*see* S. SUZUKI for campaign details); Escaped to Cebu Island (with S. SUZUKI), arriving at Cebu City, 24 March 1945; Americans landed on Cebu Island, 24 March 1945; Forced to sail in small boats for Mindanao Island (with S. SUZUKI in a separate boat); Attacked by American aircraft but survived to reach Mindanao, 14 June 1945.*

*Accounts of the date of attack vary, usually being put around 16-19 April 1945. However the date of 14 June 1945 is apparently now confirmed.

TORITA Ryuichi
Lieutenant-General; Commander of Southern Malaya Fuel Storage Depots, Singapore, October 1944.

TOSHIGE Shoji
Served in Hong Kong; Major-General by the end of the war; Tried by a British Military Tribunal for ill treatment and killing of British and Canadian POWs captured in Hong Kong; Acquitted of charges, 17 March 1947.

TOSHIO Hisao – Same as TANI Hisao

TOYAMA
Lieutenant-General; Commander of 58th Army (under 17th Area Army – Y. KOZUKI), Cheju-do Island (probably replacing S. NAGATSU), off south Korea, 1945; Surrendered 50,100 army and naval troops to representatives of American XXIV Army Corps, 30 September 1945.

TOYAMA Nobori
Lieutenant-General; Commander of 71st Division, Hunchun, Manchuria, from its activation in April 1942; Division moved to Chiamussu, October 1944.

TSUCHIHASHI (TSUCHIBASHI) Yuitsu (Yuichi)
2nd Lieutenant (infantry), December 1912; Graduated from War College, November 1920; Attached to Army General Staff, May 1921; Member of Army

General Staff, June 1922; Official duty in France, May 1924; Member of Military Affairs Bureau at War Ministry, May 1926; Battalion Commander in 1st Infantry Regiment, August 1930; Member of Military Affairs Bureau at War Ministry, August 1931; Member of Army General Staff, August 1932; Member of Military Affairs Bureau at War Ministry, August 1934; Colonel and Commander of 20th Infantry Regiment, August 1935; Military Attaché to France and, concurrently, Belgium, August 1937; Chief of Staff to 21st Army, August 1939;* Chief of 2nd Bureau (Intelligence) of Army General Staff, December (1939?); Deputy Chief of Staff to China Expeditionary Army, October 1940; Concurrently Military Attaché to China, December 1940; Lieutenant-General; Commander of 48th Division, Formosa, September 1941; Transferred with the division for the Philippines invasion (under 14th Army – M. HONMA), December 1941 – March 1942; Java invasion, 1942; Timor from 1942; Commander of Indo-China Garrison Army, November 1943 (or in 1944?); Renamed 38th Army (under the control of Southern Army), HQ Saigon, January or December 1944; Seized French Indo-China from the Vichy French Administration and French armed forces to forestall a possible American invasion, 9 March 1945 (French troops were disarmed or massacred if they resisted); Allies agreed to split Indo-China along the 16° Latitude for surrender purposes (with the north to come under China and the south under SEAC); Assembled in northern Indo-China by the end of the war, September 1945; Surrendered 38th Army and Japanese troops in northern Indo-China to Chinese General Lu Han of 1st Front Army, at Hanoi, September 1945 (The remaining forces in southern Indo-China remained under Southern Army for surrender purposes).

*Assumed to be a Major-General for this post.

TSUDA Tatsumi

Major-General; Concurrently Commander of two Home Stations for an air unit at Kikuchi and various army units at Kumamoto, both in Kumamoto Regimental District, Japan, March 1945.

TSUDA Yoshitake

Lieutenant-General; Commander of 105th Division (under 14th Area Army – S. KURODA, T. YAMASHITA), Los Banos, Luzon Island, Philippines, from its activation in July 1944; HQ at Naga on Bicol Peninsula, September 1944; HQ at Antipolo, January 1945; Responsible for the defence of northern Luzon and mountains east of Manila; Under 41st Army (S. YOKOYAMA) control, March 1945; Division virtually destroyed by the time of 14th Area Army surrender, 2 September 1945.

TSUKADA Osamau (Osami, Ko)

Major-General; Chief of Staff to Central China Area Army (under I. MATSUI), Nanking, 1937; Vice Chief of Army General Staff (under G. SUGIYAMA), c.1941; Vociferous supporter of war with America (and agreed it should start no later than 3 November 1941 but agreed with the 1 December date after naval pressure for a delay); Chief of Staff to Southern Army (under H. TERAUCHI) from its activation on 6 November 1941.

TSUKADA Rikichi

2nd Lieutenant (infantry), December 1916; Graduated from War College, November 1924; Attached to Army General Staff, December 1925; Attached to

Training Unit at Shimoshizu Army Air School, July 1927; Instructor at same school, March 1930; Staff Officer in 20th Division, August 1930; Staff Officer in 39th Infantry Brigade, September 1931; Staff Officer in Kwantung Army, Manchuria, February 1932; Attached to 7th Air Regiment, March 1933; Instructor at Hamamatsu Army Air School, August 1933; Attached to Staff Section of China Garrison Army HQ, May 1936; Lieutenant-Colonel (Air Force), March 1938; Commander of 7th Air Regiment, June 1938; Chief of Staff to 1st Air Group, December 1939; Major-General, August 1941; Commander of 3rd Air Brigade, April 1942; Chief of Staff to 3rd Air Army, February 1944; Commander of Airborne Operations Training Unit, August 1944; Commander of 1st Airborne Raiding Group (paratroops), November? 1944; Moved to Luzon Island (under 14th Area Army – T. YAMASHITA), Philippines; Commander of 'Kembu Group' with 30,000 men (when 14th Area Army forces on Luzon were split by T. YAMASHITA), 1 January 1945; Ordered to defend important airbase of Clark Field and the mountains west of the central plains of Bataan; Ordered by 14th Area Army to prevent American usage of Clark Field by fighting to the death; American XIV Corps attacked 'Kembu Group' outer defences but suffered heavy casualties for only minor gains, 27 January 1945; Americans launched major attack, 28 January 1945; Clark Field lost after heavy fighting, 31 January 1945; (Japanese losses were 2,500 by this time); Group restricted to the mountains west of Clark field with 25,000 men; Front defensive line broken by American 40th Division after heavy fighting with a further 5,000 Japanese dead, late February 1945; Lieutenant-General, March 1945; Attacked by American 43rd Division and then by the 38th Division; Group virtually destroyed by early April 1945; Ordered 'Kembu Group' to disband and fight guerrilla actions as independent units, 6 April 1945; Believed to have surrendered (with only 15,000 men left) at the end of the war, 2 September 1945.

TSUKAMOTO Makoto
Lieutenant-General; Commander of Formosan Military Police (Kempeitai), Formosa, c.1945; (See also T. NOMI).

TSUKATA
Lieutenant-General or General; Commander of 11th Army (replacing A. TADAKI), China, December 1942; Shot down and killed while flying from Hankow to Nanking to take up this appointment, 8 December 1942; Replaced (by I. YOKOYAMA).

TSUKINOKI Masao
Major-General; Commander of Nagasaki Fortress, Japan, October 1942.

TSUTSUMI Fusai
Lieutenant-General; Commander of 9th Division, Kurile Islands, from activation in April 1944.

TSUTSUMI Mikio
Lieutenant-General; Commander of 21st Army, from its activation, China; Comprised 11th, 18th, 104th Divisions plus ships and aircraft; Army shipped to Makung from Dairen, Manchuria, via Tsingtao, China, and Shanghai, China, making a forced-landing near Ao-tou in Taya Bay, Kwantung province, south China, 12 October 1938; Captured Canton, 21 October 1938; Captured Hu-men

Fortress, 23 October 1938; Captured Fu-shan and San-shui, 25 October 1938; Forced to defend the area around Canton with 2½ divisions after Chinese offensives, November 1938; Commander of 68th Division (replacing T. SUKUMA) under 11th Army (I. YOKOYAMA), China, from 1 July 1944, and during the fourth Battle of Changsha – Hengyang, mid May–early August 1944; Division in Hengyang – Leiyang area, Hunan province, September 1944; Battle of western Hunan (under 20th Army), early April–early June 1945.

UBE
Major-General; Commander of a Mixed Brigade (under Kwantung Army), Harbin area, Manchuria, by August 1945; Assisted in blowing up bacteriological warfare centre 'Detachment 731' (see S. ISHII) after removal of equipment before the Russian advance could capture it, August 1945.

UCHIDA Ginnosuke
Major-General; Commander of 118th Division, north China, September 1944?; Lieutenant-General; Commander of 116th Division (replacing O. IWANAKA?) under 20th Army during the Battle of western Hunan, China, April–early June 1945.

UCHIDA Takayuki
Lieutenant-General; Commander of 70th Division, Nanchang area, Kiangsi province, China, from its activation in April 1942; Kinhua–Hangchow area, by May 1942.

UCHIYAMA Eitaro
Lieutenant-General; Commander of 12th Army (under North China Area Army) during the Battle of central Honan, mid April–mid June 1944; Replaced (by T. TAKAMORI?); Commander-in-Chief of 15th Area Army, HQ Osaka, Japan, April 1945.

UEDA Kenkichi
General; Commander-in-Chief of Kwantung Army, Manchuria, March 1936; Concurrently Ambassador to 'Manchukuo'; Forcibly retired (and replaced by Y. UMEZU), c.1939.

UEMURA Mikio
Lieutenant-General; Commander of 57th Division, Shanshefu, Heiho province, Manchuria, March 1943; Commander of 4th Army (directly responsible to Kwantung Army under O. YAMADA) comprising 119th, 123rd, 149th Divisions; HQ Tsitsihar; Responsible for the defence of northern Manchuria; Russians invaded Manchuria, 9 August 1945; Army forced back with heavy fighting, becoming isolated from adjoining 44th Army, by 13 August 1945; Units forced to fight rear-guard actions; 119th Division and 80th IMB stood at Hailar but were defeated with 2,300 dead; Believed to have surrendered to the Russians after the official cessation of hostilities, 21 August 1945.

UEMURA Seitaro
Lieutenant-General; Chief Superviser of Prisoner-of-War (Allied) Information Bureau of War Ministry, December 1941; Objected to Premier H. TOJO's insistence that POWs must be made to work, but was overruled, April 1942; Committed suicide, 1945.

UEMURA Toshimichi

2nd Lieutenant (infantry), December 1910; Graduated from War College, November 1922; Member of Army General Staff, February 1935; Battalion Commander in 13th Infantry Regiment, July 1926; Lieutenant-Colonel and Staff Officer in 9th Division, August 1930; Colonel and Staff Officer in Formosa Army, August 1933; Commander of 24th Infantry Regiment; Section Chief of Army General Staff, August 1936; Deputy Chief of Staff to Shanghai Expeditionary Army, China, August 1937; Major-General, March 1938; Superintendent of Tokyo Army Preparatory School, March 1938; Chief of Staff to 3rd Army, March 1940; Lieutenant-General, December 1940; Commander of 29th Division, April 1941; Commander of 5th Army, Manchuria, October 1943; Commander of 36th Army, Japan, September 1944.

UENO Kanichiro

Lieutenant-General; Commander of a Home Station for shipping and infantry units at Wakayama, Japan, March 1945.

UGAKI Kazushige

Born 1868; Brother of Vice-Admiral UGAKI Matome; Graduated from Military Academy, 1891; Major, during Russo-Japanese war, 1904-5; Colonel; Commander of a Regiment in the Imperial Guards Division, 1906; General, 1925; War Minister four times (including 1924-5 and 1930-1);[1] Became embroiled in the 'March 1931 Plot' which was designed to remove him from office; Governor-General of Korea, 1931 – January 1937; Premier-designate after the fall of the Hirota cabinet but failed to form a cabinet because of lack of support by the army, January 1937;[2] Foreign Minister for four months in the first Prince Konoye cabinet, May– September 1938; Elected to the House of Councillors (Upper House of the Diet), 1953 until his death aged 87, 30 April 1956.

[1] He gained the emnity of the militarists for disbanding three army divisions which he considered to be redundant at that time. Regarded by the army as too much of a politician.
[2] Although requested by the Emperor to form a cabinet, he was prevented by the army who refused to nominate a Minister of War on the grounds that his (UGAKIs) appointment was 'detrimental to military discipline and unity in the army'.

UGAKI Matsuhiro

Major-General; Chief of Staff to 48th Division, Timor, May 1943.

UMAHACHI

Major-General; Commander of Army forces on Pakanto Island, 70 miles north of Saipan, Marianas; by-passed and isolated by American forces; Became the ranking officer in the Marianas after the deaths of Y. SAITO and Vice-Admiral C. NAGUMO, 7 July 1945; Surrendered to Americans, November? 1945; Issued orders for the surrender of the last active army unit in the Second World War – it had remained fighting on Saipan under Army Captain Oba (who finally surrendered on 1 December 1945).

UMEZU Yoshijirō 梅津美次郎

Born 1882; 2nd Lieutenant (infantry), March 1904; Graduated from War College, November 1911; Captain, March 1912; Military Student in Germany, April 1913; Military Student in Denmark, March 1915; Army General Staff, May 1917; Major, June 1918; Military Attaché to Switzerland, November 1919; Lieutenant-Colonel, February 1922; Ordance Bureau at War Ministry, March 1923; Colonel and Commander of 3rd Infantry Regiment, December 1924; Section Chief of Army General Staff, December 1926: Chief of Army Affairs Section at War Ministry, August 1928; Major-General and Commander of 1st Infantry Brigade, August 1930; Chief of General Affairs Bureau of Army General Staff, August 1931; Commander of China Garrison Army, March 1934; Lieutenant-General, August 1934; Declared an anti-Japanese movement in Hopeh province, China, was a violation of the Tangku armistice and ordered the Chinese government to withdraw (which they did) with the Signing of the 'Ho – Umezu Agreement', 10 June 1935;[1] Commander of 2nd Division, August 1935; Vice Minister of War, March 1936; Commander of 1st Army, north China, May 1938; General, August 1939; Commander-in-Chief of Kwantung Army (replacing K. UEDA), Manchuria, September 1939; Chief of Army General Staff (replacing H. TOJO), July 1944; (Remained in this post until the end of the war); Concurrently Member of Supreme War Council; Agreed with Admiral M. YONAI's proposal to request Russia to mediate for peace on Japan's behalf, 12 May 1945; Reprimanded by the Emperor at an Imperial Conference for not agreeing to a 'speedy' peace settlement, 22 June 1945; Wanted to fight on even after the dropping of the atomic bombs and the Japanese acceptance of the Potsdam declaration for unconditional surrender, 13 August 1945;[2] Requested to join an army *coup* by the 1st Imperial Guards Division to occupy the Imperial Palace to safeguard the Emperor (and prolong the war) but was evasive stating he 'did not disapprove', 14 August 1945; Signed the Instrument of Surrender on board USS *Missouri* on behalf of the Japanese armed forces, Tokyo Bay, 2 September 1945;[3] Arrested as a Class A war criminal; Indicted on 39 charges including waging an aggressive war and tried by the International Tribunal for the Far East, Tokyo, 26 April 1946–12 November 1948; Found guilty and sentenced to life imprisonment (although not in court for sentence due to illness); Died of cancer, 8 January 1949.

[1] The Tangku armistice set up a demilitarized zone between Manchuria and China.
[2] Previously he had called upon everything on Japanese soil (both physical and spiritual) for the war effort to ensure 'certain victory'.
[3] Only agreed to do this after a personal request by the Emperor.

UNO
Major-General; Surrendered 2,500 troops to Australian Lieutenant-Colonel Robson at Bandjermasin, southern Borneo, 17 September 1945.

USHIJIMA Mitsuru
Lieutenant-General; Commander of 32nd Army (under 10th Area Army – R. ANDO), Okinawa, Ryukyu Islands (replacing M. WATANABE), 8 August 1944; Ordered transfer of 9th Division to Formosa, December 1944; Lost half of 32nd's ammunition in a large explosion, December 1944 (and it was not replaced); Army consisted of 24th Division (T. AMAYIA), 62nd Division (K. ARIKAWA, T. FUJIOKA), 5th Artillery Command (K. WADA), 44th IMB (S. SUZUKI), a Tank Regiment, 19th Air Sector Command – Giving a total of 67,000 regular army and 33,000 irregular troops; Okinawa Naval Base Force (Rear-Admiral M. OTA) with 9,000 men also under 32nd Army command, plus the Okinawa Home Guard (Boeitai) of 17,000–20,000 men; HQ Shuri Castle in the south of the island; Command reorganized, February 1945; Built up the defence of the island against an expected American attack with the bulk of his forces in the south, by March 1945; Not given his own air defence; American naval forces began mine-clearing operations along the south-east coast, 24 March 1945; Kerama Retto islands

invaded by the Americans, 26-7 March 1945; American 10th Army commenced landings on mid–north-west Okinawa (Hagushi area) against little opposition, from 1 April 1945; American forces reached mid–north-east coast cutting the island in two, 3 April 1945; Mountain region of Motobu Peninsula in the north was defended to the death by 'Udo Force' (under Colonel Udo) until 20 April 1945 (with 2,000 Japanese killed); Ie Shima Island (defended by 7,000 troops) invaded by American forces, 16 April 1945; Ie Shima declared secure by Americans (with 4,706 known Japanese dead and 149 captured), 21 April 1945; American attack on main Japanese forces on Okinawa commenced the first week of April 1945; Abortive Japanese counter-attacks against the American 96th Division (in the centre) resulted in 1,584 Japanese killed, 13-14 April 1945; American 27th Division launched a massive attack but had been forced to halt because of heavy fire, underground fortifications and suicide tactics, by 20 April 1945;* Heavy enemy pressure forced a tactical Japanese withdrawal along the centre and right line by 24 April 1945; The Americans relieved their 27th and 96th Divisions with two fresh divisions by 27 April 1945; Japanese forces concentrated in the extreme south to defend the Shuri area by 27 April 1945; Persuaded by Chief of Staff I. CHO and staff to launch a 'decisive' all-out counter-attack by the whole of the remaining 32nd Army forces with 24th Division (T. AMAMIYA) in the van plus an amphibious action and co-ordinated *Kamikaze* air attack; Attack launched, 4 May 1945; Americans caught by surprise but the seaborne flanking movement by Japanese 26th Shipping Engineers failed; Heavy American artillery fire and infantry resistance stopped the attack, inflicting very heavy Japanese losses, forcing a return to the original defensive positions, 5 May 1945; Tactics became holding actions in defensively prepared positions with minor offensive infiltration raids into the American lines; Dakeshi Ridge, just north of Shuri, taken by the Americans, 11-12 May 1945; Americans launched attacks on Shuri eastern and western flanks, 14 May 1945; Bitter fighting delayed the American advance; Outskirts of Shuri reached by American 77th Division, 20 May 1945; Ordered reinforcement of north and east of Shuri defences; Agreed at a staff conference to withdraw to the Kiyamu Peninsula in the south (which was honeycombed with caves) for the final defence of the island; Withdrawal (covered by a rear-guard), 23-30 May 1945; Defensive line across the Kiyamu Peninsula complete by 4 June 1945; Oroku Peninsula (in mid west of the island) was attacked by US marines who cut off and destroyed 32nd Army reserves (formed from the naval forces under Rear-Admiral M. OTA), 4-14 June 1945; HQ established in a cave near Mabuni Village; Army split up; Notified IGHQ, Tokyo, that further resistance was no longer possible; Mabuni attacked by American 7th Division, 19 June 1945; Committed suicide (traditional *seppuku* with a dagger and was then decapitated by the HQ adjutant, at the same time as his C of S I. CHO), evening of 21 June 1945; Island declared secure by the Americans, 22 June 1945.

Note: This was the costliest operation of the Pacific war for American forces. Japanese loses estimated at 107,539 with 23,764 entombed in caves and 10,755 captured. These figures probably include 42,000 civilian casualties.

*American naval ships and army artillery opened a concentrated barrage on the 5-mile-long Shuri defence line, firing 19,000 shells, 19 April 1945. This was the greatest single concentration of artillery of the Pacific war, but the Japanese forces withstood it.

USHIROKU Jun (Gen)

Born 1884; 2nd Lieutenant (infantry) in 38th Infantry Regiment, April 1905; 53rd Infantry Regiment, January 1906; 1st Lieutenant, December 1907; Adjutant to 19th Infantry Brigade, January 1909; Attached to Training Unit of Military Academy, December 1912; Captain in 53rd Infantry Regiment, April 1915; Graduated from War College, November 1917; Assigned to Kwantung Government-General, Manchuria, September 1918; Staff Officer in 3rd Division, July 1919; Staff Officer in 5th Division, Vladivostock, Siberia, August 1919; Major, July 1921; Army General Staff, February 1923; Lieutenant-Colonel, March 1925; Kwantung Army HQ, Manchuria, August 1925; Colonel and Commander of 48th Infantry Regiment, August 1929; Staff Officer in 4th Division, August 1931; Kwantung Army HQ, Manchuria, February 1932; Major-General, March 1934; Chief of 3rd Bureau (Transport and Communications) of Army General Staff, August 1934; Chief of Personnel Affairs Bureau of War Ministry, August 1935; Various appointments until 1944 (including promotion to Lieutenant-General); General; Senior Deputy Chief of Army General Staff, February 1944; Suggested suicide tactics by soldiers carrying satchel charges on their backs because of shortages of anti-tank weapons; Idea approved by IGHQ, Tokyo, and orders issued to this effect; This resulted in severe criticism by fellow officers who thought it a useless waste of life; Concurrently Inspector-General of Military Aviation (replacing T. YASUDA) and Chief of Aviation HQ, 28 March 1944; Commander of forces on Saipan Island, Marianas; Saipan invaded by Americans, 16 June 1944;* Presumably left Saipan before its capture in late July 1944; Replaced and transferred to Manchuria (in disgrace for ordering suicide tactics by his men during the Saipan defence), July 1944; Commander-in-Chief of 3rd Area Army (under Kwantung Army – O. YAMADA), Manchuria, consisting of 30th Army (S. IIDA) and 44th Army (Y. HONGO); HQ Mukden; Russia invaded Manchuria, 9 August 1945; Ignored Kwantung Army plan to withdraw to defensive positions, but instead he ordered 44th Army to counter-attack to protect Mukden – Port Arthur line and Japanese settlers; Because he was protected by high-ranking officers in Tokyo, including ex-premier H. TOJO, this disobedience was not overruled by C in C Kwantung Army O. YAMADA; All his forces had disintergrated with heavy loses by 13 August 1945; Manchurian troops mutinied at Hsinking (Changchun) which prevented regrouping, 13 August 1945; Gave assurance to O. YAMADA that he would follow instructions (but it was to late); Unofficially authorized surrender but was countermanded by O. YAMADA until official confirmation was received from Japan; Formal Kwantung Army surrender, 21 August 1945; Surrendered to the Russians and was held as a prisoner until repatriation in 1956.

*He was probably on an inspection tour and took over temporary command since it appears he was not relieved of his post as Senior Deputy Chief of Army General Staff until July 1944.

USUI Kengo

Major-General; Commander of Muroran Defence Command, Muroran, Hokkaido, Japan, September 1943.

UTSONOMIYA

Major-General; Deputy Chief of Staff to 14th Area Army, Philippines, from 20 October 1944.*

*This posting is unconfirmed since it conflicts with that of NISHIMURA Toshio. This entry and date was obtained from *The Four Samurai* by A. Swinson (*see* Bibliography). It is of course possible that the dating for NISHIMURA Toshio is incorrect and that UTSONOMIYA replaced him.

WACHI Takaji (Takeji)

Chief of Special Service, Peking, China; Arranged the 'Marco Polo Bridge Incident', Peking, which precipitated the Sino-Japanese war, 7 July 1937 (see also K. TASHIRO); Major-General; Chief of Staff to Formosa Army; Chief of Staff to 14th Army (under M. HONMA), Philippines (replacing M. MAEDA), March or May 1942; Appeared as a defence witness in the war crimes trial of M. HONMA, Manila, Philippines, 1946.*

*He claimed that M. HONMA ordered that prisoners be 'moved' to the rear but did not specify how this was to be done, since this was left to a Colonel Takasu. He therefore did not order the infamous 'Bataan Death March'. (See also I. KAWANE.)

WADA Kosuke

Major-General; Commander of 5th Artillery Command (under 32nd Army – M. USHIJIMA) for the defence of Okinawa Island, Ryukyus, late 1944; Command consisted of 27th Tank Regiment, 1st, 23rd Medium Artillery Regiments, 100th Heavy Artillery Battery, 1st Independent Mortar Regiment (six batteries of 320mm spigot mortars firing huge 675lb shells) and other units; HQ Itokazu; Utilized in southern section to defend against an expected American attack from the south-east against the Minatogawa region, which did not materialize; Americans landed in mid–north-west of Island, 1 April 1945; Ordered to concentrate in Shuri defensive area because of American pressure from the north by 27 April 1945; Ordered to participate in an all-out counter-attack by the whole of 32nd Army commencing 4 May 1945; Heavy American artillery fire negated any success and the attack failed, 5 May 1945; Ordered to retire to Kunishi – Makabe – Madeara area; Withdrew 23-30 May 1945; Supported army resistance with heavy artillery fire; Army split up by 19 June 1945; Dead (killed or suicide) by the time Okinawa was declared secure by the Americans, 22 June 1945.

Personal facts: Regarded as a brilliant strategist.

WAKAMATSU

Believed to be a General officer; Head of General Affairs Bureau of Army General Staff, Tokyo, 1944.

WAKAMATSU Heiji

Major-General; Commander of Home Station for one infantry unit at Miyakonejo in Miyasaki Regimental District, Japan, March 1945.

WAKAMATSU Tadaichi

Lieutenant-General; Vice Minister of War at the time of the Japanese surrender, August 1945.

WAKAMATSU Yujiro

Colonel; Army Veterinary Service; Major-General; Commander of 'Hippo–Epizootic Administration of Kwantung Army', Manchuria, with 600–800 personnel (set up in 1935-6) and code-named 'Detachment 100', 1941; This was a top secret centre for research into bacteriological weapons, located near Mogatong village, 10 kilometres south of Hsinking; Directly under the control of C in C Kwantung Army (see also S. ISHII, T. TAKAHASHI); Ordered the deliberate infection of the River Derbul on the Soviet border in north Khingan province with 'glanders' and 'anthrax', 1942; Deliberately infected human subjects (prisoners) with various lethal bacteria for study purposes (any survivors were killed), 1944.

WATANABE Hiroshi

Major-General; Chief of Staff to 3rd Area Army, Tsitsihar, Manchuria, October 1943; Lieutenant-General; Commander of 47th Division, 1944; Division stationed in Hirosaki Divisional District, Japan, until September 1944; Division transferred to Woosung–Hangchow area, east China, September–October 1945; Hengyang area, central China, early 1945.

WATANABE Jotaro

General; Inspector-General of Military Education (replacing J. MAZAKI) in Admiral K. OKADA cabinet, July 1935; Assassinated by young army officers in '2-26 Insurrection' merely because he had dared to take the place of the reactionary J. MAZAKI who had much support among junior officers, 26 February 1936.*

*See K. KASHI for details of the insurrection.

WATANABE Masao

Major-General; Commander of 52nd Independent Mixed Brigade, Ponape Island, Carolines, from its activation in May 1944.

Note: Possibly same as next entry.

WATANABE Masao

Lieutenant-General; Commander of 32nd Army (under 10th Area Army), Okinawa, Ryukyu Islands, from its activation in March 1944; Army consisted of two divisions and one Mixed Brigade but later increased to four divisions; Replaced (by M. USHIJIMA), August 1944.
Note: Possibly same as last entry.

WATANABE Masaru

Major-General; Commander of 9th Field Replacement Unit, Tokyo?, February 1944; Located in Yincheng, central China, July 1944.

WATANABE Nagashi

Lieutenant-General; Commander of 47th Division (under 20th Army), during the Battle of western Hunan, China, early April–early June 1945.

WATANABE Nobuyoshi

Major-General; Commander of 5th Shipping Transport Command, April 1944; Located at Otaru, Hokkaido, Japan, November 1944; Concurrently Commander of 3rd Shipping Company, also at Otaru.

WATARI Hisao

Lieutenant-General by 1939; Killed or died in China.

WATARI Sakon

Major-General; Commander of 29th Independent Mixed Brigade, Siam, May 1944.

YAHAGI Nakao

Major-General; Chief of Staff to 25th Army, Fort de Kock, Sumatra, October 1944? – end of war; Received surrender orders on board LSI *Persimmon* at Emmahaven (the port of Padang, Sumatra), 10 October 1945.

YAMADA Eizo

Major-General; Commander of 1st Shipping Group, February 1943; Commander of army forces at Finschhafen harbour, New Guinea; Reinforced by 20th Division (S. KATAGIRI), 10 October 1943; Fortified Sattelberg (six miles from Finschhafen); Launched numerous attacks against Australians but forced to abandon Sattelberg and Finschhafen, 25 October 1943.

YAMADA Ginzo (Kingo) 山 田 金 吾

A General officer (or equivalent) known only from a surrender or transportation label on a sword with a General Officer's knot.[1] It translates as: 'RIKUGUN' (army), 'SENNIN' (full-time service), 'SHOKUTAKU' (part-time employment), 'YAMADA', 'GINZO' (or 'KINGO'), 18500 (unidentified unit code-number), OKA (code-name of 7th Area Army), 'BUTAI' (unit or organization), i.e., Yamada Ginzo in part-time/full-time army employment in a (unidentified) unit of 7th Area Army.[2]

Note: The inference from this label is that this man was a high-ranking *Gunzoku* (civilian adviser to the army). This organization had its own uniforms, insignia and officer ranks, but carried army-style swords with army-pattern sword knots. However they were not regarded as military personnel by the Japanese army. This entry has only been included since the interpretation has not been confirmed.

[1] Civilian mounted *katana* with good quality hilt fittings and civilian scabbard converted to military use. General officer's knot. 17th-century blade signed 'KOZUKE (NO) KAMI FUJIWARA JUMYO', i.e., Fujiwara Jumyo, lord of Kozuke. Now in a private collection in England.
[2] Each army unit had a code-number and code-name. The number for 7th Area Army was 1615 and the code-name was 'OKA'. The number 18500 has not been identified but is probably that of one of the subordinate units. 7th Area Army HQ was located at Singapore, Malaya, but by the end of the war, it controlled Malaya, Sumatra, Java, Borneo, and Timor area.

YAMADA Kunitaro

Lieutenant-General; Commander of 48th division (under 16th Army – Y. NAGANO), Timor and Lesser Sundas, November 1944; Placed under 2nd Army control (F. TESHIMA) after the ceasefire; Surrendered at Koepang, 3 October 1945.

Note: His sword is now in the Australian War Memorial Museum. Cat. no. AWM 20493. A *shin-guntō* with a blade signed 'TADAYOSHI' and dated 1936.

YAMADA Otozō

Born 1881; Family name Ichikawa; 2nd Lieutenant (cavalry) in 3rd Cavalry Regiment, June 1903; 1st Lieutenant, February 1905; Served with gallantry in Russo-Japanese War, 1904-5; War College, December 1909-12; Captain in 3rd Cavalry Regiment, September 1912; Army General Staff, August 1913; Instructor at Cavalry School, November 1914; Instructor at War College, January 1917; Major and Instructor at Cavalry school, June 1917; Lieutenant-Colonel at Office of Cavalry Training (Inspectorate General of Military Training), August 1922; Commander of 26th Cavalry Regiment, Toyohashi, Japan, September 1922; Colonel, August 1925; Chief of Staff to Korea Army, March 1926; Army General Staff, July 1927; Major-General and Chief of Training Branch of Cavalry school, August 1930; Commander of 4th Cavalry Brigade, Nagoya, Japan, August 1931; Chief of Army Signal School, August 1932; Chief of 3rd Bureau (Transport and

Communications) of Army General Staff, August 1933; Lieutenant-General and Chief of Personnel Bureau of Army General Staff, August 1934; Chief of 3rd Bureau of Army General Staff, August 1935; Superintendent of Military Academy, December 1935; Commander of 12th Division, HQ Tunging, Manchuria, March–December 1937; Commander of 3rd Army, HQ Mutanchiang, Manchuria, January 1938; Commander-in-Chief of China Expeditionary Army, HQ Nanking, China, December 1938–October 1939; Inspectorate General of Military Training, October 1939–July 1944; General, August 1940; Concurrently Commander-in-Chief of General Defence Command, July–December 1941; Concurrently Member of Supreme War Council, from 1943; Commander-in-Chief of Kwantung Army (replacing Y. UMEZU), Manchuria, July 1944; HQ Hsinking (Changchun); Army consisted of 21 divisions of poor quality; Four best divisions and one-third of war *matériel* transferred to other theatres; Direct controller of secret bacteriological warfare 'Detachments 100 and 731' (*see* S. ISHII, Y. WAKAMATSU); Sanctioned experiments on captured civilians; Called up a quarter of a million Japanese civilians in Manchuria as army reinforcements, from early 1944; Attended a conference at Dairen, south Manchuria, to discuss the defence of China and Manchuria with C in C China Expeditionary Army Y. OKAMURA and the Chief of General Staff Y. UMEZU, May 1945; Stated that he could not hold the Manchurian border with current strength of only eleven divisions (thirteen divisions had been transferred) by June 1945; IGHQ, Tokyo, insisted on a new defence plan with a concentration of forces in northern Korea and along the Hsinking – Tumen and Hsinking – Port Arthur railways, 30 May 1945; Activated eight new divisions and seven brigades from conscripts (who were poorly trained and ill equipped), 1 August 1945; Forces consisted of 3rd Area Army (J. USHIROKU), 1st Area Army (S. KITA) and 4th Army (M. UEMURA) giving a total of 663,000 men plus 117,000 men of the Manchukuo puppet army; Russians invaded Manchuria, 9 August 1945; 17th Area Army (Y. KOZUKI) in Korea finally assigned to Kwantung Army control after previous requests were refused by the Emperor on the grounds that it was a 'home army', 9 August 1945; Signed the orders for the destruction of all bacteriological warfare centres (and the deaths of all prisoners held there), 10 August 1945; Disobeyed by 3rd Area Army Commander J. USHIROKU who mounted a counter-attack and refused to fall back to agreed defensive positions, but was forced to sanction his actions because of his protection by high-ranking officers in Tokyo including ex-premier H. TOJO; Ordered the transfer of 'capital city' status from Hsinking to Tunghua, 9 August 1945; All forces in Manchuria disintegrated with heavy loses by 13 August 1945; Received assurances from J. USHIROKU that he would follow orders (but it was to late), 14 August 1945; Kwantung Army all but defeated by the time of the Emperor's surrender broadcast, 15 August 1945; Convened a staff conference to discuss the surrender and recommended acceptance despite opposition from those who first wanted ceasefire orders direct from IGHQ, Tokyo, 16 August 1945; Received confirmation of the surrender from Prince Takeda who flew from Tokyo to Hsinking; Chiefs of Staff of all land and air armies were informed of the surrender at Hsinking, 18 August 1945; Chief of Staff H. HATA received surrender orders from Russian C in C Far East Marshal Vasilevsky at their HQ at Jeliho, 19 August 1945; Formal surrender of Kwantung Army at Hsinking (Chanchun), 21 August 1945; Kwantung Army HQ occupied by the Russians who took complete control of all army functions and operations, 22 August 1945 (594,000 Japanese including 148 General officers surrendered, most being sent to Siberia); Tried by Russian Military tribunal at Khabarovsk for war crimes relating to bacteriological warfare and experimentation, and sentenced to 25 years in a labour correction camp, December 1949; Released in June 1956 and repatriated in ill health.

YAMADA Seiichi
Lieutenant-General; Commander of 5th Division, Kai and Aroe Islands, from October 1944 (Possibly replacing T. YAMAMOTO).

YAMADA Shigeru
Major-General; Commander of 4th Engineers Unit, June 1943; Located in north-west New Guinea, March 1944.

YAMAGATA Kurihanao (Tsuyo)
Lieutenant-General; Commander of 26th Division (under 35th Army – S. SUZUKI), Leyte Island, Philippines, arriving early November 1944 (see S. SUZUKI for campaign details); Division virtually destroyed by late December 1944.

YAMAGATA (YAMANATA) Rikao
Major-General; Commander of 21st Independent Mixed Brigade; Landed at Buna, New Guinea to protect the beaches of Gona, Buna and Sanananda (reinforcing forces under K. ODA), early December 1942; Attacked by the 7th Australian Division (and later by the American 41st Division) which captured Buna village, 14 December 1942; Sanananda captured by the enemy, 14 January 1943; Escaped in a landing craft (before all Japanese resistance ceased on 23 January 1943) after deliberately throwing out wounded Japanese soldiers from the vessel.

YAMAGUCHI Takeo
Major-General; Commander of 53rd Independent Mixed Brigade, Babelthaup, Palau Islands, from its activation in June 1944.

YAMAJI Hideo
Lieutenant-General; Commander of 3rd Armoured Division, March 1944; Engaged in Honan operations, China, March-April 1944; Later in Hsiangcheng area, Honan province, north China.

YAMAMOTO
Lieutenant-General; Commander of Ordnance Depot, Hiroshima, Japan, by August 1945; Lived on Ushita hillside, outside Hiroshima, and thus escaped injury from the atomic bomb blast, 5 August 1945; Rendered assistance to S. MATSUMURA (see also Y. FUJII).

YAMAMOTO Bin
Major-General; Principal of the Nakano (espionage and saboteur) School (replacing O. KAWAMATA), Japan, March 1945–until closure at the end of the war, September? 1945.*

*See O. KAWAMATA for details of the school and location of its branches.

YAMAMOTO Kenji
Major-General; Commander of 8th Air Division (under 6th Air Army – M. SUGAWARA); Responsible for the camouflage of aircraft on the ground

throughout Kyushu and Honshu, Japan, by March 1945; Created *Kamikaze* (suicide) units from air schools to form 8th School Special Attack Squadron, March 1945.

YAMAMOTO Kiyoe

Major-General; Commander of 5th Special Railway Command, January 1943; Located at Rangoon, Burma, February 1944; Concurrently Commander of Burma Railway Unit, March 1944.

Note: Also reported to be Acting Commander of 15th Division, Mandalay area, Burma, from February 1945, but this appears incorrect, unless the same as YAMAMOTO Seiei.

YAMAMOTO Mitsuo

Lieutenant-General; Commander of 3rd Division (under 11th Army) during the Battle of Changsha – Hengyang, China, late May–early August 1944; Engaged in the Battle of Kweilin–Liuchow, early September–mid December 1944; HQ Nanning, February 1945.

YAMAMOTO Seiei

Major-General; Chief of Staff to 33rd Army under M. HONDA (replacing T. KATAKURA), Burma, late 1944; Replaced (by R. SAWAMOTO) January? 1945; Commander of 15th Division (replacing R. SHIBATA), under 15th Army (S. KATAMURA), Burma, January? 1945;* Ordered to prevent a British thrust at Mandalay and reinforced with 119th Regiment (from 53rd Division), January 1945; Ordered by C in C 15th Army S. KATAMURA to defend Mandalay to the death with 51st, 60th, 67th Infantry Regiments; HQ Fort Dufferin, Mandalay; Mandalay Hill lost to the Gurkhas, 12 March 1945; Heavily defended Fort Dufferin; 15th Army cancelled previous order in favour of a withdrawal, 18 March 1945; Main body of 15th Division withdrew from Mandalay leaving it open for the Allies, 19 March 1945; Reached Toungoo, 19 April 1945.

*Could possibly be the same as YAMAMOTO Kiyoe.

YAMAMOTO Shigeichi (Moichiro)

Captain; Seconded to the British Army, serving with the 3rd Infantry Brigade at Bardon, Hampshire, England, 1929;[1] Major-General; Military Governor of Java, by 1945; Concurrently Chief of Staff to 16th Army (under Y. NAGANO) by the time of the cessation of hostilities, August 1945; Received surrender orders (together with NISHIMURA and Rear-Admiral M. MAEDA) from Rear-Admiral W. R. Patterson, C in C 5th Cruiser Squadron, on board HMS *Cumberland* at Tandjoenpriok (Jakarta's port), Java, 16 September 1945; Formally surrendered his sword to Lieutenant-General Sir Philip Chistison, C in C Allied Forces Netherlands East Indies, at the Dutch KPM Hall, Jakarta;[2] Surrendered another sword (together with Y. NAGANO) to Major-General D. C. Hawthorn, GOC 23rd Indian Division, Batavia, October 1945; Both were immediately arrested by order of Major-General Hawthorn for allowing arms to be handed over to Indonesian nationalists in contravention of Allied surrender orders;[3] Flown to Singapore, Malaya, for a judicial inquiry (*see also* NAKAMURA); Dismissed from command by order of Japanese Southern Army GHQ.

[1] Spoke very good English.
[2] Recognized by Christison who had served with him when he was in England. He said 'General, my shame is very great. I did so hope you would not recognise me . . . I would like you to have my family

sword which was made in Bizen in the sixteenth century'. Sir Philip, in his nineties, returned this sword to Yamamoto's widow in 1990 as a gesture of good will. Sir Philip Christison was formerly C in C Allied Land Forces South East Asia (ALFSEA) 6 July–15 August 1945.
[3] See NAGANO Yuichiro for a quotation of the actual charge.

YAMAMOTO Toshi

Major-General; Chief of Staff to 13th Army; Shanghai, China, December 1944.

YAMAMOTO Tsunoru

Major-General; Infantry Group Commander of 33rd Division (under M. YANA-GIDA), Burma, by 1944; Formed extreme right column of 33rd Division for advance against Imphal, India (known as 'Yamamoto Force'); Reinforced by a battalion from 15th Division, March 1944; Captured Witok, 19 March 1944; Moved up Kabaw Valley; Forced a British evacuation and self-destruction of their own large supply dump at Moreh, 31 March 1944; Made many attempts to capture the vital Palel airfield (approx. five miles from the Imphal plain) but failed because of the stubborn defence of the British 20th Division, April–June 1944; Driven back by British forces; Ordered by 15th Army (R. MUTAGUCHI) to withdraw into Kabaw Valley from the Shenam–Tengnoupal area, 13 July 1944; Refused to obey direct 15th Army orders and acted on his own initiative, late July 1944; Retreated with remnant and stragglers from 15th Division to Sittaung on the Chindwin River, establishing HQ at Yazagyo; Arrived 2 August 1944; Ordered to cover the retreat of 33rd Division main body but refused, sending only a token force; Commander of 72nd Independent Mixed Brigade (under direct command of 28th Army – S. SAKURAI) at Yenangyaung, Burma, from its activation in December 1944; Placed under 55th Division (T. HANAYA) and code-named 'Kantetsu Force'; Formed part of the rearguard to protect 55th Division crossing of the Irrawaddy River, May 1945.

YAMAMOTO Tsutomi

Lieutenant-General; Commander of 5th Division, Kuala Lumpur vicinity, Malaya, from May 1942; Division transferred to Ambon–Dutch New Guinea area, late 1942; Division transferred to Kai and Aroe Islands, early 1944; (Possibly replaced by S. YAMADA).*

*It has not been established whether he was still in command during these transfers.

YAMAMURA H.

Major-General; Commander of 71st Independent Mixed Brigade, Kuching area, Sarawak in Borneo, under 37th Army (M. BABA), by 1945; Surrendered to Australian Brigadier T. Eastick on board HMAS *Kapunda* off Kuching, 11 September 1945;*

*Surrendered a sword at this time. A *shin-guntō* with General Officer's knot. Blade signed 'BISHU OSAFUNE (NO) JU SUKENAGA', i.e., Sukenaga living at Osafune in Bishu. c.1830. Now in the Australian War Memorial Museum. Cat. no. AWM 20320.

YAMAOKA Shigeatsu

Born 1884; Major-General; Director of War Ministry Equipment and Supplies Bureau, c.1935; Implicated in the murder of the Chief of the Military Affairs Bureau T. NAGATA, July 1935; Sympathised with the 'Strike North' faction (i.e., against Russia) and became an embarrassment to his seniors; Posted to a field command, August 1935; Retired or discharged from the army, 1939.
Note: A keen swordsman. He was a shinto fanatic who worshipped the ghosts in

old samurai sword blades. He had a personal collection of more than one hundred historic blades. Announced the regulation that all army officers should own a sword and wear it at public ceremonies.

YAMASHITA Tomoyuki (Hobun) 山 下　　 秦 文

Born 8 November 1885 in Osugi Village, Shikoku Island; Son of a local doctor; Lived with his uncle at Koichi; Went to Kainen Middle School where he received a military education which fired his ambition; Enrolled as a Military Cadet at Hiroshima Military College, 1900?; Selected to go on to Central Military Academy, Tokyo, 1903?; 2nd Lieutenant (infantry), June 1906; Posted to 11th Infantry Regiment, Hiroshima; Entered War College and graduated in November 1916; Attached to Army General Staff, August 1917; Member of Army General Staff, February 1918; Military Student at the Japanese Embassy in Berne, Switzerland, April 1919; Military Student in Germany, July 1921; Major; Member of Military Affairs Bureau at War Ministry, Tokyo, July 1922; Instructor at War College, March 1926; Lieutenant-Colonel; Military Attaché to Vienna, Austria, and concurrently, to Hungary, February 1927; Recalled to Tokyo; Colonel; Commander of 3rd Infantry Regiment, Tokyo, August 1930; Chief of Army Affairs Section of Military Affairs Bureau (responsible for mobilization, defence and military expenditure), Tokyo, April 1931; Appointed mediator between young rebel army officers and the War Ministry in the '2-26 Insurrection', 26 February 1936; Considered sympathetic to the rebel cause by other senior officers which caused him to consider whether or not he should resign; Major-General; Commander of 40th Infantry Brigade, Korea (which was considered a punishment for his sympathetic views since it was an overseas posting), March 1936; Commander of China Mixed Brigade, August 1937; Lieutenant-General, November 1937; Chief of Staff to North China Area Army, July 1938; Commander of 4th Division, Manchuria?, September 1939; Head of 'Unit 82' (detailed planning of 'Strike South' policy against Malaya, East Indies, etc.), based on Formosa, 1940; Head of a military mission (observer team) to Germany and Italy (while concurrently still head of 'Unit 82'), December 1940;[1] Met Mussolini and Hitler, leaving Germany before the attack on Russia; Arrived in Japan, June 1941; His report recommended the unification of all Japanese armed services, improvement of the airforce and privately considered that the Japanese – Axis alliance was a poor policy; Military Councillor, June 1941; Commander of Kwantung Defence Army (including Kwantung Special Man-oeuvre Force which was a special large scale 'Strike South' exercise), Manchuria, July–November 1941;[2] Recalled to Tokyo and appointed Commander of 25th Army (replacing S. IIDA) which was completing training on Hainan Island, off south China, November 1941; Instructed to invade Malaya and seize Singapore when war was declared; Army consisted of 2nd Imperial Guards (T. NISHIMURA) which were untried in battle, 5th Division (T. MATSUI), 18th Division (R. MUTAGUCHI), 56th Division (held in reserve), 3rd Tank Brigade (80 tanks), 3rd Air Group (M. SUGAWARA), Artillery, Engineers, etc,; Sailed with 5th Division from Samah Port, Hainan, 4 December 1941; Landed at Singora, Siam, 8 December 1941; Joined by 2nd Imperial Guards Division; Other landings made at Patani and Kota Bharu, 8 December 1941; Advanced down east and west sides of Malaya, breaking the British defensive lines and incorporating seaborne out-flanking landings; 56th Division released from campaign before embarkation was necessary (for general campaign details *see* S. KAWAMURA, T. MATSUI, R. MUTAGUCHI, T. NISHIMURA); Siege of Singapore commenced on 31 January

1942; HQ north of Johore; Losses reduced 25th Army strength to 30,000 men with minimal supplies (against 100,000 well-supplied British troops who did not know of the Japanese weakness); HQ moved to the Sultan's palace, Johore; 5th Division commenced the attack on Singapore, 9 February 1942; HQ moved to Singapore Island, 10? February 1942; Japanese committed atrocities at Alexandra Military Hospital; Singapore finally surrendered, 15 February 1942 (see also T. NISHIMURA, IMAYE); Concurrently Military Commander of Malaya and Sumatra, until July 1942; Replaced (possibly by T. KUSABA); Transferred direct to Manchuria as Commander-in-Chief of 1st Area Army, Bontenko, Siberian border, before he could read his victory speech to the Emperor, July 1942;[3] HQ Hsingking; General, February 1943 (while in Manchuria); Ordered to Tokyo (after the fall of the Premier H. TOJO), August? 1944; Commander-in-Chief of 14th Area Army, (replacing S. KURODA), Philippines, September 1944; HQ Manila, Luzon Island; Army comprised four divisions on Luzon and 35th Army (S. SUZUKI) which had 16th Division on Leyte, 30th, 100th Divisions on Mindanao and 102nd Division distributed on islands to the west; Realized the Philippines would eventually be lost; Ordered 35th Army (S. SUZUKI) on Leyte Island to bear the brunt of the expected American attack without reinforcements while he prepared the defences of Luzon; Leyte invaded 20 October 1944; IGHQ, Tokyo, ordered the reinforcement of Leyte against his wishes; Reinforcement convoys to Leyte were virtually destroyed; 1st, 26th Divisions (from China) were landed with losses; Ormoc port lost; Ordered the capture of all airstrips to maintain reinforcement links but this failed; IGHQ, Tokyo, eventually realized further reinforcement was impossible and allowed the evacuation of Leyte which was undertaken from late December 1944; Luzon was reinforced with 10th, 19th, 23rd Divisions; Americans invaded Luzon, first week of January 1945; Personally commanded the defence of Luzon; Split his forces into three which comprised 'SHOBU' Group (under his personal command) in north (with 152,000 men including four divisions), HQ Baguio; 'KEMBU' Group (R. TSUKADA) in centre (with 30,000 men); 'SHIMBU' Group (newly formed 41st Army under S. YOKOYAMA) in south (with 80,000 men including two divisions); 4th Air Army (K. TOMINAGA) came under direct control of 14th Area Army, 1 January 1945; Ordered Manila to be abandoned but 41st Army was to defend it to the south; Naval troops were not under army command and disagreed with the abandonment of Manila (see Vice-Admiral D. OKOCHI, Rear-Admiral S. IWABUCHI); They refused to leave or allow themselves to be extricated and fought to the last man, committing atrocities; Manila captured by American forces, 4 March 1945; Determined to hold the Cagayan Valley to maintain food supplies and prevent American use of the airfields but was forced out; HQ moved to Bambang Village further into the mountains; Baguio captured by American army; HQ withdrawn further into Sierra Madre mountains to Kiangan; Cagayan Valley finally lost, 26 June 1945; Last HQ on Mount Prog, June 1945; Formally ordered to cease fire by HQ Southern Army (under H. TERAUCHI), 19 August 1945; Surrendered, with only 50,000 men left, to Major-General R. S. Beightler, C in C Luzon Area Command, near Kiangan, 2 September 1945; Formally signed the surrender (together with Vice-Admiral D. OKOCHI) and handed over his sword to Major General W. H. Gill, GOC American 32nd Division, at Government House, Baguio, 3 September 1945 (also present were Lieutenant General J. Wainwright, US Army, who was defeated at Corregidor, and Lieutenant-General Sir Arthur Percival who was defeated at Singapore);[4] Taken to New Bilibid prison; Tried as a Class A war criminal, Manila, 29 October 1945; 123 charges involving the deaths of 57,000 people (including naval atrocities at Manila); Guilty, and sentenced to death, 7 December 1945; Hanged at Bilibid prison, 23 February 1946.

Personal facts: Involved with the 'Imperial Way' political faction which was an utra-nationalist organization wanting to restore traditional virtues under the Emperor, free from the influence of big business and political parties. Ambitious, ruthless, highly strung and believed in Samurai traditions. Suffered a persecution complex in that he thought H. TOJO wanted to assassinate him. Had a habit of snoring and appearing to be asleep when listening to briefings. His final campaign is regarded as one of the most effective delaying actions in history. Respected by his contemporaries and said to be the best of Japanese generals.

[1] According to *A Soldier must Hang* by J. D. Potter (*see* Bibliography) he was Inspector-General of the Air Force in 1940 which conflicts with this appointment and seems incongruous since he had held no previous air force posts.
[2] This overseas posting was at the instigation of Premier H. TOJO who had become jealous of him.
[3] By order of H. TOJO who now regarded him as a rival. Although an important post, it was safe from Tokyo intrigues.
[4] The sword surrendered at Baguio was subsquently presented to West Point Military Academy. It is a *shin-guntō* with a General Officer's knot. Blade signed by FUJIWARA KANENAGA, possibly of Sagami province, c.1640-80.

YAMAUCHI Masafumi (Masabumi)

Military Attaché to Japanese Embassy, Washington, USA; Lieutenant-General; Commander of 15th Division, China; Division transferred via Siam (where it was held up for road construction duties) to Burma (under 15th Army – R. MUTAGUCHI); Crossed the Chindwin River at Thaungdut, mid March 1944; Formed southern column for the assault on Kohima from the south and Imphal from the north; Accused of delaying his advance along the Kohima–Imphal road; Shangshak taken by 31st Division (S. MIYAZAKI) instead of 15th Division, 23-5 March 1944; Became seriously ill with tuberculosis; Division ill equipped, undermanned and possessed no anti-tank weapons; Accused of cowardice by C in C 15th Army R. MUTAGUCHI who decided not to deal with him but run the division through 15th Division Chief of Staff K. OKADA; Cut the Imphal–Kohima road at Kangpoki, 3 April 1944; Thought the British were retreating which conflicted with the opinion of C of S K. OKADA; Encountered British tanks at Kemang but could not defend against them, 4 April 1944; Advance halted ten miles from Imphal at Nungishigum Hill by tanks (which almost destroyed the 3rd Battalion of 51st Regiment), 6-13 April 1944; Removed from command by order of R. MUTAGUCHI on grounds of ill health and the excessive burden of command (he was running operations from his sick bed); Told about his removal on 23 June although it had been effective from 10 June 1945; Replaced (by R. SHIBATA); Transferred to Army General Staff, Tokyo.*

*According to *Burma – The longest War* by L. Allen (*see* Bibliography). Another reference says he died of tuberculosis in the field.

YAMAWAKI Masataka

Lieutenant-General; Commander of 3rd Division (under 11th Army) during the Battle of Sui-Tsao, China, late April–mid May 1939; Engaged in the Battle of Tsaoyang–Ichang, early May–late June 1940; Commander of 37th Army, Borneo, c.1944; Confirmed an order to restrict food supplies to POWs; Confirmed the death sentence on three Australian soldiers tried for spying (who were executed 30 December 1944); Issued orders to march Australian and British POWs 165 miles from Sandakan prison camp to Ranau, but was transferred before implementation;* Replaced (by M. BABA), December 1944; Survived the war and was tried for the murder of the three Australians but was found not guilty, 1950.

*This resulted in the infamous 'Sandakan death marches'. *See* M. BABA.

YAMAZAKI

Major-General; Member of Civil Administration Department of the Army, Hong Kong, 1 January–20 February 1942; Secretariat to the Governor-General replaced Civil Admin. Dept., 1942; Probably replaced by ICHIKI at this time.

YAMAZAKI Yasuo

Lieutenant-General; Killed or died on Attu Island, Aleutians;* Presumably he was the Commander of the Aleutian Islands invasion troops, who landed 17 June 1942, or was the Garrison Commander.

*Attu was re-occupied by American forces, 30 May 1943.

YANAGAWA Heisuke

Born 1879; Educated in Germany; Lieutenant-General, December 1931; Vice Minister of War, 1932-4; Commander of Formosa Army, 1934 or 1935; Supervised amphibious landing techniques, December 1935; Retired, 26 September 1936;[1] Recalled to active service as Commander of 10th Army for the southern amphibious attack on Shanghai, August–December 1937; Commanded 6th and 14th Divisions in the attack on Nanking (under I. MATSUI Prince Y. ASAKA) and involved in the rape, massacres and looting of Nanking, China, December 1937–February 1938;[2] Head of the Asian Development Board, 16 December 1938; Appointed economic adviser to occupied China; Minister of Justice; Pro-Nazi; Leader of the nationalist 'Imperial Rule Assistance Association', January 1941; Governor-General of Sumatra where he died on 22 January 1945.[3]

[1] From *Kogun* by S. Hayashi (*see* Bibliography). Presumably recalled for 10th Army command.
[2] Disgreed with I. MATSUI's policy of constraint in China and induced his troops to view everything in China as an 'enemy'. Recalled to Japan after the massacres became known.
[3] From *Kogun* by S. Hayashi, but it could be 1944.

YANAGAWA Shinichi

Lieutenant-General; Commander of 120th Division, Tungching, Manchuria, from its activation in November 1944.

YANAGI Isamu

Major-General; Commander of 67th Infantry Brigade (in 63rd Division – M. NOZOE), Peiping (Peking), China, from the divisional activation in June 1943.

YANAGI Shigetoshi

Major-General; Commander of 1st Fuel Storage Depot, Japan, March 1944; Located at Iwakuni, Yamaguchi prefecture, Japan, December 1944.

YANAGIDA Genzō (Motozō)

Lieutenant-General; Commander of 33rd Division (under 15th Army – R. MUTAGUCHI), Burma (replacing S. SAKURAI), late 1943;* Formed part of Operation 'U-GO' (invasion of Imphal and Kohima in Assam, India); Commenced to move against Imphal, capital of Manipur State, India, 7-8 March 1944 (*see also* T. YAMAMOTO); Attempted to encircle 17th Indian Division; Tiddim (150 miles south of Imphal) was abandoned by the British, 13 March 1944; HQ moved to Kamzang village, 14 March 1944; Captured a huge British supply dump just north of Tongzang (110 miles south of Imphal) after heavy fighting, 18 March 1944; Supply dump recaptured by British 17th Indian Division, 25 March 1944; 17th Indian Division retreated over the Manipur River, 26 March 1944; Thought his losses were too heavy to continue the advance so recommended to C in C 15th Army R. MUTAGUCHI that the operation be slowed down; 15th Army and Burma Area Army were both angry and ordered him to follow the plan; Advanced recommenced, 29 March 1944; R. MUTAGUCHI wanted him court-martialled for cowardice and refused to deal with him, instead operated the division through the divisional Chief of Staff Colonel Tanaka Tetsujiro; Relieved of command by R. MUTAGUCHI and placed on the reserve list, 9 May 1944; Replaced (by N. TANAKA).

*Had no battlefield experience at this time.

YANAGITA

Major-General; Chief of Harbin Military Mission, Manchuria, c.1940.

YANIGAWA Yasushi

Lieutenant-General; Commander of 54th Depot Division, Himeji, Japan, September 1944; Supplied 10th, 17th, 54th, 84th?, 110th Divisions and 38th, 56th IMBs.

YANO Masao

Major-General; Chief of Staff to Mongolia Garrison Army, Kalgan (Changkiakow), just in north China, December 1942.

YASUDA Takeo

2nd Lieutenant, (engineers), December 1909; Graduated from Artillery and Engineering School, July 1916; Resident Officer Germany, January 1922; Major, August 1924; Instructor at Artillery and Engineering School, September 1924; Member of Research Branch of Army Signal School, May 1925; Lieutenant-Colonel, May 1929; Colonel, August 1932; Member of Research Branch of Army Signal School, April 1933; Chief of Defence Section of Military Affairs Bureau at War Ministry, December 1934; Major-General and attached to Army Air Technical Laboratories, March 1937; Chief of 2nd Bureau of Army Aeronautical Department, August 1937; Chief of Army Air Technical Laboratories, December 1938; Lieutenant-General, August 1939; Commander of 1st Air Army, June 1942; Inspector-General of Army Aviation and Chief of Army Aeronautical Department, May 1943; Favoured the use of suicide attacks by ramming enemy aircraft; Engineered an army air force command reshuffle to place officers sympathetic to *Kamikaze* (suicide) tactics in control and commenced a 'Special Attack' (i.e., suicide) training programme, March 1943; The high command and recruits were not told that such attacks were to become policy; Replaced (by T. YASUDA), March 1944; Military Councillor, March 1944; Commander of 1st Air Army (responsible for the aerial defence of eastern Honshu), HQ Tokyo, Japan, April 1945.

YASUMI Kinsaburo

Major-General; Commander of 1st Engineers Unit, July 1942; Located in Manchuria by March 1944.

YASUZAKA

Lieutenant-General; Doctor; Dissected bodies of people deliberately killed in experiments by 'Unit 731', near Pingfan Station, 20 kilometres from Harbin, Manchuria (*see* S. ISHII for details).*

*'Unit 731' was the '731st Manchurian Detachment of the Kwantung Army' set up to research bacteriological weapons.

YOKOYAMA Isamu

Born 1889; 2nd Lieutenant (infantry) in 3rd Infantry Regiment, December 1909; 1st Lieutenant, February 1913; Graduated from War College, December 1915; Army General Staff, January 1917; 3rd Infantry Regiment, April 1919; Captain, June 1919; Military Affairs Bureau at War Ministry, October 1921; Major and Resident Officer in Germany, August 1924; Economic Mobilization Bureau at War Ministry, March 1927; Lieutenant-Colonel, August 1928; Section Chief of Planning Bureau at Cabinet Resources Board, April 1929; Kwantung Army HQ, Manchuria, April 1932; Colonel, August 1932; Section Chief of Economic Mobilization Bureau at War Ministry, August 1933; Commander of 2nd Infantry Regiment, August 1934; Chief of Staff to 6th Division, March 1936; Major-General and Chief of Planning Bureau at Cabinet Resources Board, October 1937; Chief of 1st Bureau at Cabinet Planning Board, April 1939; Lieutenant-General, August 1939; Commander of 1st Division, September 1939; Commander of 4th Army, Manchuria, October 1941; Commander of 11th Army, China (replacing TSUKATA); Commander-in-Chief of Western District Army, Fukuoka, Japan, November 1944; Commander-in-Chief of 16th Area Army (formerly Western District Army) comprising 40th, 56th, 57th Armies, HQ Fukuoka, Japan, February 1945.

YOKOYAMA Nobuhiro

Major-General; Commander of 2nd Field Replacement Unit, May 1945?; Located in central and southern China.

YOKOYAMA Shizuo

2nd Lieutenant (infantry) in 24th Infantry Regiment, December 1912; Captain, February 1922; Graduated from War College, November 1925; Company Commander in 24th Infantry Regiment, December 1925; General Staff HQ, Tokyo, December 1926; Major and Member of Army General Staff, March 1928; Korea Army HQ, December 1929; Lieutenant-Colonel and Member of Army General Staff, April 1932; Official duty in Europe, September 1934; Member of Railway Sector HQ in Kwantung Army, Manchuria, March 1935; Colonel and Commander of same Sector HQ, August 1935; Assigned to Kwantung Army HQ, December 1937; Commander of 2nd Infantry Regiment, March 1938; Major-General and Commander of 2nd Field Railway Command, October 1940; Lieutenant-General, October 1941; Commander of 8th Division, June 1942; Division in Manchuria, HQ Suiyang, until August 1944; Division transferred to Luzon Island (under 14th Area Army – T. YAMASHITA), Philippines, arriving in September 1944; Divisional strength reduced by three infantry battalions which were sent to Leyte Island, December 1944; Commander of 'Shimbu Group' with 50,000–80,000 men (when 14th Area Army forces on Luzon were split by T. YAMASHITA), 1 January 1945; Ordered to defend the area from Manila to Bicol Peninsula with the main group of about 30,000 entrenched in the foothills of the Sierra Madre mountains, north-west of Manila, and the reserves in the centre;

Ordered to delay American forces south of Manila but failed; American 1st Cavalry and 6th Infantry Divisions attacked the centre on a narrow front after heavy air bombardment, 7 January 1945; Attempted to extricate Japanese naval forces fighting in Manila (see Rear-Admiral S. IWABUCHI) but failed because they did not want to be rescued, February 1945; Commander of 41st Army (which appears to have been activated in March 1945 to upgrade 'Shimbu Group'); Army consisted of 8th Division (concurrently under his own command), 10th Division (Y. OKAMOTO), 19th Division (Y. OZAKI), 23rd Division (F. NISHIYAMA), 103rd Division (Y. MURAOKA), 105th Division (Y. TSUDA), 2nd Armoured Division (Y. IWANAKA), and 1st Penetration Group – all of which were severely depleted by this time;* Underground defensive fortifications were individually destroyed by American forces after heavy fighting; Japanese counter-attack (using reserves) had been repulsed by the American 6th Division by 12 March 1945; Left flank in the south around Laguna de Bay collapsed on about 17 March 1945; Right flank in Wawa and Ipo Dams area attacked by saturation bombing (including 250,000 gallons of napalm); Ipo Dam attacked by American forces and Filipino guerrillas, 6 May 1945; Ipo Dam lost, 17 May 1945; Wawa Dam lost, 28 May 1945; Army effectively destroyed with 50 per cent losses and retreated further into the mountains; Surrendered with 6,300 men upon the official cessation of hostilities, September 1945; Gave evidence for the defence of T. YAMASHITA at war crimes trial, Manila, Philippines, 1945.

*Many of these units appear to have been dispersed to other army commands on Luzon by the end of the war.

YONAI Isamu

Major-General; Commander of Home Station for Headquarters Unit at Shikuka in Toyohara Regimental District, Japan, May 1945?

YONEYAMA Yoneshika

Major-General; Commander of 22nd Independent Mixed Brigade, Hainan Island, off south China, December 1942; Moved to Kweiping area, Kwangsi province, China.

YOSHIDA Gonpachi

Major-General; Commander of Anti-aircraft Artillery Unit, July 1943; Commander of Rangoon Anti-aircraft Artillery Unit, Burma, July 1944; Chief of Staff to 15th Army (under S. KATAMURA), Burma (replacing M. KUNOMURA), from September 1944? – end of the war, September 1945; Appears to have surrendered to Lieutenant-Colonel L. M. Coffey of British Intelligence Corps at Banpong, Siam, September 1945;[1] Participated in the formal surrender of 18th Area Army (under A. NAKAMURA) at Bangkok, 11 January 1946.[2]

[1] Surrendered a tanto (dagger with a guard) which is unusual. Good quality, having a signed blade with horimono on both sides. Silver plate on the scabbard inscribed 'Family knife of honour. Presented to Lieut. Colonel L. M. Coffey. British Int. Corps by Maj. General Gonpachi Yoshida, Chief of Staff 15th Army, Sept. 25th Banpong, Siam 1945'. Now in a private collection in Australia.
[2] Surrendered a sword (together with nineteen Generals and two Admirals) at the formal surrender of Japanese forces in Siam to Major-General G. C. Evans, GOC 7th Indian Division, at Bangkok, 11 January 1946.

YOSHIDA Hiromu

Major-General; Concurrently commander of two Home Stations for air and infantry units at Gifu and Kagamihara, both in Gifu Regimental District, Japan, March 1945.

YOSHIDA M.
Major-General; Chief of Staff to 2nd Army (under F.TESHIMA), Macassar, Celebes, by the time of the cessation of hostilities, August 1945.

YOSHIDA Minetaro
Lieutenant-General; Commander of 13th Division, south China, January 1945.

YOSHIDA Sadao
Major-General; Commander of 4th Airfield unit, January 1944; Located at Heito, Formosa, August 1944.

YOSHIDA Shin
Lieutenant-General; Commander of Kwantung Defence Army, Hsinking, Manchuria, September 1944.

YOSHIHARA (YOSHIWARA) Kane
Lieutenant-General; Commander of 20th Division (replacing J. AOKI?), eastern New Guinea, July 1944; Chief of Staff to 18th Army (under H. ADACHI), New Guinea; Sent into the mountains with 32 officers of 18th Army HQ to organize supplies and protection of the rear of 41st Division (G. MANO), 25 February 1945; Handed over these responsibilities to GOC 20th Division M. NAKAI, 5 May 1945; Given the task of establishing a self-supporting resistance group in the Sepic River area, 11 June 1945; Presumably surrendered at the end of the war.

YOSHIKAWA Nobuyoshi (Yashikata)
Major-General; Commander of part of 14th Independent Infantry Brigade (under 12th Army), China, by February 1945; Engaged in the Battle of western Honan–northern Hopeh, March–late May 1945.

YOSHINAKA Wataro
Major-General; Chief of Staff to Western District Army, HQ Fukuoka, Japan, December 1942.

YOSHIOKA Yasunori
Instructor at Military Academy, Japan; Lieutenant-Colonel; Military Attaché to the Imperial Court of (puppet) Emperor of Manchukuo Henry Pu Yi at Hsinking, Manchuria, from 1932; Lieutenant-General by August 1945; Advised Pu Yi to move the capital from Hsinking to Tunghua in accordance with Japanese wishes to avoid probable capture by the invading Russians, 9 August 1945; Moved with Pu Yi to Tunghua, 12 August 1945; Informed Pu Yi that he would be sent to Japan after the Japanese surrender; Flew via Mukden but was caught, together with Pu Yi, by the Russians before the aircraft could take off for Tokyo, 17 August 1945; Presumably imprisoned in a Siberian camp.

YOSHIRO
General officer; (Commander of?) Army Air Force, Honshu, Japan, by 1945; Ordered conversion of 4th Fighter Squadron to a *Kamikaze* (suicide) unit, Hiro air base, western Honshu, early 1945.

YOSHITA Kiyaro
Major-General; Acting Commander of 10th Air Division, near Kyoto, Japan (with responsibility for the defence of Tokyo and the Kanto Plain), c.1944; Area

bombed by American B-29s but Japanese aircraft were unable to match their ceiling to attack them; Realized the only defence was to strip fighters of guns and armour to enable them to gain the necessary height to ram the bombers;* Accordingly set up a *Kamikaze* unit with 47th Squadron, November 1944; First organized ramming attacks on B-29s in November 1945.

*Ramming became the main form of air defence.

YOSHITOMO Teiichi
Lieutenant-General; Commander in Chief of North-eastern District Army, Sendai?; Japan, February 1945.

YOSHIYUKI
Major-General, by the time of the ceasefire, August 1945.*

*Surrendered a sword. A *shin-guntō* with signed Showa-period (post-1926) blade. Taken by the Australian 7th Military History Field Team. Now in the Australian War Memorial Museum. Cat. no. ACC 7186.

YOSHIZUMI Masao
Lieutenant-General; Director of Military Affairs Bureau at War Ministry, Tokyo, Japan, by 1945; Acted as secretary at an Imperial Conference at which the Emperor personally recommended acceptance of the Allied Potsdam Declaration for Japan's unconditional surrender, Tokyo, 9 August 1945; Disagreed with the decision for peace; Approved the unofficial preparation, and release, of a public communiqué to renew offensive action against the Allies (without the official sanction of War Minister K. ANAMI and Army Chief of Staff Y. UMEZU); Prevented from releasing it by Y. UMEZU, 13 August 1945.

YOTSUIDE
Lieutenant-General; Chief of Staff to 1st Area Army (under T. YAMASHITA), Mutankiang, Manchuria, 1944.

YUGUCHI Toshitaro
Major-General; Commander of 80th Infantry Brigade (in 103rd Division – Y. MURAOKA), Baguio, Luzon Islands, Philippines, July 1944?

Imperial Japanese Navy Flag Officers 1926–45

ABE Hiroaki (Hoki, Koki)
Rear-Admiral; Commander of 8th Cruiser Squadron (heavy cruisers *Tone*, *Chikuma*), forming part of Support Force (under G. MIKAWA) in Pearl Harbor Attack Force, December 1941; Detached from main fleet during return to Japan to reinforce invasion of Wake Island, Marshalls (*see* S. KAJIOKA), 24 December 1941; 8th Cruiser Squadron formed Support Group to Darwin Strike Force (under C. NAGUMO), flagship heavy cruiser *Tone*, 19 February 1942; Commander of Support Group (to 1st Air Fleet under C. NAGUMO) comprising 8th Cruiser Squadron (heavy cruisers *Tone*, *Chikuma*) and 2nd Section of 3rd Battleship

Division (battleships *Haruna, Kirishima*) in Operation 'MI' for attempted invasion of Midway (*see* I. YAMAMOTO), May–June 1942; Assumed temporary tactical command at Battle of Midway (while C. NAGUMO transferred flag), 4 June 1942; Commander of Vanguard Force in Combined Fleet attempt to protect reinforcement convoy to Guadalcanal, Solomons, 23–5 August 1942; Commander of Battleship Division (2 battleships, 4 cruisers, 8 destroyers) forming Vanguard Force (under 2nd Fleet – N. KONDO) of Main Body at Battle of Santa Cruz Islands, 26 October 1942; Detached from 2nd Fleet as Advance Raiding Force to bombard Henderson Airfield, Guadalcanal, in support of army attack (*see* Lieutenant-General H. HYAKUTAKE); Force consisted of 2 battleships (flagship *Hiei* and *Kirishima*), light cruiser *Nagara* and 11–14 destroyers; Forces split in squall and intercepted by inferior American forces in first phase of Third Battle of the Solomon Sea (Battle of Savo Island) and forced to retreat with loss of battleship *Hiei* transferring to destroyer *Yukikaze*, 12–13 November 1942;* Wounded and relieved of command by Naval High Command for failure to complete the operation (*see also* G. MIKAWA).

* *Hiei* was the first Japanese battleship lost during the war. She was so badly damaged that she was torpedoed by the Japanese. *Kirishima* was sunk together with one heavy cruiser and seven out of eleven transports on 14 November 1942.

ABE Katsuo (Hatsuo)

Graduated from Etajima Naval College, 1912; Visited Germany and became pro-German; Rear-Admiral; Chief of Naval Affairs Bureau (replacing S. INOUYE), October 1939; Advocated signing of Tripartite Pact even though senior naval leaders opposed it; Replaced (by T. OKA), October 1940; Head of Japanese Military Mission in Berlin, 1943–5.

ABE Koso

Rear-Admiral; Commander of Transport Force of abortive Port Moresby Invasion Force in Operation 'MO' (*see* S. INOUYE), which was postponed, 8 May 1942; Naval Commander of Kwajalein, Marshall Islands, *c.* 1942; Ordered beheading of nine American prisoners on Kwajalein when they became 'a burden' to his command, 1942; Tried for execution of the Americans and sentenced to death; Hanged on Guam, 19 June 1947.

ABO Kiyokazu

Naval Attaché in London *c.*1930; (Full?) Admiral; Navy Minister (replacing T. TAKARABE), 3 October 1930; Implemented 'First Supplementary Building Programme' to increase Combined Fleet by four cruisers, 27 other smaller vessels and doubling the size of the naval air arm, 1931 (to 1936); Replaced (by Prince H. FUSHIMI), 2 February 1932.

AKIYAMA Teruo

Rear-Admiral; Commander of destroyer escort and transport convoy ('Tokyo Express') to Vila on Kolombangara Island, Solomons, with total force of ten destroyers; Sailed from Rabaul, New Britain, 5 July 1943; Split force and made successful landing with one section at lower end of Kula Gulf, 6 July 1943; Section rejoined but whole force intercepted by American warships resulting in his death when flagship destroyer *Niizuki* was sunk, 6 July 1943 (replaced by S. IZAKI).

ANDO
Captain; Commander of Tan Toey POW camp, Ambon Island, Moluccas; Ordered beatings and ill treatment of prisoners, November 1942; Rear-Admiral by the end of war; Committed suicide at Surabaya, Java, September 1945.

ARIMA Masafumi (Masabumi)
Raised in England; Attended English Public School; Started training with British Royal Navy; Rear-Admiral; Commander of 26th Air Flotilla (air maintenance unit) under 1st Air Fleet (K. TERAOKA), Philippines, c.1944; Supported formation of a 'TOKKO' (Special attack, i.e., *Kamikaze*) programme in agreement with T. ONISHI for defence of Philippines but the idea was rejected, September 1944; Repeatedly requested such action but was always refused; Deliberately set out on a personal suicide mission (to demonstrate his ardent support for such a scheme); Personally lead the second wave of a normal air attack on American Task Force Group 38–4 but deliberately crash-dived into the cruiser USS *Franklin*, 13 or 15 October 1944 (replaced by SUGIMOTO).

ARUGA (ARIGA) Kosaku
Captain; Commander of 4th Destroyer Division (part of 10th Destroyer Flotilla under S. KIMURA) which formed Destroyer Screen for 1st Air Fleet (1st Carrier Striking Force under C. NAGUMO) in Operation 'MI' during attempted invasion of Midway Island, May–June 1942; Rear-Admiral; Captain of super battleship *Yamato* (replacing N. MORISHITA), December 1942; Sailed in Operation 'TEN-ICHI' as flagship of First Special Attack Force (redesignated name of 2nd Fleet) under S. ITO, 6 April 1945;* Force attacked by American carrier aircraft and *Yamato* sunk by bombs and torpedoes; Had himself tied to the ship's wheel and went down with the ship (and S. ITO), 7 April 1945.

* Operation 'TEN-ICHI' was to be a suicidal attack by 2nd Fleet on American naval forces at Kadena off Okinawa but the loss of *Yamato* aborted the mission. *Yamato* only had enough fuel for a one-way trip and, if she survived, was to be beached to become a shore battery.

Prince ASA-AKIRA Kuni III
Born 1901; Brother of Empress Nagako; Graduated from Etajima Naval Academy, 1921; Rear-Admiral, 1942; Commanded an Air Squadron in support of Timor occupation, February 1942; Supported formation of *Kamikaze* (suicide) corps, 1944; Survived the war, running the Kuni Perfume Company and becoming a gentleman farmer.

ASAGUMA Toshihide
Vice-Admiral; Commander of naval designers at Kure, Japan, 1939; Co-designer with K. KISHIMOTO of the 'Long-lance' torpedo (which left no tell-tale wake).

BANNO
Rear-Admiral; Forcibly retired or sacked by Navy Minister M. OSUMI because he unwisely voiced an opinion against Japanese naval expansion, 1934.

BAZUDI
Rear-Admiral; Commander of Japanese forces on Penang Island, Malaya; Signed surrender of Penang (together with J. UOZUMI, Governor of Penang) on board HMS *Nelson* to Vice-Admiral H. T. C. Walker, 2 September 1945.

Note: *see* footnote to UOZUMI Jisaku.

CHIGUSA Sadao
(Rear?-) Admiral; c.Second World War.

CHUDO Kaigye
Rear-Admiral; Assistant Chief of Staff to Field Marshal H. TERAUCHI (from November 1944?); Member of surrender delegation (together with Southern Army Chief of Staff Lieutenant-General T. NUMATA) who were ordered by H. TERAUCHI to discuss surrender terms with Lieutenant-General Browning at Rangoon, Burma, 26 August 1945; (He argued that 10th Fleet Commander S. FUKUDOME should receive special treatment as naval commander, separate from Southern Army but was overruled).

CHUDŌ Kanei
Captain; Chief of British Section of Intelligence Division of Naval Affairs Bureau, 1939; Replaced (by Captain Oi Atushi), 1941; Chief of IGHQ Navy Department French Indo–China Expeditionary Committee, 1941; Returned from inspection of Thailand and Indo-China and reported that a Japanese advance could be made into these two countries without causing war with Britain or America, June 1941; Replaced August 1943; Rear-Admiral by end of war.

Marquis DAIGO Tadashige
Rear-Admiral; Commander of 5th Submarine Flotilla forming part of screen of 'Malaya Force' (under J. OZAWA) against Allied warships and for reconnaissance during Malaya invasion, flagship light cruiser *Yura*, December 1941;[1] Vice-Admiral; Operational Commander of Eastern (submarine) Attack Group, May 1942; Ordered to attack Sydney Harbour, Australia with midget submarines (which were carried to launch position by I-Class submarines); Eastern Attack Group (under Captain Sasaki Hankyu) launched three midget submarines (which were all sunk) into Sydney Harbour Bay but only sunk the depot ship HMAS *Kuttabul* and the Dutch submarine *K9*, 31 May 1942;[2] Eastern Attack Force continued to harass shipping off Australia until July 1942; Commander of 6th Fleet – Submarines (replacing S. MIWA), May 1945–end of the war.[3]

[1] Submarine *I65* of 30th Submarine Division was the first to sight and report Force Z (HMS *Prince of Wales* and *Repulse*) but lost them in a squall, 9 December 1941.
[2] *K9* was damaged beyond repair and was scrapped.
[3] This conflicts with M. NAGAI who is also reported as holding this post at the same time. It seems likely that the NAGAI entry is incorrect in this aspect.

DOI Naoji
Rear-Admiral; Commander of 32nd Special Naval Base Force, Davao, Mindanao, Philippines, October 1944.

EGUCHI Rinroku
Vice-Admiral; Possibly 1930s.

ENDŌ
(Full?) Admiral; Retired by 1945; Stated in a magazine dated April 1945 that by invading Okinawa the enemy had done just what the Japanese high command wanted them to do since the Japanese had the power to 'thrust at the enemy's vitals while letting him thrust at our vital parts'.

ENDŌ Yoshikazu
Rear-Admiral; Anglophile; Naval Attaché in Berlin, c.1940.

FUJITA

Vice-Admiral; Commander of 7th Special Naval Base Force, Lae, New Guinea, March–August 1943.

FUJITA Hisanori

Admiral; Grand Chamberlain to Emperor Hirohito by late 1944 until end of the Second World War.

FUJITA Risaburo

Vice-Admiral; Commander of 11th Special Naval Base Force, September 1943; Located in Saigon, Indo–China, March 1944.

FUJITA Ruitaro 藤田

Rear-Admiral; Commander of 11th Carrier Division attached to 3rd Fleet (see I. TAKAHASHI), 1941; Commanded part of Macassar Invasion Force (in Celebes), 8 February 1942; Commander of Seaplane Tender Group, part of Midway Island Invasion Force (2nd Fleet) under N. KONDO in Operation 'MI', May–June 1942; Vice-Admiral; Commander of Tsingtao Special Base Force, Eastern China, November 1943; Commander of South China Fleet by 1945; Signed surrender of all naval forces in Hong Kong and South China Fleet (together with Major General U. OKADA) to Rear-Admiral Sir Cecil Harcourt, at Government House, Hong Kong, 16 September 1945.*

* Surrendered his sword at Government House, Hong Kong, to Rear-Admiral Sir Cecil Harcourt after signing the surrender document, 16 September 1945. It is now in the National Maritime Museum (Cat.no. 185). A *kai-guntō* with brown tassel. Blade signed 'TENSHOZAN TAN RENBA SAKU', i.e., 'Made at the Tenshozan Forge', and is dated June 1942.

FUKUCHI Nobuo

Vice-Admiral; Secretary to three successive Naval Ministers (M. YONAI 1937–9, Z. YOSHIDA 1939–40, K. OIKAWA 1940–1).

FUKUDA Ryozo

Vice-Admiral; Commander of Takao Naval Guard District, Formosa, 1943; HQ Takao; Commander of China Area Fleet (which controlled all naval forces in China theatre), late 1944 or early 1945 (possibly replacing N. KONDO) until the end of the war; Signed surrender of all naval forces under his command (together with General Y. OKAMURA) to Chinese General Ho Ying-Chin at Central Military Academy, Nanking, China, 9 September 1945.

FUKUDOME Shigeru

Rear-Admiral; Senior naval aviation officer and Chief of Staff to Combined Fleet (under I. YAMAMOTO), replacing T. IBO, January 1940; Prepared study of air torpedo attack on Pearl Harbor (together with Commander Genda Minoru and Rear-Admiral T.ONISHI); Replaced (by M. UGAKI), April 1941; Chief of 1st Division (Operations) of Naval General Staff (replacing M. UGAKI), April 1941; Predicted, at a conference of Operations Divisional Chiefs, that the navy would lose too many ships by the end of the first year of a war successfully to carry out projected 'Southern Operations', 6 October 1941; Was alone in suggesting Japan withdraw from China and the Tripartite Pact in order to avoid war with Britain and America; Would not recognize superiority of air power even after sinking of British warships *Prince of Wales* and *Repulse* by air attack, 10 December 1941; Replaced May 1943; Chief of Staff to Combined Fleet (under M. KOGA), HQ

Palau, Caroline Islands, May? 1943; Flew to new Combined Fleet HQ in Philippines with M. KOGA (in separate aircraft); Both aircraft crashed in a storm off Cebu, 31 March/1 April 1944; Saved 'Z-plan' documents (Marianas – Carolines offensive orders. *See* Addenda to this entry); Injured his leg and rescued by Filipino fishermen then handed over to guerrillas; Claimed he was C in C Combined Fleet M. KOGA in order to obtain his release through intimidation; Japanese reprisals secured his release but the documents were obtained by the Americans; A Board of Enquiry in Tokyo acquitted him of being captured and failing to commit *hara-kiri* (suicide) in violation of *sen-jin-kun*[1] (he maintained that he merely 'encountered' guerrillas), 18 April 1944; Known to be a Vice-Admiral; Commander of 2nd Air Fleet (with 6th Base Air Force), Formosa, 15 June 1944 (training special Army–Navy torpedo aircraft unit); HQ destroyed by air attacks with many aircraft destroyed on the ground, 12–14 October 1944; Counter-attacked American fleet off Okinawa and Formosa (Japanese lost 650 aircraft against American losses of only 75 aircraft and two cruisers damaged), 15 October 1944;[2] HQ with 2nd Air Fleet and 6th Base Air Force (450 aircraft) transferred to Philippines to cover planned Operation 'SHO' (see T. KURITA), arrived at Clark Field, Luzon, 22 October 1944; Rejected request by T. ONISHI to use his aircraft on suicide missions in favour of mass attacks; Supported Operation 'SHO' (naval attack on American fleet off Leyte), lost 150 aircraft for minimal sinkings, 23–6 October 1944; Imperial approval of *Kamikaze* tactics forced him to accept the idea; Under instigation of C in C 1st Air Fleet T. ONISHI they combined 1st and 2nd Air Fleets to form Combined Base Air Corps (or South-west Area Fleet Combined Land Based Air Force); Agreed merger on the terms that he be Commander-in-Chief with T. ONISHI as Chief of Staff; The new force was a Special (*Kamikaze*) Attack Unit, 26 October 1944; (Suicide attacks were made compulsory for all pilots who were so ordered 25 October 1944); Reinforced by 12th Air Fleet from Kuriles, late October 1944; Continued *Kamikaze* sorties resulted in loss of all aircraft; Last attack on American fleet off Luzon, 6 January 1945; Wanted to fly back to Takao, Formosa (since still officially part of the Formosan Defence Force) rather than die in defence of the Philippines; Imperial GHQ disagreed, disbanded Combined Base Air Corps and Transferred him to Tokyo (remnant placed under T. ONISHI), 6 January 1945; Commander-in-Chief of 10th Area Fleet[3] comprising 1st and 2nd Southern Expeditionary Fleets and 13th Naval Air Fleet), HQ Singapore, January? 1945 (i.e., Supreme Commander of all naval forces in South East Asia but subordinate to C in C Southern Army Field Marshal H. TERAUCHI); Signed local surrender of Singapore on behalf of 1st Southern Expeditionary Fleet (together with C in C 7th Area Army General S. ITAGAKI) to Lieutenant-General Sir Philip Christison (V Corps Commander) and Rear-Admiral Holland aboard HMS *Sussex*, Singapore, 4 September 1945; Delegate (on behalf of 10th Area Fleet) at formal surrender of all Japanese forces in South East Asia to Lord Louis Mountbatten, Singapore, 12 September 1945.

Personal facts: Reserved and unexcitable. Good personality. Sharp mind. A moderate. Obeyed orders without question.

---

[1] This unwritten code of honour required all Japanese officers to commit suicide rather than submit to capture. Although unwritten it was subject to court-martial if an officer were deemed to have survived or escaped from capture.

[2] Japanese pilots reported 11 carriers, 2 battleships, 3 cruisers, 1 destroyer sunk which was accepted as true by IGHQ Tokyo.

[3] 10th Area Fleet was formed from surviving units of South-west Area Fleet which was under direct command of GHQ Tokyo until its disbandment in October/November 1944.

Addenda
'Z-plan' detailed the Combined Fleet attack to relieve Saipan which resulted in disaster at the Battle of the Philippine Sea ('Great Marianas Turkey Shoot'). Naval GHQ did not seem worried at the loss of the documents or the thought that they could end up in American hands. The plans were left virtually unchanged and the Americans were fully prepared. He denied that he had saved the documents but they were found, water-stained, in the historical section of Supreme Commander, Allied Powers, Tokyo (American archives) after the war. (Ref: *Kamikaze* by D. and P. Warner. *See* Bibliography).

FURUSE
Rear-Admiral; Hanged after war crimes trial on Luzon, Philippines, 1949.

Prince FUSHIMI Hiroyasu
Born 1875; Cousin of Emperor Hirohito; Studied in Germany and spoke fluent German; Lieutenant-Commander in Russo–Japanese war, 1904–5; Admiral; Chief of Naval General Staff (replacing K. ABO), 2 February 1932; Advocated a 'southward advance' by the navy to obtain essential materials but by peaceful means if possible, 19 September 1940; Agreed with the signing of the Tripartite Pact with Germany and Italy, September 1940; Replaced (by O. NAGANO), 9 April 1941; Admiral of the Fleet and most senior of all naval officers; Chairman of the Supreme War Council which advised the Emperor (until the end of the war); Retired from active list, 1944; Approved of the use of suicide weapons; Died 1947.

Personal facts: Nicknamed the 'long-faced prince'. Quiet. Relied on his staff. Considered something of a tyrant.

GOGA Keijiro
Vice-Admiral; Commander of Hainan Naval Guard District, Hainan Island, off south China, November 1944.

GOTO Aritomo
Rear-Admiral; Commander of 6th Cruiser Squadron; Supported Bismarck Archipelago invasion by 4th Fleet (under S. INOUYE), flagship heavy cruiser *Aoba*, January 1942; Commanded invasion force for Tulagi (capital of Solomon Islands) which landed unopposed, 3 May 1942; Commander of Covering Force in Operation 'MO' (Port Moresby invasion. *See* K. ABE, S.INOUYE, S. KAJIOKA, K. MARUSHIGE) with cruisers and light carrier *Shoho*; American air attack near Louisiade Archipelago sank *Shoho* (first Japanese carrier sunk in the war) at Battle of Coral Sea which forced a withdrawal of the Port Moresby invasion forces, 7 May 1942; Escorted Japanese transports ('Tokyo Express' under R. TANAKA) to reinforce Guadalcanal, Solomons, with three heavy cruisers (flagship *Aoba, Kurutaka, Kinugasa*) and two destroyers but defeated by American naval forces at Battle of Cape Esperance; Mortally wounded by shell burst on *Aoba* which was badly damaged with *Kurutaka* being sunk, 11 October 1942 (Command was passed to Captain K. Kijima who relinquished it to G. MIKAWA upon return to Rabaul, New Britain).

GOTO Eiji
Vice-Admiral; Commander of Ominato Naval Guard District, Japan, February 1945; HQ Ominato, Aomori province.

GOTO Hideji
Rear-Admiral; Commander of 24th Air Flotilla, c.1942.

HAMANAKA

Rear-Admiral; Surrendered 1945;* Sentenced to death by shooting after war crimes trial by Australian Military Court, Morotai Island, 15 January 1946; (Found guilty of ordering the killing of Australian prisoners of war and ill treatment of others).

* Surrendered a *kai-guntō* with *gendaitō* (hand-forged) blade signed 'KANEHISA', c.1942. Taken by Lieutenant-General R. A. C. Muir. Now in Australian War Memorial museum. Cat.no.AWM 28292.

HARA Chuichi (Tadaichi)

Rear-Admiral; Commander of 5th Carrier Division (carriers *Shokaku* and flagship *Zuikaku*), October 1941; Formed part of 1st Carrier Fleet (i.e., 1st Air Fleet) under C. NAGUMO in Pearl Harbor attack, 7 December 1941; Division detached from 1st Air Fleet, 16 April 1942; Commander of Carrier Division of Carrier Strike Force (under T. TAKAGI) in Operation 'MO' (invasion of Port Moresby, New Guinea. *See also* S. INOUYE) with carriers *Shokaku* and *Zuikaku*; Sailed from Truk; Tulagi Island, Solomons, occupied in conjunction with Strike Force (T. TAKAGI); Battle of Coral Sea (with aircraft carrier *Shokaku* badly damaged and taken back to Japan), 6–8 May 1942; Ordered to withdraw to Truk after cancellation of Operation 'MO', 15th? May 1942; Commander of Detached Carrier Strike Force (of 3rd Fleet under C. NAGUMO) with light carrier *Ryujo*, heavy cruiser *Tone* and two or three destroyers as escort force to Guadalcanal reinforcements; Attacked by American aircraft in Second Battle of Solomon Sea with loss of *Ryujo*, 24 August 1942; Commander of 4th Fleet (replacing M. KOBAYASHI), 19 June 1944–end of war; Surrendered his sword on Truk, Caroline Islands, to Vice Admiral G. P. Murray, 22 November 1945.

HARA Kanezo (Teizo, Tisia)

Rear-Admiral; Commander of 12th Special Naval Base Force, Andaman and Nicobar Islands, HQ Port Blair, South Andaman Island, June 1944; Vice-Admiral; Surrendered to Captain J.H. Blair,* DSC, RNR, at Port Blair, 9 October 1945 (also surrendering were Major General T. SATO, Staff Captain Shimazaki and Lieutenant-Colonel Tazawa); Tried as war criminal for responsibility of deaths of 213 islanders; Sentenced to death and hanged at Changi Jail, Singapore, 18 June 1946.

*Surrendered his sword at this date to Captain Blair who presented it to Trinity House, London. *Kai-guntō* with unsigned blade and *same* scabbard. It is illustrated in *Swords for Sea Service* by May and Annis, Plate no. 116.

HARA Kenzaburo

Rear-Admiral; Commander of First Surprise Attack Group for Aparri Landings, Luzon, in the Philippines, flagship light cruiser *Natori*, 10 December 1941; Commander of Third (Close) Escort Force for Western Force (under I. TAKA-HASHI) with light cruisers *Yura, Natori* and sixteen destroyers for invasion of Java, February 1942.

Note: There appears to be some confusion over whether or not this is the same as HARA Chuichi but the different locations for 8–10 December 1941 would seem to discount this.

HARADA Kaku

Captain; Commander of Special Force (Seaplane carriers), flagship *Chiyoda*, forming part of 1st Fleet (Main Force) under I. YAMAMOTO in Operation 'MI' during attempted invasion of Midway island, May–June 1942; Rear-Admiral; Commander of 33rd Naval Base Force, August 1944; Located in Central Philippines, September 1944.

HASE Shinsaburo

Rear-Admiral; Commander of Special Naval Base Force, February 1944; Located on Ambon Island, January 1945.

HASEGAWA Kiyoshi   長谷川 清

Captain; Naval Attaché in Washington, USA; Replaced (by I. YAMAMOTO), January 1925; Rear- or Vice-Admiral and Vice Navy Minister by 1936; Replaced (by I. YAMAMOTO) and returned to sea duty, late 1936; Vice-Admiral; Commander of naval units which landed 1,300 sailors and marines to protect Japanese interests just outside, and in, the International Settlement at Shanghai, China, against besieging Chinese, August 1937; Flagship cruiser *Idzumo*; Issued orders prohibiting shipping from entering Haung-P'u River (through Shanghai), and fired on Chinese troops, 13 August 1937; Supported landing by Shanghai Expeditionary Army (under General I. MATSUI), 23 August 1937; Commanded? naval support to Japanese landings by 10th Army near Fushon, Chiang-yin and Hangchow Bay in pincer movement, 5 November 1937; Shangai captured, 12 November 1937; Admiral; Military Councillor by 1940.

Note: Photographed in 1938 with a naval *Kyu-guntō* sword. A hand-forged blade (*gendaito*) made specially for him by Kurihara Akihade and dated November 1937 was obtained from China without mounts in 1985. See *The Oshigata Book* by Fuller and Gregory, published 1985, pp. 101–3.

HASHIMOTO Shintaro

Rear-Admiral; Commander of 1st Escort Force (under 'Malaya Force' – J. OZAWA) with ten destroyers, six minesweepers, three sub-chasers for invasion of Malaya, November 1941; Escorted transports for landings at Kota Bharu, northern Malaya, against opposition, 8/9 December 1941; Commander of Escort Group for Balikpapan and Bandjermasin (Borneo) Occupation Force, late January–early February 1942; Commander of 3rd Destroyer Flotilla (comprising 11th, 19th Destroyer Divisions) acting as Destroyer Screen for 1st Fleet (Main Force) under I. YAMAMOTO in Operation 'MI' during attempted invasion of Midway Island, May–June 1942; Commander of Sweeping Force in Third Battle Of Solomon Sea (3rd Phase) under N. KONDO, 14–15 November 1942; Commander of 5th Cruiser Squadron (under 10th Area Fleet – S. FUKUDOME); Killed aboard flagship cruiser *Ashigara* which was sunk in Bangka Strait, Sumatra, 8 June 1945.

HASHIMURA

Rear-Admiral; Commander of 4th Destroyer Flotilla supporting Philippines landings, December 1941.

HATAKEYAMA (HATAKIYAMA)

Rear-Admiral; Commander of the Ambon (Amboina) Island Invasion Force, consisting of 1st Kure Special Landing Party and two platoons of the Sasebo Special Marines Landing Party; Landed at Hitulama, north-east Ambon, 31 January 1942; HQ Soewakoda; Captured Laha airfield, 2 February 1942; Ordered the execution of Dutch and Australian POWs, 1, 5 and 6 February 1942; HQ Laha, 3 February 1942; Replaced (by Lieutenant-Commander Hayashi) by 17 February 1942; Killed later in the war (*see also* ICHISE).

HIRATA
Vice-Admiral; Commander of Yokosuka Naval Base, Japan, 18 October 1941.

HIRATA Noburo
Rear-Admiral; Naval aide-de-camp to Emperor Hirohito (replacing K. KATO), May 1935.

HIROSE Sueto
Rear-Admiral; Commander of Attack Force for Batan and Camiguin Islands, Philippines, 8–10 December 1941; Commander at Tarakan, Borneo, 10 January 1942; Commander of 4th Destroyer Flotilla forming part of Macassar (in Celebes) Invasion Force, 8 February 1942; Commander of 9th Naval Base Force, Sabang Island, off Northern Sumatra, by 1945; Received instructions regarding the Japanese surrender of Sabang and evacuation of Sumatra aboard HMS *London* from Commodore A.C. Poland, 31 August 1945; Moved from Sabang to Sumatra, 1 September 1945; Formally surrendered with Lieutenant-General TANABE (25th Army) at Padang to Major-General H. M. Chambers GOC 26th Indian Division, 21 October 1945; Evacuated with 9th Naval Shore Force (3,776 army and naval personnel) and Major-General S. INO (Governor of Atjek province) from Koetaradja (northern point of Sumatra) by Major E. Esmond-Jones, OC of D. Company, 2nd Battalion, Durham Light Infantry, 19 December 1945; (He was told to surrender his sword to 'British Flag Officer, Malaya', which presumably he did).

HONDA Takeo
Rear-Admiral; Commander of Aleutian Islands Submarine Supply Squadron with six *I*-Class and two *RO*-Class submarines, 1942–3.

HORI Teikichi (Takeichi)
Graduated from Etajima Naval College (1st of 200), 14 November 1904; Best friend of I. YAMAMOTO; Adviser at Washington Naval Conference where British, French, Italian, Japanese and American fleet sizes were limited and tonnages reduced, 1922; Rear- or Vice-Admiral; Chief of Naval Affairs Bureau, Tokyo, 1931; Commander of a Naval Squadron during 'Shanghai Incident', China, January 1932; Forcibly retired to reserve list aged 51 in a purge by Navy Minister M. OSUMI on false grounds of cowardice during the 'Shanghai Incident' (he delayed firing on Chinese because civilians were present) but, in reality, it was because of his continued opposition to Japanese naval expansion and support of the 1930 London Naval Limitation Agreement, December 1934; President of a large Japanese shipyard by 1941; Remained a close friend of I. YAMAMOTO until his death.

HORIUCHI Shigetada
Captain; Chief of British Section of Naval Intelligence Division of Naval Affairs Bureau, 1937–9 (replaced by K. CHUDO); Rear-Admiral by end of war.

HOSHINA (HOSHIMA) Zenshiro
Rear?-Admiral; Served under Vice Navy Minister I. YAMAMOTO, 1936–9; Chief of Mobilization and War Preparations in Navy Ministry, Tokyo, c.1941.

HOSOGAYA Boshiro (Moshiro)

Vice-Admiral; Commander of 5th Fleet based at Ominato, northern Honshu, Japan, c.1941; Commanded 5th Fleet in Operation 'AL' (invasion of Aleutian Islands), flagship heavy cruiser *Nachi*; Fleet comprised of Northern Force Main Body, 2nd Carrier Striking Force (K. KAKUTA), Attu Island Landing Force (S. OMORI), Kiska Island Landing Force (Captain Ono Takeji) and Submarine Detachment; Sailed with Main Body from Ominato, 28 May 1942; Bombed American air base at Dutch Harbor, Unalaska Island, 3 and 4 June 1942; Occupied Kiska Island 6 June 1942; Occupied Attu Island, 7 June 1942; Temporarily withdrew from Attu after American Forces moved into Adak Island; Re-occupied Attu, October 1942; Commander of reinforcement convoy and escorts to Attu, early March 1943; Repeated reinforcement convoy but wasted the chance to defeat American blockade ships at Battle of Kormandorski Island (or Attu Island) and failed to land, 26 March 1943; Relieved of command upon return to base.

HYAKUTAKE Saburo

Elder brother of Major-General HYAKUTAKE Seikichi; Admiral; Grand Chamberlain to Emperor Hirohito and a Military Councillor; 1936–44.

ICHIKAWA Noboru

Vice-Admiral; Commander of Otake Submarine School, Japan, 1945.

Note: Possibly the same as ISHIZAKI Noboru.

ICHIMARU

Rear-Admiral; Commander of 21st Naval Air Flotilla, 1941 (Disbanded 1943).

Note: Possibly the same as ICHIMARU Toshinosuke.

ICHIMARU Toshinosuke

Graduated from Naval Academy; Famous naval pilot; Limped from injury sustained in crash of experimental aircraft, 1926; Rear-Admiral; Commander of 27th Naval Air Wing, Iwo Jima (for defence of Bonin Islands) with 2,300 men, 1944; Placed under command of Lieutenant-General T. KURIBAYASHI (109th Division), June 1944; Disagreed with policy of T. KURIBAYASHI to leave the beaches undefended; Insisted that naval troops should concentrate on defence of one area only (Minamiburaki district); Compromised and built 300 pillboxes; Naval troops increased to about 7,000; Island heavily bombarded by American naval forces for six weeks, January–February 1945; American 4th and 5th Marines landed, 19 February 1945; Japanese army and naval forces destroyed by mid March 1945; HQ in a cave; Left his cave with 60 men for final suicide attack but survived, 18 March 1945; Killed when leaving his cave, 27 March 1945.*

Note: His sword has not been traced but is said to have had a blade by 'Tadayoshi' but which one is not known.

* He left a letter in the cave addressed to President Roosevelt which is now in the US Naval Academy Museum, Annapolis. It justifies the war to prevent exploitation of the Japanese by Anglo-saxons. The full text is published in *The Rising Sun* by J. Toland (*see* Bibliography).

ICHISE

Vice-Admiral; Commander of the Naval Base on Ambon Island, Moluccas, arriving June 1945; He (or a subordinate) refused to negotiate a surrender until senior Japanese commanders had surrendered, and an Australian naval party was ordered to return to Morotai without landing, 16 August 1945; Received surrender orders (together with Major General KOBORI) from Australian Brigadier Steel who instructed him to transfer all his men to Ceram, 22 September 1945; Presumably formally surrendered on Ceram; Obtained, and delivered information to an Allied War Crimes Commission which implicated other Japanese in the murder of POWs on Ambon in 1942 (see HATAKEYAMA), November 1945.

IDE Kenji
Admiral; Head of Japanese military delegation which toured England, Europe and America, 1923.

IDEMITSU Mambei
Rear-Admiral; Chief Naval aide-de-camp to Emperor Hirohito, c.1935; Principal of Naval Academy, May 1935; Commander of a port arsenal, c.1938.

IJUIN Matsuji
Captain; Captain of cruiser *Atago* in 4th Cruiser Squadron (under N. KONDO), forming part of Midway Island Invasion Force Main Body in Operation 'MI', May–June 1942; Rear-Admiral; Commander of Transport and Destroyer Escort (to establish barge staging base at Vella Lavella Island, New Georgia), in flagship destroyer *Sazanami* in Battle of Horaniu, 17 August 1943; Transport and Destroyer Escort Commander for evacuation of Vella Lavella, 6 October 1943; Commander of 3rd Destroyer Flotilla with flagship light cruiser *Sendai* and six destroyers (under S. OMORI) at Battle of Gazelle Bay (Empress Augusta Bay), Solomons, night of 2/3 November 1943; Defeated with loss of flagship *Sendai* and destroyer *Katsukaze*; rescued by Japanese submarine *I-104*.

IKEDA Iwasaburo
(Full?) Admiral; (Head of?) Naval Engineering Section, 1930s?

IMAMURA Osamu
Rear-Admiral; Commander of 2nd Naval Air Force using part of it (12th Air Flotilla) to support invasion of Malaya (see J. OZAWA), December 1941; Commander of 10th Naval Special Base Force, November 1943; Located at Singapore, March 1944.

INAGAKI
Rear-Admiral; Chief of General Affairs Bureau of Naval Air Force, c.1937.

INOGUCHI Toshihara
Rear-Admiral; Advocated peaceful solution to the war, 1944; Deputy Commander of 1st Battleship Division and Captain of super battleship *Musashi* in 1st Battleship Division (under M. UGKAI), 1944; Part of 1st Sriking Force (under T. KURITA) in Operation 'SHO.1.' (attempted decisive battle with American naval forces), Philippines; Attacked in Sibuyuan Sea (Battle of Leyte Gulf), Philippines, by American aircraft, 24 October 1944; Wounded in the attack and the ship was badly damaged; Ordered by T. KURITA to ground his ship on the nearest land to become a shore battery but she was already sinking; Gave his sword to a young ensign with a letter requesting the Emperor's forgiveness and went down with *Musashi* having refused to leave, 24/25 October 1944.

INOUYE (INOUE) Shigeyoshi (Shigemi, Seibei)

Naval Attaché in Rome, 1927–30; Rear Admiral; Chief of Staff of Yokosuka Naval Base, Japan (under M. YONAI) by 1936; Vociferous supporter of the 1930 London Naval Conference Treaty giving a fleet ration of 5:5:3 (Britain:America: Japan); Head of Naval Affairs Bureau, Tokyo, 20 September 1937; Opposed army plans to conquer China after the 'Marco Polo Bridge Incident', 1937; Vice-Admiral, November 1939; Chief of Naval Aviation Department, 1940; Predicted island-hopping strategy of the American navy in the event of war; Advocated an increase in naval air power instead of battleships but was ignored; Opposed signing of Tripartite Pact with Germany and Italy, 1940; Stated at a conference that the Japanese naval arm was too weak to fight a war with America, 3 July 1941; Replaced, 1941; Commander of 4th (Mandates) Fleet (replacing S. KAJIOKA) comprising three light cruisers, 6th Destroyer Flotilla, etc., HQ Truk, Caroline Islands, December 1941; Supported invasion of Guam, 10 December 1941, and Wake Island (see S. KAJIOKA), 23 December 1941; Bismarck (Rabaul and Kavieng) invasion (see A. GOGO, T. ONISHI), January 1942; Commander of 4th Fleet and Task Force for Operation 'MO' (invasion of Port Moresby, New Guinea, and Tulagi) which embarked from Truk to Rabaul, New Britain, 30 April 1942; Remained aboard flagship at Rabaul during the operation; Controlled five separate forces (see A. GOTO, C. HARA, S. KAJIOKA, K. MARUSHIGE, K. SHIMA, T. TAKAGI) plus 25th Air Flotilla (under S. YAMADA); Tulagi on Florida Island, Solomons, occupied (by K. SHIMA), 3 May 1942; Main Port Moresby Force was near Louisiade Archipelago, 7 May 1942; Postponed invasion attack and ordered fleet back to Rabaul, 7 May 1942 (Carrier Strike Force was defeated at Battle of Coral Sea which forced cancellation of Port Moresby attack), 8 May 1942; He was recalled 11–15 May 1942; Commandant of Etajima Naval College, c.1942–5 August 1944; Vice Minister of Navy, August 1944; Recommended peace proposals be prepared, late August 1944; Survived the war.

Personal facts: Excellent administrator. Possessed no personal ambition. Analytical mind and far-sighted. Excellent musician.

IRIFUMA Naosaburo

Vice-Admiral; Commander of 8th Naval Base Force, Rabaul, New Britain, November 1943.

ISHIDO Yuzo

Rear-Admiral; Commander of 4th Naval Guard Force (under 24th Base Force – Y. SHIBATA), Koepang, Dutch East Indies, October 1944.

ISHIKAWA

Rear-Admiral; Commander of 23rd Air Flotilla, Macassar or Kendari, Celebes, 1942.

ISHIZAKI (ISHIZAKA, ISHIZUKE) Noburo (Riku)

Rear-Admiral; Commander of Submarine Special Attack Group, Kure, Japan, 1942;* Ordered by C in C Combined Fleet (I. YAMAMOTO) to attack Allied shipping at Madagascar with midget submarines, April 1942; Sailed in *I*-Class submarines with midget submarines attached; Launched two (of three) midget submarines into Diego Suarez Bay, Madagascar, which sank the tanker *Loyalty*, and unsuccessfully attacked the battleship HMS *Ramillies*, 30 May 1942 (both midgets failed to return); Group remained at sea for two months, sinking nineteen vessels in the Mozambique Channel, June–July 1942.

Note: Possibly the same as ICHIKAWA Noboru.

* This may be the same as 8th Submarine Flotilla.

ITAGAKI Sakae
Rear-Admiral; Commander of Kure Naval Guard Force, Kure, Japan, November 1943.

ITO Seiichi
Born in Kurosaki-Hiraki village near Omuta in Fukuoka prefecture; Entered Etajima Naval Academy, 1908; Graduated (15th of 148), 1911; Graduated top of class from Naval War College, 1922; Assistant Naval Attaché, Washington, USA, 1927; Graduate of Yale University, America; Rear-Admiral; Chief of Navy Personnel Bureau of Naval General Staff, c.1940; Vice-Admiral; Vice Chief of Naval General Staff (replacing N. KONDO), 1 September 1941; Accompanied Prince Takeda (in the army) to Combined Fleet HQ, Truk, for discussions on Guadalcanal and Port Moresby operations, 3 September 1942; Member of Board of Enquiry into S. FUKUDOME, 18 April 1944; Commander of 2nd Fleet, November 1944; Recommended decommissioning of 2nd Fleet to C in C Combined Fleet (S. TOYODA) because of inactivity and losses due to American air power, March 1945; Commander of First Special Attack Force (redesignated name of 2nd Fleet) in Operation 'TEN-ICHI' ('Heaven Number One') for suicide attack on American fleet off Okinawa without air cover (see also K. ARUGA, K. KOMURA, N. MORISHITA); Sailed in flagship Yamato with light cruiser Yahagi (see also K. KOMURA) and eight destroyers from Tokuyama, Inland Sea, Japan, 6 April 1945; Mission to sink as many American ships as possible and then beach Yamato as a shore battery; One destroyer forced to return with engine trouble; Force attacked by American carrier aircraft before reaching Okinawa; Yamato crippled and sunk by torpedoes and bombs; Refused to abandon ship, locking himself in his cabin and going down with the ship (see also K. ARUGA), 7 April 1945 (the mission was subsequently abandoned).

Personal facts: Regarded as one of the best naval officers of his generation. A moderate. Approachable and pleasant personality.

ITO Yoshioka (Kenzo)
Vice-Admiral; Commander of 30th Naval Base Force, January 1944; Palau Islands, April 1944; Surrendered at Pelelieu, Palau Islands, 1945.*

* Surrendered his sword at Pelelieu to a US Marine detachment. Now in Annapolis Naval Academy Museum. Cat.no. 46.43. It is a naval kyu-guntō with scabbard and knot.

IWABUCHI (IWABACHI) Sanji
Rear-Admiral; Commander of 31st Naval Special Base Force, Manila, Philippines, under South West Area Fleet (D. OKOCHI), September? 1944; Ordered by D. OKOCHI to concentrate his force of 16,000–17,000 naval troops in Manila and defend it to the last man (even though 14th Area Army Commander T. YAMASHITA insisted Manila be declared an 'open city' to avoid fighting), January 1945;[1] Fortified many buildings and the walled citadel of Intramuros; Americans attacked from three sides with 37th, 11th Airborne and 1st Cavalry

divisions, 4 February 1945; Japanese refused to allow civilian population to evacuate the city; Half of the city taken by the Americans after fierce fighting, 7 February 1945; Refused to be extricated by assistance of 14th Area Army forces sent for this purpose; American heavy artillery fire forced surviving Japanese into Intramuros Citadel and the southern waterfront area, 12 February 1945; Those in the Intramuros Citadel had refused to release non-combatants and prisoners by 16 February 1945; Walls breached in two places and entered by American 37th division, 23 February 1945; 3,000 civilians suddenly released by Japanese in the Citadel, 23 February 1945; Intramuros finally taken after the death of the entire garrison, 25 February 1945; Fierce house-to-house fighting to the death using suicide tactics continued in remaining occupied areas of the city;[2] Japanese naval troops committed atrocities and massacres of civilians during the fighting; Last remnant killed, 3 March 1945; Committed suicide or was killed, his body never being found.

[1] Naval units remained autonomous even though all fighting had been restricted to land.
[2] Manila was virtually destroyed with an estimated 100,000 Filipino civilians killed. American casualties were 1,000 dead and 5,500 wounded. Only a handful of Japanese survived out of 16,000–17,000 men.

IWAMURA Seiichi
Captain; Senior Aide to Navy Minister, c.1933. Vice-Admiral; Chief of Naval Technical Department, c.1941; Opposed war with America and Britain; Pro-British and pro-American.

IZAKI Shunji
Rear-Admiral; Commander of reinforcement convoy 'Tokyo Express' to Vila on Kolombangara Island, Solomons (replacing T. AKIYAMA), 13 July 1943; Sailed with nine destroyers and flagship light cruiser *Jintsu*; Reached Kolombangara and successfully unloaded troops while five destroyers fought superior American naval forces at Battle of Kolombangara; Killed when *Jintsu* was sunk with 482 officers and men, 13 July 1943.

JOJIMA Takatsugu
Rear-Admiral; Attempted to persuade M. UGAKI not to commit suicide, Kyushu, Japan, 14 August 1945.

JOSHIMA Takaji
Rear-Admiral; Commander of Escort Force to reinforce Guadalcanal, Solomons, 12 October 1942; Commander of naval garrison of Shortland Islands, Solomons, 1943; Flew from his Shortland HQ to Rabaul, New Britain, to warn C in C Combined Fleet I. YAMAMOTO to cancel his tour of inspection because he thought the Americans had broken the naval code, 17 April 1943;* Commander of Reserve Carrier Force (part of 1st Mobile Fleet) at Battle of Philippine Sea, June 1944.

* This warning was ignored with the resultant death of I. YAMAMOTO.

KAJIOKA Sadamichi
Rear-Admiral; Commander of Wake Island (in Marshalls) Invasion Force (under 4th Fleet – S. INOUYE) consisting of flagship cruiser *Yubari*, destroyer force and invasion transports; Bombarded island and attempted to land but was repulsed with loss of two destroyers and damage to *Yubari*, 11 December 1941;* Withdrew to Kwajalein; Reinforced by 8th Cruiser Squadron (under H. ABE) returning from

Pearl Harbor attack and launched a second attack on the island which resulted in its occupation, 24 December 1941; Removed from command by C in C Combined Fleet I. YAMAMOTO for failure to take Wake on schedule, 24 December 1941; Commander of Port Moresby (New Guinea) Invasion Force (*see also* S. INOUYE), sailing from Rabaul, New Britain (with flagship *Yubari*, eleven transports and destroyer escort), 4 May 1942; Rendezvoused with Support Group (under K. MARUSHIGE) off Buin, Bougainville, with Covering Force (A. GOTO) nearby, 7 May 1942; Operation ordered abandoned with withdrawal to Rabaul, 7 May 1942.

* The destroyer *Hayate*, sunk by shore batteries, was the first Japanese surface warship lost in the war, 11 December 1941.

KAKUTA (KATUTA) Kakaji

Rear-Admiral; Commander of 3rd Naval Air Base covering Balikpapan and Bandjermasin, Borneo, invasions, late January–early February 1942; Commander of 2nd Carrier Division Striking Force (under 5th Fleet – B. HOSOGAWA) with two carriers (flagship *Ryujo*), two heavy cruisers and three destroyers in Operation 'AL' (invasion of Aleutians) sailing from Ominato, Honshu, Japan, 26 May 1942; Launched air attacks on Dutch Harbour, Unalaska Island, Aleutians, 3rd and 4th June 1942; Supported Kiska Island landings, 6 June 1942, and Attu Island landings, 7 June 1942 (both in Aleutians); Commander of 2nd Carrier Division (under 3rd Fleet – C. NAGUMO) with carriers *Junyo*, *Zuiho*, flagship *Hiyo*, in Guadalcanal, Solomons, operations, October, 1942; *Hiyo* returned to Truk with engine trouble, transferred flag to *Junyo*, 22 October 1942; Battle of Santa Cruz with *Zuiho* badly damaged, 26 October 1942; Returned to Truk by 30 October 1942; Vice-Admiral; Commander of 1st Air Fleet (land-based) for defence of Marianas and Philippines, HQ Tinian; Attacked American task force in support of 1st Mobile Fleet (J. OZAWA) at Battle of Marianas (Philippine Sea), 18–20 June 1944; American 4th Marine Division invaded Tinian Island in the north, 24 July 1944; Left tactical defence of island to Captain Ōya Goiichi, IJN, commanding 56th Naval Guard Force with 4,110 men (and 4,700 army troops under Colonel Ogata); American 2nd Marine Division landed, 26 July 1944; Japanese army and naval troops combined in pincer movement to attack Americans but were beaten off with severe losses (1,241 killed); Tinian town taken by Americans by 31 July 1944; Final *banzai* (suicide) attack launched 1 August 1944; Island secured by Americans, 12 August 1944; Presumed killed or suicide by this time (replaced by K. TERAOKA).

Note: By the end of the Tinian campaign the Japanese had 6,050 dead with 235 taken prisoner. American losses were 314 with 1,515 wounded.

KAMADA Michiaki

Rear-Admiral; Commander of 22nd Naval Special Base Force during defence of Balikpapan, Borneo, 1 July 1945; The 1st Battalion was broken during the first day's fighting with invading Australians; Surrendered Japanese forces in Dutch Borneo to Australian Major-General E.J. Milford, GOC 7th Australian Division aboard HMAS *Burdekim*, twenty miles south-east of Samarinda, 8 September 1945;* Sentenced to death as a war criminal at a military court at Pontianak,

* Surrendered a *kai-guntō* with knot to Major-General Milford at this ceremony. It has a 15th-century blade and 17th-century *tsuba* (guard). Now in the Australian War Memorial museum. Cat.no. AWM 20323.

Dutch Borneo, for ordering the decapitation of 1,500 west Borneo natives (who plotted against the Japanese) in 1944 plus the murder and ill treatment of 2,000 Dutch POWs on Flores Island.

KAMATA
Rear-Admiral; Commander of 2nd Special Naval Base Force, Wewak, New Guinea, January 1943.*

* 2nd Special Base Force was absorbed by 27th Special Base Force in March 1944 and he appears to have been replaced by that time.

KANAZAWA Masao
Rear-Admiral; Commander of Kure Naval District, Japan, May 1945; HQ Kure.

KATAGIRI (KATAGIEI) Eikichi
Vice-Admiral; Commander of a naval air force base in China, 1941; Chief of Naval Aviation Department, c.1941; Opposed war with Britain and America.

KATO Kanji
Inspection tour of Europe and became pro-German, 1920; Vice-President of Naval Academy; Vice-Admiral; President of Naval War College; Leader of Militant officer corps; Vehemently opposed 1922 Washington Naval Conference Treaty limiting naval tonnage (opposing T. KATO) and instead wanted to increase Japan's fleet strength, 1922; Vice Chief of Naval General Staff, c.1923; Voiced his views on the need for an increase in fleet strength, receiving the support of major Japanese industrial cartels; Commander of Yokosuka Naval Base, Japan, by 1925; Demanded to head naval delegation to London Naval Conference but was refused because of his belligerent attitude, 1930; Admiral; Chief of Staff to Navy Minister by 1930;* Furious at terms agreed at 1930 London Naval Conference for a fleet ratio of 5:5:3 (Britain:America:Japan) and appealed directly to the Emperor but was ignored; Resigned in protest (replaced by N. TANIGUCHI), 10 June 1930; Member of Supreme Military Council by 1933 (see also S. TAKAHASHI); Tried to manoeuvre naval policy, as he wanted it, through his protégé N. SUETSUGU; Supported purge of moderate senior naval officers by Navy Minister M. OSUMI, 1933–4; Supporter of 'Strike North' (against Russia) policy; Retired from active service, November 1935.

Note: An extreme militant, he is often known as 'KATO the younger' and is easily confused with KATO Tomosaburo ('KATO the elder').

* Advocated building super battleships apparently to force the Americans to follow suit so that those based in the Atlantic could not reinforce the Pacific easily because they would not be able to pass through the Panama Canal.

KATO Tadao
Admiral?; Surrendered all Ryukyu Islands at Kadena airfield on Okinawa to General Joseph Stilwell, the new American 10th Army Commander, 7 September 1945.

KATO Takayoshi
Admiral; Military Councillor by 1940.

KATO Tomosaburo
Captain or Rear-Admiral; Chief of Staff to Combined Fleet (under H. TOGO), 1905; Vice-Admiral; Commander-in-Chief of Combined Fleet, c.1914; Admiral;

Navy Minister, 1914–23; Strongly advocated '8–8 plan' (i.e., fleet with a nucleus of 8 modern battleships and 8 modern cruisers) which was finally approved in 1920; Strengthened naval air arm, 1918; Supported a reduction in naval ship building programme; Senior naval delegate at Washington Naval Conference and ratified the international decision to limit the navies of Britain, America and Japan by a reduction of tonnage, 1922; Prime Minister, 1922; Died while in this office, aged 64, 1923.

Note: A Liberal, he is often known as 'KATO the elder' and was a restraining influence on KATO Kanji ('KATO the younger'). The two are often confused.

KATSUMATA
(Full?) Admiral; *c.* Second World War; Interrogated after the war in an American bombing survey.

KIMURA Masanori (Masatomi)
Captain; Captain of cruiser *Suzuya* in 7th Cruiser Squadron (under T. KURITA) forming part of Close Support Group to Midway Island Invasion Force Main Body in Operation 'MI', May–June 1942; Rear-Admiral; Commander of 8th Escort Fleet; Sailed from Rabaul, New Britain, with six transports and four destroyers to reinforce Salamaua, New Guinea; Attacked by American aircraft and lost all transports and escorts in Battle of Bismark Sea, 3 March 1943;* Bombarded San Jose airfield, Philippines, with an 'Intrusion Force' but was defeated, 26 December 1944.

* Also reported to be eight transports and eight destroyers suffering heavy losses including four destroyers.

KIMURA Shofuku
Rear-Admiral; Commander of the most brilliant evacuation of the war, taking off 5,183 men in two cruisers and six destroyers which were loaded in 55 minutes, from Kiska Island, Aleutians (aided by fog and American errors) late July 1943.

Note: The Americans landed after six weeks of heavy bombardment of the island only to find the Japanese had evacuated the entire garrison without their knowledge.

KIMURA Susumu
Rear-Admiral; Commander of 10th Destroyer Flotilla (comprising flagship light cruiser *Nagara* and 4th, 10th, 17th Destroyer Divisions) acting as Destroyer Screen to 1st Air Fleet (under C. NAGUMO) in Operation 'MI' during attempted invasion of Midway Island, May–June 1942.

KISHI Fukuki
Rear-Admiral; Commander of Destroyer Screen* (with 9th, 20th, 24th, 27th Destroyer Divisions) for Aleutian Support (Guard) Force under S. TAKASU in Operation 'AL' (invasion of the Aleutians), May–June 1942.

*He was probably a Commander of a Destroyer Flotilla.

KISHIMOTO Kaneji
Rear-Admiral; Chief of Torpedo Department of Kure Naval Arsenal, Japan; Developed (with Captain Asaguma Toshihide) 24in diameter oxygen-fuelled 'Long Lance' torpedo which was virtually trackless, 1928–33.

KITAMURA

Rear-Admiral; Chief Paymaster to 8th Fleet; Shot down in transport aircraft which crashed into the sea (when I. YAMAMOTO who was in the first aircraft was killed) in ambush by American aircraft near Buin, Bougainville, Solomon Islands, but survived, 18 April 1943.

KOBAYASHI

Rear- or Vice-Admiral; Commander? of 14th Air Fleet, c.1944; Commanded defence of Truk, Caroline Islands, after abandonment as a main naval base; Lost numerous ships (mostly transports), and aircraft during heavy American air attacks, 16–17 February 1944.

KOBAYASHI Masashi

Vice-Admiral; Commander of 4th Fleet, 26 July 1943; Replaced (by C. HARA), June 1944.

KOBAYASHI Seizo

Admiral; Retired; Governor-General of Formosa, 1936–40; Ordered arrested by American occupation forces in Tokyo as a suspected war criminal, 2 December 1945; Held in Sugamo prison, Tokyo, but released without prosecution, 31 August 1947.

KOBAYASHI Seizaburō

Vice-Admiral; Retired by 1940; Leader of anti-British movement; An ardent nationalist.

KOBAYASHI Shosaburo

Rear-Admiral; Commander of Kasumigaura Aviation Corps, north-east of Tokyo, Japan, until December 1931;* Chief of Navy Special Service, Manchuria, from December 1931.

* A top secret establishment also known as 'Misty Lagoon Air Development Station'.

KOBAYASHI T.

Rear-Admiral; Commander of 17th Minelayer Flotilla, 1941–2.

KOGA Mineichi

Graduated from Etajima Naval College (14th of 174), 1906; Had connections with the Imperial Household; Spent much time in Europe; Approved of Naval Limitation Treaty of 1930; Vice-Admiral; Chief of 2nd Division of Naval General Staff, 1935; Considered capital ships could be adequately defended against air attack; Replaced 1937; Vice Chief of Naval General Staff, December 1937; Opposed war with America and Britain; Replaced (by N. KONDO), October 1939; Commander of 2nd Fleet, 1939; Commander of China Area Fleet, Shanghai, China, by 1941 or early 1942; Commander of Yokosuka Naval Base, Japan, 1942; Admiral; Commander-in-Chief of Combined Fleet (after death of I. YAMA-MOTO), 18 April 1943; HQ Truk, Caroline Islands; Reinforced Rabaul, New Britain, with 3rd Fleet aircraft (taken from carriers *Zuikaku, Shokaku, Zuiho*), 1 November 1943; Lost many aircraft to American carrier aircraft and ordered a withdrawal of survivors, 12 November 1943; Losses of carriers and cruisers *see* T. KURITA) forced Combined Fleet to remain at Truk; After fall of Marshall Islands it became necessary to abandon Truk as a main base (*see* KOBAYASHI), 10

February 1944; Withdrew to Palaus leaving only light forces at Truk consisting of two light cruisers, eight destroyers and auxiliaries, February 1944 (these vessels had all been sunk in harbour by 18 February 1944); Palaus abandoned as Combined Fleet advance base, early April 1944; Adopted defensive policy, wanting to hold the line of Marianas, Palaus, Western New Guinea to the death; Ordered Fleet sortie and transferred HQ to Davao, Mindanao in Philippines, to co-ordinate defence against expected American attack on the Palaus but was killed en route, crashing into the sea during a storm off Cebu, 31 March 1944* (see also S. FUKUDOME); Replaced by S. TOYODA.

Note: He had prepared plans to reorganize Combined Fleet on American lines which was immediately implemented by his successor S. TOYODA.

* News of his death was kept from the Japanese people for one month which also delayed official announcement of TOYODA's appointment.

KOJIMA Hideo
Naval Attaché in Berlin; Captain; Chief of 7th Section of Intelligence Division (Europe and Russia), 1939–41; Pro-German; Rear-Admiral by the end of the war.

Marquis KOMATSU Teruhisa
Cousin of Empress; Rear-Admiral; Dean of Naval Staff College, Tokyo, c.1941; Vice-Admiral; Commander of 6th Fleet – Submarines (replacing M. SHIMIZU), March 1941; HQ Kwajalein, Marshall Islands; Flagship light cruiser *Katori*; Advance Submarine Force consisting of 1st, 3rd, 5th Submarine Flotillas, formed screen west of Midway Island during Operation 'MI' (attempted invasion of Midway), May–June 1942; Admiral; HQ Truk, Caroline islands; Replaced (by T. TAKAGI), November 1943; After the war he was elevated to the House of Councillors (formerly 'Peers').

KOMURA Keizo
Captain; Captain of cruiser *Chikuma**in 8th Cruiser Squadron (under H. ABE) forming part of Support Group to 1st Air Fleet in Operation 'MI' (attempted invasion of Midway Island), May–June 1942; Under 3rd Fleet (C. NAGUMO) in Battle of Santa Cruz Islands, Solomons, 25 October 1942; Rear-Admiral; Chief of Staff to Mobile Strike (Carrier) Force Commander (J. OZAWA) during Operation 'SHO.1' (acting as a decoy force in attempted attack by other units on American vessels off Leyte, Philippines) at Battle of Cape Engano (Leyte Gulf), 25 October 1944; Commander of 2nd Destroyer Flotilla in 2nd Fleet (under S.ITO), flagship light cruiser *Yahagi*; Ordered to form escort of super battleship *Yamato* (see K. ARUGA, S. ITO) with eight destroyers in Operation 'TEN-ICHI' (suicide attack on American naval forces off Okinawa); Sailed from Tokuyama, Inland Sea, Japan, 6 April 1945; One destroyer dropped out with engine trouble; *Yahagi* sunk by air attack but he refused to abandon ship because it would be demeaning to be rescued by a small boat which was the only thing available; He survived and was picked up by the destroyer *Hatsushimo*, 7 April 1945; three destroyers sunk, two damaged but returned to Japan with survivors; Continued towards Okinawa with two undamaged destroyers (all that remained of 2nd Fleet) but was recalled, 7 April 1945; Returned to Sasebo, Japan.

* The *Battle of Midway* by Peter C. Smith (see Bibliography) gives him as commander of the cruiser *Chikuma* (in 8th Cruiser Division) and also as commander of the battleship *Kirishima* (in 2nd Section of 3rd Battleship Division) simultaneously. This an error and the former command appears correct.

KONDO Nobutake

Graduated from Etajima Naval College (1st of 171), 1907; Studied in Germany and became pro-German; Considered a brilliant staff officer; Rear-Admiral; Chief of Staff of 1st Division (Operations) of Naval General Staff, December 1935; Replaced (by M. UGAKI), December 1938; Vice-Admiral; Vice Chief of Naval General Staff (replacing M. KOGA), October 1939; Remained neutral about joining Tripartite Pact with Germany and Italy; Recommended by German Ambassador to Japan that the Japanese navy should attack Singapore when Germany invaded Britain, but he rejected the idea since America would be drawn into the war, March 1941; Replaced (by S. ITO), August 1941; Said to be the last Naval Attaché to London (but this is doubtful. see KONDO Taiichiro);[1] Commander of 2nd Fleet (Scouting Fleet) based on Hainan Island, southern China, 1941; Concurrently Commander of Southern Force for attack on Malaya and Dutch East Indies; Forces comprised 3rd Battle Squadron–2nd Division (battleships *Kongo, Haruna*), 4th Carrier Division (carrier *Zuiho* and later *Shoho*), 4th, 5th, 7th Cruiser Squadrons (ten cruisers), 16th Light Cruiser Squadron (three light cruisers), 2nd, 3rd, 4th, 5th Destroyer Flotillas, and 4th, 5th, 6th Submarine Flotillas (eighteen submarines); Split into 2nd Fleet (N. KONDO) for Malaya and Java invasions; Western Force (J. OZAWA) for invasion of Sumatra after Malaya was secure; Eastern and Central Forces (I. TAKAHASHI) for invasions of Menedo, Kendari, Macassar in Celebes and Dutch Borneo; Personally commanded Main Body with battleships *Haruna, Kongo,* heavy cruisers *Atago* (flagship), *Maya, Takao* and ten destroyers; Rendezvoused in Inland Sea Japan, 24 November 1941; 'Malaya Force' assembled at Samah on Hainan Island, 26 November 1941; Supported invasion of southern Siam and northern Malaya, 7–9 December 1941; Reunited with forces of J. OZAWA and T. KURITA to search for British Naval Force Z (*Prince of Wales* and *Repulse*), 10 December 1941; Formed Southern Support Force for main Eastern and Central Forces (under I. TAKAHASHI) for invasion of Java, February 1942; Commander of Support Force (battleships and cruisers) to 1st Air Fleet (under C. NAGUMO) to prevent Allied reinforcements to India, Ceylon and Australia, sinking shipping from Java (flagship heavy cruiser *Atago*) February–March 1942; Commander of Support Group (battleships and cruisers) in Operation 'C' (under C. NAGUMO) in attack on Ceylon, April 1942; Returned to Japan, 17 April 1942; Short abortive sortie to locate American carriers which launched the 'Doolittle' raid on Tokyo, 18 April 1942; Refitted for Operation 'MI' (attempted invasion of Midway Island. *See* I. YAMAMOTO);[2] Commander of 2nd Fleet (Midway Invasion Cover Force) with personal command of Main Body and 4th Cruiser Squadron; Forces comprised carrier *Zuiho*, battleships *Kongo, Hiei,* four heavy cruisers, one light cruiser and 4th Destroyer Flotilla; Sailed from Hashirajima, Inland Sea, Japan, together with 1st Air Fleet (Main Force), 29 May 1942; Ordered to support 1st Air Fleet (carriers, *See* C. NAGUMO) after their sinking at Battle of Midway and ordered to take command from C. NAGUMO, 4 June 1942; Ordered back to join 1st Fleet, 5 June 1942; Commander of Main Support Force (2nd Fleet) at Second Battle of Solomon Sea, 24 August 1942; Commander of Advance Force (2nd Fleet)[3] with one battleship (flagship) *Kirishima*, four cruisers, nine destroyers at Battle of Santa Cruz Islands, 26 October 1942; Detached section of 2nd Fleet (under H. ABE) to bombard Henderson airfield, Guadalcanal, Solomons, while he took remainder of fleet (two carriers, two battleships, four cruisers nineteen destroyers) 150 miles north of Savo Island to launch aircraft to cover Bombardment Force; Henderson Field bombardment failed to go to plan (*see* H. ABE) so he left carriers with escorts and took battleship *Kirishima*, four cruisers and nine destroyers to complete the bombardment; Intercepted by American fleet at Ironbottom Sound off Savo Island and was defeated in third phase of the Battle of Solomon Sea with loss of battleship *Kirishima*, 14–15 November 1942; Withdrew leaving Guadalcanal reinforcement force (under R. TANAKA) unsupported (*see also* G. MIKAWA); Commander of 2nd Air Fleet, defence of Gilbert Islands, 1944; Commander-in-Chief of China Area Fleet by January 1945 (possibly replaced by R. FUKUDA); In Saigon, Indo–China, at end of war, August 1945; Remained in command of Japanese naval units used by the British to fight Communist Viet Minh guerrillas in Indo–China, 1945; Surrendered a sword in an embroidered silk bag to the senior British Naval Officer at Saigon, Captain I Scott-Bell, RN, aboard HMS *Waveney*, December 1945;[4] Became a businessman after the war.

Personal facts: Liked by all officers. Punctual and methodical. Always listened to others before making a decision. A good bureaucrat.

[1] According to *Old Friends, New Enemies* by A. J. Marder (*see* Bibliography), he held the post of Naval Attaché in London, returning to Japan in November 1941. This is probably incorrect since it conflicts with KONDO Taiichiro also given in this post by the same reference work. There appears to be confusion over the names.
[2] Opposed Midway invasion plan since the island could not be supplied easily after capture.
[3] Also nominal Commander of Main Force (3rd Fleet under C. NAGUMO with three carriers and escorts) which acted independently.
[4] The blade is said to have been made in 1385. Scott-Bell personally returned this sword to KONDO in Tokyo, early June 1952.

KONDO Chimaki
Rear-Admiral; Commander of 3rd Submarine Flotilla (consisting of Submarine Tender, 13th, 19th, 30th Submarine Divisions) under 6th Fleet (T. KOMATSU) during Operation 'MI' (Midway Island invasion attempt). May–June 1942; Five submarines formed a screen between Midway and Hawaii in an attempt to intercept any American naval units.

KONDO Taiichiro
Captain; Naval Attaché in London, February 1939; Spoke Fluent English; Continually advised Tokyo that Britain would not surrender and that Germany could not successfully invade; Rear-Admiral, October 1941; Replaced, November 1941.

Note: KONDO Nobutake is also said to have held this post at this time (according to *Old Friends, New Enemies* by A.J. Marder) but this is probably the correct entry, unless they are one and the same person.

KOYONAGI Koniji (Tomiji)
Captain; Captain of battleship *Kongo* in 3rd Battleship Division (under G. MIKAWA) forming part of Midway Island Invasion Force Main Body (under N. KONDO), May–June 1942; Bombarded Henderson airfield, Guadalcanal, Solomons (accompanied by battleship *Haruna*) with devastating results, 14 October 1942; Rear-Admiral; Commanded destroyer convoy ('Tokyo Express') reinforcing Guadalcanal (replacing R. TANAKA) from late December 1942 or early 1943; GHQ, Tokyo, ordered evacuation of Guadalcanal, 4 January 1943; Commander of destroyer force which evacuated 12,000–13,000 troops of 17th Army (under Lieutenant-General H. HYAKUTAKE) using 18–22 destroyers in three separate night-time operations from Cape Esperance, 1–7 February 1942;[1]

Possibly Commander of 11th Air Fleet, Rabaul, New Britain (under South-east Area Fleet), 1944; Chief of Staff to 5th Fleet (under T. KURITA) which formed 1st Striking Force (with 1st Division) in Operation 'SHO.1', in flagship heavy cruiser *Atago*;[2] Sailed from Brunei, Borneo, 22 October 1944; *Atago* sunk, transferred with T. KURITA to super battleship *Yamato* in Suriago Straits, Philippines, 22 October 1944; Passed through San Bernardino Straits into Philippine Sea, 25 October 1944; Attacked American naval force of escort carriers ('Taffy 3') but counter-attacked by American aircraft from other 'Taffy' groups; Wounded by shrapnel; Advised T. KURITA to turn south to Leyte Gulf to attack the American 7th Fleet off Samar Island; Withdrew upon hearing of Southern Force (*see* S. NISHIMURA) losses; Survived the war.

[1] The Americans despite naval and air superiority failed to detect these evacuations until late on 9 February 1942, by which time it was too late.
[2] This appointment could possibly have been after the 'SHO.1' operation.

KUBO Kyuji
Rear-Admiral; Commander of 4th Surprise Attack Force for Legaspi landings, Luzon, Philippines, in flagship light cruiser *Nagara*, 12 December 1941; Commander of Escort Group (2nd Destroyer Flotilla) for invasion of Macassar in Celebes, flagship *Nagara*, 8 February 1942; Commander of Bali Occupation Force and involved in battle with Admiral Doorman's ABDA naval forces off Bali, 19–20 February 1942; Commander of Christmas Island invasion (190 miles south-west of Java), flagship light cruiser *Naka*, 31 March 1942.

KUDA Hisahachi
Rear-Admiral; Commander of Yokosuka Naval Guard Force, Yokosuka, Japan, August 1944.

KURIHARA Etsuzo
Rear-Admiral; Publicly supported formation of Special Attack Corps ('Kamikaze' units), May 1945.

KURITA Takeo
Graduated from Etajima Naval College (28th of 149), 1910; Torpedo specialist; Rear-Admiral; Commander of 7th Cruiser Squadron forming Main Body of Escort Force (under 'Malaya Force' – J. OZAWA) with cruisers *Mikuma, Mogami, Suzuya,* flagship *Kumano* and ten destroyers for invasion of Malaya, December 1941; Supported invasion of Southern Siam and Northern Malaya, 7–9 December 1941; Reunited with forces of J. OZAWA and N. KONDO to search for British Force Z (*Prince of Wales* and *Repulse*), 19 December 1941; Commander of Support Force for invasion of Java (under J. OZAWA), February 1942; Commanded part of 'Malaya Force' to harass shipping in Bay of Bengal (under J. OZAWA), flagship heavy cruiser *Chokai*, April 1942; Commander of Close Support Group (under 2nd Fleet – N. KONDO) with 7th and 8th Cruiser Squadrons for Operation 'MI' (occupation of Midway Island – *see* I. YAMA-MOTO); Sailed from Guam for Midway, 28 May 1942; Ordered to withdraw after hearing of carrier losses at Battle of Midway, 5 June 1942; Cruisers *Mikuma* sunk and *Mogami* severely damaged by American aircraft, 6 June 1942; Commander of 3rd Battleship Division with battleships *Haruna, Kongo*, which shelled Henderson airfield, Guadalcanal, Solomons, 14 October 1942; Vice-Admiral; Commander of Close Support Group (under 2nd Fleet) with two battleships and six destroyers at

Battle of Santa Cruz Islands, 26 October 1942; Transferred from Truk with seven heavy and one light cruisers, four destroyers plus fleet train to Rabaul, New Britain (after defeat of S. OMORI at Empress Augusta Bay), early November 1943; Five cruisers and two destroyers damaged by American air attack at Rabaul, 5 November 1943; Ordered to withdraw to Truk, Caroline Islands, by 11 November 1943; Commander of 2nd Fleet* (under 1st Mobile Fleet – J. OZAWA) comprising 1st Battle Division (M. UGAKI with battleships *Musashi, Nagato, Yamato*), 2nd Battle Division (battleships *Haruna, Kongo*), 4th Cruiser Squadron (flagship *Atago, Chokai, Maya, Takao*), 5th Cruiser Squadron (*Harugo, Myoko*), 7th Cruiser Squadron (*Chikuma, Kumano, Suzuya, Tone*), and screen of fourteen destroyers with light cruiser *Noshiro*, April 1944; Formed Van Force of 1st Mobile Fleet (under J. OZAWA) at Battle of the Marianas (Philippine Sea) with one battleship and two cruisers being damaged, 18–20 June 1944; Commander of 5th Fleet in Operation 'SHO.1' (two-pronged attack on American invasion forces off Leyte, Philippines, with hoped for decisive naval battle), October 1944; 5th Fleet comprised super battleships *Yamato, Musashi,* five battleships, eleven heavy cruisers, five light cruisers and nineteen destroyers; Flagship heavy cruiser *Atago*; Arrived at Brunei, Borneo, 20 October 1944; Sailed for Leyte Gulf, 22 October 1944; Formed 1st Striking Force of the operation; Split Force into two, retaining personal command of 1st Division Attack Force to proceed through Sibuyuan Sea and San Bernardino Strait (while Southern Force under S. NISHIMURA was to attack through the Suriago Strait); *See also* J. OZAWA, N. SAKONJU, K. SHIMA, S. TOYODA; Lost heavy cruisers *Atago, Maya*, with *Takao* badly damaged by submarines and rescued by a destroyer; Transferred flag to super battleship *Yamato* (*see also* K. KOYONAGI), 22 October 1944; Lost super battleship *Musashi* to American air attack in the Sibuyan Sea (*see* T. INOGUCHI), 24 October 1944; Heavy cruiser *Mogami* badly damaged, forced to withdraw but sunk by aircraft attack; Passed through San Bernardino Straits into Philippine Sea, 25 October 1944; Attacked American naval force of escort carriers ('Taffy 3') but counter-attacked by aircraft from other 'Taffy' groups which damaged three heavy cruisers, 26 October 1944; Turned south towards Leyte Gulf to attack American 7th Fleet landing troops but then turned north to attack American Task Force, 26 October 1944; Withdrew upon hearing of Southern Force losses (*see* S. NISHIMURA); He survived the war.

*Effectively the Main Body and core of the battle fleet.

KUROSHIMA Kumahito (Kameto)
Rear-Admiral; Under command of I. YAMAMOTO, November 1941; Involved in Pearl Harbor attack plan; Chief of 2nd Division of Naval General Staff, July 1943; Prepared list of 'special weapons' (for suicide usage) for Naval General Staff and suggested ramming ships in the hull, April 1944; Worked on the design of the 'Oka' (piloted suicide rocket bomb).

KUSAKA Jinichi (Ninichi) 草鹿 任一
Cousin of R. KUSAKA;[1] Vice-Admiral; Commander of South East Area Fleet (controlling 4th Fleet, 11th Air Fleet and naval forces in the Bismarcks, New Guinea and Solomons) from activation in December 1942; HQ Rabaul, New Britain; Involved in Guadalcanal operations, Solomons, until February 1943; Ordered by C in C Combined Fleet, I. YAMAMOTO, to reinforce New Guinea, February 1943; Reinforced convoy destroyed in Battle of Bismarck Sea, 2–5 March 1943; Took overall command of defence of New Georgia while at Rabaul

(see Major-General M. SASAKI), July–August 1943, Co-signatory of surrender of 'Japanese forces in New Guinea, New Britain, New Ireland, Bougainville and adjacent islands' on behalf of South East Area Fleet (together with Lieutenant-General H. IMAMURA) to Lieutenant-General Vernon H. Sturdee, C in C Australian First Army, in HMS *Glory* off Rabaul, New Britain, 6 September 1945;[2] Surrendered a sword at this time.[3]

[1] See footnote 1 to KUSAKA Ryūnosuke.
[2] Quoted from the formal Instrument of Surrender signed at this time.
[3] An army *shin-guntō* presented to the Australian War Memorial museum by Lady Sturdee in 1982 is said to be his sword (Cat.no. ACC 7013); Blade signed 'KANEYOSHI', 16th-century. Possibly it belonged to an army officer who surrendered at the same time (Lieutenant-General IMAMURA's sword is also in the museum). The whereabouts of his naval sword is unknown.

KUSAKA Ryūnosuke 草鹿 龍之介

Cousin of J. KUSAKA;[1] Graduated from Naval Academy, 1913; Involved in naval aviation; Captain; Captain of carrier *Hosho*; Captain of carrier *Akagi*; Commander of 24th Air Squadron, Palau, Caroline Islands; Rear-Admiral; Chief of Staff to 1st Air Fleet (carriers), Tokyo, 10 April 1941; Given Proposals prepared by T. ONISHI for Operation Z (attack on Pearl Harbor) with instructions to make it operational (assisted by Commanders Oishi and Genda for aviation expertise); Joined 1st Air Fleet (under C. NAGUMO) at Hiroshima; Sailed from Inland Sea, Japan, in fleet flagship carrier *Akagi*; Pearl Harbor attack launched, 7 December 1941; Advised C. NAGUMO to retire as planned (although a second attack was requested by others to bomb the oil storage tanks) because fleet could be at risk since the element of surprise had gone; Returned to Japan with fleet; Remained as Chief of Staff to 1st Air Fleet (under C. NAGUMO) at Battle of Midway, 5–7 June 1942; Made a personal apology to C in C Combined Fleet I. YAMAMOTO on behalf of C. NAGUMO for the failure of the Midway battle; Chief of Staff to 3rd Fleet (under C. NAGUMO);[2] Sailed with three carriers, one heavy cruiser, eight destroyers towards Guadalcanal, Solomons, in flagship *Shokaku* which was badly damaged at Battle of Santa Cruz Islands, 25 October 1942; Vice-Admiral; Commander of 11th Air Fleet (land-based), HQ Rabaul, New Britain (replacing N. TSUKAHARA), October 1942; Supported New Guinea operations and launched air attacks on Guadalcanal to support 17th Army offensive (*see* Lieutenant-General H. HYAKUTAKE); Requested reinforcements from carriers after American air attack on Rabaul but was refused, 11 October 1942; Lost many experienced pilots and aircraft by mid October 1942; Launched heavy raids on Guadalcanal, 11, 14, 18 October 1942; Last intact strike force transferred to New Guinea, 14 November 1942; Received poorly trained reinforcements; Covered naval evacuation of Japanese forces from Guadalcanal, 1–8 February 1943; Advance air bases moved back from Buka Island, Solomons, to New Georgia and Kolombangara, Solomons, February 1943; Commenced Operation 'I' to destroy American air power on Guadalcanal and New Guinea (*see also* G.MIKAWA, J. OZAWA, I. YAMAMOTO), 7–14 April 1943; Excessive claims made for American aircraft destroyed; Chief of Staff to C in C Combined Fleet S. TOYODA (replacing S. FUKUDOME), April? 1944; HQ Tokyo; Supported plan for a 'decisive naval battle' in Philippines, Saipan or Palau areas (code-name 'A-GO'), April 1944; On board flagship cruiser *Oyoda* at Yokosuka, Japan, by May 1944; Insisted Biak Island, off New Guinea, be heavily reinforced (Operation 'KON') after American landings even though he was advised that Saipan was actually the main target of American strategy, May 1944; Visited naval and army HQs on Luzon Island, Philippines, to discuss naval and air assistance for the army, December 1944; Opposed order of C in C Combined Fleet S. TOYODA to send remnant of 2nd Fleet (under S. ITO) on a suicide attack on American naval forces off Okinawa but was overruled and instructed to comply, 6 April 1945; Retained post until end of war; Assumed concurrent command of 1st, 3rd, 5th Air Fleets upon suicide of M.UGAKI, 15 August 1945; Advised his officers to accept the surrender.

[1] There is sometimes confusion over KUSAKA Ryūnosuke and KUSAKA Jinichi since they were both Vice-Admirals, both were stationed at Rabaul at the same time (for a period) and they were cousins. The latter fact was only mentioned in the *Rising Sun* by J. Toland (*see* Bibliography). For a period KUSAKA Ryūnosuke (as C in C 11th Air Fleet) was subordinate to KUSAKA Jinichi (as C in C South-east Area Fleet) at Rabaul.
[2] 3rd Fleet was formed in July 1942 (full title being 3rd Southern Expeditionary Force) and replaced 1st Air Fleet.

KUSUSE Kumagi
Vice-Admiral; (Head of?) Naval Ordnance Section; Dating uncertain.

MAEDA Tadashi (Minoru)
Rear-Admiral; Chief of 3rd Division (Intelligence) of Naval Affairs Bureau, October 1940; Undertook an inspection tour of Siam and French Indo–China and reported that a Japanese advance into these countries could be made without war with America and Britain, April 1941; Commander of 24th Naval Air Flotilla 1941; HQ Kwajalein, Marshall Islands; Flotilla comprised Chitose Air Group (on Aur and Wotje) and 14th Air Group (on Jaluit and Wotje); Formed part of Shore Based Air Group for Midway Island Expeditionary Force (under N. TSUKAHARA) in Operation 'MI' May–June 1942; Commander of naval forces in Java, HQ Batavia, and concurrently Chief of Naval Intelligence throughout Indonesia, c.1944; Actively promoted Indonesian independence under Soekarno which was declared after the Japanese surrender, before the Allied re-occupation and without their sanction, 17 August 1945; Attended surrender talks (with Major-General NISHIMURA and S. YAMAMOTO) aboard HMS *Cumberland* at Tandjoepriok (Jakarta's port) with Rear-Admiral W.R. Patterson (CO 5th Cruiser Squadron), 16 September 1945.

MARUSHIGE (MARUMO) Kuninori
Rear-Admiral; Commander of Close Cover Force in Operation 'MO' (Port Moresby Invasion. *See* S. INOUYE); Rendezvoused with Attack Force (S. KAJIOKA) off Buin, Bougainville, with total force of two light cruisers, five destroyers, one seaplane tender; Whole force near Louisiade Archipelago, 7 May 1942; Close Support Force (A. GOTO) close by; Operation cancelled after defeat of carriers in Coral Sea and withdrew to Rabaul, 7 May 1942.

MASUDA Nisuke
Rear-Admiral; Charged with murdering American airmen at Jaluit Atoll, Marshall Islands; Committed suicide 1945.

MATSUAKI Akira
Rear-Admiral; Chief of Staff to Southern Expeditionary Fleet, c.1943–end of war; HQ Surabaya, Java; Responsible for mine counter-measures in Borneo, Celebes and Java areas.

MATSUBARA

Rear-Admiral; Commander of Marcus Island;* Surrendered to Rear Admiral Whiting, USN (American Commander of Saipan) aboard destroyer USS *Bagley*, 31 August 1945.

* Remote island approximately 800 miles north-east of Saipan.

MATSUDA

Rear?-Admiral; Commander of Covering Force (with battleships *Ise, Hyuga*, carrier *Tama* and four destroyers) for Mobile Strike Decoy Force (carriers under J. OZAWA) at Battle of Cape Engano, Philippines, 25 October 1944.

MATSUHITA Hajime

Vice-Admiral; Commander of a naval squadron which visited Germany in 1934.

MATSUMURA Junichi

Vice-Admiral; Believed to be 1930s.

MATSUNAGA Sadaichi

Graduate of War College; Gunnery specialist; Rear-Admiral; Commander of 22nd Air Flotilla, south Formosa, c.1940;[1] Transferred with unit to Saigon, Indo–China, (under 11th Air Fleet), October 1941; Covered invasion of Malaya (*see* J. OZAWA) with 99 twin-engined bombers, 37 fighters and six reconnaissance aircraft; Supported invasion of southern Siam and northern Malaya, 7–9 December 1941;[2] Sent reconnaissance aircraft to locate British Naval Force Z (*Prince of Wales* and *Repulse*) but failed to make contact, 9–10 December 1941; Informed of submarine sighting of Force Z and ordered 85 torpedo and bomber aircraft of Genzan, Mihoro and Kanoya Air Groups (all temporarily attached to his command) to search and destroy which they did, sinking both capital ships for minimal losses, 10 December 1941.[3]

[1] Given as Commander of 1st Air Force in *Old Friends, New Enemies* by A. J. Marder (*see* Bibliography), but there appears to have been no such unit since 11th Air Fleet was the equivalent of an Air Force with an Air Flotilla being subordinate to it.
[2] For this campaign he was under the direct command of the surface fleet commander J. OZAWA.
[3] These sinkings broke British naval power in the Far East and, more importantly, was the death knell of battleship warfare since it showed their vulnerability to air attack.

MATSUYAMA M.

Rear-Admiral; Commander of 18th Cruiser Squadron (under 8th Fleet) for invasion of Milne Bay, New Guinea, 1942.

MIKAWA Gunichi

Vice-Admiral; Commander of Support Force (3rd Battleship Division) in Pearl Harbor Attack Force (under C. NAGUMO), 7 December 1941; Commander of Battle Squadron in Operation 'C' (attack on Colombo, Ceylon), 5 April 1942; Commander of 3rd Battleship Division (with battleships *Hiei, Kongo*) forming part of Midway Invasion Force (under N. KONDO) in Operation 'MI', May–June 1942; Commander of 8th Fleet (replacing the Outer South Seas Force), HQ Rabaul, New Britain, from its activation on 14 July 1942; Supported 17th Army landings on New Guinea, 21 July 1942; Commander of reinforcement convoy to Guadalcanal, Solomons, after American landings, 7 August 1942; Fleet sailed against American transport force at Guadalcanal with five heavy cruisers (flagship *Chokai*), two light cruisers and one destroyer, defeating American naval forces at

Battle of Savo Island (First Battle of Solomon Sea) sinking five American warships with no losses (which was the worst American naval defeat since Pearl Harbor), 8–9 August 1942;* (However he retired before attacking the transports which earned him a censure from naval GHQ); Commanded unsuccessful Reinforcement Force to Guadalcanal, 23–5 August 1942; Took command of Guadalcanal Escort Force (after death of A. GOTO in mid October 1942) and supported the supply runs (by 'Tokyo Express' under R. TANAKA) to Guadalcanal; Supported 'Tokyo Express' convoy carrying army 38th Division with six cruisers and six destroyers covering eleven transports and twelve destroyers from Rabaul; Transports ordered to withdraw temporarily to Shortland Islands because Henderson airfield (in American control) had not been bombarded by units of 2nd Fleet (see H. ABE); Ordered to use 8th Fleet to undertake bombardment on night of 13/14 November 1942; Attacked by American aircraft upon completion and retired to Shortland Islands (leaving transport force to proceed with its destroyer escort only which subsequently lost seven out of eleven transports, landing only 2,000 men); Commenced Operation 'I' to destroy American air power on Guadalcanal and New Guinea (see also R. KUSAKA, J. OZAWA, I. YAMAMOTO), 7–14 April 1943; Replaced, November 1943?; Commander of South-west Area Fleet (possibly replacing S. TAKASU), Philippines, c.1944; (Possibly replaced by D. OKOCHI, c.1944).

* This was a night fight in which the Americans lost four heavy cruisers for no Japanese losses.

MITO Hisashi
Rear-Admiral; Chief of Staff to 6th Fleet – Submarines (under T. KOMATSU), HQ Kwajalein, c.1942.

MITSUMASA Teizo
(Full?) Admiral; Commander of 2nd Combined Air Force.

MITSUNAMI Teijo (Teigo)
Vice?-Admiral; Commander of naval forces off Shanghai, China, which sunk the American gunboat USS *Panay* on the Yangtze River, near Nanking, 11 December 1937; Since there was no state of hostilities between Japan and America this caused a serious diplomatic crisis; Publicly sacked upon his return to Japan by Navy Minister M. YONAI for this action, 1938.

MIWA Shigeyoshi
Rear-Admiral; Commander of 3rd Submarine Flotilla; Vice-Admiral; Commander of 6th Fleet – Submarines (replacing T. TAKAGI. *See also* N. OWADA), July 1944; HQ Kure, Japan; Reluctant to use suicide weapons but was overruled; Formed 'Chrysanthemum Special Attack Force', Otsu, Japan, 1944; Authorized formation of 'Kongo Unit' (*I*-Class submarines carrying 'Kaiten' which were manned suicide torpedoes) to attack simultaneously certain Allied targets in Operation 'GEN', 8 December 1944; Attacks launched on Hollandia, Ulithi, Admiralties, Palau and Guam, 12 January 1945; No success with losses;* Two submarines carrying 'Kaiten' lost off Iwo Jima, Late February–early March 1945; Replaced (by T. DAIGO), May 1945 (*see also* M. NAGAI).

* One *I*-Class submarine and eight Kaiten lost at Ulithi for the sinking of only one American tanker. Eleven Kaiten were lost in the other attacks.

MORI

Rear-Admiral; Chief of Navy Works Department at Surabaya Naval Base, Java, (under 2nd Expeditionary Fleet – SHIBATA) at the time of the Japanese surrender, August 1945.

MORI Kunizo

Rear-Admiral; Commander of Kurile Islands Area Special Naval Base Force, February 1944; HQ Kataoka Bay, Kuriles, May 1944; Vice-Admiral; Commander of naval forces in Bonin Islands by end of the war;[1] Occupation by American forces was delayed until the garrison of 40,000 troops were assembled for repatriation; Surrendered his sword to Colonel Presley M. Rixley, USMC, Chichi Jima Island Commander, 13 December 1945;[2] Three junior Japanese naval officers told a United States Military Commission that he participated in a feast in a cave on Chichi Jima Island with other Japanese where they ate the flesh of an executed American prisoner of war in February 1945.

[1] The Bonin Islands were surrendered by Lieutenant-General Y. TACHIBANA.
[2] This sword is now in US Naval Academy Museum, Annapolis. It is a *kai-shuntō* with (lacquered?) scabbard. Cat.no.46.41.1.

MORISHITA Nobii (Nobue)

Rear-Admiral; Captain of super battleship *Yamato* during Leyte battle, October 1944; Replaced (by K. ARUGA); Chief of Staff to 2nd Fleet, December? 1944; Sailed in *Yamato* (*see* S.ITO) in Operation 'TEN-ICHI', 6 April 1945; Attacked by American carrier aircraft and sunk, 7 April 1945; Rescued by the Japanese destroyer *Yukikaze*.

NAGAI Mitsuru

Rear-Admiral; Commander of Base 'P' (Special Base Corps – 'Tokko' Squadron No. 1 which was a suicide unit) comprising 'Kaiten' (manned suicide torpedoes), HQ Ourazaki, south of Kure in Japan, formed September 1944; Said to be commander of 6th Fleet (submarines), possibly replacing S. MIWA, 1945–until the end of the war;* After the war he donated money for a farm for ex-Kaiten pilots at Hikari, Japan.

* This position seems unlikely since he was only a Rear-Admiral and it conflicts with T. DAIGO who is also said to have held this post at the same time.

NAGANO Osami (Shūshin)

Graduated from Etajima Naval College (2nd of 104), 1900; Served in USA 1913–14; Captain; Naval Attaché to Washington, 1920–3; Admiral, 1934; Head of Japanese delegation to Second London Naval Conference where he proposed equality of naval power with Britain and America but withdrew from the conference when it was refused, winter of 1935–6; Navy Minister (replacing M. OSUMI) in Hirota Cabinet, 1936–7; Replaced (by M. YONAI); Commander-in-Chief of Combined Fleet, 1937; Military Councillor by 1940; Chief of Naval General Staff (replacing Prince H. FUSHIMI), 9 April 1941; Supporter of 'Strike South' policy (i.e., against East Indies and Malaya); Stated at an Imperial Conference that the navy backed the army's plan to seize bases in Indo–China and Siam, 2 July 1941; Told the Emperor that Japan had oil stocks for only two years if the American oil embargo continued, 30 July 1941; Warned that American embargo and failure of negotiations over China and Indo–China required a pre-emptive Japanese attack before reserves became insufficient, September 1941;

Recommended to the Emperor that diplomacy must be tried as a first resort but war preparations were necessary, 5 September 1941; Stated at a Liaison Conference 'There is no longer time for discussion. We want action!', 4 October 1941; Ordered Combined Fleet to make battle preparations October 1941; Stated at Imperial Conference that the navy could not be ready before 20 November, 1 November 1941; Ratified that naval policy would be to attack Pearl Harbor before diplomatic negotiations were broken off to facilitate a complete surprise;* Proposed cutting Australian supply lines by taking Samoa after Pearl Harbor (but the plan of I. YAMAMOTO to engage in a decisive naval battle was preferred), April 1942; Fleet Admiral, June 1943; Concurrently Supreme Naval Adviser to the Emperor and a member of the Supreme War Council; Dismissed by Premier H. TOJO from post of Chief of the Naval General Staff when he amalgamated posts of army and navy Chiefs of Staff, February 1944; Arrested as a Class A war criminal; Tried by the International Tribunal for the Far East, Tokyo, on the main charge of waging an aggressive war, 26 April 1946; Died of pneumonia during the trial, aged 67, 5 January 1947.

Personal facts: Recognized as very clever when young. Became lazy and willing for others to do his work by 1941. Famous for napping during conferences and meetings. Impulsive. Did not receive the confidence of the Emperor or Naval General Staff.

* Even Premier H. TOJO was not informed of the Pearl Harbor operation until 30 November 1941, i.e., after the *Kido Butai* (attack force) had sailed.

NAGUMO Chuichi

Vice-Admiral; Commander of 1st Air Fleet (carriers); Flagship carrier *Akagi*; HQ Hiroshima, Japan; Issued first operational order for naval action in the event of war, 10 November 1941; Fleet assembled under the name *Kido Butai* in Inland Sea, Japan, consisting of 1st, 2nd Carrier Divisions (total of six carriers), Support Force (under G. MIKAWA) of 3rd Battleship Division and 8th Cruiser Squadron (two heavy cruisers), Scouting Force (under S. OMORI) with 1st Destroyer Flotilla (one light cruiser, nine destroyers) plus a Supply Force (eight tankers), 16 November 1941; Ships sailed at staggered intervals and re-assembled for Pearl Harbor attack (Operation 'Z'), 26 November 1941; Remained undetected and launched air attack on Pearl Harbor, Hawaii, devastating American battleships, airfields and aircraft, 8 December Japanese time (7 December American time) 1941; Ordered retirement as planned despite requests by his staff to launch a second raid aimed at fuel storage and oil tanks (he thought the element of surprise had gone and the fleet would be at risk); Fleet returned to Japan (except for 8th Cruiser Squadron which was diverted to Wake Island. *See* H. ABE, S. KAJIOKA); Reported the success of the mission to the Emperor at a personal audience; Commander of Darwin Strike Force which launched air attack on Darwin, Australia, sinking three destroyers, eight merchant ships and one sub-chaser, 19 February 1942; Sunk Allied shipping at Tjilatap, Java, late February–March 1942; Commander of Carrier Strike Force in Operation 'C' (attack on Colombo, Ceylon) which sunk two British cruisers by air attack, 5 April 1942; Attacked Trincomalee, Ceylon, 9 April 1942; Ordered to eastern Japan after American 'Doolittle' bombing raid on Japan, 18 April 1942; Returned with fleet to Japan by 23 April 1942; 1st Air Fleet refitted for Operation 'MI' (Midway Island invasion. *See* I. YAMAMOTO) to form 1st Carrier Striking Force; Sailed from Hashirajima, Japan, 27 May 1942; Personally commanded Carrier Group and 1st Carrier Division with carriers flagship *Akagi* and *Kaga* (command included 2nd Carrier Division under

T. YAMAGUCHI); Launched air attack on Midway Island, 4 July 1942; Battle of Midway with sinking by American carrier aircraft of carriers *Kaga, Soryu, Akagi*; Forcibly removed from flagship *Akagi* by his senior staff (including Chief of Staff R. KUSAKA) to light cruiser *Nagara*; Ordered remaining units to retire (temporary operational command given to H. ABE and air operations to T. YAMAGUCHI); Fourth, and last carrier, *Hiryu* (*see* T. YAMAGUCHI) sunk, 5 June 1942; Replaced as battle commander by N. KONDO (by order of C in C Combined Fleet I. YAMAMOTO who regarded him as a defeatist and too conservative); Commander of 3rd Fleet (nominally under Commander of 2nd Fleet N. KONDO, but acting independently), July 1942;[1] Personally commanded Carrier Striking Force (including two heavy cruisers and six destroyers) at Second Battle of the Solomon Sea, 24 August 1942; Ordered by C in C Combined Fleet I. YAMAMOTO to bring the American Fleet to battle by moving against American carriers off Guadalcanal, Solomons, which resulted in the Battle of Santa Cruz Islands; Personally commanded 3rd Carrier Strike Force Main Body (consisting of two heavy carriers, one heavy cruiser, one light cruiser, eight destroyers); Flagship carrier *Shokaku* damaged in the battle and forced to transfer flag to the carrier *Zuikaku*, 25–6 October 1942; Returned to Truk, Caroline Islands, 30 October 1942; Sailed for Japan in *Zuikaku* with orders to rebuild carrier group and train replacements, but replaced (by J. OZAWA) before undertaking this, mid November 1942; Commander of Sasebo Naval Base, Japan, mid November 1942; Commander of Central Pacific Area Fleet (which was a relegation posting because of his failures) from its activation, 1942?;[2] HQ Saipan Island, Marianas; By June 1944 this fleet only existed on paper; Naval units on Saipan consisted of 5th Special Naval Base Force (T. TSUJIMURA) and 1st Yokosuka Landing Force (giving a total of 6,160 men); American forces invaded Saipan, 16 June 1944; Combined with army (*see* Lieutenant-General Y. SAITO and Major-General K. IGETA) for defence of the island; Agreed at a meeting with army commanders that defence line should be formed across northern part of the island after heavy Japanese losses, 26 June 1944; Defence broken and forces split, 6 or 7 July 1944; Accounts of his death vary but an eye-witness account in Oba *The Last Samurai* (*see* Bibliography) confirms that he, Chief of Staff H. YANO and Generals K. IGETA, Y. SAITO committed ritual suicide (having ordered their aides to administer the *coup de grâce* by shooting) in a cave at Jingoku-dani (Valley of Hell) at dawn on 7 July 1945; Posthumously promoted to Admiral, 12 December 1944.

Note: His dress uniform and decorations are on display at the Yasukuni Shrine Museum, Tokyo.

[1] 1st Air Fleet was reorganized for the Philippines operations, becoming 3rd Southern Expeditionary Fleet.
[2] In theory he was in overall command of all navy and army (31st Army under Lieutenant-General H. OBATA) forces in the Marianas, but official orders to this effect were vague, making it titular only.

NAKAHARA Yoshimasa (Giichi)
Rear-Admiral; Chief of Personnel Bureau of Naval General Staff, Tokyo, Japan, 1941.

NAKAMURA Katsuhei
Rear- or Vice-Admiral; Responsible for passage of Japanese surrender party to, and from, USS *Missouri* for signing of the Instrument of Surrender, Yokohama, 2 September 1945.

Note: He could not find one seaworthy Japanese vessel of any kind so an American destroyer was provided.

NAKAMURA Toshihisa

Naval aide to Emperor Taisho, Tokyo, pre-1926; Admiral; In the Imperial Palace when it was occupied by the 1st Imperial Guards during the attempted *coup* to prevent the Japanese surrender, 14–15 August 1945.

NAKANO Tarō

Vice-Admiral; Chief of Navy Medical Bureau, c.1940.

NAKASAWA (NAKAZAWA) Tasuki (Yu-u)

Captain; Chief of 1st Section (war plans) of Naval General Staff; Opposed the Tripartite Pact with Germany and Italy, 1940; Rear-Admiral; Chief of First Division (Operations Section) of Naval General Staff, c.1944; Requested the Imperial Fleet be given the chance to fight a last-ditch suicide battle and earnestly supported the implementation of Operation 'SHO. 1' (attack on American invasion forces off Leyte, Philippines, with a hoped for decisive naval battle), October 1944; Vice-Admiral by the end of the war.

NAKASE

Rear-Admiral; Commander of carrier *Zuikaku* which was sunk at the Battle of Cape Engano, Philippines (*see* J. OZAWA), 25 October 1944; Possibly he was killed or went down with his ship.

NIMI

Vice-Admiral; Naval Commander of the Hong Kong attack and entered the city with Lieutenant-General J. SAKAI, 25 December 1941.

NIIMI Masaichi

Vice-Admiral, Second World War.

Note: Possibly same as NIMI

NIPPA Teizo

Rear-Admiral; Commander of Okinawa Naval Base until January 1945; Replaced (by M. OTA); Transferred to Formosa.

NISHIMURA Shoji (Teiji)

Rear-Admiral; Commander of 2nd Surprise Attack Force for Vigan, Luzon, Philippines with flagship light cruiser *Naka*, 11 December 1941; Commander of Escort (4th Destroyer Flotilla) of Balikpapan (Borneo) Invasion Force, 24 January 1942; Commander of Eastern Attack Force for invasion of Java, personally commanding 1st Escort Force, February 1942; Battle of Java Sea, 27 February 1942; Commander of 4th Destroyer Flotilla consisting of 2nd, 9th Destroyer Divisions and flagship light cruiser *Yura* which formed Destroyer Screen for Midway Island Invasion Force (under N. KONDO) in Operation 'MI' May–June 1942; Commander of Outer South Seas (Bombardment) Force at Third Battle of the Solomon Sea (2nd phase), 13–14 November 1942; Vice–Admiral; Commander of Southern Force (Force C) detached from 5th Fleet (1st Division Attack, or Striking, Force under T. KURITA) in Operation 'SHO. 1' (attempted decisive naval battle with American naval forces and invasion forces off Leyte, Philippines); Force consisted of two old battleships (including flagship *Yamashiro*, one heavy cruiser and four destroyers; Entered southern Suriago Strait, 24 October 1944; Lost three ships by early hours of 25 October 1944; Continued on to attack American 7th Fleet with only one battleship, one heavy cruiser and one destroyer left; Died with the entire crew of *Yamashiro* when she was sunk at the Battle of Suriago Strait (Leyte Gulf), 25 October 1944.

NISHINA Kozo
Rear-Admiral; Chief of Staff to 6th Fleet (submarines) under S. MIWA, c.1944.

NOMIYA (NOMEJA)
Rear-Admiral; Commander of a local force (garrison?) in Balikpapan area (under M. KAMADA), Borneo; Signed surrender of all Japanese forces in Balikpapan area to Australian Brigadier F.G. Wood, 25th Brigade Commander, at Tempadeong, 10 September 1945; Surrendered his sword at this time.

NOMURA Kichisaburō
Admiral; Formal visit with staff to American bases in Hawaii, 1929;[1] Naval Attaché in Washington, USA; Retired; Foreign Minister in N. ABE cabinet, October 1939; Resigned with fall of the cabinet, January 1940; Ambassador to USA, 14 February 1941; Arrived in Washington, April 1941; Attempted diplomatic negotiations to resolve difficulties of America and Japan over war in China and seizure of northern Indo–China; Offered to withdraw from Indo–China and concede some American demands subject to America lifting its embargo and unfreezing Japanese assets, but the offer was rejected because the Chinese question was unresolved, September 1941; Commenced final negotiations with American Secretary of State Cordell Hull, 7 November 1941;[2] Final offer of terms was made by the Japanese, 20 November 1941 (Americans refused and presented an unacceptable counter-proposal);[3] Ordered to deliver declaration of war but due to delay in decoding and typing it was delivered 80 minutes after the Japanese bombing of Pearl Harbor, 7 December American time (8 December Japanese time) 1941; He did know of the planned attack until after handing over the declaration of war; Confined to a Washington hotel by American security where he requested a 'samurai sword' (with which to commit suicide) but this was refused; Interned in USA but returned to Japan on an exchange ship, 20 August 1942.

[1] Senior Japanese naval officers made annual visits to American Pacific bases before the war (to gauge American power and strengthen relationships with *émigré* Japanese).
[2] Hull was already aware of his instructions because the Japanese diplomatic code had been broken for some time. However the American translation was badly at fault and misleading making Hull distrust Japanese intentions and causing an unnecessarily intransigent attitude.
[3] *The Rising Sun* by J. Toland (*see* Bibliography) states that the American demand to withdraw from China did not include Manchuria, whereas the Japanese assumed that it did. Had they known, war might have been postponed or avoided.

NOMURA Naokuni
Vice-Admiral; Chief of Naval Intelligence; Returned from Germany by submarine to report on the state of the Third Reich to Emperor Hirohito, 11 August 1943.

Note: Possibly the same as NOMURA Tadakuni.

NOMURA Tadakuni
Admiral; Naval Attaché in Berlin; Navy Minister in General H. TOJO cabinet (replacing S. SHIMADA), 17–18 July 1944.*

Note: Possibly the same as NOMURA Naokuni.

* He was Navy Minister for only 17 hours because the resignation of H. TOJO automatically forced his removal from office.

OBAYASHI Sueo
Captain; Commander of Carrier Group with carrier *Zuiho* and one destroyer (flotilla?) forming part of Main Body (under N. KONDO) of Midway Island Invasion Force in Operation 'MI', May–June 1942; Rear–Admiral; Commander of 3rd Carrier Division (Van) in 1st Mobile Fleet (under J. OZAWA), April 1944; Launched air attack on American 5th Fleet in Philippine Sea but suffered heavy losses in aircraft for little success, 19 June 1944; Returned to port; Suggested *Kamikaze* (suicide) air attacks to J. OZAWA; Survived the war.

OGATA Taketora
Full? Admiral; Minister of State; Held under house arrest pending possible war crimes trials but released without prosecution, 31 August 1947.

OGAWA Kanji
Captain; Assistant Chief of Intelligence Division of Naval General Staff, December 1940–May 1942; Rear-Admiral by the end of war.

OIKAWA (OYOKAWA, OKAWA) Koshirō
Graduated from Etajima Naval College, 1903; Superintendent of Naval College, 1931–5; Vice-Admiral; Commander of China Area Fleet, Replaced (by S. SHIMADA), May 1940; Navy Minister in second Konoye Government (replacing Z. YOSHIDA), 3 September 1940;[1] Told the Emperor at an Imperial Conference that war preparations must proceed but strenuous efforts must be made through diplomacy to avoid hostilities with America over question of China, Indo–China and embargo of essential materials, 6 September 1941; Stated at a private meeting with Premier Prince Konoye and War Minister General H. TOJO that the navy did not want war (although previously publicly agreeing with a war policy), 12 October 1941; Replaced (by S. SHIMADA) because of new premier H. TOJO, 18 October 1941; Commander of Escort Command HQ, Japan, from its activation in mid November 1943; Formed to provide escort to shipping from Japan, comprising 901st Naval Air Group and four escort carriers;[2] Navy Chief of Staff, 1944; Approved final text of report on final defence of Japanese homeland by mass suicide attacks of both military and civilian population, 6 April 1945; Resigned in protest over Emperor Hirohito's refusal to listen to American peace proposals, May 1945; Gave evidence at the International War Crimes Trials, Tokyo, 1946–8.

[1] Stated that the signing of the Tripartite Pact with Germany and Italy was essential for the well-being of Japan. He insisted that all admirals must support both the Tripartite Pact and the Japanese army move into Indo–China (which they did with reservations), 1940.
[2] The Japanese did not adopt the large convoy system favoured by the Allies since small groups of ships were thought to be faster in delivering supplies to Japanese-held islands. However large convoys were reluctantly tried from March 1943 with initial success.

Personal facts: Chinese classical scholar. Tried to please everybody. Weak character. Willing to co-operate with the army when other very senior naval officers opposed it. Tall, heavily built and handsome.

Note: OIKAWA and OYOKAWA are given as separate persons in *Eclipse of the Rising Sun* by Toshikazu Kase (*see* Bibliography), but they seem to be one and the same.

OKA Arata
Vice-Admiral; Commander of Osaka Naval Guard District, November 1944; HQ Osaka, Japan.

OKA Takasumi (Takazumi)
Born 1890; Rear-Admiral; Chief of Intelligence Division of Naval General Staff, October 1939; Opposed Tripartite Pact with Germany and Italy; Replaced, October 1940; Chief of General and Military Affairs Bureau of Navy Ministry (replacing K. ABE), 15 October 1940;* Suggested a Japanese withdrawal from China might placate America, 6 October 1941; Wrote to Premier Prince Konoye that the navy did not want war but could not express this view in public, 12 October 1941; Stated that naval policy should be to destroy key enemy bases which might be used for countering attacks including Hawaii and Australia (this idea was opposed by the army but a mutual agreement was reached to attack Port Moresby, New Guinea by 13 March 1942); Resigned or replaced, July 1944; Commander of Chinkai Naval Guard District (Korea) by September 1945; Tried by the International Tribunal for the Far East, Tokyo, as a war criminal, 26 April 1946–12 November 1948; Sentenced to life imprisonment; Paroled, 1954; Died 1973.

Personal facts: Bachelor. Pro-German and supporter of Japanese army policies.

* Believed to have been promoted to Vice-Admiral during this appointment.

OKADA Keisuke
Admiral; Navy Minister, 1927; Retired; Prime Minister (first term), 1927–32;[1] Prime Minister (second term) replacing M. SAITO, 7 July 1934; Escaped assassination attempt by hiding in cupboard in the servants' quarters of his house during the '2–26 Insurrection', his brother-in-law being killed in mistake for him, 26 February 1936;[2] Resigned, March 1936 (replaced by K. Hirota); 'Jushin' (elder statesman) and adviser to the throne by 1941; Opposed war with Britain and America; Stated at a conference with seven other Jushin and the Emperor that he did not think Japan could ensure an adequate supply of war *matériel* and voiced his opposition to Premier H. TOJO's war preparations, 29 November 1941;[3] Reported to have secretly organized a 'peace party' to sue for peace with America, 1943; Supported movement to remove Premier General H. TOJO and his cabinet and negotiate for peace, June 1944; Adviser to Premier K. SUZUKI on the formation of his cabinet, early 1945.

[1] Supported the 1930 London Naval Conference decision to limit fleet ratios to 5:5:3 (Britain:America: Japan).
[2] See Lieutenant-General K. KASHI for details of the '2–26 Insurrection'.
[3] Raised and voiced eighteen objections to war at this conference.

OKOCHI (OKAUCHI) Denshichi

Vice-Admiral; Commander of South West Area Fleet (possibly replacing G. MIKAWA), 1944; HQ Manila, Philippines, under direct command of GHQ, Tokyo; Fleet disbanded, October 1944, but he remained in command of naval forces in the Philippines; Disagreed with 14th Area Army Commander General T. YAMASHITA whose policy was to abandon Manila, on Luzon, without a fight and refused to assist in preparing defences outside the city; Instead he reinforced the city with 31st Special Naval Base Force (under S. IWABUCHI) as the army withdrew; Instructed S. IWABUCHI to defend Manila to the last man while he withdrew into the mountains with 14th Area Army; Manila taken by American forces after massacres by Japanese naval forces, 4 March 1945; Surrendered with General T. YAMASHITA at Baguio, Luzon, to Major General W.H. Gill, US Army, 2 September 1945; Gave evidence for defence of General T. YAMASHITA at his war crimes trial, Manila 1945.

Note: Surrendered a sword in 1945 (to Major General Gill?). It was Presented by General Douglas MacArthur to the US Naval Academy Museum, Annapolis. A naval *kai-guntō* with shagreen scabbard. Cat.no.45.60.

OKUDA Kikuji

Rear- or Vice-Admiral; Commander of 13th Air Corps, China, *c.*1939; Killed when his aircraft was shot down while raiding Chengtu airfield, China, 4 November 1939.

OKUVA

Vice-Admiral; Chief Medical Officer to 8th Fleet, Rabaul, New Britain; Shot down in a Betty bomber (second transport in flight carrying I. YAMAMOTO) when attacked by American fighters near Buin, Bougainville, but survived, 18 April 1943 (*see also* TAKATA).

Note: The spelling of this name is doubtful since it is not a recognizable Japanese name. Perhaps it should be; 'Okura' or 'Okuda'.

OMORI Sentaro

Rear-Admiral; Commander of Scouting Force (1st Destroyer Flotilla) which accompanied 1st Air Fleet to attack Pearl Harbor in flagship light cruiser *Abukuma*, 7 December 1941; Formed Screen of Darwin Strike Force, 19 February 1942; Part of Battle Squadron in Operation 'C' (attack on Colombo, Ceylon, under G. MIKAWA), 5 April 1942; Commander of Attu Island Landing Force (part of Operation 'AL' during invasion of Aleutian Islands under 5th Fleet – B. HOSOGAYA) with flagship *Abukuma*, four destroyers, two transports with 1,200 soldiers; Occupied Attu, 7 June 1942; Joined forces with 8th Fleet (under T. SAMEJIMA) at Rabaul, New Britain, to reinforce troops at Empress Augusta Bay, Bougainville, Solomons, October 1943; Commander of Torokina Interception Force, sailing from Rabaul to attack American invasion transports at Bougainville, 1 November 1943; Force consisted of two heavy cruisers (*Haguro*, flagship *Myoko*), two light cruisers (*Agano, Sendai*), 3rd Destroyer Flotilla with six destroyers (under M. IJUIN); Attacked by inferior American naval force of four light cruisers plus destroyers in a night attack at Battle of Empress Augusta (Gazelle) Bay, 2/3 November 1943; Defeated with loss of *Sendai*, one destroyer and four ships heavily damaged; Reported that defeat was due to superior enemy forces but when the facts became known was relieved of his command for displaying little skill and less resolution; Vice-Admiral; Commandant of Torpedo School, Yokosuka, Japan; Temporary vice-chairman of a special committee to prepare 'Special Attack Weapons' (i.e., suicide weapons), late June 1944; Chief of Staff to Special Attack Division, September 1944; Authorized first use of Special Attack Division, October 1944; Ordered 721st Air Unit to train 'Oka' (piloted rocket bomb) pilots.

ONISHI (OHNISHI) Takijirō (Takujiro, Kakijiro) 大西滝次郎

Born at Ashida village, Hikami county, Hyogo prefecture; Entered Etajima Naval Academy aged 17; Outspoken and a gambler; Attended brothels and geisha houses; Not allowed to take final examination at Naval War College for slapping a geisha and conduct unbecoming an officer; Spent two years studying in Britain; Sub-Lieutenant; Served in Japan's first seaplane tender, the *Wakimiya Maru*, 1915; Helped set up the Nakajima Aircraft Company and flew the first production model, 1916; Commander of Yokosuka Air Corps; Generally responsible for creating Japan's naval air arm (with I. YAMAMOTO); Air ace in China war; Rear-Admiral, November 1939; Supporter of naval air power and considered expenditure on capital ships a waste of money; Foremost Japanese authority on naval aviation; Chief of Staff to 11th Air Fleet; Prepared study of air attack on Pearl Harbor together with Commander Genda Minoru and S. FUKUDOME, January 1941; Totally opposed to battleship building and criticized naval planners for not concentrating on carriers; Chief of Staff to 11th Air Fleet (under N. TSUKAHARA), Philippines, c.1942; Insisted Saipan Island, Marianas, be reinforced when others considered it should be abandoned but he was overruled; Called for pilots to ram American ships during the Saipan battle, June 1944; Advocated use of island chains for airbases at expense of carriers because of shortage of skilled pilots (who could fly off carriers); Chief of Administrative Bureau of Aeronautic Weapons and Ammunition Ministry, June 1944; Vice-Admiral; Commander of 1st Air Fleet including 5th Base Air Force (replacing H. TERAOKA) being appointed on orders of Combined Fleet because he supported the 'SHO' plan (*see* S. TOYODA), Manila, Philippines, 2 October 1944; Arrived at HQ Manila, 17 October 1944; Disliked the use of suicide tactics but realized there was no other alternative; Found only fifty serviceable aircraft left; Formed first naval *Kamikaze* unit from 201st Air Group at Mabalacat airfield, Luzon (fifty miles from Manila) under Commander Tamai Asaichi, 19 October 1944; Organized four Special Attack Units (Tokko-tai) by 24 October 1944; They were named (Shikishima, Asashi, Yamazakura and Yamato); First *Kamikaze* attack on American Fleet off Philippines during Battle of Leyte Gulf (in Operation 'SHO.1') had some success but with one-third losses from 1st and 2nd (under S. FUKUDOME) Air Fleets, 25 October 1944, against the American loss of the carrier *St Lo*; On his instigation the command of 1st and 2nd Air Fleets was merged to form Combined Base Air Corps (or South-west Area Fleet Combined Land Based Air Force) as a Special Attack *Kamikaze* unit, 26 October 1944; C in C was S. FUKUDOME and Chief of Staff was T. ONISHI; Suicide attacks had been made compulsory for all pilots so ordered, 25 October 1944; Final *Kamikaze* attack by 1st Air Fleet on American Fleet off Luzon, 6 January 1945; Nearly all aircraft lost and naval troops ordered to fight with the army on Luzon; 2nd Air Fleet disbanded (*see* S. FUKUDOME) and remnant placed under the control of 1st Air Fleet; ONISHI became C in C upon withdrawal of S. FUKUDOME; He was then ordered by Combined Fleet to withdraw together with staff, pilots and radio technicians to Formosa from 8 January 1945; Formed new *Kamikazes* (Niitaka Unit) at HQ east of Takao, Formosa, from 12 January 1945; First *Kamikaze* attack on American 3rd Fleet Task Force off Formosa, 21 January 1945; Ordered to co-operate with army air forces and 4th Air Fleet (under M. UGAKI) to defeat American fleet off Okinawa, April 1945; Admiral; Vice Chief of Naval General Staff, 29 May 1945–end of war; Strenuously opposed Japan's surrender and advocated total war even after the dropping of atomic bombs; Refused to accept Japanese surrender and said at a meeting of military chiefs of staff that if twenty million men (i.e., entire male population) were recruited for Special Attack Corps (suicide corp) Japan could still emerge victorious, Tokyo, 13 August 1945; Committed traditional *seppuku* (suicide) with a sword on the night of 15 August 1945 (refusing the *coup de grâce*, he died after 12 hours, 16 August 1945).*

Note: A civilian *tachi* (long slung sword) is now in the Yasukuni Shrine Museum, Tokyo. The blade is signed 'TSUSHIMA (NO) KAMI TACHIBANA TSUNEMITSU', i.e., 'Tachibana Tsunemitsu, lord of Tsushima'. 17th-century. 1st or 2nd generations of Musashi. He is said to have committed suicide with this sword which was presumably a family heirloom. The whereabouts of his military sword has not been located.

* He left a suicide note addressed 'to the spirits of members of the Special Attack Corps' (i.e., *Kamikaze* units). The ·first paragraph reads 'I express my deep gratitude to you who have fought so well. Ever convinced of final victory, you fell gallantly as human bullets. But that conviction has not been fulfilled. With my death I desire to make atonement to the souls of my former subjects and to members of their bereaved families.'

ONISHI Shinzō
Rear-Admiral; Commander of 7th Submarine Flotilla, 1941; Supported Bismarck Archipelago invasion by 4th Fleet (under S. INOUYE), January 1942; Chief of Staff to 8th Fleet, HQ Rabaul, New Britain, c.1944.

ONO Hiroshi
Born 1883 in Aichi-ken, Japan; Graduated from Naval College, 1911; Vice-Admiral, 1934; Worked undercover, visiting Western Australia as an official of a pearl company, obtaining information from Japanese immigrants, July 1940.

ONO (OUNO) Ichiro
Rear-Admiral; Commander of naval forces attacking Amoy, Fukien–Kwantung area, China, with one battalion of 14th Fleet Marines and three battalions of Formosan Force; Landed 10 May 1938; Captured Amoy 12 May 1938.

ŌNO Takeji
Captain; Attached to Operations Division of Naval General Staff, 1939–November 1941; Rear-Admiral by the end of the war.

OSUGI (OHSUGI) Morikazu
Rear-Admiral; Commander of 23rd Special Naval Base Force, February 1944; Unit located in Macassar, Celebes, by November 1944; Vice-Admiral; Surrendered to Brigadier I. N. Dougherty at Macassar, 1945.

ŌSUMI Mineo
Admiral; Navy Minister, c.1932; Condemned shelling of Shanghai, China, by K. SHIOZAWA, January 1932; Reappointed Navy Minister, 1933; A militant;

Instigated a purge and forced the retirement of some senior naval officers (because they allegedly supported the naval limitation agreement signed at the 1930 London Naval Conference) which removed moderates from the navy, early 1934; Military Councillor by 1940; Strongly pro-German by 1940.

OTA Minoru

Captain; Commander of Special Naval Landing Force battalion in attack on Shanghai, China, August 1937; Commander of Midway Island Landing Force Transports in Transport Group (under R. Tanaka) which formed part of Midway Invasion Force in Operation 'MI', May–June 1942; Rear-Admiral; In Central Solomons, c.1943; Commander of Okinawa Naval Base Force (placed under 32nd Army – Lieutenant-General M. USHIJIMA) for defence of Okinawa, c.1944; Command comprised of Naval Base Force, 4th Surface Escort Unit and other units including torpedo-boats, midget submarines and suicide boats; American landings commenced, April 1945 (see Lieutenant-General M. USHIJIMA for campaign details); Suicide boats destroyed by American action before they could be used; Concentrated in southern section of island; Ordered to form four infantry battalions from his naval units as reserves for all-out counter-attack by 32nd Army on 4 May 1945; Attack failed, 5 May 1945; Remained in reserve in Oroku Peninsula area; Oroku area attacked by seaborne landings (American 6th Marine Division), 4 June 1945; Encircled by American forces and cut off from 32nd Army; Japanese forces destroyed; HQ in a cave was attacked, 10 June 1945; Committed suicide with his staff in underground HQ, 14 June 1945.

Note: In this phase of the battle in Okinawa there were 5,000 Japanese dead with 200 being taken as prisoners. American casualties were 1,608.

ŌTAGAKI (OHTAGAKI) Tomisaburō

Vice-Admiral; Presumably retired to become Chief Operating Officer of the Machinery Manufacturing Industrial Council, 1942.

OWADA Noburu (Noburu)

Rear-Admiral; Commander of 7th Submarine Flotilla, Truk, Caroline Islands, by 1944; Acting Commander of 6th Fleet-Submarines, when C in C T. TAKAGI was on Saipan Island (where he was killed), mid June–early July 1944; Handed over command of 6th Fleet to S. MIWA, July 1944; Commander of 2nd 'Tokko' Squadron (suicide unit), Japan, 1945; Formed as a Kaiten (manned suicide torpedo) and suicide boat unit; Trained and organized Shinyu (suicide boats containing high-explosives) for the defence of Japan.

OZAWA Jisaburō

Born in southern Kyushu, Japan; Graduated from Etajima Naval College (45th of 109), 1909; Torpedo specialist; Vice-Admiral; Commander of 2nd Southern Expeditionary Fleet, 18 October 1941; Commander of 'Malaya Force' (under Southern Force – N. KONDO) escorting 15th Army transports for the invasion of Malaya in flagship light cruiser Kashii with Main Body (under his personal command), Main Body Escort Force (T. KURITA), 1st Escort Force (S. HASHI-MOTO) and 2nd Escort Force; 'Malaya Force' assembled at Samah on Hainan Island, 26 November 1941; Left Samah with invasion transports, 4 December 1941; Landings in southern Siam and northern Malaya unopposed except at Kota Bharu, 7–8 December 1941; Closed to within about twenty miles of British Force Z (Prince of Wales and Repulse) but passed without sighting one another, 9

December 1941; Reunited with forces of N. KONDO and T. KURITA to search for Force Z, 10 December 1941; *Repulse* and *Prince of Wales* were sunk by aircraft attached to 22nd Air Flotilla (under S. MATSUNAGA) and under the direct command of 'Malaya Force' for campaign duration, 10 December 1941; Commander of Western Force (Southern Expeditionary Fleet) for invasion of Sumatra (under N. KONDO), February 1942; Commander of 2nd Expeditionary Force to harass Allied shipping in the Bay of Bengal, April 1942; Commander of 3rd Fleet (replacing C. NAGUMO), November 1942; HQ Truk, Caroline Islands; Commenced Operation 'I' to destroy American air power on Guadalcanal, Solomons and New Guinea (*see also* R. KUSAKA, G. MIKAWA, I. YAMAMOTO), 7–14 April 1943; Commander of 1st Mobile Fleet (after reorganization of the Japanese navy) which comprised 2nd Fleet (T. KURITA) and 3rd Fleet (which he personally commanded); 3rd Fleet consisted of 1st Carrier Division (carriers *Shokaku*, flagship *Zuikaku*, 2nd Carrier Division (carriers *Hiyo, Junyo, Ryujo*), 3rd Carrier Division (carriers *Chitose, Chiyoda, Zuiho*, plus two light cruisers (*Agano, Yahagi*) and fifteen destroyers, April–May 1944; Fleet sailed to reinforce Biak Island, off New Guinea, in Operation 'KON'; Thought he might bring the American Fleet into a decisive naval battle (in accordance with Combined Fleet plan 'A-GO') and was thus reinforced by the super battleships *Musahi* and *Yamato*, June 1944; Operation 'KON' was suspended when it became evident that Saipan Island in the Marianas was in fact the main American target, June 1944; Fleet recalled to Philippine Sea to take part in Operation 'A-GO'; Ordered by C in C Combined Fleet S. TOYODA to attack American naval forces in the Mariana Islands area, 15 June 1944; Launched air strike on American Task Force 58 but lost 346 aircraft (i.e., 92 per cent of his carrier aircraft) for only 15 American losses, crippling Japanese air power and also the loss of carriers *Shokaku, Taiho* and *Hiyo* sunk by torpedoes in the Battle of the Philippine Sea ('Great Marianas Turkey Shoot'), transferring flag to carrier *Zuikaku*, 19–20 June 1944; Returned to port and offered his resignation because of the defeat but it was refused by the C in C Combined Fleet; Commander of Mobile Strike (carrier) Force in Operation 'SHO. 1' (attack on American fleets off Leyte, Philippines) with carriers *Chitose, Chiyoda, Zuiho*, flagship *Zuikaku* plus two converted battle-ship/carriers, three light cruisers and eight destroyers; Sailed from Kure, Japan (*see also* T. KURITA, MATSUDA, S. NISHIMURA, K. SHIMA, S. TOYODA); Formed decoy force to lure away American 3rd Fleet northwards from Leyte, 23 October 1944; Attacked by American carrier aircraft at Battle of Cape Engano and lost all but the two converted battleship/carriers and eleven escorts, transferring flag to light cruiser *Oyoda*, 25 October 1944; Japanese naval power was then reduced to a minimum defensive capability only; Returned with remaining ships to Japan; Vice Chief of Naval General Staff, March? 1945; Opposed the use of 2nd Fleet (under S. ITO) in a suicide mission off Okinawa but was overruled; Died 1966 aged 80.

Personal facts: Taller than average for a Japanese. Regarded as the navy's premier tactician. Regarded as a first-class 'fighting admiral'. Moderate. Declined promotion to full Admiral since he claimed his country was more important than his rank.

SAICHIRO Tomonari

Rear- or Vice-Admiral; Commander of Gilbert Islands with 3rd (Special) Naval Base Force, HQ Betio Island in Tarawa Atoll, September 1942–September 1943; Replaced by K. SHIBASAKI.

Viscount SAITO Makoto

Admiral; Governor-General of Korea for a long period; Delegate (or head) of Japanese delegation at Geneva Naval Conference, Switzerland, 1927; The conference failed because of disagreement over fleet parities; Served as Navy Minister in five different governments; Retired; Prime Minister aged 74 (after assassination of Premier Inukai), 26 May 1932; Formed a military dominated cabinet which effectively meant the end of democratic party government in Japan; The cabinet fell because of a scandal involving Finance Ministry officials, 4 July 1934; Replaced by K. OKADA; Lord Privy Seal, December 1936; Assassinated in '2–26 Insurrection' aged 77, 26 February 1936.

SAKAIBARA (SAKAIHARA) Shigemitsu

Captain; Commander of 65th Guard Force (part of 4th Base Force), Wake Island, from its occupation in late December 1941; Rear-Admiral; Ordered mass executions of 98 American civilian employees of Pan American Airways, October 1943; Island bypassed by American forces; Surrendered, 4 September 1945; Tried for war crimes and hanged (together with his adjutant Lieutenant-Commander Tachibana Soichi) on Guam, 19 June 1947.

SAKAMAKI

Rear-Admiral; Commander of 2nd Carrier Division; Reinforced 26th Air Flotilla at Buin on Bougainville, Solomon Islands, July 1943; Moved to Rabaul, New Britain, after abandonment of Buin, mid October 1943.

SAKANO

Rear-Admiral; Pro-British, c.1934.

SAKONJI Seizō

Vice-Admiral; Commander of Sasebo Naval District, Japan; Head of naval delegation to London Naval Conference; Wanted parity with America and Britain but forced to settle for 5:5:3 (Britain:America:Japan) ratios;[1] He was prepared to walk out of the conference but was overruled by the Emperor who did not want Japan disgraced if she caused the conference to fail, November–December 1930;[2] Commander of 3rd Fleet; Forced into early retirement, aged 55, in a purge of senior naval officers by Navy Minister M. OSUMI, March 1934.

[1] It is uncertain if the conference came before or after his appointment with 3rd Fleet.
[2] It was unprecendented for the Emperor to order such action.

SAKONJU Naomasa 左近允 尚正

Captain; Officer commanding Hankow, China, 1940; Vice-Admiral; Commander of 16th Cruiser Squadron (forming part of South-west Area Fleet under S. TAKASU) with cruisers *Chikuma, Tone* and flagship *Aoba*; Sailed from Banka Straits to harass Allied shipping in the Indian Ocean, 28 February 1944; Ordered killings ('disposal') of 72 survivors from the ship MV *Behar* aboard *Tone*, 18 March 1944; Part of 2nd Reinforcement Group in unsuccessful attempt to reinforce Biak Island, off Dutch New Guinea, 7 June 1944; Commander of Tansport Unit to land troops on Leyte Island, Philippines, in Operation 'SHO. 1' (defence of Philippines); Successful but lost the light cruiser *Kinu*, 26 October 1944; Sentenced to death at Hong Kong for the Behar killings, September 1947.

Note: Photographed in 1940 with a civilian *katana* with a leather-covered scabbard having two suspension mounts for naval use.

SAMEJIMA Hiroichi

Rear?-Admiral; Involved in Operation 'AL' (invasion of the Aleutian Islands) in 2nd Carrier Striking Force (see K. KAKUTA); Led first flight of torpedo-bombers in attack on Dutch Harbour, Unalaska Island, Aleutians, 3 June 1942;* Returned to Dutch Harbour in June 1982 to attend a memorial unveiling to all those who suffered in the campaign.

* This island was not invaded.

Baron SAMEJIMA Tomoshige

Vice-Admiral; Chief naval aide-de-camp to Emperor Hirohito, until November 1942; Naval Air Commander at Rabaul, New Britain, December 1942;[1] Commander of a relief convoy to Kolombangara Island, off New Guinea, sailing from the Shortland Islands on flagship cruiser *Chokai* but was repulsed by American naval ships (however 2,500 troops were landed), 8–9 July 1943; Joined forces with S. OMORI to reinforce Empress Augusta Bay, Bougainville, Solomons, which culminated in the Battle of Empress Augusta (Gazelle) Bay, 2 November 1943; Commander of 8th Fleet HQ Rabaul, New Britain, October 1944–end of the war; Became isolated because of American island-hopping strategy and the loss of New Guinea; Handed over control of naval troops on Bougainville to 17th Army Commander Lieutenant-General M. KANDA, June 1945; Retained HQ and forces around Buin, Bougainville; Surrendered together with Lieutenant-General M. KANDA to Australian Lieutenant-General S. C. Savige at Torokina, Bougainville, 8 September 1945.[2]

[1] Edwin P. Hoyt in *Yamamoto* (see Bibliography) gives his command as C in C 4th Fleet, Truk, replacing S. INOUYE after 30 October 1942 which does not agree with this command location and has not been confirmed by other references.
[2] Surrendered his sword, a *kai-guntō*, at this time.

SATŌ Katsuya

Rear-Admiral; Chief of Staff to 13th Naval Base Force (under R. TANAKA), Bangkok, Siam, c.1945; Surrendered a sword to Major General G. C. Evans, GOC 7th Indian Division (together with R. TANAKA and 20 Japanese Generals) at Bangkok, 11 January 1946.

SATŌ Shiro

Rear-Admiral; Commander of forces occupying Muschu and Kairiru Islands, off New Guinea (in 18th Area Army under H. ADACHI); Surrendered to Lieutenant-General Sir H. Robertson aboard ML *805* off Muschu, 10 September 1945; Handed over his sword at this time; Returned to Yokosuka, Japan, January 1946; Shot his wife, two children and himself in despair over the defeat.

SATŌ Tsutomu

Rear-Admiral; Commander of 1st Submarine Flotilla, based at Yokosuka, Japan.

SAWAMOTO Yorio

Vice-Admiral; Vice Navy Minister (replacing T. TOYODA), 22 April 1941; Opposed war with America and Britain; Tended to be bypassed by his juniors and the Navy Minister S. SHIMADA; Presided over court of enquiry on S. FUKUDOME, Tokyo, 18 April 1944; Replaced, July 1944; Survived the war.

Personal facts: Clever, diligent with an excellent memory. More of a bureaucrat than an operational officer.

SENDA Sadatoshi

Rear-admiral; Commander of 28th Naval Base Force, north-west New Guinea, May 1944.

SHIBASAKI Keiji (Keichi)

Rear-Admiral; Commander of Gilbert Islands garrison (replacing T. SAICHIRO) with HQ on Betio Island in Tarawa Atoll, September 1943; Command consisted of 3rd (Special) Naval Base Force (formerly 6th Yokosuka Special Naval Landing Force), 7th Sasebo Special Naval Landing Force, 111th Construction Unit and a detachment of 4th Fleet Construction Department (approx 4,835 men including Korean labourers); Command also included Makin Island with a garrison of 830 men;[1] Tarawa, Makin and Nauru heavily attacked by American aircraft, 17–19 September 1943; Betio (having an airfield) was particularly heavily defended with entrenchments and underground redoubts; Tarawa invaded by American 2nd Marines with landings on Betio while under heavy fire, 20 November 1943; American penetration from the beach-head was very slow because of stiff resistance with heavy losses on both sides; Battalions of American 6th Marines landed, 21 November 1943; Airfield reached after which Japanese resistance was slowly overwhelmed with first Japanese counter-attacks repulsed with almost total losses, 22 November 1943; Japanese wiped out except for the eastern end and isolated pockets on north-west coast, by 23 November 1943; Pockets eliminated, 23 November 1943; He died (killed or suicide) but his body was never found.[2]

Note: Remainder of Japanese forces on Tarawa Atoll cleared by 28 November 1943. Japanese dead (killed or suicide) were 4,690 with only seventeen Japanese and 129 Koreans being taken prisoner. American casualties were extremely high (more than 18 per cent) with 1,115 killed, died or missing and 2,292 wounded. It was one of the bloodiest battles of the Pacific War, with unacceptable American losses.

[1] Makin Island was invaded by American forces, 20 November 1943; Declared secure, 22 November 1943; The Japanese lost the entire garrison except for one sailor and 104 Koreans.
[2] Probably killed when his command bunker received a direct shell hit.

SHIBATA

Vice-Admiral; Commander of 2nd Southern Expeditionary Fleet, Surabaya, Java, c.1945; Threatened, and stripped of his sword, by armed Indonesian nationalists at HQ Surabaya prior to the Allied re-occupation; Delegate at formal surrender of all Japanese forces in South East Asia to Lord Louis Mountbatten, Singapore, Malaya, 12 September 1945.

Note: Possibly the same as SHIBATA Yaichiro.

SHIBATA Yaichiro

Vice-Admiral; Commander of 24th Naval Base Force, Ende, Dutch East Indies, March 1944.

Note: Possibly the same as SHIBATA.

SHIMA Kiyohide

Rear-Admiral; Commander of 19th Minelaying Flotilla during invasion of Guam (see S. INOUYE), January 1942; Commander of Tulagi Invasion Force, landed 3

May 1942; Commander of Ocean and Nauru Islands Invasion Force (in Operation 'MO'. See S. INOUYE); Sailed 10 May 1942; Flagship minelayer *Okinoshima* sunk and force recalled to Rabaul, New Britain, 15 May 1942; Vice-Admiral; Commander of 2nd Striking Force; Advance Guard of 1st Mobile Fleet (under J. OZAWA) c. May 1944; Placed under South-west Area Fleet HQ, Manila, Philippines; Sailed from Pecadores as Commander of 2nd Division Attack (or Strike) Force with two heavy cruisers, one light cruiser (flagship *Abukuma*, seven destroyers in Operation 'SHO. 1' (attack on American naval forces off Leyte Islands, Philippines. See also T. KURITA, S. NISHIMURA, J. OZAWA, S. TOYODA), 21 October 1944; Formed support to Southern Force (of 1st Striking Force under S. NISHIMURA); Approached southern Surigao Straits (30–40 miles behind 1st Striking Force) but retired after light action and meeting the remnant of 1st Striking Force after its destruction, 25 October 1944; Concurrently Navy Minister and Chairman of the Military Chiefs' Organization, 1944.

SHIMADA Shigetarō

Born 1883; Graduated from Etajima Naval Academy (27th of 191), November 1904; Ensign, August 1905; 2nd Lieutenant, September 1907; Lieutenant, October 1909; Naval War College (a Class A student), December 1913; Lieutenant-Commander, December 1915; Assistant Naval Attaché to Italy, August 1916; Naval Attaché to Italy, December 1917; Staff Officer on Naval General Staff, June 1920; Commander, December 1920; Instructor at Naval War College, December 1923; Captain, December 1924; Captain of *Tama*, August 1928; Captain of battleship *Hiei*, December 1928; Rear-Admiral; November 1929; Chief of Staff to 2nd Fleet, November 1929; Chief of Staff to 1st Fleet and (concurrently?) Chief of Staff to Combined Fleet, December 1930; Commandant of Submarine School, December 1931; Chief of Staff to 3rd Fleet; February 1932; Staff Officer on Naval General Staff, June 1932; Chief of 3rd Department of Navy General Staff, June 1932; Concurrently Chief of 1st Department, November 1932; Vice-Admiral, November 1934; Vice Chief of Naval General Staff, December 1935; Commander of 2nd Fleet, December 1937; Commander of Kure Naval District, Japan, November 1938; Commander of China Area Fleet (replacing K. OIKAWA), May 1940; Admiral, November 1940; Opposed use of force to secure air and naval bases in French Indo–China, February 1941; Commander of Yokosuka Naval District, Japan, September 1941; Navy Minister in General H. TOJO cabinet (replacing K. OIKAWA), 18 October 1941; Initially expressed his opinion that war must be avoided but soon stated that it could not; Concurrently Chief of Naval General Staff (replacing O. NAGANO), 21 February 1944; Devotee of H. TOJO and sometimes called by other officers 'Tojo's brief-case carrier' or 'male bedmate'; Ordered preparation of a committee to prepare suicide weapons (*see* S. OMORI), late June 1944; Authorized formation of First Special Base Corps (to train and investigate use of suicide weapons), 10 July 1944; Relieved as Navy Minister to please political opponents of H. TOJO, July 1944; Relieved as Chief of the Naval General Staff, August 1944; Appointed to Supreme War Council, August 1944; Retired to reserve at his own request, 20 January 1945–end of war; Arrested as a Class A war criminal; Tried by the International Tribunal for the Far East, Tokyo, being indicted on 55 charges including crimes against peace, conventional war crimes and crimes against humanity, 26 April 1946–12 November 1948; Found guilty and sentenced to life imprisonment in Sugamo prison, Tokyo; Served only 7 years.

Personal facts: Tall. Very religious. A very clever man and shrewd. Charming. A 'yes man'. Always followed the advice of Prince H. FUSHIMI in important decisions. Excessive co-operation with General H. TOJO.

SHIMIZU Mitsumi
Vice-Admiral; Commander of 6th Fleet-Submarines, comprising 1st, 2nd, 3rd, Submarine Flotillas (approx. 40 subs.), 1 February 1941; Flagship cruiser *Katori* based at Kwajalein, 1942; Replaced (by T. KOMATSU), 16 March 1941.

SHINOZUKA Yoshio
Vice-Admiral; Attached to espionage service, c.1941.

SHIOZAWA Koichi
Vice?-Admiral; Commander of Yangtze Squadron, China, with fifteen cruisers, twenty destroyers, two gunboats, etc., plus two carriers; Anchored off Shanghai to defend Japanese concessions, 18 January 1932; Ordered to implement 'the right of self-defence' which became the first 'Shanghai Incident', 26 February 1932; Launched air and marine attack on Shanghai, 29 January 1932; Met unexpected opposition and was forced to request army assistance which arrived 14 February 1932; In Tokyo by 1939.

SHIRAGAWA
Admiral; Assassinated by a Korean patriot, 29 April 1932.

SHIRAISHI Kazutaka
Rear-Admiral; Chief of Staff to Southern Force (under N. KONDO) for the invasion of Malaya and Dutch East Indies, November 1941; (*see* N. KONDO for campaign details); Chief of Staff to 2nd Fleet (under N. KONDO) during Operation 'MI' (attempted invasion of Midway Island), May–June 1942.

SOSA Tanetsugu
Rear-Admiral; A spokesman for the navy, 1942.

SUETSUGU Naguma
Admiral; Fanatically anti-British and a radical; Represented Japan's military extremists; Possibly Naval Minister in first Konoye cabinet, 1937–9; Stated to Associated Press that America wished to subordinate Japan, 23 November 1941.

SUETSUGU Nobumasa
Studied English in London, 1914–15; Attached to Royal Navy Battle Cruiser HMS *Queen Mary*; Admiral; Totally opposed to 1930 London Naval Conference which ratified 5:5:3 (British:American:Japan) fleet ratios, but ordered by Navy Minister T. TAKARABE to stop announcing his opposition in public; Vice Chief of Naval General Staff (under K. KATO), c.1930; Commander-in-Chief of Combined Fleet, November 1933; Approved research on midget submarines; Officially recommended fleet parity with American; Protégé of K. KATO and attempted to introduce his militant ideas; Supported a purge of moderate senior naval officers by Navy Minister M. OSUMI, 1933–4; On reserve list and Cabinet Councillor by late 1937; Retired; Home Minister in Prince Koyone Cabinet; Died of heart disease aged 65, 29 December 1944.

SUGIMOTO
Rear-Admiral; Commander of 26th Air Flotilla (under 1st Air Fleet – T. ONISHI), Philippines, (replacing M. ARIMA), October? 1944.

SUGUIYAMA Rokuzo
Vice-Admiral; Commander of Sasebo Naval District at HQ Sasebo, Japan, November 1944.

SUMIYAMA Tokutarō
Educated at the Peers school; Graduated from Etajima Naval College, 1906; Captain; Aide-de-camp to Emperor Hirohito, 1927–32; Vice-Admiral; Vice Navy Minister (replacing I. YAMAMOTO), August 1939; Although easy-going and a moderate, he did not support Navy Minister M. YONAI in opposing the Tripartite Pact with Germany and Italy, June 1940; Replaced, September 1940.

SUZUKI Chozo
Rear-Admiral; Commander of Shanghai Special Naval Landing Force, HQ Shanghai, China, March 1944.

Baron SUZUKI Kantarō
Born 1867; Brother of General SUZUKI Takeo; Graduated from Naval Academy, 1887; Graduated from Naval War College, 1898; Lieutenant; Commander of a torpedo-boat during the Sino–Japanese war, participating in a night torpedo attack on We-hai-wei, 1898; Commander; Commander of 4th Destroyer Division which picked up survivors of the Port Arthur Blockade Squadron during the Russo–Japanese war, 1904–5; Rear-Admiral; Vice Navy Minister, 1914; Vice-Admiral, 1917; Commander of a Training Squadron, 1918; Military Councillor; Chief of Naval General Staff; Retired, Grand Chamberlain to the Emperor and Privy Councillor, January 1929–March 1936; Seriously wounded in an assassination attempt by disgruntled army officers demanding reforms in the '2–26 Insurrection', 26 February 1936; Withdrew from public life but remained as adviser to Emperor Hirohito; President of Privy Council, 10 August 1944–5 April 1945; Nominated by 'Jushin' (elder statesmen) as Premier to form a government but he refused on personal grounds; however, he was ordered to do so by the Emperor, 5 April 1945; Premier (aged 78), 7 April 1945 (replacing K. KOISO); Favoured peace but tended to sit on the fence; Soviet–Japanese neutrality pact denounced by Russia on 5 April 1945 (i.e., between the fall and formation of two cabinets); Agreed with proposals by M. YONAI that Russia should be requested to mediate for peace on Japan's behalf, 12 May 1945; Wrote a memorandum supporting the approach to Russia and recommended that Japan should be prepared to give up territories such as the northern Kuriles, Port Arthur and the South Manchurian Railway as payment to the Soviets, 14 May 1945; Member of the Supreme War Council; Wartime Emergency Measures Bill passed enabling the government to make legal decrees without recourse to the Diet (parliament) and take any draconian measures thought necessary, 22 June 1945; National Volunteer Fighting Corps Bill passed whereby the 'entire Japanese male population' was to be inducted into military service, 22 June 1945; Publicly proclaimed peace should be considered at Diet meeting but shouted down; Supreme War Council instructed by the Emperor to consider means to terminate the war, 22 June 1945; Russia rejected the request to act as an intermediary in

peace negotiations, mid July 1945; Issued press statement without prior consultation with his advisers that Japan rejected the Allied Potsdam Declaration for an 'unconditional surrender' which resulted in the dropping of atomic bombs; Soviet Union declared war on Japan, 8 August 1945; Would not decide whether or not to accept the Potsdam Declaration terms even after dropping of atomic bombs and Russian declaration of war, so took the unprecedented step of asking the Emperor personally to decide, 10 August 1945; Could not convince the cabinet to accept the Potsdam Declaration because of opposition of S. TOYODA and Generals K. ANAMI and Y. UMEZU; Acceptance of the Potsdam Declaration notified to Allies, 10 August 1945;* Allied reply did not seem to guarantee status of the Emperor which caused a crisis but was resolved by the personal intervention of the Emperor at an Imperial Conference, 14 August 1945; Escaped an assassination attempt by rebellious army officers during attempted *coup* (to protect the Emperor and prevent the Emperor's surrender broadcast), 15 August 1945; Suicide of War Minister General K. ANAMI forced his resignation and that of the cabinet, 15 August 1945 (replaced by Field Marshal Prince N. HIGA-SHIKUNI); Died 1948.

* Because of opposition by military forces to the surrender it was considered necessary to ensure that senior commanders throughout occupied areas be personally informed of the Emperor's acceptance of Allied terms. Three members of the imperial family were dispatched on 14 August 1945. They were Lieutenant-Colonel Prince Takeda Tsunenori to Korea and Manchuria; Colonel Asaka to the China Expeditionary Army and China Fleet; Prince Kanin Haruhito to Shanghai, Canton, Saigon, Singapore, Indo–China and Nanking.

TADA Takeo
Vice-Admiral; Chief of the Bureau of Naval Affairs by December 1944.

TAKAGI Sokichi
Captain; Chief of Research Section of Naval Affairs Bureau; Concluded in a report that an alliance with Germany, Italy and Russia was more favourable than isolationism or an alliance with Britain and France, 24 August 1939; Rear-Admiral; On Naval General Staff; Member of 'peace faction'; Assigned to contingency planning for possible defeat of Japan from 1940; Ordered by Navy Minister S. SHIMADA to undertake study of war capabilities and lessons learned from losses of military equipment (ships, aircraft, etc.), inability to import essential materials and effects of probable Allied bombing on the homeland, 20 September 1943; Concluded that Premier General H. TOJO was one major cause of Japan's failures and recommended that he should be removed from office; Informed three senior admirals of this opinion, February 1944; Since H. TOJO remained in office he proposed to some trusted naval captains and commanders that H. TOJO should be assassinated (however no attempt was made); also concluded that Japan could not win and should seek peace; Replaced, February 1944; Chief of Naval Training (Education) Bureau of Navy Ministry, March–August (or September) 1944; Transferred to minor post on the Naval General Staff by Navy Minister S. INOUYE on grounds of ill health, but secretly ordered to evolve peace proposals; Concluded that Japan should request Russia to negotiate on Japan's behalf; Navy Minister (in K. SUZUKI cabinet), 7 April 1945; Supported peace moves; Offered to fly to Switzerland to open surrender negotiations with the Americans but was refused permission, May 1945; Request to Russia to act as a peace negotiator failed; Resigned when the suicide of War Minister General K. ANAMI forced the resignation of the government; Retired 15 September 1945.

TAKAGI Takeo

Rear-Admiral; Commander of Covering Group (5th Cruiser Squadron) to 3rd Fleet (*see* I. TAKAHASHI), 1941; Invasion of Macassar, Celebes, 8 February 1942; Timor occupation, 20 February 1942; Vice-Admiral; Commander of Eastern Invasion Support Force, Main Body (under 2nd Fleet – I. TAKAHASHI) for Java invasion with forty transports, two heavy cruisers, one light cruiser and seven destroyers; Flagship heavy cruiser *Nachi*; Sighted by an Allied aircraft, 26 February 1942; Engaged by fifteen ships of Allied ABDA Fleet (under Rear-Admiral K.W.F.M. Doorman) at the Battle of the Java Sea; Japanese attacked with torpedoes, sinking two light cruisers, three destroyers and damaging others for no Japanese losses, 26–27 February 1942; Java invaded, 28 February 1942; Commander of Carrier Strike Force in Operation 'MO' (invasions of Port Moresby, New Guinea. *See* S. INOUYE) with two heavy carriers (*Shoho, Shokaku. See also* C. HARA), two heavy cruisers and six destroyers; one carrier badly damaged at the Battle of the Coral Sea, 7–9 May 1942; Ordered back to Truk, 11 May 1942; Commander of 5th Cruiser Squadron (cruisers *Myoko, Harugo*) under 2nd Fleet which formed Midway Invasion Cover Force Main Body (under N. KONDO) in Operation 'MI'; Sailed 29 May 1942; Ordered to withdraw, 5 June 1942; Commander of 6th Fleet-Submarines (replacing T. KOMATSU), November 1943; HQ, Truk, Caroline Islands; Said to be on Saipan Island, Marianas, when it was invaded by the Americans, 16 June 1944; Killed on Saipan during the fighting, 7 July 1944;* Replaced by S. MIWA (but *also see* N. OWADA).

* Reports of his death vary. He is also said to have been killed aboard a submarine before reaching the island.

TAKAHASHI Ibo (Sankichi, Koremochi)

Rear- or Vice-Admiral; Vice Chief of Naval General Staff (and protégé of K. KATO), 1932; A militant; Influenced the introduction of K. KATO's original proposal to devolve the right of overall naval command from the Navy Minister to the Chief of the Naval General Staff (which was ratified by the Emperor on 25 September 1933); Commander-in-Chief of the Combined Fleet, 1934–6; Stated that the Japanese navy must expand suddenly to the south as far as New Guinea, Celebes and Borneo, 10 February 1939; Chief of Staff to Combined Fleet;* Replaced (by S. FUKUDOME) and possibly retired, January 1940; (Recalled?); Commander of 3rd Fleet (Blockade and Transport Force) comprising 5th, 7th Cruiser Squadrons, 2nd, 4th Destroyer Flotillas; Formed part of Southern Force under N. KONDO, Formosa, 1941; Divided into Eastern Force (for invasions of Menedo, Kandari and Macassar in Celebes) and Central Force (for invasion of Dutch Borneo), late January–early February 1942; Commanded amphibious operations in the Banda Sea area, January 1942; Commander of Eastern and central (Western) Forces during invasion of Java and personally commanded Direct Support Force for both on flagship, heavy cruiser *Ashigara*, February 1942; Eastern Force comprised Support or Covering Group (under T. TAKAGI), First Escort Force (under S. NISHIMURA), Second Escort Force (under R. TANAKA), 1st, 2nd Naval Base Forces and 41 transports; Central (Western) Force comprised Support Force (under T. KURITA), Third Escort Force (under C. HARA), First Air Group (light carrier RYUJO) and 56 transports; Eastern Force defeated combined Allied ABDA Fleet at Battle of Java Sea (*see* T. TAKAGI), 26–7 February 1942; Completed invasion of Java without further resistance; Possibly Admiral by the end of the war; Ordered arrested by American occupation forces in Tokyo as a suspected war criminal, 2 December 1945.

* There appears to be some confusion over his rank and the timing of his appointment as Chief of Staff to Combined Fleet. Edwin P. Hoyt in *Yamamoto* (*see* Bibliography) says he was a Rear-Admiral in 1940 and retired after this post. Another reference gives him as a full Admiral when C in C Combined Fleet, 1934, while another gives him as Vice-Admiral when C in C 3rd Fleet, 1941. One would expect him to have had the rank of at least Vice-Admiral when holding the post of C in C Combined Fleet.

TAKAMA Tamotsu
Rear-Admiral; Commander of 4th Destroyer Flotilla (under 8th Fleet – G. MIKAWA); Acted as a Bombardment Force attacking Guadalcanal, Solomons, in flagship light cruiser *Yura*; Repulsed by American air attack, with the loss of *Yura*, at Battle of Santa Cruz Islands, 26 October 1942.

TAKARABE (TAKAROBE) Takeshi (Takeishi)
Admiral; Navy Minister, *c.*1930; Delegate at London Naval Conference, 1930; Supported retention of submarines as a cheap but effective weapon and wanted to increase permissible submarine tonnage for Japan over that previously agreed in the 1922 Washington Treaty but failed to get the figure required, April 1930; Forced to resign (replaced by K. ABO), 3 October 1930.

TAKASU Shirō
Vice-Admiral; President of Naval War College, *c.*1938; Commander of Aleutian Support (Guard) Force in Operation 'AL' (invasion of western Aleutian Islands) with personal command of 2nd Battleship Division (battleships *Fuso, Hyuga, Ise, Yamashiro*); Sailed from Kure, Japan (under 1st Fleet – I. YAMAMOTO); Detached to support 2nd Carrier Striking Force (K. KATUKA) in Aleutian campaign, June 1942; Commander of South-west Area Fleet, 1944 (Possibly replaced by G. MIKAWA).

TAKATA
Vice-Admiral; Doctor and personal physician to C in C Combined Fleet I. YAMAMOTO; Flew in same aircraft and was killed with I. YAMAMOTO when the flight was ambushed near Buin, Bougainville, 18 April 1943 (*see also* OKUVA).

TAKATA Toshitane
Rear-Admiral; Head of 1st Section of Military Affairs Bureau, Tokyo, 1941; Senior Staff Officer to 3rd Fleet by 1943.

TAKEDA
Rear-Admiral; Commander of southern sector units, Elebente on Bougainville, Solomon Islands, during the war.

TAKEMA Chumi
Rear-Admiral; Submarine service; Prepared plans for *Kaiten* (manned suicide torpedoes) usage and submitted it to the Imperial Naval General Staff, early 1943.

TAKESHI Takarabe – *See* TAKARABE Takeshi

TAMURA Ryukichi
Rear-Admiral; Commander of 14th Naval Base Force and 83rd Naval Garrison Unit, New Ireland; Ordered senior staff officer Lieutenant-Commander Mori

Kyoji to arrange the executions of POWs at Kavieng in the event of an enemy landing, March 1944; When this appeared imminent, 23 Australian male civilians were strangled in secret at Kavieng south wharf, 17 March 1944; Surrendered his sword together with his staff to Lieutenant-General Eather, GOC Australian 11th Division, aboard HMS *Swan* at Fangelawa Bay, New Ireland, afternoon of 19 September 1945 (The army surrendered the same day. *See* Lieutenant-General T. ITO); Tried for Kavieng killings by Australian War Crimes Tribunal in Hong Kong, 24 November–17 December 1947; Sentenced to death and hanged at Stanley Jail, Singapore, 16 March 1948.

TANAKA Kikumatsu

Captain; Captain of cruiser *Kumano* in 7th Cruiser Squadron (under T. KURITA) which formed part of Close Support Group to Midway Island Invasion Force Main Body in Operation 'MI', May–June 1942; Rear-Admiral; Commander of naval land units at Surabaya Naval base, Java (under 2nd Expeditionary Fleet – SHIBATA) at the time of the Japanese surrender, August 1945.

TANAKA Raizo

Rear-Admiral; Commander of Escort Group (comprising 2nd Destroyer Flotilla) in 3rd Fleet (*see* I. TAKAHASHI), 1941; Commander of Davao (Philippines) Attack Force, December 1941; Escort Group Commander to Timor Invasion Force in flagship light cruiser *Jintsu*, 20 February 1942; Destroyer Escort Commander of Covering Force (under T. TAKAGI) in Eastern Attack Force for Java invasion (*see also* S. NISHIMURA); Torpedoed and sank three Allied warships at Battle of Java Sea, 27 February–1 March 1942; Commander of Escort Force (2nd Destroyer Flotilla), in flagship *Jintsu*, and a Transport Group with Midway Landing Force (under 2nd Fleet – N. KONDO) in Operation 'MI', May–June 1942; Commander of Convoy Escort Force of unsuccessful Guadalcanal Reinforcement Force (8th Fleet under G.MIKAWA) suffering damage to *Jintsu* and transferring to destroyer *Suzukaze*, 25 August 1942; Commander of Destroyer Escorts to Guadalcanal reinforcement convoys ('Tokyo Express'), August–November 1942; Completed the landing of 38th Division without naval support (*see* N. KONDO) and incurred heavy losses of ships, troops and supplies, 15 November 1942; In flagship destroyer *Naganami* in Battle of Lunga Point (Tassafaronga) which was the last naval battle for Guadalcanal, 29–30 November 1942; Accompanied supply destroyers in flagship which was hit off Tulagi when he was wounded, 11 December 1942; Removed from sea command for being outspoken (relaced by K. KOYONAGI), late December 1942 or early January 1943; Commander of 13th Special Naval Base Force, October 1943; HQ Rangoon, Burma, November 1944; Came under Burma Area Army command, 18 February 1945; Left Rangoon to re-establish HQ at Moulmein, southern Burma, 1 May 1945; Transferred with HQ to Bangkok, Siam (under 18th Area Army command) until end of the war; Vice-Admiral before end of the war; Surrendered his sword to Major-General G. C. Evans, GOC 7th Indian Division, at Bangkok (together with his Chief of Staff K. SATO and twenty Generals), 11 January 1946.

TANIGUCHI Naozane

Admiral; Chief of Naval General Staff (replacing K. KATO), June 1930; Replaced (by Prince H. FUSHIMA), 1932.

TAYUI Minoru
Vice-Admiral; Commander of Maizuru Naval District, March 1945; HQ Maizuru, Japan.

TAYUI Yuzuru
Flag Officer, *c.* Second World War.

TERAOKA Kimpei
Vice-Admiral; Commander of 1st Air Fleet (replacing K. KAKUTA), Philippines, arriving 12 August 1944; HQ Clark Field, Luzon; Started a training programme for 'skip' bombing technique to be used against American invasion naval forces off the Philippines but it was abaondoned after disastrous losses during August and September 1944; Rejected *Kamikaze* tactics suggested by M. ARIMA, September 1944; Rebuilt the Air Fleet but suffered heavy losses; Partially rebuilt again, October 1944; Replaced (by T. ONISHI) on orders of C in C Combined Fleet S. TOYADA, early October 1944; Commander of 3rd Air Fleet responsible for the naval defence of Honshu Island, Japan; Lost 150 aircraft in one day (*see also* M. UGAKI), 15 February 1945; Formed *Kamakaze* unit 'Mitate No. 2' from 601st Air Group, February 1945; This unit attacked the American fleet off Iwo Jima, 21 February 1945.

TERASHIMA Ken
Rear-Admiral; Concurrently Post and Telecommunications Minister and Railway Minister in General H. TOJO cabinet, 18 October 1942; Ordered arrested by American occupation forces as a possible war criminal (for involvement in the Pearl Harbor attack), Tokyo, 12 September 1945.

TERASHIMA Takeshi
Full? Admiral; Forced to retire by 1933 because he supported the 1930 London Naval Conference Limitation Treaty.

TIDZYAKI
Vice-Admiral; Member of the Jinmukai Society (society for action), 1931.

Note: The spelling of this name is doubtful since it is not recognizable as a Japanese name and does not equate to anything similar.

TOEDA Ogasawara
Full? Admiral; Involved in the Society for the Foundation of the State (presumably a nationalist right-wing organization), *c.*1930.

Count TŌGŌ Heihachirō 東郷 平八郎
Born 1847; Samurai family of the Satsuma clan; Became a samurai and served with artillery (canon with stone shot) at Kagoshima when it was bombarded by the British Royal Navy under Admiral Kuper, 14 August 1863; Cadet in fledgling Japanese navy; Junior naval officer and learnt English, 1870; Sent to England for training with the Royal Navy, 1871; Returned to Japan and carried out survey work around the coast; First-Lieutenant, 1878; Captain of cruiser *Naniwa*,[1] firing first shots of the Sino–Japanese war (although it had not been officially declared), 25 July 1894; Part of Flying Squadron at Battle of the Yalu, defeating the Chinese fleet, 17 September 1894; Rear-Admiral, 1895; Member of Board of Admirals by

late 1895; President of Naval Technical College; Vice-Admiral by 1900; Commander of Sasebo and Maizuru naval bases, Japan; Commander-in-Chief of Main Battle Squadron in flagship battleship *Mikasa*;[2] Launched surprise attack on Port Arthur, (beginning the Russo–Japanese war), 18–19 February 1904; Blockaded Port Arthur; Drew Russian Port Arthur Squadron out to battle but they failed to engage, April 1904; Destroyed Russian Port Arthur Squadron at the Battle of the Yellow Sea, 10 August 1904; First Commander-in-Chief of newly formed Combined Fleet (with 1st, 2nd Squadrons and a 3rd Squadron of old ships), 15 October 1904; Destroyed Russian Second Pacific Squadron (formerly the Baltic Fleet) at the Battle of Tsushima (or Battle of the Sea of Japan), sinking nineteen ships, capturing seven with two scuttled, six interned in neutral ports and only four escaping (all for minor Japanese losses), 27–8 May 1905.[3] Combined Fleet placed on a peacetime footing and formerly disbanded, 21 December 1905; Senior Admiral and naval adviser;[4] Naval tutor to Prince Hirohito; Acted as a restraint on militant flag officers such as K. KATO 1914–24; Supported a reduction in Japan's naval expansion programme, 1921; Count and Fleet Admiral by the time of his death on 30 May 1934; First ever commoner to receive a state funeral, 5 June 1934.

Personal facts: Quiet. Slow to learn but determined. Studied naval tactics and regarded Admiral Lord Nelson with reverence. Greatest of all Japanese admirals. An anglophile.

[1] One of three cruisers (under Rear-Admiral Tsuboi). He sank two Chinese ships plus the British ship *Kowshing* which was under charter to the Chinese and carried Chinese troop reinforcements. The British crew were rescued but the Chinese survivors were machine-gunned in the water. This nearly created an international incident but the sinking was declared legal and no action was taken over the killings which did not seem to tarnish his reputation.
[2] *Misaka* still survives as a museum, being declared a National Monument in 1961.
[3] Flew his famous 'Z' signal ('The fate of the empire depends on this battle. Let every man do his utmost') which was used by other Japanese admirals during the Second World War.
[4] He successfully urged the dispatch of a Japanese naval squadron to the Mediterranean to serve with the Allies in 1916.

TŌGŌ Minoru
Son of Count H. TŌGŌ; Rear-Admiral by the end of the war. Became a night watchman, guarding American destroyers and submarines, at Yokosuka Naval Base, Japan, after the war.

Baron TOMIOKA Sadatoshi
Born 1900; Captain; Chief of 1st Section of 1st Division (Operations) of Naval General Staff, October 1940; Concurrently member of the 1st Committee of Navy National Defence Policy Committee; Stated he supported war with America, October 1941; Consistently refused to believe Intelligence Division reports on American national power; Replaced, January 1942; Section head in Operations Bureau of Naval General Staff, September 1943–November 1944; Rear-Admiral; Chief of Operations Bureau of Naval General Staff (possibly until the end of the war); Ordered by Chief of Naval General Staff S. TOYODA to attend the Japanese surrender signing aboard USS *Missouri*, Tokyo Bay, 2 September 1945; Edited the Japanese Naval History of the Pacific War; Member of a twelve-man commission for setting up a Japanese defence programme, 1951; Lectured at the Japanese Defence Research Institute; Died 1970.

TOTSUKA (TOZUKA) Mitsutaro

Vice-Admiral; Commander of Yokosuka Naval District Base, May 1945; HQ Yokosuka, Japan; Surrendered to Rear Admiral Robert B. Carney, USN, Chief of Staff to American 3rd Fleet, 30 August 1945.

Note: His sword is now in the American Naval Academy Museum, Annapolis. A *kai-guntō* with (lacquered?) scabbard. Cat.no. 45.65.

TOYODA Soemu

Vice-Admiral; Commander of the 4th Fleet at the time of the 'China Incident', 1937; Captured Tsingtao, China, January 1938; Commander of Kure Naval District, Japan, 1941; Did not believe the navy could win a war against America; Intensely disliked the army and made his views public, 1943; Possibly Commander of Yokosuka Naval Base, Japan; Commander-in-Chief of the Combined Fleet (replacing M. KOGA), officially announced 3 May 1944;[1] HQ Kieo University, Hiyoshi, Japan; Ordered by IGHQ to adopt aggressive policies;[2] Prepared Operation 'A-GO' (closely based on Operation 'Z' see S. FUKUDOME) to lure the American Pacific Fleet between Palau and New Guinea where Japanese carrier and land-based aircraft could destroy them; Reorganized Combined Fleet (around the nucleus of 1st Mobile Fleet – under J. OZAWA) on American lines, April–May 1944;[3] Ordered Biak Island, off Dutch New Guinea, to be held (*see* Lieutenant-General T. NUMATA) and reinforced it by Operation 'KON' which was only partially successful, June 1944; Ordered 35–50 per cent of all aircraft in the central Pacific to reinforce western New Guinea, but they could not cover the American landings on Saipan Island, Marianas, 15 June 1944; Operation 'A-GO' ended in disaster at the Battle of the Philippine Sea ('Great Marianas Turkey Shoot'. *See also* J. OZAWA) with heavy losses of Japanese aircraft, 19–20 June 1944;[4] Realized the navy was virtually defeated but decided to launch Operation 'SHO. 1' in a last-ditch gamble, October 1944;[5] Flew to Manila, Philippines, 7 October 1944; Ordered naval forces to the Philippines to prevent the American invasion of Leyte; Directed operations from Naval HQ, Tokyo; Planned to lure the American 3rd Fleet northwards with his Main Force (under J. OZAWA) while attacking invasion transports with 1st (under T. KURITA) and 2nd (under K SHIMA) Attack (Striking) Forces; Leyte to be reinforced by Transport Unit (under N. SAKONJU); Attacks failed with disastrous losses of 35 ships comprising three battleships (including super battleship *Musashi*), four carriers, ten cruisers, thirteen destroyers and five submarines in the battles of Palawan Passage, Sibuyan Sea, Surigao Straits, Samar and Cape Engano, 23–6 October 1944; The Japanese navy was thus virtually destroyed and split into two, with forces in the Inland Sea, Japan, and at Singapore, Malaya, by 26 October 1944; Ordered remnant of 2nd Fleet (under S. ITO) to undertake a suicide mission in Operation 'TEN-GO' to attack American invasion forces off Okinawa; Temporary HQ at Kanoya, Kyushu, Japan; Ordered army and naval air units to co-operate with 5th Air Fleet (under M. UGAKI) to undertake first mass *Kamikaze* attacks on American naval forces in support of Operation 'TEN-GO', 6–7 April 1945; First Special Attack Force (redesignated name of 2nd Fleet) carried out the attack without air cover and was destroyed by American air attacks, before reaching the American fleet, losing most ships including super battleship *Yamato*, 7 April 1945; Combined Fleet ceased to exist as a fighting force after this date; Concurrently Chief of Naval General Staff, May 1945; Believed that offers of peace negotiations from America via Switzerland were a trick, May 1945; Remained deliberately evasive about accepting the Allied Potsdam Declaration for unconditional surrender even after the dropping of atomic bombs and the Russian invasion of Manchuria; Wanted to fight on even after the Japanese acceptance of Potsdam Declaration, 13 August 1945; Ordered his Operations Officer S. TOMIOKA to represent him at the formal signing of the Instrument of Surrender aboard USS *Missouri*, Tokyo Bay, 2 September 1945; Arrested as a war criminal but cleared of crimes committed by naval personnel; Died of a heart attack aged 72 in 1957.

Note: He presented his sword to Admiral C. Nimitz, C in C American Pacific Fleet, at the time of his surrender. Nimitz returned the sword in 1952 as a gesture of good will.

[1] The death of M. KOGA one month earlier was kept from the Japanese public until a replacement was found. The delay was caused by the argument over who was to be appointed.
[2] Supported a 'single decisive battle' policy.
[3] Reorganization was set in motion by M. KOGA before his death. 1st Mobile Fleet (under J. OZAWA) was formed by 3rd Fleet (also under J. OZAWA) consisting of 1st, 2nd, 3rd Carrier Divisions, two light cruisers and fifteen destroyers, plus 2nd Fleet (or Main Body under T. KURITA) consisting of 1st, 2nd Battleship Divisions, 4th, 5th, 7th Cruiser Squadrons with Screen of fourteen destroyers and one light cruiser.
[4] America was aware of the general strategy and forces involved because of the capture of the original 'Z Plan' documents from S. FUKUDOME.
[5] Operation 'SHO' (Victory) was a national defence plan to throw every available ship of the 1st Mobile Fleet against American fleets if they attacked in any one of four sectors: SHO-1: Philippines; SHO-2: Formosa and the Ryukyus; SHO-3: Japanese home islands of Kyusha and Shikoku; SHO-4: Japanese home islands of Hokkaido and Kurile islands.

TOYODA Teijiro
Graduated from Etajima Naval College (1st of 171), 1905; Naval Attaché in London, 1920s; Vice-Admiral; Vice Navy Minister (under K. OIKAWA), 6 September 1940; Regarded as a moderate and a 'friend of England'; Supported the Tripartite Pact with Germany and Italy because he thought a triple alliance plus Russian assistance would keep America out of a war and bring about an early termination of the war in China, 1940; Replaced (by Y. SAWAMOTO), April 1941; Retired from active list; Minister of Commerce and Industry in second Prince Konoye Cabinet; Foreign Minister in the third Prince Konoye cabinet (replacing Y. Matsuoka), 18 or 22 July 1941; Advised Premier Konoye that negotiations with America should proceed if the Japanese army could be persuaded to withdraw from China, 12 October 1941; Resigned, 18 October 1941; Minister of Munitions in K. SUZUKI cabinet, 1945.

Personal facts: Spoke fluent English. Identified himself with the British Royal Navy which earned him much criticism. Excellent administrator.

TSUJIMURA T.
Rear-Admiral; Commander of 5th Special Naval Base Force (under Central Pacific Fleet – C. NAGUMO); HQ Saipan Island, Marianas; American forces invaded Saipan, 16 June 1944 (*see* C. NAGUMO for campaign details); Killed 16 July 1944.

TSUKAHARA Nishio (Nishizo, Fushizo)
Vice-Admiral; Commander of Combined Naval Air Fleet and concurrently Commander of the 11th Air Fleet, HQ Formosa, c.1941; 600 aircraft including those in 1st Air Fleet (carrier-based for Pearl Harbor attack) were under his command as were 550 aircraft in 11th Air Fleet (which was land-based and

comprised 21st, 23rd Air Flotillas based in Formosa and 22nd Air Flotilla, under S. MATSUNAGA, based in Indo–China); Land-based units launched air strikes on American air bases in the Philippines from 8 December 1941; Supported invasions of Malaya (by 25th Army), British Borneo, and Philippines (by 14th Army), from December 1941; Supported invasion of Dutch East Indies, early 1942; Dutch and Allied fighter power effectively destroyed in an air battle over Surabaya, Java, 19 February 1942; HQ Tinian Island, Marianas, March? 1942; Responsible for shore-based Air Group supporting Midway Island Expeditionary Forces in Operation 'MI' (see I. YAMAMOTO) with 36 aircraft embarked on 1st Air Fleet carriers (under C. NAGUMO) and main shore-based units under 24th Air Flotilla (under T. MAEDA) on the islands of Wake, Jaluit, Wotje, Aur and Kwajalein, May–June 1942; Supported 17th Army in New Guinea area from 21st July 1942; HQ transferred to Rabaul, New Britain, August 1942; Launched numerous air raids on American naval and ground forces on Guadalcanal, Solomons, August–September 1942; 11th Air Fleet made exaggerated claims for enemy ships sunk and aircraft destroyed to C in C Combined Fleet I. YAMAMOTO which were believed; Relieved of command because of malaria and dengue fever, being sent home late September or early October 1942; Replaced (by R. KUSAK); Believed to have become Commander of 3rd Fleet; Sat on a Board of Enquiry regarding S. FUKUDOME, Tokyo, April 1944.

UGAKI Kenji
Vice-Admiral; Commander of Ominato Naval Guard District by 1945; HQ Ominato port, northern Honshu, Japan; Surrendered Ominato Guard District* to Vice Admiral Frank Jack Fletcher, USN, aboard USS *Panamint* in Ominato anchorage, 10 September 1945.

* This area consisted of all of Honshu north of 40° Latitude and the entire island of Hokkaido. Formerly it also included the Kurile Islands but these were occupied by the Russians.

UGAKI Matome
Brother of General K. UGAKI; Rear-Admiral; Chief of 1st Division of Naval General Staff (replacing N. KONDO), December 1938; With five other senior naval leaders, he openly opposed the signing of the Tripartite Pact, 13 September 1940; Chief of Staff to Combined Fleet (replacing S. FUKUDOME) under I. YAMAMOTO, April 1941; Based in flagship battleship *Atago*, Kure, Japan, 1941; Concurrently Chief of Staff to 1st Air Fleet (under C. NAGUMO) for Pearl Harbor attack but remained in *Atago*, December 1941; Became convinced that air power could defeat capital ships after the sinkings of Royal Navy ships *Prince of Wales* and *Repulse*, December 1941;[1] New fleet flagship super battleship *Yamato*, 12 February 1942; Wanted to send submarines all over the Pacific in an aggressive role but was overruled by I. YAMAMOTO; Wanted to delay Port Moresby invasion because of a lack of carriers but was overruled with the resultant Battle of the Coral Sea, 8 May 1942; Silenced opposition to the Midway Island invasion plan (Operation 'MI'); Sailed for Midway in flagship *Yamato*, 29 May 1942; Returned after cancellation due to loss of carriers at the Battle of Midway; Transferred with Combined Fleet HQ to Truk, Caroline Islands, August 1942; Sent to Rabaul, New Britain, to observe combined operations to secure Guadalcanal, Solomons, 10 September 1942; Returned to Truk with unfavourable reports, late September 1942; Moved to Rabaul, New Britain (with I. YAMAMOTO) to concentrate on defending New Guinea, 1943; Accompanied I. YAMAMOTO on one-day tour of the Shortland Islands, flying in the second aircraft from Rabaul to

Ballale, off southern Bougainville, when both aircraft were shot down by American fighters, but swam ashore with a broken arm after crash-landing in the sea, 18 April 1943; Vice-Admiral by late October 1943; Commander of 1st Battleship Division (under 2nd Fleet – T. KURITA) with battleship *Nagato* and super battleships *Yamato* and *Musashi*, April 1944; HQ Tawi-Tawi in Sulu Islands, north-east Borneo; Joined forces with (and subordinate to) 1st Mobile Fleet (under J. OZAWA), 15 June 1944; Battle of Marianas (Philippine Sea), 18-20 June 1944; Formed part of 1st Strike Force in Operation 'SHO-1' (defence of Philippines. *See* S. TOYODA); Battle of Surigao Strait (Leyte Gulf) with sinking of *Musashi*, 24-5 October 1944; Commander of 5th Air Fleet from its formation, 2 February 1945 (built up to defend Okinawa) with HQ at Kanoya, northern Kyushu, Japan; Assumed concurrent tactical command of 6th Air Army (Major-General M. SUGAWARA); Ordered to attack American fleet and main American naval repair base at Ulithi Island, Carolines, (Operation 'TAN') with *Kamikazes* which was launched 11 March 1945; Attack failed with only one major strike on an American carrier, 12 March 1945; Operation 'TEN-GO' (*see* S. TOYODA) launched to attack American invasion forces off Okinawa; Attacked Amercian carriers south of Kyushu but with only minor success, 17 March 1945; Ordered a second attack including *Kamikazes* which badly damaged two US carriers, 19 March 1945; Had a squadron equipped with 'Okas' (piloted suicide rocket bombs launched from the underside of an aircraft); First 'Oka' attack from Usa Navy Base, north-eastern Kyushu, against American carriers, was a complete failure with all mother aircraft destroyed before launching the 'Okas', 19 (or 21?) March 1945; Numerous *Kamikaze* attacks launched on enemy shipping off Okinawa; Army and navy air units including those in Formosa (see T. ONISHI) were ordered to co-operate and defeat the American Okinawa invasion forces from April 1945; 3rd Air Fleet (K. TERAOKA) also transferred to his command together with 1st Air Fleet and Army 6th and 8th Air Regiments, April 1945; These were combined to form *Kikusui* ('chrysanthemum on the water') mass *Kamikaze* attack units against enemy naval forces off Okinawa as part of Operation 'TEN-GO'; First mass attack (547 navy and 188 army aircraft including *Kamikazes*)met with some success but no large capital ships were sunk, 6-7 April 1945; Second mass attack (500 aircraft including *Kamikazes* and eight 'Okas') sunk one destroyer and one LCS, damaging sixteen other ships, 16 April 1945; Third mass *Kamikaze* attack (400 aircraft including six 'Okas'), 16 April 1945; 10th Air Fleet command withdrawn, 17 April 1945; Fourth mass attack, 28 April 1945; Fifth mass attack, 3-4 May 1945; There were a total of ten mass attacks until the capture of Okinawa by the Americans, the last being on 22 June 1945; *Kamikaze* attacks continued on Allied naval forces in the Okinawa area until July 1945; Final HQ at Oita, Kyushu, Japan; Listened to the Emperor's surrender broadcast then committed suicide by a last attack on the enemy, 15 August 1945; Climbed aboard a two-seater aircraft of 701st Air Group at Oita air base carrying his sword and stripped of insignia;[2] Allowed the Warrant Officer, whose place he had taken, also to squeeze in; This was the only aircraft in the flight to carry three people; The total of eleven fighter-bombers flew off against unspecified American naval forces in the last *Kamikaze* attack of the war; Radioed base that he was going to make an attack on Okinawa (timed at 7.24pm); After the war a US sailor, Danny Rosewall, told a Japanese historian that he had seen several *Kamikazes* attacking off Iheya-ushiro-jima, north of Okinawa on that day; One aircraft, on fire, crashed on the beach; The next day he examined the wreckage and found three bodies, one of which had an 'ornate samurai sword'.[3]

Personal facts: Arrogant and humourless. A hard drinker, suffered ill health during the Guadalcanal campaign.

[1] Intended to have *Prince of Wales* and *Repulse* raised and repaired for use by the IJN since they sank in only about 30 metres of water. Soon after the sinkings a salvage ship was sent but only recovered some AA guns from *Repulse* before being diverted elsewhere, March 1942.

[2] Said to have carried a 'short samurai sword' given to him by C in C Combined Fleet I. YAMAMOTO on this last mission (reference *The Rising Sun* by J. Toland). He is thought to have been presented with a *tanto* (dirk) which was one of ten specially made (and commissioned by I. YAMAMOTO) for presentation to his Chiefs of Staff and favoured officers who had participated in the Pearl Harbor campaign. These had YAMAMOTO's signature engraved on the tang and a nine character version of the famous H. TOGO Z-signal on the blade. (Reference: Japanese Sword Society of the United States newsletter of December 1989). Presumably, in this case, it was mounted as a naval officer's dirk.

[3] This account is given in *The Fall of Japan* by Keith Wheeler (*see* Bibliography). The subsequent fate of the 'sword' is not mentioned. All other references consulted say no *Kamikaze* attacks were reported that day and that he is presumed to have crashed into the sea.

UOZUMI (UZUMI, UZUMUI, UZONI) Jisaku

Awarded British Distinguished Service Cross during the First World War; Rear-Admiral; Commander of 15th Special Naval Base Force, August 1944; Unit at Prai, Malaya, November 1944; Governor of Penang Island, Malaya, by the end of the war; Signed surrender of Penang Island (with BAZUDI, Military Commander of Penang)* aboard HMS *Nelson* to Vice-Admiral H. T. C. Walker, Deputy Commander of East Indies Fleet and Commander of 3rd Battle Squadron, 2 September 1945.

*This is given in the *History of the Second World War – The War against Japan* vol.5. (*see* Bibliography). However Stephen Harper in *Miracle of Deliverance* gives the signing 'arrangements for the British re-occupation of the island' aboard the cruiser HMS *Cleopatra* to Admiral Sir Arthur Power, C in C East Indies Fleet, 29 August 1945. It is unclear whether this was the preliminary surrender, full surrender, or is a contradiction.

WADA Misao

Vice-Admiral; Construction Supervisor of the first 'Okas' (piloted suicide rocket bombs), Yokosuka Air Arsenal, Japan, from 6 August 1944.

YAMADA Sadayoshi

Rear-Admiral; Commander of 25th Air Flotilla (land based), HQ Rabaul, New Britain; Covered Operation 'MO' (attempted invasion of Port Moresby under 4th Fleet – S. INOUYE), May 1942; Launched air strikes against American forces which occupied Tulagi (capital of Solomon Islands) and Guadalcanal, Solomons, from 7 August 1942; Provided air support for Japanese naval forces at the Battle of Eastern Solomons, 24 August 1942; Reinforced by 80 bombers and 100 fighters, 25 September 1942; Lost most of them by the end of September 1942.

YAMAGATA Seigō

Vice-Admiral; Chief of Management Division of Naval Aviation Department, c.1940.

YAMAKI Akira

Captain; Attached to Personnel Bureau of Navy Ministry, 1940; Rear-Admiral by the end of the war.

YAMAGUCHI Gisaburo (Chisaburo)

Vice-Admiral; Commander of Ryojun (i.e., Port Arthur) Special Base Force, Manchuria, March 1944; Signed surrender of all naval troops in South Korea (south of the 38° Latitude) in the Throne Room of Government House, Keijo (Seoul), Korea (together with General N. ABE and Lieutenant-General Y. KOZUKI) to Lieutenant General J. R. Hodge, US Army, and Admiral T. C. Kinkaid, USN, 9 September 1945.

YAMAGUCHI Tamon

Rear-Admiral; Commander of 2nd Carrier Division (part of 1st Air Fleet under C. NAGUMO) with carriers *Hiryu, Soryu*, October 1941;* Part of *Kido Butai* (code-name of) fleet which attacked Pearl Harbor, Hawaii, 7 December 1941; Supported operations in Banda Sea area (*see* I. TAKAHASHI), January 1942; Part of Darwin Strike Force, 19 February 1942; Commander of 2nd Carrier Division (with *Soryu* and flagship *Hiryu* in Carrier Group of 1st Air Fleet (under C. NAGUMO) in the attempted invasion of Midway Island (Operation 'MI'); Sailed from Kure, Japan; Lost the carrier *Soryu* in the Battle of Midway, 4 June 1942; Given temporary responsibility for air operations when other carriers were also sunk, 4 June 1942; Launched air attack on American carriers, severely damaging the American flagship USS *Yorktown*, 4 June 1942; Committed suicide aboard the carrier *Hiryu* when she was badly damaged and sunk in the last phase of the Battle of Midway, 5 June 1942.

*He believed implicitly in the superiority of carriers and thought older admirals, such as C. NAGUMO, did not know how to use them properly.

YAMAMOTO Eisuke
Admiral. Retired by 1935.

YAMAMOTO Isoroku 山 本 五 十 六

Born 1884 in Nagaoka, Niigata Prefecture, Honshu Island; Son of a former samurai; Real name Takano Isoroku;[1] Learned English for six years at Nagaoka Middle School, 1884-1900;[2] Won an appointment to Imperial Naval Academy, Etajima, Hiroshima, coming second highest in the national entrance examination, 1901; Studied English and specialized in naval gunnery; Graduated (7th of 191), 14 November 1904; Commissioned as an Ensign; Joined heavy cruiser *Nisshin* as a gunnery specialist and deck officer, 3 January 1905; Wounded in the thigh and lost two fingers of his left hand when a ship's gun (or possibly enemy shell) exploded during the Battle of Tsushima in the Russo-Japanese war, 26 May 1905; Yokosuka Gunnery School, Japan, 5 August 1905; Sub-Lieutenant, September 1905; Transferred to sea in the *Kagero*, 1907; Served in *Maezuru*, 1908; and *Aso*, 1909-12; With *Aso* when she formed part of a Squadron visiting the west coast of America, March–July 1909; Advanced gunnery course at Gunnery School, 1912; Gunnery officer in battleship *Shintaku*, 1913; Entered Naval Staff College at Tsukiji, Japan, 1913; Lieutenant-Commander, 1915; Graduated from Staff College with top honours, 1916; Honoured by the request of the 'Yamamoto' clan to adopt their surname and become their leader because of his impressive performance, which he accepted, becoming 'Yamamoto Isoroku', 1916;[3] Married, 31 August 1918;[4] Posted to USA, studying English and petroleum resources at Harvard University and also became interested in aviation, April 1919–summer 1921; Commander, December 1919; Instructor at Naval Staff College (realizing the possible use of naval air power), 1921; Executive Officer in cruiser *Kitakami*, August 1922; Naval Command School, late 1922; Accompanied K. IDE as an interpreter on a tour of England, Europe and USA, 1923; Captain, early 1923; Yokosuka Naval Base, Japan; Captain of cruiser *Fuji*, June 1923; On staff of

Kasumigaura Aviation Corps, Japan, autumn 1924;[5] Executive Officer and Director of Studies at same, late 1924; Japanese Naval Attaché to Washington, USA (replacing K. HASEGAWA), arriving January 1925; Recommended to the navy high command that the American celestial navigation system for carrier-borne aircraft be used; Returned to Japan, spring 1928; Captain of light cruiser *Isuzu*, summer 1928; Captain of carrier *Akagi*, 10 December 1928; Predicted air power would become the nucleus of the navy, 1928; On staff of Naval Affairs Bureau of Navy Ministry, Tokyo, late 1929; Member of naval delegation (under S. SAKONJI) to first London Naval Conference and also promoted to Rear-Admiral, November–December 1930; Chief of Technical Division of Naval Aviation Department (responsible for building up a naval airforce and implementation of a programme to increase carrier strength at the expense of battleships), 1930-3;[6] Commander of 1st Naval Air (carrier) Division, flagship carrier *Akagi*, 3 October 1933; Member of Special Committee for study of Disarmament Measures, spring 1934; Head of naval delegation to 1934 Preliminary London Naval Limitation Conference, arriving 16 October 1934; Told by Navy Minister M. OSUMI to demand fleet parity with the British and Americans, but instructed by the Emperor to attempt to gain a general disarmament; Vice-Admiral, 15 November 1934; Talks failed so returned to Japan via Berlin and Moscow, early 1935; Naval Affairs Bureau, Tokyo, 1935; Head of Naval Aviation Department, 1935; Vice Navy Minister (under O. NAGANO), December 1936;[7] Remained in post under M. YONAI, 1937; Opposed army plans to conquer China after 'Marco Polo Bridge Incident', 1937; Apologised personally to American Ambassador Grew for the sinking of the gunboat USS *Panay* by Japanese aircraft, December 1937; Replaced (by T. SUMIYAMA), August 1939; Commander-in-Chief of Combined Fleet (replacing Z. YOSHIDA), 30 August 1939;[8] Flagship battleship *Nagato*, Kagoshima base, Japan; Implemented tough training schedules, night exercises, carrier and torpedo-bomber usage; Built up Combined Fleet strength; Opposed signing of Tripartite Pact with Germany and Italy, 1940; Told Premier Prince Konoye that Japan would loose a war with America after two or three years, 1940; Staged a fleet review for the Emperor showing Japanese naval power, new ships and a fly past of 500 aircraft, Tokyo Bay, 11 October 1940; Admiral, November 1940; Conceived the idea of a pre-emptive carrier attack on the American Pacific Fleet at Hawaii with a simultaneous declaration of war (should it become necessary) and threatened to resign if this plan were dropped, 19 October 1941; Reorganized Combined Fleet structure around carriers; Held war games at Naval Staff College to finalize Pearl Harbor strike, October and November 1941; Ordered by IGHQ, Tokyo, to prepare for war with Britain, America and Holland so issued Operational Order No. 1. which specified strategy for the first phase of naval operations against Hawaii, Malaya, Philippines and Dutch East Indies, 5 November 1941; Units for Operation 'Z' (Pearl Harbor strike) sailed 19-29 November 1941; Pearl Harbor attacked by 1st Air Fleet (under C. NAGUMO and code-named 'Kido Butai') but it was regarded as a partial failure because the American carriers were not in port and oil storage facilities were untouched, 8 December Japanese time (7 December American time) 1941; Battle of the Java Sea (destroyed remaining Allied naval warships in that area), 7 February 1942; New flagship super battleship *Yamato*, 12 February 1942; Darwin, in Australia attacked by carriers (*see* C. NAGUMO), 19 February 1942; Ordered massive air and sea search for the American carriers which launched the 'Doolittle' bombing raid on Japan; 18 April 1942; Battle of the Coral Sea (*see* C. HARA, A.GOTO) with the first Japanese carrier loss of the war, 7-8 May 1942; Proposed an attack on

Midway Island in the mid Pacific to bring about a decisive naval battle with the American fleet before it could rebuild; Threatened to resign unless the Midway plan were accepted which forced Navy Chief of Staff O. NAGANO to accept it despite opposition from the Naval General Staff; Ordered by GHQ, Tokyo, to undertake Operation 'MI' (occupation of Midway) and Operation 'AL' (occupation of the western Aleutian Islands) as a combined operation, 5 May 1942; Used 1st Air Fleet (carriers under C. NAGUMO), 2nd Fleet (N. KONDO), 1st Fleet Main Body (directly under I. YAMAMOTO in flagship *Yamato*) for Operation 'MI'; 5th Fleet (B. HOSOGAWA) for Operation 'AL'; 1st Fleet sailed from Hashirajima, Inland Sea, Japan, 29 May 1942; The loss of four carriers at the Battle of Midway (*see* C. NAGUMO) forced the cancellation of Operation 'MI', 5-7 June 1942; Operation 'AL' was a success; Returned to Hashirajima, 15 June 1942; Reorganized Combined Fleet creating 3rd Fleet (under C. NAGUMO) and disbanding 1st Striking Force (i.e., 1st Air Fleet), July 1942; Dispatched 8th Fleet to Tulagi Island and Guadalcanal (both in the Solomons) and Rabaul, New Britain, to counter American invasion forces; Took personal command of the operation, sailing in *Yamato* with 2nd and 3rd Fleets for Rabaul area, 8 August 1942; Combined Fleet HQ moved to Truk, Caroline Islands, August 1942; 2nd Fleet dispatched to join 8th Fleet for Guadalcanal operations, mid August 1942; Issued orders for destruction of American land and sea forces on Guadalcanal (while remaining in flagship at Truk) which resulted in the Second Battle of the Solomon Sea (*see* H. ABE, C. HARA, N. KONDO, G. MIKAWA, C. NAGUMO, R. TANAKA), 23-5 August 1942; Stated naval plans for combined Guadalcanal operations at a meeting with Commanders of 2nd, 4th, 6th Fleets and 11th Air Fleet, 7 September 1942; Blamed the army for many failures; Opposed naval *bushido* code whereby a captain was supposed to die with his ship; This made him unpopular with those traditionalists in high command; Ordered destroyer night operations to supply Guadalcanal (*see* R. TANAKA), 30 September 1942; Dispatched 2nd, 3rd Fleets and 2nd Carrier Division from Truk to assist in major operations aimed at the recapture of Guadalcanal, 11 October 1942; Issued offensive orders to all naval forces in an attempt to stem the American superiority around Guadalcanal, 25 October 1942; Battle of Santa Cruz with two carriers damaged for the loss of one American carrier, 26 October 1942; Entire Combined Fleet assembled at Truk, 30 October 1942; Carriers *Chikuma*, *Shokaku*, *Zuiho* sent to Japan for repairs, early November 1942; Only one carrier, *Junyo*, left active; Battle of Savo Island with loss of battleship *Hiei* (*see* K. ABE), 12 November 1942; Informed by IGHQ that the evacuation of Guadalcanal could proceed with priority given to the defence of New Guinea, 3 January 1943; Evacuation of Guadalcanal undertaken, 1-8 February 1943; Reinforcement convoy taking army 51st Division to New Guinea destroyed by American air attack, 2-3 March 1943; Moved with staff to Rabaul, New Britain, to control offensive operations, early April 1943; Commenced Operation 'I' to destroy American air power on Guadalcanal and New Guinea with 11th Air Fleet (R. KUSAKA), 3rd Fleet (carriers under J. OZAWA) and 8th Fleet (G. MIKAWA), 7-14 April 1943; Launched massive naval air attack on Guadalcanal, 7 April 1943; Launched three air attacks on Port Moresby, Milne Bay and Oro Bay, all in New Guinea, mid April 1943; Warned by T. JOSHIMA that he feared the Americans had broken the Japanese naval codes and that the itinery of YAMAMOTO's planned one-day tour of inspection of the Shortland Island bases was known to them, 17 April 1943; Set out on the tour flying from Rabaul to Ballele, off southern Bougainville in a flight of two bombers and an escort of six fighters with the intention of finally returning to HQ Truk; The naval code had been broken and an ambush arranged by American fighters, with long-range tanks, from Bougainville; Intercepted, shot down and killed near Buin (*see also* OKUVA, TAKATA, M. UGAKI), 18 April 1943;[9] His remains were retrieved from the wreck, cremated and returned to Japan in the destroyer *Yugumo*; Posthumously promoted to Fleet Admiral and awarded the Grand Order of the Chrysanthemum First Class;[10] State funeral (the second ony for a commoner in Japanese history); His ashes were divided and taken to Tama cemetery, Tokyo, and a cemetery at his birthplace in Nagaoka; Replaced (by M. KOGA).

Personal facts: Calm, diffident and a professional officer. Athletic and muscular. Reputation as a clown and a story-teller. Neither smoked nor drank but kept both for visitors. Inveterate gambler on any game. Sent numerous examples of his calligraphy to students upon request. Great leader and administrator. Inspired the confidence of others, both senior and junior. Had no personal ambitions. Made his own decisions.

[1] This is an unusual name which means '5, 10, 6', i.e., '56', which was the age of his father when he was born.
[2] He kept and read a bible all through his life even though he was not a Christian.
[3] Family of Yamamoto Tatekawa of Nagaoka who was killed in the Bosshin War fighting against the re-establishment of the Emperor in 1868. Isoroku's father had been on his side. It was thought that, although a potentially brilliant staff officer, Isoroku could not rise to high rank because of his humble origin and lack of influential sponsorship. This, however, solved the problem.
[4] Eventually having four children.
[5] A top secret establishment north-east of Tokyo also known as 'Misty Lagoon Air Development Station'. Here he became regarded as a liberal who advocated untried military tactics and theories through the use of aviation in warfare. Learned to fly during this posting.
[6] Undertook development of the famous 'Zero' fighter and other aircraft for naval use.
[7] Opposed the study to build *Yamato* class super battleships but advocated carrier building for air supremecy.
[8] He was given this post by Navy Minister M. YONAI to remove him from political and shore postings in order to prevent threatened assassination by young militarists who regarded him as as 'obstructionist' and a 'moderate'.
[9] His body was found strapped in his seat but he had been hit twice by bullets which killed him. His sword, a *kai-guntō*, was with him. It was given to him by his elder brother and has a blade by the showa period swordsmith Amada Sadayoshi of Niigata.
[10] Posthumously awarded the Nazi Knight's Cross of the Iron Cross with Oakleaves and Swords, 27 May 1943. He was the only foreigner to receive this decoration.

YAMANASHI Katsunoshin

Admiral; Military Councillor; Forced into early retirement, aged 56, in a purge by Navy Minister M. OSUMI on the pretence that he supported the 1930 London Naval Conference limitation agreement, March 1933.

YAMASAKI (YAZAKI, YAZAZAKI) Shigeaki (Shigeki)

Rear-Admiral; Commander of 2nd Submarine Squadron, 1941.

YAMASHITA Gentaro

Fleet Admiral; Retired; Died 18 February 1931.

YANŌ Hideo

Captain; Captain of battleship *Nagato* in Battleship Group (1st Division) forming part of 1st Fleet (Main Force) under I. YAMAMOTO in Operation 'MI' for the attempted invasion of Midway Island, May–June 1942; Rear-Admiral; Probably Chief of Staff to Central Pacific Area Fleet (under C. NAGUMO), HQ Saipan; Committed suicide with C. NAGUMO and Generals Y. SAITO, K. IGETA on Saipan, dawn on 7 July 1944.

YANŌ Shikazo

Rear-Admiral; Chief of Staff to Commander of Wake Island Invasion Force S. KAJIOKA, December 1941.

YAZAKI (YAZAZAKI) Shigeaki – *See* YAMASAKI Shigeaki

YOKOGAWA Ichihei

Rear-Admiral; Commander of 26th Naval Special Base Force, February 1943; Located at Kau, April 1944.*

*Possibly this should be Kai Island, off southern New Guinea since Kau has not been identified on a map.

YOKOI Toshiyuki

Rear-Admiral; Chief of Staff to 5th Air Fleet (under M. UGAKI), Japan 1944; HQ Kanoya, southern Kyushu, Japan; Took off in aircraft on a suicide mission after the Emperor's surrender broadcast, 15 August 1945.*

*This seems to have been at the same time as M. UGAKI's flight from Oita airbase.

YOKOYAMA Ichiro

Language officer at Yale University, America, 1931–2; Captain; Naval Attaché in Washington, USA, September 1940 until the outbreak of war in December 1941;* Rear-Admiral; Member of Naval General Staff by 1945; Member of a delegation to Manila, Philippines (together with Major-General M. AMANO, Lieutenant-General T. KAWABE) to receive Allied requirements for execution of the surrender terms, 19-20 August 1945.

*May have become a Rear-Admiral during this posting.

YAMAMOTO Yoshio

Commander; Staff officer in China Area Fleet, c.1940; Rear-Admiral by the end of the war.

YONAI Mitsumasa

Born 1880 into a samurai family; Graduated from Etajima Naval Academy, 1901; Ensign, January 1903; Second Lieutenant, July 1904; Lieutenant, 1905; Instructor at Naval Gunnery School, 1911-12; Lieutenant-Commander, December 1912; Graduated from War College, 1913; Resident naval officer (language) in Russia, 1915-17; Commander, December 1916; Sasebo Naval District, Japan, 1917; Naval General Staff, 1918; Captain, December 1920; Rear-Admiral; Chief of Staff to 2nd Fleet, December 1925; Naval General Staff and Member of Technical Council in Naval Technical Department, December 1926; Commander of 1st Expeditionary Fleet, Yangtze River, China, December 1928; Vice-Admiral, December 1930; Commander of Chinkai Naval Station, Korea; Supported 1930 London Naval Conference Agreement ratifying 5:5:3: (Britain:America:Japan) fleet ratios; Commander of Sasebo Naval District, Japan, November 1933; Commander of 2nd Fleet, November 1934; Commander of Yokosuka Naval District, Japan, December 1935; Commander-in-Chief of Combined Fleet and concurrently Commander of 1st Fleet, December 1936-7; Navy Minister (replacing O. NAGANO) in three successive cabinets (Premiers S. HAYASHI, Prince Konoye, K. HIRANUMA) from February 1937;[1] Reinforced Shanghai, China, with marines, 1937;[2] Rejected appeals for arms restrictions and presided over fourth Navy Replenishment Program; Admiral, 1939 (or possibly 1937); Insisted Chinese island of Hainan be occupied by the Japanese; Stated at a ministerial Conference that the Japanese navy could win a war against Britain, America and France, 8 August 1939; Forced to resign as Navy Minister because of resignation of Premier K. HIRANUMA and replaced (by Z. YOSHIDA), 30 August 1939; Member of Supreme War Council, August 1939; Concurrently an Imperial Councillor; On first reserve list; Prime Minister (replacing General N. ABE), 16 January 1940;[3] Feared war with Britain and America; Forced to resign by the resignation of the army War Minister because of his continued opposition to army expansion into South-east Asia and full alliance with the axis powers (i.e., signing of the Tripartite Pact), June 1940; 'Jushin' (elder statesman) and adviser to the Emperor, c.1941; Convinced that the war between Germany and Britain would be protracted and that America must become involved, with Germany losing and Japan (if she also declared war) left fighting America alone; Opposed war at conference with seven other 'Jushin' and the Emperor where he also told General H. TOJO that he would not give an opinion as to the 'need' for war, 29 November 1941; Requested by Premier H. TOJO to join the cabinet as Navy Chief of Staff and Navy Minister to save it, but refused, July 1944; Refused a request from the 'Jushin' General N. ABE to form a cabinet, July 1944; Deputy Prime Minister (in General K. KOISO cabinet) and reinstated to the active list for concurrent post of Navy Minister, 22 July 1944; Favoured a peaceful settlement of the war; Resigned as Deputy Premier, 4 April 1945; Continued as War Minister in K. SUZUKI cabinet, 5 April 1945; Concurrently adviser to War Relief Association; Proposed that Russia be requested to mediate peace terms on Japan's behalf, 12 May 1945; Recommended acceptance of the Allied Potsdam Declaration for a Japanese unconditional surrender after dropping of atomic bombs and the Russian invasion of Manchuria even though opposed by other senior military leaders, 10 August 1945;[4] Continued as Navy Minister in Field Marshal Prince N. HIGASHIKUNI cabinet after the surrender, 16 August 1945; Enforced general naval compliance with Allied surrender requirements even though opposed by senior naval officers such as T. ONISHI, S. TOYODA and younger officers who wanted to fight on; Navy Ministry and his post abolished by American occupation forces, October 1945; Gave evidence in International Tribunal for the Far East war crimes trials, Tokyo, 1946-8; Died aged 68, 1948.

Personal facts: Kind, gentle and somewhat reserved. Spoke and read Russian. Could drink copious quantities of alcohol without noticeable effect. No personal ambition. Never compromised his principles. Usually right on policy matters. A moderate in military matters. Said by his contemporaries to be one of the three greatest admirals Japan had produced. Well respected both nationally and internationally.

[1] Initially opposed to building of *Yamato*-class super battleships but was forced to accept them.
[2] Opposed army plans to conquer China after the 'Marco Polo Bridge Incident'. Publicly sacked T. MITSUNAMI for sinking the American gunboat USS *Panay* near Nanking, China.
[3] Declared a 'non-involvement' policy in the European war but would not issue a public declaration of neutrality. Reached an agreement with European allied powers by refusing passage of returning German men of military age in Japanese ships.
[4] In June 1945 he expressed a desire to resign as Navy Minister because of his dissatisfaction with the cabinet movement towards peace but was persuaded to stay on to prevent the automatic fall of the government.

YOSHIDA Zengo
From Saga prefecture in north-west Kyushu, Japan; Graduated from Etajima Naval Academy, 1904; Vice-Admiral; Commander-in-Chief of Combined Fleet,

1937; Failed to recognize the importance of the naval air arm; Replaced (by I. YAMAMOTO), 28 August 1939; Navy Minister (replacing M. YONAI), August 1939; Supported good relations with Britain and America; Opposed the Tripartite Pact with Germany and Italy, 1940; Opposed war when Japan had only an estimated one year's supply of essential materials, 1940; Suffered a severe nervous breakdown from overwork, hospitalized and resigned, 4 September 1940; Replaced (by K. OIKAWA).

Personal facts: Stubborn, strong-willed and independent with a good sense of humour. A moderate. Distrusted aircraft and refused even to set foot in one. Hobbies were Chinese literature and calligraphy.

YOSHITOMI Setsuzō (Etuzo)

Rear-Admiral; Commander of 4th Submarine Flotilla* forming part of the screen for 'Malaya Force' (under J. OZAWA) as reconnaissance and defence against Allied warships in flagship cruiser *Kinu*, December 1941; Commander of 7th Submarine Flotilla, HQ Rabaul, New Britain, 1942; Personally reported to C in C Combined Fleet at Truk, Caroline Islands, 11 November 1942.

*Also reported as 5th Submarine Flotilla so it is unclear which is correct. One of his submarines, *I-58*, sighted and reported British Force Z (*Prince of Wales* and *Repulse*). Apparently it fired five torpedoes at *Repulse* but missed.

YUKICHI Yasuhiro

Rear-Admiral; Naval Commander of Marshall Islands, 1942; Killed during an American air attack, 1 February 1942.*

*He was the first Japanese admiral to be killed in the war.

Bibliography

Allen, Louis. *Burma, The Longest War, 1941-45.* J. M. Dent & Sons, 1984
— *Nakano School For Spies.* World War Investigator, vol. 1, No. 12. World War Investigator Publications Ltd., 1989
— *Sittang, The Last Battle.* Arrow Books Ltd., 1976
— *The End of the War in Asia.* Granada Publishing Ltd., 1976
Barber, Noël. *Sinister Twilight – The Fall of Singapore.* Arrow Books Ltd., 1988
Bateson, Charles. *The War With Japan.* Barrie & Rockliff, 1968
Bell, Leslie. *Destined Meeting.* Readers Book Club, Australia, 1959
Bennett, G. *The Loss of Prince of Wales and Repulse.* Ian Allan Ltd., 1973
Bergamini, David. *Japan's Imperial Conspiracy.* Heinemann,
Browne, C. *Tojo – The Last Banzai.* Corgi Books, 1967
Calvert, Michael. *Chindits – Long-Range Penetration.* Ballantine Books Inc., USA, 1973
Carew, Tim. *The Fall of Hong Kong.* Pan Books Ltd., 1968
Carruthers, Steven L. *Australia Under Siege* (Japanese Submarine Raiders, 1942). Solus Books. JMSR Film Production Pty. Ltd., Australia, 1982
Chamberlain, W. H. *Japan Over Asia.* Duckworth, 1938
Collier, Basil. *Japan At War.* Sidgwick & Jackson Ltd., 1975
Craig, William. *The Fall of Japan.* Pan Books Ltd., 1967
Craige, Rt Hon Sir Robert, GCMG, CB. (HM Ambassador to Japan, 1937-42). *Behind The Japanese Mask.* Hutchinson & Co., 1946
Derby, Harry. *Hand Cannons of Imperial Japan.* 1981
Dollinger, Hans. *The Decline and Fall of Nazi Germany and Imperial Japan.* Crown Publishers Inc., New York and Hamlyn Publishing Group London, 1968
Dull, Paul S. *A Battle History of the Imperial Japanese Navy, 1941-45.* Patrick Stephens Ltd., 1978
Fabricius, J. *Java Revisited.* William Heinemann, 1947

Firkins, Peter. *From Hell to Eternity.* Westward Ho Publishing Co., Western Australia, 1979
Fuller, Richard, and Gregory, Ron. *Military Swords of Japan, 1868-1945.* Arms & Armour Press, 1986
Goralski, Robert. *World War II Almanac, 1931-1945.* Hamish Hamilton Ltd., 1981
Gow, Ian. *Okinawa 1945 – The Gateway to Japan.* Doubleday & Company Inc., New York, 1985
Harper, Stephan. *Miracle of Deliverance.* 1980
Hayashi, Saburo. *Kogun, The Japanese Army in the Pacific War.* Marine Corps Association, USA, 1959
Horton, Dick. *Ring of Fire – Australian Guerrilla Operations against the Japanese in World War II.* The Macmillan Company of Australia Pty. Ltd., Melbourne, 1983
Howard, A., and Newman, E. *The Menacing Rise of Japan.* George G. Harrap & Co. Ltd., 1943
Howarth, Stephen. *Morning Glory – The Story of the Imperial Japanese Navy.* Hamish Hamilton, London, 1983
Hoyt, Edwin P. *The Kamikazes.* Panther Books, London, 1983
— *Yamamoto (The Man who planned Pearl Harbor).* McGraw-Hill, USA, 1990
Hsu Long-hsuen and Chang Ming-kai (comps.) *History of the Sino-Japanese War, 1937–1945.* Chung Wu Publishing Co., Taiwan, 1971
Jones, Don. *Oba, The Last Samurai – Saipan 1944-45.* Airlife Publishing Ltd., England, 1986
Kase, Toshikazu. *Eclipse of the Rising Sun.* Ed. David Nelson Rowe. Jonathan Cape, London, 1951
Liddell Hart, Sir Basil (Editor-in-Chief). *History of the Second World War.* Macdonald & Co. (Publishers) Ltd., 1989
Lindsay, O. *At the Going Down of the Sun.* Sphere Books Ltd., 1981
Long, Gavin. *The Final Campaigns.* Canberra Australian War Memorial, 1963
Madej, Victor W. (Ed.). *Japanese Armed Forces Order of Battle, 1937-1945,* vols. 1 and 2. Game Publishing Co., USA, 1981
— *Japanese War Mobilization and the Paci-*

fic Campaign, 1941-1945. Game Publishing Co., USA, 1985

Marder, Arthur J. Old Friend, New Enemies. Clarendon Press, 1981

Mayer, S. L. (Ed.). The Japanese War Machine. Bison Book Corpn., 1976

McKie, Ronald. The Heroes. Australia at War series

Millot, Bernard. Divine Thunder – The Life and Death of the Kamikazes. Macdonald & Co. (Publishing) Ltd., 1971

Mollo, Andrew. The Armed Forces of World War II. Orbis Publishing, 1981

Murray, M. Hunted, A Coastwatcher's Story.

Nagatsuka, R. I Was a Kamikaze. New English Library, London, 1974

Onoda, Hiroo. No Surrender – My Thirty-Year War. Andre Deutsch Ltd., London, 1975

Owen, Frank. The Fall of Singapore. Pan Books Ltd., London, 1960

Paull, Raymond. Retreat from Kokoda. Panther Books, 1960

Potter, John Deane. A Soldier Must Hang. Four Square Books, New English Library Ltd., London, 1964

Rosie, George. The British in Vietnam (How the Twenty-Five Year War Began). Panther Books, 1970

Russell of Liverpool, Lord. The Knights of Bushido. Corgi Books, 1960

Sakai, Saburo. Samurai. New English Library Ltd., London, 1974

Sekigawa, Eiichiro. Japanese Military Aviation. Purnell Book Services Ltd., London, 1974

Shiroyama, Saburo. War Criminal (The Life and Death of Hirota Koki). Kodansha International Ltd., 1977

Smith, Peter C. The Battle of Midway. New English Library Ltd., London, 1976

Spur, Russell. A Glorious Way to Die (The Kamikaze Mission of the Battleship Yamato, April 1945). Sidgwick & Jackson, London, 1982

Strabogli, RN, Lord. Singapore and After. Hutchinson & Co., 1942

Swinson, Arthur. The Four Samurai. Hutchinson & Co., 1968

Thomas, David. Battle of the Java Sea. Pan Books, London, 1968

Japan's War at Sea – Pearl Harbor to the Coral Sea. Andre Deutsch, 1978

Toland, John. The Rising Sun (The Decline and Fall of the Japanese Empire, 1936-1945). Random House, New York, 1970

Tsuji, Masanobu. Singapore – The Japanese Version. Ure Smith Pty. Ltd., Sydney, Australia, 1960

Valentine, Douglas. The Hotel Tacloban. Angus & Robertson, UK and Australia, 1985

Warner, Denis and Warner Peggy, with Sadao Seno. Kamikaze (The Sacred Warriors, 1944-45). Oxford University Press, Melbourne, 1983

Wheeler, Keith. The Fall of Japan, World War II. Time Life Books, USA, 1983

Yokoto, Yutaka. The Kaiten Weapon. Ballantine Books, 1962

History of the Second World War, vols. 1-6, Purnell & Sons Ltd., 1966

Purnell's History of the Second World War: Campaign Book No. 9:
Japan – The Final Agony, Alvin Cox, Macdonald & Co. (Publishers) Ltd., London, 1970

Purnell's History of the Second World War: Tarawa – A Legend is Born, Henry I. Shaw, Jr., 1969; Liberation of the Philippines, Stanley Falk, 1970; Okinawa – Touchstone to Victory, Benis M. Frank, 1970; Macdonald & Co. (Publishers) Ltd.

Illustrated History of World War II, Pan/Ballantine: New Georgia – Pattern for Victory, D. C. Horton, 1971; New Guinea – The Tide is Stemmed, J. Vader, 1971; Merrill's Marauders, Captain A. Baker, 1972; Guadalcanal, Island Ordeal, Graeme Kent, 1972; Pacific Onslaught (7 December 1941-7 February 1943), Paul Kennedy, 1972; Japanese High Seas Fleet, Richard Humble, 1974

The Campaign in Burma, HMSO, 1946

History of the Second World War – The War Against Japan, Vols. 3-5, HMSO, 1969

Pictorial History of Australia at War, 1939-1945, vol. 5, Australian War Memorial, Canberra, 1958

World War II, vols. 1-8. Orbis Publishing Ltd., 1972

Sea War in the Pacific (a compilation). Marshall Cavendish Ltd., London

Order of Battle of the Japanese Armed Forces (issued by Military Intelligence Division of US Army, October 1944–January 1945)

Handbook on Japanese Military Forces (US War Department Technical Manual TM-E 30-480, 1 October 1944)

Japan's Longest Day. Compiled by (Japanese) Pacific War Research Society. Souvenir Press, 1968

The Japanese Air Forces in World War II. Arms & Armour Press, 1979

The Times Handy Atlas, John Bartholomew, Selfridge & Co., London, 1935

Diary of World Events, compiled by J. A. H. Hopkins. Chronological record of the Second World War as reported day by day in American and foreign newspaper dispatches. National Advertising Co., USA, vols. 46-54 (1 July 1945-7 March 1948)

Biennial Report of the United States Army to the Secretary of War, 1 July 1943 to 30 June 1945

United States Navy at War (Final official report to the Secretary of the Navy) 1 March 1945 to 1 October 1945, by Fleet Admiral Ernest J. King

Report to the Combined Chiefs of Staff by the Supreme Allied Commander South-East Asia, 1943-1945 by Vice-Admiral The Earl Mountbatten of Burma, HMSO, 1951

Material on the trial of former servicemen of the Japanese Army charged with manufacturing and employing bacteriological weapons. Foreign Languages Publishing House, Moscow, 1950

'The Tokyo Trial'. Contemporary documentary film footage of the International Military Tribunal for the Far East war crimes trial in Tokyo, 1946-48, by Masaki Kobayashi. Produced by Kodansha Ltd. Running time five hours.

Japan Society of London, various bulletins, 1951-6

After The Battle (magazine, various issues). Battle of Britain Prints International Ltd., 1977

War Monthly (magazine, various issues). Marshall Cavendish Ltd., 1974

Syonan Shimbun (Singapore newspaper), various issues November 1943 to February 1945

Indexes

General Index

atomic bomb, 82, 100, 149, 226, 290, 297, 306; Hiroshima, 32, 85, 87, 91, 97, 233; Nagasaki, 32

bacteriological warfare, 116, 137
bacteriological warfare centres, 122; Detachments: 100, 192, 205, 229, 232; 731 (Manshu), 81, 116, 131, 133, 137, 192, 197, 224, 232, 241; Nami 8604; 192; Tama, 81; Hogoin Camp, 81
banzai attack, 106, 184, 185, 259
Bataan Death March, 104, 131, 229
Burma National Army, 31, 72, 134, 193
Bushido, 12, 13, 104, 160, 303

Chindits, 28, 29, 98, 108, 137, 150, 159, 187, 206, 215
coup d'état, 31, 83, 100, 156, 213, 275, 290

Doolittle raid, 27, 192, 196, 219, 264, 273, 302

espionage, 88, 120, 288; Nakano School, 120, 130, 190, 213, 233

Imperial Way (Kodo-ha) faction, 84, 85, 151, 218, 238
Incidents: China (Marco Polo Bridge), 24, 95, 115, 159, 186, 199, 214, 229, 256, 296, 302, 306; Lake Khasan, 25, 88, 118, 213; Manchurian (Mukden), 7, 23, 89, 94, 103, 115, 118, 122, 152; Nomonhan (Khalkyn-Gol), 25, 109, 117, 118, 140; Nonni Bridge, 23, 98; Shanghai, First, 23, 253, 288; Second, 24
Indian National Army, 72, 117, 120, 124, 134, 187, 195
Insurrection, '2-26', 84, 103, 123, 131, 151, 153, 169, 216, 218, 230, 236, 278, 284, 289

Kamikaze, 12, 30, 112, 127, 128, 155, 198, 220, 221, 234, 240, 243, 244, 246, 249, 266, 277, 280, 281, 294, 296, 299
Kempeitai, see Japanese Army, Military Police

Long Lance torpedo, 246, 261

March 1931 Plot, 139, 162, 225
Merrill's Marauders, 30, 152, 211, 212
Military Tribunals (for war crimes): Khabarovsk, 121, 131, 192, 205, 232; International for the Far East, 84, 89, 97, 100, 115, 118, 134, 139, 148, 153, 161, 182, 191, 203, 213, 219, 226, 273, 277, 278, 287, 306
Manila, 104, 139, 229, 237, 242, 279

Naval Limitation Conferences (Treaties), 24, 90, 133, 220, 253, 256, 260, 261, 262, 278, 282, 284, 288, 292, 294, 302, 304, 305
Navy Minister, 15, 191, 252, 256, 260, 272, 278, 281, 284, 285, 287, 290, 291, 297, 302, 305, 306, 307

Oka, 31, 267, 280, 299, 300
Operations, Allied: Cartwheel, 29; Rimau, 183; Japanese: A-GO, 268, 283, 296; AL, 259, 261, 279, 285, 292, 303; BAN, 125; C, 160, 264, 270, 273, 279; DAN, 124; FU-GO, 144; GEN, 271; HA-GO (or Z), 94, 187; I, 268, 271, 283, 303; KA, 106, 107; KAN, 187; KETSU-GO, 97, 127, 200; KON, 268, 283, 296; MAI, 187; MI, 245, 246, 248, 251, 252, 254, 261, 263, 264, 265, 266, 269, 270, 273, 275, 277, 282, 288, 291, 293, 298, 301, 303, 304; MO, 245, 250, 251, 256, 269, 287, 291, 300; SHO, 249, 297; SHO.1, 191, 220, 255, 263, 266, 267, 275, 280, 283, 284, 287, 296, 297, 299; SHO.2, 297; SHO.3, 297; SHO.4, 297; TAN, 299; TEN-GO, 198, 296, 299; TEN-ICHI, 246, 257, 263, 272; U-GO, 29, 113, 127, 160, 176, 191, 210, 215, 219; WA, 202; Z (Pearl Harbor), 268, 273, 300, 302; Z Plan (Marianas and Carolines), 249, 250, 296; 21, 108, 159

poison gas, 96
Potsdam Declaration, 82, 226, 244, 290, 297, 306

Rape of Nanking, 85, 88, 95, 148, 161, 165, 214, 239
Russian invasion of Manchuria, 82, 102, 103, 108, 136, 145, 155, 176, 195, 224, 232, 297, 306

Sandakan death march, 87, 144, 239
Secret Police, 96, 153, 165, 178, 214
Seppuku (ritual suicide), 83, 88, 103, 107, 143, 184, 227, 274, 281
Strike North, 84, 97, 140, 151, 162, 169, 176, 191, 235, 260
Strike South, 88, 98, 172, 191, 199, 216, 236, 272
Supreme War Council, 85, 99, 103, 123, 139, 160, 169, 199, 226, 232, 250, 260, 273, 287, 306
Surrenders, Japanese, 7, 8, 32, 34–48, 82, 83, 86, 94, 98, 99, 100, 107, 108, 111, 112, 113, 114, 118, 120, 122, 124, 125, 128, 134, 137, 138, 141, 142, 145, 146, 149, 151, 153, 158, 161, 163, 166, 174, 178, 180, 186, 190, 191, 193, 195, 203, 207, 209, 217, 221, 222, 225, 226, 228, 230, 231, 232, 234, 235, 246, 247, 248, 249, 265, 268, 269, 276, 281, 286, 293, 295, 297, 298, 300, 305
swords, details of, 78, 80, 83, 86, 87, 91, 102, 113, 119, 134, 143, 145, 147, 151, 153, 162, 166, 172, 173, 175, 179, 180, 181, 203, 207, 211, 216, 231, 235, 236, 242, 248, 251, 252, 254, 255, 257, 260, 268, 279, 281, 284, 285, 296, 299, 300, 304
swords, surrender of, 36–48, 78, 80, 87, 93, 94, 100, 102, 107, 113, 118, 119, 120, 122, 123, 124, 125, 129, 134, 137, 138, 141, 145, 146, 147, 151, 155, 162, 163, 172, 174, 175, 178, 179, 180, 181, 184, 187, 190, 191, 193, 195, 203, 207, 209, 216, 217, 219, 231, 234, 235, 238, 242, 244, 251, 257, 260, 265, 276, 279, 285, 293, 296, 297

Tripartite Pact, 26, 182, 245, 248, 250, 256, 264, 275, 277, 278, 287, 289, 298, 302, 306, 307

war crimes and criminals, 79, 83, 84, 85, 87, 89, 92, 94, 96, 97, 103, 104, 105, 113, 114, 116, 117, 118, 119, 121, 122, 131, 133, 134, 137, 138, 139, 145, 148, 153, 161, 169, 171, 173, 180, 182, 191, 192, 195, 197, 203, 204, 205, 210, 211, 214, 219, 221, 226, 229, 232, 239, 245, 246, 250, 251, 253, 255, 262, 272, 273, 278, 284, 287, 292, 293, 294, 297
war crimes trials (see also military tribunals), 87, 95, 104, 117, 119, 131, 139, 144, 148, 171, 195, 203, 205, 211, 214, 239, 245, 251, 255, 284, 293
War Minister, 14, 15, 17, 82, 84, 93, 96, 97, 118, 123, 133, 139, 181, 188, 199, 218, 220, 225, 226, 229, 277, 290, 306

Index of Battles

Land battles:

Burma Admin Box, 94, 187; Pyabwe, 102; Sittang Bend, 102

China Changsha: First, 26, 81, 92, 165, 184; Second, 26, 84, 122, 204; Third, 27, 30, 84, 110, 122, 168, 177, 204, 217; Fourth, 30, 224; Changsha – Hengyang, 81, 121, 190, 200, 234; Chekiang – Kiangsi, 192; Hsuchow, 118, 157, 172, 198, 214; Kweilin – Liuchow, 81, 121, 153, 156, 197, 201, 234; Nangchang, 112, 150, 184; Shanghai, 95, 165; Shangkao, 26, 109, 120, 186, 204; Southern Hunan, 90; Southern Kwangsi, 142; Southern Shansi, 186; Sui-Tsao, 238; Taierchuang, 25, 193; Tsaoyang – Ichang, 82, 90, 93, 132, 137, 158, 238; Western Honan – Northern Hupeh, 153, 154, 181, 189, 200, 205, 243; Western Hunan, 186, 224, 230; Western Hupei, 81; Wuhan, 218; Xuzhow, 95
Guadalcanal: Gavanga Creek, 106; Tenaru (Ilu), 106, 107
Malaya: Slim River, 149
New Guinea: Ioraibaiwa Ridge, 105; Isurava, 105;   Kokoda: First, 104; Second, 105; Oiri, 105

Naval battles:
Bismarck Sea, 28, 111, 261, 267; Cape Engano, 263, 270, 275, 283, 296; Cape Esperance, 28, 250; Coral Sea, 28, 10, 190, 250, 251, 256, 291, 298, 302; East China Sea, 31; Eastern Solomons, 28, 300; Empress Augusta (Gazelle) Bay, 29, 255, 267, 279, 285; Horianu, 255; Java Sea, 27, 275, 291, 293, 302; Kolombangara (Kula Gulf), 29, 258; Komandorski (Attu) Island, 254; Leyte Gulf, 30, 139, 255, 272, 276, 280, 296, 299; Lunga Point (Tassafaronga), 293; Malacca Strait, 32; Midway, 28, 245, 264, 266, 274, 298, 301, 303; Palawan Passage, 296; Philippine Sea (Great Marianas Turkey Shoot), 30, 250, 258, 259, 267, 283, 296, 299; Samar, 296; Santa Cruz Islands, 28, 245, 259, 263, 264, 267, 268, 274, 292, 303; Sibuyuan Sea, see Leyte Gulf; Solomon Sea: First, 28, 271; Second, 251, 264, 274, 303; Third,

245, 252, 265, 275, 303; Suriago Strait, see Leyte Gulf; Tsushima (Sea of Japan), 295, 301; Yalu, 294; Yellow Sea, 295

Index of Places

Admiralty Islands, 30, 271; Manus, 80
Aleutian Islands 28, 239, 253, 254, 259, 261, 285, 292, 303; Attu (Komandorski) Island, 29, 239, 254, 259, 279; Kiska Island, 259, 261; Unalaska Island, 259, 285
America, 27, 97, 100, 116, 120, 199, 203, 210, 212, 213, 215, 218, 238, 248, 252, 257, 272, 276, 278, 297, 302, 305; Hawaii, 209, 302; Pearl Harbor, 27, 218, 220, 248, 251, 265, 268, 273, 276, 280, 294, 298, 302
Andaman and Nicobar Islands, 41, 67, 114, 119, 251; Port Blair, 11, 41, 67, 70, 192
Australia, 27, 28, 190, 209, 247, 281; Darwin, 29, 279, 302

Biak Island, 30, 49, 50, 174, 175, 268, 283, 284, 296
Bismarcks, see New Britain
Bonin (Ogasawara) Islands, 41, 51, 105, 183, 272; Chichi Jima, 10, 41, 51, 143, 203, 272; Iwo Jima, 31, 49, 51, 143, 183, 193, 254, 271, 294
Borneo 27, 32, 41, 66, 80, 87, 129, 206, 217, 226, 235, 238, 252, 253, 259, 260, 264, 291, 298; Balikpapan, 11, 41, 87, 252, 259, 275, 276; Ranau, 87, 239; Sandakan, 87, 239
Burma 27, 28, 29, 30, 31, 32, 34, 35, 38, 41, 68, 69, 71, 72, 76, 80, 94, 98, 101, 102, 107, 108, 114, 120, 123, 125, 126, 127, 129, 133, 134, 137, 138, 146, 148, 150, 163, 164, 166, 175, 176, 181, 186, 187, 193, 194, 201, 204, 206, 208, 210, 211, 212, 215, 217; Arakan, 28, 29, 31, 71, 94, 120, 124, 127, 137, 154, 163, 186, 187; Bhamo, 31, 137; Chindwin, River, 28, 108, 178, 186, 191, 210, 235; Irrawaddy, River, 31, 94, 120, 125, 129, 134, 137, 152, 154, 163, 187, 210, 235; Lashio, 27, 108, 124; Mandalay, 31, 124, 125, 134, 194, 206, 210, 234; Maymyo, 113, 124, 142, 143, 159, 160; Meiktila, 31, 94, 101, 102, 123, 124, 134, 164, 174, 207; Mergui, 35, 36, 41, 70, 166, 208; Moulmein, 35, 68, 108, 134, 193, 206, 208, 293; Myitkyina, 28, 30, 101, 108, 127, 150, 152, 206, 212, 215; Paung, 42, 68, 137, 154, 163, 186, 193; Pegu, 125, 148, 206; Pegu Yomas, 98, 120, 134, 137, 148, 154, 163, 164, 186, 187, 193; Rangoon, 11, 27, 32, 34, 37, 38, 42, 72, 86, 94, 96, 102, 107, 108, 117, 119, 127, 133, 134, 140, 143, 148, 150, 151, 159, 160, 164, 174, 175, 180, 187, 192, 193, 208, 212, 234, 242, 247, 293; Salween, River, 30, 108, 127, 159; Shan States, 150, 151, 159, 160, 211, 212, 215; Sittang, River, 98, 102, 120, 125, 134, 137, 148, 154, 163, 164, 186, 187, 207; Tenasserim coast, 35, 98, 108, 125, 134, 137, 148, 155, 166, 187, 207; Thaton, 42, 69, 102, 129, 207; Toungoo, 125, 134, 137, 150, 208, 212, 234
Cambodia, 68, 97, 120; Phnom Penh, 68, 97, 146, 186

Caroline Islands, 8, 42, 51, 158, 191; Kusaie, 51, 95
Palau Islands, 11, 30, 47, 51, 113, 176, 249, 257, 263, 268, 271, 296; Koror Island, 129; Peleliu Island, 30, 47, 113, 158, 257
Ponape Island (Pakin Atoll), 42, 51, 230
Truk, 11, 29, 42, 48, 51, 109, 158, 209, 251, 256, 257, 259, 262, 263, 267, 274, 282, 283, 291, 298, 303, 304, 307
Ulithi Atoll, 30, 271, 299
Woleai, 42, 136
Celebes 42, 46, 65, 107, 109, 217, 291; Aroe (Aru), see Kai and Aroe Islands; Kendari, 256, 264, 291; Macassar, 11, 42, 65, 93, 217, 243, 248, 253, 256, 264, 266, 281, 291; Menedo, 42, 82, 90, 264, 291; Pirang, 109
Ceylon, 27, 270, 279
China 10, 23, 24, 25, 26, 27, 28, 29, 30, 31, 32, 34, 42, 43, 51–4, 81, 84, 85, 86, 88, 89, 90, 92, 93, 97, 98, 99, 100, 103, 105, 109, 110, 111, 112, 115, 116, 117, 118, 119, 120, 121, 122, 123, 124, 125, 126, 127, 129, 130, 131, 132, 135, 136, 137, 141, 142, 144, 145, 147, 148, 149, 150, 151, 152, 153, 154, 155, 156, 157, 158, 159, 161, 162, 164, 165, 166, 167, 168, 169, 170, 172, 173, 174, 176, 177, 178, 179, 180, 181, 184, 186, 189, 191, 195, 196, 197, 198, 199, 200, 201, 204, 205, 208, 209, 210, 212, 214, 217, 218, 222, 223, 224, 225, 226, 230, 234, 236, 238, 239, 241, 243, 248, 256, 260, 272, 277, 278, 279, 281, 296, 297, 302; Anhwei province, 204; Canton, 42, 54, 100, 128, 167, 201, 205, 210, 223, 224, 290; Chekiang Province, 24, 132, 156, 192; Chunking, 24, 26, 29, 31; Fukien province, 26, 281; Hainan Island, 8, 9, 100, 149, 196, 201, 209, 242, 250, 264, 282, 305; Hankow, 24, 25, 43, 51, 99, 121, 126, 130, 165, 172, 178, 180, 190, 192, 284; Honan province, 25, 30, 31, 52, 98, 102, 111, 126, 131, 135, 165, 172, 174, 183, 193, 196, 199, 201, 224, 233; Hopeh province, 135, 140, 173, 208, 226; Hsuchow, 43, 118, 142, 158, 183, 185, 198; Hunan province, 26, 30, 121, 135, 144, 156, 161; Hupeh province, 26, 31, 52, 86, 132, 154, 158, 159, 183; Kiangsi province, 110, 224; Kiangsu province, 52, 92, 142, 158, 169, 177, 183, 185; Kwangsi province, 31, 32, 142, 177, 242; Kwantung province, 54, 141, 223, 281; Nanking, 24, 26, 34, 42, 43, 52, 53, 85, 88, 95, 103, 111, 116, 118, 132, 137, 148, 149, 160, 165, 180, 190, 192, 198, 204, 214, 222, 232, 239, 248, 290, 306; Peking (Peiping), 24, 43, 52, 95, 126, 129, 130, 131, 158, 165, 170, 172, 174, 196, 199, 205, 214, 218, 229, 239; Shanghai, 23, 43, 53, 85, 95, 114, 119, 121, 148, 149, 162, 165, 169, 179, 192, 213, 214, 235, 239, 252, 253, 271, 281, 290, 305; Shansi province, 24, 52, 82, 96, 97, 98, 102, 110, 112, 119, 153, 161, 165, 175, 200; Shantung province, 25, 53, 90, 105, 154, 161, 162, 172, 177, 209, 214
East Indies, see Indonesia
England, 83, 103, 111, 130, 136, 144, 175, 178, 212, 215, 245, 264, 265, 288
Flores Islands, see Indonesia
Formosa, 8, 9, 23, 34, 42, 44, 54, 57, 62, 83, 98, 101, 111, 117, 133, 136, 168, 170, 173, 180, 195, 209, 220, 221, 222, 223 226, 236, 243, 248, 249, 262, 270, 275, 281, 291, 297, 298, 299
France, 90, 99, 101, 103, 159, 170, 186, 194, 222
Germany, 24, 26, 95, 97, 100, 115, 127, 128, 132, 136, 161, 162, 168, 182, 216, 218, 236, 245, 247,

263, 270, 276, 277
Gilbert Islands 59, 69, 265, 283, 286; Makin Island, 27, 29, 49, 59, 286; Nauru Island, 286; Tarawa Atoll, 27, 29, 49, 69, 286; Betio Island, 69, 283, 286
Guam, see Mariana Islands

Halmahera Island, see Moluccas
Hong Kong, 10, 27, 44, 80, 85, 86, 107, 117, 119, 136, 179, 185, 188, 210, 211, 221, 239, 248, 275, 293

India 83, 103, 124, 127, 144, 154, 164, 175, 199; Assam, 29, 108, 113, 127, 143, 154, 159, 160; Imphal, 30, 71, 72, 86, 96, 98, 109, 113, 119, 127, 140, 143, 159, 160, 176, 178, 187, 191, 210, 239, 240; Kohima, 29, 30, 72, 96, 109, 127, 140, 143, 154, 160, 176, 178, 187, 191, 206, 239; Bengal, 94, 127, 187
Indo-China 8, 26, 31, 32, 34, 42, 44, 68, 71, 83, 88, 110, 123, 125, 146, 152, 162, 171, 176, 177, 180, 181, 199, 217, 218, 220, 222, 247, 269, 272, 277, 287, 290, 298; Hanoi, 88, 162, 170, 177, 222; Saigon, 11, 43, 44, 63, 68, 70, 84, 109, 131, 135, 142, 146, 172, 174, 198, 211, 216, 222, 248, 265, 270, 295
Indonesia (East Indies) 90, 106, 217, 265, 298, 302; Bali, 266; Christmas Island, 266; Flores Islands, 260; Ende, 11, 286, Java, 27, 44, 66, 86, 88, 99, 103, 124, 126, 130, 144, 147, 162, 166, 171, 180, 184, 217, 222, 234, 251, 264, 266, 275, 291, 293; Bandoeng, 44, 66, 126, 145; Batavia, 44, 66, 95, 126, 162; Surabaya (Soerabaja), 11, 66, 70, 119, 166, 272, 286, 293, 298; Lesser Sunda Islands, 66, 217, 231; Lombok Island, 217; Sumatra, 27, 32, 39, 48, 66, 67, 86, 100, 113, 120, 172, 176, 181, 209, 217, 237, 252, 253, 283; Fort de Kock, 67, 210, 230; Koeta Radja (Koetaradja), 48, 113, 253; Medan, 67, 143; Pedang, 39, 40, 48, 67, 181, 209, 230; Palembang, 67, 86, 167; Sabang Island, 70, 253
Italy, 26, 29, 86, 195, 256, 287
Iwo Jima, see Bonin Islands

Japan 8, 9, 23, 31, 32, 34, 44, 54–8, 79, 81, 84, 85, 86, 88, 89, 90, 91, 93, 95, 97, 98, 99, 100, 101, 103, 104, 108, 109, 110, 113, 114, 115, 116, 117, 118, 121, 122, 124, 127, 128, 129, 130, 137, 139, 140, 142, 143, 147, 150, 152, 153, 155, 156, 157, 158, 160, 161, 163, 165, 166, 168, 169, 171, 173, 174, 176, 177, 178, 186, 188, 189, 190, 193, 195, 197, 198, 199, 200, 215, 218, 224, 225, 228, 229, 230, 233, 234, 239, 240, 241, 242, 243, 244, 253, 254, 258, 264, 274, 277, 282, 295, 296, 297, 299, 302, 304, 305; Aomori, 55, 105, 150, 200, 250; Chiba, 55, 56, 86, 195; Fukuoka, 204, 243; Hiroshima, 8, 32, 57, 85, 87, 91, 95, 97, 106, 149, 188, 192, 233; Inland Sea, 257, 263, 264, 268, 296, 303; Kumamoto, 57, 132, 222; Kure, 8, 12, 31, 246, 256, 257, 260, 271, 272, 283, 298; Kyoto, 116, 135, 140, 165, 167, 203, 243; Maizuru, 8, 115, 140, 294; Nagano, 95, 101; Nagasaki, 32, 150; Nagoya, 56, 91,128, 168, 185, 231; Ominato, 254, 298; Osaka, 9, 57, 84, 103, 137, 142, 193, 205, 278; Sakhalin Island, 23, 34, 46, 55; Sasebo, 8, 150, 274; Sendai, 55, 57, 84, 91, 115, 177, 193, 197, 212, 244; Tokyo, 27, 31, 32, 55, 56, 58, 81, 82, 83, 86, 92, 93, 95, 96, 100, 103, 104, 109, 112, 113, 116, 118, 119, 120, 121, 123, 127, 128, 133, 140, 141, 151, 153, 155, 156,

158, 161, 165, 169, 172, 174, 175, 180, 181 188, 193, 194, 195, 196, 200, 202, 204, 205, 210, 211, 212, 213, 215, 218, 219, 226, 228, 229, 232, 236, 240, 241, 243, 253, 256, 262, 263, 264, 268, 273, 275, 281, 287, 292, 296, 302, 304, 306; Tokyo Bay, 34, 44, 99, 131, 161, 226, 295, 297; Yokohama, 200, 274; Yokosuka, 253, 260, 262, 285, 296, 301, 305

Kai and Aroe (Aru) Islands, 11, 65, 145, 217, 223, 305

Kairiru and Muschu Islands, 44, 285

Korea 9, 23, 25, 34, 42, 44, 45, 46, 58, 59–61, 79, 93, 97, 108, 116, 118, 121, 122, 129, 142, 145, 152, 153, 173, 177, 183, 189, 206, 215, 236, 278, 284, 300; Cheju-do, 45, 58, 162, 221; Keijo (Seoul), 45, 58, 59, 79, 142, 196, 205, 301

Kurile Islands, 10, 11, 34, 46, 55, 140, 194, 198, 199, 201, 223, 272, 289

Kwajalein, see Marshall Islands

Madagascar, 256

Makin Island, see Gilbert Islands

Malaya 11, 27, 32, 45, 46, 67, 90, 92, 97, 98, 112, 113, 114, 125, 126, 130, 142, 146, 149, 159, 167, 171, 172, 174, 176, 177, 179, 198, 199, 201, 208, 209, 216, 217, 221; 236, 237, 247, 252, 255, 265, 266, 270, 282, 283, 293, 298, 300, 302; Bidor, 45, 174, 177; Johore, 45, 67, 114, 171, 237; Johore Bahru, 149, 175; Kluang, 46, 67, 149, 159, 210; Kuala Lumpur, 45, 86, 90, 114, 118, 149; Penang Island, 11, 45, 70, 114, 119, 149, 217, 246, 300; Singapore, 11, 27, 34, 45, 66, 67, 70, 85, 86, 89, 92, 112, 113, 114, 118, 120, 129, 130, 134, 135, 147, 149, 152, 159, 160, 162, 166, 171, 175, 180, 183, 184, 199, 210, 214, 216, 217, 234, 236, 237, 249, 251, 255, 286, 290, 296

Manchuria (Manchukuo) 8 10, 23, 24, 25, 32, 46, 59–61, 79, 81, 82, 85, 86, 88, 89, 91, 93, 96, 98, 99, 100, 102, 103, 105, 106, 108, 109, 112, 115, 116, 117, 120, 121, 122, 127, 128, 131, 132, 133, 136, 137, 142, 144, 145, 147, 150, 152, 153, 155, 156, 158, 159, 160, 161, 163, 167, 170, 172, 173, 176, 180, 184, 189, 193, 194, 195, 197, 200, 201, 204, 205, 208, 209, 212, 213, 217, 218, 220, 221, 223, 224, 225, 226, 228, 229, 232, 236, 237, 239, 240, 241, 243, 244, 262, 289; Changchun, see Hsinking; Harbin, 46, 116, 131, 224, 240, 242; Hsinking (Changchun), 34, 46, 59, 60, 96, 97, 108, 123, 158, 204, 209, 228, 232, 243; Khalka, River, 25, 26, 93, 140; Mukden, 23, 60, 89, 94, 103, 115, 117, 118, 161, 201, 213, 215; Mutanchiang, 59, 60 95, 101, 136, 195, 209, 232; Nomonhan (Khalkyn-Gol), 110, 165; Pingfan, 116, 133, 137; Port Arthur (Ryojun), 9, 97, 103, 289, 295, 300; Sunwu, 116, 171, 181, 206; Tsitsihar, 23, 60, 82, 103, 158, 173, 224, 230; Tungan, 60, 81, 145, 168

Marcus Island, 46, 270

Mariana Islands 51, 70, 191, 207, 259, 263, 283; Guam, 27, 30, 51, 105, 106, 176, 204, 207, 208, 245, 271, 284, 286; Pagan, 51; Rota, 51; Saipan, 11, 30, 51, 90, 107, 176, 184, 225, 228, 274, 280, 282, 291, 296, 297, 304; Tinian, 30, 70, 259, 298

Marshall Islands 59; Eniwetok Atoll, 29, 170; Brown Island, 170; Engebi Island, 29, 170; Parry Island, 170; Jaluit, 51, 269; Kwajalein, 8, 29, 49, 59, 245, 258, 263, 269, 271, 288, 298; Maloelap, 51; Mereyon, 51; Wotje, 51, 269, 298

Midway Island, 27, 245, 246, 248, 252, 255, 261, 263, 264, 265, 266, 268, 270, 274, 275, 277, 282,

291, 293, 298, 303, 304

Moluccas: **46**; Ambon (Amboina) Island, 11, 119, 137, 145, 217, 25; Ceram Island, 46, 65, 113, 207; Halmahera Island, 65, 109, 110, 115, 117, 204, 206; Morotai Island, 46, 107, 217, 252, 255

Mongolia, 25, 89, 90, 93, 102, 110, 142,170, 172, 213, 218; Chahar province, 24, 86, 89; Jehol province, 24, 89, 172, 180

Nauru Island, 46, 51, 187

New Britain (and Bismarcks): 27, 46, 63, 148, 185, 250, 256, 268, 281; Rabaul, 11, 46, 63, 93, 104, 105, 121, 129, 141, 147, 155, 185, 186, 188, 190, 196, 250, 256, 258, 259, 262, 267, 268, 281, 284, 285, 287, 298, 300, 303, 307

New Caledonia: Noumea, 27

New Guinea, 11, 28, 46, 63, 65, 79, 80, 82, 83, 84, 104, 105, 106, 124, 128, 145, 154, 164, 165, 177, 185, 190, 197, 208, 209, 217, 231, 233, 243, 261, 263, 267, 268, 270, 271, 291, 296, 298, 303; Aitape, 63, 79, 80, 83, 147, 165, 298; Buna: 28, 79, 105, 177, 233; Cape Wom, 46, 80; Finschhafen, 79, 124, 131; Gona, 79, 104, 177; Hansa Bay, 147, 164; Hollandia, 63, 79, 117, 147, 167, 271; Lae, 28, 79, 167, 248; Port Moresby, 28, 104, 209, 245, 250, 251, 256, 259, 269, 291, 303; Sepic River, 79, 164, 243; Wewak, 11, 78, 79, 80, 147, 164, 165, 167, 260; New Ireland, 27, 46, 119, 268, 292, 293; Fangelawa Bay, 46; Kavieng, 11, 293

Nomonhan, see Manchuria

Ocean Island, 46, 51, 287; Mili (Mille), 46, 51

Ogasawara Islands, see Bonin Islands

Okinawa, see Ryukyu Islands

Palaus, see Caroline Islands

Philippines 27, 30, 32, 47, 98, 103, 107, 109, 110, 112, 122, 135, 136, 137, 138, 141, 144, 146, 147, 152, 159, 161, 163, 175, 180, 183, 191, 205, 208, 212, 217, 220, 221, 222, 229, 237, 246, 249, 252, 253, 255, 261, 266, 270, 271, 275, 277, 283, 293, 294, 297, 298, 302; Batan Island, 204; Bohol Island, 92; Cebu Island, 29, 92, 125, 147, 157, 202, 221, 249, 263; Iloito, 92; Jolo Islands, 203; Leyte Gulf, 30, 266, 267, 276, 299; Leyte Island, 92, 109, 125, 146, 157, 202, 221, 233, 237, 263, 275, 283, 284, 287, 296; Ormoc, 125, 146; Tacloban, 146; Lingayen Gulf, 31, 103, 121, 173, 190, 220; Luzon Island, 11, 27, 47, 84, 104, 109, 110, 121, 122, 131, 157, 159, 163, 173, 177, 179, 183, 190, 194, 200, 222, 223, 237, 241, 244, 249, 250, 251, 266, 275, 280, 294; Baguio, 47, 84, 159, 173, 220, 237; Bataan peninsula, 27, 103, 104, 110, 112, 131, 135, 136, 146, 157, 161, 163, 190; Corregidor, 27, 28, 31, 104; Manila, 11, 31, 32, 47, 78, 81, 82, 84, 88, 96, 103, 104, 110, 128, 130, 148, 172, 173, 206, 214, 216, 220, 229, 237, 238, 242, 257, 258, 279, 280, 287, 296, 305; Mindanao Island, 11, 32, 101, 157, 202, 221, 263; Davao, 11, 82, 95, 157, 247, 263; Suriago, 157; Suriago Straits, 266, 287; Mindoro Island, 109; Panay Island, 92; San Bernardino Strait, 267; Visayan Islands, 32, 92, 129, 141; Negros Island, 92, 141

Russia (Soviet Union), 23, 24, 26, 31, 32, 47, 86, 96, 122, 128, 130, 161, 189, 220, 226, 289, 290, 306; Siberia, 25, 86, 218; Vladivostock, 84, 96, 228

Ryukyu Islands, 10, 31, 54, 62, 83, 155, 297; Ie Shima Island, 227; Okinawa, 31, 32, 47, 49, 54, 62, 81, 82, 85, 88, 91, 102, 155, 165, 168, 201, 203, 226, 227, 229, 230, 246, 247, 257, 260, 263, 268, 275, 281, 282, 283, 296, 299

Saipan, *see* Mariana Islands
Siam (Thailand) 27, 32, 47, 48, 68, 72, 94, 125, 126, 130, 134, 151, 166, 175, 208, 210, 211, 217, 230, 236, 266, 269, 270, 272, 282; Bangkok, 27, 47, 67, 68, 70, 80, 94, 114, 122, 125, 135, 141, 146, 151, 166, 174, 178, 190, 191, 195, 208, 242, 285, 293; Banpong (Bampong), 47, 242; Hadyai (Ha'adyai), 47; Ubon, 48, 68, 100
Solomon Islands 27, 28, 29, 48, 63, 106, 132, 185, 255, 256; Bougainville, 11, 29, 48, 63, 81, 88, 121, 123, 132, 146, 155, 185, 259, 262, 268, 279, 285, 292, 299, 303, 304; Buka Island, 268; Florida Island, 28; Guadalcanal, 28, 93, 106, 121, 129, 130, 141, 147, 155, 169, 188, 190, 191, 200, 210, 211, 245, 250, 251, 258, 259, 264, 265, 266, 268, 270, 271, 274, 292, 293, 298, 300, 303; Kula Gulf, 29, 245; New Georgia, 29, 121, 189, 190, 255, 265, 268; Arundel Island, 189; Choiseul Island, 190; Kolombangara Island, 189, 190, 245, 258, 268, 285; Munda, 189; Rendova Island, 189; Savo Island, 264, 265; Shortland Islands, 106, 258, 271, 285, 298, 303; Tulagi Island, 106, 250, 251, 286, 293, 300, 303
Sulu Islands: Tawi-Tawi, 299
Sumatra, *see* Indonesia
Switzerland, 90, 115, 127, 179, 220, 225, 236, 290

Tarawa, *see* Gilbert Islands
Thailand, *see* Siam
Timor, 27, 48, 66, 119, 217, 222, 225, 231, 246, 293
Truk, *see* Caroline Islands

Wake Island, 27, 48, 51, 244, 256, 258, 259, 284, 298, 305

Vietnam, 68

Index of Japanese Armed Forces

ARMY
Army Groups

China Expeditionary Army, 25, 31, 42, 51–4, 97, 101, 111, 118, 138, 172, 173, 180, 187, 188, 192, 197, 201, 212, 218, 222, 232, 290
General Army: 1st, 55, 56, 89, 128, 199, 213; 2nd, 57, 91, 97, 188
Kwantung Army, 23, 24, 26, 32 46, 58, 59–61, 79, 86, 89, 91, 93, 96, 97, 99, 100, 103, 105, 106, 109, 111, 115, 116, 117, 118, 121, 122, 123, 128,

131, 133, 136, 144, 145, 150, 151, 152, 153, 156, 158, 159, 160, 161, 167, 169, 172, 176, 180, 184, 188, 192, 195, 196, 201, 205, 209, 210, 211, 218, 220, 223, 224, 226, 228, 229, 232, 241
Southern Army, 26, 44, 45, 49, 63–9, 70, 71, 84, 86, 88, 96, 103, 108, 109, 111, 113, 114, 118, 120, 124, 127, 133, 134, 135, 143, 155 163, 164, 166, 172, 174, 206, 211, 216, 221, 222, 234, 237, 249
Korea (Chosen) Army, 97, 99, 108, 118, 121, 122, 137, 139, 152, 170, 173, 216, 217, 231, 241
Area Armies: 1, 59, 86, 136, 145, 195, 232, 237; **2,** 50, 63, 66, 79, 82, 93, 109, 111, 137, 167, 174, 186, 217; **3,** 60, 102, 108, 120, 145, 228, 230, 232; **5,** 54, 55, 93, 99; **6,** 43, 51, 52, 155, 178, 180; **7,** 45, 66, 86, 89, 114, 135, 145, 162, 183, 209, 214, 231, 249; **8,** 46, 63, 106, 111, 126, 155, 185, 189, 190, 196; **10,** 44, 54, 62, 83, 226, 230, 252; **11,** 55, 91, 200, 215, 220; **12,** 55, 56, 89, 91, 200, 205, 213; **13,** 56, 179, 200; **14,** 64, 65, 81, 107, 109, 121, 138, 141, 144, 155, 157, 161, 172, 173, 179, 202, 204, 220, 222, 223, 237, 241, 257, 258, 279; **15,** 57, 58, 127, 224; **16,** 57, 58, 241; **17,** 58, 59, 61, 118, 142, 162, 221, 232; **18,** 45, 47, 68, 72, 80, 94, 100, 122, 124, 134, 138, 141, 146, 151, 166, 174, 178, 190, 191, 195, 242, 285; Burma Area Army, 42, 45, 68, 69, 71, 72, 96, 101, 102, 107, 108, 113, 117, 119, 124, 125, 127, 133, 140, 143, 146, 148, 150, 151, 160, 164, 166, 181, 187, 192, 193, 194, 206, 212, 240, 293; Central China Area Army, 85, 95, 148, 222; Central Defence Army, 129; Central District Army, 57, 127, 129, 142, 188; East Central District Army, 57, 91; Eastern District Army, 55, 83, 91, 130, 156, 200, 205, 212, 213, 215, 220; North China Area Army, 52, 79, 118, 126, 127, 129, 157, 170, 172, 180, 181, 186, 190, 196, 199, 204, 205, 214, 216, 224, 236; Northern Army, 94, 99, 215; Northern District Army, 99; North-eastern District Army, 55, 115, 212, 244; South China Area Army, 83, 167, 220; Western District Army, 57, 91, 171, 185, 241, 243
Armies: 1, 43, 52, 96, 108, 126, 130, 153, 156, 172, 196, 200, 226, 244; **2,** 46, 65, 66, 82, 93, 99, 115, 121, 142, 145, 165, 172, 194, 217, 231, 243; **3,** 59, 86, 127, 136, 155, 157, 158, 167, 205, 225, 232; **4,** 60, 159, 171, 224, 232, 241; **5,** 60, 89, 109, 125, 136, 138, 146, 192, 195, 197, 215, 225; **6,** 43, 53, 142, 156, 189, 197, 198; **10,** 24, 85, 148, 239; **11,** 43, 52, 53, 81, 82, 84, 90, 92, 93, 105, 109, 110, 112, 121, 123, 132, 137, 142, 150, 153, 155, 156, 158, 165, 168, 172, 177, 178, 180, 184, 186, 198, 200, 204, 212, 217, 223, 224, 234, 238, 241; **12,** 43, 52, 136, 153, 172, 181, 205, 224, 243; **13,** 43, 53, 149, 162, 172, 192, 235; **14,** 47, 88, 103, 110, 111, 112, 122, 129, 131, 135, 136, 137, 144, 146, 151, 157, 159, 161, 163, 183, 184, 205, 212, 222, 228, 229, 298; **15,** 29, 30, 47, 68, 71, 72, 95, 97, 98, 101, 108, 113, 114, 123, 124, 125, 127, 129, 133, 134, 138, 142, 150, 151, 153, 159, 160, 164, 166, 171, 175, 176, 178, 186, 187, 191, 194, 195, 201, 206, 208, 210, 211, 212, 215, 234, 235, 238, 239, 240, 242, 282; **16,** 44, 66, 89, 94, 97, 111, 119, 145, 162, 171, 180, 231, 234; **17,** 45, 48, 63, 81, 93, 106, 107, 111, 122, 129, 132, 141, 146, 147, 155, 169, 188, 200, 268, 270, 285, 298; **18,** 28, 46, 63, 78, 79, 80, 82, 83, 84, 105, 111, 112, 122, 124, 127, 147, 167, 177, 178, 197, 211, 243; **19,** 82, 113, 137, 140, 156, 207; **20,** 43, 52, 101, 130, 178, 186, 224,

230; **21,** 83, 172, 223; **22,** 83, 172, 223; **23,** 42, 43, 53, 85, 111, 119, 140, 143, 185, 188, 197, 201, 205, 210; **25,** 48, 66, 89, 90, 97, 100, 108, 112, 125, 129, 142, 144, 146, 149, 159, 171, 172, 181, 184, 198, 199, 201, 202, 209, 210, 230, 236, 237, 298; **27,** 54, 55, 201; **28,** 41, 42, 68, 71, 72, 94, 98, 102, 120, 124, 127, 134, 137, 154, 163, 180, 186, 187, 193, 207, 235; **29,** 45, 66, 68, 89, 113, 114; **30,** 60, 108, 228; **31,** 48, 51, 107, 114, 158, 175, 183, 184, 203, 207, 209: **32,** 62, 81, 82, 83, 85, 88, 91, 102, 155, 201, 226, 227, 229, 230; **33,** 42, 69, 71, 98, 101, 102, 124, 125, 127, 129, 134, 150, 151, 152, 164, 166, 186, 193, 206, 207, 212, 234, 282; **34,** 61, 108, 121, 142, 145, 188; **35,** 64, 92, 95, 101, 141, 144, 146, 147, 157, 202, 203, 221, 233, 237; **36,** 55, 122, 213, 225; **37,** 41, 46, 66, 80, 87, 144, 206, 217, 235, 238; **38,** 43, 67, 68, 131, 146, 186, 222; **39,** 68, 94, 166; **40,** 57, 168, 241; **41,** 65, 121, 159, 173, 179, 184, 200, 222, 237, 242; **43,** 43, 53, 105; **44,** 60, 102, 176, 224, 228; **50,** 55, 105; **51,** 55, 173, 213; **52,** 56, 195, 213; **53,** 56, 81, 101, 213; **54,** 56, 138; **55,** 57, 95; **56,** 57, 150, 166, 194, 241; **57,** 57, 114, 171, 241; **58,** 45, 58, 121, 162, 221; **59,** 57, 91, 97, 149; Army of the Decisive Battle (Kesshōgun), 101, 207; Central China Expeditionary Army, 96, 115, 118, 127; China Garrison Army, 89, 129, 164, 167, 181, 223, 226; Formosa (Garrison) Army, 96, 129, 148, 210, 216, 225, 229, 239; Indo-China Expeditionary Army, 164; Indo-China Garrison Army, 145, 222; Kwantung Defence Army, 60, 103, 236, 243; Mongolia Garrison Army, 43, 53, 142, 170, 199, 211, 240; North China Garrison Army, 95, 126, 214; Shanghai Expeditionary Army (Force), 25, 85, 95, 104, 136, 148, 160, 180, 199, 225, 252; Siberian Expeditionary Army, 84, 86, 108; Singapore Garrison Army, see Garrisons, Singapore; South China Expeditionary Army, 164, 210; Tohoku District Army, 91; Tokai District Army, 179; Tokyo Bay Defence Army (Corps), 56, 213; Tokyo Defence Army, 56, 109, 213

Divisions Armoured: **1,** 55, 105; **2,** 65, 121, 179, 200; **3,** 53, 233; **4,** 55, 163; Depot: **1,** 173, **2,** 156; **3,** 168; **4,** 125, 205; **5,** 95; **6,** 132; **8,** 104; **10,** 175; **11,** 104; **12,** 217; **19,** 183; **20,** 197; **30,** 205; **51,** 197; **51,** 197; **54,** 240; **56,** 109; Imperial Guards: 128, 145, 172, 176, 216, 217, 225; **1,** 56, 81, 85, 100, 118, 156, 213, 226, 275; **2 (Konoe),** 66, 82, 108, 112, 118, 138, 143, 160, 171, 209, 220, 236; **3,** 56, 132, 158; Infantry: **1,** 64, 80, 97, 125, 146, 151, 168, 202, 217, 221, 241; **2,** 67, 71, 102, 106, 129, 134, 141, 146, 147, 164, 169, 173, 180, 187, 188, 2097, 226; **3,** 43, 53, 90, 92, 99, 123, 133, 153, 172, 178, 195, 198, 217, 228, 234, 238; **4,** 43, 47, 68, 87, 90, 99, 104, 108, 129, 134, 137, 153, 161, 179, 212, 216, 236; **5,** 46, 65, 83, 111, 118, 126, 130, 139, 145, 149, 166, 171, 181, 216, 217, 228, 233, 235, 236, 237; **6,** 63, 81, 84, 90, 95, 106, 112, 121, 122, 126, 137, 195, 206, 214, 239, 241; **7,** 54, 99, 140, 185; **8,** 65, 91, 101, 151, 170, 195, 208, 241, 242; **9,** 54, 95, 99, 114, 223, 225, 226; **10,** 64, 65, 88, 95, 103, 117, 175, 179, 193, 237, 242; **11,** 57, 196, 205, 223; **12,** 54, 101, 127, 132, 139, 146, 199, 209, 232; **13,** 43, 52, 81, 90, 123, 212, 243; **14,** 47, 51, 89, 96, 113, 126, 158, 173, 176, 189, 239; **15,** 43, 68, 72, 90, 98, 124, 125, 134, 151, 153, 160, 178, 181, 191, 194, 206, 212, 234, 235, 238; **16,** 64, 88, 91, 103, 115,

146, 152, 157, 163, 165, 167, 168, 175, 184, 202, 203, 221, 237; **17,** 63, 90, 111, 185; **18,** 69, 71, 72, 80, 101, 102, 108, 124, 125, 137, 149, 150, 159, 160, 164, 179, 185, 186, 206, 207, 208, 211, 223, 236; **19,** 65, 88, 142, 177, 183, 213, 237, 242; **20,** 63, 79, 80, 83, 84, 124, 126, 129, 130, 154, 164, 165, 194, 223, 231, 243; **21,** 67, 152, 161, 177, 210; **22,** 43, 47, 48, 67, 68, 100, 123, 154, 181, 197, 205; **23,** 25, 64, 170, 173, 204, 237, 242; **24,** 62, 81, 82, 88, 168, 177, 226, 227; **25,** 57, 81, 126; **26,** 64, 93, 202, 221, 233, 237; **27,** 43, 51, 103, 123, 149, 208, 215; **28,** 62, 83, 145; **29,** 51, 170, 207, 225; **30,** 64, 90, 94, 157, 158, 202, 237; **31,** 42, 69, 72, 124, 125, 129, 143, 153, 160, 191, 206, 238; **32,** 65, 115; **33,** 47, 52, 68, 71, 72, 81, 98, 108, 125, 134, 138, 150, 159, 160, 164, 186, 191, 204, 207, 208, 210, 211, 235, 239; **34,** 43, 53, 120, 177, 186, 198, 204; **35,** 65, 109, 195, 217; **36,** 65, 110, 122, 186, 204, 217; **37,** 47, 67, 68, 79, 114, 161, 191; **38,** 63, 106, 111, 119, 121, 141, 185, 188, 211, 271, 293; **39,** 60, 86, 90, 108, 158, 188, 189, 200; **40,** 53, 82, 84, 132, 198; **41,** 63, 78, 79, 80, 84, 90, 147, 243; **42,** 55, 189, 194, 199; **43,** 51, 184; **44,** 55, 193; **46,** 46, 67, 114, 140; **47,** 43, 51, 105, 116, 182, 186, 230; **48,** 65, 66, 78, 103, 110, 163, 217, 222, 225, 231; **49,** 42, 69, 71, 72, 101, 102, 124, 134, 164, 206, 207; **50,** 54, 117; **51,** 63, 79, 80, 128, 159, 164, 167, 185, 303; **52,** 51, 158; **53,** 69, 71, 98, 101, 102, 107, 125, 164, 187, 193, 194, 206, 234; **54,** 42, 68, 71, 124, 134, 137, 153, 163, 187, 193; **55,** 42, 67, 68, 71, 72, 94, 102, 104, 108, 120, 138, 150, 151, 159, 160, 163, 186, 187, 188, 208, 235; **56,** 47, 66, 68, 71, 72, 101, 102, 108, 124, 148, 150, 151, 152, 160, 185, 207, 236; **57,** 57, 65, 224; **58,** 43, 52, 123, 138, 156, 174, 198; **59,** 61, 90, 105, 145, 162, 188, 214; **60,** 43, 53, 85, 138, 149, 169; **61,** 43, 53, 102, 149; **62,** 62, 85, 91, 165, 226; **63,** 60, 102, 103, 174, 186, 188, 239; **64,** 43, 51, 92, 120, 179, 186; **65,** 43, 53, 142, 158, 183, 185, 195, 198; **66,** 54, 136; **68,** 183, 186, 200, 224; **69,** 43, 51, 53, 97, 149, 153, 205; **70,** 43, 53, 173, 198, 224; **71,** 54, 66, 221; **72,** 55, 177, 195; **73,** 56, 128; **77,** 57, 176; **79,** 59, 158; **81,** 55, 139; **84,** 56, 155, 178; **86,** 57, 114, 186; **88,** 55; **89,** 55; **91,** 55, 198; **93,** 55, 198; **94,** 45, 67, 113, 114, 167; **96,** 58; **100,** 64, 95, 132, 157, 202, 237; **101,** 184; **102,** 64, 92, 141, 202, 237; **103,** 65, 84, 159, 210, 242, 244; **104,** 43, 54, 125, 185, 201, 210, 223; **105,** 65, 118, 131, 173, 222, 242; **106,** 150, 165; **107,** 60, 79, 102; **108,** 61, 120, 126, 196, 214; **109,** 51, 82, 143, 193, 203, 254; **110,** 43, 52, 98, 135, 181, 205, 214; **111,** 58, 121; **112,** 59, 158, 167; **114,** 43, 52, 98, 153, 168, 178, 198, 200; **115,** 52, 199, 205; **116,** 52, 121, 186, 224; **117,** 60, 102, 103, 188, 201, 205; **118,** 43, 53, 224; **119,** 60, 224; **120,** 59, 239; **121,** 58; **122,** 60; **123,** 60, 124; **124,** 60, 195; **125,** 60, 108; **126,** 60, 195; **127,** 59, 158; **128,** 59, 155, 158; **129,** 42, 54, 210; **130,** 42, 54, 210; **131,** 54; **132,** 43, 52; **133,** 43, 53, 132, 149, 156; **134,** 60; **135,** 60, 195; **136,** 61; **137,** 61, 145; **138,** 60, 108, 221; **139,** 60, 221; **140,** 56; **142,** 55; **143,** 56; **144,** 57; **145,** 57; **146,** 57; **147,** 56; **148,** 60, 108; **149,** 60, 224; **150,** 58; **151,** 55; **152,** 56; **153,** 56; **154,** 57; **155,** 57; **156,** 57; **157,** 55; **160,** 58; **161,** 43, 53, 198; **162,** 147; **201,** 55; **202,** 55; **205,** 57; **206,** 57; **209,** 55; **212,** 57; **214,** 55; **216,** 57; **221,** 55; **222,** 55; **229,** 56; **230,** 57, 91; **231,** 57, 91; **234,** 56; **255,** 57; **303,** 57; **308,**

55; **312**, 57; **316**, 56; **320**, 59; **321**, 56; **322**, 55; **344**, 57; **351**, 57; **354**, 56; **355**, 56; **Brigades** Amphibious: **1**, 170; **2**, 208; Cavalry: **1**, 143; **2**, 143; **3**, 125, 145; **4**, 52, 189, 231; Field Artillery: **1**, 195; **4** Heavy, 90, 96; Independent Infantry: **1**, 53; **2**, 53, 97; **5**, 52; **6**, 53; **7**, 52, 110; **8**, 54, 126; **10**, 53, 119; **11**, 52, 154; **12**, 52, 159; **13**, 54, 177; **14**, 52, 168; **18**, 132; Independent Mixed: **1**, 53, 140; **2**, 53, 143, 193; **3**, 52, 175; **4**, 57, 106; **5**, 53; **6**, 53, 204; **8**, 53, 208; **9**, 53; **12**, 54; **17**, 135; **19**, 54, 141; **20**, 204; **21**, 53, 177, 233; **22**, 41, 52, 54, 242; **23**, 54, 196; **24**, 69, 72, 98, 186; **25**, 48, 66, 181; **26**, 67; **27**, 66, 130; **28**, 66, 119; **29**, 47, 67, 190, 210, 230; **34**, 68; **35**, 39, 40, 67, 114; **36**, 67, 114, 119; **37**, 41, 67, 114, 192; **38**, 48, 63, 106, 132; **39**, 63, 186, 223; **40**, 46, 63; **43**, 55, 194; **44**, 62, 82, 201, 226; **45**, 62, 155; **47**, 184; **48**, 207; **49**, 51; **50**, 51, 136; **51**, 51, 109; **52**, 51, 230; **53**, 51, 233; **54**, 64, 101, 202; **55**, 64, 202, 203; **56**, 41, 80, 87; **57**, 90, 217; **58**, 64, 183, 190; **59**, 62; **60**, 63; **61**, 64; **62**, 53; **64**, 63; **65**, 63, 111, 148; **66**, 53; **68**, 64, 144, 202; **69**, 55; **70**, 67, 114, 177; **71**, 66, 87, 235; **72**, 69, 72, 235; **75**, 54, 195; **76**, 54; **80**, 60, 224; **81**, 52; **84**, 53; **85**, 52; **86**, 52; **87**, 52; **88**, 52; **89**, 53; **90**, 52; **91**, 52; **92**, 52, 131; **98**, 57; **102**, 54; **103**, 54; **105**, 69, 72, 134, 148, 157; **107**, 57; **109**, 51; **118**, 57; **122**, 57; **125**, 57; **126**, 57; **158**, 166; Infantry: **1**, 83, 151, 162, 226; **5**, 99, 212; **8**, 84; **9**, 89, 130; **12**, 166, 185; **14**, 243; **19**, 216; **21**, 199; **23**, 208; **24**, 194, 218; **27**, 217; **29**, 181; **32**, 103; **35**, 129; **39**, 167, 172; **40**, 111, 142, 236; **51**, 174; **52**, 138; **53**, 214; **54**, 162; **55**, 169; **56**, 85; **60**, 97; **61**, 173; **63**, 165; **65**, 110, 157, 163; **66**, 186; **67**, 239; **69**, 120; **70**, 179; **72**, 142, 158; **73**, 198; **75**, 132; **77**, 141; **79**, 65, 84; **80**, 179, 244; **81**, 173; **82**, 131; **83**, 178; **84**, 98; **99**, 132; **105**, 157; **107**, 173; **121**, 118; 3 Imperial Guards, 95; Tank: **1**, 105; **3**, 236; **5**, 190 **Garrisons** Bangkok, 68; Hainan Island, 54; Hunchung, 137; Kyoto, 115; Singapore (Singapore Garrison Army), 130, 170; Tokyo, 99, 188

Garrison Units 1, 110, 117; **2**, 130; **11**, 161; **32**, 178; **41**, 93; 1 **Border**, 167; **4 Border**, 81; **6 Border**, 138; **15 Border**, 196; North China Special, 43, 53, 126, 170; North Seas (Hokkai), 153; Peking (Peiping), 159; Penghu, 44; Tientsin, 135

Independent Garrison Units 2, 52; **4**, 53; **5**, 83; **6**, 52; **7**, 181; **9**, 53, 83, 185; **11**, 53; **12**, 53; **13**, 52; Manchuria, 164

Miscellaneous units
Army General Staff: 20, 79, 82, 83, 84, 85, 88, 89, 90, 91, 92, 96, 99, 103, 105, 106, 108, 109, 110, 111, 115, 118, 122, 123, 125, 127, 128, 129, 133 135, 136, 137, 139, 141, 142, 144, 146, 150, 151, 155, 156, 159, 160, 162, 165, 168, 172, 173, 174, 175, 176, 178, 180, 181, 185, 188, 189, 194, 196, 199, 201, 203, 204, 209, 211, 212, 214, 215, 218, 220, 221, 222, 225, 226, 228, 229, 231, 232, 235, 238, 240, 241, 273
Army Intelligence, 89; Unit 82, Formosa Army Research Station: 98, 133, 236
Artillery Commands, **1**, 206; **5**, 62, 226, 229; **9**, 196; Artillery, Field, 42, 82; Artillery, Group, 8, 91; 24, 168.

Chemical Weapons Branch (Warfare), 145, 170

Detachments: Nanto (southeast), 63, 189; South

Seas, 104, 105, 119; **2**, 95; **5**, 177
Forces: Chu (Burma), 94; 1 Field, 206; Hong Kong Defence, 54, 80; KAN I (Burma), 148; Kanjo (Burma), 163; Kantetsu (Burma), 235; Kayashima (China), 132; Koba (Burma), 137; Manchuria (Manchukuo) Defence, 161; Matsuyama (Burma), 151; Miyake (New Guinea), 154, 165; Murakami (China), 158; Sakura (Burma), 188; Sepik (Burma), 188; Sepik (New Guinea) 9, 197; Shimbu (Burma), 94, 163; Udo (Okinawa), 227; Yamamoto (Burma), 235
Gendarmerie, *see* Military Police
Groups Kembu (Philippines), 65, 223, 237; 1 Penetration, 242; 1 Raiding, 65; Shimbu (Philippines), 65, 237, 241, 242; Shobu (Philippines), 65, 237; Tokyo Bay, 175

Home Stations, 84, 86, 90, 91, 93, 95, 100, 101, 109, 110, 117, 121, 124, 130, 135, 143, 150, 153, 156, 157, 158, 161, 163, 166, 167, 168, 177, 178, 182, 185, 193, 195, 197, 200, 204, 222, 225, 229, 242

Kempei (Kempeitai), *see* Military Police

Medical and Veterinary, 116, 121, 122, 140, 163, 204
Military Education, 15, 97, 101, 170, 230
Academies Military, 81, 89, 136, 137, 146, 150, 151, 160, 164, 168, 173, 193, 194, 196, 198, 218, 228, 232, 243; Military Medical, 116, 121 159; Military Preparatory, 146, 168, 175, 194; Military Reserve, 193; Colleges: Staff, 84, 132; War, 79, 86, 90, 91, 109, 112, 115, 125, 128, 133, 136, 146, 155, 156, 159, 162, 168, 170, 172, 175, 176, 181, 189, 203, 210, 213, 231, 236, 241; Schools: Artillery, 90, 129, 133, 195, 240; Cavalry, 125, 152, 156, 231; Infantry, 101, 107, 108, 111, 127, 164, 170, 173, 194; Tank, 179, 220; Training: Artillery, 96, 195; Inspectorate of Military, 15, 21, 83, 89, 96, 111, 127, 136, 173, 179, 199, 201, 211, 216, 231, 232; Military, 84, 115, 122, 133, 144, 151, 162, 171, 172, 194
Military Police (Kempei, Kempeitai, Gendarmerie), 11, 44, 91, 100, 113, 121, 126, 130, 135, 137, 145, 148, 156, 161, 166, 173, 181, 195, 197, 212, 218, 223
Railways 97; Field Railway Command (Corps): **2**, 47, 94, 158; **4**, 192; Siam, 47, 141; Southern Army, 114; Field Railway Corps, Siam, 47, 141; Railway Transport Command: **1**, 152; **4**, 145; **6**, 208; Kwantung Army, 79, 241; Special Railway Corps: **4**, 47, 80; **5**, 234
Shipping 192; Groups: **1**, 231; **11**, 203; **13**, 93; Transport Command: 209; **2**, 119; **3**, 112; **5**, 230; Army Maritime, 87
Technical Army Technical Department, 99, 170; Army Technical Research Institutes: **6**, 183; **9**, 93
Transport Field Transport Command: **2**, 47, 123, 124; **3**, 137; **5**, 204; **6**, 170; **7**, 194; **11**, 100; **12**, 214; **13**, 122; **14**, 42; **16**, 92
Japanese Army Air Force (service) 139; Army Aeronautical Department: 82, 96, 99, 139, 188, 196, 198, 199, 215, 240; Army Air Groups: Air General Army, Japan, 58, 127; Kanto Command, Manchuria, 218; Air Armies: **1**, 58, 127, 240; **2**, 61, 127, 128; **3**, 45, 67, 135, 175, 198, 217, 223; **4**, 65, 82, 111, 112, 141, 183, 215, 220, 237; **5**, 58, 59, 127, 196; **6**, 58, 127, 155, 198, 233, 299; **10**, 220; Air Training, 198; Air Divisions

(Groups): **1**, 90, 127, 198, 233; **2**, 90, 175, 215; **3**, 90, 142, 236; **4**, 65, 194, 215; **5**, 67, 71, 97, 103, 108, 135, 175, 186, 215; **7**, 67, 90, 93, 135; **8**, 54, 220, 233; **9**, 67, 90, 93, 135, 209; **10**, 58, 127, 243; **11**, 58, 127; **12**, 58, 90, 93, 127, 215; **13**, 54; **27**, 174; **30**, 58; **51**, 58, 127; **52**, 58, 127; **53**, 58; **55**, 67, 135; Air Brigades: **2**, 198, **3**, 198, 223; **7**, 128; **10**, 175; **22**, 152; Air Schools: Aheno, 175; Hamamatsu, 128, 215, 223; Shimoshizu, 198, 223; 1 Airborne Raiding Group (paratroops), 223; Aviation Weaponry Bureau, 90; Inspector-General of the Air Force (Army Aviation), 15, 82, 89, 128, 218, 228, 240; **2** Joint Air Group, 89, 93

Navy:
Combined Fleet, 10, 217, 245, 248, 249, 257, 262, 263, 268, 273, 280, 287, 291, 296, 298, 302, 303; Commander-in-Chief of, 198, 256, 257, 258, 259, 260, 262, 267, 268, 269, 272, 274, 283, 288, 291, 292, 294, 295, 296, 298, 302, 305, 306, 307
Area Fleets Central Pacific, 10, 274, 297, 304; China Area, 10, 42, 188, 248, 262, 265, 277, 287, 290, 305; North-east Area, 10; South-east Area, 10, 46, 267, 269; South-west Area, 19, 47, 249, 257, 271, 279, 284, 287, 292; **10** Area, 45, 49, 70, 47, 249, 252
Fleets 1, 8, 251, 252, 264, 287, 292, 303, 304, 305; 1 Mobile, 10, 258, 259, 267, 277, 283, 287, 296, 297, 299; 1 Special Attack, *see* 2 Fleet; **2**, 8, 10, 245, 246, 247, 257, 262, 263, 264, 266, 267, 269, 271, 272, 274, 283, 287, 291, 293, 296, 297, 299, 303, 305; **3**, 8, 248, 284, 287, 291, 292, 293; **4** (Mandates), 8, 10, 11, 41, 250, 251, 256, 258, 262, 267, 281, 285, 286, 296, 300, 303; **5**, 8, 10, 254, 259, 266, 267, 275, 279; **6** (Submarines), 8,10, 22, 247, 263, 265, 271, 272, 276, 282, 288, 291, 303; **8**, 10; South China, 44, 248; Southern Expeditionary: **1**, 10, 45, 70, 249; **2**, 10, 45, 70, 217, 249, 272, 282, 283, 293; **3**, 10, 251, 259, 262, 265, 268, 269, 274, 283, 292, 297, 298, 303; **4**, 10
Divisions Battleship: **1**, 255, 297, 299, 304; **2**, 270, 292, 297; **3**, 245, 263, 265, 273; Carrier: **1**, 273, 283, 297, 302; **2**, 259, 273, 283, 284, 297, 301, 303; **3**, 277, 283, 297; **4**, 264; **5**, 251; **11**, 248;
Flotillas Destroyer: **1**, 273; **2**, 263, 264, 266, 291, 293; **3**, 252, 255, 264, 279; **4**, 252, 253, 264, 275, 291, 292; **5**, 264; **10**, 246, 261; Minelayer: **17**,267; **19**, 286; Submarine: **1**, 263, 285, 288; **2**, 288; **3**, 263, 265, 271, 288; **4**, 264, 307; **5**, 247, 263, 264, 307; **6**, 264; **7**, 281, 282, 307; **8**, 257
Squadrons Cruiser: **2**, 304; **4**, 255, 264, 267, 297; **5**, 252, 264, 267, 291, 297; **6**, 250; **7**, 261, 264, 266, 291, 293, 297; **8**, 244, 258, 263, 266, 273; **16**, 264, 284; **18**, 280; Yangtze, 288
Base Forces 1, 11, 291; **2** (Special), 11, 260, 291; **3** (Special), 11, 69, 283, 286; **4** (Special), 11, 284; **5** (Special), 11, 274, 297; **6**, 11, 59; **7** (Special), 11, 248; **8**, 11, 256; **9**,11, 48, 70, 253; **10** (Special), 11, 70, 255; **11** (Special), 11, 70, 248; **12** (Special), 11, 41, 70, 251; **13** (Special), 11, 47, 70, 285, 293; **14**, 11, 292; **15** (Special), 11, 70, 300; **21** (Special), 11; **22** (Special), 11, 259; **23** (Special), 11, 281; **24** (Special), 11, 256, 286; **25** (Special), 11; **26** (Special), 11, 305; **27** (Special), 11, 260; **28**, 11, 50, 286; **30**, 11, 257; **31** (Special), 11, 257, 279; **32** (Special), 11, 247; **33**, 11, 252; Ambon Special, 252; Amoy Special, 10; Bako Special, 10; Chichijima Area Special, 10;

Hong Kong Area Special, 10; Kurile Islands Area Special, 10, 11, 272; Okinawa Area, 10; Okinawa Special, 62, 226, 282; Rashin Special, 10; Ryojun (Port Arthur) Special, 10; Shanghai Special, 10; Tsingtao Special, 10, 248; Yangtze River Special, 10
Bases: Maizuru, Japan, 8, 294, 295; Okinawa, 275; Ryojun (Port Arthur), Manchuria, 8, 79; Sasebo, Japan, 274, 295, 305; Surabaya, Japan, 166, 271, 293; Truk, *see* Caroline Islands; Yokosuka, Japan, 253, 260, 262, 285, 295, 296, 301, 305; Guard Districts: Chinkai, Korea, 8, 278; Hainan Island, China, 8, 250; Ominato, Japan, 8, 44, 250, 298; Osaka, Japan; 8, 278; Takao, Formosa, 8, 248; Guard Force: **4**, 256; **13**, 14£; **17**, 35, 41, 70; **19**, 50; **56**, 259; **65**, 284; Kure, 257; Yokosuka, 266
Japanese Navy Miscellaneous Units
Escort Command, Japan, 277; Kaiten, 271, 272, 282, 292; Landing Forces: Attu Island, 279; Kure: **1**, Special, 252; **7**, 106; Midway Island, 282; Sasebo: **5**, 105; **6**, 106; **7** Special, 69, 286; Shanghai Special, 289; Yokosuka Special: **1**, 274; **5**, 177; **6**, 286; Midget Submarines: 274, 256, 288; Naval Affairs Bureau: 245, 247, 269, 290, 302; Naval Arsenal, Kure, 246, 261; Naval Education, 290; Etajima Naval College, 256, 277; Naval Staff College, 263, 301, 302; Naval Technical College, 295; Naval War College, 260, 280, 287, 292; Otake Submarine School, 254, 287; Yokosuka Gunnery School, 301, 305; Yokosuka Torpedo School, 280; Naval Forces: Darwin Strike, 244, 279, 301; Malaya, 247, 252, 264, 266, 282, 283, 307; Midway Invasion, *see* Operations, MI; Naval General Staff, 191, 248, 250, 257, 260, 262, 264, 267, 272, 273, 274, 275, 277, 278, 281, 283, 287, 288, 289, 290, 292, 293, 295, 296, 298, 305; Naval Intelligence, 253, 276, 277, 278, 281, 295; Tokyo Express, 106, 245, 250, 258, 265, 271, 293
Japanese Naval Air Force
Air Arsenal, Yokosuka, 300
Air Fleets 1 (1st Striking Force) carriers, 8, 10, 12, 244, 246, 249, 251, 261, 263, 264, 268, 269, 273, 274, 279, 280, 289, 294, 297, 298, 299, 301, 302, 303; **1** (land-based), 259, 269, 280; **2**, 249, 255, 265, 280; **3**, 269, 294, 299; **4**, 281; **5**, 269, 296, 299, 305; **10**, 299; **11**, 8, 10, 266, 267, 268, 269, 270, 297, 298, 303; **12**, 10, 249, 280; **13**, 10, 70, 249; **14**, 10, 262; Combined Base Air Corps (South-west Area Fleet Combined Land-Based Air Force), 249, 280; Pearl Harbor Attack Force (Kido Butai), *see* 1 Air Fleet (1st Striking Force), carriers
Base Air Force 3, 259; **5**, 280; **6**, 249
Air Flotillas (Squadrons) 12, 255; **21**, 254, 298; **22**, 270, 283, 298; **23**, 256, 298; **24**, 250, 268, 269, 298; **25**, 256, 300; **26**, 246, 284, 289
Air Groups 14, 269; **201**, 280; **601**, 294; **701**, 299; **901**, 277; Chitose, 269; Genzen, 270; Kanoya, 270; Mihoro, 270; Kasumigaura Aviation Corps (Misty Lagoon), 262, 302; Naval Aviation Department, 256, 260, 300, 302; Special Attack, 246, 266, 280; Special Attack Units (Tokko-tai): 282, **721**, 280; Asashi, 280; Mitate, 294; Niitaka, 281; Shikishima, 280; Yamato, 280; Yamazakura, 280
Japanese Naval Vessels *Abukuma*, 279, 287; *Agano*, 279, 283; *Akagi*, 268, 273, 274, 302; *Aoba*, 250, 284; *Ashigara*, 252, 291; *Aso*, 301;

Atago, 255, 264, 266, 267, 298; *Chikuma*, 111, 244, 263, 267, 284, 303; *Chitose*, 283; *Chiyoda*, 251, 283; *Chokai*, 266, 267, 270, 285; *Fuji*, 301; *Fuso*, 292; *Harugo*, 267, 279, 291; *Haruna*, 245, 264, 265, 267; *Hatsushimo*, 263; *Hayate*, 259; *Hiei*, 245, 264, 270, 287, 303; *Hiryu*, 274, 301; *Hiyo*, 259, 283; *Hosho*, 268; *Hyuga*, 270, 292; *Idzumo*, 252; *Ise*, 270, 292; *Isuzu*, 302; *Jintsu*, 258, 293; *Junyo*, 259, 283, 303; *Kaga*, 273, 274; *Kagero*, 301; *Kashii*, 282; *Katori*, 263, 288; *Katsukaze*, 255; *Kinu*, 284, 307; *Kinugasa*, 250; *Kirishima*, 245, 263, 264, 265; *Kitakami*, 301; *Kongo*, 264, 265, 267, 270; *Kumano*, 266, 267, 293; *Kurutaka*, 250; *Maezuru*, 301; *Maya*, 264, 267; *Mikasa*, 295; *Mikuma*, 266; *Mogami*, 266, 267; *Musashi*, 90, 255, 267, 283, 296, 299; *Myoko*, 267, 279, 291; *Nachi*, 254, 291;

Naganami, 293; *Nagara*, 245, 261, 266, 274; *Nagato*, 267, 299, 302, 304; *Naka*, 266, 275; *Naniwa*, 294; *Nashi*, 12; *Natori*, 251; *Niizuki*, 245; *Nisshin*, 301; *Noshiro*, 267; *Okinoshima*, 287; *Oyoda*, 268, 283; *Ryujo*, 251, 283; *Sazanami*, 255; *Sendai*, 255, 279; *Shintaku*, 301; *Shoho*, 250, 264, 291; *Shokaku*, 251, 262, 268, 274, 283, 291, 303; *Soryu*, 274, 301; *Suzukaze*, 293; *Suzuya*, 261, 266, 267; *Taiho*, 283; *Takao*, 264, 267; *Tama*, 270, 287; *Tone*, 244, 251, 267, 284; *Wakimiya* Maru, 280; *Yahagi*, 257, 263, 283; *Yamashiro*, 276, 292; *Yamato*, 90, 246, 257, 263, 266, 267, 272, 283, 296, 298, 299, 302, 303, 306; *Yubari*, 258, 259; *Yugumo*, 304; *Yukikaze*, 245, 272; *Yura*, 247, 275, 292; *Zuiho*, 259, 262, 264, 277, 283, 303; *Zuikaku*, 251, 262, 274, 275, 283